NP285

ADMIRALTY LIST OF RADIO SIGNALS

VOLUME 5

THIRD EDITION

2022

GLOBAL MARITIME DISTRESS AND SAFETY SYSTEM (GMDSS)

IMPORTANT - SEE RELATED ADMIRALTY PUBLICATIONS

Notices to Mariners (Annual, Permanent, Preliminary and Temporary); **Symbols and Abbreviations used on Paper Charts** (NP5011); **ADMIRALTY Guide to ENC Symbols used in ECDIS** (NP5012); **The Mariner's Handbook** (NP100, especially Chapters 1 and 2 on the use, accuracy and limitations of charts); **Sailing Directions** (Pilots); **List of Lights** and **Fog Signals**; **List of Radio Signals** and **Tide Tables** (or their digital equivalents).

KEEP CHARTS AND PUBLICATIONS UP TO DATE AND USE THE LARGEST SCALE CHART APPROPRIATE

PUBLISHED BY THE UK HYDROGRAPHIC OFFICE

DIRECTIONS FOR UPDATING THIS VOLUME

Subsequent updates to this book will be included in Section VI of the Weekly Edition of ADMIRALTY Notices to Mariners, copies of which can be obtained from authorised ADMIRALTY distributors, or from the UKHO Website admiralty.co.uk/msi

A cumulative list of updates is published quarterly in Section VI and provides a summary list of the entries in the current editions which have been updated. New or extensively altered material is intended to be pasted over the existing material. Shorter updates should be made in manuscript. The Weekly Edition number is shown on all updates. The appropriate indexes and diagrams should also be updated if necessary.

RECORD OF UPDATES

This Volume should only be used once fully updated by Section VI Notices to Mariners. The inclusion of updates in this Volume should be recorded in the following table:

NEW EDITION First Updates	

Weekly Notices to Mariners (Section VI)

ANNUAL NOTICES TO MARINERS

Attention is called to the following ADMIRALTY Notices to Mariners which are published annually and contain information of particular interest to the users of ADMIRALTY List of Radio Signals:

03   Safety of British Merchant Ships in periods of peace, tension, crisis or conflict.
05   Firing Practice and Exercise Areas.
20   Mandatory Expanded Inspections - EU Directive 2009/16/EC.

The content of annual ADMIRALTY Notices to Mariners 04 is included in NP285, ADMIRALTY List of Radio Signals, Global Maritime Distress and Safety System (GMDSS).

CONTENTS

CONTENTS

CONTENTS

PREFACE

The Third Edition (2022) of ALRS Volume 5 contains the latest information received by the UKHO.

All reasonable effort has been made to ensure that this Volume contains all of the information obtained and assessed by the UKHO by the date of publication. Information received after that date will be included in Section VI of the Weekly Edition of ADMIRALTY Notices to Mariners.

This edition supersedes the Second Edition (2021) which is cancelled.

PURPOSE OF ADMIRALTY RADIO SIGNALS

ADMIRALTY List of Radio Signals (ALRS) provides a comprehensive source of information on all aspects of Maritime Radio Communications. The purpose of this Volume is to provide information on the following topics:

Worldwide Communications Requirements for the Global Maritime Distress and Safety System (GMDSS)

Distress Communications and Operational Procedures

SOLAS Regulations

Extracts from ITU Regulations

Navtex and Maritime Safety Information

Distress and Search & Rescue (incorporating MRCC & MRSC Contacts)

Worldwide Operational DSC Ranges and Search and Rescue (SAR) Regions

HOW TO REPORT NEW OR SUSPECTED DANGERS TO NAVIGATION OR CHANGES OBSERVED IN AIDS TO NAVIGATION

A Hydrographic Note, Form H102, with instructions, is contained in the back of the Weekly Edition of ADMIRALTY Notices to Mariners. This form can also be downloaded from the UKHO Website. The form should be used to report all observations, including new or suspected dangers to navigation or changes to aids to navigation.

FEEDBACK

Feedback on this publication is most welcome and should be addressed to Customer Services and marked for the attention of ADMIRALTY List of Radio Signals and Marketing.

UKHO CONTACT DETAILS

Customer Services
ADMIRALTY
The UK Hydrographic Office
Admiralty Way
TAUNTON
Somerset
TA1 2DN
United Kingdom
email: customerservices@ukho.gov.uk
Tel: +44 (0)1823 484444
Website: admiralty.co.uk

Enquiries regarding the content of ADMIRALTY List of Radio Signals should be made to the contact listed above clearly stating "For the attention of ALRS".

HOW TO OBTAIN ADMIRALTY CHARTS AND PUBLICATIONS

A complete list of ADMIRALTY Charts and Publications (both paper & digital), together with a list of authorised ADMIRALTY distributors for their purchase, is contained in the *"Catalogue of ADMIRALTY Charts and Publications"* (NP131), published annually. The ADMIRALTY Digital Catalogue is available to download free of charge from the UKHO Website.

Details of authorised ADMIRALTY distributors can also be obtained free of charge from Customer Services.

RELATED ADMIRALTY PUBLICATIONS AND THEIR CONTENTS

ADMIRALTY Notices to Mariners (NMs):
- Weekly Notices to Mariners
  - Navigationally significant changes to nautical charts, lights and fog signals, Radio Signals and Sailing Directions
  - Reprint of all Radio Navigational Warnings in force and a summary of charts and publications being published.
- Cumulative List of Notices to Mariners
  - Published in January and July of each year
  - A list of all nautical charts available and a complete list of all NMs affecting them during the previous two years.
- Annual Summary of Notices to Mariners
  - Published at the beginning of the year in two parts
  - Annual Notices to Mariners, Temporary and Preliminary NMs
  - Cumulative summary of updates to Sailing Directions.

For more information, please visit admiralty.co.uk/msi

The Mariner's Handbook:
- Information on nautical charts and their use
- Operational information and regulation
- Tides and currents
- Characteristics of the sea
- Basic meteorology
- Navigation in ice
- Hazards and restrictions to navigation

ADMIRALTY Sailing Directions (Pilots):
- Waterway directions
- Port facilities
- Directions for port entry
- Navigational hazards
- Buoyage
- Climate information.

ADMIRALTY List of Radio Signals:
- Maritime Radio Stations
- Radio Aids to Navigation
- Time
- Maritime Safety Information
- Radio Weather Services
- Global Maritime Distress and Safety System (GMDSS)
- Pilot Services
- Vessel Traffic Services
- Port Operations
- Ship Reporting Systems.

ADMIRALTY List of Lights:
- Lighthouses, lightships, fog signals and other lights of navigational significance.
- Equivalent foreign language light descriptions
- International number
- Characteristics
- Light elevation and structure height in metres
- Range of light
- Description of structure.

ADMIRALTY Tidal Publications:
- Tide Tables
  - Daily predictions of time and height of high and low waters at Standard Ports
  - Time and height differences for Secondary Ports
  - Harmonic constants where known
  - Supplementary Tables including Land Levelling to Chart Datum connections where known.
- Tidal Stream Atlases
  - Major tidal streams for selected waters of north west Europe
  - Direction and rate of tidal streams at hourly intervals.

For more information, please visit admiralty.co.uk

GENERAL INFORMATION

Copyright
ADMIRALTY Charts and Publications are protected by Crown Copyright. They are derived from Crown Copyright information and from copyright information published by other organisations. They may not be reproduced in any material form (including photocopying or storing by electronic means) without prior permission, which may be sought by applying, in the first instance, to the Copyright Manager, UK Hydrographic Office, Admiralty Way, Taunton, Somerset, TA1 2DN, United Kingdom.

Times
Times quoted are in Universal Time (UT) unless otherwise stated, and are reckoned from 0000 (midnight) to 2400. The term UT is gradually replacing Greenwich Mean Time (GMT); the abbreviation UT(GMT) will be used to indicate the general equivalence of the two terms. GMT will be retained as the term for the time within Standard Time Zone 0 (Zero).

Geographical Positions
Geographical positions of radio aids to navigation are normally given by the controlling authority. In some cases they are in accordance with the ADMIRALTY Chart. If bearings are taken to radio aids, it should be remembered that, in some cases, the positions quoted are only approximate.

Radio aids to navigation are ascribed to a coastal state purely to indicate to the mariner where to look for the feature. This publication is not an authority on either the ownership of such or sovereignty of features on which they are constructed.

Bearings
Bearings are given from seaward and refer to the true compass.

Names
Names in ADMIRALTY List of Radio Signals are spelt in accordance with the principles and systems approved by the Permanent Committee on Geographical Names for British Official Use.
A second name may be given in parentheses in the following circumstances:
1. if the retention of a superseded rendering will facilitate cross-reference to related publications;
2. if, in the case of a name that has changed radically, the retention of the former one will aid recognition;
3. if it is decided to retain an English conventional name in addition to the present official rendering.

Diagrams
Diagrams will be updated by weekly Notices to Mariners when significant changes are required. Otherwise diagrams will be corrected for the next new edition.

Telephone Numbers
National Direct Dialling (NDD) prefixes are shown in brackets (0). This digit should only be dialled when calling from within that country.

Reporting Changes
In the interests of safe navigation, mariners and others are invited to notify the UK Hydrographic Office (UKHO) of any information which would be useful towards the updating of ADMIRALTY Charts and Publications. Early advice, with supporting particulars of newly discovered dangers, the establishment of, or changes to any aids to navigation is specially requested. Copies of forms H102, H102a and H102b, designed for such notification are contained in the weekly editions of ADMIRALTY Notices to Mariners. Additional copies can be obtained free of charge from the UKHO. In addition, user feedback on our products in terms of format, content, availability and any other aspects is always welcome.

General Disclaimer
The UKHO makes no representation as to the fitness, quality or suitability of the products or services supplied by any person other than the Office and advertised herein and no endorsement of, or connection of the Office with, such products or services is to be inferred from such advertisement. The product names mentioned are the trademarks, registered trademarks or service marks owned or used by the relevant companies or bodies. The names are used within this publication solely for descriptive purposes and no connection of such products or services within the UKHO is to be inferred nor is any representation or endorsement, expressed or implied, made by the UKHO as to fitness, quality or suitability of the products or services bearing those names. The delimitation of areas and boundaries shown in Nautical Publications, graphics or textual format, is not related to and shall not prejudice the delimitation of any boundary between States.

Laws and Regulations Appertaining to Navigation
While, in the interests of the safety of shipping, the UKHO makes every endeavour to include in its hydrographic publications details of the laws and regulations of all countries appertaining to navigation, it must be clearly understood:-
(a) that no liability whatever can be accepted for failure to publish details of any particular law or regulation.
(b) that publication of the details of a law or regulation is solely for the safety and convenience of shipping and implies no recognition of the domestic or international validity of the law or regulation.

ABBREVIATIONS AND GLOSSARY

The following list gives the meaning of abbreviations and a glossary of terms and definitions used in ALRS products.

A	Aerodrome, airfield, etc.
A1A	Continuous wave telegraphy, Morse code.
A1B	Amplitude modulation telegraphy with automatic reception, without using a modulating subcarrier.
A2A	Telegraphy by the on-off keying of a tone modulated carrier, Morse code: double sideband.
A3E	Telephony using amplitude modulation: double sideband.
A9W	Composite emission: double sideband e.g. a combination of telegraphy and telephony.
AAIC	Accounting Authority Identification Code.
Absorption	The loss of energy from a radio wave. Mostly occurs in the D region.
ACO	Aircraft Co-Ordinator.
ADRS	ADMIRALTY Digital List of Radio Signals.
AFTN	Aeronautical Fixed Telecommunications Network.
AIS	Automatic Identification System.
AIS SART	AIS Search And Rescue Transmitter.
Alert data	Generic term for COSPAS-SARSAT 406 MHz alert data derived from 406 MHz distress beacon information. Alert data may contain beacon position and other beacon information such as beacon identification data and coded information.
Almanac	A set of parameters included in the GPS satellite navigation message that is used by a receiver to predict the appropriate location of a satellite.
ALRS	ADMIRALTY List of Radio Signals.
AM	Amplitude Modulation.
AMVER	Automated Mutual-Assistance VEssel Rescue system.
AOH	After Office Hours.
AOR-E	Atlantic Ocean Region (East), coverage area of Inmarsat satellite.
AOR-W	Atlantic Ocean Region (West), coverage area of Inmarsat satellite.
approx	Approximate.
Apr	April.
APR	Automated Position Report.
ARCC	Aeronautical Rescue Coordination Centre. A centre nominated by the national SAR agency to which an Inmarsat Land Earth Station (LES) normally routes distress calls.
ARQ	Automatic Repetition reQuest (mode of telex operation for point to point working between two stations).
ASCII	American Standard Code for Information Interchange, see Kilobit(s).
ASIC	Application Specific Integrated Circuit.
ASM	Application Specific Messages. An extension of AIS whereby the VDL is used for additional purposes such as weather, tides, planned routes, pilotage etc.
ATBA	Area To Be Avoided.
AtoN	Aid to Navigation.
ATS	Air Traffic Services.
Aug	August.
AUT	Automatic Station or observation made by automatic equipment.
Autolink RT	Any vessel fitted with Autolink RT equipment is able to make a radiotelephone call, using direct dialling on VHF, MF or HF frequencies, through any coast radio station operating an Autolink RT service.
AVISO	Notice.
AVURNAVE	AVisos URgentes a los NAVEgantes.
AVURNAVS	AVis URgents aux NAVigateurS.
AWOS	Automatic Weather Observing System.
AWS	Automatic Weather Station.
Baud	A measure of the rate of transfer of binary messages (1 bit/second = 1 baud for most purposes).
BBC	British Broadcasting Corporation.
BC Code	Code of safe practice for Solid Bulk Cargo.
BCD	Binary Code Decimal.
Bcst	Broadcast.
Bit	A single unit of binary data (see Kilobit).
BMS	Bulletins Météorologique Spéciaux.
Bn	Beacon.
BOA	Beam Over All.

bps	Bits per second (transmission rate).
BPSK	Bi Phase Shift Keying.
brg	bearing.
Broadcasting- satellite service	A radiocommunication service in which signals transmitted or retransmitted by space stations are intended for direct reception by the general public.
Broadcasting service	A radiocommunication service in which the transmissions are intended for direct reception by the general public.
BSH	Bundesamtes für Seeschifffahrt und Hydrographie.
Byte	The collection of bits that make up a binary word.
C	Coastal station.
°C	Degrees Celsius.
CCR	Coast Radio Station — Spain.
CDMA	Code Division Multiple Access.
CES	Coast Earth Station. See LES.
CG	Coastguard.
CGAS	Coastguard Aviation Station.
Ch, Ch/s	Channel (As in VHF Ch).
Cm	Centimetre.
CNIS	Channel Navigation Information Service. A 24 hour information service provided by MRCC Dover for vessels using the Dover Strait TSS.
CNOSS	Centre National Opérationnel de Surveillance et de Sauvetage (National centre of operations for surveillance and maritime rescue MRCC) in France and Francophone countries.
CNW	Coastal Navigational Continued Warning.
COLREGS	Convention on the International Regulations for Preventing Collisions at Sea, 1972.
COMMCOM	Communications Command (formally CAMSLANT). This is the central controlling station for all US Coastguard HF broadcasts and communications.
Cont	Continuous.
(Cont)	Continued.
Contracting Government	A signatory to the 1974 Safety of Life at Sea Convention.
COSPAS-SARSAT system	A satellite - aided search and rescue system based on low-altitude near-polar-orbiting satellites and designed to locate distress beacons transmitting on the frequencies 406 MHz and 121·5 MHz. **COSPAS** is an acronym for the Russian words "**CO**asmicheskaya **S**istyema **P**oiska **A**variynikh **S**udov", which translates to "Space System for the Search of Vessels in Distress". **SARSAT** is an acronym for **S**earch **A**nd **R**escue **S**atellite-**A**ided **T**racking. The system uses 4 geosynchronous satellites. GEOSAR's and 5 low-earth polar orbit satellites LEOSARs.
CPRNW	The Commission on Promulgation of Radio Navigational Warnings.
CROSS	Centre Régional Opérationnel de Surveillance et de Sauvetage (Regional centre of operations for surveillance and maritime rescue MRCC) in France and Francophone countries.
CRS	Coast Radio Station. A land station in the maritime mobile service.
CSS	Coordinator Surface Search.
D7W	Emission in which the main carrier is amplitude and angle, modulated either simultaneously or in a pre- established sequence combined with two or more channels containing quantized or digital information.
dB	decibels.
dBW	decibel watts.
Dec	December.
DF	Direction-finding.
DGNSS	Differential Global Navigation Satellite Systems.
DGPS	Differential Global Positioning System. For a full explanation see the SATELLITE NAVIGATION SYSTEMS section.
Distress Alerting	Rapid and successful reporting of a distress incident to a unit which can provide or coordinate assistance.
Distress Call	The spoken word "MAYDAY" made three times followed by the name of the vessel three times which prefaces the distress message.
Distress Message	Consists of the following; The distress signal MAYDAY, the name and or callsign of the vessel in distress, the vessel's position, the nature of the distress, the type of assistance required, and any other information which may assist in facilitating the rescue.
Distress Phase	A situation wherein there is a reasonable certainty that a vessel or other craft, including an aircraft or a person, is threatened by grave or imminent danger and requires immediate assistance.
Distress-Priority Request Message	A ship-to-shore request message containing priority indication 3, the highest priority of ship-to-shore calls.

DOM-TOM	Départements d'outre-mer — Territoires d'outre-mer.
D Region	The lowest region of the ionosphere where most HF absorption occurs. Present during daylight hours only.
DSC	Digital Selective Calling system. A technique using digital codes which enables a radio station to establish contact with, and transfer information to, another station or group of stations utilising HF, MF and VHF bands.
DSHA	Dangerous Substances in Harbour Areas.
DST	Daylight Saving Time. For a full explanation see the LEGAL TIME section.
DUT1	Is the value of the predicted difference between UTC and UT1. For a full explanation see the UNIVERSAL TIME and RADIO TIME SIGNALS sections.
DWD	Deutscher Wetterdienst.
DWT	Dead Weight Tonnage.
E	East.
ECDIS	Electronic Chart Display and Information Service.
EEZ	Exclusive Economic Zone.
EGC	Enhanced Group Calling means the broadcast of coordinated MSI and SAR related information to a defined geographical area using a recognized mobile satellite service.
EMSA	European Maritime Safety Agency.
ENID	EGC Network Identification Code used in the EGC FleetNET Service.
Ephemeris data	Tabulated information fromwhich the location of a satellite (e.g.: COSPAS–SARSAT) relative to the Earthmay be determined for any time within a specified time interval.
EPIRB	Emergency Position-Indicating Radio Beacon. A station in the mobile service, the emissions of which are intended to facilitate search and rescue operations.
EPIRB registration database	A register established and maintained for the purpose of: (a) establishing a readily accessible and up-to-date satellite EPIRB data register containing essential SAR information particular to individual EPIRBs for the use by SAR authorities; and (b) providing readily accessible access to essential SAR data by recognized SAR authorities in the processing of distress situations.
ESV	Eath Station on board a vessel.
ETA	Estimated Time of Arrival.
ETD	Estimated Time of Departure.
EU	European Union.
ext	Extension.
°F	Degrees Fahrenheit.
F1B	Single channel using frequency modulation containing quantised or digital information without the use of a modulating sub carrier. Frequency shift keying, used in DSC systems.
F3E	Telephony using frequency modulation.
Fax	Facsimile.
FDPSO	Floating, Drilling, Production, Storage and Offloading.
Feb	February.
FEC	Forward Error Correction.
FIR	Flight Information Region.
FleetNET	An Inmarsat EGC broadcast facility.
FM	Frequency Modulation.
FPSO	Floating, Production, Storage and Offloading.
Fri	Friday.
FSO	Floating, Storage and Offloading.
FSK	Frequency Shift Keying.
FTP	Anonymous File Transfer Protocol (INTERNET).
Fx	Frequency.
G2B	Phase modulation (automatic reception). A single channel containing quantized or digital information with the use of modulating sub-carrier.
G3E	Phase modulation telephony.
GBAS	Ground Based Augmentation System.
Gateway	Terrestrial part of a mobile satellite system that acts as an interface between the network and other communication networks.

General communications	Those communications between ship stations and shore-based stations which concern the management and operation of the ship, normally taken to mean public correspondence to the exclusion of safety, distress and urgency messages. These communications may be conducted on the appropriate frequencies.
GEOSAR	COSPAS-SARSAT GEostationary Orbiting Search And Rescue satellite system.
Geostationary- Satellite Orbit	The orbit of a geosynchronous satellite whose circular and direct orbit lies in the plane of the Earth's equator.
GHz	Gigahertz.
GLA	General Lighthouse Authority.
GLONASS	**GLO**bal'naya **NA**vigatsionnaya **S**putnikovaya **S**istema.
GMDSS	**G**lobal **M**aritime **D**istress and **S**afety **S**ystem; a global communications service based upon automated systems, both satellite based and terrestrial, to provide distress alerting and promulgation of maritime safety information for mariners.
GMPRS	Geo-mobile Packet Radio Service.
GMT	Greenwich Mean Time.
GNSS	Global Navigation Satellite System.
GPS	Global Positioning System.
GroundWave	The radio wave which propagates close to the Earth's surface. Severe signal losses due to ground resistance limit the range of ground waves to about 100 km over land and 300 km over sea for the lowest HF frequencies. The ground waves for the higher HF frequencies cover much shorter distances.
GSM	Global System for Mobile Communications.
gt	Gross Tonnage.
h	Hours.
H	Heliport.
H+...	Commencing at...minutes past the hour (UTC).
H24	Continuous.
H3E	Telephony: single sideband, full carrier.
H9W	Composite emission: single sideband, full carrier; composite systemwith one or more channels containing quantized or digital information together with one or more channels containing analogue information (e.g. combination of telegraphy and telephony).
HAZREP	HAZardous incident REPort. Near miss incident or breach of the COLREGS.
HAZMAT	HAZardous MATerial. Reporting requirements for vessels carrying dangerous or polluting cargoes.
Hd	Head.
HF	High Frequency (3 - 30 MHz).
Hi+	At...minutes past odd hours (UTC).
HJ	Day service only.
HM	Her Majesty's.
HMCG	Her Majesty's Coastguard.
HN	Night service only.
Hp+	At...minutes past even hours (UTC).
hPa	Hectopascal; unit of pressure used in meteorological work, supersedes the millibar (1 mb = 100 pascals = 1 hPa).
Hr	Harbour.
Hr Mr	Harbour Master.
HSD	High Speed Data.
HW	High Water.
HX	No specific hours or fixed intermittent hours.
HY/A	Seaplane base.
HYDROLANT	US Navigational Warnings for the Atlantic and contiguous areas outside NAVAREA IV.
HYDROPAC	US Navigational Warnings for areas outside Navarea XII.
Hz	Hertz.
I	Island.
IAC	International Analysis Code.
IALA	International Association of Lighthouse Authorities.
IAMSAR	International Aeronautical and Maritime Search And Rescue Manual. This manual is published every three years and is a mandatory publication for all SOLAS vessels.
IBC Code	International Bulk Carriers Code, means the International Code for construction and equipment of Ships carrying dangerous chemicals in bulk.
ICAO	International Civil Aviation Organization.

Ident	Identification Signal.
IERS	International Earth Rotation Service.
IHO	International Hydrographic Organization.
IMDG Code	International Maritime Dangerous Goods Code.
IMN	Inmarsat Mobile Number.
IMO	International Maritime Organization.
IMSO	International Mobile Satellite Organization.
INF Code	International code for the safe carriage of Irradiated Nuclear Fuel.
Inmarsat	The organisation established by the Convention on the International Mobile Satellite Organization (Inmarsat) adopted on 3 September 1976.
Inmarsat C	Operating since 1991 to complement Inmarsat A, provides a global low cost two-way data communications network using a small terminal and omni-directional antenna - suitable for vessels of any size, low power-consumption. This system provides the services of global two-way store-and-forward messaging, distress alerting, reception of MSI, EGCSafetyNET and FleetNET. Inmarsat C is capable of data reporting and polling and is used extensively for SSAS and LRIT reporting.
Inmarsat FleetBroadband	Provides broadband and voice services simultaneously on a global basis. A compact antenna used in conjunction with three different terminal types can offer standard IP of up to 432bps, and streaming IP of up to 256 kbps. A distress facility is standard for all terminals.
Inmarsat GAN	(Global Area Network) supporting high speed data, ISDN compatible service @ 64 kbit/s.
Inmarsat mini-C	mini-C offers the same primary functions as Inmarsat C through a lower-power terminal. It is also GMDSS compatible and meets the requirements for Ship Security Alert Systems (SSAS).
Inop	Inoperative.
Int	International.
International Alphabet Number 5 (IA5)	(Also known as ASCII, IRA5 & ISO646) — a standard alpha-numeric character set based on 7-bit binary codes.
International Atomic Time	see TAI.
International DSC frequencies	Frequencies designated in the Radio Regulations for exclusive use for DSC on an international basis.
International NAVTEX Service	The coordinated broadcast and automatic reception of Maritime Safety Information by means of narrow-band direct-printing on 518 kHz. See also: NAVTEX.
IOPP	International Oil Pollution Prevention.
IOR	Indian Ocean Region, coverage area of Inmarsat satellite.
IPS	Ionospheric Prediction Service.
IR	Infra-red.
Iridium	Mobile Satellite Service Provider (Iridium Communications Inc.).
Iridium Safety Gateway	The central system responsible for managing GMDSS communications within the Iridium Network
ISDN	Integrated Service Digital Network.
ISL	Interstation Signalling Links, used to pass information between LESs and the NCSs in an Ocean Region.
ISPS	International Ship and Port facility Security. The IMO adopted changes to SOLAS in December 2002, as part of agreeing the new ISPS code, within the changes, a Ship Security Alert System (SSAS) was specified. The ISPS Code came into effect on 1 July 2004.
ISSC	International Ship Security Certificate.
ITOFAR	Interrogated Time Offset Frequency Agile Racon.
ITU	International Telecommunication Union.
ITZ	Inshore Traffic Zone.
J2B	Single sideband suppressed carrier containing quantised or digital information with the use of a modulating sub carrier used in DSC systems.
J3E	Telephony using amplitude modulation: single sideband, suppressed carrier.
Jan	January.
JCG	Japan Coast Guard.
JCOMM	The Joint WMO-IOC Technical Commission on Oceanography and Marine Meteorology.
JRCC	Joint Rescue Coordination Centre. A Rescue Coordination Centre responsible for both aeronautical and maritime search and rescue.
Jul	July.
Jun	June.
kbps	kilobit per second.
kHz	Kilohertz.

Kilobit (Kbits)	1 Kbit = 1024 bits = 128 characters (a character in ASCII is a letter, digit or a special character, represented by a byte or a group of 8 bits). This code is used in computer-to-computer communication.
km	Kilometre(s).
kW	Kilowatt(s).
L	Lightship.
L1	GPS primary frequency, 1575·42 MHz.
L2	GPS secondary frequency, 1227·60 MHz.
LANBY	Large Navigational Buoy.
Lat	Latitude.
LBP	Length Between Perpendiculars.
Ldg	Leading.
LEO	Low Earth Orbit.
LEOSAR	COSPAS-SARSAT Low Earth Orbit Search and Rescue polar orbiting satellite system.
LES	Land Earth Station. An earth station in the fixed-satellite service or, in the maritime mobile-satellite service, located at the specified fixed point on land to provide a feeder link for the maritime mobile-satellite service. This may also be referred to as a Coast Earth Station (CES).
LESO	Land Earth Station Operator. An Inmarsat service provider which owns and operates the LES.
LF	Low Frequency (30 - 300 kHz).
LH	Lighthouse.
LOA	Length Over All.
Local Warning	A navigational warning which covers inshore waters, often within the limits or jurisdiction of a harbour or port authority.
Locating	The finding of ships, aircraft, units or persons in distress.
Locating signals	Transmissions intended to facilitate the finding of a mobile unit in distress or the location of survivors using DF or 9 GHz radar.
Londonlength	Approximate length between the stem and the stern x 96%.
Long	Longitude.
LORAN	LOng RAnge Navigation.
LORAN-C	LOng RAnge Navigation-C. This is a low frequency electronic position fixing system.
LPG	Liquefied Petroleum Gas.
LPS	Local Port Service.
LRIT	Long Range Identification and Tracking. The new regulation on LRIT is included in SOLAS Chapter V on Safety of Navigation. The Maritime Safety Committee (MSC 81), adopted a new SOLAS Amendment on LRIT (MSC.202 (81)). This amends SOLAS Chapter V, Regulation 19-1 and requires that ships shall be fitted with equipment to transmit automatically the LRIT information (ship's ID, position, date/time of position). LRIT data can be provided, using Inmarsat C, mini-C or D+
LT	Local Time.
Lt	Light.
Lt F	Light Float.
Lt Ho	Light House.
Lt V	Light Vessel.
LUT	Local User Terminal. A ground receiving station which receives alert data from COSPAS and SARSAT satellites.
LW	Low Water.
m	Metre(s).
M	Mountain Station.
MAFOR	Maritime Forecast Code.
Mar	March.
MAREP	Mariner Reporting Program.
Maritime Distress Channel	An Inmarsat satellite channel between a ship in distress and a Land Earth Station.
Maritime mobile service	A mobile service between coast stations and ship stations, or between ship stations, or between associated on board communication stations; survival craft stations and Emergency Position-Indicating Radiobeacon (EPIRB) stations may also participate in this service.
Maritime mobile-satellite service	A mobile-satellite service in which Mobile Earth Stations are located onboard ships; survival craft stations and emergency position-indicating radiobeacon stations may also participate in this service.
Maritime SAR plan	A Search and Rescue plan developed by coastal States.
MARPOL	International Convention for the Prevention of Pollution from Ships, 1973.

MAS	Maritime Assistance Service.
Mar	March.
MBM	Multi Buoy Mooring.
MCA	Maritime and Coastguard Agency.
MCC	Mission Control Centre. A COSPAS-SARSAT ground system element which receives alert data from its local user terminal(s) and distributes that information to affiliated SAR points of contact or forwards it to other MCCs. The MCC may also receive alert data from another MCC and receive and distribute COSPAS-SARSAT system information.
MCC service area	The area for which an MCC accepts responsibility for the distribution of COSPAS-SARSAT alert data. The service area includes sub-areas serviced by SAR points of contact (SPOCs).
MCS	Master Control Station.
MCTS	Marine Communications and Traffic Services.
MDR	Marine Domain Awareness.
MEDILINK	MEDIcal LINK call.
MENAS	Middle East Navigation Aids Service.
MES	Mobile Earth Station — Inmarsat device installed on a ship (or on fixed installation in a marine environment) to enable the user to communicate to and from shore-based subscribers, via a selected satellite and LES.
Met	Meteorological.
METAREA	METeorological AREA: A geographical sea area established for the purose of coordinating the broadcast of marine meteorological information within the IMO/WMO WWMIWS. The limits are similar to the NAVAREAs within the World-Wide Navigational Warning Service.
METAREA Coordinator	The authority charged with coordinating marine meteorological information broadcasts by one or more National Meteorological Services, or appropriate national authority, acting as Preparation or Issuing Services within the METAREA.
MF	Medium frequency (300 - 3000 kHz).
MGN	Marine Guidance Note. Issued by the MCA.
MHz	Megahertz.
MID	Maritime Identification Digits.
MIN	Marine Information Note. Issued by the MCA.
min(s)	Minute(s).
MKD	Minimum Keyboard Display.
MMSI	Maritime Mobile Service Identity.
MOB	Man overboard.
Mon	Monday.
MOU	Memorandum of Understanding.
MPDS	Mobile Packet Data Service.
MRCC	Maritime Rescue Coordination Centre.
MRSC	Maritime Rescue coordination Sub-Centre.
ms	Millisecond(s).
m/s	Metres per Second.
MSI	Maritime Safety Information. Navigational and meteorological warnings, meteorological forecasts, distress alerts and other urgent safety related information broadcast to ships.
MSK	Minimum Shift Keying.
MSL	Mean Sea Level.
MSLP	Mean Sea Level Pressure.
MSN	Merchant Shipping Notice. Issued by the MCA.
mt	Metric Tonnes.
Multipath	Signal arrival at a receiver's antenna by way of two or more different paths such as direct, line-of-sight path and one that includes reflections from nearby objects.
N	North.
n mile	International nautical mile.
n/a, N/A	Not Applicable.
National Coordinator	The national authority charged with collating and issuing coastal warnings within a national area of responsibility.
National Hydrographic Office	A National organisation responsible for collecting and distributing navigational warnings.
National Meteorological Office	A National organisation responsible for collecting and distributing meteorological warnings and forecasts.
National NAVTEX service	The coordinated broadcast and automatic reception of Maritime Safety Information by means of narrow-band direct-printing using frequencies other than 518 kHz and languages as decided by the Administration concerned. See also: NAVTEX and International NAVTEX service..

NAVAREA	NAVigational AREA: One of the sea areas into which the world's oceans are divided for the dissemination of navigational and meteorological warnings.
NAVAREA Coordinator	The authority charged with coordinating, collating and issuing NAVAREA warnings for a designated NAVAREA.
NAVAREA warning	Long- range warning broadcasts issued by an area coordinator of the world-wide navigational warning service for his area and broadcast by CRS(s) or LES(s) to cover the whole of the area, for which the area coordinator is responsible, and parts of an adjacent area.
NAVDAT	A digital system for the broadcasting of Navigational Data on the 500 kHz frequency. ITU-R M.2010 refers.
NAVIP	Navigational Warning (Russia). NAVIPs contain information about dangers to navigation in the coastal waters of countries other than Russia and the high seas areas. NAVIPs are broadcast in Russian.
NAV-msg	Navigation Message. A 37,500-bit data message included in the GPS signal. The message, sent at a rate of 50 bits per second, includes the satellite ephemeris, clock data, almanac and other information about the satellites and their signals.
NAVTEX	Narrow-Band Direct-Printing telegraphy system for transmission of navigational and meteorological warnings and urgent information to ships. See also: International NAVTEX Service.
NAVTEX Coordinator	The authority charged with operating and managing one or more NAVTEX stations broadcasting maritime safety information as part of the International NAVTEX service.
NAVTEX Service Area	A unique and precisely defined sea area for which maritime safety information is provided from a particular NAVTEX transmitter.
NAV warning	NAVAREA warning.
NBDP	Narrow-Band Direct-Printing; automated telegraphy as used by the NAVTEX system and telex-over-radio.
NCC	Network Control Centre.
NCS	Network Coordination Station (for Inmarsat).
NCSR	IMO Sub-committee for Navigation, Communications and Search & Rescue.
NE	North East.
NM	Notice to Mariners.
NMOC	National Maritime Operations Centre
Nov	November.
NP	Nautical Publication.
NS or **ns**	Nanosecond.
NSR	Northern Sea Route.
nt	Net Tonnage.
NW	North West.
OBS	The station accepts messages concerning weather observations by ships.
OCC	Operations Control Centre (for Inmarsat).
Occas	Occasional.
Oct	October.
OFCOM	Office of Communication.
On-scene communications	Communications between the ship in distress and assisting units.
OSC	On-Scene Coordinator. The commander of a rescue unit designated to coordinate surface search and rescue operations within a specified search area.
OTF	Optimum Transmitting Frequency.
P	Pilot-balloon; upper wind observations by optical tracking of a free balloon.
PA	Position Approximate.
Paired frequencies	Frequencies which are associated in pairs; each pair consisting of one transmitting and one receiving frequency.
PEC	Pilotage Exemption Certificate.
PFSO	Port Facility Security Officer.
PLB	Personal Locator Beacon.
PMO	Port Meteorological Office(r).
PNT	Position, Navigation and Timing.
POB	Persons On Board — total number of.
Polar Orbiting Satellite Service	A service which is based on polar orbiting satellites which receive and relay distress alerts from satellite EPIRBs and which provides their position.
POR	Pacific Ocean Region, coverage area of Inmarsat satellite.

Port Operations Service	A maritime mobile service in or near a port between coast stations and ship stations or between ship stations, in which messages are restricted to those relating to the operational handling, the movement and safety of ships and, in emergency, to the safety of persons. It does not include public correspondence.
Positioning	Establishing the geographical place of the unit in distress (normally expressed in degrees and minutes of latitude and longitude).
PRIP	Coastal Warning (Russia). PRIPs contain information for the safety of navigation in the coastal waters of Russia and the Arctic Ocean. PRIPs are broadcast by maritime radio stations in Russian. NAVTEX coastal warnings are transmitted in English.
PSK	Phase Shift Keying.
PSTN	Public switched Telephone Network.
Pt	Point.
PTTI	Precise Time and Time Interval.
Public Correspondence	Any telecommunication which the offices and stations must, by reason of their being at the disposal of the public, accept for transmission.
PV	Pilot Vessel.
QHM	Queen's Harbour Master.
R	Radiosonde; atmospheric pressure, temperature and humidity observations in the upper air obtained by electronic means.
Racon	RAdar BeaCON.
Radiolocation- Satellite Service	A radiodetermination satellite service used for the purpose of radiolocation.
Radio Regulations	Means the Radio Regulations annexed to, or regarded as being annexed to, the most recent International Telecommunication Convention which is in force at any time.
RANP	Regional Air Navigation Plan.
RCC	Rescue Coordination Centre. A unit responsible for promoting efficient organisation of search and rescue (SAR) services and for coordinating the conduct of SAR operations within a SAR region.
RCF	Remote Communications Facility. This is a term used by the US Coastguard to describe HF radio stations that are remotely controlled by Communications Command (COMMCOM) – (NMN).
Rep	Reported.
Rescue unit	A unit composed of trained personnel provided with equipment suitable for the expeditious conduct of SAR operations.
RF or RFx	Radio Frequency.
RG	Radio Direction-finding Station.
RR	ITU Radio Regulations (as amended).
RSC	Rescue Sub-Centre. A subordinate to the Rescue Coordination Centre, established to complement the latter according to particular provisions of the responsible authorities.
RT	Radio telephony.
RTCM	Radio Technical Commission for Maritime services.
RTCM SC-104	The special committee of the Radio Technical Commission for Marine Services that developed recommended standards for DGPS.
RT (HF)	Radio Telephony (High Frequency).
RT (MF)	Radio Telephony (Medium Frequency).
RTTY	Radio Teletype.
Rx	Receiver.
RX	Retransmission.
S.	Saint.
s	Second(s).
S	South.
SafetyCast	International Iridium SafetyCast service means the coordinated broadcast and automatic reception of Maritime Safety Information and Search and Rescue related information via the Enhanced Group Call system, using the English language.
SafetyNET	The International SafetyNET Service (provided by Inmarsat Global Ltd), which comprises the coordinated broadcast and automatic reception of Maritime Safety Information via the Enhanced Group Call (EGC) system, using the English language.
SAR	Search And Rescue.
SAR Convention	International Convention on Search and Rescue 1979.
SARSAT	Serch And Rescue Satellite Aided Tracking.
SART	Search And Rescue Transponder.
SAS	Satellite Access Station.

Sat	Saturday.
Satellite Network Operations Centre (SNOC)	A terrestrial part of the Iridium mobile-satellite system which controls the Iridium satellites and manages the Iridium system overall.
SATNAV	SATellite NAVigation.
SBAS	Satellite Based Augmentation Systems.
SBM	Single Buoy Mooring.
SBP	Shore Based Pilotage.
SBT	Segregated Ballast Tanks.
SC	SAR Coordinator.
SCADA	Supervisory Control and Data Acquisition.
sdwt	Summer Dead Weight Tonnes.
SE	South East.
Sea Area A1, A2, A3 and A4	Under the GMDSS the (radio) equipment required to be carried by ships is determined in principle by the ship's area of operation; these areas are designated as 'Sea Area A1', 'Sea Area A2', 'Sea Area A3' or 'Sea Area A4'.
Search And Rescue (SAR) region	An area of defined dimensions within which search and rescue services are provided.
Sec	Seconds.
Sep	September.
Seq	Sequence.
SES	Ship Earth Station, see **MES**.
SHIPPOS	SHIP POSition Reporting Service.
Ship station	A mobile station in the maritime mobile service located on board a vessel which is not permanently moored, other than a survival craft station.
Sig	Signal.
Single frequency	The same frequency used for transmission and reception.
SITOR	Simplex Telex Over Radio.
SITREP	SITuation REPort.
SMC	SAR Mission Controller.
SMS	Short Messaging Service.
SNAC	Single Network Access Code.
Solar Cycle	Solar activity changes over a period of, on average, 11 years. At solar maximum, the solar activity is high and so too the EUV (Extreme Ultra-Violet) radiation output which affects the ionosphere. At solar minimum, the opposite is true.
SOLAS	The International Convention on the Safety Of Life at Sea 1974 (SOLAS), as amended.
Sous-CROSS	Sous-Centres Régionaux Opérationels de Surveillance et de Sauvetage (Regional sub-centre of operations for surveillance and maritime rescue, MRSC).
SPM	Single Point Mooring.
SPOC	SAR Point Of Contact. In the COSPAS-SARSAT system mission control centres (MCCs), rescue coordination centres (RCCs) and other established and recognized national points of contact which can accept responsibility for the coordination of the rapid and effective transfer of alert data to enable the rescue of people in distress.
SPS	Standard Position Service. The GPS single receiver (stand-alone) positioning service available to any user on a continuous world wide basis.
SRR	Search and Rescue Region. An area of defined dimensions within which search and rescue services are provided.
SRS	SAR Sub-region.
SRU	Search and Rescue Unit.
SSAS	Ship Security Alert System. Resolution XI-2/6 states that the Ship Security Alert System shall provide ships with two alarm buttons, which can be activated in case of a piracy or terrorist attack. The alarm is a covert signal, no sound and no flashing lights.
SSB	Single SideBand.
SST	Sea Surface Temperature.
Stn, STN	Station.
Sun	Sunday.
Survival craft	A craft capable of sustaining the lives of persons in distress from the time of abandoning ship.
SW	South West.
SWL	Safe Working Load.
System information	In the COSPAS-SARSAT system tabulated data (ephemeris and time calibration) that affect the determination of distress beacon locations using the satellite sub-track; current status of all system elements; information related to interference.

TAI	International Atomic Time is determined by the comparison of the reading of very accurate (better than 1 microsecond a day) atomic clocks located at national observatories throughout the world. Unlike UT1, TAI does not change with variations in the rate of the Earth's rotation. TAI provides the most accurate and uniform unit of time interval for scientific purposes. The fundamental unit of TAI is the SI second, defined as "the duration of 9 192 631 770 periods of the radiation corresponding to the transition between two hyperfine levels of the ground state of the cesium 133 atom".
TBC	To Be Confirmed.
TBD	To Be Determined.
Tel	Telephone.
Teleport	A terrestrial part of the Iridium mobile-satellite system which communicates between the Iridium satellites and the gateway and Satellite Network Operations Centre terrestrial parts.
Thurs	Thursday.
Time Calibration	Data used to relate the SARSAT satellite time code in an alert message to the actual elapsed time from a known satellite time epoch.
TLX	Telex.
TMAS	The maritime TeleMedical Assistance Service.
TOR	Telex Over Radio.
Tr	Tower.
TSS	Traffic Separation Scheme.
TTAC	Telemetry, Tracking and Control.
Tues	Tuesday.
Tx	Transmitter; Transmission.
UHF	Ultra High Frequency (300 - 3000 MHz).
UIR	Upper flight Information Region.
UK	United Kingdom.
UKHO	UK Hydrographic Office.
ULCC	Ultra Large Crude Carrier.
UT	Universal Time.
UT0	Uncorrected Universal Time.
UT1	UT0 corrected for polar variation.
UT2	UT0 corrected for polar and seasonal variations.
UTC	Coordinated Universal Time is a composite time scale, broadcast in many radio time signals. UTC corresponds exactly in rate with TAI but differs from it by an integral number of seconds. UTC is adjusted by the insertion or deletion of seconds (positive or negative leap seconds) to ensure that the departure of UTC from UT1 does not exceed +/- 0·9 seconds. Stations listed in the Radio Time Signals section of this volume broadcast time signals in the UTC time scale unless otherwise indicated in the station entry. Leap seconds are notified in advance as corrections to TABLE 1 within the RADIO TIME SIGNALS section.
VDES	A VHF Data Exchange System which together with a satellite component (VDE-SAT) is designed to augment AIS and provide intership and ship-shore data exchange and other related applications.
VDL	VHF Data Link. A set of frequencies, messages and protocols forming a maritime information exchange; used for AIS and associated applications.
VHF	Very High Frequency (30 - 300 MHz).
VLCC	Very Large Crude Carrier.
VLF	Very Low Frequency (3 - 30 kHz).
VOS	Voluntary Observing Ship Programme.
VSAT	Very Small Aperture Terminal.
VTM	Vessel Traffic Management.
VTMIS	Vessel Traffic Management and Information System.
VTMS	Vessel Traffic Management System.
VTS	Vessel Traffic Service.
W	West; Watt; Radiowind; upper wind observations by tracking of a free balloon by electronic means
Wed	Wednesday.
wef	With effect from.
WMO	World Meteorological Organization.
WP	Wind Profiler.
WT	Radio (Wireless) Telegraphy.
WT (HF)	Radio (Wireless) Telegraphy (High Frequency).
WT (MF)	Radio (Wireless) Telegraphy (Medium Frequency).

WWMIWS	World-Wide Met-Ocean Information and Warning Service. A service established by the International Maritime Organisation and World Meteorological Organisation for the purpose of coordinating the transmission of met-ocean Maritime Safety Information in geographical areas.
WWNWS	World-Wide Navigational Warning Service. A service established by the International Maritime Organization and International Hydrographic Organization for the purpose of coordinating the transmissions of radio navigational warnings in geographical areas.
www	World-Wide Web (INTERNET).
µs	Microsecond(s).
Note:	In the WMO Station tables P, R and W are combined as necessary to indicate simultaneous upper-air observations of the different types.

NOTES

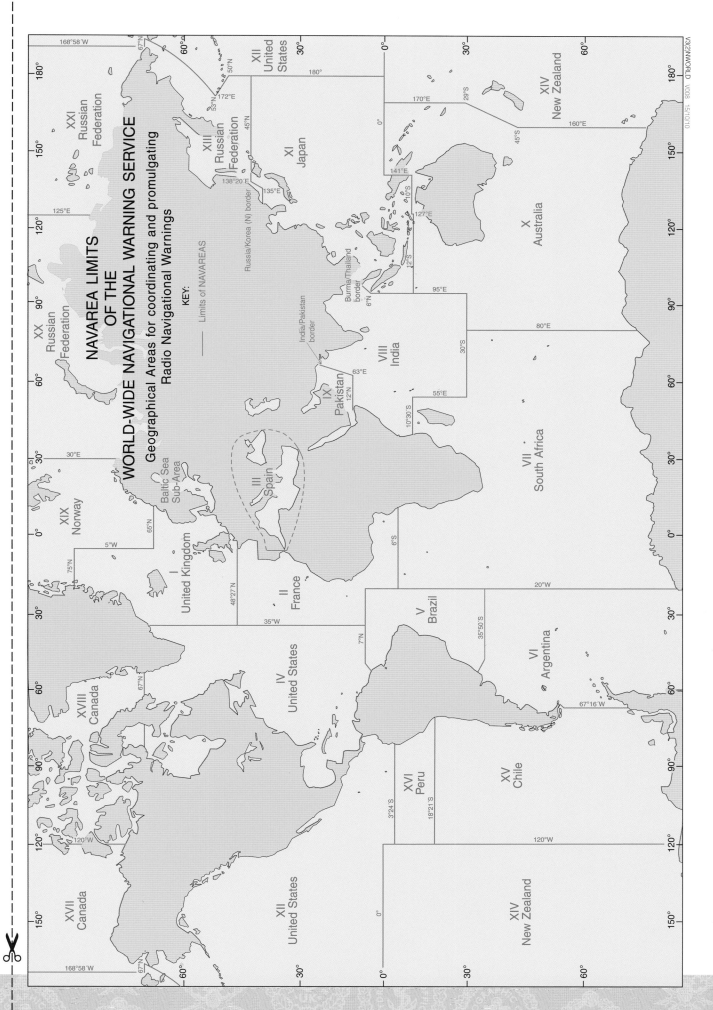

NAVAREA LIMITS
OF THE
WORLD-WIDE NAVIGATIONAL WARNING SERVICE

Geographical Areas for coordinating and promulgating
Radio Navigational Warnings

KEY:

—— Limits of NAVAREAS

GLOBAL MARITIME DISTRESS AND SAFETY SYSTEM (GMDSS)

INTRODUCTION

The concept of a GMDSS began at the International Maritime Organization (IMO) in 1973. It entered into force in February 1999, following a 7- year introductory period. The requirement for ships to comply with the GMDSS is prescribed by SOLAS Chapter IV and applies to all passenger vessels and all cargo vessels over 300 GT, if on international voyages.

The GMDSS has been constructed according to the IMO Master Plan, historically published annually but superseded in 2019 by the GISIS (Global Integrated Shipping Information System) GISIS. The IMO have granted public access to GISIS on a registration basis via the IMO website: https://gisis.imo.org/

The GISIS GMDSS module follows the same structure as the Master Plan and shows the detail behind the world network. Information contained in GISIS is maintained by IMO Member States who have administrators authorised to make changes, update and submit information. Details are also included of Rescue Coordination Centres (RCCs), each responsible for a given Search and Rescue Region (SRR).

Each RCC is able to initiate Maritime Safety Information (MSI), which is broadcast in telex format via satellite and/or terrestrial radio.

GMDSS communication between ships and the RCCs is carried out using satellite and/or terrestrial radio sub-systems. The satellite sub-systems provide communications between ships and shore, and the terrestrial sub-systems provide for both ship-shore and ship-ship communications (see Figure 1).

The satellite sub-systems include earth stations for all the GMDSS satellite services and for the Cospas-Sarsat service – the former provides both GMDSS and commercial services, the latter provides a distress alerting system which responds to signals from a portable transmitter known as an Emergency Position-Indicating Radio Beacon (EPIRB). The satellite sub-systems are described later in this volume.

It will be seen that the world has been equipped with many HF radio stations for long-range working, and several hundred MF and VHF stations for shorter ranges, each of which is listed in the ALRS suite of publications.

The GMDSS terrestrial component uses an automatic calling device to make initial contact, after which communications are carried out by voice or telex (Narrow-Band Direct-Printing or NBDP) according to normal radio procedures. The automatic calling system is known as Digital Selective Calling (DSC).

Many types of vessel, regardless of size, are not required to comply with GMDSS even when on an international voyage. This includes fishing vessels, warships, pleasure yachts not engaged in trade, wooden ships of primitive build, ships not propelled by mechanical means and vessels in the Great Lakes. There is no internationally agreed standard of service for these vessels, although some countries encourage their non-GMDSS vessels to participate in the GMDSS on a voluntary basis.

Provision of distress and safety services for non-GMDSS vessels is determined by individual flag states, and many countries continue to provide Maritime Safety services of a non-GMDSS nature. These are fully described in ALRS Volume 1 (which includes telemedical assistance services), Volume 3 (maritime safety services) and Volume 6 (which includes ship reporting procedures).

The GMDSS is, in effect, interleaved with pre-existing systems, which have not been prohibited in any way, but merely made optional.

The maritime communication procedures, GMDSS and non-GMDSS, are contained in the Radio Regulations 2020 published by the ITU. The procedures for initiating and responding to DSC calls are described in the latest ITU Recommendation M.541.

The various components which make up a DSC call are described in the latest ITU Recommendation M.493, the body of which is summarised later in this Section.

GMDSS watch keeping at sea must be maintained in accordance with SOLAS Regulations 12 and 16. The latter requires that a primary GMDSS operator shall be nominated to carry primary responsibility for communications during distress incidents. The provisions of STCW 95 must also be observed. The main consideration being that when shipboard communications are not in progress, the radio operator (usually the bridge watchkeeper) is required to monitor two essential conditions:

1. That the equipment is operational (i.e. switched on) and
2. That it is correctly set up to perform the nine GMDSS functions required by SOLAS, described below.

This is achieved by carrying out regular statutory tests. STCW 95 also requires that the primary GMDSS operator must be nominated on the ship's emergency muster list and adds further duties such as ensuring that GMDSS communications are conducted according to IMO and ITU procedures and that any necessary instruction is given to other operators.

The GMDSS, like all communication systems, continues to evolve with advancing technology. For example the identifying number of ITU Recommendation M.493-14 indicates the fourteenth version of the recommendation. Additionally, the following two IMO Committees publish circulars from time to time, to modify procedures and technical standards.

1. Navigation, Communication Search and Rescue (NCSR)
2. The Maritime Safety Committee (MSC)

It can be seen from the above that the GMDSS facilities, regulations and procedures are contained in several publications, e.g. IMO SOLAS Chapter IV; IMO GMDSS Handbook; IAMSAR Manual; STCW 95 Guidance on Radio Watchkeeping; ITU Radio Regulations and other ITU publications.

The extracts reproduced in ALRS Volume 5 should always be read in conjunction with the full authoritative regulations. In the case of any discrepancy, the latest version of the source document or regulation will prevail.

Basic concept of the Global Maritime Distress and Safety System

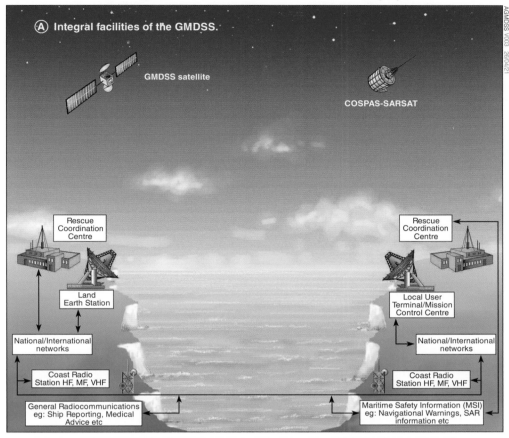

Ⓐ Integral facilities of the GMDSS.

GMDSS satellite

COSPAS-SARSAT

Rescue Coordination Centre

Rescue Coordination Centre

Land Earth Station

Local User Terminal/Mission Control Centre

National/International networks

National/International networks

Coast Radio Station HF, MF, VHF

Coast Radio Station HF, MF, VHF

General Radiocommunications eg: Ship Reporting, Medical Advice etc

Maritime Safety Information (MSI) eg: Navigational Warnings, SAR information etc

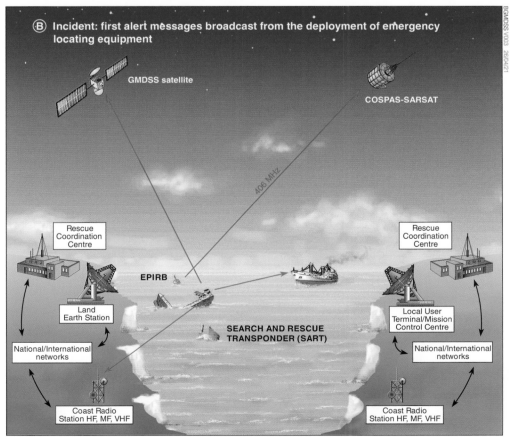

Ⓑ Incident: first alert messages broadcast from the deployment of emergency locating equipment

GMDSS satellite

COSPAS-SARSAT

406 MHz

Rescue Coordination Centre

Rescue Coordination Centre

EPIRB

Land Earth Station

Local User Terminal/Mission Control Centre

National/International networks

National/International networks

SEARCH AND RESCUE TRANSPONDER (SART)

Coast Radio Station HF, MF, VHF

Coast Radio Station HF, MF, VHF

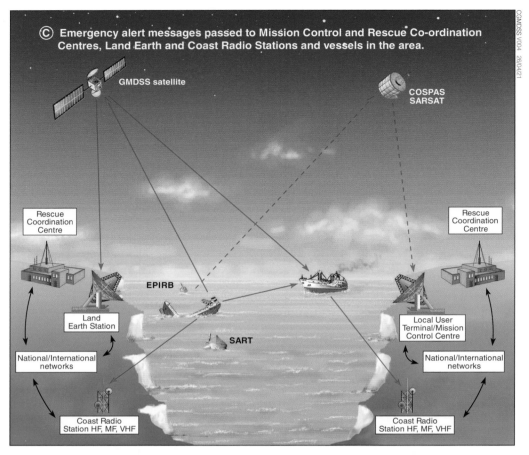

© Emergency alert messages passed to Mission Control and Rescue Co-ordination Centres, Land Earth and Coast Radio Stations and vessels in the area.

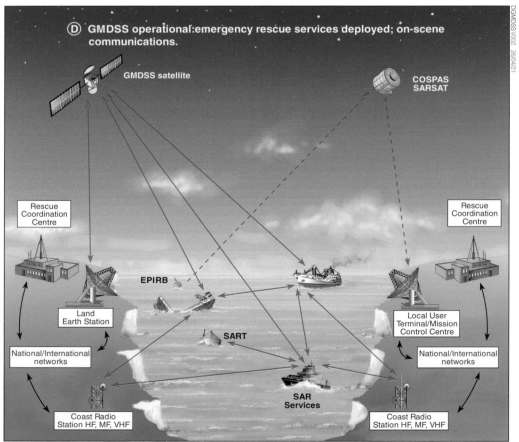

Ⓓ GMDSS operational:emergency rescue services deployed; on-scene communications.

Continued on next page

OPERATIONAL DETAILS

The type of equipment to be carried by each vessel, together with its maintenance arrangements and operating personnel is determined by a vessel's area of operation. Four Sea Areas have been defined according to the coverage of VHF, MF, HF Coast Radio Services and Inmarsat Services as follows.

DESCRIPTIONS OF GMDSS SEA AREAS

Sea Area Description	Distance	Radio	Frequencies	EPIRBs	Survival Craft
A1: Within range of at least one VHF Coast Station in which continuous DSC alerting is available.	Depends on antenna height at shore-based VHF station, around 20-50 n miles	VHF	156·525 MHz (Ch 70) for DSC, 156·8 MHz (Ch 16) RT	406 MHz Cospas-Sarsat	9 GHz radar transponder (SART); VHF portable radio (Ch 16 and one other frequency)
A2: An area excluding Sea Area A1, within the radiotelephone range of at least one MF Coast Station in which continuous DSC alerting is available.	About 50-250 n miles	MF VHF	As above, plus, 2187·5 kHz DSC, 2182 kHz RT, 2174·5 kHz NBDP, 518 kHz NAVTEX	406 MHz Cospas-Sarsat	as above
A3: An area excluding Sea Areas A1 and A2, within the coverage of an Inmarsat geostationary satellite in which continuous alerting is available.	In the range of: 76°N-76°S	HF or Satellite MF VHF	As above, plus 1·5-1·6 GHz alerting or as A1 and A2 plus all HF frequencies	406 MHz Cospas-Sarsat	as above
A4: An area outside Sea Areas A1, A2 and A3.	North of approximately 76°N or South of approximately 76°S	HF MF VHF		406 MHz Cospas-Sarsat	as above

BASIC EQUIPMENT FOR SOLAS SHIPS
(minimum requirements including duplication of equipment)

(SOLAS 1974, as amended, Chapter IV and IMO Resolution A.702(17))

Equipment	A1	A2	A3 Inmarsat Solution	A3 HF Solution	A4
VHF with DSC	X	X	X	X	X
DSC watch receiver Ch 70	X	X	X	X	X
MF telephony with MF DSC		X	X		
DSC watch receiver 2187·5 kHz		X	X		
Inmarsat Ship Earth Station with EGC receiver			X		
MF/HF telephony with DSC and NBDP				X	X
DSC watch receiver MF/HF				X	X
Duplicated VHF with DSC			X	X	X
Duplicated Inmarsat Ship Earth Station			X		
Duplicated MF/HF telephony with DSC and NBDP					X
NAVTEX receiver 518 kHz	X	X	X	X	X
EGC receiver	X[1]	X[1]		X	X
Float-free satellite EPIRB	X	X	X	X	X
Radar transponder Search and Rescue Transponder (SART)	X[2]	X[2]	X[2]	X[2]	X[2]
Hand held GMDSS VHF transceiver	X[3]	X[3]	X[3]	X[3]	X[3]

Continued overleaf

Equipment	A1	A2	A3 Inmarsat Solution	A3 HF Solution	A4
For passenger ships the following has applied since 1st July 1997					
"Distress panel" (SOLAS Ch.IV/6.4 and 6.6)	X	X	X	X	X
Automatic updating of position to all relevant radiocommunication equipment (SOLAS Ch.IV/6.5). This also applies for cargo ships from 1st July 2002 (Chapter IV, new Regulation 18)	X	X	X	X	X
Two-way-on-scene radiocommunication on 121·5 or 123·1 MHz from the navigating bridge (SOLAS Ch.IV/7.5)	X	X	X	X	X

[1] Outside NAVTEX coverage area.
[2] Cargo ships between 300 and 500 gt.: 1 set. Cargo ships of 500 gt. and upwards and passenger ships: 2 sets.
[3] Cargo ships between 300 and 500 gt.: 2 sets. Cargo ships of 500 gt. and upwards and passenger ships: 3 sets.

Recommended installation

In order to meet all requirements and recommendations concerning the location of all units included in a GMDSS radio installation, it is recommended to establish either a "radio work station" in connection with the navigating bridge, or a separate "communication office" outside the navigation bridge with remote controls on the bridge. It must be emphasised, however, that the suggestions in sub-sections below are to be considered as guidelines only. Other solutions and combinations are equally acceptable as long as the general requirements and recommendations outlined are fulfilled. (SOLAS 1974, as amended, Chapter IV, COM/Circ. 105 and ISO 8468: 1990(E)) An antenna plan should be available as per COMSAR/Circ.32 and SN/Circ.227.

Radio workstation

1. The work station should be located in the aft of the navigation bridge so that the navigator can operate the radio equipment whilst maintaining a view of the navigation aids / screens or equipment. If the work station and the rest of the navigation bridge are separated by a wall, it must be made of glass or fitted with windows. There must be no lockable door between the workstation and the navigation bridge.
2. When the work station is being used during night time, a curtain must be provided in order to avoid dazzling effect from the lights.
3. All mandatory radio equipment (except mandatory VHF) should be located in the radio work station. Watch receivers may alternatively be located elsewhere on the navigation bridge.
   Note: It is essential that satisfactory watch (clearly audible signals/visual alarms) can be maintained at the position from which the ship is normally navigated. If it is not possible to maintain satisfactory watch, alarm indicators on MF or MF/HF and Inmarsat equipment, including EGC printer, must be located outside this work station. (A.807(19) Annex item 3.2 regarding EGC, and A.610(15), A.806(19) Annex D, item 8, regarding MF and MF/HF DSC requirements, and SOLAS 1997 Chapter IV.12 regarding watch-keeping requirements)
4. MF/HF RF power amplifiers should be located in a separate and screened room. Antenna tuners should, as a general rule, be located outdoors below the antenna.

Communication office

1. The communication office may be located as required by the shipping company, e.g. in connection to the Captain's office. It should be possible to make public calls and perform general radiocommunications on MF or HF and/or through satellite from the communication office, if such calls cannot be made from a suitable location elsewhere on the ship.
2. All equipment for written correspondence, as well as telephone services for MF/HF and Inmarsat, should be located in the communication office.
3. The remote operation panels for the mandatory equipment must be located in a central position on the navigation bridge, in order to fulfil the requirements for transmitting distress alerts from the navigation bridge.
   Note: Consideration should also be given to the requirements for navigational safety communication and subsequent distress communications on MF or HF. When MF/HF DSC is included in the mandatory basic or duplicated radio equipment, it must be possible to conduct distress and safety communications from the navigating position, and the MF/HF DSC controller must be installed in this position. (IMO Resolutions A.804(19) and A.806(19))
4. Watch receivers and NAVTEX/EGC receivers should be located on the navigation bridge.
5. VHF transceivers with DSC used for navigational safety should be located in the front of the navigation bridge.

Ships with Integrated Bridge System (IBS)

1. Ships constructed to satisfy the IBS requirements for single-manned navigating bridge should have the operation panels for mandatory GMDSS equipment installed as close to the conning position as possible.
2. Equipment for the transfer of radiotelephone calls via radio (VHF, MF or MF/HF) or satellite to other areas of the ship should be placed close to the other GMDSS equipment near the conning position.
3. It should be possible also to operate printed communications (data communications via radio and/or Inmarsat) from other areas of the ship.

Ships with Integrated Radio Communication Systems (IRCS)

1. The IRCS is a system in which individual radiocommunication equipment and installations are used as sensors, i.e. without the need for their own control units, providing outputs to and accepting inputs from the operator's position, called work stations. Such work stations are called "GMDSS work stations" if they include control and monitoring of all equipment and installations provided on a ship for the GMDSS which are also suitable for general radiocommunications. The IRCS workstation should be installed in a console located in a central position on the navigation bridge. Transmitting and receiving equipment may be located outside the navigation bridge.
2. The IRCS should comprise at least two GMDSS work stations each connected to each GMDSS radiocommunication sensor over a network or connection system. At least two printers should be installed. All requirements laid down in SOLAS 1974, as amended, Chapter IV, should be fulfilled. (IMO Resolution A.811(19)).

Drawings

General

Specified drawings (plan of the radio installation) should be prepared well before the work on a new building or reconstruction of ships or offshore units is stated. Insufficient or missing drawings may result in deficiencies during radio survey and could lead to expensive repair costs later (IMO Resolution A.746(18), section 8).

For the radio installation the following drawings should be prepared:

1. Antenna drawing:
2. Radio arrangement drawing (all equipment including fuse locations); and
3. Wiring diagram (to include fuses for all equipment).

For new buildings the antenna and radio arrangement drawings should at least be of size 1:50.

Approved "as installed" wiring diagram, radio arrangement, as well as antenna drawings, should be kept available on board the ship for presentation during radio survey, etc.

Antenna drawings

Antenna drawings should show all antennas seen from fore or aft position, the port or starboard position and from above. This applies to the following antennas:

1. All transmitting antennas including location of antenna tuner;
2. All receiving antennas including GNSS antennas;
3. Radar antennas;
4. Satellite communication antennas; and
5. The location of float-free EPIRBs.

Changes in the antenna arrangement

When changes are made in the antenna arrangement, modified antenna drawings should be prepared.

An example antenna plan is shown below.

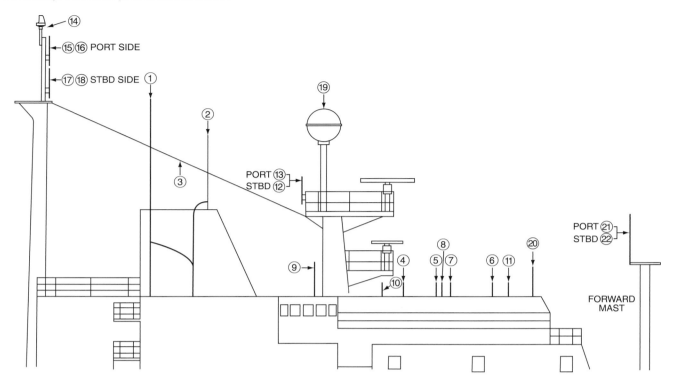

① TRANSMIT WHIP ANT. (MAIN)	⑨ VHF R/T (SAILOR RT2048) ANT.	⑰ VHF R/T No.2
② TRANSMIT WHIP ANT. (DUPLICATION)	⑩ NAVTEX REC. ANT.	⑱ VHF DSC No.2
③ TRANSMIT WIRE ANT. (DUPLICATION)	⑪ PASSIVE RECEIVE ANT.	⑲ GMDSS Satellite antenna
④ ACTIVE RECEIVE WHIP ANT.	⑫ SHIP TO SHORE DIPOLE ANT.	⑳ NAVTRAC TRIMBLE GPS ANT.
⑤ PASSIVE RECEIVE WHIP ANT.	⑬ SHIP TO AIR DIPOLE ANT.	㉑ ACTIVE RECEIVE ANT.
⑥ SATELLITE PICTURE RECEIVE ANT.	⑭ INMARSAT 'C' ANT.	㉒ ACTIVE RECEIVE ANT.
⑦ ASHTEC 3D GPS ANT.	⑮ VHF R/T No.1	
⑧ ASHTEC 3D GPS ANT.	⑯ VHF DSC No.1	

Connection of external located data terminal to mandatory Inmarsat C ship earth station in the GMDSS

If the operators of the vessel wish to connect the mandatory Inmarsat C terminal to the ship's PC-network or to an outside located data terminal, all mandatory GMDSS requirements in accordance with SOLAS 1974, as amended, shall always be fulfilled.

In that case, the dedicated printer should be connected permanently to the mandatory Inmarsat terminal's printer port.

A manually operated and duly marked switch, located near the Inmarsat terminal, should be installed to disconnect the Inmarsat terminal from the external equipment.

SUB-SYSTEMS

The GMDSS is composed of several "sub-systems" which are coordinated through Rescue Coordination Centres to provide all the required functions needed to ensure safety at sea. The main sub-systems can be grouped as follows:

1) The Digital Selective Calling (DSC) System

This is an automatic calling system which makes the initial contact between two stations, groups of stations or stations in a selected area. The caller composes a short message which is transmitted directly to the receiving station(s). Dedicated radio frequencies have been allocated for this purpose in the VHF, MF and HF bands for short, medium and long ranges respectively.

An alarm sounds when a call is received. The received information is displayed on a small screen, often abbreviated in a way which needs to be interpreted. Among other things it indicates the purpose of the call and may direct the operator to a radiotelephone or radiotelex channel for subsequent communications.

If the caller is in distress, the ship's position and nature of distress are included in the DSC alert. For distress and urgency situations, the alarm sounds continuously until the received information has been read by the operator and action taken.

DSC Distress alerts received by shore stations are usually automatically and immediately routed to the nearest Rescue Coordination Centre (RCC).

Some shore stations, such as ZSC (Cape Town Radio), manually route alerts to the MRCC.

2) The Satellite Communication System

Inmarsat and Iridium are commercial enterprise and currently the only approved providers of GMDSS maritime communications and services. Other providers may offer such services in the future, subject to authorisation by IMO.

Inmarsat offer a full range of general communication and network solutions. Geographical coverage is between 76°N and 76°S.

Satellite Ship Earth Station (SES)

1. If the equipment is the main station or duplicated equipment, it must be possible to activate the distress alert from the navigation bridge (SOLAS 1974, as amended, Chapter IV.10.3).
2. The terminal and telephone, if any, may be placed in a "radio work station" in connection with the navigation bridge or in a separate communication office.
3. The satellite terminal and/or external printers may also be located elsewhere in the ship. Note: - Attention should be made to IMO Resolution A807(19), Annex 3.2 regarding Inmarsat C, which has the following text: "It should be possible to initiate and make distress calls from the position from which the ship is normally navigated and from at least one other position designated for distress alerting". The words "one other position designated for distress alerting" is only actually for ships which have defined an additional place/room on board to be such "other position". Normally it will be accepted that Inmarsat C equipment is installed in the "radio work station" if it is provided with facilities for conducting distress alerts from the navigation bridge. It is, however, recommended that the Inmarsat C terminal, including additional equipment, should be located on the navigation bridge in order to make it possible to conduct follow-up distress communication from this position.

3) The Maritime Safety Information (MSI) System

MSI includes navigational and meteorological warnings, meteorological forecasts and other urgent or safety-related messages of importance to all vessels at sea and may also include updates for electronic charts. Broadcast are by MF telex (known as NAVTEX) for local MSI, by Inmarsat SafetyNET (II) for Inmarsat C and Fleet Safety SES's, by Iridium SafetyCast for Iridium LT-3100S SES, or HF telex (NBDP) for long-range MSI.

Not all countries have an established NAVTEX service, in which case local warnings are broadcast using Inmarsat, Iridium or HF telex (NBDP) (see Maritime Safety Information section for further details).

4) The EPIRB (Emergency Position-Indicating Radio Beacon) System

All SOLAS compliant vessels are required to carry an appropriate EPIRB. Satellite alerting by EPIRB is carried out through the Cospas-Sarsat network.

The Cospas-Sarsat network provides full global coverage via a series of satellites in polar orbit, supplemented by an additional series in geostationary orbit. The polar orbiting satellites can determine the EPIRB's position by the Doppler method; this does not require a position input at the EPIRB but it might take a few hours to accurately determine the location.

The geostationary satellites relay the EPIRB signal to earth with no delay, but are unable to determine position by Doppler method; however, they will relay the position if the EPIRB is a model which incorporates a GPS or manually entered position.

For ships engaged in voyages exclusively in Sea Area A1 the carriage of a satellite EPIRB may be replaced by an EPIRB which is capable of transmitting a distress alert using DSC on VHF Ch 70 and follows up with a SART signal. It is the SART signal which provides the electronic position indication. The DSC distress alert indicates "EPIRB emission" instead of specifying the nature of distress. Ships receiving this type of DSC distress alert should take extra care to search for a SART on their 3 cm X-band (9 GHz) radar equipment as described in SN/Circ. 197.

Satellite float-free EPIRB

The satellite float-free EPIRB should be located/installed so that the following requirements are fulfilled:

- The EPIRB should - with greatest possible probability - float free and avoid being caught in railings, superstructure etc., if the ship sinks.
- The EPIRB should be located so that it may be easily released manually and brought to the survival craft by one person. It should therefore not be located in a radar mast or any other place which can only be reached by vertical ladder. (SOLAS 1974, as amended, Chapters IV.7.1.6, 8.1.5.2, 9.1.3.1, 10.1.4.1, 10.2.3.1 and IMO Resolutions A.763(18), A.810(19), and A.812(19)).

Note: A float-free EPIRB may also be used to fulfil the requirements for one piece of equipment (of two), which is capable of transmitting distress alert to shore from or near the navigation bridge of the ship. Under such conditions the float-free EPIRB must fulfil the following additional requirements with regards to location/installation:

- The EPIRB must be installed in the vicinity of the navigation bridge, i.e. on the wings of the navigation bridge. Access via vertical ladder should not be accepted. A location on the top of the wheelhouse may be accepted to fulfil the requirement if accessible by stairs. (SOLAS 1974, as amended, Chapter IV/7 and Com/circ. 105) or
- It may be possible to activate the EPIRB remotely from the bridge. If remote activation is used, the EPIRB should be installed so that it has unobstructed hemispherical line of sight to the satellites. (COM /Circ. 105)

Note: It should be considered that the main function of the EPIRB is float-free activation. If the additional requirements mentioned above cannot be met without reducing the reliability of the float-free activation, priority must be given to this requirement. Alternatively, two float-free EPIRBs should be installed.

- The EPIRB should be equipped with a buoyant lanyard suitable for use as a tether to life raft etc. Such buoyant lanyard should be so arranged as to prevent it being trapped in the ship's structure. (IMO Resolution A.810(19))
- The EPIRB should be marked with the ship's call sign, serial number of EPIRB, MMSI number (if applicable), 15 Hex ID, and battery expiry date.

EPIRBs: False alerts

The false activation of a 406 MHz EPIRB which is not immediately detected onboard, will result in RCCs attempting to contact the ship. If contact is not established very quickly, full SAR procedures can often be initiated. This can place a heavy burden on people in SAR organisations, including volunteers. Moreover, there is a chance that a false distress alert will coincide with an actual distress situation, resulting in SAR resources being delayed in responding to a real distress. It can result in ships being diverted, and may involve helicopters or long distance flights by fixed-wing aircraft if the position indicated is in mid-ocean.

5) The SART (Search And Rescue Transponder) System

The SART is a portable radar transceiver, primarily intended to be deployed on survival craft. When it receives a 9 GHz (3 cm) radar signal (i.e. from a searching radar), it switches on its transmitter and radiates a own special signal. This is seen as a series of 12 dots on all radar screens within range. The dot nearest to the screen centre is the SART's location. Aircraft are sometimes fitted with 9 GHz marine radar for marine SAR operations.

6) The Future of the GMDSS

The GMDSS is currently undergoing a process of review, see World Radiocommunication Conference at the end of this section.

FUNCTIONAL REQUIREMENTS OF THE GMDSS

SOLAS requires GMDSS equipment to be capable of performing the following nine radiocommunications functions.

EXISTING USER NEEDS RELATING TO SOLAS REGULATION IV/4

User needs									
SOLAS regulation IV/4 Functional requirements	SOLAS regulation IV/7 to IV/11								
	VHF-DSC	SART	NAVTEX	EGC	EPIRB	MF/DSC	Inmarsat SES	HF/ DSC	Two-way VHF
1 Transmitting ship-to-shore alerts	X				X	X	X	X	
2 Receiving shore-to-ship distress alerts	X					X	X	X	
3 Transmitting and receiving ship-to-ship distress alerts	X					X		X	
4 Transmitting and receiving search and rescue coordinating communications	X					X	X	X	
5 Transmitting and receiving on-scene communications	X					X	X		X
6 Transmitting and receiving signals for locating		X			X				
7 Transmitting and receiving Maritime Safety Information			X	X		X	X		
8 Transmitting and receiving general radiocommunications to and from shore-based radio systems or networks	X					X	X	X	X
9 Transmitting and receiving bridge-to-bridge communications	X					X		X	X
Note: Ships are required to be provided with means for two-way on-scene radiocommunications on aeronautical frequencies in accordance with SOLAS regulations III/6									

1. Transmission of ship-to-shore distress alerts by at least two separate and independent means, each using a different radiocommunication service;

Details for each individual vessel are to be found on its Safety Radio Certificate. On a Sea Area A1 vessel, for example (which always remains within DSC range of a shore VHF station) the primary means would be the VHF DSC, and the secondary means could be an EPIRB. In the case of a Sea Area A4 ship, the primary means would have to be HF DSC and the secondary means a 406 MHz EPIRB.

2. Reception of shore-to-ship distress alerts;

If, for example, a vessel sends a distress signal via an EPIRB or an Inmarsat C satellite terminal, other vessels in the vicinity will not become aware of the distress until the shore authorities relay the distress details by directing a DSC distress relay call and/or a satellite call to all vessels within an appropriate geographical area.

3. Transmission and reception of ship-to-ship distress alerts;

A vessel in distress can alert other vessels in the vicinity by sending a DSC distress alert on VHF and MF, simultaneously if desired, and follow it up with a distress (MAYDAY) voice message on Ch 16 or 2182 kHz. Note that HF DSC is for long-range work and is intended primarily for alerting the shore-based authorities, especially if there are no vessels in the vicinity.

4. Transmission and reception of search and rescue coordinating communications;

Vessels must be able to perform the functions described in the IAMSAR Manual. For suitably equipped vessels, this might include the use of radiotelex (more properly called Narrow-Band Direct-Printing - NBDP) between the vessels involved in a search in broadcast FEC mode.

5. Transmission and reception of on-scene communications;

"On-scene communications" are short to medium range communications carried out during the course of a search and rescue operation. For this purpose, vessels must be able to communicate with aircraft, as well as with other vessels and the shore, using the dedicated GMDSS frequencies for voice and NBDP distress communications.

The "on-scene" frequencies for radiotelephone are:-

VHF (F3E/G3E)	Ch 16 (distress & safety communications) and Ch 06 (intership and ship-aircraft communications)
VHF (A3E)	121·5 & 123·1 MHz (ship-aircraft communications - compulsory for passenger vessels)
MF (J3E)	2182 kHz (distress & safety communications)
HF (J3E)	3023 kHz (ship-aircraft), 4125 kHz (ship-shore, ship-ship) and 5680 kHz (ship-aircraft)

To avoid confusion and unnecessary interventions, any DSC transmissions on MF or HF related to distress incidents, and intended to be received by other ships in general, should be addressed precisely to the geographical area involved.

6. Transmission and reception of signals for locating

Locating and homing signals in the GMDSS are provided by radar beacons (SARTs) and EPIRBs as described above.

7. Transmission and reception of Maritime Safety Information (MSI);

The GMDSS supports three independent systems for broadcasting MSI to ships, viz: (1) NAVTEX on MF for coastal areas, (2) Transmission over satellite by a GMDSS satellite Service Provider for long-range purposes, either using the SafetyNET or SafetyCast services and (3) HF telex on the 8 GMDSS frequencies allocated for MSI. MSI for coastal areas not covered by NAVTEX are broadcast via GMDSS satellite communication and/or HF telex. For full details of stations providing MSI services which are part of the GMDSS and also outside of the GMDSS, refer to ALRS Volume 3 (NP283).

8. Transmission and reception of general radiocommunications to and from shore-based radio systems or networks;

The GMDSS provides facilities for all types of commercial and personal communications. GMDSS radio operators need to be familiar with voice and data communications, email and the internet and connecting through commercial telecommunication networks.

9. Transmission and reception of bridge-to-bridge communications;

This refers to the SOLAS requirement that access to VHF communication equipment must be available from the position at which the vessel is normally navigated. The equipment must include operation on Ch 13, the frequency reserved for intership communications relating to the Safety of Navigation.

AVAILABILITY OF RADIO EQUIPMENT (see SOLAS Regulation 15 in Chapter IV)

There are three options, viz: (1) at-sea maintenance; (2) shore-based maintenance; and (3) duplication of equipment.

- Sea Areas A1 and A2 vessels must nominate one option.
- Sea Areas A3 and A4 vessels must nominate two options.
- A shore-based maintenance contract must be acceptable to the authorities of the vessel's flag state.

Details of which options apply to each vessel are entered on the Safety Radio Certificate.

RADIO PERSONNEL REQUIREMENTS

The requirements of Radio personnel are specified in ITU Articles Chapter VII Regulations 47 (Operator's certificates), Regulation 48 (Personnel) and in The International Convention for the Safety of Life at Sea (SOLAS), 1974 Chapter IV Regulation 16.

Radio Operator certification
Certification of operators is a flag state matter but different categories of operator are recognised and the requirements for each is contained in Article 47 of the ITU Radio Regulations. Some of the categories in the ITU regulations cover non-SOLAS vessels and only four relate specifically to most commercial ships. These four categories of certificates, which are also part of GMDSS rules, in descending order of requirements are:

First-class radio electronic certificate.
Second-class radio electronic certificate.
General operator's certificate (GOC).
Restricted operator's certificate (ROC).
There are different types of GMDSS qualifications, currently these are:

First Class Radio-Electronic Certificate;
Second Class Radio-Electronic Certificate; and
GMDSS General Operator's Certificate
ROC (Restricted Operators Certificate)
Those holding the last two certificate types are considered as operators only. The GMDSS General Operator's Certificate is a non-technical qualification, designed for navigating officers. It is normally awarded after a ten-day course and examination. Most ships must have two or more crew holding GOCs with the ROCs only recognised for ships limited to coastal service.

For stations on board vessels which sail solely within range of a VHF coast station (Sea Area A1), taking into account SOLAS requirements, a holder of a First or Second Class Radio-Electronic Certificate or a General Operator's or Restricted Operator's Certificate.

For stations on board vessels which sail beyond the range of VHF coast stations (Sea Areas A2, A3 and A4), taking into account the requirements of SOLAS, a holder of a First or Second Class Radio-Electronic Certificate or a General Operator's Certificate.

STCW 95 further requires that all deck officers shall hold an appropriate qualification to operate radiocommunications equipment. In cases where equipment is fitted over and above the minimum requirements, a higher standard of operator certification may also be required, to ensure that the operator knowledge requirements match the actual equipment comprising the radio installation.

In the case of the GOC, the usual certificate held by deck officers on GMDSS vessels, Article 47 of the Radio Regulations indicates that candidates for certification must give proof of the following knowledge requirements:-

1. Detailed practical knowledge of the operation of all the GMDSS sub-systems and equipment.
2. Ability to send and to receive correctly by radiotelephone and direct-printing telegraphy (radiotelex).
3. Detailed knowledge of the regulations applying to radiocommunication, knowledge of the documents relating to charges for radiocommunications and knowledge of those provisions of SOLAS which relate to radio.
4. Sufficient knowledge of one of the working languages of the ITU (French, English or Spanish). Candidates should be able to express themselves satisfactorily in that language, both orally and in writing.

In respect of language skills, the standard of competence set for STCW 95 overrides the French and Spanish options in the Radio Regulations by requiring knowledge, understanding and proficiency in "the English language both written and spoken for the communication of information relevant to the safety of life".

GMDSS training courses are expected to conform to the syllabus set out in the IMO Model Course. The current edition (1.25) was published in 2015.

THE TERRESTRIAL COMMUNICATION SYSTEM

Compliance with the Radio Regulations is important, and RR15.19 requires that *"infringements of the Radio Regulations shall be reported ...... by the ...... stations ...... detecting them"* , and a form for submitting such reports is printed at Appendix 9 in the ITU Manual. If infringements are reported, penalties might be levied upon the licensee of the station, i.e. the shipowner.

Sometimes, a Radio Regulation will briefly state that communications shall be carried out in accordance with one of the ITU Recommendations; the actual Recommendation, which can be quite lengthy, can be found in another part of the ITU Manual.

The following ITU-R Recommendations, are of particular interest to the GMDSS:

M.493-14	Describes the structure and content of DSC calls	**(outlined below, refer to ITU Manual)**
M.541-9	Sets out operational procedures for DSC calls in five Annexes	**(see Section 5 "Operational Procedures for use of DSC Equipment in the Maritime Mobile Service)**
M.1171	Describes radiotelephone procedures	**(refer to ITU Manual)**
M.492-6	Describes the radiotelex system	**(refer to ITU Manual)**

THE DIGITAL SELECTIVE CALLING (DSC) SUB-SYSTEM

DSC is a calling system that provides for distress, urgency and safety communications and also offers comprehensive facilities for routine communications, e.g. to initiate and to keep watch for automatic phone calls between ship and shore subscribers. The operator sets up calls using a DSC controller, and the controller is connected to a transceiver. Sometimes both are contained in a single unit.

In each MF/HF band, there is a dedicated frequency for DSC calls relating to distress, urgency and safety. Separate frequencies have been assigned for Routine Calls which are not permitted on the distress frequencies. The frequency 2177 kHz has been nominated for ship-ship Routine Calls. Theoretically, a ship may call another ship on any of the Routine DSC frequencies, but since they all use paired frequencies (one for transmit, the other for receive), intership calling by this method is impractical. The VHF band is different, and the same frequency (Ch 70) is used for all categories of DSC calls.

Before Routine Calls and Test Calls are transmitted, it should be verified that the frequency is not being used by another station. On newer equipment, Routine Calls are automatically blocked until the frequency is free.

One of the duties of the bridge watchkeeper is to ensure that the VHF DSC is keeping automatic watch on Ch 70, and that the MF/HF DSC is programmed to scan at least three of the six MF/HF distress and safety frequencies, i.e. 2 MHz, 8 MHz and one other band deemed to be suitable at the time (e.g. 12 MHz by day and 4 MHz by night, or as decided by the operator).

Commercial (Routine) frequencies and the Intership frequency may also be scanned but normally, this requires a separate DSC unit because the distress watch must be continuous. This is usually achieved by using a dedicated DSC watch receiver.

After a distress alert has been sent by DSC, subsequent communications are always carried out on the distress frequency in the same band. For example if a DSC distress alert is sent on 8 MHz, a subsequent voice MAYDAY message (the distress call) will be sent on the 8 MHz RT frequency (8291 kHz, or Ch 833).

In contrast to the distress alert, the DSC format for Urgency and Safety Calls requires the operator to enter a frequency to be used for the subsequent voice message. Normally, this would be the associated distress frequency, but a working frequency may be used instead, e.g. if a coast station needs to transmit lengthy messages.

DSC signals can sometimes be received over greater ranges than the subsequent voice transmission because they have a narrow bandwidth and are less affected by certain types of noise that affect voice signals. Thus a successful DSC call does not mean that subsequent RT signals on the same frequency band will be of intelligible quality or even heard at all. With this in mind, a DSC call can be acknowledged by a return DSC call. Such an acknowledgement can include a suggested change of frequency for subsequent communications.

STRUCTURE AND CONTENT OF THE DSC CALL (ITU-R Recommendation M493-14 (2015))

The Distress Alert

A distress alert is defined in the Radio Regulations as either a terrestrial DSC call using the unique Distress Format (described below), or a satellite call which also has a special Distress Format to gain priority over the satellite link.

In newer equipment, distress alerts are immediately followed by an additional signal giving higher resolution position.

The additional signal is known as an "expansion sequence".
If the expansion sequence follows a distress alert it will also follow acknowledgements and relays.
Older equipment does not recognise the expansion sequence.

A full description of all DSC call sequences can be found in Tables A1 - 4.1 to A1 - 4.10 in ITU-R Recommendation M493-14 (2015).

The full document contains over 61 pages. The following is a plain language summary of the main points.

DSC calls are composed of "symbols", which are actually "numbers" (00 – 127), signalled as a series of 10 tones each.

The sequence of symbols differs for each type of DSC call, and the meaning of each symbol depends on its position in the DSC call.

e.g. If symbol "100" appears in the "Category" part of a call, it means "Routine";
if it appears in the "Nature of Distress" part of a call, it means "Fire, explosion".

Components of the DSC call

A DSC call consists of nine sections, i.e.

1)	Dot Pattern	to temporarily stop receivers from scanning and perform bit synchronisation
2)	Phasing Signal	to perform character synchronisation
3)	Format Specifier	programs the receiver so that it can interpret the symbols which follow

4)	Address	the address of the receiving station (MMSI or Geographical Area)
5)	Category	informs the receiving operator whether the call is distress, urgency, safety or routine
6)	Self-ID	the calling station's MMSI
7)	Messages	"message elements" (additional information), which may be keyed in by the operator
8)	End-of-Sequence	symbol indicates whether the call is an acknowledgement of a DSC call
9)	Error Check Symbol	a "checksum" number for the whole message

The DSC call lasts for about 7 seconds on MF/HF, and about 0·6 seconds on VHF making the cancellation during transmission of a VHF DSC call very difficult. MF/HF DSC calls are long enough to allow termination during transmission.

The main features of the above nine components are described below in more detail.

Note 1: The DSC call does not contain a date/time group to indicate time of transmission. The receiving DSC set has to be programmed with its own date and time, which will be applied to messages as they are received.

Note 2: The operator does not necessarily have to key in every item of every DSC call. The DSC equipment is designed to insert essential components automatically. This reduces the number of entries to be keyed in or selected by the operator.

1) The Dot Pattern

This is simply a series of alternating high and low tones, which will cause receiving equipment to stop scanning and "listen" to the forthcoming DSC call. The dot pattern is also used to synchronise the receiver to the precise rate at which the bits are being transmitted (bit synchronisation). On MF/HF the dot pattern lasts for 2 seconds. For this reason, watchkeeping receivers must be able to scan all six distress frequencies within 2 seconds.

2) The Phasing Signal

The signal arriving at a DSC receiver is nothing more than a stream of high and low tones, arriving at a steady and pre-determined rate (100 Baud on MF/HF, 1200 Baud on VHF DSC). Just as the dot pattern tells the receiver precisely how fast the bits are arriving, the phasing sequence tells the receiver exactly where to start separating them into groups of ten. Having found the correct starting point, the receiver continues to separate the incoming stream of highs and lows into groups of ten at exactly the right places. On MF/HF the phasing signal takes about 1·2 seconds.

3) The Format Specifier

Can be any one of the following six alternatives:

1. Distress
2. All Ships
3. Individual station
4. Groups of stations
5. Stations in a Geographical Area
6. Automatic phone call.

Different types of call contain different numbers of symbols and in different sequences. In other words, each type of message has a different format. The Format Specifier "tells" the receiver the exact order in which these symbols will be sent. For example the 27th symbol might be a part of the sending station's MMSI or it might be a Telecommand, or something else, depending on the format of the call.

When defining a Geographical Area, the northernmost latitude is entered first, and the southernmost latitude is defined by indicating how many degrees further south it is. Likewise, the westernmost longitude is entered first and the easternmost longitude is defined by indicating how many degrees further eastward it is. This was always necessary with earlier model DSC units, but under current standard the DSC will also accept a circular distance for own ship's position, and will default to a radius of 500 n miles unless changed by the operator. The equipment will automatically convert this to a rectangular area.

4) The Address

This is either the MMSI of the receiving station (or group of stations) or a Geographical Area. A DSC receiver detecting its own MMSI or Geographical Area will continue to receive the rest of the sequence. Otherwise, it will return to watchkeeping mode. If the Format Specifier was for Distress or All Ships, the receiver will always continue to receive the rest of the DSC call. Address symbols are therefore unnecessary and are omitted from these two types of call.

5) The Category

This indicates to the receiving operator how important the message is and therefore what procedures need to be followed. There are four Categories: Distress, Urgency, Safety and Routine. A previous Category of Ships Business has been abolished. The receiver will display the Category as part of the message.

6) The Self-ID

The calling station's MMSI is automatically included in all DSC calls regardless of format. This is in accordance with RR19.4 which requires that all maritime mobile transmissions must be accompanied by station identification.

7) The Messages

Additional information known as "message elements" keyed in by the operator, can indicate the purpose, nature or location of the call, and provide frequency / channel information regarding subsequent communications .

A. Message elements for Distress Format only

The Distress Format contains four "message elements" as follows:-

1. Nature of Distress: selected by the operator from a list of up to 12, including Piracy and Man Overboard. The use of the distress alert and subsquent use of the term MAYDAY is now authorised for MOB (Man Overboard) events provided that the person is "threatened by grave and imminent danger and requires immediate assistance" as described in the ITU Radio Regulations Article 32, Section II, paragraph A1. A footnote implies that the use of the Urgency category may be more appropriate in particular circumstances.
2. Position of vessel in distress. The position should be updated automatically, but may be entered manually for older equipment. If the position data is not known, or has not been updated within 4 hours, the position is signalled as digit "9" repeated ten times.
3. UTC Time means the time that the position was valid. Note that this time is not the same as the equipment's internal date and time setting, which can be set to any Time Zone. If the UTC time is incorrect, rescue parties might start searching in the wrong position. If the internal clock is incorrect, the date and time displayed with incoming DSC calls will be incorrect.
4. Indicates whether subsequent communications will be RT (J3E) or NBDP (F1B-FEC).

If the operator does not enter any of the above information, the equipment will automatically send the following:

Nature of distress "undesignated" Position: "9999999999"
Time: "8888" Ongoing traffic "J3E" (single side-band radiotelephone)

Note: The four 8s and ten 9s might be translated into a text phrase by some receivers.

B. Message elements for All Other Formats

Three important types of DSC call contain 5 "message elements"

These are Distress Acknowledgement, Distress Relay and Distress Relay Acknowledgment.

"Message element 0" is the MMSI of the vessel in distress; Message elements 1-4 are the same as in the original distress alert.

Other calls contain 2 or 3 "message elements" as follows:

1. Two Telecommands
2. Position or Working Frequency (or neither)
3. The phone number when making an autophone call UTC time when sending position in response to a Position Request.

These "message elements" are briefly described below.

Message element 1: Two Telecommands (selected by the person making the call)

- The **First Telecommand** is selected from a list of approximately 24. It usually indicates the class of emission to be used in subsequent communications. It can also indicate that the call is a "distress acknowledgement" or a "distress relay". These are not "distress alerts" as defined above because they do not follow the Distress Format. **However they include the details of the vessel in distress, therefore they must only be sent on the authority of the Master.** Among other things, the First Telecommand can also be "Test", "Position" or "Polling". If it is "Test" the station receiving the call will send an automatic acknowledgement to indicate a successful test sequence. The "Position" telecommand is used to request the receiving ship to send its position by return DSC call (DSC equipment can do this automatically, if enabled). The "Polling" telecommand is only for use by coast stations wishing to call a ship with commercial traffic; if the ship is in range and scanning the coast stations frequency, it will send a "Polling acknowledgement" (if enabled) so that the coast station knows it can go ahead with the traffic.

- The **Second Telecommand** is selected from a different list. Two of them are for use in war zones; one of them indicates that the vessel is a Hospital Ship (see "Medical Transports" at RR33 in the ITU Manual), and the other indicates that the vessel is identifying itself as a Neutral Vessel (refer to ITU Manual "Resolution 18 relating to the procedure for identifying and announcing the position of ships and aircraft of States not parties to an armed conflict"). This lengthy title is abbreviated in various ways depending on the manufacturer's interpretation, e.g. "Res 18" or "Ships and aircraft". Older models of DSC automatically offer the two war zone telecommands when the operator composes a DSC call, but in future models they will be available from a setup menu instead of being offered as a regular choice. Other Second Telecommands may be used when responding to an incoming call (e.g. "unable to comply", "busy", "cannot use channel" etc), or when composing the Auto Phone Format to prepare the shore equipment for automatic dialling.

Message element 2: Position or Working Frequency

If a working frequency is entered by the operator, equipment at the receiving station may automatically be set to the channel or frequencies nominated by the sender. Obviously this facility must be used with some care to avoid interfering with equipment on other vessels.

If a position is entered, the called station is obliged to reply **by DSC** and indicate a working frequency, or indicate inability and a reason for declining to communicate.

Message element 3: Phone number or UTC time

When the Format Specifier indicates an Automatic Phone Call, the symbols appearing in this part of the call will be routed to the automatic dialling equipment. If the DSC call is a response to a Position Request, this part of the call will indicate the UTC time that the position was valid. In all other cases, message element 3 is omitted.

8) The End-of-Sequence (EOS) Symbol

The EOS symbol signifies the end of the call. Usually it is signalled as symbol "127" which simply means "end of call". But it can also be used to request an acknowledgement by DSC. In this case the EOS is signalled as symbol "117" Acknowledge RQ, and the receiver is obliged to send a DSC acknowledgement, either manually or automatically (a function which can be enabled or disabled). The EOS symbol for the mandatory acknowledgement is symbol "122" (Acknowledge BQ). This enables the original caller to be certain that the call was received. This can be useful because DSC signals are usually received at greater ranges than radiotelephone signals in the same band – e.g. on VHF reception range could be 30 miles for DSC but only 25 miles for the subsequent RT signals. The RQ and BQ symbols only appear with Individual Formats and Autophone calls.

9) The Error Check Symbol

The final character, sometimes known as an Error Check Character (ECC), provides an error check by a method known as "checksum". Checksum is a method of error-checking in which every character is given a number. The numbers are added up by the transmitter and sent as a final group. The receiver then adds up numbers corresponding to the characters actually received. If the receiver's checksum calculation corresponds to the transmitted checksum number, the message has probably been received without error. The checksum is one of three error-detecting techniques used in DSC. The two other methods are (a) "time diversity" and (b) 10-bit coding. "Time diversity" means that each character is repeated a short time after the first transmission - deemed correct if they are both received identically. "10-bit coding" means that a 10-bit signal is used for each symbol instead of the usual 7 bits. The extra 3 bits tell the receiver how many "highs" and "lows" should have been in the first 7-bits. If they correspond, the character is deemed as correct.

Note: The DSC call does not contain a date/time group. The times recorded for transmitted and received calls is the time which is entered into the DSC equipment by the operator. Modern equipment is required to have GNSS input which should be UTC as per RR Article 2.

Classes of DSC

Class A   MF/HF - all functions

Class B   MF and/or VHF - all functions

Class D   VHF – minimum distress, urgency and safety functions, limited routine functions.

Class E   MF and or HF – minimum distress urgency and safety functions, limited routine functions

Class H   VHF HANDHELD – minimum distress, urgency and safety functions, limited routine. Somewhat similar to Class D, but contains a GNSS receiver.

Class M   Man Overboard – distress functions only, contains AIS and GNSS receiver.

Class M can work as an "open loop" system, in which case it sends a "man overboard" Distress Alert to all stations, or as a "closed loop" system, in which case it sends a Distress Alert Relay addressed to "Individual" or "Group". In both cases, upon activation, it will transmit "position and time unknown". When the internal GNSS receiver has determined an accurate position it will send another Alert or Relay including the position with expansion sequence.

Classes C, F and G lacked certain distress and safety functions and are no longer authorised.

The different classes of DSC send and receive different types of DSC call. The sections below are a summary of the tables in ITU-R M493-14 which describe in detail the types of DSC call made by different classes of equipment.

Distress Alert Attempts

The ITU Recommendations refer to "distress alert attempts" and indicate that on MF/HF a DSC distress alert may be sent as a "single frequency call attempt" or a "multi-frequency call attempt".

1) Multi-frequency call attempt (the default HF setting)

A single 7·2 second Distress Alert is transmitted on up to six frequencies in succession, within the space of 1 minute. Modern MF/HF DSC equipment – unlike the earlier models – is required to use the multi-frequency method as factory default, with "undesignated" nature of distress. After sending this type of distress alert, it is necessary to wait for a DSC Distress Acknowledgement from a coast station. Once the distressed person has determined the frequency band on which the acknowledgement was received, the voice distress procedure will then take place on the relevant distress frequency for radiotelephone signals, e.g. if the DSC distress acknowledgement was received on 8414·5 kHz, the voice distress message will follow on 8291 kHz. Coast stations are required to send the DSC distress acknowledgement on all HF distress channels on which it was received. Therefore the distressed vessel may receive acknowledgements on more than one frequency. The choice of subsequent channel must then be decided by the ship's operator.

2) Single frequency call attempt

Although the default setting is for multi-frequency, the operator can choose to set up a single frequency distress call attempt if desired. In this case, the 7·2 second call sequence is sent 5 times in a single uninterrupted burst thereby increasing the probability that it will be received at the first attempt. The burst of 5 alerts may be followed immediately by a 1·8 second "expansion sequence" which repeats the position with increased precision. The total transmission time for a distress alert would then be 38 seconds. Older equipment may not receive the expansion sequence but the distress alert will be received normally. The single-frequency alert may be followed by a voice (or telex) distress message without necessarily waiting for a DSC Distress Acknowledgement. If there is no response it would be necessary to repeat the process on another frequency.

Human machine interface (HMI) and automated DSC procedures

The Recommendation specifies several default settings, automated procedures and other features which DSC equipment must now offer to the user, e.g.

- DROBOSE (Distress Relay On Behalf Of Someone Else). This function allows the operator to relay a DSC Distress Alert. The default address is always Individual, but the operator may change this to "All Ships" on VHF, and to "Geographical Area" on MF/HF. The geographic area limit defaults to a circle of 500 nautical mile radius from own ship.

- The default distress alert attempt is "undesignated" for the nature of distress, "radiotelephony" for the communication mode and, on HF, the transmission uses the multi-frequency method including all six bands.

- A distress cancel facility. A ship sending a false alert firstly acknowledges its own alert. This is done by pressing a "cancel" button which becomes available after a distress alert has been sent. In the case of a multi-frequency alert, the acknowledgement will be transmitted on all six frequencies. The operator must then follow the correct "cancel procedure" and perform a voice (or telex) cancellation on each band. The text for the voice cancellations will appear on the display screen to guide the operator.

- All alarms start softly and increase in volume if not silenced.

- Distinctive 2-tone alarm for distress and urgency. Alarm will always activate if distress position is "unknown" or is higher than 70° latitude; otherwise only if the position is within 500 nautical miles from own ship.

- Duplicate distress relays addressed to all ships or geographic areas will not activate the alarm if received within 1 hour of the original distress relay.

- If the DSC controller is in a menu which disables the receiver, it switches itself back to watchkeeping mode after 10 minutes of inactivity.

- DSC transmission is disabled if MMSI is not stored in memory and a warning will be displayed. Once stored, user is unable to change MMSI without manufacturer's assistance.

- Ability to disable automatic channel switching.

- Automatic tuning of the radio for subsequent communications.

- Warnings appear when the operator attempts to do anything that does not follow the IMO and ITU guidelines.

- Use of plain language, e.g. "radiotelephone" instead of "J3E".

- Equipment will automatically propose the next step when composing a DSC call, with defaults offered to avoid operator error.

- Display to indicate own ship's position and whether it is manual, internal or external.

- Automatic position updating – alarm to sound after maximum 4 hours of non-operation. Positions older than 24 hours to be automatically erased.

Testing of DSC equipment

A test is considered successful when a DSC call to another station is followed by a DSC acknowledgement received from that other station. To facilitate this, the "Test Call" facility has been developed such that both ship and coast station equipment can provide an automatic response on VHF, MF or HF (see sections above).

When testing, it is necessary to first ascertain whether the station to be called is maintaining a DSC watch on the intended frequency. If using HF coast stations, the World Chartlet showing HF DSC Stations (Figure 13) will be of assistance in selecting a suitable station. If testing is between ships, it should be remembered that some vessels may have disabled the automatic acknowledgement facility.

If the equipment has been set up to automatically acknowledge individually addressed polling, position request, or test DSC messages, no alarm should sound and the automated procedure should self-terminate.

MMSI NUMBERS (Edited extract from Rec. ITU-R M.585-7)

Annex 1 - Maritime mobile service identities.
Section 1

Assignment of identification to ship station.

1. Ships participating in the maritime radio services *(participating in search and resuce operations and other safety-related communications, automatic identification system (AIS) aids to navigation, and craft associated with a parent ship)* should be assigned a nine digit unique ship station identity in the format $M_1I_2D_3X_4X_5X_6X_7X_8X_9$ where in the first three digits represent the Maritime Identification Digits (MID) and X is any figure from 0 to 9. The MID denotes the administration having jurisdiction over the ship station so identified.
2. Restrictions may apply with respect to the maximum number of digits, which can be transmitted on some national telex and/or telephone networks for the purpose of ship station identification.
3. The maximum number of digits that could be transmitted over the national networks of many countries for the purpose of determining ship station identity was six. The digits carried on the network to represent the ship station identity are referred to as the "ship station number" in this text and in the relevant ITU-R Recommendations. The use of the techniques described below should have made it possible for the coast stations of such countries to engage in the automatic connection of calls to ship stations.

   To obtain the required nine digit ship station identity a series of trailing zeros would have to be added automatically to the ship station number by the coast station in order to complete a shore-originated telephone call, for example, carried over the public switched telephone network:

   $$\text{ship station number: } M_1I_2D_3X_4X_5X_6$$

   $$\text{ship station identity: } M_1I_2D_3X_4X_5X_60_70_80_9$$

4. In accordance with the above, and the relevant ITU-T Recommendations, a numbering plan was instituted for Inmarsat Standard B, C and M systems, which also requires that MMSI with three trailing zeros be assigned to ships fitting standard B, C and M ship earth stations.
5. The above restrictions do not necessarily apply to Inmarsat C systems, as they are not diallable terminals from the public switched telephone network but are only data terminals.
6. With respect to Inmarsat Standard B and M systems and as long as the above restrictions apply, ships reasonably expected to be affected by the above limitations should only be assigned ship station identities with $X_7X_8X_9 = 000$.
7. Group ship station call identities for calling simultaneously more than one ship are formed as follows:

   $$0_1M_2I_3D_4X_5X_6X_7X_8X_9$$

   Where the first figure is zero and X is any figure from 0 to 9. The MID represents only the territory or geographical area of the administration assigning the group ship station call identity and does not therefore prevent group calls to fleets containing more than one ship nationality.
8. With the evolution of global mobile-satellite systems, ship earth stations are able to participate in international public correspondence telecommunication services. Ship earth stations having this functionality may be assigned international telecommunication numbers that have no direct correspondencee with the ship station MMSI. Those authorized to assign the numbers, names and addresses associated with such ship earth stations should maintain a record of the cross reference relationships with the MMSI, for example in an appropriate database. For the purposes of GMDSS the details of these relationships should be made available to authorized entities such as but not limited to the Rescue Coordination Centres (RCC)[1] Such availability should be on an automatic basis, 24 hours per day, 365 days per year.

---

[1] IMO Resolution a.1001(25) requires that distress priority communications in these systems should, as far as possible, be routed automatically to an RCC.

Section 2
Assignment of identification to coast station

1. Coast stations and other stations on land participating in the maritime radio services (participating in search and rescue operations using digital selective calling equipment in accordance with Recommendation ITU-R M.493 should use their 9-digit numerical identities transmitted as a 10-digit address / self-identity, normally with a digit 0 added at the end of the identity - see also Recommendation ITU-R M.1080) should be assigned a nine-digit unique coast station identity in the format $0_10_2M_3I_4D_5X_6X_7X_8X_9$ where the digits 3, 4 and 5 represent the MID and X is any figure from 0 to 9. The MID reflects the administration having jurisdiction over the coast station or coast earth station.

2. As the number of coast stations decreases in many countries, an administration may wish to assign an MMSI of the format above to harbour radio stations, pilot stations, system identities and other stations participating in the maritime radio services. The stations concerned should be located on land or on an island in order to use the 00MIDXXXX format.

3. The administration may use the sixth digit to further differentiate between certain specific uses of this class of MMSI, as shown in the example applications below:

    (a) 00MID1XXX Coast radio stations

    (b) 00MID2XXX Harbour radio stations

    (c) 00MID3XXX Pilot stations, etc.

    (d) 00MID4XXX AIS Repeater stations

4. This format scheme creates blocks of 999 numbers for each category of station, however the method is optional and should be used only as a guidance. Many other possibilities exist if the administration concerned wishes to augment the scheme.

5. Group coast station call identities for calling simultaneously more than one coast station are formed as a subset of coast station identities, as follows:

$$0_1 0_2 M_3 I_4 D_5 X_6 X_7 X_8 X_9$$

6. Where the first two figures are zeros and X is any figure from 0 to 9. The MID represents only the territory or geographical area of the administration assigning the group coast station call identity. The identity may be assigned to stations of one administration which are located in only one geographical region as indicated in the relevant ITU-T Recommendations.

7. The combination $0_1 0_2 M_3 I_4 D_5 0_6 0_7 0_8 0_9$ should be reserved for a Group Coast station Identity and should address all 00MIDXXXX stations within the administration. The administration may further augment this use with additional group call identities, i.e. 00MID1111, etc.

8. For the purpose of the GMDSS the details of these MMSI assignments should be made available to authorized entities such as, but not limited to, RCC. Such availability should be on an automatic basis, 24 hours per day, 365 days per year.

9. The combination $0_1 0_2 0_3 0_4 0_5 0_6 0_7 0_8 0_9$ is reserved for all coast station identities and should address all VHF 00XXXXXXX stations. It is not applicable to MF or HF coast stations.

Section 3

Assignment of identification to aircraft

1. When an aircraft is required to use maritime mobile service identities for the purposes of search and rescue operations and other safety-related communications with stations in the maritime mobile service, the responsible administration should assign a nine-digit unique aircraft identity, in the format $1_1 1_2 1_3 M_4 I_5 D_6 X_7 X_8 X_9$ where the digits 4, 5 and 6 represent the MID and X is any figure from 0 to 9. The MID represents the administration having jurisdiction over the aircraft call identity.

2. The format shown above will accommodate 999 aircraft per MID. If the administration concerned has more search and resuce (SAR) aircraft than 999 they may use an additional country code (MID) if it is already assigned by the ITU.

3. The administration may use the seventh digit to differentiate between certain specific uses of this class of MMSI, as shown in the example applications below:

    (a) 111MID1XX Fixed-wing aircraft

    (b) 111MID5XX Helicopters

4. This format scheme creates blocks of 99 numbers for each of the category of stations, however, the method shown here is optional.

5. The combination $1_1 1_2 1_3 M_4 I_5 D_6 0_7 0_8 0_9$ should be reserved for a Group Aircraft Identity and shoud address all 111MIDXXX stations within the administration. The administration may further augment this with additional Group Call identities, i.e. 111MID111, etc.

6. For the purpose of search and rescue the details of these MMSI assignments should be made available to authorized entities such as, but not limited to, RCC. Such availability should be on an automatic basis, 24 hours per day, 365 days per year.

7. The MMSI assigned to aircraft should also be avaiilable from the ITU MARS database (see RR No. 20.16).

Section 4

Assignment of identification to automatic identification systems aids to navigation

1. When a means of automatic identification is required for a station aiding navigation at sea, the responsible administration should assign a nine-digit unique number in the format $9_1 9_2 M_3 I_4 D_5 X_6 X_7 X_8 X_9$ where the digits 3, 4 and 5 represent the MID and X is any figure from 0 to 9. The MID represents the administration having jurisdiction over the call identity for the navigational aid.

2. The format shown above applies to all types of aids to navigation (AtoN) as listed in the most recent version of Recommendation ITU-R M.1371, see AIS Message 21 parameter "Type of aids to navigation" and the associated table for the parameter. This format is used for all AIS stations for the transmission of messages that relate to AtoN. In the case where an AIS base station is co-located with an AIS AtoN station the messages related to the base station operation should be assigned an identification number in the format of a freeform number identity which uses the 3-digit prefix.

3. The format scheme shown above will accommodate 10,000 AtoNs per MID. If the administration concerned has more than 10,000 they may use an additional country code (MID) if it is already assigned by the ITU giving a further 10,000 identities.

4. The administration may use the sixth digit to differentiate between certain specific uses of the MMSI, as shown in the example applications below:

    (a) 99MID1XXX Physical AIS AtoN

    (b) 99MID6XXX Virtual AIS AtoN

5. This format scheme creates blocks of 999 numbers for each category of station, however the method shown here is optional and should only be used as a guidance.

6. In addition to the use of the sixth digit to differentiate between specific navigational aids as explained above, the seventh digit may be used for national purposes, to define areas where the AIS AtoNs are located or types of AIS AtoN to the discretion of the administration concerned.
7. The details of these MMSI assignments should be made available but not limited to the International Association of Marine Aids to Navigation and Lighthouse Authorities (IALA) and appropriate national authorities.
8. The assigned MMSI to aids of navigation should also be available from the ITU MARS database (see RR No. 20.16).

Section 5

Assignment of identification to craft associated with a parent ship

Craft associated with a parent ship, need unique identification. These crafts which participate in the maritime mobile service should be assigned a nine-digit unique number in the format $9182M_3I_4D_5X_6X_7X_8X_9$ where the digits 3, 4 and 5 represent the MID and X is any figure from 0 to 9. The MID represents the administration having jurisdiction over the call identity for the craft associated with a parent ship.

This numbering format is only valid for devices on board craft associated with a parent ship. A craft may carry multiple devices which would be identified by the MMSI assigned to the craft. These devices may be located in lifeboats, life-rafts, rescue-boats or other craft belonging to a parent ship.

A unique MMSI should be assigned for each craft associated with a parent ship and will have to be separately registered and linked to the MMSI of the parent ship.

The format scheme shown above will accommodate 10,000 crafts associated with parent ships per MID. If the administration concerned has more than 10,000 they may use an additional country code (MID) if it is already assigned by the ITU giving a further 10,000 identities.

The assigned MMSI to these craft associated with a parent ship should also be available from the ITU MARS database (see RR No. 20.16).

Annex 2 - Maritime identities used for other maritime devices for special purposes

These identities use MID numbering resources, but have special uses defined in each of the sections below.

Section 1

Assignment of identities for handheld VHF transceivers with digital selective calling and global navigation satellite system

A handheld VHF transceiver with DSC and GNSS may require a unique identification showing that this device has restricted battery capacity and restricted coverage area. This may give additional information in an emergency case.

The handheld VHF transceiver with DSC and GNSS should be used exclusively in the maritime mobile service.

Handheld VHF transceivers with DSC and GNSS participating in the maritime mobile services should be assigned a unique 9-digit number in the format $81M_2I_3D_4X_5X_6X_7X_8X_9$ where digits 2, 3 and 4 represents the MID and X is any figure from 0 to 9. The MID represents the administration assigning the identity to the handheld transceiver.

The procedure and criteria for assignment and registration of these identities should be left to the administration concerned.

Some mimimum of procedures for registration of this identity should be observed:

*   All identities in this category should be registered by the national authority concerned, and the local RCC or MRCC should be able to access the data on a 24 hours-per-day, 7 days-per-week basis. In systems that have automatic distress priority, this information should be automatically forwarded to an RCC.
*   The re-use of this identity should follow the guidance within Annex 3 of this Recommendation.

The administration may use the 5th digit to differentiate between certain specific uses / users of the maritime identity. However, this method is optional and for national use only.

Section 2

Devices using a freeform number identity

These identities, which use the 3-digit prefix (allocated from the table of maritime identification digits), are used to identify maritime radio equipment like the AIS-SART, MOB and EPIRB-AIS and similar equipment needing identification.

1. Automatic identification system-search and rescue transponder
The AIS-SART should use an identity:

$$9_1 7_2 0_3 X_4 X_5 Y_6 Y_7 Y_8 Y_9$$

(where X_4X_5 = manufacturer ID 01 to 99, $Y_6Y_7Y_8Y_9$ = the sequence number 0000 to 9999. When reaching 9999 the manufacturer should restart the sequence numbering at 0000)

2. Man overboard

The MOB (Man overboard) device transmits DSC and / or AIS should use an identity:

$$9_1 7_2 2_3 X_4 X_5 Y_6 Y_7 Y_8 Y_9$$

(where $X_4 X_5$ = manufacturer ID 01 to 99, $Y_6 Y_7 Y_8 Y_9$ = the sequence number 0000 to 9999. When reaching 9999 the manufacturer should restart the sequence numbering at 0000)

3. Emergency Position indicating radio beacon-automatic identification system

The EPIRB-AIS should use an identity:

$$9_1 7_2 4_3 X_4 X_5 Y_6 Y_7 Y_8 Y_9$$

(where $X_4 X_5$ = manufacturer ID 01 to 99, $Y_6 Y_7 Y_8 Y_9$ = the sequence number 0000 to 9999. When reaching 9999 the manufacturer should restart the sequence numbering at 0000)

The user identity of the EPIRB-AIS indicates the identity of the homing device of the EPIRB-AIS, and not the MMSI of the ship.

Annex 3 - Assignment, management and conversation of maritime identities.

Section 1

Maritime Mobile Service Identities

Administrations should employ the following measures to manage the limited identity resource, particularly for the re-use of MMSI with three trailing zeros, in order to avoid depletion of MID and the corresponding MMSI series:

(a) Implement effective national procedures for identity assignment and registration;
(b) Provide the Radiocommunication Bureau with regular updates of assigned MMSI numbers in conformity with RR No. 20.16;
(c) Ensure that when ships move from the flag of registration of one administration to that of another administration, all of the assigned means of ship station identification, including the MMSI, are reassigned as appropriate and that the changes are notified to the Radiocommunication Bureau as soon as possible (see RR No. 20.16);
(d) An MMSI assignment could be considered for re-use after being absent from two successive editions of List V of the ITU service publications or after a period of two years, whichever is greater.

Section 2

Maritime identities used for other maritime devices for special purposes

Administrations, when assigning maritime identities to handheld VHF transceivers with DSC and GNSS, should employ all available measures to effectively manage the limited identity resource.

(a) The format scheme used for assigning VHF transceiver identities, will accommodate 100,000 VHF transceivers per MID. When the administration concerned has assigned identities to 100,000 VHF transceivers with DSC and GNSS, it may use an additional country code (MID), if it is already assigned by the ITU, giving a further 100,000 identities. 10 Rec. ITU-R M.585-7.
(b) When an administration determines it has a need for additional allocation of a MID, because it has exhausted more than 80% of its allocated MID resource, it should communicate a written formal application to the Director, Radiocommunication Bureau to request allocation of an additional MID.

WATCHKEEPING

Vessels, while at sea, must maintain a continuous watch appropriate to the sea area in which the vessel is sailing using:

1. VHF DSC Ch 70.
2. MF DSC distress and safety frequency 2187·5 kHz.
3. DSC distress and safety frequency 8414·5 kHz and at least one other HF DSC frequency appropriate to local time and ship's position relative to the nearest DSC coast station.
4. SOLAS vessels, where practical, should maintain a watch on VHF Ch 13 for communications related to the safety of navigation.
5. A continuous watch for MSI broadcasts must also be kept on the appropriate service for the area in which the ship is sailing, by:
    (a) NAVTEX
    (b) GMDSS Satellite Service providers MSI delivery service
    (c) HF MSI

Note 1: Weather and Navigational Warnings are also transmitted at fixed times throughout the day by a variety of non-GMDSS coast stations on MF, HF and VHF. See ALRS Volume 3 (NP 283).

Note 2: In Sea Areas A3 and A4, the purpose of VHF and MF is to attract the attention of other ships in the vicinity; this is why DSC watch keeping receivers must remain operational at all times, and in all sea areas.

RADIOTELEPHONE PROCEDURES

The frequency 2182 kHz is an international distress frequency for radiotelephony, see ITU Regulations, ITU-R M.541-9, Article Res. 32-2 & RR52-11 of the Radio Regulations.

For distress purposes, communications are carried out on a single frequency so that all parties can hear both sides of any conversation. Radiotelephone transmissions at MF and HF always use (upper) single side band modulation (class of emission: J3E) and at VHF use frequency / phase modulation (class of emission: F3E / G3E). Operators are referred to the ITU Manual for full details of Distress, Urgency and Safety procedures, as well as those for commercial operations.

The RT distress frequencies are not used exclusively for distress and safety purposes. Both VHF Ch 16 and 2182 kHz may be used for calling and reply, although such transmissions must be kept at a minimum and, in the case of Ch 16, be no more than 1 minute in duration. Also, 4125 kHz and 6215 kHz may be used for call and reply at powers below 1 kW. it is essential, in accordance with Recommendation ITU-R M.1171, to listen for a reasonable period, to make sure that no distress traffic is being sent, before transmitting on any of the carrier frequencies 2182 kHz, 4125 kHz, 6215 kHz, 8291 kHz, 12290 kHz, 16420 kHz and 156·8 MHz (Ch 16).

The carrier frequencies 12290 kHz and 16420 kHz used to be the ship frequency for Channels 1221 and 1621; they were used as routine calling frequencies for ships to coast stations in much the same way as 2182 kHz.These two frequencies have now been strictly limited to GMDSS use between ship and Rescue Coordination Centres only. The frequencies for routine radiotelephone calling are now 12359 kHz and 16537 kHz for both ship and coast stations.

RADIOTELEX (NBDP) PROCEDURES

All telex signals use a binary system. Over landlines (cables), they consist of two voltages, "high" and "low" sometimes called "1's" and "0's". But voltages can not be sent by radio so a modem is used to change them into two tones which can then be transmitted. The tones are only 170 Hz apart and thus occupy a narrow bandwidth, giving rise to the abbreviation NBDP (Narrow Band Direct Printing). The receiving modem changes the tones back into voltages to drive the equipment at the receiving end.

As required by RR33, all telex messages must be preceded by at least one "carriage return", one "line feed" and one "letter shift". The terms "carriage return" and "line feed" hark back to the days of manual typewriters when the paper was shifted up a line while the paper "carriage" was being pushed to the start of the next line, an operation rarely seen since the advent of computers. The "letter shift" is required because the telex code can deal with either letters or figures but not both together; it has to be switched between the letter code and the figure code. This is because it is a 5-unit code - i.e. each character is represented by 5 "bits", which allows for 32 different combinations of "high" and "low" - only enough for the letters of the alphabet plus a few other essential items. It is necessary to press a special key called a "figure shift" which makes the telex send figures and punctuation symbols, until the "letter shift" is pressed once again to return to letters. On computer keyboards, the "Enter" key performs all three functions in a single keystroke, and when changing between letters and figures the shift keys are operated automatically by the computer.

In radiotelex, each character is represented by 7 tones. There are 128 possible combinations but only those which have "3 lows" and "4 highs" are used. There are 35 such combinations - enough for the standard telex code plus three extra for use as control signals. If the received character does not have 3 lows and 4 highs, the receiving station will send a control signal requesting a repeat until it is received correctly – hence ARQ (Automatic ReQuest for repetition). ARQ is only possible between two stations synchronised together using rapid alternations between transmission and reception. ARQ provides error-free text because the likelihood of a low tone becoming a high tone and a low tone becoming a high tone in the same group is virtually zero. But it is not possible to use ARQ to send messages to a large number of stations at the same time, e.g. for distress and safety purposes. In these cases, the only suitable method is to send the message twice; a character will be printed only if it is received identically on both transmissions. This is called Forward Error Correction (FEC) – a misnomer, because although errors can be detected, they are not corrected at all.

Operational Procedures are detailed in ITU-R M.492-6 (in the ITU Manual). It describes the use of (ARQ) and (FEC), and how to set up a call with a coast station using "free channel" signals. Ships' telex terminals usually offer two types of ARQ call; one which makes the equipment wait for a "free" signal before transmitting the call, and one which transmits the call immediately, regardless of whether or not the called station has traffic in progress. Care should be taken to ensure that the correct choice is made.

ITU-R M.492-6 refers to two other Recommendations, i.e. M.476 and M.625. The former specifies (among other things) that vessels should be issued with a 5-digit "Selcall" number for automatic reception of incoming calls. M.625 came later and authorised use of the vessel's MMSI number. Thus, ships terminals may be programmed to respond to both Selcall and MMSI numbers. It also specified that the ARQ mode should allow 32 repeats (with characters being sent in groups of three) before breaking off contact, slightly different from M.476 which said "after a predetermined time of continuous repetition".

All three Recommendations remain valid for backwards compatibility.

GENERAL BUSINESS AND COMMERCIAL COMMUNICATIONS

General communications are one of the nine functions of the GMDSS. The emphasis of general communications in the GMDSS has shifted to Narrow-Band Direct-Printing (NBDP) techniques, otherwise known as telex, in preference to voice communications. Coast stations providing these services are included in ALRS Volume 1 (NP281).

It is possible to make telex calls to any subscriber to the International Telex Network by using the MF/HF or satellite communications equipment forming part of the GMDSS installation.

In the modern business environment telex communications have several advantages over telephone communications, e.g.

- Messages can be prepared in advance, ensuring that no essential information is overlooked.
- A telex message is regarded as a written document and is legally accepted as such in many countries.
- The exchange of answerback codes acts as confirmation that the message has been received at the destination.
- Messages can be received at any time, regardless of the presence of an operator.
- Many coast stations and coast earth stations offer "Store and Forward" or electronic mail type of facilities, whereby a telex message can be left on a computer for onward transmission to either a single or multiple addressees or in an electronic mail box for later retrieval.
- Many coast stations and coast earth stations also offer services whereby messages can be accepted from ships over the telex network, for onward delivery as a radiotelegram or telefax.

Operators should note that procedures for Maritime Commercial Working, including radiograms and radiotelexograms as well as telephone and telex calls, are contained in Recommendations published by the ITU Telecommunication Committee (ITU-T, as distinct from ITU-R).

ITU-T Recommendation F.110 is particularly relevant, but ITU-T Recommendations F.1, F.60 and E.141 also describe internationally agreed commercial procedures for telegrams, telex and telephone calls respectively. The Recommendations are printed in the ITU Manual.

ITU-T Recommendation D.90 deals with charges and the settlement of accounts. Among other things it indicates that if one land station relays traffic between two mobiles, two land station charges are collected. This applies to satellite and terrestrial services alike.

RADIO REGULATIONS

GMDSS operators are required to have a detailed knowledge of the Radio Regulations. A brief reference is made to the content of some of them below.

RR2	Date and time to be UTC, Gregorian Calendar; date format dd/mm/yy.
RR4	Use minimum power; stations in distress can use any means at their disposal to attract attention.
RR15	How to avoid causing interference; infringement reports.
RR17	Deliberate interception of third-party traffic prohibited; existence of traffic intercepted accidentally not to be divulged.
RR19	All transmissions to carry ID signals; formation of call signs and MMSI numbers.
RR20	List of documents, descriptions of ITU Manuals.
RR30	Ships to comply with non-GMDSS procedures at AP13; land mobiles can use GMDSS in remote/uninhabited areas.
RR31	Always listen on GMDSS frequencies before transmitting; minimum testing, use artificial antennae and low power.
RR32	Distress procedures; RT signals to be slow and distinct; no action against ship or mariner reporting false alert.
RR33	Urgency/Safety procedures; for telex, use FEC with:- a carriage return, a line feed signal, a letter shift signal and the safety signal.
RR49	Radio inspectors to see ship's licence and operator's certificates; give report of inspection to Master before leaving vessel.
RR50	Radio station to have accurate UTC clock; radio log to be kept in UTC.
RR52	Max RT power for ship station is 1·5 kW; max 25 W for VHF; use J3E and comply with ITU-R M.1173 (USB only).
RR54	DSC and Selcall procedures to be as per ITU-R Recommendations.
RR56	NBDP Procedures as per ITU-R M.492-6; use ARQ between 2 stations.
RR57	RT procedures as per ITU-R M.1171; use duplex for phone calls if possible.

World Radiocommunication Conference

The World Radio Conference 2019 was held in Sharm el-Sheikh, Egypt 28 October to 22 November 2019.
The significant items on the agenda and their outcomes were:

AI 1.8 – **Maritime GMDSS**
- To consider possible regulatory actions to support Global Maritime Distress Safety Systems (GMDSS) modernization and to support the introduction of additional satellite systems into the GMDSS, in accordance with Resolution 359 (Rev.WRC-15)
- **Issue A: Modernisation of GMDSS**
- Issue A outcome was in line with the European preferences;
- Introduction of MF frequencies for international NAVDAT in RR Article 5 and for the introduction of the HF NAVDAT frequencies in RR Appendix 17
- Europe opposed the introduction of the MF frequencies for international NAVDAT in RR Appendix 15 and the introduction of the HF NAVDAT frequencies in RR Appendix 15 at this WRC

- **Issue B: Regulatory action due to the introduction of additional satellite systems into the GMDSS by IMO**
- A primary allocation to the mobile maritime-satellite service for both uplink and downlink direction in 5 MHz, namely 1621.35-1626.35 MHz.
- Provisions to provide protection to radioastronomy operating in the adjacent band were also agreed.

AI1.9.1 – Maritime AIS
- To consider, based on the results of ITU-R studies
- 1.9.1 - Maritime autonomous devices regulatory actions within the frequency band 156-162.05 MHz for autonomous maritime radio devices to protect the GMDSS and automatic identifications system (AIS), in accordance with Resolution 362 (WRC-15);
- There was early consensus on the frequency allocations for AMRD group A and AMRD group B that are operated with AIS technology (Group A channel 70 for digital selective calling and on channels AIS1 and AIS2 for automatic identification system, with Group B in the bands of RR Appendix 18). A note in the plenary minutes addressed AMRD group B using technology other than AIS.

AI 1.9.2 – Maritime VDES
- To consider, based on the results of ITU-R studies
- 1.9.2 - VDES Satellite modifications of the Radio Regulations, including new spectrum allocations to the maritime mobile-satellite service (Earth to space and space-to-Earth), preferably within the frequency bands 156.0125-157.4375 MHz and 160.6125-162.0375 MHz of Appendix 18, to enable a new VHF data exchange system (VDES) satellite component, while ensuring that this component will not degrade the current terrestrial VDES components, applications specific messages (ASM) and AIS operations and not impose any additional constraints on existing services in these and adjacent frequency bands as stated in recognizing d) and e) of Resolution 360 (Rev.WRC-15)

A new secondary allocation to the VDE-SAT uplink and downlink within the frequency bands of Appendix 18, with an additional provision on the use of the MMSS (space-to-Earth) downlink subject to agreement under RR No. 9.21 in Azerbaijan, Belarus, China, Korea (Rep. of), Cuba, the Russian Federation, the Syrian Arab Republic, the Dem. People's Rep. of Korea, South Africa and Viet Nam.

GMDSS will also feature on the next WRC to be held in 2023.

COMMUNICATIONS SYSTEMS FOR USE IN THE GMDSS

TERRESTRIAL COMMUNICATIONS

Long-Range Service

Use of HF provides a long-range service in both the ship-to-shore and shore-to-ship directions. In areas covered by a GMDSS satellite communication system, it can be used as an alternative to satellite communications and outside these areas (**GMDSS Sea Area A4**) it provides the only long-range communication capability. HF frequencies have been designated in the 4, 6, 8, 12 and 16 MHz bands.

Digital Selective Calling (DSC) forms the basis of distress alerting and safety communications. Distress and safety communications following a DSC call can be performed by radiotelephony or radio telex (Narrow Band Direct Printing - NBDP).

Automated HF Radio Test Call Facilities have been activated by the US Coast Guard. An Automated Digital Selective Calling Answering System (ADSCAS) facility for responding to HF-DSC test calls is available on 4 MHz only.

The HF DSC section contains details of stations in addition to the United States which offer test call facilities.

Medium-Range Service

A medium-range service is provided on frequencies in the 2 MHz band. In the ship-to-shore, ship-to-ship and shore-to-ship directions 2187·5 kHz will be used for distress alerts, urgency and safety calls using DSC, and 2182 kHz will be used for distress urgency and safety traffic by radiotelephony, including SAR coordinating and on-scene communications. 2174·5 kHz will be used for radio telex (NBDP) distress, urgency and safety traffic.

Short-Range Service

VHF provides short-range service on the frequencies:

- 156·525 MHz (Ch 70) for distress, urgency and safety alerts using DSC, and
- 156·800 MHz (Ch 16) for distress and safety traffic by radiotelephony, including SAR coordinating and on-scene communications.

SATELLITE COMMUNICATIONS

Introduction
(The UKHO gratefully acknowledges the assistance of both Inmarsat and Iridium in compiling the following sections and for their kind permission to reproduce some of the images that follow.)

Satellite communication is a key element of the Global Maritime Distress and Safety System (GMDSS).

The International Maritime Satellite Organisation (IMSO) was established by the IMO to oversee maritime satellite service providers within the GMDSS. IMSO works on behalf of the maritime community to ensure that new satellite service providers meet all the criteria required of a GMDSS satellite service provider.

The Inmarsat system, which employs geostationary satellites and operates in the 1·5 - 1·6 GHz frequency band, provides ships fitted with suitable Inmarsat Mobile Earth Stations (MESs) a means of distress alerting, Voice Distress, receiving Maritime Safety Information, Priority Messaging, LRIT, SSAS, Inmarsat Safety Services and a capability for two-way general communications using voice, data and messaging.

The Inmarsat International SafetyNET service is used for broadcast of Maritime Safety Information (MSI) and Search and Rescue (SAR) related information to all ships in various geographical areas covered by Inmarsat's geostationary satellites, including those not covered by the NAVTEX system.

The Iridium satellite system is the latest system to gain approval by the IMO for the provision of GMDSS services.

A polar-orbiting Cospas-Sarsat satellite system, operating in the 406 - 406·1 MHz frequency band, and the use of 406 MHz satellite EPIRBs provides one of the main means of distress alerting and for determining the position of distress alerts in the GMDSS.

INMARSAT

OVERVIEW

Inmarsat has been a leader in global satellite communications for more than 40 years and operates its own secure satellite fleet, and ground infrastructure across L-Band, Ka-Band and S-Band. The Inmarsat network provides global coverage between 76° North and 76° South with its geostationary satellites.

Inmarsat Satellite Services

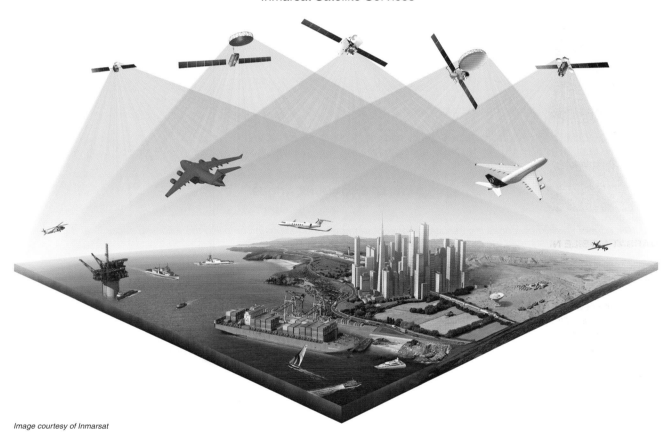

Image courtesy of Inmarsat

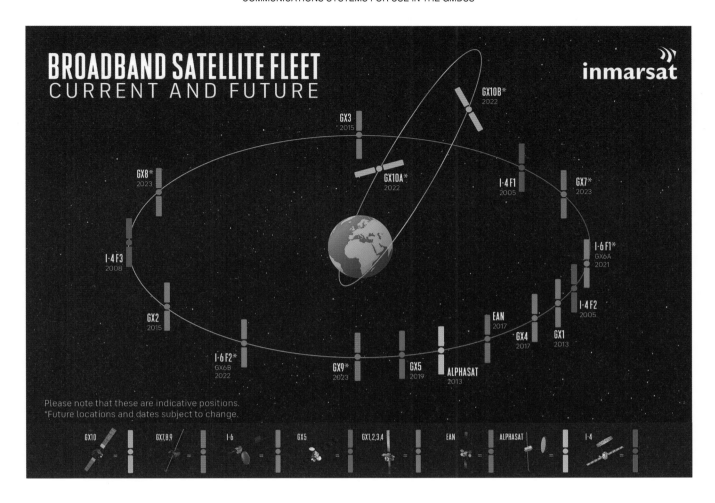

INMARSAT MOBILE NUMBERS (IMN)

Each communication system uses a distinctive Inmarsat Number which allows the functionality to be recognised from the number allocated to a specific terminal:

Terminals with GMDSS Capability:
- **Inmarsat C:** *Nine (9) digits beginning with 4 followed by 3-digit MID (Maritime Identification Digits)*
- **Inmarsat Mini-C:** *Nine (9) digits beginning with 4 followed by 3-digit MID (Maritime Identification Digits)*
- **Fleet Safety -** *ICCID number between 18-22 digits associated with a voice number starting with (+870) 77...*
- **Inmarsat SNAC:** *Calls from the terrestrial telephone network (PSTN) to an Inmarsat network are made using the Inmarsat +870 international dialling code.*

Ship Earth Stations (SES)

Inmarsat offers ship earth stations (SES) within the GMDSS and also shore-side systems to NAVAREA, METAREA and Maritime Rescue Coordination Centres (MRCC's). This provision exceeds the minimum requirement as specified by the IMO. Inmarsat provides 2 SES designed to provide approved GMDSS compliant functions required by ships conforming to the SOLAS Convention.

INMARSAT C MES and Mini-C MES

Inmarsat C is the original satellite communications system primarily used for distress alerting and reception of MSI from all 21 NAV/METAREAs and shore-to-ship distress alert relay messages. A two-way store and forward system that can handle data and messages up to 32KB, plus commercial email. Inmarsat C is also utilised for other IMO services such as Ship Security Alerting System (SSAS), Vessel Monitoring System (VMS) and Long-Range Identification and Tracking of ships (LRIT).

Distress Alert: Inmarsat C terminals are equipped with a Distress-Alerting feature, which automatically generates and sends a Distress Alert, incorporating the ships position, time the position was acquired, MMSI number and the ships Inmarsat Mobile Number, to 1 of Inmarsat's 14 Inmarsat C associated Rescue Coordination Centres (RCC) when the dedicated Distress Button is pressed. The procedure for sending a Distress Alert is similar to that for DSC. The dedicated distress button is pressed and held. If there is time to enter information, the system allows entry of the Nature of Distress. The Distress Alert is acknowledged by the LES and automatically sent to the RCC. The Inmarsat Network Operation Centre (NOC) monitors every Distress Alert to ensure positive delivery and action.

Distress Message: After the distress alert is sent and an acknowledgement received, a more detailed Distress Message may be sent to provide more detailed information about the distress incident and Search and Rescue (SAR) coordination. This distress priority message should be sent through the same LES as the Distress Alert and will be automatically routed to the same RCC.

Urgency priority: Inmarsat C terminals can utilise the Inmarsat Urgency priority shortcodes that provide the vessel with Medical Advice (32), Medical Assistance (38) and Maritime Assistance (39). When entering the shortcodes 32, 38, or 39, the user can enter a text-based message that will automatically be delivered to the appropriate medical facility or maritime agency with full Urgency priority over the Inmarsat network.

Safety priority: Inmarsat C can also be used to provide Meteorological (41) and Navigational (42) reporting, this is transmitted to the relevant shore-side authorities using Safety priority.

Maritime Safety Information: Inmarsat C terminals can automatically receive MSI through the Enhanced Group Call system. These messages are meteorological warnings and forecasts, navigational warnings and Search and Rescue broadcasts. These messages are promulgated by IMO EGC Certified MSI providers to NAVAREAs / METAREAs (see figures 5 and 7) or user-defined areas such as coastal, circular or rectangular areas.

All 21 NAVAREA and METAREA Co-ordinators broadcast MSI through the Inmarsat SafetyNET or SafetyNET II system. All IMO Certified Search and Rescue authorities also broadcast through the Inmarsat SafetyNET / SafetyNET II system ensuring MSI and SAR related information is received on the Inmarsat C terminals in every NAV/METAREA.
The Inmarsat C and Mini C NAVAREA and METAREA coverage diagrams are located in the EGC SYSTEMS section of this publication.

Diagram page 213
Diagram page 214

INMARSAT C LES AND ASSOCIATED RCCS

Country	LES Name	LES Operator	Region	LES ID	Associated RCC	RCC Emergency contact email	RCC Emergency phone
Netherlands	Burum	Inmarsat Solutions	AOR-W	002	MRCC UK	ukmrcc@hmcg.gov.uk	+44 (0) 1326 317575 or +44 (0) 2038172548
				012	JRCC Den Helder	ccc@kustwacht.nl	+31 223 542 300
			AOR-E	102	MRCC UK	ukmrcc@hmcg.gov.uk	+44 (0) 1326 317575 or +44 (0) 2038172548
				112	JRCC Den Helder	ccc@kustwacht.nl	+31 223 542 300
			POR	202	MRCC UK	ukmrcc@hmcg.gov.uk	+44 (0) 1326 317575 or +44 (0) 2038172548
				212	RCC Australia	rccaus@amsa.gov.au	+61 2 62306811
			IOR	302	MRCC UK	ukmrcc@hmcg.gov.uk	+44 (0) 1326 317575 or +44 (0) 2038172548
				312	RCC Australia	rccaus@amsa.gov.au	+61 2 62306811
Norway	Eik	Comsat, Marlink	AOR-W	001	USCG Norfolk	DO5-SMB-CAA-LANT30cc@uscg.mil	+1 757 398 6700
				004	JRCC Stavanger	operations@jrcc-stavanger.no or opinsp@jrcc-stavanger.no	+47 51 64 60 00 or +47 51646002
			AOR-E	101	USCG Norfolk	DO5-SMB-CAA-LANT30cc@uscg.mil	+1 757 398 6700
				104	JRCC Stavanger	operations@jrcc-stavanger.no or opinsp@jrcc-stavanger.no	+47 51 64 60 00 or +47 51646002
			POR	201	USCG Alameda	rccalameda1@uscg.mil	+1 510-437-3701 or +1 510 437 3700
				204	JRCC Stavanger	operations@jrcc-stavanger.no or opinsp@jrcc-stavanger.no	+47 51 64 60 00 or +47 51646002
			IOR	301	JRCC Stavanger	operations@jrcc-stavanger.no or opinsp@jrcc-stavanger.no	+47 51 64 60 00 or +47 51646002
				304	JRCC Stavanger	operations@jrcc-stavanger.no or opinsp@jrcc-stavanger.no	+47 51 64 60 00 or +47 51646002
Japan	Yamaguchi	KDDI	AOR-W	003	Opr. Centre, Tokyo	jcg-op@mlit.go.jp	+81 3 3591 9812 or +81 3 3591 9000
			AOR-E	103	Opr. Centre, Tokyo	jcg-op@mlit.go.jp	+81 3 3591 9812 or +81 3 3591 9000
			POR	203	Opr. Centre, Tokyo	jcg-op@mlit.go.jp	+81 3 3591 9812 or +81 3 3591 9000
			IOR	303	Opr. Centre, Tokyo	jcg-op@mlit.go.jp	+81 3 3591 9812 or +81 3 3591 9000
Italy	Fucino	Telecom Italia	AOR-E	105	CG Rome	imrcc-ssas@mit.gov.it	+39 06 59648187
			IOR	335	CG Rome	imrcc-ssas@mit.gov.it	+39 06 59648187
India	BSNL	BSNL	IOR	306	MRCC Mumbai	mrcc-west@indiancoastguard.nic.in	+91 22 24316558
			POR	206	MRCC Mumbai	mrcc-west@indiancoastguard.nic.in	+91 22 24316558
China	Beijing	MCN	POR	211	MRCC Beijing	cnmrcc@msa.gov.cn	+86-10-65292221
			IOR	311	MRCC Beijing	cnmrcc@msa.gov.cn	+86-10-65292221
Russian Federation	Nudol	Marsat	POR	217	MRCC Vladivostok	vldvmrcc@pma.ru	+7 4232 227782, +7 4232 495522, +7 4232 497401
			IOR	317	MRCC Moscow	smrcc@morflot.ru	+7 495 626 1052
France	Aussaguel	Marlink	AOR-W	021	CROSS Griz-Nez	gris-nez@mrccfr.eu	+33 3 21 87 21 87
			AOR-E	121	CROSS Griz-Nez	gris-nez@mrccfr.eu	+33 3 21 87 21 87
			POR	221	CROSS Griz-Nez	gris-nez@mrccfr.eu	+33 3 21 87 21 87
			IOR	321	CROSS Griz-Nez	gris-nez@mrccfr.eu	+33 3 21 87 21 87
Vietnam	Hai Phong	Vishipel	POR	230	MRCC Vietnam	rescuevietnam@yahoo.com.vn or rescue-dept@vinamarine.gov.vn	+ 84 4 3768 3050

Telex Services

Telex services are still available on the Inmarsat C SES however, users wishing to utilise this service should check for available shore side terrestrial services that contine to provide Telex services.

INMARSAT FLEET SAFETY

Fleet Safety brings GMDSS safety services to FleetBroadband and Fleet One users by connecting a Maritime Safety Terminal (MST). This is the first and only IP-based voice and data GMDSS ship earth station. In addition to hosting GMDSS and Inmarsat Safety services, Fleet Safety is also capable of Ship Security Alert System (SSAS), LRIT, VMS, high-speed internet connections and simultaneous voice and data. Seamless coverage and 99.9% network availability ensure that the service is always available. Inmarsat's many years of safety experience ensures that ships are provided with robust and reliable communications platform.

GMDSS SERVICES

Distress Alert: Fleet Safety routes Distress Alerts directly to one of 50+ IMO recognised Inmarsat associated MRCCs using the RescueNET system. Distress alerts reach the closest MRCC within seconds, not minutes. New 3-stage notifications provide additional reassurance that the Distress has been sent, delivered and read by an approved MRCC.

Voice Distress: Giving choice to the user, Fleet Safety allows the user to send a Distress Alert if there is no time permitting to speak on the phone, alternatively, by pressing the Voice Distress Button the user's phone is connected directly to one of Inmarsat's global MRCCs with Distress Priority. The called MRCC is also provided with the vessel information including position via a data connection to ensure additional accuracy.

Distress Message: As with Inmarsat C, Fleet Safety allows the user to create a Distress Message to provide additional information after the Distress Alert has been sent. Fleet Safety provides this function with the 3-stage notification and delivery within seconds.

Urgency priority Data: Using the interactive interface, the user can select Medical Advice, Medical Assistance, or Maritime Assistance, create a message and send it directly to the correct authority automatically.

Urgency priority Voice: Provides direct voice connections for medical advice and assistance as well as maritime assistance.

Safety Priority messages: Fleet Safety enables users to update authorities on Navigational and Meteorological egents in real time through the interactive display.

Maritime Safety Information: Maritime Safety Information is available from all IMO EGC certified NAVAREA, METAREA and MRCC's. With additional filtering and a quick set-up interface, the user can select which adjacent areas they want to receive information from.

In addition to the IMO GMDSS services, Fleet Safety provides additional enhanced Inmarsat Safety Services:

On-demand Maritime Safety Information: This enables the user to search for any vital Maritime Safety Information broadcasts they may have missed and download them directly onto their MST.

Distress Chat: Distress priority text chat room between the vessel in distress, assisting vessels and MRCCs. The MRCC can include multiple vessels and multiple MRCCs into a Distress Chat. This service provides an extra layer of coordination when in distress or assisting with a SAR operation.

Distress Vessel Tracking: If a vessel equipped with Fleet Safety gets into a distress situation, the Inmarsat MRCC dealing with the distress can activate the vessel tracking system to ensure rescue services are directed to the correct position the first time.

The Fleetbroadband NAVAREA and METAREA footprint diagrams are located in the EGC SYSTEMS section of this publication.

Fleet Safety

FLEETBROADBAND

FleetBroadband provides voice and data globally via the L-Band constellation and ground network, which maintains over 99.9% network availability. The reliability of the L-band service means it provides unlimited back-up to Inmarsat's high-speed service, ensuring seamless global mobility.

FleetBroadband currently offers 505 Emergency Calling as standard for non-SOLAS vessels, simply dialing '505' puts vessels directly in contact with an MRCC free of charge for emergency calls. Virtually all telecommunication services found in offices ashore are available to ships equipped with Inmarsat Fleet Xpress, FleetBroadband or Fleet One services.

Various sized antennas are available to suit any size of vessel; these services deliver high speed, high quality, reliable and automatic communications via telephone, facsimile, data and e-mail.

FleetBroadband

FLEET XPRESS
This delivers high data speeds of the Global Xpress Ka-band network with the proven reliability of L-band to offer excellent speed, continuous connectivity and performance. It allows vessel efficiencies and performance in real-time and provides users access to the Inmarsat Fleet Data system. It does this by enabling the growth of Internet of Things (IoT) and onboard sensors to resolve queries and make operational decisions.

Fleet Xpress provides a continuous, consistent service as traffic is seamlessly handed across spot beams and between Inmarsat's satellites around the world. Switching between satellites is handled by a tracking system that acquires the new satellite as a vessel moves into its coverage footprint. This is all done automatically to ensure seamless coverage and without the need for any intervention or manual actions by the crew. In the event of a degradation in the Ka-band signal, the service will automatically switch to FleetBroadband on the L-band network, resulting in no break in service. Inmarsat's Land Earth Stations (LES) are fully redundant, so vessels will remain in contact without needing to chase satellites.

SHORE-SIDE SERVICES
Inmarsat offers several shore-side services to enhance further the requirements of the GMDSS. These include SafetyNET, SafetyNET II and RescueNET.

SafetyNET: An international automatic reception satellite-based service for the promulgation of Maritime Safety Information, navigational and meteorological warnings, meteorological forecasts, Search and Rescue related information and other urgent safety-related messages to ALL Inmarsat GMDSS SES including Inmarsat C, Mini C and Fleet Safety. Information providers submit their messages to an Inmarsat LES for broadcast over a defined geographical area with a priority of Safety, Urgency or Distress. These messages are received automatically by Inmarsat SES in the intended broadcast area (or adjacent area if selected by the vessel).

SafetyNET II: An enhancement to the current SafetyNET system, and provides a user-friendly, interactive web interface for Maritime Safety Information providers to create their Maritime Safety Information messages and deliver them simultaneously over multiple Inmarsat networks. New features of SafetyNET II include enhanced scheduling of messages, manual cancelation, message report creation, monitoring of each broadcast and API access.
As a part of the Inmarsat GMDSS modernization programme, SafetyNET II was developed, enabling registered information providers to prepare and issue MSI and SAR coordination messages directly to the Inmarsat C Network Coordination Station (NCS) and Inmarsat FleetBroadband (FB) Satellite Access Stations (SAS) for simultaneous broadcast to safety enabled Inmarsat-C, Mini-C and Fleet Safety terminals.

RescueNET: A new bespoke safety service tailored specifically for RCCs. This intuitive and interactive service delivers fast, reliable and IMO-approved Search and Rescue (SAR) communications in Ship-to-Shore and Shore-to-Ship directions. Services available to Inmarsat approved RescueNET users:
- Reception of Distress Alerts (Fleet Safety to RescueNET)
- Broadcast of Distress Alert Relay (Shore-to-Ship Distress Alert) to Inmarsat C, Mini C and Inmarsat Fleet Safety SES
- Broadcast Search and Rescue Co-ordination messages to Rectangular or Circular area to Inmarsat C, Mini C and Fleet Safety SES
- Priority Messaging (Ship-to-Shore and Shore-to-Ship)
- RCC information look-up tools
- Vessel information look-up tools
- Distress vessel tracking
- Distress Chat

This service is only available to IMO GISIS registered MRCC's approved by Inmarsat.

INMARSAT GMDSS SERVICES

Transmitting Ship-to-Shore Distress Alerts

The Inmarsat system provides priority access to satellite communications channels in emergency situations. Ship's terminals with distress capability are able to initiate and transmit a distress alert by pressing a dedicated distress button and the alert is automatically delivered by the Inmarsat system to a Maritime Rescue Coordination Centre (MRCC). Distress alert transmissions are automatically recognized within the network and a satellite channel is instantly assigned. In addition, a distress priority message can also be sent from a terminal to give more information to the addressed MRCC about the distress event and to ask for required assistance. If all satellite channels happen to be busy, one of them will be pre-empted and allocated to the SES which initiated distress alert or distress priority message. The processing of such calls is completely automatic and does not involve any human intervention. The Inmarsat NOC personnel, however, are notified of the reception and passing through of a distress alert or distress priority message by audio/visual alarms.

To ensure all distress urgency and safety communications are communicated and with the correct priority, each priority message or broadcast is closely monitored by the Inmarsat network. If any form of anomaly is detected, the Inmarsat NOC, LES and NCS personnel are alerted and take immediate action to ensure all messages and alerts are received correctly by the appropriate MRCC. Follow up action with the MRCC's is also initiated to offer additional support if required.

The distress priority applies not only with respect to the imminent allocation of satellite channels but also to the automatic routing of the call to the appropriate rescue authority. All interconnects into the Inmarsat network, including NCS, LES and MSS have dedicated lines and additonal redundancies to ensure the highest level of reliability. MRCC's are responsible for providing suitable connections into the network, however Inmarsat makes available dedicated lines where required.

Distress alert is initiated by the ship's crew by using the dedicated distress button that requires two independent actions to activate alert. On activation the equipment instantaneously transmits the distress alert that is automatically routed to a competent rescue authority. This also avoids the need for the SES operator to select the telephone or e-mail of the MRCC thereby eliminating possible human error. The establishment of this end-to-end connection, being completely automatic and on a priority basis, takes only a few seconds.

The procedure described above is the primary means of ship-to-shore distress alerting in the Inmarsat system. It should be noted, however, that Inmarsat-equipped ships may also contact any MRCC of their choice by following the calling procedure for routine priority calls. In this case, the complete international telephone number or e-mail address has to be used.

A major benefit of the Inmarsat satellite system is that it eliminates the need for dedicated frequencies to be used for distress and safety communications. Distress messages made through the Inmarsat system use the existing communication protocol on a priority basis to ensure an immediate connection.

Receiving Shore-to-Ship Distress Alerts Through The Inmarsat SafetyNET II Service

The EGC (Enhanced Group Call) receiver is an integral part of an Inmarsat C, Mini-C MES and Fleet Safety, that is used to automatically receive Maritime Safety Information (MSI) and SAR related information addressed to various geographical areas. All ships navigating in the addressed area receive MSI and SAR related messages automatically. Shore-to-Ship distress alert (relay) is part of the SAR related information and broadcast to all ships by certified MRCCs upon receiving an initial distress alert from a ship. Distress alert relay is addressed to a circular area around the ship in distress and all ships within the addressed area automatically receive it. When a distress alert relay or distress priority message is received, visual and audible alarms will be provided on the ship's terminal which can only be acknowledged manually.

Transmitting and Receiving Search and Rescue (SAR) Coordinating Communications

For the coordination and control of SAR operations, MRCCs require communications with the ship in distress as well as with other units participating in the operation. The methods and modes of communication (terrestrial, satellite, telephone & telex) used will be governed by the capabilities available onboard the ship in distress as well as those onboard assisting units. Where some or all are equipped with satellite terminals, the advantage of the Inmarsat system for rapid, reliable communications including receipt of SAR communications can be achieved. Advances in the Inmarsat Fleet Safety technology have enabled greater SAR coordination through the Distress Chat function, this now enables the controlling MRCC, the vessel in distress and other assets, such as MRCC's and Fleet Safety vessels, to all coordinate together over a free Distress Priority network.

Those MRCCs that are registered with the IMO EGC Coordinating Panel as providers of SAR communications are able to use Inmarsat RescueNET services and broadcast SAR information to all ships navigating in the addressed areas. All Inmarsat GMDSS terminals, Inmarsat C, Mini-C and Fleet Safety will automatically receive these broadcasts if their position is inside the addressed area.

RescueNET is an Inmarsat safety service provided to MRCCs to enable swift, reliable and approved Search and Rescue communications in both Ship-to-Shore, Shore-to-Ship directions as well as coordination between MRCCs. These services include:

- Reception of Distress Alerts
- Broadcast of Distress Alert Relay
- MSI Broadcast Search and Rescue Co-ordination messages to rectangular and circular areas
- Priority Messaging
- RCC lookup
- Vessel lookup
- Distress Chat

For MRCCs that are not SafetyNET certified, RescueNET offers simplified features.
RescueNET offers a reliable interlinking of MRCCs which is important as a distress message may be in an area between suitable MRCCs that cover thousands of miles of ocean. In these cases, prompt relay of the distress messages to all the MRCCs involved is essential by any communications means, whether landlines, terrestrial radio networks or satellite links.

Transmitting and Receiving Maritime Safety Information
Maritime Safety Information (MSI) is defined by IMO as navigational and meteorological warnings, meteorological forecasts and other urgent safety-related messages to ships. MSI is promulgated to ships via the Enhanced Group Call (EGC) system operated by Inmarsat. All IMO Certified EGC NAV/MET and SAR authorities broadcast over the SafetyNET or SafetyNET II services, ensuring all Inmarsat GMDSS SES receive vital MSI globaly.

Transmitting and Receiving On-Scene Communications
On-scene communications are mainly those between the ship in distress, assisting ships, and SAR on-scene Coordinator. These communications are normally short-range communications which are made on the VHF or MF distress and safety frequencies in the GMDSS. However, ships fitted with Inmarsat SES could use satellite communications as a supplement to their VHF and MF facilities.

Transmitting and Receiving General Communications
IMO define general radiocommunications as operational and public correspondence traffic other than distress, urgency and safety messages conducted by radio. General communications may be carried out by utilizing Inmarsat C, Mini-C, Fleet Safety and Inmarsat FleetBroadband systems as well as terrestrial radiocommunication systems.

IRIDIUM GMDSS SERVICES

General Information
Iridium offers global voice and data communications coverage. Iridium's 66 low-Earth orbiting (LEO) cross-linked satellites operate as a fully meshed network. Iridium serves all the navigable waters of the world, including the polar regions which are currently GMDSS Sea Area A4.

The satellite constellation provides the communication links between the MESs and the teleport(s), which are interconnected to the gateways. The gateways serve as the switching centre, routing all communications into and from terrestrial networks, such as the Public Switched Telephone Network (PSTN). The gateway also locates, identifies and tracks subscribers for mobility management, and records user activity for billing purposes. These components are illustrated and explained further below:

Iridium offers a range of communication services to fulfil the functional requirements of the GMDSS. The IMO recognized Iridium's compliance with Resolution A.100(25) and recognized this in Resolution MSC.451(99) on 24 May 2018

The Iridium Global Mobile-Satellite System

Iridium Satellite LLC owns and operates a mobile satellite system providing global digital communications. The major components of the Iridium mobile-satellite system are:
- The space segment, consisting of 66 operational satellites and additional in-orbit spare satellites.
- The ground segment, consisting of satellite teleports (teleports) for the transfer of voice and data communications between the gateways and the satellite constellation, and gateways which provide connection to terrestrial voice and data networks.
- Mobile earth stations (MES), which consist of a satellite modem which is incorporated into a commercial product (the ship earth station), and an externally installed antenna.

Global coverage with overlapping satellite beams

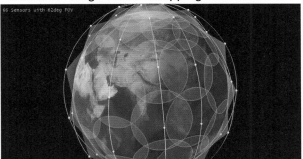

Image courtesy of Iridium

Ship Earth Stations:
A new range of GMDSS-compliant ship-borne equipment has been developed to meet the IMO's Performance standards for a ship earth station for use in the GMDSS contained in resolution MSC.434(98), and the IEC's testing requirements of international standard IEC 16097-16:2019, Global maritime distress and safety system (GMDSS) - Part 16: Ship earth stations operating in mobile-satellite systems recognized for use in the GMDSS - Operational and performance requirements, methods of testing and required test results.

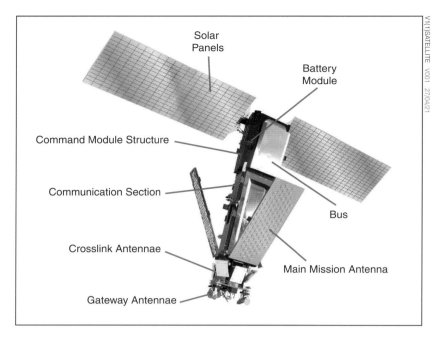

Iridium constellation showing Inter-Satellite Links

Image courtesy of Iridium

The Space Segment

The constellation of 66 operational Low Earth Orbit (LEO) satellites enables user terminal-to-user terminal, user terminal-to-gateway, and gateway-to-user terminal communications. The 66 satellites are evenly distributed in six orbital planes with a polar (86.4°) inclination, with on-orbit spare satellites. The satellites orbit the Earth at an altitude of 780 km and take approximately 100 minutes to complete one orbit. In addition to the 66 operational satellites, Iridium maintains an additional nine in-orbit spare satellites. These have the same capabilities as the operational satellites, and all are operating nominally.

The satellites support three types of communication links – satellite-to-satellite, satellite-to-teleport, and satellite-to-MES. Each satellite communicates with the satellite immediately ahead and behind in its orbital plane (north/south) and to the nearest satellite in each of the two adjacent orbital planes (east/west) using a K-band link. The Iridium system is currently the only mobile-satellite system employing this cross-linked satellite architecture. As a result, an MES is not required to be within the same satellite footprint as a gateway in order to gain access to the network.

The satellite-to-MES link uses an L-band antenna system. This projects 48 spot beams, or cells, on the Earth, with each beam being approximately 400 km (approximately 250 miles, or 220 nautical miles) in diameter. Each satellite antenna has a "footprint" with a diameter of approximately 4,500 km (approximately 2,800 miles or 2,500 nautical miles). Adjacent satellite footprints overlap on the Earth's surface, enabling seamless global coverage from pole to pole. The overlapping coverage provided by the cross-linked satellites operates as a fully meshed network.

About once every minute, the cell for an MES is provided by a different beam on the same satellite (the cellular look down antenna has 48 spot beams). About once every six minutes, the cell transitions to a beam on an adjacent satellite. Special processing called a handoff ensures that communication sessions are maintained.

The Satellite Network Operations Center (SNOC) manages the satellite constellation and provides network management over the entire Iridium system. The SNOC communicates with the satellites through Telemetry, Tracking and Control (TTAC) facilities. In addition to controlling communications between the SNOC and the satellites, the TTAC sites track the Iridium satellites and receive telemetry data from them.

The Ground Segment

Iridium currently operates teleports at geographically diverse locations around the globe, as part of the commercial network. The teleports use a Ka-band link to interconnect the satellite constellation with the Iridium gateways for the transfer of communications to and from Iridium user terminals.

IRIDIUM GATEWAY & GROUND STATION LOCATIONS

Operating as a switching centre, the primary gateway provides the connection between the Iridium network and terrestrial-based networks. Additional gateways also provide such connections. Each gateway controls system access, call setup, mobility management, billing, tracking and maintaining all information pertaining to user terminals, such as user identity and geo-location.

Iridium communication services recognised by IMO for use in the GMDSS

Iridium offers a range of communication services to fulfil the functional requirements of the GMDSS.
The recognized Iridium services specified in resolution MSC.451(99) are:
- Iridium Safety Voice
- Iridium Safety Messaging
- Iridium SafetyCast

The Iridium SafetyCast service was recognized as "Enhanced Group Calling" at the time of adoption of MSC.451(99), but renamed commercially afterwards. "Enhanced Group Calling" is reserved as an IMO generic term, recognized providers will use a commercial name.

Operational Status - summary
On 15 December 2020, Iridium announced the readiness and availability of the Iridium Safety Voice and Safety Messaging as operational, with the USCG RCC Norfolk Virginia serving as the primary associated RCC for the global region, and the RCC Alameda California serving as the backup (secondary) associated RCC.

The Iridium SafetyCast enhanced group calling system was declared ☐live☐ for all authorised and registered providers of Maritime Safety Information (MSI) and registered SAR authorities to use. Their declarations of operational status are within their discretion and dependent upon their own operational procedures, and will be declared publicly by them according to their national Notices to Mariners and national publications.

Further information may be obtained from the IMO website at , which contains modules for the Global SAR Plan and the GMDSS Master Plan. The GMDSS Master Plan module in GISIS provides necessary information to identify the coverage area and necessary details for MSI and SAR related information broadcast services related to each NAVAREA and METAREA. The GMDSS Master Plan module is accessible to all registered Public Account holders (any member of the public who is registered with an IMO Web account).

Additionally, the IHO currently published the Operational Status of the SafetyCast MSI service on it's website:
Changes to this information, as new RCCs become associated with the Iridium system, and as NAVAREA and METAREA Coordinators declare their operational status, will also be included in Notices to Mariners at the appropriate time.

Prioritisation of GMDSS communications
The Iridium network permits ship-to-shore, shore-to-ship and ship-to-ship calls for maritime safety communications. It provides for four levels of prioritization of all calls and performs pre-emption of lower priority communications, if necessary. It is necessary to ensure that the prioritization of traffic is protected against inadvertent or malicious misuse.

Distress traffic (alerts or calls) from ship to shore are initiated by a dedicated distress button which automatically assigns the priority. Urgency and safety priorities from ship to shore can be assigned by other features, such as short-codes or soft-keys, as the manufacturer of the ship earth station might include.

Prioritized traffic from shore to ship promulgated by authorized users, including such as an RCCs or registered information providers such as a NAVAREA or METAREA Coordinators is protected by secure means.

Distress Alerting and Calling

Iridium worked closely with the United States Coast Guard (USCG) from 2019 to date to prepare Iridium and the USCG tested the Iridium GMDSS service procedures and processes, verifying the alert processing and distribution, the automated failover process from the primary RCC to the backup (secondary) RCC, the procedures for the adding of new associated RCCs, and the EGC broadcasting of SAR related information.

In cooperation with the USCG and with the SAR authorities of Australia, New Zealand, Norway, and the United Kingdom, Iridium conducted further testing of its GMDSS SAR service and procedures prior to declaring the Iridium GMDSS SAR service operational. Iridium has defined enrolment procedures for RCCs desiring to become Iridium GMDSS associated RCCs.

The USCG has taken responsibility for SAR notifications for the Iridium GMDSS initially. RCCs may request to become Iridium-associated RCCs using the Iridium enrolment process and providing a copy of the enrolment request to the USCG. The full enrolment process has three stages:

Stage 1 requires a certificate from the IMO EGC Coordinating Panel and permits the RCC to email distress alert relays and EGC SAR related information broadcasts to the Iridium GMDSS service. Distress alerts are received via relay from an associated RCC.
Stage 2 provides:
1   Use of the Iridium GMDSS RCC interface to receive and send Distress and other safety traffic through the Iridium GMDSS from terminals where the specific RCC has been "addressed" (on top of Stage 1 capability); and
2   Details of the RCC being sent to all Iridium GMDSS terminals so that the RCC can be manually selected in a terminal ("addressed") and therefore all GMDSS traffic for that terminal be sent to the RCC in question.
Stage 3 provides: the establishment of an area of responsibility for the RCC; and the ability to receive the RCC to receive and send distress and other safety traffic through the Iridium GMDSS from terminals where the specific RCC has not been "addressed" and the terminal is in the RCC's area of responsibility (on top of Stage 2 capability).
Advancing to Stage 2 and Stage 3 requires that the RCC meets additional minimum requirements. At each stage, appropriate testing and exercises with other RCCs to confirm operations and procedures is required.

To advance to Stage 3, the RCC also needs to declare their associated SAR region for the Iridium GMDSS service. By definition, the SAR region (SRR) is "an area of defined dimensions associated with an RCC within which search and rescue services are provided". The RCC declared SRR for the Iridium GMDSS service should align with its defined SRR in the Global SAR Plan module in the Global Integrated Shipping Information System (GISIS). However, by agreement, a national authority may serve as the associated RCC for multiple RCC SRRs. The issue of having accurate SRR descriptions in a centrally accessible repository is critical to ensuring the proper distribution of distress alerts and that no gaps in coverage exist.

The USCG has taken initial responsibility for SAR notifications for the Iridium GMDSS on a global basis. As the primary associated RCC, the USCG intends to monitor the enrolment process, ensure adherence to the process, and promote full coverage for Iridium GMDSS distress alerts.

Table of Associated RCCs

Iridium Gateway	Associated RCC	SRR	Address	Contact details
Tempe, Arizona, USA	JRCC Norfolk (USA)	Global (Primary or First RCC))	Commander (ACC) Atlantic Area US Coast Guard 431 Crawford St. Portsmouth VA 23704 United States	Tel: +1 757 398 6700 Fax: +1 757 398 6775 E-mail: lantwatch@uscg.mil
Tempe, Arizona, USA	JRCC Alameda (USA)	Global (Secondary or back-up)	Pacific Area Command Central US Coast Guard Bldg. 51-2 Coast Guard Island Alameda CA 94501-5100 United States	Tel: +1 510 437 3701 Fax: +1 510 437 3017 E-mail: rccalameda@uscg.mil
Tempe, Arizona, USA	NMOC (RCC) Fareham (UK)	SRR being confirmed and registered with IMO	Unit 12 Kites Croft Business Park, Fareham PO14 4LW United Kingdom	Tel: +44 344 382 0025
Tempe, Arizona, USA	RCC Stavanger (Norway)	SRR being confirmed and registered with IMO	Hovedredningssentralen Sør-Norge Postboks 13 4097 Sola Norway	Tel: +47 51 51 70 00
Tempe, Arizona, USA	JRCC New Zealand (New Zealand)	SRR being confirmed and registered with IMO	41 Percy Cameron Street Avalon Lower Hutt 5011, New Zealand	Tel: +64 4577 8030
Tempe, Arizona, USA	JRCC Australia (Australia)	SRR being confirmed and registered with IMO	82 Northbourne Avenue Braddon ACT 2612 Australia	Tel: +61 2 623 06811

The United States Coast Guard, acting as the "first RCC" (and back-up RCC) in accordance with the SAR Convention and the IAMSAR Manual, receives all non-addressed (geographically allocated) distress alerts. Addressed distress alerts are delivered directly to the associated RCC the alert was addressed to, but even in ☐addressed☐ cases, the United States Coast Guard still acts as the back-up RCC and remains in standby to engage if the addressed RCC does not respond to the distress alert. This ensures delivery of a distress alert to an RCC in any circumstances. If the location of the distress is outside of the SAR Region of Responsibility of the first RCC, the first RCC will then coordinate with the responsible SAR Authority in whose SRR the event is occurring to alert the responsible RCC.

Changes to this information, as new RCCs become associated with the Iridium system, will be included in Notices to Mariners at the appropriate time.

Medical Advice and Assistance
For any medical advice or assistance, the RCCs listed above all provide medical assistance and may be contacted in first instance.
It is possible to programme the ship earth station with other services' contact details if desired. One well known example is the Centro Internazionale Radio Medico (Italy) who offer multilingual medical advice worldwide. See ALRS NP281 for further details.

Further Information and Contact Details
Questions concerning the operation of the Iridium GMDSS system, including the Distress and SafetyCast services, should be addressed to:
Maritime Safety Services
Iridium Satellite LLC
1750 Tysons Boulevard, Suite 1400
McLean, VA
22102 USA
email: maritime.safety@iridium.com

COSPAS-SARSAT SYSTEM
The Cospas-Sarsat (COSPAS: Space System for the Search of Vessels in Distress; SARSAT: Search And Rescue Satellite-Aided Tracking) System provides distress alert and location information to Search and Rescue (SAR) services for aviation, maritime and land users in distress, with no discrimination. It is free of charge for the persons in distress. This objective is accomplished through the use of satellite systems which relay or process the transmissions of distress radiobeacons operating on 406 MHz.

Cospas-Sarsat is a joint international satellite-aided SAR system established by organisations in Canada, France, Russia and the United States, which has 43 countries and organisations contributing to the operation and management of the system.

The carriage of a float-free satellite EPIRB operating on the 406 MHz in the Cospas-Sarsat system is required on all SOLAS vessels operating in Sea Areas A1, A2, A3 and A4.

Basic Concept of the System
The basic Cospas-Sarsat System concept is given in Figure 4. There are, at present, three types of distress beacons, namely Emergency Locator Transmitters (ELTs) (aviation), Emergency Position-Indicating Radio Beacons (EPIRBs) (maritime) and Personal Locator Beacons (PLBs) (land). These beacons transmit signals that are detected by Cospas-Sarsat polar-orbiting and geostationary satellites equipped with suitable receivers/processors. The signals are then relayed to a ground receiving station, termed a Local User Terminal (LUT), which processes the signals. An alert is then relayed, together with location data and other information as available, through a Mission Control Centre (MCC), either to a national Rescue Coordination Centre (RCC), another MCC or to the appropriate SAR authority to initiate SAR activities. The current spacecraft availability status and the list of operational MCC's and LUT's is available from the Cospas-Sarsat Website at: www.cospas-sarsat.org

System Operation
From January to December 2020 the Cospas-Sarsat System provided assistance in rescuing at least 2278 persons in 951 SAR events.

406 MHz Beacons
406 MHz beacons were specifically designed to be processed by Cospas-Sarsat satellites. The performance of 406 MHz satellite EPIRBs was the reason these devices were selected for the GMDSS and included in the 1988 amendments to the 1974 SOLAS Convention. At the end of 2020 there were about 1,935,000 devices. The estimated 2020 global 406-MHz beacon population computed using the registration-rate method was about 2,534,000 units. The estimated 2020 global 406-MHz beracon population computed using the results of the beacon manufacturer survey was about 1,899,000 units.
All information on Cospas-Sarsat type-approved 406-MHz beacons and a list of 406-MHz beacon manufacturers are available on the Cospas-Sarsat website at www.cospas-sarsat.int.

406 MHz beacons transmit a 0·5 second burst approximately every 50 seconds. Included in this burst is a digital message which uniquely identifies each beacon thereby enabling the Cospas-Sarsat System to:

- Categorically distinguish between beacon signals and other transmissions (e.g. interference);
- Obtain information about the operator of the beacon that might be critical to any rescue mission; and
- Uniquely identify and track specific distress events in the presence of several events active simultaneously.

Cospas-Sarsat has developed and maintains its own 406 MHz beacon specification which it makes available, free of charge, to administrations, international organisations, and individuals to use as appropriate. In addition, Cospas-Sarsat implements a beacon type approval process, in which 406 MHz beacon models are tested at approved test facilities to confirm their conformance to the specifications. Upon successfully completing all these tests, Cospas-Sarsat awards the beacon model a type approval certificate. It is this certificate that assures the public and administrations that the beacon design/type has been proven to work with the system.

406 MHz EPIRB False alerts
Resolution 9 (Revision WRC-12) states that the procedure for dealing with EPIRB false alerts is now to immediately stop the transmission and contact the appropriate Rescue Coordination Centre through a coast station or Land Earth Station and cancel the distress alert. The previous advice was to cancel the alert after the EPIRB had been located. In 2018 the SAR false alert rate was 96.8%, i.e. about one real alert in 32 alerts received.

406 MHz Beacon Registration
Because a beacon may be transmitting from anywhere in the world, each beacon should be registered whereby the serial number of the beacon, together with any other relevant information, is included in a suitable registration database. Information encoded in the 406 MHz beacon message includes information on the specific database's location. It is vitally important that the registration

authorities are informed promptly of any changes affecting the information given on the registration cards, e.g. change of vessel, change of ownership, loss, theft etc.

Owners of vessels are advised to contact the relevant flag state to establish the registration procedures. Cospas-Sarsat operates an International 406 MHz Beacon Registration Database (IBRD). As of 10 October 2019, there were 82,704 beacons registered in IBRD (77,869 on 1 September 2018) from 148 Administrations (new in 2019 was Nauru). The IBRD is freely available to users with no access to national registration facilities and to Administrations who wish to avail themselves of the facility to make their national beacon registration data more available to SAR services. Individual beacon owners may register their beacons and select their own passwords during the registration process, provided use of the IBRD is permitted by their national Administration. Cospas-Sarsat is in the process of redesigning the IBRD user interface. The user interface will be easier to understand and navigate, and will provide better support for new technologies such as "second generation beacons" (SGBs) and the Return Link Service (RLS) functionality, which provides confirmation to a user that their beacon distress signal has been successfully received. The new IBRD should be available online in 2020.

Beacons from any country that does not operate a national beacon registry may be registered in the International 406 MHz Beacon Registration Database (www.406registration.com).
SAR Services who wish to search the IBRD for these beacons should contact the Cospas-Sarsat Secretariat to obtain a user name and password for the IBRD (mail@cospas-sarsat.int)

For a full list of countries and their beacon registration details, see www.406registration.com/countriessupported.aspx. Contact details within this table will indicate if an EPIRB may be registered with the IBRD as is the case for BURUNDI (MID #609).
BULGARIA (MID #207) for example is registered with MRCC Varna (comprehensive contact details displayed).

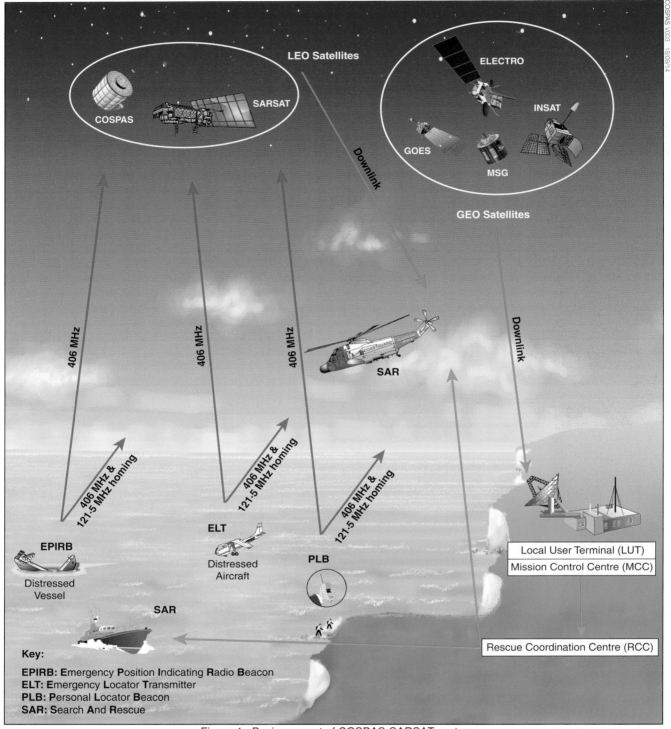

Figure 4 - Basic concept of COSPAS-SARSAT system

Cospas-Sarsat Space Segment

Cospas-Sarsat uses Search and Rescue (SAR) instruments on satellites in Low-altitude Earth Orbit (LEO), Geostationary Earth Orbit (GEO) and Medium Earth Orbit (MEO). These space segments are known respectively as LEOSAR, GEOSAR and MEOSAR. The 406 MHz beacon messages are partially processed on board the LEOSAR satellites, then directly transmitted on the satellite downlink as well as being stored on board for re-transmission in the global mode. Satellites in the GEOSAR system only relay 406 MHz transmissions for ground processing.

SARSAT satellites are also equipped with a 406 MHz repeater instrument which relays beacon signals directly for ground processing.

Please refer to the COSPAS-SARSAT website at: www.cospas-sarsat.int for up to the minute satellite data.

GEOSAR Space Segment

Seven geostationary satellites operating at full operational capability (FOC) and under active tracking by earth stations comprise the GEOSAR space segment: the United Sates' GOES-15 (135°W) and GOES-16 (75°W); the Indian INSAT-3D (82°W) and INSAT-3DR (74°W); and EUMETSAT's MSG-1 (41.5°E), MSG-3 (9.5°E) and MSG-4 (0°). Eight other satellites are in "sparing" roles or under test: GOES-13, GOES-14, GOES-17, GSAT-17, MSG-2, Electro-L No. 2, Louch-5A and Louch-5V.

COSPAS-SARSAT combined LEOSAR - GEOSAR operations

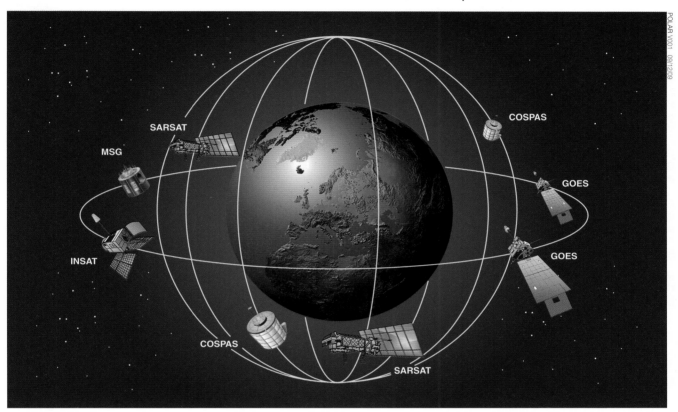

LEOSAR Space Segment

The LEOSAR system configuration comprises five satellites, Sarsat-7, Sarsat-10, Sarsat-11, Sarsat-12 and Sarsat-13, placed in near-polar orbits from 700 to 1,000 km altitude and equipped with SAR instrumentation at 406 MHz. Planned LEOSAR launches include provision by the Russian Federation for three Meteor-M satellites with Cospas SAR instruments on board. For the latest Cospas-Sarsat satellite configuration please refer to:
http://cospas-sarsat.int/en/system-overview/detailed-cospas-sarsat-system-description
Each satellite makes a complete orbit of the earth around the poles in about 100 minutes, travelling at a velocity of 7 km per second. The satellite views a "swath" of the earth over 6,000 km wide as it circles the globe, giving an instantaneous "field of view" about the size of a continent. When viewed from the earth, the satellite crosses the sky in about 15 minutes, depending on the maximum elevation angle of the particular pass. The satellite's low-altitude results in a low uplink power requirement, a pronounced Doppler shift, and short intervals between successive passes. The near-polar orbit results in complete world coverage over a period of time.

The satellites of the LEOSAR Space Segment consist of:

- A 406 MHz repeater unit on Sarsat satellites designed for re-transmission of distress signals to a ground receiving station located within its current footprint; and
- A receiver-processor and memory unit (SARP) on COSPAS and SARSAT satellites designed to receive, process and store signals received on 406 MHz for re-transmission directly to a ground station in its footprint, or to any other station located around the world.

Combined 406 MHz LEOSAR-GEOSAR System Concept

The major advantage of the 406 MHz system is the provision of global earth coverage using a limited number of polar-orbiting satellites in low-altitude earth orbit. However, the use of satellites in low-altitude earth orbit does not permit, as noted above, continuous coverage. This results in possible delays in the reception of the alert. By the nature of the polar orbits, the waiting time for detection by the LEOSAR system is greater in equatorial regions than at higher latitudes. In contrast, geostationary satellites provide continuous coverage of a large area centred on the equator with a near-immediate alerting capability.

Access to the geostationary satellite can be masked due to ground relief or obstructions, particularly on land, at high latitudes, and GEOSAR satellites do not provide coverage of the polar regions. On the other hand, LEOSAR satellites will eventually come into visibility of any beacon at the surface of the earth, whatever the terrain and the obstructions which may mask the distress transmission. Therefore, in terms of coverage, the specific characteristics of LEOSAR and GEOSAR systems are clearly complementary.

LOCAL USER TERMINALS (LUTs) AND MISSION CONTROL CENTRES (MCCs)

LEOSAR Local User Terminals (LEOLUTs)
The configuration and capabilities of each LEOLUT vary to meet the specific requirements of countries, but the COSPAS and SARSAT satellite downlink signal formats ensure inter-operability between the various satellites and all LUTs meeting Cospas-Sarsat specifications. All Cospas-Sarsat LEOLUTs must, as a minimum, process the output of the 406 MHz receiver-processor system (SARP) which provides the 406 MHz global coverage.

Each transmission is detected and the Doppler shift information calculated. The Doppler shift (using the relative motion between the satellite and the beacon) is used to locate beacons in the LEOSAR system. The carrier frequency transmitted by the beacon is reasonably stable during the period of mutual beacon-satellite visibility, and the low-altitude near-polar orbit of the LEOSAR satellites optimize the Doppler location process. A similar type of processing is also applied to the 406 MHz signals in the 406 MHz repeater band (SARP) which can be processed by LEOLUTs either separately or combined with the 406 MHz SARP data.

Processing of 406 MHz SARP data is relatively straightforward since the Doppler shifted frequency is measured and time-tagged on-board the spacecraft. All 406 MHz data received from the satellite memory on each pass can be processed within a few minutes of pass completion.

GEOSAR Local User Terminals (GEOLUTs)
GEOLUTs receive and process distress alerts from 406 MHz beacons relayed by the geostationary satellites of the GEOSAR system and provide permanent monitoring of the frequency band. 19 GEOLUTs are operational.

Almost as soon as a beacon is activated in the monitored GEOSAR satellite coverage area, it can be detected by the LUT. As there is no relative movement between a transmitting beacon and the satellite, it is not possible to use the Doppler effect to calculate the beacon position. However, when location information provided by external or internal navigation devices is included in the digital message of a 406 MHz beacon, this position data can be sent with the alert message to the MCC for re-transmission to the appropriate point of contact.

Mission Control Centres (MCCs)
Cospas-Sarsat mission control centres (MCCs) have been set up in most of those countries or organisations operating at least one LUT. Their main functions are to:

- Collect, store and sort the data from LUTs and other MCCs;
- Provide data exchange within the Cospas-Sarsat system; and
- Distribute alert and location data to associated RCCs or SPOCs.

MCCs in the system are interconnected through appropriate networks for the distribution of system information and alert data.

LEOSAR Ground Segment Status
For the latest details please refer to Cospas-Sarsat documentation contained on their website:
http://cospas-sarsat.int/en/documents-pro/system-data

MEOSAR Space Segment
Over time there will be more than 70 MEOSAR satellites, and the MEOSAR system will become the dominant space-segment capability of Cospas-Sarsat.

SAR Point of Contact (SPOC)
Each MCC distributes Cospas-Sarsat alert data to its national RCCs and to designated SAR Points of Contact (SPOCs) in the countries which are included in its Service Area. A SPOC is generally a national RCC that can accept or assume responsibility for handling Cospas-Sarsat distress alerts located within its national area of responsibility for SAR, defined as its Search and Rescue Region. Contact details for a number of Cospas-Sarsat SPOC's may be found in the Distress, Search and Rescue section of this book.

System developments MEOSAR
The most recent space segment augmentation for Cospas-Sarsat is MEOSAR.

MEOSAR over time will have more than 70 satellites in a medium earth orbit. The MEOSAR system offers a relatively large footprint and with sufficient satellite motion relative to a ground position will permit the use of Doppler measurement to assist with determining a distress beacon's location.

Operational distribution of MEOSAR alert data began in December 2016 when the system was classified as being in the early operational capability (EOC) phase.

The MEOSAR system was anticipated to achieve full operational capability (FOC) in 2020.

Further Information

For detailed information concerning the COSPAS-SARSAT System, see website www.cospas-sarsat.int

Contacts:
Telephone: +1 514 5007999
Fax: +1 514 5007996
E-mail: mail@cospas-sarsat.int

SOLAS REGULATIONS

Introduction

All the ships to which the 1974 SOLAS Convention, as amended, applies, are required to carry the GMDSS radio equipment, depending on the sea areas in which they operate.

One of the basic principles on which the GMDSS carriage requirements is based is a functional requirement to ensure the capability of transmitting ship-to-shore distress alerts by at least two separate and independent means. The capability of performing other communications functions is also required. There are specific carriage requirements for ships according to the sea area(s) in which they operate.

Carriage requirements for GMDSS radio equipment can be summarized as follows:

- Sea Area A1 ships will carry VHF equipment and either a satellite EPIRB or a VHF EPIRB;
- Sea Area A2 ships will carry VHF and MF equipment and a satellite EPIRB;
- Sea Area A3 ships will carry VHF, MF, a satellite EPIRB and either HF or satellite communication equipment;
- Sea Area A4 ships will carry VHF, MF and HF equipment and a satellite EPIRB; and
- all ships will carry equipment for receiving MSI broadcasts.

Regulations

The following extracts are taken from the SOLAS consolidated edition 2014, CHAPTER IV - Radiocommunications - Part C - Ship requirements. The regulation and paragraph numbers correspond to those in the original volume.

Regulation 6

Radio Installations

1. Every ship shall be provided with radio installations capable of complying with the functional requirements prescribed by **Regulation 4** throughout its intended voyage and, unless exempted under **Regulation 3**, complying with the requirements of **Regulation 7** and, as appropriate for the sea area or areas through which it will pass during its intended voyage, the requirements of either **Regulation 8**, **9**, **10** or **11**.

2. Every radio installation shall:

.1 be so located that no harmful interference of mechanical, electrical or other origin affects its proper use, and so as to ensure electromagnetic compatibility and avoidance of harmful interaction with other equipment and systems;

.2 be so located as to ensure the greatest possible degree of safety and operational availability;

.3 be protected against harmful effects of water, extremes of temperature and other adverse environmental conditions;

.4 be provided with reliable, permanently arranged electrical lighting, independent of the main and emergency sources of electrical power, for the adequate illumination of the radio controls for operating the radio installation; and

.5 be clearly marked with the call sign, the ship station identity and other codes as applicable for the use of the radio installation.

3. Control of the VHF radiotelephone channels, required for navigational safety, shall be immediately available on the navigation bridge convenient to the conning position and, where necessary, facilities should be available to permit radiocommunications from the wings of the navigation bridge. Portable VHF equipment may be used to meet the latter provision.

4. In passenger ships, a distress panel shall be installed at the conning position. This panel shall contain either one single button which, when pressed, initiates a distress alert using all radiocommunication installations required on board for that purpose or one button for each individual installation. The panel shall clearly and visually indicate whenever any button or buttons have been pressed. Means shall be provided to prevent inadvertent activation of the button or buttons. If the satellite EPIRB is used as the secondary means of distress alerting and is not remotely activated, it shall be acceptable to have an additional EPIRB installed in the wheelhouse near the conning position.

5. In passenger ships, information on the ship's position shall be continuously and automatically provided to all relevant radiocommunication equipment to be included in the initial distress alert when the button or buttons on the distress panel is pressed.

6. In passenger ships, a distress alarm panel shall be installed at the conning position. The distress alarm panel shall provide visual and aural indication of any distress alert or alerts received on board and shall also indicate through which radiocommunication service the distress alerts have been received.

Regulation 7

Radio Equipment: General

1. Every ship shall be provided with:

.**1** a VHF radio installation capable of transmitting and receiving:

.**1.1** DSC on the frequency 156·525 MHz (channel 70). It shall be possible to initiate the transmission of distress alerts on channel 70 from the position from which the ship is normally navigated[1], and

.**1.2** radiotelephony on the frequencies 156·300 MHz (channel 06), 156·650 MHz (channel 13) and 156·800 MHz (channel 16);

.**2** a radio installation capable of maintaining a continuous DSC watch on VHF channel 70 which may be separate from, or combined with, that required by subparagraph **1.1**[1];

.**3** a radar transponder capable of operating in the 9 GHz band,which:

.**3.1** shall be so stowed that it can be easily utilised; and

.**3.2** may be one of those required by **Regulation III/6.2.2** for a survival craft;

.**4** a receiver capable of receiving international NAVTEX service broadcasts if the ship is engaged on voyages in any area in which an international NAVTEX service is provided;

.**5** a radio facility for reception of maritime safety information by the Inmarsat enhanced group calling system[2] if the ship is engaged on voyages in any area of Inmarsat coverage but in which an international NAVTEX service is not provided. However, ships engaged exclusively on voyages in areas where an HF direct-printing telegraphy maritime safety information service is provided and fitted with equipment capable of receiving such service, may be exempt from this requirement[3].

.**6** subject to the provisions of **Regulation 8.3**, a satellite emergency position-indicating radio beacon (satellite EPIRB)[4] which shall be:

.**6.1** capable of transmitting a distress alert either through the polar orbiting satellite service operating in the 406 MHz band or, if the ship is engaged only on voyages within Inmarsat coverage, through the Inmarsat geostationary satellite service operating in the 1·6 GHz band[5];

.**6.2** installed in an easily accessible position;

.**6.3** ready to be manually released and capable of being carried by one person into a survival craft;

.**6.4** capable of floating free if the ship sinks and of being automatically activated when afloat; and

.**6.5** capable of being activated manually.

2. Every passenger ship shall be provided with means for two-way on-scene radiocommunications for search and rescue purposes using the aeronautical frequencies 121·5 MHz and 123·1 MHz from the position from which the ship is normally navigated.

[1] Certain ships may be exempted from this requirement (see regulation 9.4).

[2] Refer to Resolution A. 7011 (17) concerning carriage of Inmarsat enhanced group. all SafetyNET receivers under the GMDSS.

[3] Refer to the Recommendation on promulgation of maritime safety information adopted by the Organization by resolution A. 705 (17).

[4] Refer to Resolution A. 616 (15) concerning search and rescue homing capability.

[5] Subject to the availability of appropriate receiving and processing ground facilities for each ocean region covered by Inmarsat satellites.

Regulation 8

Radio Equipment: Sea Area A1

1. In addition to meeting the requirements of **Regulation 7**, every ship engaged on voyages exclusively in Sea Area A1 shall be provided with a radio installation capable of initiating the transmission of ship-to-shore distress alerts from the position from which the ship is normally navigated, operating either:

.**1** on VHF using DSC; this requirement may be fulfilled by the EPIRB prescribed by paragraph **3**, either by installing the EPIRB close to, or by remote activation from, the position from which the ship is normally navigated; or

.**2** through the polar orbiting satellite service on 406 MHz; this requirement may be fulfilled by the satellite EPIRB, required by **Regulation 7.6.1**, either by installing the satellite EPIRB close to, or by remote activation from, the position from which the ship is normally navigated; or

.3 if the ship is engaged on voyages within coverage of MF coast stations equipped with DSC, on MF using DSC; or

.4 on HF using DSC; or

.5 through the Inmarsat geostationary satellite service; this requirement may be fulfilled by:

.5.1 an Inmarsat ship earth station[1]; or

[1] This requirement can be met by Inmarsat ship earth stations capable of two-way communications, such as Fleet-77 (Resolution A.808(19) and MSC. 130(75) or Inmarsat C (Resolution A.807(19), as ammended) ship earth stations. Unless otherwise specified, this footnote applies to all requirements for an Inmarsat ship earth station prescribed by this chapter.

.5.2 the satellite EPIRB, required by **Regulation 7.6.1**, either by installing the satellite EPIRB close to, or by remote activation from, the position from which the ship is normally navigated.

2. The VHF radio installation, required by **Regulation 7.1.1**, shall also be capable of transmitting and receiving general radiocommunications using radiotelephony.

3. Ships engaged on voyages exclusively in Sea Area A1 may carry, in lieu of the satellite EPIRB required by **Regulation 7.6.1**, an EPIRB which shall be:

.1 capable of transmitting, a distress alert using DSC on VHF channel 70 and providing for locating by means of a radar transponder operating in the 9 GHz band;

.2 installed in an easily accessible position;

.3 ready to be manually released and capable of being carried by one person into a survival craft;

.4 capable of floating free if the ship sinks and being automatically activated when afloat; and

.5 capable of being activated manually.

Regulation 9

Radio Equipment: Sea Areas A1 and A2

1. In addition to meeting the requirements of **Regulation 7**, every ship engaged on voyages beyond Sea Area A1, but remaining within Sea Area A2, shall be provided with:

.1 an MF radio installation capable of transmitting and receiving, for distress and safety purposes, on the frequencies:

.1.1 2187·5 kHz using DSC; and

.1.2 2182 kHz using radiotelephony;

.2 a radio installation capable of maintaining a continuous DSC watch on the frequency 2187·5 kHz which may be separate from, or combined with, that required by subparagraph **1.1**; and

.3 means of initiating the transmission of ship-to-shore distress alerts by a radio service other than MF operating either:

.3.1 through the polar orbiting satellite service on 406 MHz; this requirement may be fulfilled by the satellite EPIRB, required by **Regulation 7.6.1**, either by installing the satellite EPIRB close to, or by remote activation from, the position from which the ship is normally navigated; or

.3.2 on HF using DSC; or

.3.3 through the Inmarsat geostationary satellite service; this requirement may be fulfilled by:

.3.3.1 the equipment specified in paragraph **3.2**; or

.3.3.2 the satellite EPIRB, required by **Regulation 7.6.1**, either by installing the satellite EPIRB close to, or by remote activation from, the position from which the ship is normally navigated.

2. It shall be possible to initiate transmission of distress alerts by the radio installations specified in paragraphs **1.1** and **1.3** from the position from which the ship is normally navigated.

3. The ship shall, in addition, be capable of transmitting and receiving general radiocommunications using radiotelephony or direct-printing telegraphy by either:

.1 a radio installation operating on working frequencies in the bands between 1,605 kHz and 4,000 kHz or between 4,000 kHz and 27,500 kHz. This requirement may be fulfilled by the addition of this capability in the equipment required by paragraph **1.1**; or

.2 an Inmarsat ship earth station.

4. The Administration may exempt ships constructed before 1 February 1997, which are engaged exclusively on voyages within sea area A2, from the requirements of **Regulations 7.1.1.1** and **7.1.2** provided such ships maintain, when practicable, a continuous listening watch on VHF channel 16. This watch shall be kept at the position from which the ship is normally navigated

Regulation 10

Radio Equipment: Sea Areas A1, A2 and A3

1. In addition to meeting the requirements of **Regulation 7**, every ship engaged on voyages beyond Sea Areas A1 and A2, but remaining within Sea Area A3, shall, if it does not comply with the requirements of paragraph 2, be provided with:

.1 an Inmarsat ship earth station capable of:

.1.1 transmitting and receiving distress and safety communications using direct-printing telegraphy;

.1.2 initiating and receiving distress priority calls;

.1.3 maintaining watch for shore-to-ship distress alerts, including those directed to specifically, defined geographical areas;

.1.4 transmitting and receiving general radiocommunications, using either radiotelephony or direct-printing telegraphy; and

.2 an MF radio installation capable of transmitting and receiving, for distress and safety purposes, on the frequencies:

.2.1 2187·5 kHz using DSC; and

.2.2 2182 kHz using radiotelephony; and

.3 a radio installation capable of maintaining a continuous DSC watch on the frequency 2187·5 kHz which may be separate from or combined with that required by subparagraph **.2.1**; and

.4 means of initiating the transmission of ship-to-shore distress alerts by a radio service operating either:

.4.1 through the polar orbiting satellite service on 406 MHz; this requirement may be fulfilled by the satellite EPIPB, required by **Regulation 7.6.1**, either by installing the satellite EPIRB close to, or by remote activation from, the position from which the ship is normally navigated; or

.4.2 on HF using DSC; or

.4.3 through the Inmarsat geostationary satellite service, by an additional ship earth station or by the satellite EPIRB required by **Regulation 7.6.1**, either by installing the satellite EPIRB close to, or by remote activation from, the position from which the ship is normally navigated;

2. In addition to meeting the requirements of **Regulation 7**, every ship engaged on voyages beyond Sea Areas A1 and A2, but remaining, within Sea Area A3, shall, if it does not comply, with the requirements of paragraph **1**, be provided with:

.1 an MF/HF radio installation capable of transmitting and receiving, for distress and safety purposes, on all distress and safety frequencies in the bands between 1,605 kHz and 4,000 kHz and between 4,000 kHz and 27,500 kHz:

.1.1 using DSC;

.1.2 using radiotelephony; and

.1.3 using direct-printing telegraphy; and

.2 equipment capable of maintaining DSC watch on 2187·5 kHz, 8414·5 kHz and on at least one of the distress and safety DSC frequencies 4207·5 kHz, 6312 kHz, 12577 kHz or 16804·5 kHz; at any time, it shall be possible to select any of these DSC distress and safety frequencies. This equipment may be separate from, or combined with, the equipment required by subparagraph **.1**; and

.3 means of initiating the transmission of ship-to-shore distress alerts by a radiocommunication service other than HF operating either:

.3.1 through the polar orbiting satellite service on 406 MHz; this requirement may be fulfilled by the satellite EPIRB, required by **Regulation 7.6.1**, either by installing the satellite EPIRB close to, or by remote activation from, the position from which the ship is normally navigated; or

.3.2 through the Inmarsat geostationary satellite service; this requirement may be fulfilled by:

> **.3.2.1** an Inmarsat ship earth station; or

> **.3.2.2** the satellite EPIRB, required by **Regulation 7.6.1**, either by installing the satellite EPIRB close to, or by remote activation from, the position from which the ship is normally navigated; and

> **.4** in addition, ships shall be capable of transmitting and receiving general radiocommunications using radiotelephony or direct-printing telegraphy by an MF/HF radio installation operating on working frequencies in the bands between 1,605 kHz and 4,000 kHz and between 4,000 kHz and 27,500 kHz. This requirement may be fulfilled by the addition of this capability in the equipment required by subparagraph **.1**.

3. It shall be possible to initiate transmission of distress alerts by the radio installations specified in paragraphs **1.1**, **1.2**, **1.4**, **2.1** and **2.3** from the position from which the ship is normally navigated.

4. The Administration may exempt ships constructed before 1 February 1997, and engaged exclusively on voyages within Sea Areas A2 and A3, from the requirements of **Regulations 7.1.1.1** and **7.1.2** provided such ships maintain, when practicable, a continuous listening watch on VHF channel 16. This watch shall be kept at the position from which the ship is normally navigated.

Regulation 11

Radio Equipment: Sea Areas A1, A2, A3 and A4
1. In addition to meeting the requirements of **Regulation 7**, ships engaged on voyages in all sea areas shall be provided with the radio installations and equipment required by **Regulation 10.2**, except that the equipment required by **Regulation 10.2.3.2** shall not be accepted as an alternative to that required by **Regulation 10.2.3.1**, which shall always be provided. In addition, ships engaged on voyages in all sea areas shall comply with the requirements of **Regulation 10.3**.

2. The Administration may exempt ships constructed before 1 February 1997, and engaged exclusively on voyages within Sea Areas A2, A3 and A4, from the requirements of **Regulations 7.1.1.1** and **7.1.2** provided such ships maintain, when practicable, a continuous listening watch on VHF channel 16. This watch shall be kept at the position from which the ship is normally navigated.

Regulation 12

Watches
1. Every ship, while at sea, shall maintain a continuous watch:

> **.1** on VHF DSC channel 70, if the ship, in accordance with the requirements of **Regulation 7.1.2**, is fitted with a VHF radio installation;

> **.2** on the distress and safety DSC frequency 2,187·5 kHz, if the ship, in accordance with the requirements of **Regulation 9.1.2** or **10.1.3**, is fitted with an MF radio installation;

> **.3** on the distress and safety DSC frequencies 2,187·5 kHz and 8,414·5 kHz and also on at least one of the distress and DSC frequencies 4,207·5 kHz, 6,312 kHz, 12,577 kHz or 16,804·5 kHz, appropriate to the time of day and the geographical position of the ship, if the ship, in accordance with the requirements of **Regulation 10.2.2** or **1.1.1**, is fitted with an MF/HF radio installation. This watch may be kept by means of a scanner receiver;

> **.4** for satellite shore-to-ship distress alerts, if the ship in accordance with the requirements of **Regulation 10.1.1**, is fitted with an Inmarsat ship earth station.

2. Every ship, while at sea, shall maintain a radio watch for broadcasts of maritime safety information on the appropriate frequency or frequencies on which such information is broadcast for the area in which the ship is navigating.

3. Until 1 February 1999 or until such other date as may be determined by the Maritime Safety Committee[1], every ship while at sea shall maintain, when practicable, a continuous listening, watch on VHF channel 16. This watch shall be kept at the position from which the ship is normally navigated.

[1] The Maritime Safety Committee decided (resolution MSC.131(75)) that all GMDSS ships, while at sea, shall continue to maintain, when practicable, continuous listening watch on VHF channel 16.

Regulation 13

Sources of Energy
1. There shall be available at all times, while the ship is at sea, a supply of electrical energy sufficient to operate the radio installations and to charge any batteries used as part of a reserve source or sources of energy for the radio installations.

2. A reserve source or sources of energy shall be provided on every ship, to supply radio installations, for the purpose of conducting distress and safety radiocommunications, in the event of failure of the ship's main and emergency sources of electrical power. The reserve source or sources of energy shall be capable of simultaneously operating the VHF radio installation required by **Regulation 7.1.1** and, as appropriate for the sea area or sea areas for which the ship is equipped, either the MF radio installation required by **Regulation 9.1.1**, the MF/HF radio installation required by **Regulation 10.2.1** or **11.1**, or the Inmarsat Ship Earth Station required by **Regulation 10.1.1** and any of the additional loads mentioned in paragraphs **4**, **5** and **8** for a period of at least:

.1 1h on ships provided with an emergency source of electrical power, if such source of power complies fully with all relevant provisions of **Regulation II-1/42** or **43**, including the supply of such power to the radio installations; and

.2 6h on ships not provided with an emergency source of electrical power complying fully with all relevant provisions of **Regulation II-1/42** or **43**, including the supply of such power to the radio installations.[1]

The reserve source or sources of energy need not supply independent HF and MF radio installations at the same time.

[1] For guidance, the following formula is recommended for determining the electrical load to be supplied by the reserve source of energy, for each radio installation required for distress conditions: ½ of the current consumption necessary for transmission + the current consumption necessary for reception + the current consumption of any additional loads.

3. The reserve source or sources of energy shall be independent of the propelling power of the ship and the ship's electrical system.

4. Where, in addition to the VHF radio installation, two or more of the other radio installations, referred to in paragraph **2**, can be connected to the reserve source or sources of energy they shall be capable of simultaneously supplying, for the period specified, as appropriate, in paragraph **2.1** or **2.2**, the VHF radio installation and:

.1 all other radio installations which can be connected to the reserve source or sources of energy at the same time; or

.2 whichever of the other radio installations will consume the most power, if only one of the other radio installations can be connected to the reserve source or sources of energy at the same time as the VHF radio installation.

5. The reserve source or sources of energy may be used to supply the electrical lighting required by **Regulation 6.2.4**.

6. Where a reserve source of energy consists of a rechargeable accumulator battery or batteries:

.1 a means of automatically charging such batteries shall be provided which shall be capable of recharging them to minimum capacity requirements within 10 h; and

.2 the capacity of the battery or batteries shall be checked, using an appropriate method[1], at intervals not exceeding 12 months, when the ship is not at sea.

[1] One method of checking the capacity of an accumulator battery is to fully discharge and recharge the battery, using normal operating current and period (e.g. 10 h). Assessment of the charge condition can be made at any time, but it should be done without significant discharge of the battery when the ship is at sea.

7. The siting and installation of accumulator batteries which provide a reserve source of energy shall be such as to ensure:

.1 the highest degree of service;

.2 a reasonable lifetime;

.3 reasonable safety;

.4 that battery temperatures remain within the manufacturer's specifications whether under charge or idle; and

.5 that when fully charged, the batteries will provide at least the minimum required hours of operation under all weather conditions

8. If an uninterrupted input of information from the ship's navigational or other equipment to a radio installation required by this chapter, including the navigation receiver referred to in **Regulation 18**, is needed to ensure its proper performance, means shall be provided to ensure the continuous supply of such information in the event of failure of the ship's main or emergency source of electrical power.

Regulation 14

Performance Standards
1. All equipment to which this chapter applies shall be of a type approved by the Administration. Such equipment shall conform to appropriate performance standards not inferior to those adopted by the Organization[1].

[1] Refer to the following resolutions adopted by the Organization:

.1 Resolution A.525(13): Performance standards for narrow-band direct-printing telegraph equipment for the reception of navigational and meteorological warnings and urgent information to ships.

.2 Resolution A.694(17): General requirement, for shipborne radio equipment forming part of the global maritime distress and safety system (GMDSS) and for electronic navigational aids.

.3 Resolution A.808(19): Performance standards for ship earth stations capable of two-way communications and resolution A.570(14): Type approval of ship earth stations and MSC.130(75): Performance standards for Inmarsat ship earth stations capable of two-way communications.

.4 Resolution A.803(19): Performance standards for shipborne VHF radio installations capable of voice communications and digital selective calling, as amended, and resolution MSC.68(68), annex 1 (valid for equipment installed on or after 1 January 2000).

.5 Resolution A.804(19): Performance standards for shipborne MF radio installation capable of voice communication and digital selective calling, as amended, and Resolution MSC.68(68) annex 2 (valid for equipment installed on or after 1 January 2000).

.6 Resolution A.806(19): Performance standards for shipborne MF/HF radio installations, capable of voice communication, on, narrow-band direct-printing and digital selective calling, as amended, and Resolution MSC.68(68) annex 3 (valid for equipment installed on or after 1 January 2000).

.7 Resolution A.810(19): Performance standards for float-free satellite emergency position-indicating radio beacons (EPIRBs) operating on 406 MHz and MSC.120(74): Adoption of amendments to performance standards for float-free satellite emergency position-indicating radio beacons (EPIRBs) operating on 406 MHz (Resolution A.810(19)) (see also Assembly Resolution A.696(17)): Type approval of satellite emergency position-indicating radio beacons (EPIRBs) operating in the COSPAS-SARSAT system).

.8 Resolution A.802(19): Performance standards for survival craft radar transponders for use in search and rescue operations.

.9 Resolution A.805(19): Performance standards for float-free VHF emergency position-indicating radio beacons.

.10 Resolution A.807(19): Performance standards for Inmarsat C ship earth stations capable of transmitting and receiving direct-printing communications as amended and resolution MSC.68(68), annex 3 (valid for equipment installed on or after 1 January 2000), and Resolution A.570(14): Type approval of ship earth stations.

.11 Resolution A.664(16): Performance standards for enhanced group call equipment.

.12 Resolution A.812(19): Performance standards for float-free satellite emergency position-indicating radio beacons operating through the geostationary Inmarsat satellite system 1.6 GHz

.13 Resolution A.662(16): Performance standards for float-free release and activation arrangements for emergency radio equipment.

.14 Resolution A.699(17): System performance standard for the promulgation and coordination of maritime safety information using high-frequency narrow-band direct-printing.

.15 Resolution MSC.148(77): Adoption of the revised performance standards for narrow-band direct-printing telegraph equipment for the reception of navigational and meteorological warnings and urgent information to ships (NAVTEX).

.16 Resolution A.811(19): Performance standards for a shipborne integrated radiocommunication system (IRCS) when used in the GMDSS.

.17 Resolution MSC.80(70) annex 1: Performance standards for on-scene (aeronautical) two-way portable VHF radiotelephone apparatus.

Regulation 15

Maintenance Requirements

1. Equipment shall be so designed that the main units can be replaced readily, without elaborate recalibration or readjustment.

2. Where applicable, equipment shall be so constructed and installed that it is readily accessible for inspection and on-board maintenance purposes.

3. Adequate information shall be provided to enable the equipment to be properly operated and maintained, taking into account the recommendations of the Organization[1].

[1] Refer to the Recommendation on general requirements for shipborne radio equipment forming part of the global maritime distress and safety system and for electronic navigational aids adopted by the Organization by Resolution A.694(17) and to Resolution A.813(19) on general requirements for electromagnetic compatibility (EMC) for all electrical and electronic ship's equipment and to MSC/Circ. 862: clarification of certain requirements in IMO performance standards for GMDSS equipment.

4. Adequate tools and spares shall be provided to enable the equipment to be maintained.

5. The Administration shall ensure that radio equipment required by this chapter is maintained to provide the availability of the functional requirements specified in regulation 4 and to meet the recommended performance standards of such equipment.

6. On ships engaged on voyages in Sea Areas A1 and A2, the availability shall be ensured by using such methods as duplication of equipment, shore-based maintenance or at-sea electronic maintenance capability, or a combination of these, as may be approved by the Administration.

7. On ships engaged on voyages in Sea Areas A3 and A4, the availability shall be ensured by using a combination of at least two methods such as duplication of equipment, shore-based maintenance or at-sea electronic maintenance capability, as may be approved by the Administration, taking into account the recommendations of the Organization[1].

[1] Refer to Resolution A.702(17) concerning radio maintenance guidelines for the Global Maritime Distress and Safety System related to Sea Areas A3 and A4.

8. While all reasonable steps shall be taken to maintain the equipment in efficient working order to ensure compliance with all the functional requirements specified in **Regulation 4**, malfunction of the equipment for the general radiocommunications required by **Regulation 4.8** shall not be considered as making a ship unseaworthy or as a reason for delaying the ship in ports where repair facilities are not readily available, provided the ship is capable of performing all distress and safety functions.

9. Satellite EPIRBs shall be tested at intervals not exceeding 12 months for all aspects of operational efficiency with particular emphasis on frequency stability, signal strength and coding. However, in cases where it appears proper and reasonable, the Administration may extend this period to 17 months. The test may be conducted on board the ship or at an approved testing or servicing station.

Regulation 16

Radio Personnel

1. Every ship shall carry personnel qualified for distress and safety radiocommunication purposes to the satisfaction of the Administration[1]. The personnel shall be holders of certificates specified in the Radio Regulations as appropriate, any one of whom shall be designated to have primary responsibility for radiocommunications during distress incidents.

[1] Refer to the STCW Code chapter IV, section B-IV/2

2. In passenger ships, at least one person qualified in accordance with paragraph **1** shall be assigned to perform only radiocommunication duties during distress incidents.

Regulation 17

Radio Records

A record shall be kept, to the satisfaction of the Administration and as required by the Radio Regulations of all incidents connected with the radiocommunications service which appear to be of importance to safety of life at sea.

Regulation 18

Position-updating

All two-way communications equipment carried on board a ship to which this chapter applies which is capable of automatically including the ship's position in the distress alert shall be automatically provided with this information from an internal or external navigation receiver, if either is installed. If such a receiver is not installed, the ship's position and the time at which the position was determined shall be manually updated at intervals not exceeding 4 hours, while the ship is under way, so that it is always ready for transmission by the equipment.

Ship Carriage Requirements

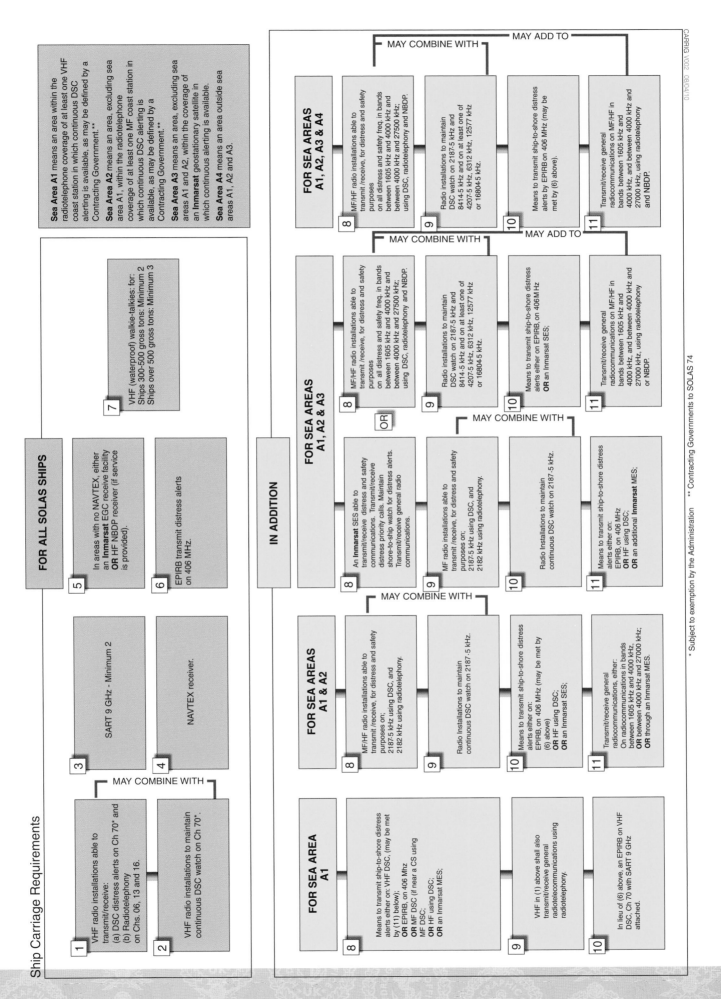

CARRIG V002 08/04/10

Sea Area A1 means an area within the radiotelephone coverage of at least one VHF coast station in which continuous DSC alerting is available, as may be defined by a Contracting Government.**

Sea Area A2 means an area, excluding sea area A1, within the radiotelephone coverage of at least one MF coast station in which continuous DSC alerting is available, as may be defined by a Contracting Government.**

Sea Area A3 means an area, excluding sea areas A1 and A2, within the coverage of an Inmarsat geostationary satellite in which continuous alerting is available.

Sea Area A4 means an area outside sea areas A1, A2 and A3.

FOR ALL SOLAS SHIPS

1. VHF radio installations able to transmit/receive:
(a) DSC distress alerts on Ch 70* and
(b) Radiotelephony on Chs. 06, 13 and 16.

2. VHF radio installations to maintain continuous DSC watch on Ch 70*.

MAY COMBINE WITH

3. SART 9 GHz - Minimum 2

4. NAVTEX receiver.

5. In areas with no NAVTEX, either an Inmarsat EGC receive facility OR HF NBDP receiver (if service is provided).

6. EPIRB transmit distress alerts on 406 MHz.

7. VHF (waterproof) walkie-talkies: for:
Ships 300-500 gross tons: Minimum 2
Ships over 500 gross tons: Minimum 3

IN ADDITION

FOR SEA AREA A1

8. Means to transmit ship-to-shore distress alerts either on: VHF DSC, (may be met by (11) below);
OR EPIRB, on 406 Mhz
OR MF DSC (if near a CS using MF DSC;
OR HF using DSC;
OR an Inmarsat MES;

9. VHF in (1) above shall also transmit/receive general radiotelecommunications using radiotelephony.

10. In lieu of (6) above, an EPIRB on VHF DSC, Ch 70 with SART 9 GHz attached.

MAY COMBINE WITH

FOR SEA AREAS A1 & A2

8. MF/HF radio installations able to transmit/receive, for distress and safety purposes on;
2187.5 kHz using DSC, and 2182 kHz using radiotelephony.

9. Radio Installations to maintain continuous DSC watch on 2187·5 kHz.

10. Means to transmit ship-to-shore distress alerts either on:
EPIRB, on 406 MHz (may be met by (6) above)
OR HF using DSC;
OR an Inmarsat SES;

11. Transmit/receive general radiocommunications, either:
On radiocommunications in bands between 1605 kHz and 4000 kHz,
OR between 4000 kHz and 27000 kHz;
OR through an Inmarsat MES.

MAY COMBINE WITH

FOR SEA AREAS A1, A2 & A3

8. An Inmarsat SES able to transmit/receive distress and safety communications. Transmit/receive distress priority calls. Maintain shore-to-ship watch for distress alerts. Transmit/receive general radio communications.

OR

9. MF radio installations able to transmit/receive, for distress and safety purposes on:
2187·5 kHz using DSC, and 2182 kHz using radiotelephony.

10. Radio Installations to maintain continuous DSC watch on 2187·5 kHz.

11. Means to transmit ship-to-shore distress alerts either on:
EPIRB, on 406 MHz
OR HF using DSC;
OR an additional Inmarsat MES;

MAY COMBINE WITH

FOR SEA AREAS A1, A2 & A3

8. MF/HF radio installations able to transmit/receive, for distress and safety freq. in bands between 1605 kHz and 4000 kHz and between 4000 kHz and 27500 kHz; using DSC, radiotelephony and NBDP.

9. Radio installations to maintain DSC watch on 2187.5 kHz and 8414.5 kHz and on at least one of 4207.5 kHz, 6312 kHz, 12577 kHz or 16804.5 kHz.

10. Means to transmit ship-to-shore distress alerts either on EPIRB, on 406M Hz OR an Inmarsat SES;

11. Transmit/receive general radiocommunications on MF/HF in bands between 1605 kHz and 4000 kHz, and between 4000 kHz and 27000 kHz, using radiotelephony or NBDP.

MAY ADD TO

MAY COMBINE WITH

FOR SEA AREAS A1, A2, A3 & A4

8. MF/HF radio installations able to transmit/receive, for distress and safety purposes on all distress and safety freq, in bands between 1605 kHz and 4000 kHz and between 4000 kHz and 27500 kHz; using DSC, radiotelephony and NBDP.

9. Radio installations to maintain DSC watch on 2187.5 kHz and 8414.5 kHz and on at least one of 4207.5 kHz, 6312 kHz, 12577 kHz or 16804.5 kHz.

10. Means to transmit ship-to-shore distress alerts by EPIRB on 406 MHz (may be met by (6) above).

11. Transmit/receive general radiocommunications on MF/HF in bands between 1605 kHz and 4000 kHz, and between 4000 kHz and 27000 kHz, using radiotelephony and NBDP.

MAY ADD TO

* Subject to exemption by the Administration   ** Contracting Governments to SOLAS 74

NOTES

PART A - DISTRESS COMMUNICATIONS

After any GMDSS equipment has been installed, the necessary operating instructions should be given to the appropriate personnel, specifically pointing out operating procedures for the equipment in question. It is important that operating instructions should be as clear and precise as possible in order that they are easy to understand.

Radio equipment used for transmitting distress alerts should be so designed that it should not be possible to transmit a distress alert unless the distress button is deliberately depressed. It is strongly recommended that personnel have full knowledge of the GMDSS and the consequences of transmitting a false alert. To reduce the chance of false alerts, routine testing of GMDSS equipment should only be undertaken under the direct supervision of the person responsible for communications.

To take maximum advantage of GMDSS, Masters should ensure that all crew members who may be required to send a distress alert are instructed and knowledgeable in the operation of all relevant radio equipment on the vessel. Such instruction should also be given, periodically, on-board the vessel to all relevant crew members by the person responsible for communications.

The following diagram could form the basis for the standard procedures for distress message routeing procedures. This may be displayed or be readily available at the control position for the radio installations.

Figure 8 - GMDSS operating guidance for Masters of ships in distress situations

RADIO DISTRESS COMMUNICATIONS			
	Digital Selective Calling (DSC)	Radiotelephone	Radiotelex
VHF	Ch 70	Ch 16	
MF	2187·5 kHz	2182 kHz	2174·5 kHz
HF4	4207·5 kHz	4125 kHz	4177·5 kHz
HF6	6312 kHz	6215 kHz	6268 kHz
HF8	8414·5 kHz	8291 kHz	8376·5 kHz
HF12	12577 kHz	12290 kHz	12520 kHz
HF16	16804·5 kHz	16420 kHz	16695 kHz

1. EPIRB SHOULD BE FLOAT-FREE AND ACTIVATE AUTOMATICALLY IF IT CANNOT BE TAKEN INTO SURVIVAL CRAFT
2. WHERE NECESSARY, SHIPS SHOULD USE ANY APPROPRIATE MEANS TO ALERT OTHER SHIPS
3. NOTHING ABOVE IS INTENDED TO PRECLUDE THE USE OF ANY AND ALL AVAILABLE MEANS OF DISTRESS ALERTING

V001 09/12/09 GMDSS

These procedures are intended for guidance only and may be amended to suit the specific equipment available. The diagram should be continuously updated in line with the latest GMDSS recommendations. Particular attention should be given to Note 3 in the above example.

Distress relays and acknowledgements have the same priority as the original alert and must only be sent on the Master's authority.

Ships must not send DSC relays for DSC alerts received on MF and VHF. Relays of HF alerts by DSC must be initiated manually, and must be sent only to coast stations, after a minimum delay of 5 minutes.

Extract from IMO COMSAR/Circ.17

Use of GMDSS equipment for transmission of general radio communications is one of the functional requirements in SOLAS Chapter IV, regulation 4. Regular use of GMDSS equipment helps to develop operator competency and ensure equipment availability. If ships use other radio communication systems for the bulk of their business communications, they should adopt a regular programme of sending selected traffic or test messages via GMDSS equipment to ensure operator competency and equipment availability and to help reduce the incidence of false alerts. This policy extends to all GMDSS equipment suites including Digital Selective Calling on VHF, MF and HF, to the Inmarsat C system, and to any duplicated VHF and long-range communications facilities.

Extract from IMO COMSAR/Circ.35

MSC 78 endorsed COMSAR 8 view that the regular use of DSC equipment as described in COMSAR/Circ.17 should be encouraged. However, the ITU Sector for Radio communications had indicated that excessive test calls on DSC distress and safety frequencies were overloading the system to the point where interference to distress and safety calls had become a cause for concern.

In view of the above, and as a matter of urgency, Administrations concerned are urged to co-operate in managing and reducing the number of test calls on MF/HF DSC distress and safety frequencies.

To achieve this, live testing on DSC distress and safety frequencies with coast stations should be limited to once a week. A background on the need for DSC test calls is described in COM/Circ.106.

PART B - FALSE ALERTS

False alerts caused by the inadvertent or incorrect operation of GMDSS equipment can put a significant burden on Search and Rescue Centres. The chances of false alerts coinciding with an actual distress situation are very real and as a consequence, search and rescue resources could be delayed in responding to a real distress.

Most false alerts are caused as a result of human error; the flow chart Figure 9 is intended as guidance for use in the event of either a known or suspected false alert having been transmitted. (See Annex to ITU Resolution 349 (WRC-12))

As well as the problems caused by the inadvertent transmission of an alert on DSC, Inmarsat C and by 406 MHz EPIRBs, the acknowledgement of a DSC distress alert on 2187·5 kHz can lead to the broadcast of a large number of unnecessary DSC calls. The following procedures should therefore be followed.

NOTE 1: Any vessel may use any frequency in any system to inform the appropriate authorities that a false alert has been transmitted and should be cancelled.

NOTE 2: From Resolution 349 (REV. WRC-12) If DSC equipment is capable of cancellation, cancel the alert in accordance with the most recent version of ITU-R M.493

MF

(a) A vessel operating in an A2 Sea Area which receives a MF DSC distress alert on 2187·5 kHz should not transmit a DSC acknowledgement, notwithstanding any prompt on the DSC equipment; it can be assumed the alert will have been heard and acknowledged by a coast station (this might not be obvious to the receiving vessel if it is beyond the reception range of the coast station). Therefore, following receipt of a DSC distress alert or distress relay, radio operators should listen on 2182 kHz for further distress traffic and (subject to the Master's instructions) acknowledge using RT. Assistance should then be rendered as required and appropriate.

(b) A vessel operating outside of an A2 Sea Area which receives a distress alert which is, beyond doubt, in its vicinity, should send an acknowledgement as soon as possible using RT on 2182 kHz. If further DSC distress alerts are heard from the same source, a DSC acknowledgement may be sent. RCCs should be informed through a coast radio station or LES and assistance rendered as required and appropriate.

HF

(a) On receipt of an HF DSC distress alert a vessel should not transmit an acknowledgement. Radio operators must listen out on the RT and NBDP distress and safety traffic frequencies associated with the distress and safety calling frequencies on which the alert was received.

(b) If subsequent DSC distress alerts are received, or it is clear there has been no acknowledgement by a coast radio station, the vessel must relay the distress alert to the appropriate coast radio station or RCC, NOT TO ALL STATIONS.

No action will normally be taken against any vessel or mariner for reporting and cancelling a false distress alert. However, in view of the serious consequences of false alerts, and the strict ban on their transmission, Governments may prosecute in cases of repeated violations.

Procedures for False Alert cancellations

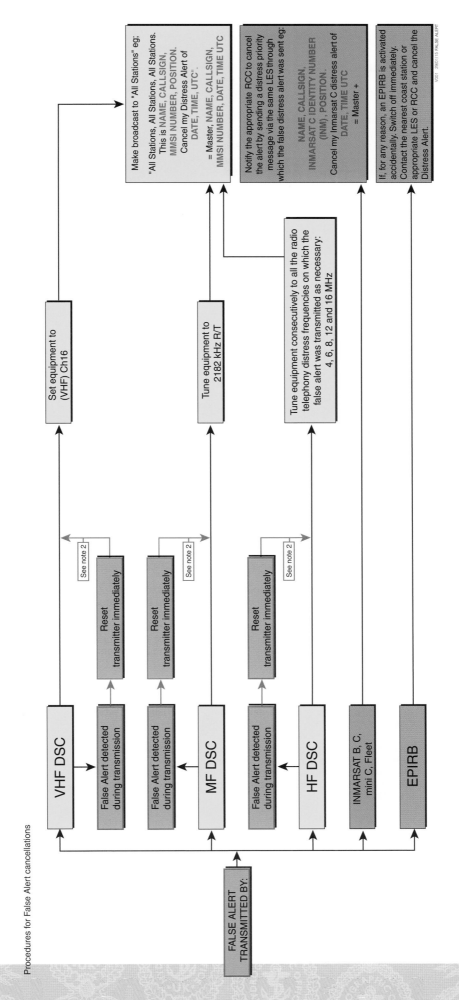

IMO GUIDELINES FOR AVOIDING FALSE DISTRESS ALERTS

Extracts from IMO *Resolution A.814 (19)*

Companies, Masters and seafarers should, as appropriate:
1. Ensure that all GMDSS certificated personnel responsible for sending a distress alert have been instructed about, and are competent to operate, the particular radio equipment on the ship;
2. Ensure that the person or persons responsible for communications during distress incidents give the necessary instructions and information to all crew members on how to use GMDSS equipment to send a distress alert;
3. Ensure that as part of each "abandon ship" drill, instruction is given on how emergency equipment should be used to provide GMDSS functions;
4. Ensure that GMDSS equipment testing is only undertaken under the supervision of the person responsible for communications during distress incidents;
5. Ensure that GMDSS equipment testing or drills are never allowed to cause false distress alerts;
6. Ensure that encoded identities of satellite EPIRBs, which are used by SAR personnel responding to emergencies, are properly registered in a database accessible 24h a day or automatically provided to SAR authorities (Masters should confirm that their EPIRBs have been registered with such a database, to help SAR services identify the ship in the event of distress and rapidly obtain other information which will enable them to respond appropriately);
7. Ensure that EPIRB, Inmarsat and DSC registration data is immediately updated if there is any change in information relating to the ship such as owner, name or flag, and that the necessary action is taken to re-program the ship's new data in the GMDSS equipment concerned;
8. Ensure that, for new ships, positions for installing EPIRBs are considered at the earliest stage of ship design and construction;
9. Ensure that satellite EPIRBs are carefully installed in accordance with manufacturers' instructions and using qualified personnel (sometimes satellite EPIRBs are damaged or broken due to improper handling or installation. They must be installed in a location that will enable them to float free and automatically activate if the ship sinks. Care must be taken to ensure that they are not tampered with or accidentally activated. If the coding has to be changed or the batteries serviced, manufacturer's requirements must be strictly followed. There have been cases where EPIRB lanyards were attached to the ship so that the EPIRB could not float free; lanyards are only to be used by survivors for securing the EPIRB to a survival craft or person in water);
10. Ensure that EPIRBs are not activated if assistance is already immediately available (EPIRBs are intended to call for assistance if the ship is unable to obtain help by other means, and to provide position information and homing signals for SAR units);
11. Ensure that, if a distress alert has been accidentally transmitted, the ship makes every reasonable attempt to communicate with the RCC by any means to cancel the false distress alert;
12. Ensure that, if possible, after emergency use, the EPIRB is retrieved and de-activated; and
13. Ensure that when an EPIRB is damaged and needs to be disposed of, if a ship is sold for scrap, or if for any other reason a satellite EPIRB will no longer be used, the satellite EPIRB is made inoperable, either by removing its battery and, if possible, returning it to the manufacturer, or by demolishing it.

Note: If the EPIRB is returned to the manufacturer, it should be wrapped in tin foil to prevent transmission of signals during shipment.

PART C - DSC RELAY PROCEDURES

The purpose of the distress alerting procedures is to ensure that those vessels able to assist in a rescue are informed. There is no advantage in broadcasting the news of a distress incident to all vessels irrespective of their location and capabilities.

The normal course of events is that the RCC which receives a distress alert then goes on to initiate the transmission of a shore-to-ship distress relay whenever necessary. The need for the RCC to analyse the circumstances of the received distress alerts and decide on what further action is required is the reason why DSC distress alerts should only ever be acknowledged or relayed by DSC by the responsible RCC or CRS.

The procedures for relaying a distress alert by a vessel acting alone should therefore be used with extreme care and only where absolutely necessary. The automatic facility to relay a DSC distress alert fitted on the first generation of DSC equipment resulted in frequent false alerts, which were regularly propagated in a self-perpetuating chain far beyond the immediate area of the distress incident. This facility is no longer available on new DSC equipment.

However, there may be circumstances where the procedures for broadcasting a distress relay could be of value. For example, there is the danger that the initial alert did not reach the shore-based authorities or a ship or aircraft may be observed to be in danger but incapable of sending a distress alert by itself. Perhaps an emergency incident only becomes known to a single ship, which is not in a position to render assistance. The philosophy of handling distress incidents is that the alert and call for assistance should only be made when no immediate help is available.

If, for example, a helicopter ditches close to a ship or oil platform in calm weather and all on board are rescued promptly, there will be little to gain in alerting all vessels and stations regardless of whether they could offer useful assistance. News of the incident must of course be sent to those able to assist directly with medical treatment and evacuation, and any resulting pollution or navigational hazards must be notified to the responsible authorities. However, any standard commercial vessels in the area are unlikely to be in a position to offer anything more in the way of assistance, meaning that no additional benefit could be obtained by disturbing their voyages.

Acknowledgement of a distress alert should be by a shore-based station. Subsequent actions and communications should be controlled by the assigned RCC. In normal circumstances it should not be necessary for a vessel to relay a distress alert. In order to avoid confusion and delay, vessels must monitor the distress frequency to be certain that the original alert was not received by a shore station before initiating a distress relay.

When a ship station may relay a distress alert
1. Distress alert or call not acknowledged by a coast station

A coast station should acknowledge a DSC distress alert within 5 minutes. If there seems to be no response then ships may send an acknowledgement to the station in distress on RT. However, if there is no reply from the station in distress, and the DSC alert is repeated, it will be necessary to assume responsibility for ensuring that shore-based authorities are informed. The repeat of the DSC alert indicates that the vessel in distress did not receive a DSC acknowledgement from a coast station.

The immediate action in such a case is to send a DSC acknowledgement using the same distress frequency on which the distress alert was received. The DSC acknowledgement will cancel the automatic control function for repeating DSC distress alerts, thus preventing any further automatic re-transmissions of the distress. It is then essential to inform the nearest coast station directly by any suitable means of communication.

The next step depends on how the distress alert was received. Vessels receiving a DSC distress alert on VHF or MF are not permitted to relay the call by DSC under any circumstances, although they may relay by other means.

Particular care is needed when a distress alert is received on HF at a considerable distance from the incident to avoid making unnecessary or confusing transmissions in response. A vessel receiving a DSC alert from another vessel on any of the HF DSC frequencies shall:

- NOT ACKNOWLEDGE
- Set watch on the appropriate RT and Telex frequencies
- If there is no sign of an acknowledgement by a coast station within 5 minutes, and no distress communications are heard between a coast station and the vessel in distress, then the receiving station must relay the distress alert ashore by any means available, but to coast stations only.

A rarer circumstance could be when a ship station receives an RT distress call, but no subsequent acknowledgement from a coast station or other vessel is heard. This is only likely to occur on VHF Ch 16, because this is the only channel still nominated for maintaining an aural watch for distress traffic. In such a case, any means available should be used to make a distress relay to the nearest coast station.

2. Ship or aircraft in distress is unable to send a distress alert

Stations not in distress which learn that a vessel, aircraft or other vehicle is in distress (for example, by a radio or cell-phone call or by observation), may transmit a DSC distress relay and a Mayday Relay on RT, as appropriate, on behalf of the other vessel, but only in the following circumstances:

- When the station in distress is not itself in a position to transmit a distress alert or message, and
- When the Master or other person responsible for the station not in distress considers that further help is necessary.

Procedures for sending a distress relay
In no case is a ship permitted to transmit an all ships DSC distress relay call on receipt of a DSC distress alert on either VHF or MF channels. If no aural watch is being maintained by nearby coast stations on the relevant RT Channel (2182 kHz, VHF Ch 16), the appropriate coast station should be contacted by sending an individual DSC distress relay call addressed solely to that coast station. However, if an aural watch is being maintained then an RT distress relay call should be made to the coast station.

However, it may be appropriate to address the call to all ships, or all ships in a certain geographical area in the case that a distress relay call is transmitted on behalf of another ship or mobile unit.

Summary of procedures:

1. Mayday relay RT procedure:
The distress relay call sent by radiotelephony consists of:

- The distress signal "MAYDAY RELAY" spoken three times;
- The words "THIS IS" or "DE" (spoken as "DELTA ECHO"), in case of language difficulties
- The call sign, name or other identification of the relaying station spoken three times;
- Complete repetition of the ORIGINAL DISTRESS MESSAGE.

Vessels making a distress relay call should ensure that a suitable CRS or RCC is informed of the original distress communications. If relaying specifically to a LES, an Inmarsat terminal set to distress priority (level 3) could also be used.

Note 1: If the station in distress could not be identified, and you therefore have to originate the distress message as well, then you must not use the name of your own station, i.e., you would say 'Unidentified Trawler' or 'Unidentified Helicopter'.

Note 2: Under the regulations governing mandatory listening watch keeping, a distress relay by radiotelephony can only be effective if sent on VHF Ch 16.

2. DSC distress relay call procedure:

If circumstances permit, a DSC distress relay call using DSC may be transmitted as follows:

- Tune the transmitter to the DSC distress channel (2187·5 kHz, VHF Ch 70)
- Select the distress relay call format on the DSC equipment,
- Key in or select on the DSC equipment keyboard:
  - the 9-digit identity of the appropriate coast station, All Ships Call (VHF) or Geographic Area Call (MF/HF), as appropriate to the circumstances,
  - the 9-digit identity of the ship in distress, if known,
  - the nature of distress,
  - the latest position of the ship in distress, if known,
  - the time (in UTC) the position was valid (if known),
  - type of subsequent distress communication (telephony);
- Transmit the DSC distress relay call;
- Prepare for the subsequent distress traffic by tuning the transmitter and the radiotelephony receiver to the distress traffic channel in the same band, i.e. 2182 kHz and VHF Ch 16, while waiting for the DSC distress acknowledgement.

Note 1: No DSC relay call to shipping generally on VHF or MF is ever permitted in response to a DSC alert.

Note 2: A DSC relay call addressed directly to a coast station should only be made if there is no possibility to make a distress relay call using RT.

3. Regulatory guidance on distress relays:

COMSAR Circular 25 (15 March 2001) sets out the recommended procedures (now included in Recommendation ITU-R M.541-9) regarding the transmissions of distress relays and acknowledgements in five key points:

1. Distress relays and acknowledgements of all types should only be sent on the Master's authority.
2. Ships should not acknowledge DSC alerts by sending a return DSC call; they should acknowledge only by RT.
3. Ships receiving a DSC distress alert on VHF or MF are not permitted to relay the call by DSC under any circumstances (they may relay by other means).
4. Ships may send a DSC distress alert (on behalf of another vessel), only if the following two conditions both apply:
   (a) The ship in distress is not itself able to transmit its own distress alert, and
   (b) The Master of the ship considers that further help is necessary.
5. This requires use of the call sequence for Distress Relay. It should be addressed to "all ships" or to the appropriate coast station.

Note 1: Item 1 is particularly important as there is a general perception that the Master's authority only applies to the distress alert. This may be partly due to the terms of RR 32.3 and the many publications which allude to it. As well, there is the fact that DSC receivers are required to store at least 20 distress alerts and just 5 Ordinary Calls. Distress Relays and Acknowledgements do not follow the Distress Format and are therefore stored as "Ordinary" calls, perhaps implying that they have a lower priority.

Note 2: Item 4 is more stringent than RR 32.16-18, which allows for either of the two quoted conditions, rather than both.

ITU Regulations

Operating procedures for Distress Relay calls are found in ITU-R M541-9 as follows

> Annex 1 - Procedures for Distress, Urgency and Safety Calls: Paragraph **3.4**
> Annex 3 - Ship Station Procedures (MF, HF and VHF): Paragraphs **1.4**, **1.5**, **1.6**, **6.1.4**, **6.1.5**, and **6.1.6**
> Annex 4 - Coast Station DSC Procedures (MF HF and VHF): Paragraphs **1.3-4** and **6.1.3**

In order to understand all the procedures, the full text of the above Regulations should be fully consulted.

Distress Acknowledgements

The procedures for Distress Acknowledgements follow a basically similar pattern to those for Distress Relays. Coast stations are required to acknowledge by DSC (immediately on VHF, after a delay of 1 to 2¾ minutes MF and HF). Ships must not normally acknowledge by DSC unless instructed to do so by a RCC; instead they acknowledge distress traffic by voice on the appropriate RT frequency. The reason is that a DSC Acknowledgement disables the distressed vessel's automatic repeat transmissions - these are no longer necessary when the distress alert has been received by a coast station because the RCC has been informed.

OPERATIONAL PROCEDURES FOR THE USE OF DSC EQUIPMENT IN THE MARITIME MOBILE SERVICE

SUMMARY

Rec. ITU-R M.541-10:

The Recommendation contains the operational procedures for digital selective-calling (DSC) equipment whose technical characteristics are given in Recommendation ITU-R M.493. The Recommendation contains six annexes. In Annexes 1 and 2 the provisions and procedures are described for distress, urgency and safety calls and for routine calls, respectively. In Annexes 3 and 4 the operational procedures for ships and for coast stations and Man overboard devices are described and Annex 6 lists the frequencies to be used for DSC.

The following definitions are used throughout this Recommendation:

Single frequency: the same frequency is used for transmission and reception;

Paired frequencies: frequencies which are associated in pairs; each pair consisting of one transmitting and one receiving frequency;

International DSC frequencies: those frequencies designated in the RR for exclusive use for DSC on an international basis;

National DSC frequencies: those frequencies assigned to individual coast stations or a group of stations on which DSC is permitted (this may include working frequencies as well as calling frequencies). The use of these frequencies must be in accordance with the RR;

Automatic DSC operation at a ship station: a mode of operation employing automatic tunable transmitters and receivers, suitable for unattended operation, which provide for automatic call acknowledgements upon reception of a DSC and automatic transfer to the appropriate working frequencies;

Call attempt: one or a limited number of call sequences directed to the same stations on one or more frequencies and within a relatively short time period (e.g. a few minutes). A call attempt is considered unsuccessful if a calling sequence contains the symbol RQ at the end of the sequence and no acknowledgement is received in this time interval.

ANNEX 1
PROVISIONS AND PROCEDURES FOR DISTRESS, URGENCY AND SAFETY CALLS

1   INTRODUCTION

The terrestrial elements of the GMDSS adopted by the 1988 Amendments to the International Convention for SOLAS, 1974, are based on the use of DSC for distress and safety communications.

1.1   **Method of calling**

The provisions of RR Chapter VII are applicable to the use of DSC in cases of distress, urgency or safety.

2   DIGITAL SELECTIVE CALLING DISTRESS ALERT

The DSC distress alert provides for alerting, self-identification, ship's position including time, and nature of distress as defined in the RR (see RR Chapter VII).

3   PROCEDURES FOR DIGITAL SELECTIVE CALLING DISTRESS ALERTS

3.1   **Transmission by a mobile unit in distress**

3.1.1   The DSC equipment should be capable of being pre-set to transmit the distress alert on at least one distress alerting frequency.

3.1.2   The distress alert shall be composed in accordance with Recommendation ITU-R M.493. Although the equipment may be able to automatically include the ship's position information and the time the position was valid, if this information is not available to the equipment then the operator has to manually enter the ship's position and time at which it was valid. Enter the nature of distress as appropriate.

3.1.3   **Distress alert attempt**

At MF and HF a distress alert attempt may be transmitted as a single frequency or a multi-frequency call attempt. At VHF only single frequency call attempts are used.

3.1.3.1   **Single frequency call attempt**

A distress alert attempt should be transmitted as 5 consecutive calls on one frequency. To avoid call collision and the loss of acknowledgements, this call attempt may be transmitted on the same frequency again after a random delay of between 3 ½ and 4 ½ min from the beginning of the initial call. This allows acknowledgements arriving randomly to be received without being blocked by retransmission. The random delay should be generated automatically for each repeated transmission, however it should be possible to override the automatic repeat manually.

At MF and HF, single frequency call attempts may be repeated on different frequencies after a random delay of between 3 ½ and 4 ½ min from the beginning of the initial call. However, if a station is capable of receiving acknowledgements continuously on all distress frequencies except for the transmit frequency in use, then single frequency call attempts may be repeated on different frequencies without this delay.

3.1.3.2 **Multi-frequency call attempt**

A distress alert attempt may be transmitted as up to 6 consecutive (see Note 1) calls dispersed over a maximum of 6 distress frequencies (1 at MF and 5 at HF). Stations transmitting multi-frequency distress alert attempts should be able to receive acknowledgements continuously on all frequencies except for the transmit frequency in use, or be able to complete the call attempt within 1 min.

Multi-frequency call attempts may be repeated after a random delay of between 3 ½ and 4 ½ min from the beginning of the previous call attempt.

[1] A VHF call may be transmitted simultaneously with an MF/HF call.

3.1.4 **Distress**

In the case of distress the operator should transmit a distress alert as described in Annex 3

3.2 **Reception**

The DSC equipment should be capable of maintaining a reliable watch on a 24-hour basis on appropriate DSC distress alerting frequencies.

3.3 **Acknowledgement of distress alerts**

Acknowledgements of distress alerts should be initiated manually.

Acknowledgements should be transmitted on the same frequency as the distress alert was received.

3.3.1 Distress alerts should normally be acknowledged by DSC only by appropriate coast stations. Coast stations should, in addition, set watch on radiotelephony and, if the "mode of subsequent communication" signal in the received distress alert indicates teleprinter, also on narrow-band direct-printing (NBDP) (see Recommendation ITU-R M.493). In both cases, the radiotelephone and NBDP frequencies should be those associated with the frequency on which the distress alert was received.

3.3.2 Acknowledgements by coast stations of DSC distress alerts transmitted on MF or HF should be initiated with a minimum delay of 1 min after receipt of a distress alert, and normally within a maximum delay of 2 ¾ min. This allows all calls within a single frequency or multi-frequency call attempt to be completed and should allow sufficient time for coast stations to respond to the distress alert. Acknowledgements by coast stations on VHF should be transmitted as soon as practicable.

3.3.3 The acknowledgement of a distress alert consists of a single DSC distress acknowledgement call and includes the identification of the ship whose distress alert is being acknowledged.

3.3.4 Ships receiving a DSC distress alert from another ship should set watch on an associated radiotelephone distress and safety traffic frequency and acknowledge the call by radiotelephony (see RR Nos. 32.28 – 32.35).

3.3.5 The automatic repetition of a distress alert attempt should be terminated automatically on receipt of a DSC distress acknowledgement.

3.3.6 When distress, urgency, and safety traffic cannot be successfully conducted using radiotelephony, an affected station may indicate its intention to conduct subsequent communications on the associated frequency for NBDP telegraphy.

3.4 **Distress alert relays**

Distress alert relays should be initiated manually.

3.4.1 A distress alert relay should use the call format for distress alert relays as specified in Recommendation ITU-R M.493 and the calling attempt should follow the procedures described in § 3.1.3 to 3.1.3.2 for distress alerts, except that the distress relay is sent manually as a single call on a single frequency. Ship stations not provided with the DSC distress alert relay function should relay the alert by radio telephony.

3.4.2 Any ship, receiving a distress alert on an HF channel which is not acknowledged by a coast station within 5 min, should transmit an individual distress alert relay addressed to the appropriate coast station.

3.4.3 Distress alert relays transmitted by coast stations, or by ship stations addressed to more than one vessel, should be acknowledged by ship stations using radiotelephony. Distress alert relays transmitted by ship stations should be acknowledged by a coast station transmitting a "distress alert relay acknowledgement call" in accordance with the procedures for distress acknowledgements given in § 3.3 to 3.3.3.

4 **PROCEDURES FOR DIGITAL SELECTIVE CALLING URGENCY AND SAFETY CALLS**

4.1 DSC, on the distress and safety calling frequencies, should be used by coast stations to advise shipping, and by ships to advise coast stations and/or ship stations, of the impending transmission of urgency, vital navigational and safety messages, except where the transmissions take place at routine times. The call should indicate the working frequency which will be used for the subsequent transmission of an urgent, vital navigational or safety message.

4.2 The announcement and identification of medical transports should be carried out by DSC transmission, using appropriate distress and safety calling frequencies. Such calls should use the call format for an urgency or safety call of the type medical transport and be addressed to all ships at VHF and Geographic Area at MF/HF.

4.3 The operational procedures for urgency and safety calls should be in accordance with the relevant parts of Annex 3, § 2.1 or 2.2 and § 3.1 or 3.2.

5 **TESTING THE EQUIPMENT USED FOR DISTRESS AND SAFETY CALLS**

Testing on the exclusive DSC distress and safety calling frequencies should be limited as far as possible. VHF, MF and HF test calls should be in accordance with Recommendation ITU-R M.493 and the call may be acknowledged by the called station. Normally there would be no further communication between the two stations involved.

ANNEX 2
PROVISIONS AND PROCEDURES FOR ROUTINE CALLS

1   FREQUENCY/CHANNELS

1.1   As a rule, paired frequencies should be used at HF and MF, in which case an acknowledgement is transmitted on the frequency paired with the frequency of the received call. In exceptional cases for national purposes a single frequency may be used. If the same call is received on several calling channels, the most appropriate shall be chosen to transmit the acknowledgement. A single frequency channel should be used at VHF.

1.2   **International calling**

The paired frequencies listed in RR Appendix **17** and in Annex 5 of this Recommendation should be used for international DSC calling at HF.

1.2.1   At HF and MF international DSC frequencies should only be used for shore-to-ship calls and for the associated call acknowledgements from ships fitted for automatic DSC operation where it is known that the ships concerned are not listening to the coast station's national frequencies.

1.2.2   All ship-to-shore DSC calling at HF and MF should preferably be done on the coast station's national frequencies.

1.3   **National calling**

Coast stations should avoid using the international DSC frequencies for calls that may be placed using national frequencies.

1.3.1   Ship stations should keep watch on appropriate national and international channels. (Appropriate measures should be taken for an even loading of national and international channels.)

1.3.2   Administrations are urged to find methods and negotiate terms to improve the utilization of the DSC channels available, e.g.:
– coordinated and/or joint use of coast station transmitters;
– optimizing the probability of successful calls by providing information to ships on suitable frequencies (channels) to be watched and by information from ships to a selected number of coast stations on the channels watched on-board.

1.4   **Method of calling**

1.4.1   The procedures set out in this section are applicable to the use of DSC techniques, except in cases of distress, urgency or safety, to which the provisions of RR Chapter VII are applicable.

1.4.2   The call shall contain information indicating the station or stations to which the call is directed, and the identification of the calling station.

1.4.3   The call should also contain information indicating the type of communication to be set up and may include supplementary information such as a proposed working frequency or channel; this information shall always be included in calls from coast stations, which shall have priority for that purpose.

1.4.4   An appropriate digital selective calling channel chosen in accordance with the provisions of RR Nos. **52.128** to **52.137** or Nos. **52.145** to **52.153** as appropriate, shall be used for the call.

2   OPERATING PROCEDURES

The technical format of the call sequence shall be in conformity with the relevant ITU-R Recommendations.

The reply to a DSC call requesting an acknowledgement shall be made by transmitting an appropriate acknowledgement using DSC.

Acknowledgements may be initiated either manually or automatically. When an acknowledgement can be transmitted automatically, it shall be in conformity with the relevant ITU-R Recommendations.

The technical format of the acknowledgement sequence shall be in conformity with the relevant ITU-R Recommendations.

For communication between a coast station and a ship station, the coast station shall finally decide the working frequency or channel to be used.

The forwarding traffic and the control for working for radiotelephony shall be carried out in accordance with Recommendation ITU-R M.1171.

Prior to a transmission the transmitting device should check as far as possible that no other call is in progress.

2.1   **Coast station initiates call to ship station (see Note 1)**

If a ship station has to be called, the coast station selects the appropriate MMSI or Maritime identity of the terminal, frequency band and transmitter site, if available.

[1] See Recommendations ITU-R M.689 and ITU-R M.1082 for further details of procedures applicable only to the semi-automatic/automatic services.

2.1.1   Assuming DSC is appropriate, the call is composed by the coast station as follows:
– format specifier,
– address of the ship,
– category,
– telecommand information,
– working frequency information in the message part of the sequence, if appropriate,
– usually end of sequence signal "RQ". However, if the coast station knows that the ship station cannot respond or the call is to a group of ships the frequency is omitted and the end of sequence signal should be 127, in which case the following procedures (§ 2.2) relating to an acknowledgement are not applicable.

2.1.2   The coast station verifies the calling sequence.

The call shall be transmitted once on a single appropriate calling channel or frequency only. Only in exceptional circumstances may a call be transmitted simultaneously on more than one frequency.

2.1.3   The coast station operator chooses the calling frequencies which are most suitable for the ship's location.

2.1.3.1   The coast station initiates the transmission of the sequence on one of the frequencies chosen. Transmission on any one frequency should be limited to no more than 2 call sequences separated by intervals of at least 45 s to allow for reception of an acknowledgement from the ship.

2.1.3.2   If appropriate, a call attempt may be transmitted, which may include the transmission of the same call sequence on other frequencies (if necessary with a change of working frequency information to correspond to the same band as the calling frequency) made in turn at intervals of not less than 5 min, following the same pattern as in § 2.1.3.1.

2.1.4   If an acknowledgement is received further transmission of the call sequence should not take place.

The coast station shall then prepare to transmit traffic on the working channel or frequency it has proposed.

2.1.5   When a station called does not reply, the call attempt should not normally be repeated until after an interval of at least 15 min. The same call attempt should not be repeated more than five times every 24 h. The aggregate of the times for which frequencies are occupied in one call attempt, should normally not exceed 1 min.

2.2   **The following procedures apply at the ship**

2.2.1   Upon receipt of a calling sequence at the ship station, the received message should be displayed.

2.2.2   When a received call sequence contains an end of sequence signal "RQ", an acknowledgement sequence should be composed and transmitted.

The format specifier and category information should be identical to that in the received calling sequence.

2.2.3   If the ship station is not equipped for automatic DSC operation, the ship's operator initiates an acknowledgement to the coast station after a delay of at least 5 s but no later than 4 ½ min of receiving the calling sequence, using the ship-to-shore calling procedures detailed in § 2.2. However the transmitted sequence should contain a "BQ" end of sequence signal in place of the "RQ" signal.

If such an acknowledgement cannot be transmitted within 5 min of receiving the calling sequence then the ship station should instead transmit a calling sequence to the coast station using the ship-to-shore calling procedure detailed in § 2.2.

2.2.4   If the ship is equipped for automatic DSC operation, the ship station automatically transmits an acknowledgement with an end of sequence signal "BQ". The start of the transmission of this acknowledgement sequence should be within 30 s for HF and MF or within 3 s for VHF after the reception of the complete call sequence.

2.2.5   If the ship is able to comply immediately the acknowledgement sequence should include a telecommand signal which is identical to that received in the calling sequence indicating that it is able to comply.

If no working frequency was proposed in the call, the ship station should include a proposal for a working frequency in its acknowledgement.

2.2.6   If the ship is not able to comply immediately the acknowledgement sequence should include the telecommand signal 104 (unable to comply), with a second telecommand signal giving additional information (see Recommendation ITU-R M.493).

At some later time when the ship is able to accept the traffic being offered, the ship station initiates a call to the coast station using the ship-to-shore calling procedures detailed in § 2.3.

2.2.7   If a call is acknowledged indicating ability to comply immediately and communication between coast station and ship station on the working channel agreed is established, the DSC call procedure is considered to be completed.

2.2.8   If the ship station transmits an acknowledgement which is not received by the coast station then this will result in the coast station repeating the call (in accordance with § 2.1.5). In this event the ship station should transmit a new acknowledgement.

2.3   **Ship station initiates call to coast station (see Note 1)**

This procedure should also be followed both as a delayed response to a call received earlier from the coast station (see § 2.2.2) and to initiate traffic from the ship station.

[1] See Recommendations ITU-R M.689 and ITU-R M.1082 for further details of procedures applicable only to the semi-automatic/automatic services.

2.3.1   Assuming a DSC is appropriate the call is transmitted by the ship station as follows:

– key in or select on the DSC equipment,
– format specifier,
– address,
– telecommand information,
– working frequency, or position (for MF/HF only) information in the message part of the sequence if appropriate,
– telephone number required (semi-automatic/automatic connections only),
– the ship station automatically inserts the category, self-identification and "end of sequence" signal RQ.

2.3.2   The ship station verifies the calling sequence.

2.3.3   The ship station selects the single most appropriate calling frequency preferably using the coast station's nationally assigned calling channels, for which purpose it shall send a single calling sequence on the selected frequency.

2.3.4   If a called station does not reply, the call sequence from the ship station should not normally be repeated until after an interval of at least 5 min for manual connections, or 5 s or 25 s in the case of semi-automatic/automatic VHF or MF/HF connections respectively. These repetitions may be made on alternative frequencies if appropriate. Any subsequent repetitions to the same coast station should not be made until at least 15 min have elapsed.

2.3.5   The coast station should transmit an acknowledgement, after a delay of at least 5 s but not later than 4 ½ min for manual connections, or, within 3 s for semi-automatic/automatic connections, containing the format specifier, the address of the ship, the category, the coast station self-identification and:

– if able to comply immediately on the working frequency suggested, the same telecommand and frequency information as in the call request;
– if no working frequency was suggested by the ship station then the acknowledgement sequence should include a channel/frequency proposal;
– if not able to comply on the working frequency suggested but able to comply immediately on an alternative frequency, the same telecommand information as in the call request but an alternative working frequency;
– if unable to comply immediately the telecommand signal 104 with a second telecommand signal giving additional information. For manual connections only, this second telecommand signal may include a queue indication.

The end of sequence signal "BQ" should also be included.

2.3.6   For manual connections, if a working frequency is proposed in accordance with § 2.3.4 but this is not acceptable to the ship station, then the ship station should immediately transmit a new call requesting an alternative frequency.

2.3.7   If an acknowledgement is received further transmission of the same call sequence should not take place. On receipt of an acknowledgement which indicates ability to comply, the DSC procedures are complete and both coast station and ship station should communicate on the working frequencies agreed with no further exchange of DSC calls.

2.3.8   If the coast station transmits an acknowledgement which is not received at the ship station then the ship station should repeat the call in accordance with § 2.3.4.

2.4   **Ship station initiates call to ship station**

The ship-to-ship procedures should be similar to those given in § 2.3, where the receiving ship station complies with the procedures given for coast stations, as appropriate, except that, with respect to § 2.3.1, the calling ship should always insert working frequency information in the message part of the calling sequence.

ANNEX 3
OPERATIONAL PROCEDURES FOR SHIPS FOR DIGITAL SELECTIVE CALLING COMMUNICATIONS ON MF, HF AND VHF

Introduction

Procedures for DSC communications on MF and VHF are described in §§ 1 to 5 below.
The procedures for DSC communications on HF are in general the same as for MF and VHF. Special conditions to be taken into account when making DSC communications on HF are described in § 6 below.

1   **DISTRESS**

1.1   **Transmission of digital selective calling distress alert**

A distress alert should be transmitted if, in the opinion of the Master, the ship or a person is in distress and requires immediate assistance.

A DSC distress alert should as far as possible include the ship's last known position and the time (in UTC) when it was valid. The position and the time should be included automatically by the ship's navigational equipment if this information is not included it should be inserted manually.

The DSC distress alert attempt is transmitted as follows:

– tune the transmitter to the DSC distress channel (2187.5 kHz on MF, channel 70 on VHF) if not done automatically by the ship station.
– if time permits, key in or select on the DSC equipment
– the nature of distress,
– the ship's last known position (latitude and longitude) if not provided automatically,
– the time (in UTC) the position was valid if not provided automatically,
– type of subsequent distress communication (telephony),

in accordance with the DSC equipment manufacturer's instructions;

– transmit the DSC distress alert;
– prepare for the subsequent distress traffic by tuning the transmitter and the radiotelephony receiver to the distress traffic channel in the same band, i.e. 2182 kHz on MF, channel 16 on VHF, while waiting for the DSC distress acknowledgement.

1.2   **Actions on receipt of a distress alert**

Ships receiving a DSC distress alert from another ship should normally not acknowledge the distress alert by DSC since acknowledgement of a DSC distress alert by use of DSC is normally made by coast stations only (see Annex 1 § 3.3.4 and Annex 3 § 6.1.4).

If a ship station continues to receive a DSC distress alert on an MF or VHF channel, a DSC acknowledgement should be transmitted to terminate the call only after consulting with a rescue coordination centre (RCC) or a coast station (CS) and being directed to do so.

Ships receiving a DSC distress alert from another ship should also defer the acknowledgement of the distress alert by radiotelephony for a short interval, if the ship is within an area covered by one or more coast stations, in order to give the coast station time to acknowledge the DSC distress alert first.

Ships receiving a DSC distress alert from another ship shall:

– watch for the reception of a distress acknowledgement on the distress channel (2187.5 kHz on MF and channel 70 on VHF);

– prepare for receiving the subsequent distress communication by tuning the radiotelephony receiver to the distress traffic frequency in the same band in which the DSC distress alert was received, i.e. 2182 kHz on MF, channel 16 on VHF;

– in accordance with the provisions of RR No. 32.23 acknowledge the receipt of the distress alert by transmitting a message by radiotelephony on the distress traffic frequency in the same band in which the DSC distress alert was received, i.e. 2182 kHz on MF, channel 16 on VHF.

1.3   **Distress traffic**

On receipt of a DSC distress acknowledgement the ship in distress should commence the distress traffic by radiotelephony on the distress traffic frequency (2182 kHz on MF, channel 16 on VHF) in accordance with the provisions of RR Nos. **32.13C** and **32.13D**.

1.4   **Transmission of a digital selective calling distress alert relay**

In no case is a ship permitted to transmit an all ships DSC distress alert relay on receipt of a DSC distress alert on either VHF or MF channels. If no aural watch is present on the relative channel (2 182 kHz on MF, channel 16 on VHF), the coast station should be contacted by sending an individual DSC distress alert relay.

1.4.1   **Transmission of a DSC distress relay call on behalf of someone else**

A ship knowing that another ship is in distress shall transmit a DSC distress alert relay if:

– the ship in distress is not itself able to transmit the distress alert,

– the Master of the ship considers that further help is necessary.

In accordance with RR No. **32.19B** the DSC distress alert relay on behalf of somebody else should preferably be addressed to an individual CS or RCC.

The DSC distress alert relay is transmitted as follows:

– select the distress alert relay format on the DSC equipment,

– key in or select on the DSC equipment:

– the 9-digit identity of the appropriate coast station or in special circumstances all ships call (VHF). Geographic area call (MF/HF),

– the 9-digit identity of the ship in distress, if known,

– the nature of distress,

– the latest position of the ship in distress, if known,

– the time (in UTC) the position was valid (if known),

– type of subsequent distress communication (telephony);

– transmit the DSC distress alert relay;

– prepare for the subsequent distress traffic by tuning the transmitter and the radiotelephony receiver to the distress traffic channel in the same band, i.e. 2182 kHz on MF and channel 16 on VHF, while waiting for the DSC distress acknowledgement.

1.5   **Acknowledgement of a digital selective calling distress alert relay received from a coast station**

Coast stations, after having received and acknowledged a DSC distress alert, may if necessary, retransmit the information received as a DSC distress alert relay, addressed to all ships (VHF only), all ships in a specific geographical area (MF/HF only), or a specific ship.

Ships receiving a distress alert relay transmitted by a coast station shall not use DSC to acknowledge the call, but should acknowledge the receipt of the call by radiotelephony on the distress traffic channel in the same band in which the relay call was received, i.e. 2182 kHz on MF, channel 16 on VHF.

Acknowledge the receipt of the distress alert relay by transmitting a message, in accordance with the provisions of RR No. **32.23**, by radiotelephony on the distress traffic frequency in the same band in which the DSC distress alert relay was received.

1.6   **Acknowledgement of a digital selective calling distress relay call received from another ship**

Ships receiving a distress alert relay from another ship shall follow the same procedure as for acknowledgement of a distress alert, i.e. the procedure given in § 1.2 above.

1.7   **Cancellation of an inadvertent digital selective calling distress alert**

A station transmitting an inadvertent DSC distress alert shall cancel the distress alert using the following procedure:

1.7.1   Immediately cancel the distress alert by transmitting a DSC self-cancel on all the frequencies where the inadvertent DSC distress alert was transmitted, if the ship station is capable hereof. A DSC self-cancel is a distress acknowledgement where the self-id and the distress id is identical as defined in Recommendation ITU-R M.493.

1.7.2   Subsequently cancel the distress alert aurally over the telephony distress traffic channel associated with each DSC channel on which the "distress alert" was transmitted, by transmitting a message in accordance with the provisions of RR No. **32.53E**.

1.7.3   Monitor the telephony distress traffic channel associated with the DSC channel on which the distress was transmitted, and respond to any communications concerning that distress alert as appropriate.

2   **URGENCY**

2.1   **Transmission of urgency messages**

Transmission of urgency messages shall be carried out in two steps:

– announcement of the urgency message,

– transmission of the urgency message.

The announcement is carried out by transmission of a DSC urgency call on the DSC distress calling channel (2187.5 kHz on MF, channel 70 on VHF).

The urgency message is transmitted on the distress traffic channel (2182 kHz on MF, channel 16 on VHF).

The DSC urgency call may be addressed to all stations at VHF, or a geographic area at MF/HF, or to a specific station. The frequency on which the urgency message will be transmitted shall be included in the DSC urgency call.

The transmission of an urgency message is thus carried out as follows:

Announcement:

– select the appropriate calling format on the DSC equipment (all ships (VHF only), geographical area (MF/HF only) or individual);
– key in or select on the DSC equipment:

    – specific area or 9-digit identity of the specific station, if appropriate,
    – the category of the call (urgency),
    – the frequency or channel on which the urgency message will be transmitted,
    – the type of communication in which the urgency message will be given (radiotelephony), in accordance with the DSC equipment manufacturer's instructions;
    – transmit the DSC urgency announcement.

Transmission of the urgency call and message:

– tune the transmitter to the frequency or channel indicated in the DSC urgency announcement;
– transmit the urgency call and message in accordance with the provisions of RR No. 33.12.

2.2   **Reception of an urgency message**

Ships receiving a DSC urgency call announcing an urgency message addressed to more than one station shall NOT acknowledge the receipt of the DSC call, but should tune the radiotelephony receiver to the frequency indicated in the call and listen to the urgency message.

3   **SAFETY**

3.1   **Transmission of safety messages**

Transmission of safety messages shall be carried out in two steps:

– announcement of the safety message,
– transmission of the safety message.

The announcement is carried out by transmission of a DSC safety call on the DSC distress calling channel (2187.5 kHz on MF, channel 70 on VHF).

In accordance with RR No. **33.32** safety messages should preferably be transmitted on a working frequency in the same band(s) as those used for the safety call or announcement.

The DSC safety call may be addressed to all ships (VHF only), ships in a specific geographical area (MF/HF only), or to a specific station.

The frequency on which the safety message will be transmitted shall be included in the DSC call.

The transmission of a safety message is thus carried out as follows:

Announcement:

– select the appropriate calling format on the DSC equipment (all ships (VHF only), geographical area (MF/HF only), or individual);
– key in or select on the DSC equipment:
– specific area or 9-digit identity of specific station, if appropriate,
– the category of the call (safety),
– the frequency or channel on which the safety message will be transmitted,
– the type of communication in which the safety message will be given (radiotelephony),in accordance with the DSC equipment manufacturer's instructions;
– transmit the DSC safety announcement.

Transmission of the safety call and message:

– tune the transmitter to the frequency or channel indicated in the DSC safety call;
– transmit the safety call and message in accordance with the provisions of RR No. 33.35.

3.2   **Reception of a safety message**

Ships receiving a DSC safety call announcing a safety message addressed to more than one station shall NOT acknowledge the receipt of the DSC safety call, but should tune the radiotelephony receiver to the frequency indicated in the call and listen to the safety message.

4   **PUBLIC CORRESPONDENCE**

4.1   **Digital selective calling channels for public correspondence**

4.1.1   VHF

VHF DSC channel 70 is used for DSC for distress and safety purposes as well as for DSC for public correspondence.

4.1.2   MF

International and national DSC channels separate from the DSC distress and safety calling channel 2187.5 kHz are used for digital selective-calling on MF for public correspondence.

Ships calling a coast station by DSC on MF for public correspondence should preferably use the coast station's national DSC channel.

The international DSC channel for public correspondence may as a general rule be used between ships and coast stations of different nationality. The ships transmitting frequency is 2189.5 kHz, and the receiving frequency is 2177 kHz.

The frequency 2177 kHz is also used for DSC between ships for general communication

4.2 Transmission of a digital selective calling call for public correspondence to a coast station or another ship

A DSC call for public correspondence to a coast station or another ship is transmitted as follows:

– select the format for calling a specific station on the DSC equipment;
– key in or select on the DSC equipment:
– the 9-digit identity of the station to be called,
– the category of the call (routine),
– the type of the subsequent communication (normally radiotelephony),
– a proposed working channel if calling another ship. A proposal for a working channel should NOT be included in calls to a coast station; the coast station will in its DSC acknowledgement indicate a vacant working channel, in accordance with the DSC equipment manufacturer's instructions;
– transmit the DSC call.

4.3 Repeating a call

A DSC call for public correspondence may be repeated on the same or another DSC channel, if no acknowledgement is received within 5 min.
Further call attempts should be delayed at least 15 min, if acknowledgement is still not received.

4.4 Acknowledgement of a received call and preparation for reception of the traffic

On receipt of a DSC call from a coast station or another ship, a DSC acknowledgement is transmitted as follows:

– select the acknowledgement format on the DSC equipment,
– transmit an acknowledgement indicating whether the ship is able to communicate as proposed in the call (type of communication and working frequency),
– if able to communicate as indicated, tune the transmitter and the radiotelephony receiver to the indicated working channel and prepare to receive the traffic.

4.5 Reception of acknowledgement and further actions

When receiving an acknowledgement indicating that the called station is able to receive the traffic, prepare to transmit the traffic as follows:

– tune the transmitter and receiver to the indicated working channel;
– commence the communication on the working channel by:
– the 9-digit identity or call sign or other identification of the called station,
– "this is",
– the 9-digit identity or call sign or other identification of own ship.

It will normally rest with the ship to call again a little later in case the acknowledgement from the coast station indicates that the coast station is not able to receive the traffic immediately.

In case the ship, in response to a call to another ship, receives an acknowledgement indicating that the other ship is not able to receive the traffic immediately, it will normally rest with the called ship to transmit a call to the calling ship when ready to receive the traffic.

5 TESTING THE EQUIPMENT USED FOR DISTRESS AND SAFETY

Testing on the exclusive DSC distress and safety calling frequency 2187.5 kHz should be limited as far as possible.

Test calls should be transmitted by the ship station and acknowledged by the called station. Normally there would be no further communication between the two stations involved.

A VHF and MF test call to a station is transmitted as follows:

– key in or select the format for the test call on the DSC,
– key in the 9-digit identity of the station to be called,
– transmit the DSC test call,
– wait for acknowledgement.

6 SPECIAL CONDITIONS AND PROCEDURES FOR DIGITAL SELECTIVE CALLING COMMUNICATION ON HF
General

The procedures for DSC communication on HF are – with some additions described in §§ 6.1 to 6.3 below – equal to the corresponding procedures for DSC communications on MF/VHF.

Due regard to the special conditions described in § 6.1 to 6.3 should be given when making DSC communications on HF.

6.1 Distress

6.1.1 Transmission of digital selective calling distress alert and choice of HF bands

In sea areas A3 and A4 a DSC distress alert on HF is intended to be received by coast stations and a DSC distress alert on MF/VHF is intended to be received by other ships in the vicinity.

The DSC distress alert should as far as possible include the ship's last known position and the time (in UTC) it was valid. If the position and time is not inserted automatically from the ship's navigational equipment, it should be inserted manually.

Propagation characteristics of HF radio waves for the actual season and time of the day should be taken into account when choosing HF bands for transmission of DSC distress alert.

As a general rule the DSC distress channel in the 8 MHz maritime band (8414.5 kHz) may in many cases be an appropriate first choice.

Transmission of the DSC distress alert in more than one HF band will normally increase the probability of successful reception of the alert by coast stations.

DSC distress alert may be sent on a number of HF bands in two different ways:

a) either by transmitting the DSC distress alert on one HF band, and waiting a few minutes for receiving acknowledgement by a coast station;

if no acknowledgement is received within 3 min, the process is repeated by transmitting the DSC distress alert on another appropriate HF band etc.;

b) or by transmitting the DSC distress alert at a number of HF bands with no, or only very short, pauses between the calls, without waiting for acknowledgement between the calls.

It is recommended to follow procedure a) in all cases, where time permits to do so; this will make it easier to choose the appropriate HF band for commencement of the subsequent communication with the coast station on the corresponding distress traffic channel.

Transmitting the DSC distress alert on HF:

– tune the transmitter to the chosen HF DSC distress channel (4207.5, 6312, 8 414.5, 12577, 16804.5 kHz);
– follow the instructions for keying in or selection of relevant information on the DSC equipment as described in § 1.1;
– transmit the DSC distress alert.

In special cases, for example in tropical zones, transmission of DSC distress alert on HF may, in addition to ship-to-shore alerting, also be useful for ship-to-ship alerting

6.1.2   **Preparation for the subsequent distress traffic**

After having transmitted the DSC distress alert on appropriate DSC distress channels (HF, MF and/or VHF), prepare for the subsequent distress traffic by tuning the radiocommunication set(s) (HF, MF and/or VHF as appropriate) to the corresponding distress traffic channel(s).

Where multiple frequency call attempts are transmitted the corresponding distress traffic frequency should be 8291 kHz.

If method b) described in § 6.1.1 has been used for transmission of DSC distress alert on a number of HF bands:

– take into account in which HF band(s) acknowledgement has been successfully received from a coast station;
– if acknowledgements have been received on more than one HF band, commence the transmission of distress traffic on one of these bands, but if no response is received from a coast station then the other bands should be used in turn.

The distress traffic frequencies are (see RR Appendix **15**, Table **15-1**):

HF (kHz):

| Telephony | 4125 | 6215 | 8291 | 12290 | 16420 |
| Telex | 4177.5 | 6268 | 8376.5 | 12520 | 16695 |

MF (kHz):

| Telephony | 2182 |
| Telex | 2174.5 |

VHF: Channel 16 (156.800 MHz).

6.1.3   **Distress traffic**

The procedures described in § 1.3 are used when the distress traffic on MF/HF is carried out by *radiotelephony*.

The following procedures shall be used in cases where the distress traffic on MF/HF is carried out by *radiotelex*:

– The forward error correcting (FEC) mode shall be used;
– all messages shall be preceded by:
– at least one carriage return,
– line feed,
– one letter shift,
– the distress signal "MAYDAY";
– The ship in distress should commence the distress telex traffic on the appropriate distress telex traffic channel as follows:
– carriage return, line feed, letter shift,
– the distress signal "MAYDAY",
– "this is",
– the 9-digit identity and call sign or other identification of the ship,
– the ship's position if not included in the DSC distress alert,
– the nature of distress,
– any other information which might facilitate the rescue.

6.1.4   **Actions on reception of a digital selective calling distress alert on HF from another ship**

Ships receiving a DSC distress alert on HF from another ship shall *not* acknowledge the alert, but should:

– watch for reception of a DSC distress acknowledgement from a coast station;
– while waiting for reception of a DSC distress acknowledgement from a coast station:
prepare for reception of the subsequent distress communication by tuning the HF radiocommunication set (transmitter and receiver) to the relevant distress traffic channel in the same HF band in which the DSC distress alert was received, observing the following conditions:
– if radiotelephony mode was indicated in the DSC distress alert, the HF radiocommunication set should be tuned to the radiotelephony distress traffic channel in the HF band concerned;
– if telex mode was indicated in the DSC distress alert, the HF radiocommunication set should be tuned to the radiotelex distress traffic channel in the HF band concerned. Ships able to do so should additionally watch the corresponding radiotelephony distress channel;
– if the DSC distress alert was received on more than one HF band, the radiocommunication set should be tuned to the relevant distress traffic channel in the HF band considered to be the best one in the actual case. If the DSC distress alert was received successfully on the 8 MHz band, this band may in many cases be an appropriate first choice;
– if no distress traffic is received on the HF channel within 1 to 2 min, tune the HF radiocommunication set to the relevant distress traffic channel in another HF band deemed appropriate in the actual case;
– if no DSC distress acknowledgement is received from a coast station within 5 min, and no distress communication is observed going on between a coast station and the ship in distress:
– inform a RCC via appropriate radiocommunications means, transmit a DSC distress alert relay if instructed to do so by a RCC or a coast station.

6.1.5 Transmission of digital selective calling distress alert relay

In case it is considered appropriate to transmit a DSC distress alert relay:

– distress alert relays on HF should be initiated manually;
– follow the procedures described in § 6.1.1 above (except the call is sent manually as a single call on a single frequency) and should preferably be addressed to an individual rescue coordination centre or coast station;
– follow the instructions for keying in or selection of call format and relevant information on the DSC equipment as described in § 1.4;
– transmit the DSC distress alert relay.

6.1.6 Acknowledgement of a HF digital selective calling distress alert relay received from a coast station

Ships receiving a DSC distress alert relay from a coast station on HF, addressed to all ships within a specified area, should NOT acknowledge the receipt of the relay alert by DSC, but by *radiotelephony* on the telephony distress traffic channel in the same band(s) in which the DSC distress relay call was received.

6.2 Urgency

Transmission of urgency messages on HF should normally be addressed:

– either to all ships within a specified geographical area,
– or to a specific coast station.

Announcement of the urgency message is carried out by transmission of a DSC call with category urgency on the appropriate DSC distress channel.

The transmission of the urgency message itself on HF is carried out by radiotelephony or radiotelex on the appropriate distress traffic channel in the same band in which the DSC announcement was transmitted.

6.2.1 Transmission of DSC announcement of an urgency message on HF

– choose the HF band considered to be the most appropriate, taking into account propagation characteristics for HF radio waves at the actual season and time of the day; the 8 MHz band may in many cases be an appropriate first choice;
– key in or select call format for either geographical area call or individual call on the DSC equipment, as appropriate;
– key in or select relevant information on the DSC equipment keyboard as described in § 2.1;
– transmit the DSC call; and
– if the DSC call is addressed to a specific coast station, wait for DSC acknowledgement from the coast station. If acknowledgement is not received within a few minutes, repeat the DSC call on another HF frequency deemed appropriate.

6.2.2 Transmission of the urgency message and subsequent action

– tune the HF transmitter to the distress traffic channel (telephony or telex) indicated in the DSC announcement;
– if the urgency message is to be transmitted using radiotelephony, follow the procedure described in § 2.1;
– if the urgency message is to be transmitted by radiotelex, the following procedure shall be used:
– use the forward error correcting (FEC) mode unless the message is addressed to a single station whose radiotelex identity number is known;
– commence the telex message by:
– at least one carriage return, line feed, one letter shift,
– the urgency signal "PAN PAN",
– "this is",
– the 9-digit identity of the ship and the call sign or other identification of the ship,
– the text of the urgency message.

Announcement and transmission of urgency messages addressed to all HF equipped ships within a specified area may be repeated on a number of HF bands as deemed appropriate in the actual situation.

6.3 Safety

The procedures for transmission of DSC safety announcement and for transmission of the safety message are the same as for urgency messages, described in § 6.2, *except* that:

– in the DSC announcement, the category SAFETY shall be used,
– in the safety message, the safety signal "SECURITE" shall be used instead of the urgency signal "PAN PAN".

ANNEX 4
OPERATIONAL PROCEDURES FOR COAST STATIONS FOR DIGITAL SELECTIVE CALLING COMMUNICATIONS ON MF, HF AND VHF

Introduction

Procedures for DSC communications on MF and VHF are described in §§ 1 to 5 below.

The procedures for DSC communications on HF are in general the same as for MF and VHF. Special conditions to be taken into account when making DSC communications on HF are described in § 6 below.

1   DISTRESS[1]

1.1   **Reception of a digital selective calling distress alert**

The transmission of a distress alert indicates that a mobile unit (a ship, aircraft or other vehicle) or a person is in distress and requires immediate assistance. The distress alert is a digital selective call using a distress call format.

Coast stations in receipt of a distress alert shall ensure that it is routed as soon as possible to an RCC. The receipt of a distress alert is to be acknowledged as soon as possible by the appropriate coast station.

[1]These procedures assume that the RCC is sited remotely from the DSC coast station; where this is not the case, appropriate amendments should be made locally.

1.2   **Acknowledgement of a digital selective calling distress alert**

The coast station shall transmit the distress acknowledgement on the distress calling frequency on which the call was received.

The acknowledgement of a DSC distress alert is transmitted as follows:

– key in or select on the DSC equipment (see Note 1):
– distress alert acknowledgement,
– 9-digit identity of the ship in distress,
– nature of distress,
– distress coordinates,
– the time (in UTC) when the position was valid.

[1]Some or all of this information might be included automatically by the equipment;

– transmit the acknowledgement;
– prepare to handle the subsequent distress traffic by setting watch on radiotelephony and, if the "mode of subsequent communication" signal in the received distress alert indicates teleprinter, also on NBDP, if the coast station is fitted with NBDP. In both cases, the radiotelephone and NBDP frequencies should be those associated with the frequency on which the distress alert was received (on MF 2182 kHz for radiotelephony and 2174.5 kHz for NBDP, on VHF 156.8 MHz/channel 16 for radiotelephony; there is no frequency for NBDP on VHF).

1.3   **Transmission of a digital selective calling distress alert relay**

Coast stations shall initiate and transmit a distress alert relay in any of the following cases:

– when the distress of the mobile unit has been notified to the coast station by other means and a broadcast alert to shipping is required by the RCC; and
– when the person responsible for the coast station considers that further help is necessary (close cooperation with the appropriate RCC is recommended under such conditions).

In the cases mentioned above, the coast station shall transmit a shore-to-ship distress alert relay addressed, as appropriate, to all ships (VHF only), to a geographical area (MF/HF only) or to a specific ship.

The distress alert relay shall contain the identification of the mobile unit in distress, its position and other information which might facilitate rescue.

The distress alert relay is transmitted as follows:

– key in or select on the DSC equipment (see Note 1 of § 1.2 of this Annex):
– distress alert relay,
– the format specifier (all ships (VHF only), geographical area (MF/HF only), or individual station),
– if appropriate, the address of the ship, or geographical area,
– 9-digit identity of the ship in distress, if known,
– nature of distress,
– distress coordinates,
– the time (in UTC) when the position was valid;
– transmit the distress alert relay;
– prepare for the reception of the acknowledgements by ship stations and for handling the subsequent distress traffic by switching over to the distress traffic channel in the same band, i.e. 2 182 kHz on MF, 156.8 MHz/channel 16 on VHF.

1.4   **Reception of a distress alert relay**

If the distress alert relay is received from a ship station, coast stations on receipt of the distress alert relay shall ensure that the call is routed as soon as possible to an RCC. The receipt of the distress alert relay is to be acknowledged as soon as possible by the appropriate coast station using a DSC distress alert relay acknowledgement addressed to the ship station. If the distress relay call is received from a coast station, other coast stations will normally not have to take further action.

2   URGENCY

2.1   **Transmission of a digital selective calling announcement**

The announcement of the urgency message shall be made on one or more of the distress and safety calling frequencies using DSC and the urgency call format.

The DSC urgency call may be addressed to all ships (VHF only), to a geographical area (MF/HF only), or to a specific ship. The frequency on which the urgency message will be transmitted after the announcement shall be included in the DSC urgency call.

The DSC urgency call is transmitted as follows:

– key in or select on the DSC equipment (see Note 1 of § 1.2 of this Annex):
– the format specifier (all ships call (VHF), geographical area (MF/HF only), or individual station),
– if appropriate, the address of the ship, or geographical area,
– the category of the call (urgency),
– the frequency or channel on which the urgency message will be transmitted,
– the type of communication in which the urgency message will be transmitted (radiotelephony);
– transmit the DSC urgency call.

After the DSC announcement, the urgency message will be transmitted on the frequency indicated in the DSC call.

3   SAFETY

3.1   **Transmission of a digital selective calling announcement**

The announcement of the safety message shall be made on one or more of the distress and safety calling frequencies using DSC and the safety call format.

The DSC safety call may be addressed to all ships (VHF only), to a geographical area (MF/HF only), or to a specific ship. The frequency on which the safety message will be transmitted after the announcement shall be included in the DSC safety call.

The DSC safety call is transmitted as follows:

– key in or select on the DSC equipment (see Note 1 of § 1.2 of this Annex):
– the format specifier (all ships call (VHF only), geographical area (MF/HF only), or individual station),
– if appropriate, the address of the ship, or geographical area,
– the category of the call (safety),
– the frequency or channel on which the safety message will be transmitted,
– the type of communication in which the safety message will be transmitted (radiotelephony);
– transmit the DSC safety call.

After the DSC announcement, the safety message will be transmitted on the frequency indicated in the DSC call.

4   PUBLIC CORRESPONDENCE

4.1   **Digital selective calling frequencies/channels for public correspondence**

4.1.1   VHF

The frequency 156.525 MHz/channel 70 is used for DSC for distress and safety purposes. It may also be used for calling purposes other than distress and safety, e.g. public correspondence.

4.1.2   MF

For public correspondence national and international frequencies are used which are different from the frequencies used for distress and safety purposes.

When calling ship stations by DSC, coast stations should use for the call, in the order of preference:

– a national DSC channel on which the coast station is maintaining watch;
– the international DSC calling channel, with the coast station transmitting on 2177 kHz and receiving on 2189.5 kHz. In order to reduce interference on this channel, it may be used as a general rule by coast stations to call ships of another nationality, or in cases where it is not known on which DSC frequencies the ship station is maintaining watch.

4.2   **Transmission of a digital selective calling call to a ship**

The DSC call is transmitted as follows:

– key in or select on the DSC equipment (see Note 1 of § 1.2 of this Annex):
– the 9-digit identity of the ship to be called,
– the category of the call routine,
– the type of subsequent communication (radiotelephony),
– working frequency information;
– transmit the DSC call.

4.3   **Repeating a call**

Coast stations may transmit the call twice on the same calling frequency with an interval of at least 45 s between the two calls, provided that they receive no acknowledgement within that interval.

If the station called does not acknowledge the call after the second transmission, the call may be transmitted again on the same frequency after a period of at least 30 min or on another calling frequency after a period of at least 5 min.

4.4   **Preparation for exchange of traffic**

On receipt of a DSC acknowledgement with the indication that the called ship station can use the proposed working frequency, the coast station transfers to the working frequency or channel and prepares to receive the traffic.

4.5   **Acknowledgement of a received digital selective calling call**

Acknowledgements shall normally be transmitted on the frequency paired with the frequency of the received call. If the same call is received on several calling channels, the most appropriate channel shall be chosen for transmission of the acknowledgement.

The acknowledgement of a DSC call is transmitted as follows:

– key in or select on the DSC equipment (see Note 1 of § 1.2 of this Annex):
– the format specifier (individual station),
– 9-digit identity of the calling ship,
– the category of the call routine,
– if able to comply immediately on the working frequency suggested by the ship station, the same frequency information as in the received call,
– if no working frequency was suggested by the calling ship station, then the acknowledgement should include a channel/frequency proposal,
– if not able to comply on the working frequency suggested, but able to comply immediately on an alternative frequency, the alternative working frequency,
– if unable to comply immediately the appropriate information in that regard;
– transmit the acknowledgement after a delay of at least 5 s, but not later than 4 ½ min.

After having transmitted the acknowledgement, the coast station transfers to the working frequency or channel and prepares to receive the traffic.

5   Testing the equipment used for distress and safety calls

Perform VHF, MF and HF test calls in accordance with Recommendation ITU-R M.493.

Acknowledgement of a DSC test call

The coast station should acknowledge test calls.

6   SPECIAL CONDITIONS AND PROCEDURES FOR DIGITAL SELECTIVE CALLING COMMUNICATION ON HF

General

The procedures for DSC communication on HF are – with some additions described in § 6.1 to 6.3 below – equal to the corresponding procedures for DSC communications on MF/VHF.

Due regard to the special conditions described in § 6.1 to 6.3 should be given when making DSC communications on HF.

6.1   Distress

6.1.1   Reception and acknowledgement of a digital selective calling distress alert on HF

Ships in distress may in some cases transmit the DSC distress alert on a number of HF bands with only short intervals between the individual calls.

The coast station shall transmit DSC acknowledgement on all HF DSC distress channels on which the DSC distress alert was received in order to ensure as far as possible that the acknowledgement is received by the ship in distress and by all ships which received the DSC distress alert.

6.1.2   Distress traffic

The distress traffic should, as a general rule, be initiated on the appropriate distress traffic channel (radiotelephony or NBDP) in the same band in which the DSC distress alert was received.

For distress traffic by NBDP the following rules apply:

– all messages shall be preceded by at least one carriage return, line feed, one letter shift and the distress signal MAYDAY;
– FEC broadcast mode should be used.

6.1.3   Transmission of digital selective calling distress alert relay on HF

HF propagation characteristics should be taken into account when choosing HF band(s) for transmission of DSC distress alert relay.

IMO Convention ships equipped with HF DSC for distress and safety purposes are required to keep continuous automatic DSC watch on the DSC distress channel in the 8 MHz band and on at least one of the other HF DSC distress channels.

In order to avoid creating on board ships uncertainty regarding on which band the subsequent establishment of contact and distress traffic should be initiated, the HF DSC distress alert relay should be transmitted on one HF band at a time and the subsequent communication with responding ships be established before eventually repeating the DSC distress alert relay on another HF band.

6.2   Urgency

6.2.1   Transmission of urgency announcement and message on HF

For urgency messages by NBDP the following apply:

– the urgency message shall be preceded by at least one carriage return, line feed, one letter shift, the urgency signal PAN PAN and the identification of the coast station;
– FEC broadcast mode should normally be used.

ARQ mode should be used only when considered advantageous to do so in the actual situation and provided that the radiotelex number of the ship is known.

6.3   Safety

6.3.1   Transmission of safety announcements and messages on HF

For safety messages by NBDP the following apply:

– the safety message shall be preceded by at least one carriage return, line feed, one letter shift, the safety signal SECURITE and the identification of the coast station;
– FEC broadcast mode should normally be used.

ARQ mode should be used only when considered advantageous to do so in the actual situation and provided that the radiotelex number of the ship is known.

ANNEX 5
MAN OVERBOARD DEVICES USING VHF DSC

Introduction

MOB devices using DSC operate on VHF channel 70. The devices are also fitted with an Automatic Identification System (AIS) transmitter. Technical and operational characteristics are described in Recommendations ITU-R M.493 and ITU-R M.1371.

1   DSC ALERT

MOB devices may be activated manually or automatically if a person falls overboard. The device will transmit a DSC distress alert upon activation. The alert message is a distress alert with the nature of distress field set to *man overboard* and the subsequent communications field set to *no information*.

There are no voice communications from MOB devices.

MOB devices may operate in either:

– open loop mode, with the DSC distress alert addressed to all stations – i.e. a standard distress alert; or
– closed loop mode, with the DSC distress alert relay message addressed to a specific station or group of stations – normally the parent vessel.

In both cases, the AIS transmitter is activated and transmits AIS Man Overboard messages.

2   IDENTIFICATION

MOB devices are programmed with a distinctive maritime identifier, coded in accordance with Recommendation ITU-R M.585.

3   POSITION UPDATING

MOB devices are fitted with an integrated electronic position fixing device. However, it should be noted that the initial distress alert from a MOB device will not contain a position and time, as the integrated electronic position fixing device will not have locked onto the satellite constellation.

As soon as the internal electronic position fixing device is able to provide an accurate position and time, the MOB device will transmit a further DSC distress alert and an AIS message with the position and time from the position fixing device automatically inserted.

4   ACKNOWLEDGMENT

MOB devices are fitted with a DSC receiver for reception of acknowledgment messages.

An acknowledgment message causes the MOB device to stop transmitting DSC alerts. Accordingly, DSC acknowledgment messages should only be sent when the Master or person in charge of the recovery vessel considers it prudent to do so.

The MOB device will continue transmitting its position via AIS until manually turned off or the battery is exhausted.

As with other VHF DSC distress alerts, DSC acknowledgments to open loop MOB device alerts are normally only sent by coast stations, or under direction of a coast station. However, the recovery vessel may send a DSC acknowledgment message if the person in the water has been recovered.

Once the person in the water is recovered, the MOB device shall be switched off as soon as possible and an announcement cancelling the distress alert made on VHF channel 16.

5   CANCELLATION OF AN INADVERTENT DISTRESS ALERT

A station transmitting an inadvertent distress alert from a MOB device shall cancel the distress alert using the following procedure:

– immediately turn off the MOB device, which causes a DSC self-cancel message to be sent automatically;
– cancel the distress alert aurally on VHF channel 16;
– monitor VHF channel 16, and respond to any communications concerning that distress alert as appropriate.

ANNEX 6
FREQUENCIES USED FOR DIGITAL SELECTIVE CALLING

1   **The frequencies used for distress, urgency, and safety purposes using DSC are as follows (RR Appendix 15):**

2187.5   kHz

4207.5   kHz

6312   kHz

8414.5   kHz

12577   kHz

16804.5   kHz

156.525   MHz[1]

[1] The frequency 156.525 MHz may also be used for DSC purposes other than distress, urgency, and safety.

2   **The frequencies assignable on an international basis to ship and coast stations for DSC, for purposes other than distress, urgency, and safety, are as follows[2]:**

2.1   **Ship stations[2]**

2177[3]	2189.5		kHz
4208	4208.5	4209	kHz
6312.5	6313	6313.5	kHz
8415	8415.5	8416	kHz
12577.5	12578	12578.5	kHz
16805	16805.5	16806	kHz
18898.5	18899	18899.5	kHz
22374.5	22375	22375.5	kHz
25208.5	25209	25209.5	kHz
		156.525	MHz

2.2   **Coast stations[2]**

2177			kHz
4219.5	4220	4220.5	kHz
6331	6331.5	6332	kHz
8436.5	8437	8437.5	kHz
12657	12657.5	12658	kHz
16903	16903.5	16904	kHz
19703.5	19704	19704.5	kHz
22444	22444.5	22445	kHz
26121	26121.5	26122	kHz
		156.525	MHz

[2] The following (kHz) paired frequencies (for ship/coast stations) 4208/4219.5, 6312.5/6331, 8415/8436.5, 12577.5/12657, 16805/16903, 18898.5/19703.5, 22374.5/22444 and 25208.5/26121 are the first choice international frequencies for DSC (see RR Appendix **17**).

[3] The frequency 2177 kHz is available to ship stations for intership calling only.

3   **In addition to the frequencies listed in § 2 above, appropriate working frequencies in the following bands may be used for DSC (see RR Chapter II, Article 5):**

1606.5 – 3400   kHz   (Regions 1 and 3)

1605.5 – 3400   kHz   (Region 2) (For the band 1605 – 1625 kHz, see RR No. **5.89**)

4000 – 27500   kHz

156 – 162.025   MHz

NOTES

Actions by ships upon reception of **VHF** / **MF** DSC distress alert

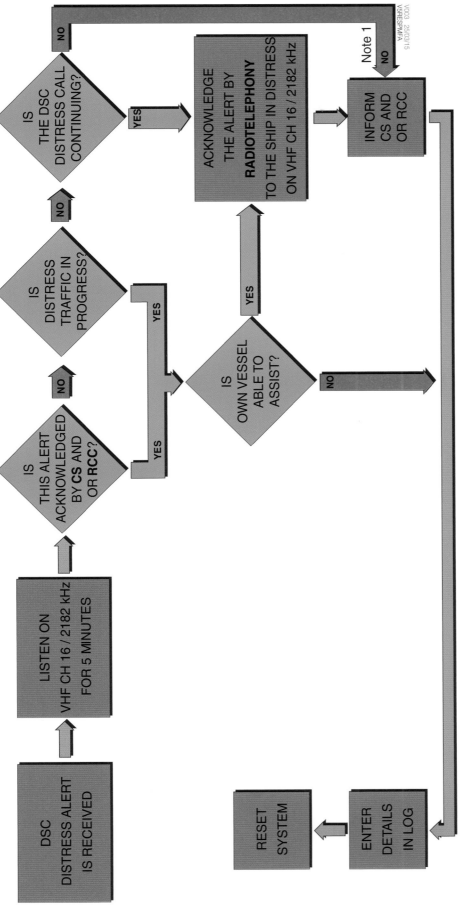

REMARKS:

Note 1: Appropriate or relevant RCC and/or Coast Station shall be informed accordingly. If further DSC alerts are received from the same source and the ship in distress is beyond doubt in the vicinity, a DSC acknowledgement may, after consultation with an RCC or coast station, be sent to terminate the call.

Note 2: In no case is a ship permitted to transmit an all ships DSC distress relay call on receipt of a DSC distress on either VHF or MF channels. If no aural watch is present on the relative channel (2182 kHz on MF, Ch16 on VHF), the coast station should be contacted by sending an individual DSC distress relay call.

CS = Coast Station   RCC = Rescue Coordination Centre

V003 25/03/15
V5RESPMFA

Actions by ships upon reception of **HF** DSC distress alert

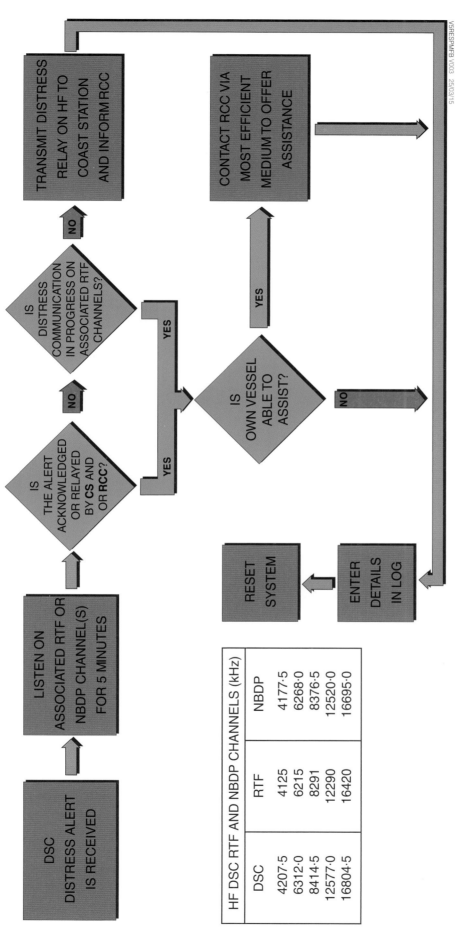

HF DSC RTF AND NBDP CHANNELS (kHz)		
DSC	RTF	NBDP
4207·5	4125	4177·5
6312·0	6215	6268·0
8414·5	8291	8376·5
12577·0	12290	12520·0
16804·5	16420	16695·0

Note 1: If it is clear the ship or person in distress are not in the vicinity and/or other craft are better placed to assist, superfluous communications which could interfere with search and rescue activities are to be avoided. Details should be recorded in the appropriate logbook.

Note 2: The ship should establish communications with the station controlling the distress as directed and render such assistance as required and appropriate.

Note 3: Distress relay calls should be initiated manually

CS = Coast Station   RCC = Rescue Coordination Centre

V5RESPMFB V003 25/03/15

83

GUIDANCE ON DISTRESS ALERTS

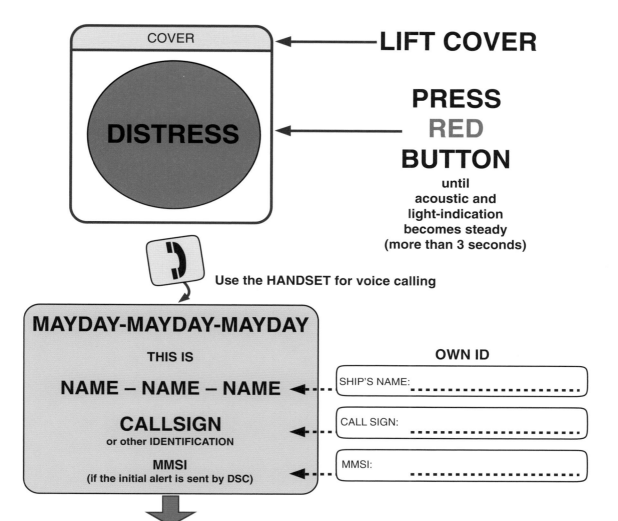

LIFT COVER

COVER

DISTRESS

PRESS
RED
BUTTON
until
acoustic and
light-indication
becomes steady
(more than 3 seconds)

Use the HANDSET for voice calling

MAYDAY-MAYDAY-MAYDAY

THIS IS

NAME – NAME – NAME

CALLSIGN
or other IDENTIFICATION

MMSI
(if the initial alert is sent by DSC)

OWN ID

SHIP'S NAME: ....

CALL SIGN: ....

MMSI: ....

MAYDAY

NAME of the **VESSEL** in distress
CALLSIGN or other **IDENTIFICATION**
MMSI
(if the initial alert is sent by DSC)

POSITION

given as **latitude** and **longitude**
or
If latitude and longitude ane not known
or if time is insufficient,
In relation to a known geographical location

NATURE of distress

Kind of **ASSISTANCE** required

Any other useful **INFORMATION**

DISTRESS and COMMUNICATION FREQUENCIES

	DSC	Radiotelephony	NBDP
VHF	Channel 70	Channel 16	- - - - -
MF	2187.5 kHz	2182 kHz	2174.5 kHz
HF4	4207.5 kHz	4125 kHz	4177.5 kHz
HF6	6312.0 kHz	6215 kHz	6268.0 kHz
HF8	8414.5 kHz	8291 kHz	8376.5 kHz
HF12	12577.0 khz	12290 kHz	12520.0 kHz
HF16	16804.5 kHz	16420 kHz	16695.0 kHz

Remember to use the correct HF-procedure
Don't forget your EPIRB is the secondary means of alerting

SEARCH AND RESCUE RADAR TRANSPONDER

INTRODUCTION

A Search and Rescue radar Transponder (SART) is a means within the GMDSS for locating vessels in distress or their survival craft. The SART operates in the 9 GHz frequency band and generates a series of response signals on being interrogated by any ordinary 9 GHz X band shipborne radar or suitable airborne radar. No modification is required to vessels' radar equipment. SARTs can be either portable (for use on-board vessel or carrying to survival craft), permanently installed on the vessel and in the survival craft or operate in a float-free position. They may also be incorporated into a float-free satellite EPIRB.

OPERATIONAL AND TECHNICAL CHARACTERISTICS

When activated in a distress situation, a SART responds to radar interrogation by transmitting a swept frequency signal which generates as a line of 12 blip code on a radar screen outward from the SART's position along its line of bearing. Displayed on the Plan Position Indicator (PPI), the spacing between each pair of dots will be 0·6 n miles. In order to distinguish the SART from other responses it is preferable to use a radar scale between 6 and 12 n miles. This will assist in differentiating between the SART and other responses. As the search craft approaches to within about 1 n mile of the SART, the blip dots will change into wide arcs, and even become complete circles as the SART is closed and becomes continually triggered. This is a useful warning to the search craft to slow down! This distinctive and unique radar signal is easily recognized and is therefore much easier to spot than a single echo such as from a radar reflector. Moreover, the fact that the SART is actually a transmitter means that the return pulses can be as strong as echoes received from much larger objects. Any radar bandwidth of less than 5 MHz will attenuate the SART signal slightly, so it is preferable to use a medium bandwidth to ensure optimum detection of the SART. The specific Radar Operating Manual should be consulted about the particular radar parameters and bandwidth selection. The SART also provides a visual or audible indication of its correct operation and will also inform survivors when it is interrogated by a radar.

The SART should have sufficient battery capacity to operate in the stand-by condition for 96 hours followed by a minimum 8 hours of transmission while being interrogated by a radar. It should also be able to operate under ambient temperatures of -20°C to + 55°C.

A SART, built to the latest specifications, will have excellent receiver sensitivity and will detect the high power pulses from a search radar at a much greater range than its relatively weak return pulses which will be detected by the radar. The limiting range is therefore determined by the return path.

Three main factors will affect the range at which a SART will be detected on a ship's radar screen:

1. THE TYPE OF RADAR USED AND HOW IT IS OPERATED

Clearly, some radars are better than others. Larger vessels will have higher gain antennæ, set higher above sea level. The radar receiver performance is also very important and should be optimised by following the procedures described in paragraphs 5 and 6 in the **Safety of Navigation Circular 197**.

2. THE WEATHER CONDITIONS

A flat calm will affect performance due to multi-path propagation - radar pulses being reflected from the surface of the sea.

High waves may result in reception at greater distances due to occasional elevation of both radar and SART; however, detection will be sporadic due to masking of the signal in the troughs.

Elimination of sea and rain clutter will depend on the radar used, and the skill of the operator, as for normal radar operations.

3. THE MOUNTING OF THE SART ON THE SURVIVAL CRAFT

The mounting of the SART is the one factor over which the SART user has some control. For maximum range an unobstructed mounting as high as possible is required.

The IMO Recommended Performance Standard for the SART calls for a range of "up to at least 5 nautical miles", for a SART mounted 1m above sea level. This assumes a search radar complying with IMO requirements, with its antenna 15m above sea level. Tests have shown the importance of maintaining the SART antenna height of at least 1m above sea level; the following results which give some indication on the degrading of the detection range, were obtained with a SART in a survival craft:

a	SART lying flat on the floor	range 1·8 n miles
b	SART standing upright on the floor	range 2·5 n miles
c	SART floating in the water	range 2·0 n miles

Survivors are advised not to deploy a SART and a radar reflector on the same survival craft because the reflector may obscure the SART.

A well mounted SART in moderate weather conditions is capable of giving a detection range of over 10 n miles to a large vessel radar. A poorly mounted SART, perhaps operated inside a liferaft or floating in the sea, may provide little better than visual search range to a small fishing boat radar.

Line-of-sight problems are much less of a problem for airborne detection of SARTs. With the increased sensitivity of the latest SARTs, compatible radars should have no problem in picking up SARTs at ranges up to 40 n miles, given an initial search height of 3000 ft.

Basic concept of the Search And Rescue radar Transponder (SART)

SART V002 08/04/10

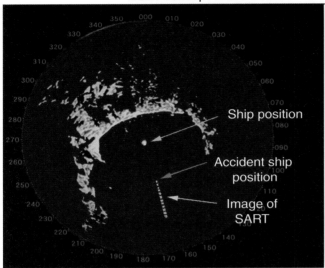

Ship position

Accident ship position

Image of SART

Radar Display showing the SART 12 dot blip code

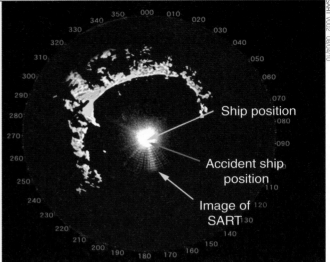

Ship position

Accident ship position

Image of SART

As the search craft approaches to within about 1n mile of the SART the 12 dots change to wide arcs

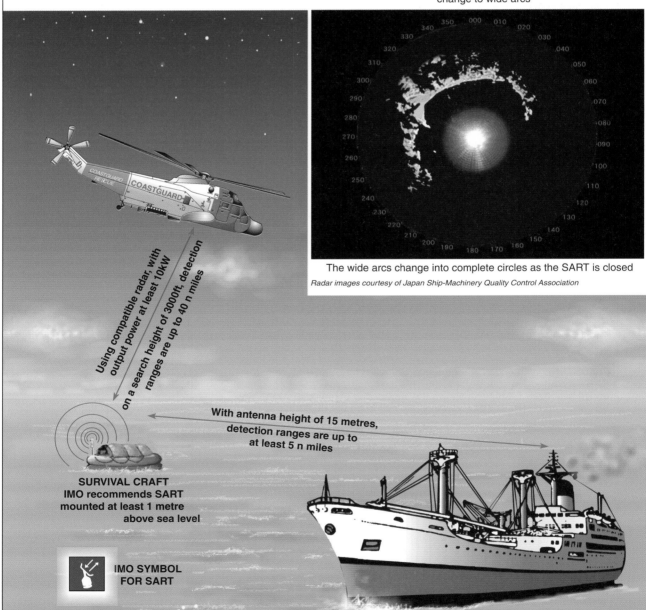

The wide arcs change into complete circles as the SART is closed

Radar images courtesy of Japan Ship-Machinery Quality Control Association

Using compatible radar, with output power at least 10kW on a search height of 3000ft, detection ranges are up to 40 n miles

With antenna height of 15 metres, detection ranges are up to at least 5 n miles

SURVIVAL CRAFT
IMO recommends SART mounted at least 1 metre above sea level

IMO SYMBOL FOR SART

OPERATION OF MARINE RADAR FOR SART DETECTION

Safety of Navigation Circular 197
WARNING: A SART will only respond to an X-Band (3cm) radar. It will not be seen on an S-Band (10 cm) radar.

Introduction
1. A Search and Rescue Transponder (SART) may be triggered by any X-Band (3 cm) radar within a range of approximately 8 n miles. Each radar pulse received causes it to transmit a response which is swept repetitively across the complete radar frequency band. When interrogated, it first sweeps rapidly (0·4 μsec) through the band before beginning a relatively slow sweep (7·5 μsec) through the band back to the starting frequency. This process is repeated for a total of twelve complete cycles. At some point in each sweep, the SART frequency will match that of the interrogating radar and be within the pass band of the radar receiver. If the SART is within range, the frequency match during each of the 12 slow sweeps will produce a response on the radar display, thus a line of 12 dots equally spaced by about 0·64 n miles will be shown.

2. When the range to the SART is reduced to about 1 n mile, the radar display may show also the 12 responses generated during the fast sweeps. These additional dot responses, which also are equally spaced by 0·64 n miles, will be interspersed with the original line of 12 dots. They will appear slightly weaker and smaller than the original dots.

Radar Range Scale
3. When looking for a SART it is preferable to use either the 6 or 12 n mile range scale. This is because the total displayed length of the SART response of 12 (or 24) dots may extend approximately 9·5 n miles beyond the position of the SART and it is necessary to see a number of response dots to distinguish the SART from other responses.

SART Range Errors
4. When responses from only the 12 low frequency sweeps are visible (when the SART is at a range greater than about 1 n mile), the position at which the first dot is displayed may be as much as 0·64 n miles beyond the true position of the SART. When the range closes so that the fast sweep responses are seen also, the first of these will be no more than 150 metres beyond the true position.

Radar Bandwidth
5. This is normally matched to the radar pulse length and is usually switched with the range scale and the associated pulse length. Narrow bandwidths of 3-5 MHz are used with long pulses on long range scales and wide bandwidths of 10-25 MHz with short pulses on short ranges.

6. A radar bandwidth of less than 5 MHz will attenuate the SART signal slightly, so it is preferable to use a medium bandwidth to ensure optimum detection of the SART. The Radar Operating Manual should be consulted about the particular radar parameters and bandwidth selection.

Radar Side Lobes
7. As the SART is approached, side lobes from the radar antenna may show the SART responses as a series of arcs or concentric rings. These can be removed by the use of the anti-clutter sea control although it may be operationally useful to observe the side lobes as they may be easier to detect in clutter conditions and also they will confirm that the SART is near to own ship.

Detuning the Radar
8. To increase the visibility of the SART in clutter conditions, the radar may be detuned to reduce the clutter without reducing the SART response. Radars with automatic frequency control may not permit manual detune of the equipment. Care should be taken in operating the radar in the detuned condition as other wanted navigational and anti-collision information may be removed. The tuning should be returned to normal operation as soon as possible.

Gain
9. For maximum range SART detection the normal gain setting for long range detection should be used i.e., with a light background noise speckle visible.

Anti-clutter Sea Control
10. For optimum range SART detection this control should be set to the minimum. Care should be exercised as wanted targets in sea clutter may be obscured. Note also that in clutter conditions the first few dots of the SART response may not be detectable, irrespective of the setting of the anti-clutter sea control. In this case, the position of the SART may be estimated by measuring 9·5 n miles from the furthest dot back towards own ship.

11. Some sets have automatic / manual anti-clutter sea control facilities. Because the way in which the automatic sea control functions may vary from one radar manufacturer to another, the operator is advised to use manual control initially until the SART has been detected. The effect of auto sea control on the SART response can then be compared with manual control.

Anti-clutter Rain Control
12. This should be used normally (i.e. to break up areas of rain) when trying to detect a SART response which, being a series of dots, is not affected by the action of the anti-clutter rain circuitry. Note that Racon responses, which are often in the form of a long flash, will be affected by the use of this control.

13. Some sets have automatic / manual anti-clutter rain control facilities. Because the way in which the automatic rain control functions may vary from one radar manufacturer to another, the operator is advised to use manual initially until the SART has been detected. The effect of the auto rain control on the SART response can then be compared with manual control.

Note:
The automatic rain and sea clutter controls may be combined in a single 'auto-clutter' control, in which case the operator is advised to use the manual controls initially until the SART has been detected, before assessing the effect of auto.

AIS-SART (Automatic Identification System - Search and Rescue Transmitter)

In January 2010 the AIS-SART was adopted into the GMDSS regulations as an alternative to the Radar-SART.

An internal GPS module provides position data which is combined with the pre-programmed unique ID code and transmitted using the international AIS channels (AIS 1 - 161·975 MHz and AIS 2 - 162·025 MHz) in the maritime VHF band.

Any vessel or station currently able to detect an AIS signal will also detect an AIS-SART.

The information transmitted by the AIS-SART provides both identification and location.

Identification consists of a unique 9 digit MMSI ID code, the first three digits will be "970", the remaining 6 digits are made up of a 2 digit manufacturers code and the unit's unique 4 digit serial number.

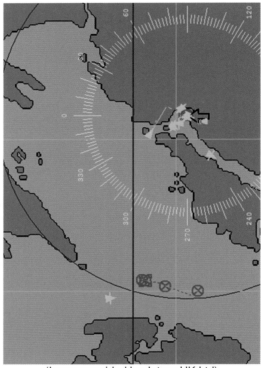

(Image provided by Jotron UK Ltd)

AIS-SART performance
During the sea level testing phase of AIS-SART development it was established that accurate AIS-SART detection was achieved between 8 - 10 n miles. An accurate position displayed on a vessels electronic map system is achievable from one transmission of 26 ms.

Further AIS-SART testing proved that accurate detection from helicopters and aircraft extended the AIS-SART range to about 130 n miles depending on the altitude of the search aircraft.

EPIRB-AIS
EPIRB-AIS devices will be displayed in the same way as an AIS-SART.

The user identity of the EPIRB-AIS indicates the identity of the AIS transmitter of the EPIRB-AIS and not the MMSI of the ship.

This section contains extracts from relevant sections of the ITU Radio Regulations 2020. Some of the extracts are abridged. Please see the full ITU Radio Regulations 2020 for the associated notes and additional references contained within tables and text.

ARTICLE 30 – General provisions

Section I – Introduction

30.1 This Chapter contains the provisions for the operational use of the global maritime distress and safety system (GMDSS), whose functional requirements, system elements and equipment carriage requirements are set forth in the International Convention for the Safety of Life at Sea (SOLAS), 1974, as amended. This Chapter also contains provisions for initiating distress, urgency and safety communications by means of radiotelephony on the frequency 156·8 MHz (VHF channel 16). (WRC-07)

30.2 No provision of these Regulations prevents the use by a mobile station or a mobile earth station in distress of any means at its disposal to attract attention, make known its position, and obtain help.

30.3 No provision of these Regulations prevents the use by stations on board aircraft, ships engaged in search and rescue operations, land stations, or coast earth stations, in exceptional circumstances, of any means at their disposal to assist a mobile station or a mobile earth station in distress.

Section II – Maritime provisions

30.4 The provisions specified in this Chapter are obligatory in the maritime mobile service and the maritime mobile-satellite service for all stations using the frequencies and techniques prescribed for the functions set out herein. (WRC-07)

30.5 The International Convention for the Safety of Life at Sea (SOLAS), 1974, as amended, prescribes which ships and which of their survival craft shall be provided with radio equipment, and which ships shall carry portable radio equipment for use in survival craft. It also prescribes the requirements which shall be met by such equipment.

30.6 Ship earth stations located at rescue coordination centres may be authorized by an administration to communicate for distress and safety purposes with any other station using bands allocated to the maritime mobile-satellite service, when special circumstances make it essential, notwithstanding the methods of working provided for in these Regulations.

30.7 Mobile stations of the maritime mobile service may communicate, for safety purposes, with stations of the aeronautical mobile service. Such communications shall normally be made on the frequencies authorized, and under the conditions specified in Section 1 of Article 31.

Section III – Aeronautical provisions

30.8 The procedure specified in this Chapter is obligatory for communications between stations on board aircraft and stations of the maritime mobile-satellite service, wherever this service or stations of this service are specifically mentioned.

30.9 Certain provisions of this Chapter are applicable to the aeronautical mobile service, except in the case of special arrangements between the governments concerned.

30.10 Mobile stations of the aeronautical mobile service may communicate, for distress and safety purposes, with stations of the maritime mobile service in conformity with the provisions of this Chapter.

30.11 Any station on board an aircraft required by national or international regulations to communicate for distress, urgency or safety purposes with stations of the maritime mobile service that comply with the provisions of this Chapter, shall be capable of transmitting and receiving class J3E emissions when using the carrier frequency 2182 kHz, or class J3E emissions when using the carrier frequency 4125 kHz, or class G3E emissions when using the frequency 156·8 MHz and, optionally, the frequency 156·3 MHz.

30.11A Aircraft, when conducting search and rescue operations, are also permitted to operate digital selective calling (DSC) equipment on the VHF DSC frequency 156·525 MHz, and automatic identification system (AIS) equipment on the AIS frequencies 161·975 MHz and 162·025 MHz. (WRC-07).

Section IV – Land mobile provisions

30.12 Stations of the land mobile service in uninhabited, sparsely populated or remote areas may, for distress and safety purposes, use the frequencies provided for in this Chapter.

30.13 The procedure specified in this Chapter is obligatory for stations of the land mobile service when using frequencies provided in these Regulations for distress and safety communications.

ARTICLE 31 - Frequencies for the GMDSS

Section I – General

31.1 The frequencies to be used for the transmission of distress and safety information under the GMDSS are contained in Appendix 15, In addition to the frequencies listed in Appendix 15, ship stations and coast stations should use other appropriate frequencies for the transmission of safety messages and general radiocommunications to and from shore-based radio systems or networks. (WRC-07)

31.2 Any emission causing harmful interference to distress and safety communications on any of the discrete frequencies identified in Appendix 15 is prohibited. (WRC-07)

31.3 The number and duration of test transmissions shall be kept to a minimum on the frequencies identified in Appendix 15; they shoud be coordinated with a competent authoritiy as necessary, and, wherever practicable, be carried out on artificial antennas or with reduced power. However, testing on the distress and safety calling frequencies should be avoided, but where this is unavoidable, it should be indicated that these are test transmissions.

31.4 Before transmitting for other than distress purposes on any of the frequencies identified in Appendix 15 for distress and safety, a station shall, where practicable, listen on the frequency concerned to make sure that no distress transmission is being sent.

31.5 Not used.

Frequencies below 30 MHz

From Appendix 15 (Rev. WRC-19)
Table 15-1

Frequency (kHz)	Description of usage	Notes
490	MSI	490 kHz is used exclusively for Maritime Safety Information (MSI). (WRC-03)
518	MSI	518 kHz is used exclusively by the international NAVTEX system.
* 2174·5	NBDP-COM	
* 2182	RTP-COM	The frequency 2182 kHz uses class of emission J3E.
* 2187·5	DSC	
3023	AERO-SAR	The aeronautical carrier (reference) frequencies 3023 kHz and 5680 kHz may be used for intercommunication between mobile stations engaged in coordinated search and rescue operations, and for communication between these stations and participating land stations in accordance with the provisions of Appendix 27 RR.
* 4125	RTP-COM	The carrier frequency 4125 kHz may be used by aircraft stations to communicate with stations of the maritime mobile service for distress and safety purposes, including search and rescue.
* 4177·5	NBDP-COM	
* 4207·5	DSC	
4209·5	MSI	The frequency 4209·5 kHz is exclusively used for NAVTEX-type transmissions. (See Resolution 339, Rev.WRC-07)
4210	MSI-HF	
5680	AERO-SAR	See 3023 kHz above.
* 6215	RTP-COM	
* 6268	NBDP-COM	
* 6312	DSC	
6314	MSI-HF	
* 8291	RTP-COM	
* 8376·5	NBDP-COM	
* 8414·5	DSC	
8416·5	MSI-HF	
* 12290	RTP-COM	
* 12520	NBDP-COM	
* 12577	DSC	
12579	MSI-HF	
* 16420	RTP-COM	
* 16695	NBDP-COM	
16804·5	DSC	
16806·5	MSI-HF	
19680·5	MSI-HF	
22376	MSI-HF	
26100·5	MSI-HF	

Legend:

AERO-SAR   These aeronautical carrier (reference) frequencies may be used for distress and safety purposes by mobile stations engaged in coordinated search and rescue operations.

DSC   These frequencies are used exclusively for distress and safety calls using Digital Selective Calling in accordance with the Radio Regulations. (WRC-07)

MSI   In the maritime mobile service, these frequencies are used exclusively for the transmission of Maritime Safety Information (MSI) (including meteorological and navigational warnings and urgent information) by coast stations to ships, by means of narrow-band direct-printing telegraphy.

MSI-HF   In the maritime mobile service, these frequencies are used exclusively for the transmission of high seas MSI by coast stations to ships by means of narrow-band direct-printing telegraphy.

NBDP-COM   These frequencies are used exclusively for distress and safety communications (traffic) by narrow-band direct-printing telegraphy.

RTP-COM   These carrier frequencies are used for distress and safety communications (traffic) by radiotelephony.

* Except as provided in these Radio Regulations, any emission capable of causing harmful interference to distress, alarm, urgency or safety communications on the frequencies denoted by an asterisk (*) is prohibited. Any emission causing harmful interference to distress and safety communications on any of the discrete frequencies identified in this Appendix is prohibited. (WRC-07)

Frequencies above 30 MHz (VHF/UHF)

From Appendix 15 (Rev. WRC-19)
Table 15-2

Frequency (MHz)	Description of usage	Notes
* 121·5	AERO-SAR	The aeronautical emergency frequency 121·5 MHz is used for the purposes of distress and urgency for Radio Telephony by stations of the aeronautical mobile service using frequencies in the band between 117·975 MHz and 137 MHz. This frequency may also be used for these purposes by survival craft stations. Use of the frequency 121·5 MHz by emergency position-indicating radio beacons shall be in accordance with Recommendation ITU-R M.690-3. Mobile stations of the maritime mobile service may communicate with stations of the aeronautical mobile service on the aeronautical emergency frequency 121·5 MHz for the purposes of distress and urgency only, and on the aeronautical auxiliary frequency 123·1 MHz for coordinated search and rescue operations, using class A3E emissions for both frequencies. They shall then comply with any special arrangement between governments concerned by which the aeronautical mobile service is regulated.
123·1	AERO-SAR	The aeronautical auxiliary frequency 123·1 MHz, which is auxiliary to the aeronautical emergency frequency 121·5 MHz, is for use by stations of the aeronautical mobile service and by other mobile and land stations engaged in coordinated search and rescue operations. Mobile stations of the maritime mobile service may communicate with stations of the aeronautical mobile service on the aeronautical emergency frequency 121·5 MHz for the purposes of distress and urgency only, and on the aeronautical auxiliary frequency 123·1 MHz for coordinated search and rescue operations, using class A3E emissions for both frequencies. They shall then comply with any special arrangement between governments concerned by which the aeronautical mobile service is regulated.
** 156·3	VHF Ch 06	The frequency 156·3 MHz may be used for communication between ship stations and aircraft stations engaged in coordinated search and rescue operations. It may also be used by aircraft stations to communicate with ship stations for other safety purposes (see also Note *f* in Appendix 18).
* 156·525	VHF Ch 70	The frequency 156·525 MHz is used in the maritime mobile service for distress and safety calls using digital selective calling.
*** 156·650	VHF Ch 13	The frequency 156·650 MHz is used for ship-to-ship communications relating to the safety of navigation in accordance with the Radio Regulations (see note *k* in Appendix 18).
* 156·8	VHF Ch 16	The frequency 156·8 MHz is used for distress and safety communications by Radio Telephony. Additionally, the frequency 156·8 MHz may be used by aircraft stations for safety purposes only.
* 161·975	AIS-SART VHF CH AIS 1	AIS 1 is used for AIS search and rescue transmitters (AIS-SART) for use in search and rescue operations.
* 162·025	AIS-SART VHF CH AIS 2	AIS 2 is used for AIS search and rescue transmitters (AIS-SART) for use in search and rescue operations.
* 406 – 406·1	406-EPIRB	This frequency band is used exclusively by satellite EPIRBs in the Earth-to-space direction.
1530 – 1544	SAT-COM	In addition to its availability for routine non-safety purposes, the band 1530 – 1544 MHz is used for distress and safety purposes in the space-to-Earth direction in the maritime mobile-satellite service. GMDSS distress, urgency and safety communications have priority in this band.

Continued on next page

* 1544 – 1545	D&S-OPS	Use of the band 1544 – 1545 MHz (space-to-Earth) is limited to distress and safety operations, including feeder links of satellites needed to relay the emissions of satellite EPIRBs to earth stations and narrow-band (space-to-Earth) links from space stations to mobile stations.
1621.35 – 1626·5	SAT-COM	In addition to its availability for routine non-safety purposes, the frequency band 1621.35 – 1626·5 MHz is used for distress and safety purposes in the Earth-to-space and space-to-Earth directions in the maritime mobile-satellite service. GMDSS distress, urgency and safety communications have priority in this band over non-safety communications within the same satellite system. (WRC-19)
1626·5 – 1645·5	SAT-COM	In addition to its availability for routine non-safety purposes, the band 1626·5 – 1645·5 MHz is used for distress and safety purposes in the Earth-to-space direction in the maritime mobile-satellite service. GMDSS distress, urgency and safety communications have priority in this band.
* 1645·5 – 1646·5	D&S-OPS	Use of the band 1645·5 – 1646·5 MHz (Earth-to-space) is limited to distress and safety operations.
9200 – 9500	SARTS	This frequency band is used by radar transponders to facilitate search and rescue.

Legend:

AERO-SAR These aeronautical carrier (reference) frequencies may be used for distress and safety purposes by mobile stations engage in coordinated search and rescue operations.

D&S-OPS The use of these bands is limited to distress and safety operations of satellite Emergency Position-Indicating Radio Beacons (EPIRBs).

SAT-COM These frequency bands are available for distress and safety purposes in the maritime mobile-satellite service.

VHF Ch # These VHF frequencies are used for distress and safety purposes. The channel number (Ch #) refers to the VHF Channel as listed in the Radio Regulations, which should also be consulted.

AIS These frequencies are used by automatic identification systems (AIS), which should operate in accordance with the most recent version of Recommendation ITU-R M.1371. (WRC-07)

* Except as provided in these Regulations, any emission capable of causing harmful interference to distress, alarm, urgency or safety communications on the frequencies denoted by an asterisk (*) is prohibited. Any emissioin causing harmful interference to distress and safety communications on any of the discrete frequencies identified in Appendix 15 is prohibited. (WRC-07)

** From note f in Appendix 18: the frequencies 156·300 MHz (Channel 06), 156·525 MHz (Channel 70), 156·800 MHz (Channel 16), 161·975 MHz (AIS 1) and 161·025 MHz (AIS 2) may also be used by aircraft stations for the purposes of search and rescue operations and other safety-related communication. (WRC-07)

*** From note k in Appendix 18: Channel 13 is designated for use on a worldwide basis as a navigation safety communication channel, primarily for intership navigation safety communications. It may also be used by the ship movement and port operations service subject to the national regulations of the administrations concerned.

Section II – Survival Craft Stations

31.6 Equipment for radiotelephony use in survival craft stations shall, if capable of operating on any frequency in the bands between 156 MHz and 174 MHz, be able to transmit and receive on 156·8 MHz and at least one other frequency in these bands.

31.7 Equipment for transmitting locating signals from survival craft stations shall be capable of operating in the 9200 – 9500 MHz band.

31.8 Equipment with DSC facilities for use in survival craft shall, if capable of operating:

31.9 a) in the bands between 1606·5 kHz and 2850 kHz, be able to transmit on 2187·5 kHz;

31.10 b) in the bands between 4000 kHz and 27500 kHz, be able to transmit on 8414·5 kHz;

31.11 c) in the bands between 156 MHz and 174 MHz, be able to transmit on 156·525 MHz.

Section III – Watch-Keeping

31.12 A – Coast stations

31.13 Those coast stations assuming a watch-keeping responsibility in the GMDSS shall maintain an automatic digital selective calling watch on frequencies and for periods of time as indicated in the information published in the List of Coast Stations and Special Service Stations (List IV). (WRC-07)

31.14 B – Coast earth stations

31.15 Those coast earth stations assuming a watch-keeping responsibility in the GMDSS shall maintain a continuous automatic watch for appropriate distress alerts relayed by space stations.

31.16 C – Ship stations

31.17 Ship stations, where so equipped, shall, while at sea, maintain an automatic digital selective calling watch on the appropriate distress and safety calling frequencies in the frequency bands in which they are operating. Ship stations, where so equipped, shall also maintain watch on the appropriate frequencies for the automatic reception of transmissions of meteorological and navigational warnings and other urgent information to ships. (WRC-07)

31.18 Ship stations complying with the provisions of this Chapter should, where practicable, maintain a watch on the frequency 156·8 MHz (VHF channel 16). (WRC-07)

31.19 D – Ship earth stations

31.20 Ship earth stations complying with the provisions of this Chapter shall, while at sea, maintain watch except when communicating on a working channel.

ARTICLE 32 - Operational Procedures for Distress and Safety Communications in the Global Maritime Distress and Safety System (GMDSS) (WRC-07)

Section I – General

32.1 Distress communications rely on the use of terrestrial MF, HF and VHF radiocommunications and communications using satellite techniques. Distress communications shall have absolute priority over all other transmissions. The following terms apply:

(a) The distress alert is a digital selective call (DSC) using a distress call format in the bands used for terrestrial radiocommunication, or a distress message format, in which case it is relayed through space stations.
(b) The distress call is the initial voice or text procedure.
(c) The distress message is the subsequent voice or text procedure.
(d) The distress alert relay is a DSC transmission on behalf of another station.
(e) The distress call relay is the initial voice or text procedure for a station not itself in distress. (WRC-07)

32.2 The distress alert shall be sent through a satellite either with absolute priority in general communication channels, on exclusive distress and safety frequencies reserved for satellite EPIRBs in the Earth-to-space direction or on the distress and safety frequencies designated in the MF, HF and VHF bands for digital selective calling (see Appendix 15). (WRC-07)

32.2A The distress call shall be sent on the distress and safety frequencies designated in the MF, HF and VHF bands for radiotelephony. (WRC-07)

32.3 The distress alert or call and subsequent messages shall be sent only on the authority of the person responsible for the ship, aircraft or other vehicle carrying the mobile station or the mobile earth station. (WRC-07)

32.4 All stations which receive a distress alert or call transmitted on the distress and safety frequencies in the MF, HF and VHF bands shall immediately cease any transmission capable of interfering with distress traffic and prepare for subsequent distress traffic. (WRC-07)

32.5 Distress alerts or distress alert relays using DSC should use the technical structures and content set forth in the most recent version of Recommendations ITU-R M.493 and ITU-R M.541. (WRC-07)

32.5A Each administration shall ensure that suitable arrangements are made for assigning and registering identities used by ships participating in the GMDSS, and shall make registration information available to rescue coordination centres on a 24-hour day, 7-day week basis. Where appropriate, administrations shall notify responsible organisations immediately of additions, deletions and other changes in these assignments. Registration information submitted shall be in accordance with Resolution 340 (WRC-97). (WRC-07)

32.5B Any GMDSS shipboard equipment which is capable of transmitting position coordinates as part of a distress alert and which does not have an integral electronic position-fixing system receiver shall be interconnected to a separate navigation receiver, if one is installed, to provide that information automatically. (WRC-07)

32.6 Transmissions by radiotelephony shall be made slowly and distinctly, each word being clearly pronounced to facilitate transcription.

32.7 The phonetic alphabet and figure code in Appendix 14 and the abbreviations and signals in accordance with the most recent version of Recommendation ITU-R M.1172 should be used where applicable[1]. (WRC-03)

Section II – Distress Alerting and Distress Calling (WRC-07)

32.8 A – General

32.9 The transmission of a distress alert or a distress call indicates that a mobile unit[2] or person[3] is threatened by grave and imminent danger and requires immediate assistance. (WRC-07)

32.10 The distress alert shall provide[4] the identification of the station in distress and its position.

32.10A A distress alert is false if it was transmitted without any indication that a mobile unit or person was in distress and required immediate assistance (see No. 32.9). Administrations receiving a false distress alert shall report this infringement in accordance with Section V of Article 15, if that alert:
  (a) was transmitted intentionally;
  (b) was not cancelled in accordance with No. 32.53A and Resolution 349 (Rev. WRC-19);
  (c) could not be verified as a result of either the ship's failure to keep watch on appropriate frequencies in accordance with the Radio Regulations, or its failure to respond to calls from an authorized rescue authority;
  (d) was repeated; or
  (e) was transmitted using a false identity.
Administrations receiving such a report shall take appropriate steps to ensure that the infringement does not recur. No action should normally be taken against any ship or mariner for reporting and cancelling a false distress alert. (WRC-19)

32.10B Administrations shall take practicable and necessary steps to ensure the avoidance of false distress alerts, including those transmitted inadvertently. (WRC-07)

---

[1] The use of the Standard Marine Communication Phrases and, where language difficulties exists, the International Code of Signals, both published by the International Maritime Organization (IMO), is also recommended.

[2] Mobile unit: a ship, aircraft or other vehicle.

[3] In this Article, where the case is of a person in distress, the application of the procedures may require adaptation to meet the needs of the particular circumstances.

[4] The distress alert may also contain information regarding the nature of the distress, the type of assistance required, the course and speed of the mobile unit, the time that this information was recorded and any other information which might facilitate rescue.

32.11B – Transmission of a distress alert or a distress call (WRC-07)

B1 – Transmission of a distress alert or a distress call by a ship station or a ship earth station (WRC-07)

32.12 Ship-to-shore distress alerts or calls are used to alert rescue coordination centres via coast stations or coast earth stations that a ship is in distress. These alerts are based on the use of transmissions via satellites (from a ship earth station or a satellite EPIRB) and terrestrial services (from ship stations and EPIRBs). (WRC-07)

32.13 Ship-to-ship distress alerts are used to alert other ships in the vicinity of the ship in distress and are based on the use of Digital Selective Calling in the VHF and MF bands. Additionally, the HF band may be used. (WRC-07)

32.13A Ship stations equipped for Digital Selective Calling procedures may transmit a distress call and distress message immediately following the distress alert in order to attract attention from as many ship stations as possible. (WRC-07)

32.13B Ship stations not equipped for Digital Selective Calling procedures shall, where practical, initiate the distress communications by transmitting a radio telephony distress call and message on the frequency 156·8 MHz (VHF Channel 16). (WRC-07)

32.13BA The radiotelephone distress signal consists of the word MAYDAY pronounced as the French expression "m'aider". (WRC-07)

32.13C 1) The distress call sent on the frequency 156·8 MHz (VHF Channel 16) shall be given in the following form:

  – the distress signal MAYDAY spoken three times;

  – the name of the vessel in distress spoken three times;

  – the words THIS IS;

  – the call sign or other identification;

  – the MMSI (if the initial alert has been sent by DSC). (WRC-12)

32.13D 2) The distress message which follows the distress call should be given in the following form, taking into account Nos. 32.6 and 32.7:

  – the distress signal MAYDAY;

  – the name of the vessel in distress;

  – the call sign or other identification;

  – the MMSI (if the initial alert has been sent by DSC);

– the position, given as the latitude and longitude, or if the latitude and longitude are not known or if time is insufficient, in relation to a known geographical location;

– the nature of the distress;

– the kind of assistance required;

– any other useful information. (WRC-12)

32.13E DSC procedures use a combination of automated functions and manual intervention to generate the appropriate distress call format in the most recent version of Recommendation ITU-R M.541. A distress alert sent by DSC consists of one or more distress alert attempts in which a message format is transmitted identifying the station in distress, giving its last recorded position and, if entered, the nature of the distress. In MF and HF bands, distress alert attempts may be sent as a single-frequency attempt or a multi-frequency attempt on up to six frequencies within one minute. In VHF bands, only single-frequency call attempts are used. The distress alert will repeat automatically at random intervals, a few minutes apart, until an acknowledgement sent by DSC is received. (WRC-07)

B2 – Transmission of a shore-to-ship distress alert relay or a distress call relay (WRC-07)

32.14 A station or a rescue coordination centre which receives a distress alert or call and a distress message shall initiate the transmission of a shore-to-ship distress alert relay addressed, as appropriate, to all ships, to a selected group of ships, or to a specific ship, by satellite and/or terrestrial means. (WRC-07)

32.15 The distress alert relay and the distress call relay shall contain the identification of the mobile unit in distress, its position and all other information which might facilitate rescue. (WRC-07)

B3 – Transmission of a distress alert relay or a distress call relay by a station not itself in distress (WRC-07)

32.16 A station in the mobile or mobile-satellite service which learns that a mobile unit is in distress (for example, by a radio call or by observation) shall initiate and transmit a distress alert relay or a distress call relay on behalf of the mobile unit in distress once it has ascertained that any of the following circumstances apply: (WRC-07)

32.17 a) on receiving a distress alert or call which is not acknowledged by a coast station or another vessel within 5 minutes. (WRC-07)

32.18 b) on learning that the mobile unit in distress is otherwise unable or incapable of participating in distress communications, if the Master or other person responsible for the mobile unit not in distress considers that further help is necessary. (WRC-07)

32.19 The distress relay on behalf of a mobile unit in distress shall be sent in a form appropriate to the circumstances (see Nos. **32.19A** to **32.19D**) using either a distress call relay by radiotelephony (see Nos. **32.19D** and **32.19E**), an individually addressed distress alert relay by DSC (see No. **32.19B**), or a distress priority message through a ship earth station. (WRC-07)

32.19A A station transmitting a distress alert relay or a distress call relay in accordance with Nos. **32.16** to **32.18** shall indicate that it is not itself in distress. (WRC-07)

32.19B A distress alert relay sent by DSC should use the call format, as found in the most recent version of Recommendations ITU-R M.493 and ITU-R M.541, and should preferably be addressed to an individual coast station or rescue coordination centre[5]. (WRC-07)

32.19C However, a ship shall not transmit a distress alert relay to all ships by digital selective calling on the VHF or MF distress frequencies following receipt of a distress alert sent by Digital Selective Calling by the ship in distress. (WRC-07)

32.19D When an aural watch is being maintained on shore and reliable ship-to-shore communications can be established by radiotelephony, a distress call relay is sent by radiotelephony and addressed to the relevant coast station or rescue coordination centre[6] on the appropriate frequency. (WRC-07)

32.19E The distress call relay sent by radiotelephony should be given in the following form:

– the distress signal "MAYDAY RELAY" spoken three times;

– the words "ALL STATIONS" or coast station name, as appropriate spoken three times;

– the words "THIS IS";

– the name of the relaying station spoken three times;

– the call sign or other identification of the relaying station;

– the MMSI (if the initial alert has been sent by DSC) of the relaying station (the vessel not in distress). (WRC-12)

32.19F This call shall be followed by a distress message which shall, as far as possible, repeat the information[7] contained in the original distress alert or distress message. (WRC-07)

32.19G When no aural watch is being maintained on shore, or there are other difficulties in establishing reliable ship-to-shore communications by radiotelephony, an appropriate coast station or rescue coordination centre may be contacted by sending an individual distress alert relay by DSC, addressed solely to that station and using the appropriate call formats. (WRC-07)

32.19H In the event of continued failure to contact a coast station or rescue coordination centre directly, it may be appropriate to send a distress call relay by radiotelephony addressed to all ships, or to all ships in a certain geographical area. (WRC-07)

32.20 C – Receipt and acknowledgement of distress alerts and distress calls (WRC-07)

C1 – Procedure for acknowledgement of receipt of distress alerts or a distress call (WRC-07)

32.21 Acknowledgement of receipt of a distress alert, including a distress alert relay, shall be made in the manner appropriate to the method of transmission of the alert and within the time-scale appropriate to the role of the station in receipt of the alert. Acknowledgement by satellite shall be sent immediately. (WRC-07)

32.21A When acknowledging receipt of a distress alert sent by DSC[8], the acknowledgement in the terrestrial services shall be made by DSC, radiotelephony or narrow-band direct-printing telegraphy as appropriate to the circumstances, on the associated distress and safety frequency in the same band in which the distress alert was received, taking due account of the directions given in the most recent versions of Recommendations ITU-R M.493 and ITU-R M.541. (WRC-07)

32.21B Acknowledgement by DSC of a distress alert sent by DSC addressed to stations in the maritime mobile service shall be addressed to all stations[8]. (WRC-07)

32.22 (SUP - WRC-07)

32.23 When acknowledging by radiotelephony the receipt of a distress alert or a distress call from a ship station or a ship earth station, the acknowledgement should be given in the following form:

- the distress signal "MAYDAY";

- the name followed by the call sign, or the MMSI or other identification of the station sending the distress message;

- the words "THIS IS";

- the name and call sign or other identification of the station acknowledging receipt;

- the word "RECEIVED";

- the distress signal "MAYDAY". (WRC-12)

32.24 When acknowledging by narrow-band direct-printing telegraphy the receipt of a distress alert from a ship station, the acknowledgement should be given in the following form:

- the distress signal "MAYDAY";

- the call sign or other identification of the station sending the distress alert;

- the word "DE";

- the call sign or other identification of the station acknowledging receipt of the distress alert;

- the signal "RRR";

- the distress signal "MAYDAY". (WRC-07)

32.25 (SUP - WRC-07).

[5] Vessels making a distress alert relay or a distress call relay should ensure that a suitable coast station or rescue coordination centre is informed of any distress communications previously exchanged. (WRC-07)

[6] Vessels making a distress call relay should ensure that a suitable coast station or rescue coordination centre is informed of any distress communications previously exchanged. (WRC-07)

[7] If the station in distress cannot be identified, then it will be necessary to originate the distress message as well, using, for example, terms such as "Unidentified trawler" refer to the mobile unit in distress. (WRC-07)

[8] In order to ensure that no unnecessary delay occurs before the shore-based authorities become aware of a distress incident, the acknowledgement by DSC to a distress alert sent by DSC shall normally only be made by a coast station or a rescue coordination centre. An acknowledgement by DSC will cancel any further automated repetition of the distress alert using DSC. (WRC-07)

C2 – Receipt and acknowledgement by a coast station, a coast earth station or a rescue coordination centre (WRC-07)

32.26 Coast stations and the appropriate coast earth stations in receipt of distress alerts or distress calls shall ensure that they are routed as soon as possible to a rescue coordination centre. In addition, receipt of a distress alert or a distress call is to be acknowledged as soon as possible by a coast station, or by a rescue coordination centre via a coast station or an appropriate coast earth station. A shore-to-ship distress alert relay or a distress call relay (see Nos. **32.14** and **32.15**) shall also be made when the method of receipt warrants a broadcast alert to shipping or when the circumstances of the distress incident indicate that further help is necessary. (WRC-07)

32.27 A coast station using DSC to acknowledge a distress alert shall transmit the acknowledgement on the distress calling frequency on which the distress alert was received and should address it to all ships. The acknowledgement shall include the identification of the ship whose distress alert is being acknowledged. (WRC-07)

C3 – Receipt and acknowledgement by a ship station or ship earth station (WRC-07)

32.28 Ship or ship earth stations in receipt of a distress alert or a distress call shall, as soon as possible, inform the master or person responsible for the ship of the contents of the distress alert. (WRC-07)

32.29 In areas where reliable communications with one or more coast stations are practicable, ship stations in receipt of a distress alert or a distress call from another vessel should defer acknowledgement for a short interval so that a coast station may acknowledge receipt in the first instance. (WRC-07)

32.29A Ship stations in receipt of a distress call sent by radiotelephony on the frequency 156·8 MHz (VHF Channel 16) shall, if the call is not acknowledged by a coast station or another vessel within 5 minutes, acknowledge receipt to the vessel in distress and use any means available to relay the distress call to an appropriate coast station or coast earth station. (WRC-07)

32.30 Ship stations operating in areas where reliable communications with a coast station are not practicable and which receive a distress alert or call from a ship station which is, beyond doubt, in their vicinity, shall, as soon as possible and if appropriately equipped, acknowledge receipt to the vessel in distress and inform a rescue coordination centre through a coast station or coast earth station. (see also Nos. 32.16 to 32.19H). (WRC-07)

32.31 However, in order to avoid making unnecessary or confusing transmissions in response, a ship station, which may be at a considerable distance from the incident, receiving an HF distress alert, shall not acknowledge it but shall observe the provisions of Nos. **32.36** to **32.38**), and shall, if the distress alert is not acknowledged by a coast station within 5 minutes, relay the distress alert, but only to an appropriate coast station or coast earth station (see also Nos. **32.16** to **32.19H**). (WRC-07)

32.32 A ship station acknowledging receipt of a distress alert sent by DSC should, in accordance No. **32.29** or No. **32.30**: (WRC-07)

32.33 a) in the first instance, acknowledge receipt of the distress alert by using radiotelephony on the distress and safety traffic frequency in the band used for the alert, taking into account any instructions which may be issued by a responding coast station; (WRC-07)

32.34 b) if acknowledgement by radiotelephony of the distress alert received on the MF or VHF distress alerting frequency is unsuccessful, acknowledge receipt of the distress alert by responding with a Digital Selective Call on the appropriate frequency.

32.34A However, unless instructed to do so by a coast station or a rescue coordination centre, a ship station may only send an acknowledgement by DSC in the event that:

(a) no acknowledgement by DSC from a coast station has been observed; and
(b) no other communication by radiotelephony or narrow-band direct-printing telegraphy to or from the vessel in distress has been observed; and
(c) at least five minutes have elapsed and the distress alert by DSC has been repeated (see No. 32.21A.1). (WRC-07)

32.35 A ship station in receipt of a shore-to-ship distress alert relay or distress call relay (see No. **32.14**) should establish communication as directed and render such assistance as required and appropriate. (WRC-07)

32.36 D – Preparation for handling of distress traffic

32.37 On receipt of a distress alert or a distress call, ship stations and coast stations shall set watch on the radiotelephone distress and safety traffic frequency associated with the distress and safety calling frequency on which the distress alert was received. (WRC-07)

32.38 Coast stations and ship stations with narrow-band direct-printing equipment shall set watch on the narrow-band direct-printing frequency associated with the distress alert if it indicates that narrow-band direct-printing is to be used for subsequent distress communications. If practicable, they should additionally set watch on the radiotelephone frequency associated with the distress alert frequency. (WRC-07)

Section III – Distress Traffic

32.39 A – General and search and rescue coordinating communications

32.40 Distress traffic consists of all messages relating to the immediate assistance required by the ship in distress, including search and rescue communications and on-scene communications. The distress traffic shall as far as possible be on the frequencies contained in Article **31**.

32.41 (SUP - WRC-07).

32.42 For distress traffic by radiotelephony, when establishing communications, calls shall be prefixed by the distress signal MAYDAY.

32.43 Error correction techniques in accordance with relevant ITU-R Recommendations shall be used for distress traffic by direct-printing telegraphy. All messages shall be preceded by at least one carriage return, a line feed signal, a letter shift signal and the distress signal MAYDAY.

32.44 Distress communications by direct-printing telegraphy should normally be established by the ship in distress and should be in the broadcast (Forward Error Correction) mode. The ARQ mode may subsequently be used when it is advantageous to do so.

32.45 The rescue coordination centre responsible for controlling a search and rescue operation shall also coordinate the distress traffic relating to the incident or may appoint another station to do so. (WRC-07)

32.46 The rescue coordination centre coordinating distress traffic, the unit coordinating search and rescue operations or the coast station involved may impose silence on stations which interfere with that traffic. This instruction shall be addressed to all stations or to one station only, according. to circumstances. In either case, the following shall be used:

32.47 a) in radiotelephony, the signal SEELONCE MAYDAY, pronounced as the French expression "silence, m'aider";

32.48 b) in narrow-band direct-printing telegraphy normally using Forward Error Correcting mode, the signal SEELENCE MAYDAY. However, the ARQ mode may be used when it is advantageous to do so.

32.49 Until they receive the message indicating that normal working may be resumed, all stations which are aware of the distress traffic and which are not taking part in it and which are not in distress, are forbidden to transmit on the frequencies in which the distress traffic is taking place.

32.50 A station of the mobile service which, while following distress traffic is able to continue its normal service, may do so when the distress traffic is well established and on condition that it observes the provisions in the above paragraph and that it does not interfere with distress traffic.

32.51 When distress traffic has ceased on frequencies which have been used for distress traffic, the station controlling the search and rescue operation shall initiate a message for transmission on these frequencies indicating that distress traffic has finished. (WRC-07)

32.52 1. In radiotelephony, the message referred to in the above paragraph consists of:

- the distress signal "MAYDAY";
- the call "ALL STATIONS" spoken three times;
- the words THIS IS;
- the name of the station sending that message spoken three times;
- the call sign or other identification of the station sending the message;
- the time of handing in of the message;
- the MMSI (if the initial alert has been sent by DSC), the name and the call sign of the mobile station which was in distress;
- the words SEELONCE FEENEE pronounced as the French words "silence fini". (WRC-12)

32.53 In direct-printing telegraphy, the message referred to above consists of:

- the distress signal "MAYDAY";
- the call "CQ";
- the word "DE";
- the call sign or other identification of the station sending the message;
- the time of handing in of the message;
- the name and call sign of the mobile station which was in distress; and
- the words "SILENCE FINI".

32.53A Cancellation of an inadvertent distress alert (WRC-07)

32.53B A station transmitting an inadvertent distress alert or call shall cancel the transmission. (WRC-07)

32.53C An inadvertent DSC alert shall be cancelled by DSC, if the DSC equipment is so capable. The cancellation should be in accordance with the most recent version of Recommendation ITU-R M.493. In all cases, cancellation shall also be transmitted by radiotelephone in accordance with **32.53E**. (WRC-07)

32.53D An inadvertent distress call shall be cancelled by radiotelephone in accordance with the procedure in **32.53E**. (WRC-07)

32.53E Inadvertent distress transmissions shall be cancelled orally on the associated distress and safety frequency in the same band on which the distress transmission was sent, using the following procedure:

- the call "ALL STATIONS" spoken three times;
- the words "THIS IS";
- the name of the vessel spoken three times;
- the call sign or other identification;
- the MMSI (if the initial alert has been sent by DSC);
- the words "PLEASE CANCEL MY DISTRESS ALERT OF" followed by the time in UTC.

Monitor the same band on which the inadvertent distress transmission was sent and respond to any communications concerning that distress transmission as appropriate. (WRC-12)

32.54 B – On-scene communications

32.55 On-scene communications are those between the mobile unit in distress and assisting mobile units, and between the mobile units and the unit coordinating search and rescue operations.

32.56 Control of on-scene communications is the responsibility of the unit coordinating search and rescue operations. Simplex communications shall be used so that all on-scene mobile stations may share relevant information concerning the distress incident. If direct-printing telegraphy is used, it shall be in the forward error correcting mode.

32.57 The preferred frequencies in radiotelephony for on-scene communications are 156·8 MHz and 2182 kHz. The frequency 2174·5 kHz may also be used for ship-to-ship on-scene communications using, narrow-band direct-printing telegraphy in the forward error correcting mode.

32.58 In addition to 156·8 MHz and 2182 kHz, the frequencies 3023 kHz, 4125 kHz, 5680 kHz, 123·1 MHz and 156·3 MHz may be used for ship-to-aircraft on-scene communications.

32.59 The selection or designation of on-scene frequencies is the responsibility of the unit coordinating search and rescue operations. Normally, once an on-scene frequency is established, a continuous aural or teleprinter watch is maintained by all participating on-scene mobile units on the selected frequency.

32.60 C – Locating and homing signals
32.61 Locating signals are radio transmissions intended to facilitate the finding of a mobile unit in distress or the location of survivors. These signals include those transmitted by searching units, and those transmitted by the mobile unit in distress, by survival craft, by float-free EPIRBs, by satellite EPIRBs and by search and rescue radar transponders to assist the searching units.

32.62 Homing signals are those locating signals which are transmitted by mobile units in distress, or by survival craft, for the purpose of providing searching units with a signal that can be used to determine the bearing to the transmitting stations.

32.63 Locating signals may be transmitted in the following frequency bands:

> 117·975 – 136 MHz;
> 156 – 174 MHz;
> 406 – 406·1 MHz; and
> 9200 – 9500 MHz. (WRC-07)

ARTICLE 33 – Operational Procedures for Urgency and Safety Communications in the Global Maritime Distress and Safety System (GMDSS)

Section I – General

33.1. Urgency and safety communications include: (WRC-07)

33.2. a) navigational and meteorological warnings and urgent information;

33.3. b) ship-to-ship safety of navigation communications;

33.4 c) ship reporting communications;

33.5 d) support communications for search and rescue operations;

33.6 e) other urgency and safety messages; and

33.7 f) communications relating to the navigation, movements and needs of ships and weather observation messages destined for an official meteorological service.

33.7A Urgency communications shall have priority over all other communications, except distress. (WRC-07)

33.7B Safety communications shall have priority over all other communications, except distress and urgency. (WRC-07)

Section II – Urgency Communications

33.7C The following terms apply:

(a) The urgency announcement is a Digital Selective Call using an urgency call format[1] in the bands used for terrestrial radiocommunication, or an urgency message format, in which case it is relayed through space stations.
(b) The urgency call is the initial voice or text procedure.
(c) The urgency message is the subsequent voice or text procedure. (WRC-07)

---

[1] The format of urgency calls and urgency messages should be in accordance with the relevant ITU-R Recommendations. (WRC-07)

33.8 In a terrestrial system, urgency communications consist of an announcement, transmitted using Digital Selective Calling, followed by the urgency call and message transmitted using radiotelephony, narrow-band direct-printing or data. The announcement of the urgency message shall be made on one or more of the distress and safety calling frequencies specified in Section I of Article **31** using either Digital Selective Calling and the urgency call format or, if not available, radio telephony procedures and the urgency signal. Announcements using Digital Selective Calling should use the technical structure and content set forth in the most recent version of Recommendations ITU-R M.493 and ITU-R M.541. A separate announcement need not be made if the urgency message is to be transmitted through the maritime mobile satellite service. (WRC-07)

33.8A Ship stations not equipped for Digital Selective Calling procedures may announce an urgency call and message by transmitting the urgency signal by radiotelephony on the frequency 156·8 MHz (Channel 16), while taking into account that other stations outside VHF range may not receive the announcement. (WRC-07)

33.8B In the maritime mobile service, urgency communications may be addressed either to all stations or to a particular station. When using digital selective calling techniques, the urgency announcement shall indicate which frequency is to be used to send the subsequent message and, in the case of a message to all stations, shall use the "All Ships" format setting. (WRC-07)

33.8C Urgency announcements from a coast station may also be directed to a group of vessels or to vessels in a defined geographical area. (WRC-07)

33.9 The urgency call and message shall be transmitted on one or more of the distress and safety traffic frequencies specified in Section I of Article 31. (WRC-07)

33.9A However, in the maritime mobile service, the urgency message shall be transmitted on a working frequency:

   a) in the case of a long message or a medical call; or
   b) in areas of heavy traffic when the message is being repeated.

An indication to this effect shall be included in the urgency announcement or call. (WRC-07)

33.9B In the maritime mobile-satellite service, a separate urgency announcement or call does not need to be made before sending the urgency message. However, if available, the appropriate network priority access settings should be used for sending the message. (WRC-07)

33.10 The urgency signal consists of the words PAN PAN. In radiotelephony each word of the group shall be pronounced as the French word "panne".

33.11 The urgency call format and the urgency signal indicate that the calling station has a very urgent message to transmit concerning the safety of a mobile unit or a person. (WRC-07)

33.11A Communications concerning medical advice may be preceded by the urgency signal. Mobile stations requiring medical advice may obtain it through any of the land stations shown in the List of Coast Stations and Special Service Stations. (WRC-07)

33.11B Urgency communications to support search and rescue operations need not be preceded by the urgency signal. (WRC-07)

33.12 The urgency call should consist of:

   – the urgency signal "PAN PAN" spoken three times;
   – the name of the called station or "ALL STATIONS" spoken three times;
   – the words "THIS IS";
   – the name of the station transmitting the urgency message spoken three times;
   – the call sign or any other identification;
   – the MMSI (if the initial announcement has been sent by DSC),

followed by the urgency message or followed by the details of the channel to be used for the message in the case where a working channel is to be used.

In radiotelephony, on the selected working frequency, the urgency call and message consist of the fiollowing, taking into account Nos **32.6** and **32.7**;

   – the urgency signal "PAN PAN" spoken three times;
   – the name of the called station or "ALL STATIONS" spoken three times;
   – the words "THIS IS";
   – the name of the station transmitting the urgency message spoken three times;
   – the call sign or any other identification;
   – the MMSI (if the initial announcement has been sent by DSC),
   – the text of the urgency message. (WRC-12)

33.13 In narrow-band direct-printing, the urgency message shall be preceded by the urgency signal (see No. **33.10**) and the identification of the transmitting station.

33.14 The urgency call format or urgency signal shall be sent only on the authority of the person responsible for the ship, aircraft or other vehicle carrying the mobile station or mobile earth station. (WRC-07)

33.15 The urgency call format or the urgency signal may be transmitted by a land station or a coast earth station with the approval of the responsible authority.

33.15A Ship stations in receipt of an urgency announcement or call addressed to all stations shall not acknowledge. (WRC-07)

33.15B Ship stations in receipt of an urgency announcement or call of an urgency message shall monitor the frequency or channel indicated for the message for at least five minutes. If, at the end of the five minute monitoring period, no urgency message has been received, a coast station should, if possible, be notified of the missing message. Thereafter, normal working may be resumed. (WRC-07)

33.15C Coast and ship stations which are in communication on frequencies other than those used for the transmission of the urgency signal or the subsequent message may continue their normal work without interruption, provided that the urgency message is not addressed to them nor broadcast to all stations. (WRC-07)

33.16 When an urgency announcement or call and message was transmitted to more than one station and action is no longer required, an urgency cancellation should be sent by the station responsible for its transmission.
The urgency cancellation should consist of:

   – the urgency signal "PAN PAN" spoken three times;
   – The words "ALL STATIONS" spoken three times;
   – the words "THIS IS";
   – the name of the station transmitting the urgency message spoken three times;
   – the call sign or any other identification;
   – the MMSI (if the initial announcement has been sent by DSC),
   – The words "PLEASE CANCEL URGENCY MESSAGE OF" followed by the time in UTC. (WRC-12)

33.17 Error correction techniques in accordance with relevant ITU-R Recommendations shall be used for urgency messages by direct-printing telegraphy. All messages shall be preceded by at least one carriage return, a line feed signal, a letter shift signal and the urgency signal PAN PAN.

33.18 Urgency communications by direct-printing telegraphy should normally be established in the broadcast (forward error correction) mode. The ARQ mode may subsequently be used when it is advantageous to do so.

Section III – Medical Transports

33.19 The term "medical transports", as defined in the 1949 Geneva Conventions and Additional Protocols, refers to any means of transportation by land, water or air, whether military or civilian, permanent or temporary, assigned exclusively to medical transportation and under the control of a competent authority, of a party to a conflict or of neutral States and of other States not parties to an armed conflict, when these ships, craft and aircraft assist the wounded, the sick and the shipwrecked.

33.20 For the purpose of announcing and identifying medical transports which are protected under the above-mentioned Conventions, the procedure of Section II of this article is used. The urgency signal shall be followed by the addition of the single word MEDICAL in narrow-band direct-printing and by the addition of the single word MAY-DEE-CAL pronounced as in French "medical", in radiotelephony. (WRC-07)

33.20A When using Digital Selective Calling techniques, the urgency announcement on the appropriate Digital Selective Calling distress and safety frequencies shall always be addressed to all stations on VHF and to a specified geographical area on MF and HF and shall indicate "Medical transport" in accordance with the most recent version of Recommendations ITU-R M.493 and ITU-R M.541. (WRC-07)

33.20B Medical transports may use one or more of the distress and safety traffic frequencies specified in Section I of Article 31 for the purpose of self-identification and to establish communications. As soon as practicable, communications shall be transferred to an appropriate working frequency. (WRC-07)

33.21 The use of the signals described in the above paragraph indicates that the message which follows concerns a protected medical transport. The message shall convey the following data: (WRC-07)

33.22 a) call sign or other recognized means of identification of the medical transport;

33.23 b) position of the medical transport;

33.24 c) number and type of vehicles in the medical transport;

33.25 d) intended route;

33.26 e) estimated time en route and of departure and arrival, as appropriate;

33.27 f) any other information, such as flight altitude, radio frequencies guarded, languages used and secondary surveillance radar modes and codes.

33.28 (SUP - WRC-07).

33.29 (SUP - WRC-07).

33.20 The use of radiocommunications for announcing and identifying medical transports is optional; however, if they are used, the provisions of the above Regulations and particularly this Section and of Articles 30 and 31 shall apply.

Section IV – Safety Communications

33.30A The following terms apply:

(a) the safety announcement is a Digital Selective Call using a safety call format in the bands used for terrestrial radiocommunication or a safety message format, in which case it is relayed through space stations;
(b) the safety call is the initial voice or text procedure;
(c) the safety message is the subsequent voice or text procedure. (WRC-07)

33.31 In a terrestrial system, safety communications consist of a safety announcement, transmitted using digital selective calling, followed by the safety call and message transmitted using radiotelephony, narrow-band direct-printing or data. The announcement of the safety message shall be made on one or more of the distress and safety calling frequencies specified in Section I of Article **31** using either digital selective calling techniques and the safety call format, or radiotelephony procedures and the safety signal. (WRC-07)

33.31A However, in order to avoid unnecessary loading of the distress and safety calling frequencies specified for use with digital selective calling techniques:

(a) safety messages transmitted by coast stations in accordance with a predefined timetable should not be announced by digital selective calling techniques;
(b) safety messages which only concern vessels sailing in the vicinity should be announced using radiotelephony procedures. (WRC-07)

33.31B In addition, ship stations not equipped for Digital Selective Calling procedures may announce a safety message by transmitting the safety call by radiotelephony. In such cases the announcement shall be made using the frequency 156·8 MHz (VHF Channel 16), while taking into account that other stations outside VHF range may not receive the announcement. (WRC-07)

33.31C In the maritime mobile service, safety messages shall generally be addressed to all stations. In some cases, however, they may be addressed to a particular station. When using Digital Selective Calling techniques, the safety announcement shall indicate which frequency is to be used to send the subsequent message and, in the case of a message to all stations, shall use the "All Ships" format setting. (WRC-07)

33.32 In the maritime mobile service, the safety message shall, where practicable, be transmitted on a working frequency in the same band(s) as those used for the safety announcement or call. A suitable indication to this effect shall be made at the end of the safety call. In the case that no other option is practicable, the safety message may be sent by radiotelephony on the frequency 156·8 MHz (VHF Channel 16). (WRC-07)

33.32A In the maritime mobile-satellite service, a separate safety announcement or call does not need to be made before sending the safety message. However, if available, the appropriate network priority access settings should be used for sending the message. (WRC-07)

33.33 The safety signal consists of the word SÉCURITÉ. In radiotelephony, it shall be pronounced as in French.

33.34 1) The safety call format or the safety signal indicates that the calling station has an important navigational or meteorological warning to transmit. (WRC-07)

33.34A 2) Messages from ship stations containing information concerning the presence of cyclones shall be transmitted, with the least possible delay, to other mobile stations in the vicinity and to the appropriate authorities through a coast station, or through a rescue coordination centre via a coast station or an appropriate coast earth station. These transmissions shall be preceded by the safety announcement or call. (WRC-07)

33.34B 3) Messages from ship stations, containing information on the presence of dangerous ice, dangerous wrecks, or any other imminent danger to marine navigation, shall be transmitted as soon as possible to other ships in the vicinity, and to the appropriate authorities through a coast station, or through a rescue coordination centre via a coast station or an appropriate coast earth station. These transmissions shall be preceded by the safety announcement or call. (WRC-07)

33.35 The complete safety call should consist of the following, taking into account Nos. **32.6** and **32.7**:

- the safety signal "SÉCURITÉ" spoken three times;
- the name of the called station or "ALL STATIONS" spoken three times;
- the words "THIS IS";
- the name of the station transmitting the safety message spoken three times;
- the call sign or any other identification;
- the MMSI (if the initial announcement has been sent by DSC),

followed by the safety message or followed by the details of the channel to be used for the message in the case where a working channel is to be used.

In radiotelephony, on the selected working frequency, the safety call and message should consist of:

- the safety signal "SÉCURITÉ" spoken three times;
- the name of the called station or "ALL STATIONS" spoken three times;
- the words "THIS IS";
- the name of the station transmitting the safety message spoken three times;
- the call sign or any other identification;
- the MMSI (if the initial announcement has been sent by DSC),
- the text of the safety message. (WRC-12)

33.36 In narrow-band direct-printing, the safety message shall be preceded by the safety signal (see No. **33.33**) and the identification of the transmitting station.

33.37 Error correction techniques in accordance with relevant ITU-R Recommendation shall be used for safety messages by direct-printing telegraphy. All messages shall be preceded by at least one carriage return, a line feed signal, a letter shift signal and the safety signal SÉCURITÉ.

33.38 Safety communications by direct-printing telegraphy should normally be established in the broadcast (forward error correction) mode. The ARQ mode may subsequently be used when it is advantageous to do so.

33.38A Ship stations in receipt of a safety announcement using digital selective calling techniques and the "All Ships" format setting, or otherwise addressed to all stations, shall not acknowledge. (WRC-07)

33.38B Ship stations in receipt of a safety announcement or safety call and message shall monitor the frequency or channel indicated for the message and shall listen until they are satisfied that the message is of no concern to them. They shall not make any transmission likely to interfere with the message. (WRC-07)

Section V – Transmission of Maritime Safety Information

(Maritime safety information includes navigational and meteorological warnings, meteorological forecasts and other urgent messages pertaining to safety normally transmitted to or from ships, between ships and between ship and coast stations or land earth stations.)

33.39 A – General

33.39A (SUP - WRC-07).

33.39B (SUP - WRC-07).

33.40 (SUP - WRC-07).

33.41 The mode and format of the transmissions mentioned in Nos. **33.43**, **33.45**, **33.46** and **33.48** shall be in accordance with the relevant ITU-R Recommendations.

33.42 B – International NAVTEX system

33.43 Maritime safety information shall be transmitted by means of narrow-band direct-printing telegraphy with forward error correction using the frequency 518 kHz in accordance with the international NAVTEX system (see Appendix **15**).

33.44 C – 490 kHz and 4209·5 kHz

33.45 The frequency 490 kHz may be used, for the transmission of maritime safety information by means of narrow-band direct-printing telegraphy with forward error correction.

33.46 The frequency 4209·5 kHz is used exclusively for NAVTEX-type transmission by means of narrow-band direct-printing telegraphy with forward error correction.

33.47 D – High seas maritime safety information

33.48 Maritime safety information is transmitted by means of NBDP telegraphy with forward error correction using the frequencies 4210 kHz, 6314 kHz, 8416·5 kHz, 12579 kHz, 16806·5 kHz, 19680·5 kHz, 22376 kHz and 26100·5 kHz.

33.49 E – Maritime safety information via satellite

33.50 Maritime safety information may be transmitted via satellite in the maritime mobile-satellite service using the band 1530 – 1545 MHz and 1621.35 - 1626.5 MHz (see Appendix **15**). (WRC-19)

Section VI – Intership Navigation Safety Communications

33.51 Intership navigation safety communications are those VHF radiotelephone communications conducted between ships for the purpose of contributing to the safe movement of ships.

33.52 The frequency 156·650 MHz is used for intership navigation safety communications (see also Appendix **15** and note k) in Appendix **18**).

Section VII – Use of Other Frequencies for Safety (WRC-07)

33.53 Radiocommunications for safety purposes concerning ship reporting communications, communications relating to the navigation, movements and needs of ships and weather observation messages may be conducted on any appropriate communications frequency, including those used for public correspondence. In terrestrial systems, the bands 415 – 535 kHz (see Article 52), 1606·5 – 4 000 kHz (see Article 52), 4000 – 27500 kHz (see Appendix 17), and 156 – 174 MHz (see Appendix 18) are used for this function. In the maritime mobile-satellite service, frequencies in the bands 1530 – 1544 MHz, 1621.35 - 1626.5 MHz and 1626·5 – 1645·5 MHz are used for this function as well as for distress alerting purposes. (see No. 32.2) (WRC-19)

33.54 (SUP - WRC-07).

33.55 (SUP - WRC-07).

ARTICLE 34 – Alerting Signals in the Global Maritime Distress and Safety System (GMDSS)

Section I – Emergency Position-Indicating Radio Beacon (EPIRB) and Satellite EPIRB Signals

34.1 The Emergency Position-Indicating Radio Beacon signal in the band 406 – 406·1 MHz shall be in accordance with Recommendation ITU-R M.633-4. (WRC-12)

Section II – Digital Selective Calling

34.2 The characteristics of the "distress call" in the digital selective calling system should be in accordance with the most recent version of Recommendation ITU-R M.493. (WRC-12)

NOTES

THE MANAGEMENT OF VHF

The proper use of VHF channels at sea makes an important contribution to navigational safety. In accordance with the ITU Radio Regulations:

(a) Channel 16 (156·8 MHz) may only be used for distress, urgency and very brief safety communications and for calling to establish communications which should then be conducted on a suitable working channel.

(b) On VHF channels allocated to the port operations service the only messages permitted are restricted to those relating to the operational handling, the movement and safety of ships and, in emergency, to the safety of persons. The use of these channels for ship-to-ship communications may cause serious interference to communications related to the movement and safety of shipping in congested port areas.

VHF equipment is frequently operated by persons not trained in its proper use though the ITU Radio Regulations require that the service of every ship radio-telephone station shall be controlled by an operator holding a certificate issued or recognized by the Government concerned.

World Radiocommunication Conference 2015 (WRC-15) approved measures to enhance maritime communications systems.

New applications for data exchange, using AIS technology, are intended to improve the safety of navigation. New allocations were made in the bands 161·9375-161·9625 MHz and 161·9875-162·0125 MHz to the maritime mobile-satellite service (MMSS). Studies will continue on the compatibility between MMSS in the downlink in the band 161·7875-161·9375 MHz and the incumbent services in the same adjacent frequency bands.

The following guidelines have been prepared and, if followed, should ensure that VHF channels are used correctly.

Proper Use of VHF Channels at Sea (An extract from the IMO Resolution A.474 (XII))

GUIDELINES ON THE USE OF VHF AT SEA

1 VHF COMMUNICATION TECHNIQUE

1.1 Preparation

Before transmitting, think about the subjects which have to be communicated and, if necessary, prepare written notes to avoid unnecessary interruptions and ensure that no valuable time is wasted on a busy channel.

1.2 Listening

To avoid unnecessary and irritating interference, listen before transmitting to make certain that the channel is not already in use.

Resolution 331 (REV. WRC-12) The International Maritime Organisation (IMO) is of the view that SOLAS ships, while at sea, should be required to keep a listening watch on VHF Channel 16, for the forseeable future with a view to providing:

— a distress alerting and communication channel for NON SOLAS ships and;

— bridge to bridge communications.

1.3 Discipline

VHF equipment should be used correctly and in accordance with the Radio Regulations. The following in particular should be avoided:

1.3.1 calling on Channel 16 for purposes other than distress, urgency and very brief safety communications when another calling channel is available;

1.3.2 communications not related to safety and navigation on port operation channels;

1.3.3 non-essential transmissions, e.g. needless and superfluous signals and correspondence;

1.3.4 transmitting without correct identification;

1.3.5 occupation of one particular channel under poor conditions;

1.3.6 use of offensive language.

1.4 Repetition

Repetition of words and phrases should be avoided unless specifically requested by the receiving station.

1.5 Power Reduction

When possible, the lowest transmitter power necessary for satisfactory communication should be used.

1.6 Automatic Identification Sytems (AIS)

AIS is used for the exchange of data in ship-to-ship communications and also in communication with shore-based facilities. The purpose of AIS is to help identify vessels; assist in target tracking; simplify information exchange (e.g. reduce verbal reporting); and provide additional information to assist situation awareness. AIS may be used together with VHF voice communications. AIS should be operated in accordance with resolution A.917(22) - Guidelines for the onboard operational use of shipborne Automatic Identification Systems (AIS).

1.7 Communications with shore stations

1.7.1 Instructions given on communication matters by shore stations should be obeyed.

1.7.2 Communications should be carried out on the channel indicated by the shore station. When a change of channel is requested, this should be acknowledged by the ship.

1.7.3 On receiving instructions from a shore station to stop transmitting, no further communications should be made until otherwise notified (the shore station may be receiving distress or safety messages and any other transmissions could cause interference).

1.8 Communications with other ships

1.8.1 VHF Channel 13 is designated by the Radio Regulations for bridge-to-bridge communications. The ship called may indicate another working channel on which further transmissions should take place. The calling ship should acknowledge acceptance before changing channels.

1.8.2 The listening procedure outlined in paragraph 1.2 should be followed before communications are commenced on the chosen channel.

1.9 Distress communications

1.9.1 Distress calls/messages have absolute priority over all other communications. When hearing them all other transmissions should cease and a listening watch should be kept.

1.9.2 Any distress call/message should be recorded in the ship's log and passed to the Master.

1.9.3 On receipt of a distress message, if in the vicinity, immediately acknowledge receipt. If not in the vicinity, allow a short interval of time to elapse before acknowledging receipt of the message in order to permit ships nearer to the distress to do so.

1.10 Calling

1.10.1 In accordance with the Radio Regulations Channel 16 may only be used for distress, urgency and very brief safety communications and for calling to establish other communications which should then be conducted on a suitable working channel.

1.10.2 Whenever possible, a working frequency should be used for calling.

If a working frequency is not available, VHF Channel 16 may be used for calling, provided it is not occupied by a distress call/message.

1.10.3 In case of difficulty to establish contact with a ship or shore station, allow adequate time before repeating the call. Do not occupy the channel unnecessarily and try another channel.

1.11 Changing channels

If communications on a channel are unsatisfactory, indicate change of channel and await confirmation.

1.12 Spelling

If spelling becomes necessary (e.g. descriptive names, call signs, words which could be misunderstood) use the spelling table contained in the International Code of Signals and the Radio Regulations and the IMO Standard Marine Communication Phrases (SMCP).

1.13 Addressing

The words "I" and "You" should be used prudently. Indicate to whom they refer.

Example:

Seaship, this is Port Radar, do you have a Pilot? Port Radar, this is Seaship, yes I do have a Pilot.

1.14 Watchkeeping

Every ship, while at sea, is required to maintain watches (Regulation on Watches in Chapter IV of SOLAS, 1974, as amended). Continuous watchkeeping is required on VHF DSC Channel 70 and also when practicable, a continuous listening watch on VHF Channel 16.

2 VHF COMMUNICATION PROCEDURE

2.1 Calling

When calling a shore station or another ship, say the name of that shore station once (twice if considered necessary in heavy radio traffic conditions) followed by the phrase "THIS IS" and the ship's name twice, indicating the channel in use.

Example:

Port City, this is Seastar, Seastar, on Channel 14.

2.2 Exchange of messages

2.2.1 When communicating with a ship whose name is unknown but whose position is known, that position may be used. In this case the call is addressed to all ships.

Example:

Hello "ALL SHIPS", this is Pastoria, Pastoria. Ship approaching number four buoy, I am passing Belinda Bank Light.

2.2.2 Where a message is received and only acknowledgement of receipt is needed, say "received". Where a message is received and acknowledgement of the correct message is required, say "received, understood", and repeat message if considered necessary.

Example:

Message: *Your berth will be clear at 08.30 hours.*

Reply: *Received, understood. Berth clear at 08.30 hours.*

2.2.3 Where appropriate, the following message should be sent:

"Please use/ I will use IMO Standard Marine Communication Phrases".

When language difficulties exist which cannot be resolved by use of IMO Standard Marine Communication Phrases, the International Code of Signals should be used.

In this case the word "INTERCO" should precede the groups of the International Code of Signals.

Example:

"Please use/I will use the International Code of Signals".

2.2.4 Where the message contains instructions or advice, the substance should be repeated in the reply.

Example:

Message: *Advise you pass astern of me.*

Reply: *I will pass astern of you.*

2.2.5 If a message is not properly received, ask for it to be repeated by saying *"Say again"*.

2.2.6 If a message is received but not understood, say *"Message not understood"*.

2.2.7 If it is necessary to change to a different channel say *"Change to channel ...."* and wait for acknowledgement before carrying out the change.

2.2.8 During exchange of messages, a ship should invite a reply by saying *"over"*.

2.2.9 The end of a communication is indicated by the word *"out"*.

3 STANDARD MESSAGES

3.1 Since most ship-to-shore communications are exchanges of information, it is advisable to use standard messages which will reduce transmission time.

3.2 Commonly used standard messages are given in the IMO Standard Marine Communication Phrases (SMCP), which should be used whenever possible.

Reference Documents

- SOLAS Convention, 1974, as amended, Chapter IV on Radiocommunications.
- Radio Regulations, Appendix 18, Table of Transmitting Frequencies in the VHF Maritime Mobile Band.
- Resolution A.917(22) on Guidelines for the Onboard Operational Use of Shipborne Automatic Identification Systems (AIS).

- Resolution A.918(22) on IMO Standard Marine Communication Phrases (SMCP).
- Resolution A.801(19) Provision of Radio Services for the Global Maritime Distress and Safety System (GMDSS)

RANGE OF VHF

The transmitting and receiving range of VHF signals is limited, in theory, it is line of sight transmission. The range may be affected to some degree by barometric pressure and/or increased humidity which often gives greater ranges than normally attained through the refraction of the transmission.

This atmospheric refraction results in the radio waves tending to follow curved rather than straight line paths. VHF radio waves experience a degree of refraction making the radio horizon greater than the visible horizon. This bending or refraction arises from a change of wave speed as the waves propagate through the atmosphere with the waves changing direction towards the region of lower wave speed. The amount of bending or refraction depends upon the rate at which the wave speed changes and is termed the refractive index. This is influenced by the air and its variation with height, other factors include pressure, temperature and humidity.

Another significant factor in determining range is, the height above sea level of the transmitting and receiving aerials. It should also be noted that a transmitter and a receiver within radio sight does not automatically guarantee that an acceptable signal will be received. Good reception will depend, amongst other things, on the power of the transmission, the sensitivity of the receiver, the quality and position of the transmitting and receiving aerials. The table below illustrates some approximate VHF ranges that can be obtained from a variety of transmitting and receiving situations.

The radio horizon calculations used to establish the ranges are obtained from Annex 3 of Resolution A.801(19) and use the following formula to calculate the range "A" in n miles:

$A = 2.5 (\sqrt{H}(\text{in metres}) + \sqrt{h}(\text{in metres}))$ or

$A = 1.23 (\sqrt{H}(\text{in feet}) + \sqrt{h}(\text{in feet}))$

H is the height of the coast station VHF receiving antenna;

h is the height of the ship's transmitting antenna.

This formula applies to line-of-sight cases but is not considered adequate for cases where both antenna are at low level.

Antenna Heights and Approximate Theoretical Radio Horizons

Antenna Height m (ft)	Radio Horizon, n miles	Antenna Height m (ft)	Radio Horizon, n miles
1.5 (5)	3	30.5 (100)	12
3.0 (10)	4	91.4 (300)	21
4.6 (15)	5	152.4 (500)	28
6.1 (20)	6	213.4 (700)	33
9.2 (30)	7	274.3 (900)	37
12.2 (40)	8	304.8 (1000)	39
15.3 (50)	9	609.6 (2000)	55
22.9 (75)	11	914.4 (3000)	67

The radio horizon table above illustrates approximate VHF range over open water (smooth earth).

To calculate the communication distance between say a small craft with an antenna height of 9.2m / 30ft and a coast station with a land based antenna height of 213m / 700ft the radio horizon for both antenna systems are added together, in this case 7 n miles and 33 n miles which equates to 40 n miles. Theoretically therefore, if the two stations are inside a 40 n miles radius they should be able to communicate.

Antenna location is particularly important because VHF RT, DSC and AIS all work on the same frequency band and are therefore particularly subject to interference between antennas as well as fron other metallic structures. Such interference can distort the radiation patterns and severely weaken transmission and reception in certain directions.

THE USE OF MOBILE TELEPHONES IN DISTRESS AND SAFETY COMMUNICATIONS

The use of mobile telephones in the marine environment offshore is now well established, with users in all areas of the commercial, fishing and leisure communities.

Incidents have occurred where vessels requiring assistance from rescue services have used the inland emergency service, or alternatively telephoned direct to request assistance. (e.g. Lifeboat services). This procedure through a mobile telephone is **strongly discouraged.**

Use of mobile telephones by-passes the existing dedicated well-established international marine distress communications systems.

Mobile telephone coverage offshore is limited and does not afford the same extensive safety coverage as VHF Channel 16. Consequently a greater risk exists of communications difficulties or even a complete breakdown if an accident should occur at the edge of a cell coverage area.

Subsequent on-scene communications would be restricted and delayed if mobile telephone communications were exclusively maintained throughout. There is always a risk that elements of vital information could be lost or misinterpreted by the introduction of further relay links in the communication chain. Mobile telephones are also highly susceptible to failure due to water ingress.

It is not possible to communicate direct to another vessel able to render assistance unless that vessel is also fitted with a mobile telephone and the telephone number is known. Requests for assistance cannot be monitored by other vessels in a position to render assistance. Valuable time would be lost whilst the relevant Coastguard Rescue Coordination Centre receives and then re-broadcasts the information to all ships on the appropriate distress channel(s).

In the interests of Safety Of Life At Sea (SOLAS), owners of vessels are urged to carry MARINE communications equipment onboard and to use this medium as the primary means of Distress and Safety communications.

Typical VHF ranges

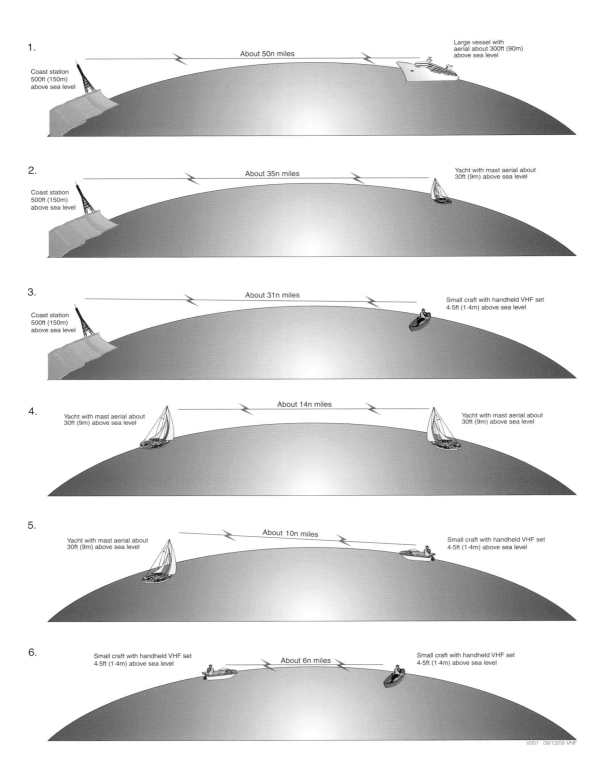

1.

Coast station 500ft (150m) above sea level

About 50n miles

Large vessel with aerial about 300ft (90m) above sea level

2.

Coast station 500ft (150m) above sea level

About 35n miles

Yacht with mast aerial about 30ft (9m) above sea level

3.

Coast station 500ft (150m) above sea level

About 31n miles

Small craft with handheld VHF set 4·5ft (1·4m) above sea level

4.

Yacht with mast aerial about 30ft (9m) above sea level

About 14n miles

Yacht with mast aerial about 30ft (9m) above sea level

5.

Yacht with mast aerial about 30ft (9m) above sea level

About 10n miles

Small craft with handheld VHF set 4·5ft (1·4m) above sea level

6.

Small craft with handheld VHF set 4·5ft (1·4m) above sea level

About 6n miles

Small craft with handheld VHF set 4·5ft (1·4m) above sea level

V001 09/12/09 VHF

Continued on next page

Table of Transmitting Frequencies in the VHF Maritime Mobile Band - Appendix 18 (REV. WRC-15)

Channel designators		Notes	Transmitting frequencies (MHz)		Inter Ship	Port operations and ship movement		Public correspondence
			Ship stations	Coast stations		Single frequency	Two frequency	
	60	m)	156.025	160.625		x	x	x
01		m)	156.050	160.650		x	x	x
	61	m)	156.075	160.675		x	x	x
02		m)	156.100	160.700		x	x	x
	62	m)	156.125	160.725		x	x	x
03		m)	156.150	160.750		x	x	x
	63	m)	156.175	160.775		x	x	x
04		m)	156.200	160.800		x	x	x
	64	m)	156.225	160.825		x	x	x
05		m)	156.250	160.850		x	x	x
	65	m)	156.275	160.875		x	x	x
06		f)	156.300		x			
	2006	r)	160.900	160.900				
	66	m)	156.325	160.925		x	x	x
07		m)	156.350	160.950		x	x	x
	67	h)	156.375	156.375	x	x		
08			156.400		x			
	68		156.425	156.425		x		
09		i)	156.450	156.450	x	x		
	69		156.475	156.475	x	x		
10		h), q)	156.500	156.500	x	x		
	70	f), j)	156.525	156.525	Digital Selective Calling for Distress, Safety and Calling			
11		q)	156.550	156.550		x		
	71		156.575	156.575		x		
12			156.600	156.600		x		
	72	i)	156.625		x			
13		k)	156.650	156.650	x	x		
	73	h), i)	156.675	156.675	x	x		
14			156.700	156.700		x		
	74		156.725	156.725		x		
15		g)	156.750	156.750	x	x		
	75	n), s)	156.775	156.775		x		
16		f)	156.800	156.800	Distress, Safety and Calling			
	76	n), s)	156.825	156.825		x		
17		g)	156.850	156.850	x	x		
	77		156.875		x			
18		m)	156.900	161.500		x	x	x
	78	m)	156.925	161.525		x	x	x
1078			156.925	156.925		x		
	2078	mm)	161.525	161.525		x		
19		m)	156.950	161.550		x	x	x
1019			156.950	156.950		x		
	2019	mm)	161.550	161.550		x		

Continued overleaf

	79	m)	156.975	161.575		x	x	x
1079			156.975	156.975		x		
	2079	mm)	161.575	161.575		x		
20		m)	157.000	161.600			x	x
1020			157.000	157.000		x		
	2020	mm)	161.600	161.600		x		
	80	y), wa)	157.025	161.625		x	x	x
21		y), ywa	157.050	161.650		x	x	x
	81	y), wa)	157.075	161.675		x	x	x
22		y), wa)	157.100	161.700		x	x	x
	82	x), y), wa)	157.125	161.725		x	x	x
23		x), y), wa)	157.150	161.750		x	x	x
	83	x), y), wa)	157.175	161.775		x	x	x
24		w), ww), x), xx)	157.200	161.800		x	x	x
1024		w), ww), x), xx)	157.200					
	2024	w), ww), x), xx)	161.800	161.800	x (digital only)			
	84	w), ww), x), xx)	157.225	161.825		x	x	x
1084		w), ww), x), xx)	157.225					
	2084	w), ww), x), xx)	161.825	161.825	x (digital only)			
25		w), ww), x), xx)	157.250	161.850		x	x	x
1025		w), ww), x), xx)	157.250					
	2025	w), ww), x), xx)	161.850		x (digital only)			
85		w), ww), x), xx)	157.275	161.875		x	x	x
1085		w), ww), x), xx)	157.275					
	2085	w), ww), x), xx)	161.875	161.875	x (digital only)			
26		w), ww), x)	157.300	161.900		x	x	x
1026		w), ww), x)	157.300					
	2026	w), ww), x)		161.900				
86		w), ww), x)	157.325	161.925		x	x	x
1086		w), ww), x)	157.325					
	2086	w), ww), x)		161.925				
27		z), zx)	157.350	161.950			x	x
1027		z), zx)	157.350	157.350				
	2027*	z)	161.950	161.950				
87		z), zz)	157.375	161.975		x		
28		z), zx)	157.400	162.000			x	x
1028		z), zz)	157.400	157.400				

Continued on next page

	2028*	z)	162.000	162.000				
	88	z), zz)	157.425	157.425		x		
AIS 1		f), l), p)	161.975	161.975				
AIS 2		f), l), p)	162.025	162.025				

* From 1 January 2019, channel 2027 will be designated ASM 1 and channel 2028 will be designated ASM 2.

From Appendix 18 (REV. WRC-15)

Note: For assistance in understanding the Table, see notes *a)* to *zz)*. (WRC-15)

NOTES REFERRING TO THE TABLE

General notes

a. Administrations may designate frequencies for the following purposes; intership, port operations and ship movement services for use by light aircraft and helicopters to communicate with ships or participating coast stations in predominantly maritime support operations, under the conditions specified in Nos. **51.69, 51.73, 51.74, 51.75, 51.76, 51.77** and **51.78**. However, the use of the channels which are shared with public correspondence shall be subject to prior agreement between interested and affected administrations.

b. The channels of the present Appendix, with the exception of channels 06, 13, 15, 16, 17, 70, 75 and 76, may also be used for high-speed data and facsimile transmissions, subject to special arrangement between interested and affected administrations.

c. The channels of the present Appendix, with the exception of channels 06, 13, 15, 16, 17, 70, 75 and 76, may be used for direct-printing telegraphy and data transmission, subject to special arrangement between interested and affected administrations. (WRC-12)

d. The frequencies in this table may also be used for radiocommunications on inland waterways in accordance with the conditions specified No. **5.226**.

e. Administrations may apply 12·5 kHz channel interleaving on a non-interference basis to 25 kHz channels, in accordance with the most recent version of Recommendation ITU-R M.1084 provided:

— it shall not affect the 25 kHz channels of the Appendix maritime mobile distress and safety frequencies, especially the channels 06, 13, 15, 16, 17, 70, AIS 1 and AIS 2, nor the technical characteristics mentioned in Recommendation ITU-R M.489-2 for those channels;

— implementation of 12·5 kHz channel interleaving and consequential national requirements shall be subject coordination with affected administrations. (WRC-12)

Specific notes

f. The frequencies 156·300 MHz (channel 06), 156·525 MHz (channel 70), 156·800 MHz (channel 16), 161·975 MHz (AIS 1) and 162·025 MHz (AIS 2) may also be used by aircraft stations for the purpose of search and rescue operations and other safety-related operations. (WRC-07)

g. Channels 15 and 17 may also be used for on-board communications provided the effective radiated power does not exceed 1 W, and subject to the national regulations of the administration concerned when these channels are used in its territorial waters.

h. Within the European Maritime Area and in Canada, these frequencies (channels 10, 67 & 73) may also be used, if so required, by the individual administrations concerned, for communication between ship stations, aircraft stations and participating land stations engaged in coordinated search and rescue and anti-pollution operations in local areas, under the conditions specified in Nos. **51.69, 51.73, 51.74, 51.75, 51.76, 51.77** and **51.78**.

i. The preferred first three frequencies for the purpose indicated in note *a)* are 156·450 MHz (channel 09), 156·625 MHz (channel 72) and 156·675 MHz (channel 73).

j. Channel 70 is to be used exclusively for digital selective calling for distress, safety and calling.

k. Channel 13 is designated for use on a worldwide basis as a navigation safety communication channel, primarily for intership navigation safety communications. It may also be used for the ship movement and port operations service subject to the national regulations of the administrations concerned.

l. The channels (AIS 1 and AIS 2) are used for an automatic ship identification system (AIS) capable of providing worldwide operation, unless other frequencies are designated on a regional basis for this purpose. Such use should be in accordance with the most recent vesion of Recommendation ITU-R M.1371. (WRC-07) *ll*   These channels may be operated as single frequency channels, subject to coordination with affected administrations. The following conditions apply for single frequency usage:

- The lower frequency portion of these channels may be operated as single frequency channels by ship and coast stations.

- Transmission using the upper frequency portion of these channels is limited to coast stations.

- If permitted by administrations and specified by national regulations, the upper frequency portion of these channels may be used by ship stations for transmission. All precautions should be taken to avoid harmful interference to channels AIS 1, AIS 2, 2027* and 2028*. (WRC-15)

* From 1 January 2019, channel 2027 will be designated ASM 1 and channel 2028 will be designated ASM 2.

mm.   Transmission on these channels is limited to coast stations. If permitted by administrations and specificed by national regulations, these channels may be used by ship stations for transmission. All precautions should be taken to avoid harmful interference to channels AIS 1, AIS 2, 2027* and 2028*. (WRC-15)

* From 1 January 2019, channel 2027 will be designated ASM 1 and channel 2028 will be designated ASM 2.

n.   With the exception of AIS, the use of these channels (75 and 76) should be restricted to navigation-related communications only and all precautions should be taken to avoid harmful interference to channel 16 by limiting the output power to 1 W. (WRC-12)

o.   (SUP - WRC-12)

p.   Additionally AIS 1 and AIS 2 may be used by the mobile-satellite service (Earth-to-space) for the reception of AIS transmissions from ships. (WRC-07)

q.   When using these channels (10 and 11), all precautions should be taken to avoid harmful interference to channel 70. (WRC-07)

r.   In the maritime mobile service, this frequency is reserved for experimental use for further applications or systems (e.g. new AIS applications, man over board systems, etc.). If authorized by administrations for experimental use, the operation shall not cause harmful interference to, or claim protection from, stations operating in the fixed and mobile service. (WRC-12)

s.   Channels 75 and 76 are also allocated to the mobile-satellite service (Earth-to-space) for the reception of long-range AIS broadcast messages from ships (Message 27; see the most recent version of Recommendation ITU-R M.1371). (WRC-12)

t.   (SUP - WRC-15)

u.   (SUP - WRC-15)

v.   (SUP - WRC-15)

w.   In Regions 1 and 3 (i.e. except N. & S. America):

Until 1 January 2017, the frequency bands 157·200-157·325 MHz and 161·800-161·925 MHz (corresponding to channels 24, 84, 25, 85, 26 and 86) may be used for digitally modulated emissions, subject to coordination with affected administrations. Stations using these channels or frequency bands for digitally modulated emissions shall not cause harmful interference to, or claim protection from, other stations operating in accordance with Article **5**.

From 1 January 2017, the frequency bands 157·200-157·325 MHz and 161·800-161·925 MHz (corresponding to channels 24, 84, 25, 85, 26 and 86) are identified for the utilization of the VHF Data Exchange System (VDES) described in the most recent version of Recommendation ITU-R M.2092. These frequency bands may also be used for analogue modulation described in the most recent version of Recommendation ITU-R M.1084 by an administration that wishes to do so, subject to not causing harmful interference to, claiming protection from other stations in the maritime mobile service using digitally modulated emissions and subject to coordination with affected administrations. (WRC-15) *wa.* In Regions 1 and 3 (i.e. except N. & S. America):

Until 1 January 2017, the frequency bands 157·025-157·175 MHz and 161·625-161·775 MHz (corresponding to channels 80, 21, 81, 22, 82, 23 and 83) may be used for digitally modulated emissions, subject to coordination with affected administrations. Stations using these channels or frequency bands for digitally modulated emissions shall not cause harmful interference to, or claim protection from, other stations operating in accordance with Article 5.

From 1 January 2017, the frequency bands 157·025-157·100 MHz and 161·625-161·700 MHz (corresponding to channels 80, 21, 81 and 22) are identified for utilization of the digital systems described in the most recent version of Recommendation ITU-R M.1842 using multiple 25 kHz contiguous channels.

From 1 January 2017, the frequency bands 157·150-157·175 MHz and 161·750-161·775 MHz (corresponding to channels 23 and 83) are identified for utilization of the digital systems described in the most recent version of Recommendation ITU-R M.1842 using two 25 kHz contiguous channels. From 1 January 2017, the frequencies 157.125 MHz and 161.725 MHz (corresponding to channel 82) are identified for the utilization of the digital systems described in the most recent version of Recommendation ITU-R M.1842.

The frequency bands 157.025-157.175 and 161.625-161.775 MHz (corresponding to channels 80, 21, 81, 22, 82, 23 and 83) can also be used for analogue modulation described in the most recent version of Recommendation ITU-R M.1084 by an administration that wishes to do so, subject to not claiming protection from other stations in the maritime mobile service using digitally modulated emissions and subject to coordination with affected administrations. (WRC-15)

ww. In Region 2 (i.e. N. and S. America), the frequency bands 157·200-157·325 and 161·800-161·925 MHz (corresponding to channels 24, 84, 25, 85, 26 and 86) are designated for digitally modulated emissions in accordance with the most recent version of Recommendation ITU-R M.1842.

In Canada and Barbados, from 1 January 2019 the frequency bands 157.200-157.157.275 and 161.800-161.875 MHz (corresponding to channels 24, 84, 25 and 185) may be used for digitally modulated emissions, such as those described in the most recent version of Recommendation ITU-R M.2092, subject to coordination with affected administrations. (WRC-15)

x. From 1 January 2017 in Angola, Botswana, Eswatini, Lesotho, Madagascar, Malawi, Mauritius, Mozambique, Namibia, Democratic Republic of the Congo, Seychelles, South Africa, Tanzania, Zambia and Zimbabwe, the frequency bands 157·125-157·325 and 161·725-161·925 MHz (corresponding to channels 82, 23, 83, 24, 84, 25, 85, 26 and 86) are designated for digitally modulated emissions.

From 1 January 2017, in China, the frequency bands 157·150-157·325 and 161·750-161·925 MHz (corresponding to channels 23, 83, 24, 84, 25, 85, 26 and 86) are designated for digitally modulated emissions. (WRC-12)

xx. From 1 January 2019, the channels 24, 84, 25 and 85 may be merged in order to form a unique duplex channel with a bandwith of 100 kHz in order to operate the VDES terrestrial component described in the most recent version of Recommendation ITU-R M.2092. (WRC-15)

y. These channels may be operated as single or duplex frequency channels, subject to coordination with affected administrations. (WRC-12)

z. Until 1 January 2019, these channels may be used for possible testing of future AIS applications without causing harmful interference to, or claiming protection from, existing applications and stations operating in the fixed and mobile services.

From 1 January 2019, these channels are each split into two simplex channels. The channels 2027 and 2028 designated as ASM 1 and ASM 2 are used for application specific messages (ASM) as described in the most recent version of Recommendation ITU-R M.2092. (WRC-15)

zx. In the United States, these channels are used for communication between ship stations and coast stations for the purpose of public correspondence. (WRC-15)

zz. From 1 January 2019, channels 1027, 1028, 87 and 88 are used as single-frequency analogue channels for port operation and ship movement. (WRC-15)

NOTES

VHF DSC, LIST OF COAST STATIONS FOR SEA AREA A1

(See diagrams at end of section)
N/A = Not applicable
TBD = To be decided

			Range	
Country Station	MMSI	Position	(n miles)	Status (*Associated RCCs*)
(1)	(2)	(3)	(4)	(5)

BELGIUM

ANTWERPEN	002050485	51°12'·52N 4°18'·80E	25	Operational (*MRCC Oostende*)
OOSTENDE	002050480	51°14'·03N 2°55'·75E	N/A	
Remotely controlled stations:-				
Zeebrugge		51°20'·11N 3°12'·17E	25	

CHANNEL ISLANDS (UK)

GUERNSEY COASTGUARD	002320064	49°26'·18N 2°35'·84W	50	Operational
JERSEY COASTGUARD MRCC	002320060	49°10'·84N 2°06'·84W	35	Operational

DENMARK

LYNGBY	002191000	55°45'·95N 12°28'·50E	N/A	Operational (*JRCC Denmark*)
Remotely controlled stations:-				Operational (*JRCC Denmark*)
Als		54°57'·92N 9°33'·25E	41	
Anholt		56°42'·98N 11°30'·94E	28	
Årsballe (Bornholm)		55°08'·95N 14°52'·73E	42	
Blåvand (Rx)		55°33'·47N 8°05'·00E	33	
Bovbjerg		56°31'·72N 8°10'·10E	34	
Fornæs		56°26'·84N 10°56'·72E	32	
Frejlev		57°00'·25N 9°49'·58E	44	
Hanstholm		57°06'·55N 8°39'·00E	34	
Hirtshals		57°31'·45N 9°57'·88E	31	
Karleby		54°52'·35N 11°11'·83E	36	
København/Lynetten		55°41'·83N 12°36'·80E	29	
Læsø		57°16'·14N 11°03'·16E	34	
Mern (Møn)		55°03'·18N 11°59'·37E	45	
Røsnæs		55°44'·15N 10°55'·12E	35	
Skagen (Tx/Rx)		57°44'·35N 10°34'·55E	29	
Varde (Tx)		55°39'·42N 8°40'·28E	53	
Vejby		56°04'·72N 12°07'·76E	30	
Vejle		55°40'·55N 9°30'·25E	42	

ESTONIA

TALLINN	002761000	59°27'·84N 24°21'·42E	N/A	Operational (*JRCC Tallinn*)
Remotely controlled stations:-				Operational (*JRCC Tallinn*)
Aabla		59°35'·12N 25°31'·45E	30	
Dirhami		59°12'·43N 23°30'·35E	30	
Eisma		59°33'·60N 26°17'·53E	30	
Kõpu		58°55'·12N 22°11'·89E	35	
Merivälja		59°29'·70N 24°50'·58E	30	
Orissaare		58°33'·51N 23°04'·00E	35	
Pärnu		58°22'·66N 24°34'·54E	35	
Ruhnu		57°48'·24N 23°15'·50E	28	
Suuremõisa		58°52'·10N 22°57'·53E	28	
Suurupi		59°27'·68N 24°22'·63E	30	
Toila		59°24'·90N 27°31'·78E	32	
Torgu		57°58'·67N 22°04'·75E	28	
Tõstamaa		58°18'·43N 23°59'·72E	30	
Undva		58°30'·89N 21°55'·29E	30	

FAROE ISLANDS (Denmark)

TÓRSHAVN	002311000	62°00'·87N 6°48'·01W	N/A	Operational (*MRCC Tørshavn*)
Remotely controlled stations:-				Operational (*MRCC Tørshavn*)
Eiðiskollur		62°18'·91N 7°06'·27W	53	
Hálsurin		62°13'·53N 6°36'·82W	45	
Hesturin		61°25'·42N 6°45'·29W	58	
Klubbin		62°20'·38N 6°19'·32W	69	
Mykines		62°06'·28N 7°35'·18W	64	
Slættafjall		62°20'·01N 6°47'·44W	50	
Sornfelli		62°04'·09N 6°58'·05W	74	
Støðlafjall		62°10'·22N 6°44'·75W	64	

(1)	(2)	(3)	(4)	(5)
FINLAND				
HELSINKI MRSC	002302000	60°09'·95N 24°57'·86E	N/A	Operational *(MRSC Helsinki)*
				Operational *(MRSC Helsinki)*
Remotely controlled stations:-				
Emäsalo		60°12'·23N 25°37'·48E	25	
Haapasaari		60°17'·23N 27°11'·18E	25	
Hanko		59°46'·22N 22°56'·52E	35	
Isosaari		60°06'·24N 25°03'·83E	25	
Jussarö		59°49'·43N 23°34'·58E	25	
Kotka		60°27'·16N 26°53'·59E	30	
Orrengrund		60°16'·47N 26°26'·65E	25	
Porkkala		60°01'·37N 24°20'·36E	25	
Virolahti		60°27'·35N 27°43'·35E	25	
TURKU	002300230	60°09'·78N 21°42'·55E	23	Operational *(MRSC Helsinki)*
				Operational *(MRSC Helsinki)*
Remotely controlled stations:-				
Espoo		60°10'·66N 24°38'·41E	42	
Geta		60°23'·20N 19°50'·85E	38	
Hammarland		60°11'·37N 19°44'·28E	37	
Hanko		59°50'·24N 22°56'·09E	29	
Järsö		60°01'·14N 20°00'·06E	38	
Kaarina		60°22'·60N 22°20'·30E	42	
Kotka		60°27'·27N 26°56'·98E	29	
Kristiinankaupunki		62°16'·63N 21°24'·10E	37	
Kruunupyy		63°44'·10N 23°30'·55E	42	
Li		65°32'·33N 25°15'·66E	29	
Mustasaari		63°12'·52N 21°32'·01E	29	
Raahe		64°40'·99N 24°32'·05E	30	
Utö		59°46'·85N 21°22'·08E	31	
Uusikaupunki		60°48'·40N 21°29'·00E	29	
Virolahti		60°36'·32N 27°50'·20E	33	
TURKU MRCC	002301000	60°26'·40N 22°13'·60E	N/A	Operational *(MRCC Turku)*
				Operational *(MRCC Turku)*
Remotely controlled stations:-				
Brändö		60°24'·82N 21°02'·79E	30	
Dragsfjärd		59°48'·74N 22°19'·11E	25	
Eckero		60°12'·91N 19°19'·14E	25	
Geta		60°23'·04N 19°50'·85E	35	
Hailuoto		65°01'·80N 24°36'·32E	30	
Järsö		60°01'·14N 20°00'·06E	35	
Kalajoki		64°11'·41N 24°45'·01E	40	
Keminmaa		65°49'·48N 24°29'·87E	30	
Kökar		59°55'·73N 20°51'·60E	25	
Kokkola		63°49'·96N 23°08'·30E	35	
Kristiinankaupunki		62°16'·14N 21°24'·22E	35	
Kustavi		60°38'·36N 21°13'·12E	25	
Kuusisto		60°22'·61N 22°20'·10E	40	
Mantyluoto		61°35'·58N 21°27'·69E	30	
Pyharanta		61°05'·19N 21°18'·21E	25	
Raippaluoto		63°21'·81N 21°18'·49E	35	
Utö		59°46'·86N 21°22'·13E	35	
FRANCE (Atlantic and English Channel Coasts)				
CORSEN (CROSS) MRCC	002275300	48°24'·85N 4°47'·28W	27	Operational *(MRCC Corsen)*
Remotely controlled stations:-				Operational *(MRCC Corsen)*
Bodic		48°47'·99N 3°02'·86W	25	
Cap Fréhel		48°41'·05N 2°19'·13W	28	
Crozon		48°15'·00N 4°30'·00W	31	
Île de Batz		48°44'·78N 4°00'·69W	25	
Pointe du Raz		48°02'·33N 4°43'·91W	24	
Stiff		48°28'·56N 5°03'·17W	33	
GRIS-NEZ (CROSS) MRCC	002275100	50°52'·09N 1°34'·96E	23	Operational *(MRCC Gris-Nez)*
Remotely controlled stations:-				Operational *(MRCC Gris-Nez)*
Dunkerque		51°03'·36N 2°20'·35E	22	
Saint-Frieux		50°36'·52N 1°36'·50E	38	
St-Valéry-en-Caux		49°51'·81N 0°41'·99E	29	
JOBOURG (CROSS) MRCC	002275200	49°41'·04N 1°54'·40W	42	Operational *(MRCC Jobourg)*
Remotely controlled stations:-				Operational *(MRCC Jobourg)*
Antifer		49°41'·01N 0°09'·92E	33	
Gatteville		49°41'·82N 1°15'·93W	26	
Granville		48°50'·06N 1°36'·81W	22	
Ver-sur-Mer		49°20'·00N 0°31'·00W	25	

(1)	(2)	(3)	(4)	(5)
GERMANY				
BREMEN MRCC	002111240	53°04'·26N 8°48'·48E	25	
Remotely controlled stations:-				Operational (MRCC Bremen)
Baltic Sea Coast				
Bastorf		54°07'·91N 11°41'·61E	26	
Damp		54°35'·01N 10°01'·31E	22	
Darsser Ort		54°28'·49N 12°30'·26E	12	
Greifswalder Oie		54°14'·49N 13°54'·58E	18	
Holnis		54°51'·71N 9°34'·41E	16	
Marienleuchte		54°29'·71N 11°14'·30E	21	
Rügen		54°34'·32N 13°39'·49E	34	
Stralsund		54°18'·36N 13°07'·10E	22	
Travemünde		53°57'·72N 10°52'·87E	24	
Waterneverstorf		54°20'·00N 10°36'·17E	22	
North Sea Coast				
Blumenthal		53°11'·72N 8°33'·55E	18	
Borkum		53°35'·32N 6°39'·72E	18	
Cuxhaven		53°51'·83N 8°37'·58E	22	
Helgoland		54°10'·82N 7°52'·99E	21	
Kampen		54°56'·77N 8°20'·44E	21	
Norderney		53°42'·54N 7°13'·79E	18	
Stade		53°50'·08N 9°18'·40E	15	
Wangerooge		53°47'·41N 7°51'·43E	17	
Westerhever		54°22'·40N 8°38'·41E	18	
IRELAND				
DUBLIN (COAST GUARD MRCC)	002500300		N/A	Operational (MRCC Dublin)
Remotely controlled stations:-				Operational (MRCC Dublin)
Carlingford		54°04'·80N 6°19'·24W	40	
Dublin		53°22'·40N 6°04'·15W	40	
Mine Head		51°59'·55N 7°35'·19W	30	
Rosslare		52°18'·93N 6°33'·77W	44	
Wicklow Head		52°57'·93N 5°59'·93W	30	
MALIN HEAD (COAST GUARD MRSC)	002500100	55°21'·80N 7°20'·39W	N/A	Operational (MRSC Malin Head)
Remotely controlled stations:-				Operational (MRSC Malin Head)
Belmullet		54°15'·97N 10°03'·40W	25	
Clew Bay		53°46'·07N 9°32'·01W	20	
Clifden		53°30'·39N 9°56'·23W	50	
Donegal Bay		54°22'·15N 8°31'·22W	30	
Glen Head		54°43'·63N 8°42'·68W	47	
Malin Head VHF Aerial		55°21'·32N 7°16'·46W	49	
VALENTIA (COAST GUARD MRSC)	002500200	51°55'·80N 10°20'·95W	N/A	Operational (MRSC Valentia)
Remotely controlled stations:-				Operational (MRSC Valentia)
Bantry		51°38'·41N 10°00'·10W	60	
Cork		51°50'·91N 8°27'·62W	40	
Galway		53°17'·51N 9°06'·75W	40	
Mizen Head		51°33'·36N 9°32'·59W	55	
Shannon		52°31'·44N 9°36'·34W	50	
Valentia VHF Aerial		51°52'·04N 10°20'·06W	54	
LATVIA				
RĪGA MRCC & RĪGA RESCUE RADIO	002750100	57°01'·94N 24°05'·29E	25	Operational (MRCC Rīga)
Remotely controlled stations:-				
Akmenrags (Rx)		56°50'·00N 21°03'·00E	20	
Jaunupe		57°32'·00N 21°41'·00E	20	
Jurmalciems		56°18'·00N 20°59'·00E	20	
Kolka		57°45'·00N 22°35'·00E	20	
Mērsrags		57°22'·00N 23°07'·00E	20	
Užava (Tx)		57°13'·00N 21°26'·00E	20	
Vitrupe		57°36'·00N 24°24'·00E	25	
LITHUANIA				
KLAIPĖDA MRCC	002770330	55°43'·13N 21°06'·05E	21	Operational (MRCC Klaipėda)
Remotely controlled stations:-				Operational (MRCC Klaipėda)
Nida		55°18'·00N 20°59'·00E	27	
Šhventoji		56°01'·00N 21°05'·00E	21	

(1)	(2)	(3)	(4)	(5)
NETHERLANDS				
NETHERLANDS COASTGUARD (DEN HELDER)	002442000			
Remotely controlled stations:-				Operational *(JRCC Den Helder)*
Appingedam (Tx)		53°20'·13N 6°51'·55E	25	
Den Helder		52°57'·25N 4°47'·66E	25	
Hoorn		52°38'·65N 5°05'·90E	25	
IJmuiden		52°27'·63N 4°35'·00E	25	
Kornwerderzand		53°04'·15N 5°20'·32E	25	
Renesse		51°44'·10N 3°49'·30E	25	
Scheveningen		52°05'·68N 4°15'·45E	25	
Schiermonnikoog		53°28'·54N 6°09'·32E	25	
Schoorl		52°43'·00N 4°38'·70E	25	
West Terschelling (Rx)		53°21'·43N 5°12'·83E	25	
Westkapelle		51°31'·75N 3°26'·83E	25	
Wezep		52°26'·83N 5°59'·85E	25	
Woensdrecht		51°26'·23N 4°20'·22E	25	

(1)	(2)	(3)	(4)	(5)

NORWAY

NORWEGIAN COASTAL RADIO SOUTH	002570000			
Remotely controlled stations:-				Operational *(JRCC South Norway Stavanger)*

Central Area (South of 63°00´N)

Ålesund (Aksla)	62°28'·57N 6°10'·75E	38	
Aurland	60°54'·35N 7°11'·52E	21	
Bangsberg (Mjøsa)	60°50'·77N 10°53'·85E	45	
Bergen (Lindås)	60°34'·63N 5°19'·73E	59	
Bergen (Rundemanen)	60°24'·77N 5°21'·93E	65	
Brattvåg (Gamlemstveten)	62°34'·52N 6°19'·12E	68	
Bremanger	61°50'·40N 4°59'·22E	63	
Fosnavåg (Nerlandshorn)	62°20'·95N 5°33'·18E	51	
Geiranger	62°07'·37N 7°11'·48E	49	
Gudvangen	60°52'·00N 6°50'·78E	16	
Gulen	61°02'·06N 5°09'·30E	63	
Gullfaks A (The North Sea)	61°10'·90N 2°11'·43E	26	
Hareid (Hjørungnes)	62°21'·53N 6°07'·40E	19	
Hellesylt (Ljønibba)	62°05'·02N 6°53'·48E	26	
I. Hardanger (Grimo)	60°24'·37N 6°38'·17E	69	
Kinn	61°33'·42N 4°45'·50E	44	
Måløy (Raudeberg)	61°59'·23N 5°09'·08E	32	
Molde	62°45'·16N 7°07'·97E	51	
Nordfjordeid (Sagtennene)	61°53'·40N 6°06'·50E	74	
Ørskogfjellet	62°30'·95N 6°52'·33E	60	
Oseberg A (The North Sea)	60°29'·90N 2°50'·05E	26	
Snorre (The North Sea)	61°27'·25N 2°09'·07E	26	
Sogndal (Storehogen)	61°10'·38N 7°07'·15E	80	
Sotra (Pyttane)	60°19'·09N 5°06'·54E	53	
Tingvoll (Reinsfjell)	62°55'·85N 7°55'·62E	49	

Northern Area (South of 65°30´N)

Åsgård B (The North Sea)	65°07'·02N 6°47'·60E	26	
Buholmraen (Yttervag)	64°17'·83N 10°17'·90E	26	
Draugen (The North Sea)	64°21'·25N 7°47'·35E	26	
Heidrun (The North Sea)	65°19'·75N 7°19'·60E	26	
Kristiansund (Varden)	63°06'·95N 7°42'·75E	28	
Litlefonni (Tjeldbergodden)	63°22'·80N 8°42'·92E	50	
Mosvik (Skavlen)	63°46'·32N 10°57'·05E	52	
Namsos (Spillumsaksla)	64°26'·53N 11°32'·27E	50	
Ørland (Kopparen)	63°48'·40N 9°44'·30E	55	
Rørvik (Falkhetta)	64°52'·75N 11°13'·53E	36	
Stjørdal (Forbordsfjell)	63°31'·62N 10°53'·27E	57	

Southern Area (South of 60°00´N)

Arendal (Hisøy)	58°26'·02N 8°44'·63E	23	
Bjerkreim (Urdalsnipa)	58°37'·99N 5°57'·64E	66	
Drammen (Bukten)	59°40'·38N 10°26'·02E	22	
Draupner (The North Sea)	58°11'·29N 2°28'·26E	30	
Ekofisk (The North Sea)	56°32'·56N 3°13'·03E	30	
Farsund	58°04'·32N 6°44'·67E	29	
Halden (Hoyås)	59°10'·52N 11°25'·67E	46	
Haugesund (Steinsfjeld)	59°25'·30N 5°19'·67E	47	
Heimdal (The North Sea)	59°34'·42N 2°13'·63E	30	
Kristiansand (Dolsveden)	58°08'·15N 8°08'·02E	33	
Lifjell (Sandnes)	58°55'·19N 5°47'·38E	43	
Lindesnes (Skibmannsheia)	58°01'·26N 7°03'·42E	40	
Lista (Storefjell)	58°09'·22N 6°42'·67E	52	
Oslo (Tryvann)	59°59'·08N 10°40'·20E	60	
Porsgrunn (Vealøs)	59°14'·17N 9°51'·93E	56	
Risør (Ranvikheia)	58°42'·83N 9°12'·47E	21	
Sleipner A (The North Sea)	58°22'·00N 1°54'·42E	30	
Stavanger (Bokn)	59°13'·19N 5°25'·67E	50	
Stavanger (Ullandhaug)	58°56'·42N 5°42'·40E	40	
Stord (Kattnakken)	59°52'·43N 5°29'·63E	74	
Ula (The North Sea)	57°06'·67N 2°50'·82E	30	
Valhall (The North Sea)	56°16'·65N 3°23'·63E	28	

(1)	(2)	(3)	(4)	(5)
POLAND				
POLISH RESCUE RADIO	002618102			
Remotely controlled stations:-				
Czołpino		54°43'·10N 17°14'·50E	25	
Gąski		54°14'·60N 15°52'·40E	23	
Gdańsk		54°22'·20N 18°46'·70E	23	
Jarosławiec		54°32'·40N 16°32'·60E	24	
Kikut		53°58'·90N 14°34'·80E	29	
Krynica Morska		54°22'·90N 19°25'·30E	24	
Niechorze		54°05'·70N 15°03'·90E	25	
Police		53°33'·90N 14°35'·10E	24	
Rozewie		54°49'·80N 18°20'·20E	28	
Stilo		54°47'·20N 17°44'·00E	29	
RUSSIA (Baltic Coast)				
KALININGRAD	002734417	54°53'·00N 19°56'·00E	28.6	Operational *(MRCC Kaliningrad)*
SANKT PETERBURG	002733700	59°52'·67N 30°13'·01E	27	Operational *(MRCC Sankt Peterburg)*
Remotely controlled stations:-				Operational *(MRCC Sankt Peterburg)*
Gogland		60°00'·70N 27°00'·38E	20	
Gorki		59°48'·00N 28°30'·00E	35	
Primorsk		60°20'·20N 28°43'·10E	30	
Vysotsk		60°35'·00N 28°33'·00E	35	
SWEDEN				
SWEDEN JRCC	002653000		N/A	Operational *(JRCC Sweden)*
Remotely controlled stations:-				Operational *(JRCC Sweden)*
Bäckefors		58°49'·37N 12°12'·18E	53	
Fårö (Gotland)		57°51'·73N 19°01'·97E	30	
Gävle		60°37'·85N 17°07'·75E	43	
Göteborg		57°41'·57N 12°03'·40E	50	
Gotska Sandön		58°22'·54N 19°13'·94E	27	
Grimeton		57°06'·33N 12°23'·42E	42	
Halmstad		56°47'·40N 12°56'·28E	57	
Härnösand		62°36'·53N 17°57'·70E	42	
Helsingborg		56°03'·17N 12°42'·53E	32	
Hoburgen (Gotland)		56°56'·20N 18°13'·48E	31	
Hörby		55°48'·22N 13°43'·15E	54	
Hudiksvall		61°42'·44N 16°51'·24E	60	
Jönköping		57°46'·19N 14°15'·02E	49	
Kalix		65°56'·26N 23°30'·97E	44	
Kalmar		56°40'·97N 16°33'·87E	34	
Karlskrona		56°10'·45N 15°36'·09E	29	
Karlstad		59°23'·72N 13°22'·96E	37	
Kivik		55°40'·08N 14°09'·48E	44	
Luleå		65°36'·39N 22°08'·69E	31	
Mjällom		62°59'·14N 18°23'·57E	49	
Motala		58°35'·31N 15°05'·79E	45	
Nacka (Stockholm)		59°17'·85N 18°10'·38E	50	
Norrköping		58°40'·59N 16°28'·06E	48	
Ölands S Udde		56°14'·02N 16°27'·30E	28	
Östhammar		60°15'·81N 18°04'·24E	49	
Skellefteå		64°46'·69N 20°57'·07E	49	
Södertälje		59°13'·41N 17°37'·24E	34	
Strömstad		58°56'·11N 11°11'·16E	30	
Sundsvall		62°24'·03N 17°28'·40E	41	
Sv Högarna		59°26'·63N 19°30'·09E	21	
Torö		58°49'·24N 17°50'·65E	31	
Trollhättan		58°17'·40N 12°16'·81E	36	
Uddevalla		58°22'·46N 11°49'·22E	51	
Umeå		63°50'·42N 19°49'·36E	60	
Väddö		59°58'·10N 18°50'·38E	36	
Västerås		59°38'·60N 16°24'·20E	45	
Västervik		57°43'·26N 16°25'·56E	50	
Visby (Gotland)		57°35'·58N 18°22'·24E	44	

(1)	(2)	(3)	(4)	(5)
UNITED KINGDOM				
ABERDEEN MRCC	002320004		N/A	Operational (Aberdeen MRCC)
Remotely controlled stations:-				Operational (Aberdeen MRCC)
Banff		57°38′·67N 2°31′·49W	31	
Craigkelly		56°04′·32N 3°14′·00W	42	
Fifeness		56°16′·70N 2°35′·29W	20	
Foyers		57°14′·41N 4°30′·73W	44	
Gregness		57°07′·65N 2°03′·22W	23	
Inverbervie		56°51′·10N 2°15′·68W	35	
Peterhead		57°29′·86N 1°48′·94W	27	
Rosemarkie		57°37′·99N 4°04′·41W	43	
St Abbs Crosslaw		55°54′·46N 2°12′·31W	42	
Windy Head		57°38′·91N 2°14′·67W	42	
BELFAST MRCC	002320021			
Remotely controlled stations:-				Operational (Belfast MRCC)
Black Mountain		54°35′·00N 6°01′·30W	52	
Caldbeck		54°46′·35N 3°05′·25W	51	
Greenock		55°55′·45N 4°48′·14W	21	
Kilchiaran		55°45′·90N 6°27′·29W	35	
Law Hill		55°41′·75N 4°50′·52W	39	
Limavady		55°06′·56N 6°53′·18W	53	
Orlock Head		54°40′·42N 5°35′·06W	22	
Rhu Stafnish		55°22′·27N 5°31′·93W	42	
Slieve Martin		54°05′·61N 6°09′·61W	61	
Snaefell		54°15′·83N 4°27′·66W	69	
South Knapdale		55°55′·06N 5°27′·79W	61	
Spanish Head		54°04′·02N 4°45′·81W	37	
West Torr		55°11′·91N 6°05′·68W	16	
DOVER MRCC	002320010		N/A	Operational (Dover MRCC)
Remotely controlled stations:-				Operational (Dover MRCC)
Bawdsey		51°59′·61N 1°24′·49E	24	
Bradwell		51°43′·98N 0°53′·36E	17	
Clacton		51°46′·87N 1°08′·47E	63	
Dover (Langdon Battery)		51°08′·25N 1°20′·15E	34	
North Foreland		51°22′·53N 1°26′·73E	23	
Shoeburyness		51°31′·38N 0°46′·57E	15	
FALMOUTH MRCC	002320014		N/A	Operational (Falmouth MRCC)
Remotely controlled stations:-				Operational (Falmouth MRCC)
Bude		50°49′·00N 4°33′·00W	24	
Combe Martin		51°10′·05N 4°02′·83W	46	
Dartmouth		50°21′·30N 3°35′·20W	29	
East Prawle		50°13′·14N 3°42′·55W	34	
Falmouth		50°08′·71N 5°02′·73W	24	
Hartland Point		51°01′·21N 4°31′·34W	33	
Ilfracombe		51°12′·93N 4°05′·23W	27	
Land's End		50°08′·10N 5°38′·10W	43	
Lizard		49°57′·86N 5°12′·46W	27	
Rame Head		50°19′·03N 4°13′·18W	33	
Scillies		49°55′·73N 6°18′·23W	25	
St Ives		50°13′·12N 5°28′·58W	18	
Trevose Head		50°32′·91N 5°01′·99W	28	
HOLYHEAD MRCC	002320018	53°18′·97N 4°37′·96W	15	Operational (Holyhead MRCC)
Remotely controlled stations:-				Operational (Holyhead MRCC)
Great Orme		53°19′·97N 3°51′·21W	41	
Langthwaite		54°01′·95N 2°45′·74W	41	
Liverpool		53°29′·83N 3°03′·47W	16	
Moel-y-Parc		53°13′·23N 3°18′·81W	59	
Rhiw		52°50′·00N 4°37′·82W	50	
South Stack		53°18′·54N 4°41′·17W	35	

(1)	(2)	(3)	(4)	(5)
UNITED KINGDOM				
HUMBER MRCC	002320007		N/A	Operational *(Humber MRCC)*
Remotely controlled stations:-				Operational *(Humber MRCC)*
Boulby		54°33'·76N 0°50'·59W	20	
Caister		52°39'·55N 1°42'·96E	20	
Cullercoats		55°04'·40N 1°27'·80W	25	
Easington		53°39'·15N 0°05'·85E	22	
Flamborough		54°07'·08N 0°05'·21W	25	
Langham		52°56'·53N 0°57'·24E	24	
Lowestoft		52°28'·60N 1°45'·65E	20	
Mablethorpe		53°18'·64N 0°15'·82E	31	
Newton		55°31'·01N 1°37'·21W	22	
Ravenscar		54°23'·83N 0°30'·35W	42	
Skegness		53°08'·94N 0°20'·69E	18	
Trimingham		52°54'·59N 1°20'·60E	29	
JRCC UK	002320011	50°48'·51N 1°12'·66W	25	Operational *(JRCC UK)*
Remotely controlled stations:-				Operational *(JRCC UK)*
Beer Head		50°41'·46N 3°06'·41W	35	
Berry Head		50°23'·97N 3°29'·04W	25	
Bincleaves		50°36'·10N 2°27'·00W	16	
Boniface Down		50°36'·22N 1°12'·03W	43	
Fairlight		50°52'·27N 0°38'·74E	33	
Hengistbury Head		50°42'·91N 1°45'·53W	21	
Newhaven		50°46'·94N 0°02'·99E	25	
Portland (Grove)		50°32'·92N 2°25'·18W	31	
Selsey		50°43'·81N 0°48'·23W	18	
LONDON MRSC	002320063			
Remotely controlled stations:-				Operational *(London MRSC)*
Crystal Palace		51°25'·45N 0°04'·49W	50	
MILFORD HAVEN MRCC	002320017	51°42'·50N 5°03'·20E	20	Operational *(Milford Haven MRCC)*
Remotely controlled stations:-				Operational *(Milford Haven MRCC)*
Blaenplwyf		52°21'·59N 4°06'·14W	47	
Dinas		52°00'·25N 4°53'·68W	43	
Gower		51°34'·13N 4°17'·41W	15	
Mumbles Hill		51°34'·15N 3°59'·05W	28	
Severn Bridge (W)		51°36'·72N 2°38'·77W	33	
St Hilary		51°27'·43N 3°24'·18W	42	
St Annes Head		51°41'·00N 5°10'·58W	25	
Tenby		51°41'·67N 4°41'·28W	28	
SHETLAND MRCC	002320001		N/A	Operational *(Shetland MRCC)*
Remotely controlled stations:-				Operational *(Shetland MRCC)*
Ben Tongue		58°29'·68N 4°23'·80W	50	
Collafirth Hill		60°32'·00N 1°23'·50W	45	
Compass Head		59°51'·99N 1°16'·41W	32	
Dunnet Head		58°40'·29N 3°22'·58W	30	
Durness		58°33'·86N 4°44'·13W	25	
Fitful Head		59°54'·34N 1°23'·02W	47	
Lerwick		60°08'·92N 1°08'·43W	25	
Noss Head		58°28'·75N 3°03'·08W	21	
Saxa Vord		60°49'·74N 0°50'·46W	46	
Thrumster		58°23'·64N 3°07'·43W	38	
Wideford Hill		58°59'·30N 3°01'·31W	45	

(1)	(2)	(3)	(4)	(5)
UNITED KINGDOM				
STORNOWAY MRCC	002320024		N/A	Operational *(Stornoway MRCC)*
Remotely controlled stations:-				Operational *(Stornoway MRCC)*
Arisaig		56°55'·14N 5°49'·81W	35	
Barra		57°00'·66N 7°30'·42W	34	
Butt of Lewis		58°27'·69N 6°13'·86W	28	
Clettraval		57°37'·08N 7°26'·81W	36	
Forsnaval		58°12'·77N 7°00'·35W	42	
Glengorm		56°37'·92N 6°07'·95W	47	
Melvaig		57°50'·58N 5°46'·92W	47	
Portnaguran		58°14'·80N 6°09'·81W	23	
Pulpit Hill		56°24'·24N 5°29'·15W	35	
Rodel		57°44'·81N 6°57'·30W	27	
Scoval		57°27'·92N 6°42'·13W	43	
Skriag		57°23'·18N 6°14'·53W	56	
Tiree		56°30'·23N 6°57'·84W	34	
Torosay		56°27'·49N 5°43'·76W	57	

NAVAREA II

Country Station	MMSI	Position	Range (n miles)	Status *(Associated RCCs)*
(1)	(2)	(3)	(4)	(5)
BENIN				
COTONOU	006100001	6°28'·00N 2°21'·00E	29	Operational

CANARIAS, ISLAS (Spain)

The Las Palmas (CCR) Coast Radio Station remotely controls stations on Islas Canarias and mainland Spain, located in both NAVAREA II and NAVAREA III regions. The whole network is displayed in each NAVAREA section for completeness.

Station	MMSI	Position	Range	Status
LAS PALMAS	002241026			
Remotely controlled stations:-				
Arrecife				
Orzola		29°13'·01N 13°28'·70W	47	Operational *(MRCC Las Palmas)*
Yaiza		28°55'·12N 13°47'·04W	52	Operational *(MRCC Las Palmas)*
Fuerteventura				
Fuerteventura (Gran Montaña)		28°24'·41N 14°02'·68W	55	Operational *(MRCC Las Palmas)*
Gomera				
Gomera		28°04'·98N 17°07'·10W	35	Operational *(MRCC Tenerife)*
Gran Canaria				
Las Palmas VHF		27°57'·52N 15°33'·49W	75	Operational *(MRCC Tenerife)*
Hierro				
Hierro (Tiñor)		27°47'·65N 17°56'·17W	69	Operational *(MRCC Tenerife)*
La Palma				
La Palma		28°38'·89N 17°49'·55W	75	Operational *(MRCC Tenerife)*
Tenerife				
Tenerife (Igueque)		28°18'·40N 16°30'·15W	75	Operational *(MRCC Tenerife)*
LAS PALMAS MRCC	002240995	28°08'·82N 15°25'·12W	30	Operational *(MRCC Las Palmas)*
Remotely controlled stations:-				Operational *(MRCC Las Palmas)*
La Isleta		28°10'·44N 15°25'·14W	30	
TENERIFE MRCC	002241007	28°28'·91N 16°14'·39W	35	Operational *(MRCC Tenerife)*

CAPE VERDE

Station	MMSI	Position	Range	Status
SÃO VICENTE DE CABO VERDE	006170000		N/A	
Remotely controlled stations:-				
Ilha de Santiago		15°02'·13N 23°37'·23W	70	Operational
Ilha de São Vicente		16°52'·12N 24°56'·02W	65	Operational
Ilha do Sal		16°45'·26N 22°56'·34W	33	Operational

(1)	(2)	(3)	(4)	(5)
FRANCE (Atlantic and English Channel Coasts)				
ÉTEL (CROSS) MRCC	002275000	47°39'·73N 3°12'·11W	26	Operational *(MRCC Étel)*
Remotely controlled stations:-				
Armandèche		46°42'·00N 1°55'·00W	20	
Beg Melen (Île de Groix)		47°39'·15N 3°30'·11W	24	
Biarritz		43°29'·63N 1°33'·23W	25	
Cap Ferret		44°37'·83N 1°15'·12W	22	Operational *(MRCC Étel)*
Chassiron		46°02'·82N 1°24'·65W	21	
Contis		44°05'·61N 1°19'·01W	23	
Hourtin		45°08'·54N 1°09'·57W	23	
Kerrouault		47°26'·99N 2°29'·69W	33	
Le Talut (Belle-Île)		47°17'·67N 3°13'·10W	27	
Penmarc'h		47°47'·85N 4°22'·49W	22	
Royan		45°38'·00N 1°01'·00E	28	
Saint-Sauveur (Île d'Yeu)		46°41'·65N 2°19'·80W	23	
GHANA				
TEMA	006270000	5°38'·00N 0°00'·00E	60	Operational *(Harbour Master's Office, Accra)*
Remotely controlled stations:-				Operational *(Harbour Master's Office, Accra)*
Ada		5°46'·83N 0°37'·13E	60	
Aflao		6°07'·00N 1°11'·00E	60	
Axim		4°52'·00N 2°14'·00W	60	
Cape Coast		5°07'·00N 1°15'·00W	60	
Half Assini		5°03'·00N 2°53'·00W	60	
Takoradi		4°54'·00N 1°45'·00W	60	
Winneba		5°21'·00N 0°37'·00W	60	
IVORY COAST				
ABIDJAN	006191000		N/A	Operational *(MRCC Abidjan)*
Remotely controlled stations:-				Operational *(MRCC Abidjan)*
Abidjan		5°19'·57N 4°01'·03W	50	
Gran Lahou		5°15'·77N 5°00'·65W	50	
Kouakro		5°15'·77N 3°29'·43W	50	
Marcory		5°21'·70N 3°57'·80W	50	
San Pedro		4°44'·33N 6°37'·50W	50	
Sassandra		4°57'·12N 6°05'·50W	50	
Tabou		4°24'·70N 7°21'·73W	50	
PORTUGAL				
Full DSC coverage has not yet been attained on Mainland Portugal.				
LISBOA MRCC	002630100	38°40'·78N 9°19'·34W	N/A	Operational *(MRCC Lisboa)*
Remotely controlled stations:-				Operational *(MRCC Lisboa)*
Arga		41°47'·80N 8°42'·60W	60	
Candeeiros		39°32'·90N 8°52'·00W	40	
Foia		37°18'·70N 8°36'·00W	60	
Freita		40°52'·80N 8°16'·30W	65	
Monte Figo		37°06'·00N 7°49'·80W	45	
Monte Funchal		38°54'·70N 9°16'·40W	45	
Picoto		38°26'·20N 9°08'·30W	40	
SENEGAL				
DAKAR MRCC	006631008	14°39'·00N 17°28'·00W	30	Operational *(MRCC Dakar)*
Remotely controlled stations:-				Operational *(MRCC Dakar)*
Cap Skirring	006630008	12°24'·15N 16°45'·36W	30	
Cayar	006630004	14°54'·00N 17°07'·00W	30	
Fass Boye	006630003	15°15'·00N 16°50'·00W	30	
Joal	006630007	14°09'·37N 16°50'·00W	30	
Saint-Louis	006630002	16°01'·48N 16°30'·61W	30	
SPAIN (North Coast)				
The primary responsibility for the receipt of VHF DSC distress alerts for Spain (North Coast) is carried out via CORUÑA Remote Stations. The facilities maintained at other MRCCs and MRSCs are only complementary to the Coast Radio Stations network.				
BILBAO MRCC	002240996	43°20'·78N 3°01'·90W	30	Operational *(MRCC Bilbao)*

(1)	(2)	(3)	(4)	(5)
SPAIN (North Coast)				
CORUÑA	002241022			
Remotely controlled stations:-				
Coruña				
Ares		43°27'·10N 8°17'·09W	35	Operational (*MRSC Coruña*)
Boal		43°27'·39N 6°49'·23W	63	Operational (*MRCC Gijón*)
Cabo Ortegal		43°43'·03N 7°53'·88W	47	Operational (*MRCC Finisterre*)
Finisterre				
Finisterre (Muxia)		43°04'·63N 9°13'·51W	38	Operational (*MRCC Finisterre*)
La Guardia		41°53'·42N 8°52'·25W	40	Operational (*MRCC Finisterre*)
Vigo		42°18'·95N 8°42'·27W	56	Operational (*MRSC Finisterre*)
Machichaco				
Bilbao		43°22'·35N 2°45'·75W	55	Operational (*MRCC Bilbao*)
Cabo Peñas		43°29'·53N 5°56'·49W	52	Operational (*MRCC Gijon*)
Jaizquibel		43°20'·61N 1°51'·43W	50	Operational (*MRCC Bilbao*)
Santander		43°17'·47N 4°08'·63W	60	Operational (*MRCC Santander*)
CORUÑA MRCC	002240992		N/A	Operational (*MRSC Coruña*)
Remotely controlled stations:-				Operational (*MRSC Coruña*)
Cabo Prioriño Chico		43°27'·54N 8°20'·39W	30	
Coruña		43°22'·14N 8°23'·11W	35	
FINISTERRE MRCC	002240993	42°42'·20N 8°59'·03W	40	Operational (*MRCC Finisterre*)
Remotely controlled stations:-				Operational (*MRCC Finisterre*)
Monte Beo		43°20'·26N 8°50'·17W	40	
Monte Taume		42°36'·24N 9°02'·73W	40	
Monte Xastas		43°01'·72N 9°16'·57W	40	
GIJÓN MRCC	002240997	43°33'·56N 5°42'·01W	30	Operational (*MRCC Gijón*)
SANTANDER MRCC	002241009	43°28'·38N 3°43'·27W	30	Operational (*MRSC Santander*)
VIGO MRCC	002240998	42°14'·48N 8°43'·71W	30	Operational (*MRSC Vigo*)
SPAIN (South Coast)				
CÁDIZ MRCC	002241011	36°32'·09N 6°17'·45W	30	Operational (*MRSC Cádiz*)
HUELVA MRCC	002241012	37°15'·30N 6°57'·56W	30	Operational (*MRSC Huelva*)

NAVAREA III

Country Station	MMSI	Position	Range (n miles)	Status (*Associated RCCs*)
(1)	(2)	(3)	(4)	(5)
ALGERIA				
ALGER	006052110	36°44'·60N 3°10'·85E	50	Operational (*CNOSS Alger*)
ANNABA	006053814	36°54'·00N 7°46'·00E	50	Operational (*CROSS Jijel*)
BEJAÏA	006053815	36°45'·00N 5°04'·00E	50	Operational (*CROSS Jijel*)
Note Operational 0800-1800 LT				
CHERCHELL	006052111	36°36'·50N 2°11'·49E	50	Operational (*CNOSS Alger*)
DELLYS	006052112	36°55'·00N 3°53'·00E	50	Operational (*CNOSS Alger*)
GHAZAOUET	006054119	35°06'·00N 1°51'·00W	50	Operational (*CROSS Oran*)
Note Operational 0800-1800 LT				
MOSTAGANEM	006054118	35°56'·00N 0°06'·00E	50	Operational (*CROSS Oran*)
ORAN	006054117	35°44'·82N 0°34'·33W	50	Operational (*CROSS Oran*)
SKIKDA	006053816	36°52'·00N 6°54'·00E	50	Operational (*CROSS Jijel*)
Note Operational 0800-1800 LT				
TÉNÈS	006052113	36°30'·00N 1°19'·32E	50	Operational (*CNOSS Alger*)
Note Operational 0800-1800 LT				
AZERBAIJAN				
BAKU	004231000 004232000	40°21'·21N 49°49'·87E	25	Operational (*Azerbaijan LRIT NC*)
Remotely controlled stations:-				Operational (*Azerbaijan LRIT NC*)
Alyat		39°54'·29N 49°24'·95E	25	
Astara		38°34'·67N 48°48'·39E	30	
Chilov		40°19'·63N 50°36'·74E	30	
Neftchala		39°17'·69N 49°14'·05E	25	
Siyazan		41°02'·88N 49°02'·27E	30	
Yalama		41°50'·25N 48°35'·92E	25	

(1)	(2)	(3)	(4)	(5)
BULGARIA				
VARNA	002070810	43°15'·00N 27°57'·00E	53	Operational *(MRCC Varna)*
				Operational *(MRCC Varna)*
Remotely controlled stations:-				
Beloslav		43°11'·00N 27°41'·00E	N/A	
Bourgas		42°29'·36N 27°28'·53E	23	
Emine		42°43'·13N 27°52'·18E	48	
Kaliakra		43°22'·79N 28°28'·12E	30	
Kichevo		43°15'·83N 27°57'·60E	53	
Peak Kitka		42°18'·46N 27°45'·50E	44	
CANARIAS, ISLAS (Spain)				

The Las Palmas (CCR) Coast Radio Station remotely controls stations on Islas Canarias and mainland Spain, located in both NAVAREA II and NAVAREA III regions. The whole network is displayed in each NAVAREA section for completeness.

(1)	(2)	(3)	(4)	(5)
LAS PALMAS	002241026	28°09'·44N 15°24'·85W	N/A	Operational *(MRCC Tenerife)*
Remotely controlled stations:-				
Tarifa (Southern Spain)				
Cádiz		36°38'·18N 6°09'·09W	35	Operational *(MRCC Tarifa)*
Huelva		37°12'·42N 7°01'·20W	35	Operational *(MRCC Tarifa)*
Málaga		36°29'·22N 5°12'·38W	75	Operational *(MRCC Tarifa)*
Motril		36°49'·02N 3°24'·36W	75	Operational *(MRCC Almeria)*
Tarifa		36°07'·52N 5°45'·80W	47	Operational *(MRCC Tarifa)*
CROATIA				
DUBROVNIK	002380300	42°39'·50N 18°05'·23E	30	Operational *(MRCC Rijeka)*
DUBROVNIK MRSC	002387800	42°39'·50N 18°05'·40E	15	Operational *(MRSC Dubrovnik)*
PLOČE MRSC	002383350	43°03'·00N 17°26'·00E	10	Operational *(MRSC Ploče)*
RIJEKA	002380200	45°20'·00N 14°25'·50E	30	Operational *(MRCC Rijeka)*
RIJEKA MRCC	002387010	45°19'·43N 14°26'·46E	15	Operational *(MRCC Rijeka)*
ŠIBENIK MRSC	002387500	43°43'·80N 15°53'·80E	7	Operational *(MRSC Šibenik)*
SPLIT	002380100	43°30'·40N 16°26'·37E	70	Operational *(MRCC Rijeka)*
				Operational *(MRCC Rijeka)*
Remotely controlled stations:-				
Ćelavac		44°15'·60N 15°47'·40E	80	
Hum (Lastovo Island)		42°45'·00N 16°51'·50E	40	
Hum (Vis Island)		43°01'·79N 16°06'·83E	70	
Kamenjak		44°46'·38N 14°47'·37E	50	
Labištica		43°34'·70N 16°12'·90E	80	
Razromir		45°14'·38N 14°40'·99E	60	
Savudrija		45°29'·41N 13°29'·46E	30	
Srd		42°39'·01N 18°06'·64E	50	
Susak		44°30'·88N 14°18'·09E	50	
Učka		45°17'·25N 14°12'·18E	90	
Ugljan		44°04'·30N 15°09'·57E	40	
Uljerje		42°53'·65N 17°28'·67E	70	
Vidova Gora		43°16'·77N 16°37'·07E	50	
SPLIT MRSC	002387040	43°30'·40N 16°26'·37E	10	Operational *(MRSC Split)*
ZADAR MRSC	002387400	44°07'·11N 15°13'·32E	7	Operational *(MRCC Zadar)*
CYPRUS				
CYPRUS	002091000		N/A	Operational *(JRCC Larnaca)*
				Operational *(JRCC Larnaca)*
Remotely controlled stations:-				
Chionistra		34°56'·47N 32°53'·72E	150	
Fanos		35°00'·36N 34°01'·82E	100	
Kremni		34°45'·51N 33°14'·95E	100	
Lara		34°57'·86N 32°22'·53E	100	
EGYPT (Mediterranean Coast)				
AL ISKANDARĪYAH (ALEXANDRIA)	006221111	31°11'·96N 29°51'·88E	22.7	Operational *(RCC Cairo)*
Remotely controlled stations:-				
Aḍ Ḍab`ah		31°04'·83N 28°26'·42E	27.5	
Al `Alamayn (El' Alamein)		30°49'·30N 28°59'·73E	24.8	
Balṭim		31°33'·22N 31°05'·24E	27	
Burg Rashīd		31°26'·81N 30°21'·50E	27	
Marsá Maṭrūḥ		31°21'·00N 27°14'·00E	22.7	
Ra's al Ḥikmah		31°06'·88N 27°49'·64E	24.8	
Sīdī Kurayr (Sidi Kerir)		31°02'·19N 29°38'·94E	24.8	

(1)	(2)	(3)	(4)	(5)
EGYPT (Mediterranean Coast)				
PORT SAID (BŪR SA`ĪD)	006221113		21.1	Operational (*RCC Cairo*)
Remotely controlled stations:-				Operational (*RCC Cairo*)
Al `Arīsh		31°07'·00N 33°48'·00E	27	
Bi'r al `Abd		31°01'·00N 33°00'·00E	27	
Ismailia (Al Ismā`īlīyah)		30°36'·00N 32°16'·00E	24.3	
Ra's al Barr		31°30'·00N 31°50'·00E	27	
Ra's az Za`farānah		29°07'·00N 32°39'·00E	27	
Suez (As Suways)		29°58'·00N 32°33'·00E	21.6	
FRANCE (Mediterranean Coast)				
CORSE (SOUS-CROSS) MRSC	002275420		N/A	Operational (*MRCC La Garde / MRSC Corse*)
Remotely controlled stations:-				Operational (*MRCC La Garde / MRSC Corse*)
Conça		41°44'·30N 9°23'·26E	45	
Ersa		42°58'·15N 9°22'·80E	54	
La Punta		41°57'·21N 8°41'·94E	63	
Piana		42°14'·28N 8°37'·27E	58	
Serra di Pigno		42°41'·66N 9°23'·97E	70	
Serragia		41°30'·89N 8°58'·67E	48	
LA GARDE (CROSS) MRCC	002275400		N/A	Operational (*MRCC La Garde*)
Remotely controlled stations:-				Operational (*MRCC La Garde*)
Espiguette		43°29'·27N 4°08'·43E	15	
Mont Coudon		43°09'·63N 6°00'·49E	60	
Pic de l 'Ours		43°28'·58N 6°54'·33E	52	
Pic Neoulos		42°29'·00N 2°57'·00E	79	
Planier		43°11'·93N 5°13'·84E	21	
GEORGIA				
BAT'UMI MRSC	002130200	41°38'·77N 41°38'·97E	15	Operational (*MRCC Georgia*)
GEORGIA MRCC	002130100	41°38'·80N 41°39'·13E	30	Operational (*MRCC Georgia*)
KULEVI MRSC	002130400	42°16'·52N 41°38'·08E	15	Operational (*MRCC Georgia*)
P'OT'I MRSC	002130300	42°09'·33N 41°39'·06E	15	Operational (*MRCC Georgia*)
GIBRALTAR (UK)				
GIBRALTAR (VTS & SAR)	002361001	36°08'·90N 5°21'·90W	25	Operational (*VTS Gibraltar*)
GREECE				
OLYMPIA	002371000	37°36'·00N 21°29'·17E	N/A	Operational (*JRCC Piræus*)
Remotely controlled stations:-				
Ándros		37°55'·87N 24°46'·30E	55	
Astypálaia		36°35'·98N 26°26'·43E	59	
Brochas Kritis		35°19'·00N 25°44'·00E	65	
Chíos		38°22'·57N 26°02'·73E	78	
Faistós		34°59'·62N 25°12'·42E	84	
Géráneia		38°01'·25N 23°07'·87E	98	
Kárpathos		35°28'·33N 27°09'·95E	66	
Kefallinía		38°08'·47N 20°39'·52E	107	
Kérkyra		39°44'·80N 19°52'·36E	82	
Knosós		35°16'·87N 24°56'·13E	87	
Kýthira		36°15'·95N 23°02'·83E	52	
Lichada		38°51'·68N 22°52'·78E	60	
Límnos		39°54'·31N 25°04'·76E	59	
Mílos		36°40'·60N 24°22'·93E	78	
Moustákos		35°18'·69N 23°36'·67E	84	
Mytilíni		39°04'·37N 26°21'·25E	84	
Párnis		38°10'·27N 23°43'·65E	98	
Pátmos		37°18'·08N 26°32'·50E	46	
Petalídion		36°55'·75N 21°51'·53E	83	
Pílion		39°24'·27N 23°03'·12E	104	
Póros		37°28'·05N 23°26'·23E	73	
Ródos		36°16'·25N 27°56'·07E	78	
Sfendámion		40°25'·15N 22°31'·10E	41	
Siteía		35°04'·23N 26°11'·53E	75	
Skýros		38°52'·70N 24°33'·02E	68	
Sýros		37°27'·45N 24°55'·69E	57	
Thásos		40°43'·85N 24°39'·72E	90	
Thíra		36°22'·09N 25°27'·84E	66	
Tsoukalás		40°22'·00N 23°28'·00E	68	
IRAN (Caspian Sea)				
AMĪRĀBĀD	004225601	36°51'·04N 48°17'·00E	30	Operational

(1)	(2)	(3)	(4)	(5)
IRAN (Caspian Sea)				
ANZALĪ	004225500	37°28'·06N 49°27'·06E	30	Operational
Remotely controlled stations:-				Operational
Kiyashahr		37°26'·38N 49°57'·08E	30	
NEKĀ'	004224602	36°50'·32N 53°16'·17E	30	Operational
NOW SHAHR	004225600	36°39'·05N 51°30'·05E	30	Operational
ISRAEL (Mediterranean Coast)				
H̱EFA JRCC	004280001	32°49'·00N 35°00'·00E	64	Operational (JRCC H̱efa)
Remotely controlled stations:-				Operational (JRCC H̱efa)
Ashdod	004280002	31°49'·80N 34°39'·75E	30	
ISRAEL (Red Sea Coast)				
EILAT	004280003	29°31'·57N 34°56'·06E	50	Operational (JRCC H̱efa)
Note Remotely controlled from H̱efa (Haifa).				
ITALY				
PALERMO	002470002	38°08'·39N 13°20'·61E	N/A	Operational
Remotely controlled stations:-				
Lampedusa		35°29'·98N 12°36'·09E	27	Operational (MRSC Palermo)
Adriatic Coast				
Abbate Argento		40°52'·00N 17°17'·00E	54	Operational (MRSC Bari)
Casa d'Orso		41°49'·10N 15°59'·44E	70	Operational (MRSC Bari)
Monte Calvario		42°04'·62N 14°39'·63E	52	Operational (MRSC Ancona)
Sicilia (North Coast)				
Cefalù		38°01'·00N 13°57'·00E	55	Operational (MRSC Palermo)
Erice		38°02'·14N 12°35'·43E	70	Operational (MRSC Palermo)
Forte Spuria		38°16'·10N 15°37'·32E	33	Operational (MRSC Catania)
Monte Pellegrino		38°09'·76N 13°21'·50E	68	Operational (MRSC Palermo)
Ustica		38°42'·35N 13°10'·50E	43	Operational (MRSC Palermo)
Sicilia (South Coast)				
Campolato Alto		37°16'·50N 15°12'·17E	32	Operational (MRSC Catania)
Gela		37°04'·50N 14°13'·57E	25	Operational (MRSC Palermo)
Monte Lauro		37°07'·00N 14°50'·00E	70	Operational (MRSC Catania)
Monte San Calogero		37°31'·00N 13°07'·00E	65	Operational (MRSC Palermo)
Siracusa		37°06'·00N 15°12'·00E	42	Operational (MRSC Catania)
Sicilian Channel				
Pantelleria		36°46'·85N 12°00'·29E	70	Operational (MRSC Palermo)
South Coast				
Capo Colonna		39°01'·88N 17°09'·60E	37	Operational (MRSC Reggio Calabria)
Capo dell'Armi		37°57'·35N 15°40'·82E	30	Operational (MRSC Reggio Calabria)
Monte Sardo		39°52'·00N 18°20'·00E	39	Operational (MRSC Bari)
Monte Titolo		39°59'·84N 16°35'·88E	55	Operational (MRSC Reggio Calabria)
Monteparano		40°26'·49N 17°25'·16E	35	Operational (MRSC Bari)
Punta Stilo		38°26'·86N 16°34'·66E	26	Operational (MRSC Reggio Calabria)
West Coast				
Capri		40°32'·86N 14°14'·37E	50	Operational (MRSC Napoli)
Monte Mancuso		39°00'·52N 16°13'·05E	70	Operational (MRSC Reggio Calabria)
Posillipo (Napoli)		40°51'·60N 14°12'·03E	36	Operational (MRSC Napoli)
Serra del Tuono		39°55'·17N 15°50'·03E	70	Operational (MRSC Reggio Calabria)
Varco del Salice		40°17'·00N 15°02'·00E	69	Operational (MRSC Napoli)

(1)	(2)	(3)	(4)	(5)
ITALY				
ROMA RADIO	002470001	41°47'·00N 12°27'·00E	N/A	Operational
Remotely controlled stations:-				
Punta Campu Spina		39°22'·47N 8°34'·02E	70	Operational *(MRSC Cagliari)*
Adriatic Coast				
Conconello		45°40'·42N 13°47'·93E	53	Operational *(MRSC Trieste)*
Forte Garibaldi		43°36'·33N 13°31'·83E	39	Operational *(MRSC Ancona)*
Monte Cero		45°15'·30N 11°40'·13E	58	Operational *(MRSC Venezia)*
Monte Conero		43°32'·93N 13°36'·33E	64	Operational *(MRSC Ancona)*
Monte Secco		42°58'·00N 13°51'·00E	39	Operational *(MRSC Ancona)*
Piancavallo		46°05'·47N 12°32'·43E	70	Operational *(MRSC Trieste)*
Ravenna Bassette		44°27'·12N 12°13'·17E	20	Operational *(MRSC Ravenna)*
Silvi		42°33'·87N 14°05'·53E	44	Operational *(MRSC Ancona)*
Sardegna				
Badde Urbara		40°09'·43N 8°37'·75E	70	Operational *(MRSC Cagliari)*
Margine Rosso		39°13'·62N 9°14'·03E	22	Operational *(MRSC Cagliari)*
Monte Limbara		40°51'·20N 9°09'·84E	70	Operational *(MRSC Cagliari)*
Monte Moro		41°06'·43N 9°30'·72E	57	Operational *(MRSC Cagliari)*
Monte Serpeddi		39°22'·00N 9°17'·82E	70	Operational *(MRSC Cagliari)*
Monte Tului		40°16'·00N 9°35'·00E	70	Operational *(MRSC Cagliari)*
Osilo		40°44'·17N 8°40'·38E	70	Operational *(MRSC Cagliari)*
Porto Cervo		41°08'·17N 9°32'·35E	24	Operational *(MRSC Cagliari)*
West Coast				
Castellaccio		44°25'·75N 8°55'·98E	53	Operational *(MRSC Genova)*
Formia		41°15'·08N 13°35'·97E	30	Operational *(MRSC Roma)*
Gorgona		43°25'·60N 9°53'·62E	47	Operational *(MRSC Livorno)*
Monte Argentario		42°23'·60N 11°09'·86E	70	Operational *(MRSC Livorno)*
Monte Bignone		43°52'·16N 7°44'·57E	70	Operational *(MRSC Genova)*
Monte Cavo		41°45'·25N 12°42'·62E	70	Operational *(MRSC Roma)*
Monte Nero		43°29'·42N 10°21'·65E	51	Operational *(MRSC Livorno)*
Monte Paradiso		42°05'·00N 11°51'·00E	52	Operational *(MRSC Roma)*
Zoagli		44°20'·37N 9°15'·52E	38	Operational *(MRSC Genova)*
KAZAKHSTAN				
AKTAU		43°36'·15N 51°13'·25E	20	Operational *(MRCC Astrakhan)*
BAUTINO		44°32'·33N 50°16'·22E	20	Operational *(MRCC Astrakhan)*
LEBANON				
BEYROUTH	004501000	33°51'·00N 35°32'·00E	23	Operational *(Lebanese Army)*
MALTA				
MALTA RCC	002150100	35°51'·30N 14°29'·30E	50	Operational *(RCC Malta)*
MONTENEGRO				
BAR	002620001	42°03'·13N 19°08'·87E	50	Operational *(MRCC Bar)*
Remotely controlled stations:-				Operational *(MRCC Bar)*
Obosnik	002620002	42°24'·60N 18°36'·64E	50	
ROMANIA				
CONSTANŢA	002640570		N/A	Operational *(Constanţa Harbour Master)*
Remotely controlled stations:-				Operational *(Constanţa Harbour Master)*
Agigea		44°06'·18N 28°37'·49E	25	
Enisala		44°51'·64N 28°50'·64E	44	
Mahmudia		45°05'·25N 29°04'·23E	43	
Sfîntu Gheorghe		44°53'·95N 29°36'·18E	21	
Sulina		45°08'·88N 29°45'·55E	23	
Tuzla		43°59'·45N 28°39'·98E	27	
RUSSIA (Black Sea Coast)				
NOVOROSSIYSK MRCC	002734411	44°41'·00N 37°47'·00E	26	Operational *(MRCC Novorossiysk)*
Remotely controlled stations:-				Operational *(MRCC Novorossiysk)*
Anapa		44°50'·00N 37°21'·00E	52	
Doob		44°36'·00N 37°58'·00E	51	
SOCHI	002731108	43°32'·00N 39°51'·00E	67	Operational *(MRCC Novorossiysk)*
TAGANROG	002734487	47°12'·10N 38°56'·80E	23	Operational *(MRSC Taman)*
Remotely controlled stations:-				Operational *(MRSC Taman)*
Lotspost		47°06'·00N 38°19'·00E	21.6	
TAMAN MRSC	002734446			
Remotely controlled stations:-				Operational *(MRSC Taman)*
Temryuk		45°19'·82N 37°13'·87E	28	
TUAPSE	002734413	44°07'·00N 39°03'·00E	46.4	Operational *(MRCC Novorossiysk)*

(1)	(2)	(3)	(4)	(5)
RUSSIA (Black Sea Coast)				
YEYSK	002734422	46°43'·00N 38°16'·00E	23	Operational *(MRSC Taman)*
				Operational *(MRSC Taman)*
Remotely controlled stations:-				
Kosa Dolgaya		46°40'·00N 37°45'·00E	25	
Primorsko-Akhtarsk		46°02'·00N 38°11'·00E	25	
RUSSIA (Caspian Sea)				
ASTRAKHAN MRCC	002734419	46°18'·00N 47°58'·00E	22.5	Operational *(MRCC Astrakhan)*
				Operational *(MRCC Astrakhan)*
Remotely controlled stations:-				
Iskusstvennyi VHF		45°23'·00N 47°47'·00E	25	
Olja		45°47'·00N 47°33'·00E	20	
MAKHACHKALA	002734423	42°59'·00N 47°30'·00E	23	Operational *(MRCC Astrakhan)*
SLOVENIA				
KOPER MRCC	002780200	45°32'·90N 13°43'·50E	14	Operational *(MRCC Koper)*
				Operational *(MRCC Koper)*
Remotely controlled stations:-				
Izola		45°32'·36N 13°39'·39E	35	
SBI		45°32'·67N 13°41'·21E	30	
Slavnik		45°32'·00N 13°58'·50E	85	

SPAIN (Mediterranean Coast)

The primary responsibility for the receipt of VHF DSC distress alerts for Spain (Mediterranean Coast) is carried out via Valencia (CCR) Coast Radio Station and its remotely controlled stations with VHF capability. The facilities maintained at the various MRCCs and MRSCs are only complementary to the Coast Radio Stations network.

(1)	(2)	(3)	(4)	(5)
ALGECIRAS MRCC	002241001	36°07'·39N 5°26'·55W	30	Operational *(MRSC Algeciras)*
ALMERÍA MRCC	002241002			
Remotely controlled stations:-				Operational *(MRCC Almería)*
Almería		36°49'·84N 2°28'·01W	30	
Cabo Gata		36°43'·30N 2°11'·57W	30	
BARCELONA MRCC	002240991	41°20'·09N 2°08'·54E	40	Operational *(MRCC Barcelona)*
CARTAGENA MRCC	002241003	37°34'·89N 0°57'·97W	30	Operational *(MRSC Cartagena)*
CASTELLÓN MRCC	002241016	39°58'·19N 0°01'·26E	30	Operational *(MRSC Castellón)*
TARRAGONA MRCC	002241006	41°05'·41N 1°13'·50E	30	Operational *(MRSC Tarragona)*
VALENCIA	002241024	39°25'·80N 0°28'·59W	N/A	Operational
Remotely controlled stations:-				
Alicante		38°19'·39N 0°42'·00W	35	Operational
Cabo de Gata				
Cabo de Gata		36°59'·34N 2°22'·99W	74	Operational *(MRCC Almería)*
Melilla		35°17'·70N 2°56'·06W	35	Operational *(MRCC Almería)*
Cabo la Nao				
Aguilas (Conil) (Cartagena)		37°29'·42N 1°33'·80W	55	Operational *(MRSC Valencia)*
Cabo de La Nao		38°39'·13N 0°16'·33W	75	Operational *(MRCC Valencia)*
Castellón		40°05'·21N 0°01'·95E	57	Operational *(MRCC Castellon)*
Ibiza (San José)		38°55'·02N 1°16'·72E	40	Operational *(MRCC Palma, MRCC Valencia, MRCC Cartagena)*
Palma				
Barcelona		41°25'·10N 2°06'·92E	51	Operational *(MRCC Barcelona)*
Begur		41°56'·93N 3°12'·55E	38	Operational *(MRCC Barcelona)*
Cadaqués		42°18'·13N 3°15'·01E	45	Operational *(MRCC Barcelona)*
Menorca		39°59'·13N 4°06'·85E	41	Operational *(MRCC Palma)*
Palma		39°44'·07N 2°42'·79E	66	Operational *(MRCC Palma)*
Tarragona		41°14'·99N 1°03'·44E	68	Operational *(MRSC Tarragona)*
VALENCIA MRCC	002241004	39°26'·63N 0°19'·73W	30	Operational *(MRCC Valencia)*

SPAIN (South West Coast)

(1)	(2)	(3)	(4)	(5)
TARIFA MRCC	002240994	36°01'·05N 5°34'·90W	30	Operational *(MRCC Tarifa)*

Note The primary responsibility for the receipt of MF DSC distress alerts for Spain (South Coast) is carried out via Las Palmas. The facility maintained at MRCC Tarifa is only complementary to the Coast Radio Stations network.

(1)	(2)	(3)	(4)	(5)
Remotely controlled stations:-				Operational *(MRCC Tarifa)*
Cape Trafalgar		36°11'·52N 6°01'·25W	30	
Punta Almina		35°53'·91N 5°16'·89W	30	

SYRIA

(1)	(2)	(3)	(4)	(5)
AL LĀDHIQĪYAH (LATAKIA)	004680011	35°30'·05N 35°46'·50E	50	Operational
ȚARȚŪS (TARTOUS)	004680012	34°54'·00N 35°53'·00E	50	Operational

(1)	(2)	(3)	(4)	(5)
TURKEY				
ANTALYA	002713000	36°09'·17N 32°26'·72E	N/A	Operational *(MSRCC Ankara)*
Remotely controlled stations:-				Operational *(MSRCC Ankara)*
Anamur		36°02'·27N 32°45'·57E	50	
Antalya		36°09'·17N 32°26'·72E	50	
Bodrum		37°04'·06N 27°26'·37E	50	
Çobandede		36°31'·13N 36°15'·32E	50	
Dilektepe		37°31'·72N 27°15'·52E	50	
Kazakin		36°50'·25N 29°05'·75E	50	
Markiz		36°16'·37N 30°26'·13E	50	
Ören		37°02'·21N 27°57'·19E	50	
Palamut		36°45'·43N 28°13'·00E	50	
Yumrutepe		36°15'·22N 29°27'·47E	50	
ISTANBUL	002711000	40°59'·00N 28°49'·00E	50	Operational *(MSRCC Ankara)*
Remotely controlled stations:-				Operational *(MSRCC Ankara)*
Akçakoca		40°58'·45N 31°12'·23E	50	
Akdağ		38°33'·00N 26°30'·00E	50	
Ayvalik		39°18'·48N 26°41'·43E	50	
Bandirma		40°21'·18N 27°53'·68E	50	
Çamlica		41°01'·85N 29°04'·25E	50	
Kayalidağ		39°57'·97N 26°38'·15E	50	
Keltepe(Kartepe)		40°38'·60N 30°06'·05E	50	
Mahyadaği		41°47'·65N 27°37'·48E	50	
Şarköy		40°41'·32N 27°10'·68E	50	
SAMSUN	002712000	41°23'·18N 36°11'·37E	50	Operational *(MSRCC Ankara)*
Remotely controlled stations:-				Operational *(MSRCC Ankara)*
Akçabat		41°04'·22N 39°27'·17E	50	
Dikmentepe		40°55'·50N 38°16'·15E	50	
Dütmen		41°26'·88N 35°28'·88E	50	
İnebolu		41°53'·45N 33°43'·10E	50	
Pazar		41°08'·93N 40°49'·12E	50	
Yildiztepe		41°05'·72N 37°01'·67E	50	
Zonguldak		41°23'·65N 31°49'·93E	50	
UKRAINE				
BERDYANS'K	002723672	46°45'·08N 36°46'·50E	20	Operational *(MRSC Berdyansk)*
KERCH MRSC	002723632	45°25'·90N 36°34'·42E	25	Temporarily Suspended *(MRCC Odesa)*
MARIUPOL' MRSC	002723650	47°03'·30N 37°30'·40E	20	Operational *(MRSC Berdyansk)*
ODESA MRCC	002723660	46°22'·65N 30°44'·87E	23	Operational *(MRCC Odesa)*
UKRAINE				
SEVASTOPOL MRSC	002723678	44°34'·00N 33°25'·00E	92	Temporarily Suspended *(MRCC Odesa)*

NAVAREA IV

Country Station	MMSI	Position	Range (n miles)	Status *(Associated RCCs)*
(1)	(2)	(3)	(4)	(5)
BERMUDA (UK)				
BERMUDA	003100001	32°22'·82N 64°40'·97W	30	Operational *(RCC / Bermuda Harbour)*
CANADA (Arctic Coast, Atlantic Coast and Saint Lawrence River)				
HALIFAX (CANADIAN COAST GUARD)	003160016	44°41'·04N 63°36'·60W	N/A	Operational *(JRCC Halifax)*
Remotely controlled stations:-				Operational *(JRCC Halifax)*
Cape Blomidon		45°13'·92N 64°24'·08W	40	
Chebogue		43°44'·67N 66°07'·29W	40	
Ecum Secum		44°57'·89N 62°08'·94W	40	
Grand Manan		44°36'·05N 66°54'·37W	40	
Kingsburg		44°16'·59N 64°16'·83W	40	
Lockeport		43°39'·82N 65°07'·78W	40	
Red Head		45°14'·01N 65°59'·06W	40	
Sambro		44°28'·34N 63°37'·23W	40	
Scotch Mountain		45°45'·80N 65°47'·60W	40	
Shannon Hill		44°41'·05N 63°36'·58W	40	
Tiverton		44°23'·67N 66°13'·60W	40	

(1)	(2)	(3)	(4)	(5)
CANADA (Arctic Coast, Atlantic Coast and Saint Lawrence River)				
LABRADOR (GOOSE BAY) (CANADIAN COAST GUARD)	003160022	53°18'·20N 60°31'·45W	40	Operational *(JRCC Halifax)*
Remotely controlled stations:-				Operational *(JRCC Halifax)*
Cartwright		53°43'·63N 56°58'·10W	40	
Comfort Cove		49°16'·43N 54°52'·53W	40	
Conche		50°53'·68N 55°53'·05W	40	
Fox Harbour (Labrador)		52°22'·17N 55°39'·70W	40	
Hopedale		55°27'·45N 60°12'·55W	40	
L'Anse aux Meadows		51°34'·33N 55°29'·45W	40	
Nain		56°32'·82N 61°42'·82W	40	
Twillingate		49°41'·17N 54°48'·00W	40	
LES ESCOUMINS (CANADIAN COAST GUARD)	003160026	48°19'·07N 69°25'·22W	40	Operational *(MRSC Québec)*
Remotely controlled stations:-				
Cap à l'Est		48°22'·96N 70°41'·21W	40	Operational *(MRSC Québec)*
Cap-aux-Meules		47°23'·23N 61°51'·67W	40	Operational *(JRCC Halifax)*
Carleton		48°08'·00N 66°07'·33W	40	Operational *(JRCC Halifax)*
Forillon		48°50'·03N 64°15'·50W	40	Operational *(JRCC Halifax)*
Grosses-Roches		48°54'·83N 67°06'·61W	40	Operational *(MRSC Québec)*
Harrington Harbour		50°30'·00N 59°29'·28W	40	Operational *(JRCC Halifax)*
Havre St-Pierre		50°16'·25N 63°40'·73W	40	Operational *(JRCC Halifax)*
La Romaine		50°12'·95N 60°41'·22W	40	Operational *(JRCC Halifax)*
Lac D'aigle		50°17'·35N 66°18'·68W	40	Operational *(MRSC Québec)*
Mont-Joli		48°36'·42N 68°13'·55W	40	Operational *(MRSC Québec)*
Mont-Louis		49°12'·88N 65°46'·44W	40	Operational *(MRSC Québec)*
Natashquan		50°08'·67N 61°48'·00W	40	Operational *(JRCC Halifax)*
Newport		48°13'·62N 64°47'·55W	40	Operational *(JRCC Halifax)*
Point Heath		49°05'·08N 61°42'·15W	40	Operational *(JRCC Halifax)*
Rivière du Loup		47°45'·58N 69°36'·20W	40	Operational *(MRSC Québec)*
Sacré Coeur		48°12'·83N 69°52'·23W	40	Operational *(MRSC Québec)*
PLACENTIA (CANADIAN COAST GUARD)	003160019	47°17'·00N 53°59'·00W	N/A	Operational *(JRCC Halifax)*
Remotely controlled stations:-				Operational *(JRCC Halifax)*
Arnold's Cove		47°46'·38N 53°59'·98W	40	
Bay L'Argent		47°32'·00N 54°51'·77W	40	
Cape Bonavista		48°41'·80N 53°05'·30W	40	
Cape Pine		46°36'·95N 53°32'·03W	40	
Cuslett		46°58'·47N 54°09'·25W	40	
Fortune Head		47°04'·03N 55°50'·87W	40	
Freshwater		47°15'·76N 53°59'·04W	40	
Hermitage		47°33'·57N 55°56'·32W	40	
Lumsden		49°17'·23N 53°35'·08W	40	
St. John's		47°36'·67N 52°40'·02W	40	
St. Lawrence		46°55'·10N 55°22'·72W	40	
Victoria		47°49'·90N 53°18'·08W	40	
PORT AUX BASQUES (CANADIAN COAST GUARD)	003160018	47°34'·32N 59°07'·96W	N/A	Operational *(JRCC Halifax)*
Remotely controlled stations:-				Operational *(JRCC Halifax)*
Bonne Bay		49°36'·17N 57°57'·40W	40	
Mount Moriah		48°58'·12N 58°02'·82W	40	
Pine Tree		48°35'·33N 58°39'·90W	40	
Pointe Riche		50°41'·98N 57°24'·32W	40	
Ramea Island		47°30'·75N 57°24'·52W	40	
Table Mountain		47°41'·23N 59°16'·43W	40	
QUÉBEC (CANADIAN COAST GUARD)	003160027		N/A	Operational *(MRSC Québec)*
Remotely controlled stations:-				Operational *(MRSC Québec)*
L'Acadie		45°19'·28N 73°18'·57W	40	
Lauzon		46°48'·78N 71°09'·57W	40	
Mont Bélair		46°49'·37N 71°29'·75W	40	
Mont Rigaud		45°27'·00N 74°17'·80W	40	
Mont Saint-Bruno		45°33'·42N 73°19'·55W	40	
Montmagny		46°55'·70N 70°30'·75W	40	
Trois-Rivières		46°23'·82N 72°27'·21W	40	

(1)	(2)	(3)	(4)	(5)
CANADA (Arctic Coast, Atlantic Coast and Saint Lawrence River)				
SYDNEY (CANADIAN COAST GUARD)	003160017		N/A	Operational *(JRCC Halifax)*
Remotely controlled stations:-				Operational *(JRCC Halifax)*
Cape Egmont		46°24'·13N 64°08'·03W	40	
Cape North		47°00'·63N 60°25'·68W	40	
Cheticamp		46°34'·65N 60°59'·17W	40	
Fox Island		45°19'·78N 61°04'·76W	40	
Kilkenny Lake		46°13'·48N 60°10'·10W	40	
Montague		46°11'·67N 62°39'·58W	40	
North Cape		47°03'·45N 63°59'·81W	40	
Point Escuminac		47°04'·42N 64°47'·88W	40	
Port Caledonia		46°11'·16N 59°53'·64W	40	
St. Columba		45°59'·28N 60°51'·60W	40	
CANADA (Great Lakes)				
PRESCOTT (CANADIAN COAST GUARD)	003160029	44°42'·40N 75°31'·10W	N/A	Operational *(JRCC Trenton)*
Remotely controlled stations:-				Operational *(JRCC Trenton)*
Cardinal		44°47'·28N 75°25'·34W	40	
Cobourg		44°03'·98N 78°12'·68W	40	
Cornwall		45°01'·10N 74°43'·78W	40	
Fonthill		43°03'·18N 79°18'·70W	40	
Kingston		44°15'·77N 76°40'·65W	40	
Orillia		44°34'·67N 79°17'·67W	40	
Trafalgar		43°29'·68N 79°43'·80W	40	
SARNIA (CANADIAN COAST GUARD)	003160030	43°01'·68N 82°11'·15W	N/A	
Remotely controlled stations:-				Operational *(JRCC Trenton)*
Great Lakes				
Bald Head		47°39'·79N 84°47'·69W	40	
Grande Pointe		42°23'·43N 82°24'·28W	40	
Horn		48°49'·04N 87°21'·25W	40	
Killarney		45°58'·09N 81°29'·36W	40	
Kincardine		44°07'·03N 81°41'·40W	40	
Leamington		42°04'·17N 82°39'·97W	40	
Meaford		44°30'·95N 80°34'·00W	40	
Pointe au Baril		45°33'·88N 80°19'·03W	40	
Port Burwell		42°34'·97N 80°36'·23W	40	
Rabbit Mountain		48°26'·03N 89°18'·10W	40	
Rondeau		42°25'·37N 81°50'·67W	40	
Sarnia (Camlachie)		43°01'·68N 82°11'·15W	40	
Sault Ste. Marie (Gros Cap)		46°32'·27N 84°34'·92W	40	
Silver Water (Manitoulin Island)		45°54'·05N 82°54'·83W	40	
Tobermory		45°09'·60N 81°29'·75W	40	
Wiarton		44°44'·83N 81°06'·73W	40	
COLOMBIA (Caribbean Coast)				
BARRANQUILLA	007300301	11°01'·30N 74°47'·68W	23	Operational *(MRCC Caribe)*
Remotely controlled stations:-				Operational *(MRCC Caribe)*
Puerto Velero		10°56'·90N 75°02'·45W	18	
CARTAGENA	007300501	10°25'·21N 75°33'·01W	32	Operational *(MRCC Caribe)*
COVEÑAS	007300901	9°24'·70N 75°40'·32W	26	Operational *(MRCC Caribe)*
PROVIDENCIA	007301201	13°22'·36N 81°22'·22W	21	Operational *(MRCC San Andrés)*
SAN ANDRÉS	007300701	12°31'·30N 81°43'·51W	22	Operational *(MRCC San Andrés)*
Remotely controlled stations:-				Operational *(MRCC San Andrés)*
Loma		12°32'·00N 81°43'·82W	34	
SANTA MARTA	007300401	11°12'·89N 74°13'·95W	25	Operational *(MRCC Caribe)*
Remotely controlled stations:-				Operational *(MRCC Caribe)*
Riohacha		11°32'·97N 72°54'·82W	16	
TURBO	007300801	8°04'·88N 76°44'·05W	23	Operational *(MRCC Caribe)*
Remotely controlled stations:-				Operational *(MRCC Caribe)*
Cerro Azul		8°07'·99N 76°33'·05W	55	
CURAÇAO				
CURAÇAO (JRCC)	003061000		N/A	Operational *(JRCC Curaçao)*
Remotely controlled stations:-				Operational *(JRCC Curaçao)*
Aruba (Hudishibana)		12°36'·70N 70°02'·93W	25	
Aruba (Jamanota)		12°29'·00N 69°56'·00W	25	
Bonaire (Seru Largu)		12°11'·69N 68°16'·69W	25	
Curaçao (Seru Gracia)		12°20'·00N 69°08'·00W	25	
Curaçao (Tafelberg)		12°04'·14N 68°49'·93W	25	

(1)	(2)	(3)	(4)	(5)
MARTINIQUE (France)				
CROSS ANTILLES-GUYANE (CROSS-AG)	003475000			
FORT-DE-FRANCE MRCC				
Remotely controlled stations:-				
Fort-de-France		14°36'·00N 61°05'·00W	32	
Guadeloupe				
Basse-Terre (Morne á Louis)		16°11'·18N 61°44'·97W	75	
Basse-Terre (Piton Ste Rose)		16°19'·90N 61°45'·72W	54	
Basse-Terre (Vieux Fort)		15°57'·37N 61°42'·05W	43	
Marie-Galante (Beauregard)		15°53'·80N 61°15'·68W	41	
Martinique				
Bellefontaine (Morne Capot)		14°41'·18N 61°08'·78W	62	
Caravelle (Morne Pavillon)		14°45'·31N 60°54'·72W	43	
Grande Rivière (Beauséjour)		14°52'·23N 61°10'·37W	38	
Le Marin (Morne Acca)		14°27'·56N 60°54'·06W	43	
Saint Martin				
Pic Paradis		18°04'·51N 63°03'·02W	58	

MEXICO (Caribbean and Gulf Coast)

The local VHF DSC Stations Cayo Arcas, Isla Contoy, Isla Holbox, Isla Mujeres, Lerma, Matamoros, Mezquital, Playa Linda and Tuxpan assist with SAR communications within their individual coastal areas.
The Mexican Navy is responsible for coordinating Search and Rescue operations within the limits of the Exclusive Economic Zone of Mexico in the Gulf of Mexico, Caribbean Sea and Pacific Ocean.

(1)	(2)	(3)	(4)	(5)
CAYO ARCAS	003450974	20°13'·00N 91°58'·00W	20	Operational (MRSC Cayo Arcas)
CHETUMAL	003451120	18°31'·48N 88°16'·80W	80	Operational (MRCC Chetumal)
CIUDAD DEL CARMEN	003450710	18°38'·51N 91°50'·05W	80	Operational (MRSC Lerma-Campeche)
COATZACOALCOS	003450320	18°08'·85N 94°25'·11W	80	Operational (MRCC Veracruz)
COZUMEL	003451110	20°28'·28N 86°58'·18W	80	Operational (MRSC Isla Cozumel)
ISLA CONTOY MRSC	003451175	21°30'·00N 86°48'·00W	20	Operational (MRSC Isla Contoy)
ISLA HOLBOX MRSC	003451174	21°32'·00N 87°17'·00W	20	Operational (MRSC Isla Holbox)
ISLA MUJERES MRSC	003451171	21°14'·00N 87°00'·00W	20	Operational (MRSC Isla Mujeres)
LERMA MRSC	003450772	19°49'·00N 90°35'·00W	20	Operational (MRSC Lerma)
MATAMOROS MRSC	003450172	25°44'·00N 97°33'·00W	20	Operational (MRSC Matamoros)
MEZQUITAL MRSC	003450173	25°15'·00N 97°27'·00W	20	Operational (MRSC Mezquital)
PLAYA LINDA MRSC	003451176	21°08'·00N 86°47'·00W	20	Operational (MRSC Playa Linda)
PROGRESO	003450910	21°16'·40N 89°42'·83W	80	Operational (MRSC Yukalpeten)
TAMPICO	003450110	22°12'·74N 97°51'·40W	80	Operational (MRCC Ciudad Madero)
TUXPAN MRCC (Mexican Navy - 1st Region)	003450372	20°57'·00N 97°22'·00W	20	Operational (MRSC Tuxpan)
VERACRUZ	003450310	19°06'·53N 96°08'·03W	80	Operational (MRCC Veracruz)

TRINIDAD AND TOBAGO

(1)	(2)	(3)	(4)	(5)
NORTH POST (TRINIDAD)	003621001	10°44'·71N 61°33'·80W	50	Operational (MRCC Port of Spain)
Remotely controlled stations:-				
Brigand Hill		10°30'·00N 61°04'·00W	50	
French Fort		11°12'·00N 60°43'·00W	50	
Point Fortin		10°11'·00N 61°41'·00W	50	
Runnymede		11°16'·00N 60°42'·00W	50	

UNITED STATES (Atlantic Coast)

(1)	(2)	(3)	(4)	(5)
BOSTON SECTOR (US COAST GUARD)	003669901	42°22'·11N 71°03'·14W	20	Operational (JRCC Boston)
CHARLESTON SECTOR (US COAST GUARD)	003669907	32°46'·42N 79°56'·64W	20	Operational (JRCC Miami)
DELAWARE BAY SECTOR (US COAST GUARD)	003669905	38°56'·68N 74°53'·03W	20	Operational (JRCC Norfolk)
JACKSONVILLE SECTOR (US COAST GUARD)	003669962	30°23'·27N 81°26'·06W	20	Operational (JRCC Miami)
LONG ISLAND SOUND SECTOR (US COAST GUARD) (NEW HAVEN)	003669931	41°16'·33N 72°54'·26W	20	Operational (JRCC Boston)
MARYLAND NATIONAL CAPITAL REGION SECTOR (US COAST GUARD)	003669961	39°12'·26N 76°34'·09W	20	Operational (JRCC Norfolk)
MIAMI SECTOR (US COAST GUARD)	003669919	25°46'·25N 80°08'·69W	20	Operational (JRCC Miami)
NEW YORK SECTOR (US COAST GUARD)	003669929	40°36'·25N 74°03'·70W	20	Operational (JRCC Boston)
NORTH CAROLINA SECTOR (US COAST GUARD)	003669906	34°11'·78N 77°56'·04W	20	Operational (JRCC Norfolk)
NORTHERN NEW ENGLAND SECTOR (US COAST GUARD) (SOUTH PORTLAND)	003669921	43°38'·68N 70°14'·77W	20	Operational (JRCC Boston)
SOUTHEASTERN NEW ENGLAND (US COAST GUARD) (WOODS HOLE)	003669928	41°31'·24N 70°40'·03W	20	Operational (JRCC Boston)
VIRGINIA SECTOR (US COAST GUARD)	003669922	36°53'·02N 76°21'·15W	20	Operational (JRCC Norfolk)

(1)	(2)	(3)	(4)	(5)
UNITED STATES (Gulf Coast)				
CORPUS CHRISTI SECTOR (US COAST GUARD)	003669916	27°42'·08N 97°16'·73W	20	Operational (JRCC New Orleans)
HOUSTON-GALVESTON SECTOR (US COAST GUARD)	003669915	29°43'·78N 95°15'·44W	20	Operational (JRCC New Orleans)
KEY WEST SECTOR (US COAST GUARD)	003669918	24°32'·90N 81°47'·19W	20	Operational (JRCC Miami)
MOBILE SECTOR (US COAST GUARD)	003669914	30°39'·11N 88°03'·49W	20	Operational (JRCC New Orleans)
NEW ORLEANS SECTOR (US COAST GUARD)	003669908	29°57'·15N 90°02'·24W	20	Operational (JRCC New Orleans)
ST PETERSBURG SECTOR (US COAST GUARD)	003669917	27°45'·69N 82°37'·62W	20	Operational (JRCC Miami)

Each of the DSC VHF Stations shown represents a U. S. Coast Guard Sector Command Center. These Sector Command Centers, among other equipment and functions, utilize and control equipment at the site indicated as well as at several remote radio communication facilities that comprise a segment of a VHF FM Communications system that provides voice on Channel 16 (156·8 MHz) and Digital Selective Calling on Channel 70 (156·525 MHz) coverage to a minimum of 20 miles off shore throughout the continental United States, the Great Lakes, the State of Hawaii, Puerto Rico and selected other U.S. Territories. Construction is ongoing to provide similar coverage to selected portions of the State of Alaska's coastline.

NAVAREA V

Country Station	MMSI	Position	Range (n miles)	Status (Associated RCCs)
(1)	(2)	(3)	(4)	(5)
NONE				

NAVAREA VI

Country Station	MMSI	Position	Range (n miles)	Status (Associated RCCs)
(1)	(2)	(3)	(4)	(5)
ANTARCTICA				
BAHÍA FILDES (ANTÁRTICA CHILENA MRSC)	007250450	62°12'·09S 58°57'·67W	15	Operational (MRCC Punta Arenas)
BAHÍA PARAÍSO	007250470	64°49'·38S 62°51'·37W	15	Operational (MRSC Antarctica Chilena)
ARGENTINA				
BUENOS AIRES (Prefectura Naval)	007010001	34°36'·17S 58°22'·03W	35	Operational (MRCC Rio de La Plata)
COMODORO RIVADAVIA (Prefectura Naval)	007010008	45°50'·81S 67°28'·99W	35	Operational (MRSC Comodoro Rivadavia)
MAR DEL PLATA (Prefectura Naval)	007010003	38°02'·24S 57°32'·29W	35	Operational (MRSC Mar del Plata)
RIO GALLEGOS (Prefectura Naval)	007010010	51°37'·39S 69°12'·71W	35	Operational (MRSC Río Gallegos)
ROSARIO (Prefectura Naval)	007010004	32°52'·21S 60°41'·25W	35	Operational (MRSC Rosario)
SAN BLAS (Prefectura Naval)	007010006	40°33'·00S 62°14'·10W	35	Operational (MRSC Bahía Blanca)
ZÁRATE (Prefectura Naval)	007010020	34°05'·21S 59°00'·42W	35	Operational (MRSC Tigre)
CHILE				
CABO ESPÍRITU SANTO, LIGHT	007250410	52°39'·53S 68°36'·70W	24	Operational (MRCC Punta Arenas)
PUNTA DUNGENESS, LIGHT	007250400	52°23'·69S 68°25'·84W	21	Operational (MRCC Punta Arenas)
URUGUAY				
MONTEVIDEO ARMADA	007703870		N/A	Operational (MRCC Uruguay)
Note Temporarily inoperative until further notice.				
Remotely controlled stations:-				Operational (MRCC Uruguay)
Armada Radio		34°56'·11S 56°09'·63W	30	
Carmelo (CWC22)		34°00'·50S 58°17'·70W	30	
Chafalote		34°26'·11S 57°26'·19W	30	
Colonia (CWC23)		34°28'·20S 57°51'·10W	30	
Piriápolis (CWC33)		34°52'·80S 55°16'·20W	30	
Santa Teresa		34°00'·90S 53°33'·47W	30	

NAVAREA VII

Country Station (1)	MMSI (2)	Position (3)	Range (n miles) (4)	Status (Associated RCCs) (5)
NONE				

NAVAREA VIII

Country Station (1)	MMSI (2)	Position (3)	Range (n miles) (4)	Status (Associated RCCs) (5)
BURMA				
AYEYARWADY MRCC	005061411	16°45'·98N 96°11'·77E	50	Operational (MRCC Ayeyarwady)
MYEIK	005060200	12°26'·00N 98°36'·00E	50	Operational (MRCC Yangon)
YANGON	005060100	16°42'·00N 96°17'·00E	50	Operational (MRCC Yangon)
INDIA (Andaman and Nicobar Region)				
CAMPBELL BAY MRSC	004194408	7°00'·70N 93°55'·50E	30	Operational (MRCC Port Blair)
DIGLIPUR MRSC	004194407	13°18'·01N 93°04'·47E	25	Operational (MRCC Port Blair)
PORT BLAIR MRCC	004194409	11°40'·63N 92°45'·89E	30	Operational (MRCC Port Blair)
INDIA (Eastern Region (Including Bay of Bengal))				
CHENNAI MRCC	004194401	13°05'·98N 80°17'·89E	25	Operational (MRCC Chennai)
HALDIA MRSC	004194404	22°02'·00N 88°06'·00E	25	Operational (MRCC Chennai)
MANDAPAM MRSSC	004194406	9°17'·00N 79°05'·00E	20	Operational (MRCC Chennai)
PĀRĀDIP MRSC	004194403	20°16'·18N 86°40'·08E	25	Operational (MRCC Chennai)
TUTICORIN MRSC	004194405	8°45'·01N 78°11'·45E	20	Operational (MRCC Chennai)
VISHAKHAPATNAM MRSC	004194402	17°41'·00N 83°17'·00E	20	Operational (MRCC Chennai)
INDIA (North Western Region)				
DAMAN CGAS	004192201	20°25'·00N 72°52'·00E	25	Operational (MRCC Mumbai)
OKHA MRSC	004192207	22°28'·08N 69°04'·55E	20	Operational (MRCC Mumbai)
PORBANDAR MRSC	004192202	21°37'·51N 69°37'·22E	25	Operational (MRCC Mumbai)
INDIA (Western Region)				
GOA MRSC	004192206	15°24'·74N 73°47'·68E	25	Operational (MRCC Mumbai)
KOCHI MRSC (Cochin)	004192205	9°58'·00N 76°16'·00E	20	Operational (MRCC Mumbai)
MUMBAI MRCC	004192203	18°55'·00N 72°49'·80E	25	Operational (MRCC Mumbai)
NEW MANGALORE MRSC	004192204	12°56'·22N 74°48'·29E	25	Operational (MRCC Mumbai)
MAURITIUS				
MAURITIUS	006452700		N/A	Operational
Remotely controlled stations:-				
Albion		20°12'·00S 57°24'·00E	30	Operational (MRCC Mauritius)
Belle Mare		20°11'·00S 57°46'·00E	30	Operational (MRCC Mauritius)
Cap Malheureux		19°59'·00S 57°36'·00E	30	Operational (MRCC Mauritius)
Souillac		20°30'·00S 57°31'·00E	30	Operational (MRCC Mauritius)

NAVAREA IX

Country Station (1)	MMSI (2)	Position (3)	Range (n miles) (4)	Status (Associated RCCs) (5)
EGYPT (Red Sea Coast)				
AL QUSAYR	006221112		N/A	Operational (RCC Cairo)
Remotely controlled stations:-				Operational (RCC Cairo)
Al Quşayr		26°06'·00N 34°17'·00E	28.1	
Dhahab		28°29'·00N 34°30'·00E	22.7	
Hurghada (Al Ghardaqah)		27°15'·00N 33°48'·00E	28.1	
Ra's Ghārib		28°22'·00N 33°04'·00E	28.1	
Safājah		26°45'·00N 33°56'·00E	28.1	
Sharm-El-Sheikh (Sharm ash Shaykh)		27°52'·00N 34°18'·00E	23.8	
Zaytīyah		27°49'·00N 33°35'·00E	28.6	
IRAN				
`ASALŪYEH	004225202	27°28'·05N 52°36'·05E	30	Operational
ĀBĀDĀN	004224102	30°19'·81N 48°16'·93E	30	Operational
ABŪ MŪSÁ	004225310	25°52'·31N 55°01'·03E	30	Operational
AFTAB	004224311	26°43'·17N 53°55'·52E	30	Operational
ARVAND KENĀR	004225106	29°58'·07N 48°30'·45E	30	Operational
BANDAR-E EMĀM KHOMEYNĪ	004225100	30°25'·49N 49°03'·87E	30	Operational (MRCC Bandar 'Abbās)

(1)	(2)	(3)	(4)	(5)
IRAN				
BANDAR-E SHAHĪD BĀHONAR	004224301	27°09'·04N 56°12'·82E	30	Operational
BANDAR-E SHAHĪD RAJĀ'Ī	004225300	27°06'·15N 56°04'·41E	30	Operational *(MRCC Bandar 'Abbās)*
BŪSHEHR	004225200	28°58'·90N 50°50'·07E	30	Operational
CHĀBAHĀR	004225400	25°20'·03N 60°38'·90E	30	Operational
DAYYER	004225203	27°50'·00N 51°55'·00E	30	Operational
DEYLAM	004225205	30°03'·00N 50°09'·00E	30	Operational
GENĀVEH	004225206	29°34'·00N 50°34'·00E	30	Operational
JĀSK	004225308	25°38'·57N 57°46'·38E	30	Operational
KHĀRK	004225201	29°13'·50N 50°20'·22E	30	Operational
KHORRAMSHAHR	004225101	30°26'·42N 48°10'·15E	30	Operational
LĀVAR-E SĀḤELĪ	004225204	28°15'·11N 51°16'·01E	30	Operational
LENGEH	004224302	26°33'·03N 54°53'·08E	30	Operational
QESHM	004224304	26°56'·86N 56°17'·09E	30	Operational
QEYS	004224303	26°33'·99N 54°00'·27E	30	Operational
TIĀB	004225309	27°07'·00N 56°52'·00E	30	Operational
IRAQ				
UMM QAṢR	004250001	30°02'·15N 47°57'·16E	30	Operational
KUWAIT				
AL KUWAYT (KUWAIT)	004472188	29°23'·86N 47°38'·80E	N/A	Operational
PAKISTAN				
KARACHI	004634060	24°50'·40N 66°58'·30E	30	Operational *(MRCC Karachi)*
SAUDI ARABIA				
JEDDAH	004030000		N/A	
Remotely controlled stations:-				Operational *(RCC Jeddah)*
Jeddah		21°14'·85N 39°09'·72E	30	
Sharm Abhur (Site 1)		21°43'·00N 39°06'·00E	33	
East Region				
Ad Dammām		26°26'·17N 50°06'·60E	33	
Al' Azīzīyah		26°14'·81N 50°09'·96E	33	
Al Jubayl (Jubail)		27°00'·17N 49°39'·54E	33	
Rās al Khafjí		28°26'·35N 48°29'·79E	33	
North Region				
Al Wajh		26°14'·14N 36°28'·12E	33	
Dubā		27°21'·00N 35°42'·00E	33	
Rābigh		22°48'·00N 39°01'·00E	33	
Umm Lajj		25°01'·00N 37°16'·20E	33	
Yanbu		24°05'·08N 38°02'·95E	33	
South Region				
Al Birk		18°12'·55N 41°32'·22E	35	
Al Lith		20°08'·00N 40°16'·00E	35	
Al Qunfudhah		19°07'·00N 41°05'·50E	33	
Al Shaqiq		17°43'·00N 42°01'·00E	35	
Al Shoaibah		20°40'·00N 39°31'·98E	35	
Jīzan		16°52'·92N 42°32'·53E	35	
UNITED ARAB EMIRATES				
EMIRATES	004700000		N/A	Operational *(RCC Abu Dhabi)*
Remotely controlled stations:-				Operational *(RCC Abu Dhabi)*
Abu Dhabi (Abū Ẓabī)		24°27'·57N 54°21'·29E	25	
Ar Ru'ays (Ruwais)		24°06'·00N 52°44'·00E	25	
Fujairah (Fujayrah)		25°07'·79N 56°20'·98E	25	
Jebel Ali (Mīnā' Jabal 'Ālī)		25°01'·73N 55°07'·55E	25	
Khawr Fakkān		25°21'·03N 56°22'·07E	25	
Ras al Khaimah (Ra's al Khaymah)		25°47'·43N 55°58'·72E	25	
Umm al Quwain (Umm al Qaywayn)		25°32'·29N 55°32'·46E	25	
Zirku (Jazīrat Zarakkūh)		24°53'·06N 53°04'·18E	25	

NAVAREA X

Country Station	MMSI	Position	Range (n miles)	Status (*Associated RCCs*)
(1)	(2)	(3)	(4)	(5)

NEW CALEDONIA (France)

NOUMÉA MRCC	005401000			
Remotely controlled stations:-				Operational (*MRCC Nouméa*)
Belep		19°44'·92S 163°40'·63E	43	
Boulouparis (Mont Do)		21°45'·24S 166°00'·00E	85	
Bourail		21°27'·25S 165°22'·08E	69	
Canala		21°29'·34S 165°52'·36E	76	
Île des Pins		22°35'·77S 167°27'·07E	15	
Koumac		20°27'·57S 164°12'·90E	66	
La Roche Maré		21°28'·40S 168°02'·09E	24	
Lifou		21°05'·68S 167°23'·38E	31	
Nouméa		22°15'·69S 166°27'·03E	33	
Ouvéa		20°39'·12S 166°32'·08E	22	
Poro		21°18'·92S 165°45'·54E	60	
Pouébo (Mandjelia)		20°24'·11S 164°31'·48E	75	
Prony (Oungone)		22°19'·05S 166°55'·31E	61	
Tadine Maré		21°34'·45S 167°53'·20E	30	
Touho		20°47'·85S 165°13'·73E	58	
Voh		20°57'·18S 164°41'·60E	45	
Yaté		22°10'·67S 166°56'·31E	42	

SOLOMON ISLANDS

HONIARA	005570001	9°25'·81S 159°57'·43E	20	Operational (*MRCC Honiara*)

NAVAREA XI

Country Station	MMSI	Position	Range (n miles)	Status (*Associated RCCs*)
(1)	(2)	(3)	(4)	(5)

CHINA

DALIAN	004121300	38°50'·69N 121°31'·09E	25	Operational (*MRCC Liaoning*)
FUZHOU	004122600	26°03'·00N 119°18'·00E	25	Operational (*MRCC Fujian*)
GUANGZHOU	004123100	23°09'·00N 113°29'·00E	25	Operational (*MRCC Guangdong*)
HAIKOU	004123500	20°01'·00N 110°17'·00E	25	Operational (*MRSC Haikou*)
HONG KONG MARINE RESCUE	004773500	22°12'·57N 114°15'·03E	50	Operational (*MRCC Hong Kong*)
Remotely controlled stations:-				Operational (*MRCC Hong Kong*)
Tai Mo Shan (main)		22°24'·56N 114°07'·46E	50	
LIANYUNGANG	004122300	34°44'·00N 119°21'·00E	25	Operational (*MRCC Lianyungang*)
NINGBO	004122400	30°01'·00N 121°36'·00E	25	Operational (*MRSC Ningbo*)
QINGDAO	004122200	36°10'·00N 120°28'·00E	25	Operational (*MRSC Qingdao*)
QINHUANGDAO	004121200	39°54'·66N 119°36'·37E	25	Operational (*MRCC Hebei*)
SHANGHAI	004122100	31°06'·00N 121°32'·00E	25	Operational (*MRCC Shanghai*)
TIANJIN	004121100	39°03'·00N 117°25'·50E	25	Operational (*MRCC Tianjin*)
XIAMEN	004122700	24°29'·63N 118°04'·59E	25	Operational (*MRSC Xiamen*)
YANTAI	004121400	37°25'·00N 121°30'·00E	25	Operational (*MRSC Yantai*)
ZHANJIANG	004123300	21°11'·00N 110°24'·00E	25	Operational (*MRSC Zhanjiang*)

INDONESIA (Bali)

BENOA	005250014	8°45'·18S 115°13'·08E	25	Operational (*MRSC Denpasar*)

Note This station is not H24. Hours of service are 0000-1200.

GILIMANUK	005251555	8°10'·68S 114°26'·08E	25	Operational (*MRSC Denpasar*)

INDONESIA (Halmahera)

NAMLEA	005250096	2°16'·62N 128°11'·88E	25	Operational (*MRSC Ambon*)

Note This station is not H24. Operational hours are 0400-0800.

TERNATE	005250020	0°47'·30N 127°21'·13E	25	Operational (*MRSC Ternate*)

INDONESIA (Jawa)

CIGADING	005250033	5°56'·08S 106°00'·38E	25	Operational (*MRSC Jakarta*)
CILACAP	005250030	7°44'·47S 108°59'·80E	25	Operational (*MRSC Semarang*)
CIREBON	005250032	6°43'·00S 108°34'·33E	25	Operational (*MRSC Bandung*)
JAKARTA	005250000	6°07'·47S 106°51'·27E	25	Operational (*MRSC Jakarta*)
KALIANGET	005251514	7°03'·00S 113°56'·00E	25	Operational (*MRSC Surabaya*)
MENENG	005251518	8°07'·55S 114°23'·85E	25	Operational (*MRSC Surabaya*)
SEMARANG	005250008	6°57'·61S 110°23'·55E	25	Operational (*MRSC Semarang*)

(1)	(2)	(3)	(4)	(5)
INDONESIA (Jawa)				
SURABAYA	005250001	7°13'·08S 112°44'·13E	25	Operational *(MRSC Surabaya)*
TEGAL	005251513	6°51'·18S 109°08'·27E	25	Operational *(MRSC Semarang)*
INDONESIA (Kalimantan)				
BALIKPAPAN	005250009	1°15'·73S 116°49'·22E	25	Operational *(MRSC Balikpapan)*
BANJARMASIN	005251520	3°19'·67S 114°35'·58E	25	Operational *(MRSC Banjarmasin)*
BATULICIN	005251523	3°25'·92S 116°00'·23E	25	Operational *(MRSC Banjarmasin)*
KETAPANG	005251503	1°48'·73S 109°57'·40E	25	Operational *(MRSC Pontianak)*
KUMAI	005251522	2°45'·17S 111°43'·18E	25	Operational *(MRSC Banjarmasin)*
PONTIANAK	005250016	0°01'·43S 109°18'·10E	25	Operational *(MRSC Pontianak)*
SAMARINDA	005251524	0°30'·50S 117°09'·20E	25	Operational *(MRSC Balikpapan)*
SAMPIT	005251521	2°32'·33S 112°56'·78E	25	Operational *(MRSC Banjarmasin)*
SINTETE	005251565	1°11'·70N 109°03'·63E	25	Operational *(MRSC Pontianak)*
TANJUNG SANTAN	005251554	0°02'·00S 117°31'·00E	25	Operational *(MRSC Balikpapan)*
TARAKAN	005250017	3°17'·47N 117°35'·42E	25	Operational *(MRSC Balikpapan)*
INDONESIA (Kep Sula)				
SANANA	005250025	2°03'·00S 125°58'·00E	25	Operational *(MRSC Ambon)*
INDONESIA (Lombok)				
LEMBAR	005250022	8°43'·68S 116°04'·38E	25	Operational *(MRSC Mataram)*
INDONESIA (Maluka)				
SAUMLAKI	005251531	7°58'·25S 131°18'·32E	25	Operational *(MRSC Ambon)*
TUAL	005251530	5°37'·77S 132°44'·77E	25	Operational *(MRSC Ambon)*
INDONESIA (Nusa Tenggara)				
BIMA	005251516	8°26'·55S 118°42'·52E	25	Operational *(MRSC Mataram)*
ENDE	005251517	8°50'·80S 121°40'·42E	25	Operational *(MRSC Kupang)*
MAUMERE	005251518	8°37'·00S 122°13'·08E	25	Operational *(MRSC Kupang)*
WAINGAPU	005251564	9°39'·18S 120°17'·58E	25	Operational *(MRSC Kupang)*
INDONESIA (Papua)				
AGATS	005251532	5°32'·17S 138°07'·67E	25	Operational *(MRSC Timika)*
BIAK	005250031	1°11'·09S 136°04'·67E	25	Operational *(MRSC Biak)*
BINTUNI	005250026	2°07'·18S 133°30'·07E	25	Operational *(MRSC Manokwari)*
FAK-FAK	005250026	2°56'·03S 132°17'·93E	25	Operational *(MRSC Sorong)*
JAYAPURA	005250007	2°31'·11S 140°43'·29E	25	Operational *(MRSC Jayapura)*
MANOKWARI	005250023	0°51'·93S 134°04'·58E	20	Operational *(MRSC Manokwari)*
MERAUKE	005250021	8°28'·78S 140°23'·63E	25	Operational *(MRSC Merauke)*
SERUI	005251567	1°53'·20S 136°14'·45E	25	Operational *(MRSC Biak)*
SORONG	005250011	0°53'·05S 131°16'·48E	25	Operational *(MRSC Sorong)*
INDONESIA (Riau)				
NATUNA	005251505	3°40'·00N 108°07'·73E	25	Operational *(MRSC Tanjung Pinang)*
INDONESIA (Seram)				
AMBOINA	005250006	3°41'·84S 128°11'·06E	25	Operational *(MRSC Ambon)*
INDONESIA (Sulawesi)				
BAUBAU	005251526	5°29'·23S 122°34'·52E	25	Operational *(MRSC Kendan)*
BITUNG	005250005	1°27'·42N 125°11'·19E	25	Operational *(MRSC Menado)*
KENDARI	005250019	3°58'·00S 122°34'·33E	25	Operational *(MRSC Kendari)*
MAKASSAR	005250002	5°06'·57S 119°26'·33E	25	Operational *(MRSC Makassar)*
MANADO	005251529	1°29'·72N 124°50'·42E	25	Operational *(MRSC Menado)*
PANTOLOAN	005250018	0°39'·90S 119°44'·75E	25	Operational *(MRSC Palu)*
PAREPARE	005251525	4°01'·05S 119°37'·73E	25	Operational *(MRSC Makassar)*
POSO	005251527	1°22'·85S 120°45'·32E	25	Operational *(MRSC Palu)*
TAHUNA	005250024	3°35'·33N 125°30'·17E	25	Operational *(MRSC Menado)*
TOLI-TOLI	005251528	1°03'·13N 120°48'·05E	25	Operational *(MRSC Palu)*
INDONESIA (Sumatera)				
AIR BANGIS	005251558	0°12'·33N 99°22'·33E	25	Operational *(MRSC Padang)*
BATU AMPAR	005250012	1°09'·45N 104°00'·87E	25	Operational *(MRSC Tanjung Pinang)*
BELAWAN	005250003	3°43'·28N 98°40'·13E	25	Operational *(MRSC Medan)*
BENGKALIS	005250034	1°28'·65N 102°06'·57E	25	Operational *(MRSC Pekanbaru)*
BENGKULU	005250062	3°53'·98S 102°18'·53E	25	Operational *(MRSC Bengkulu)*
DABO SINGKEP	005251559	0°30'·17S 104°34'·00E	25	Operational *(MRSC Tanjung Pinang)*
DUMAI	005250004	1°41'·17N 101°27'·33E	25	Operational *(MRSC Pekanbaru)*

(1)	(2)	(3)	(4)	(5)
INDONESIA (Sumatera)				
GUNUNG SITOLI	005251556	1°16'·88N 97°37'·27E	25	Operational *(MRSC Medan)*
JAMBI	005251510	1°36'·40S 103°34'·87E	25	Operational *(MRSC Jambi)*
KUALA LANGSA	005251562	4°31'·63N 98°01'·08E	25	Operational *(MRSC Banda Aceh)*
KUALA TANJUNG	005251504	3°21'·72N 99°26'·39E	25	Operational *(MRSC Medan)*
KUALA TUNGKAL	005251511	0°49'·38S 103°27'·50E	25	Operational *(MRSC Pekanbaru)*
LHOKSEUMAWE	005251503	5°12'·68N 97°02'·35E	25	Operational *(MRSC Banda Aceh)*
MUNTOK	005250546	2°03'·37S 105°09'·07E	25	Operational *(MRSC Pangkal Pinang)*
PALEMBANG	005251507	2°58'·13S 104°46'·93E	25	Operational *(MRSC Palembang)*
PANGKAL BALAM	005251508	2°06'·12S 106°07'·82E	25	Operational *(MRSC Tanjung Pinang)*
PANGKALAN SUSU	005251563	4°06'·80N 98°12'·35E	25	Operational *(MRSC Medan)*
PANJANG	005250013	5°28'·29S 105°19'·23E	25	Operational *(MRSC Lampung)*
RENGAT	005251560	0°28'·48S 102°41'·17E	25	Operational *(MRSC Pekanbaru)*
SABANG	005251501	5°52'·83N 95°19'·97E	25	Operational *(MRSC Banda Aceh)*
SEI KOLAK KIJANG	005250029	0°51'·07N 104°36'·52E	25	Operational *(MRSC Tanjung Pinang)*
SELAT PANJANG	005251561	1°01'·25N 102°43'·17E	25	Operational *(MRSC Pekanbaru)*
SIBOLGA	005250028	1°44'·48N 98°46'·59E	25	Operational *(MRSC Medan)*
SIPORA	005250047	2°12'·12S 99°41'·28E	25	Operational *(MRSC Padang)*
TANJUNG BALAI ASAHAN	005251552	2°58'·00N 99°48'·40E	25	Operational *(MRSC Medan)*
TANJUNG PANDAN	005251553	2°44'·63S 107°37'·78E	25	Operational *(MRSC Pangkal Pingang)*
TANJUNG UBAN	005251506	1°04'·05N 104°13'·47E	25	Operational *(MRSC Tanjung Pinang)*
TAPAK TUAN	005251502	3°16'·32N 97°09'·80E	25	Operational *(MRSC Banda Aceh)*
TELUK BAYUR	005250075	1°00'·17S 100°21'·92E	25	Operational *(MRSC Padang)*
TELUK DALAM	005251557	0°33'·87N 97°49'·08E	25	Operational *(MRSC Padang, MRSC Medan)*
INDONESIA (Timor)				
KUPANG	005250010	10°12'·82S 123°37'·08E	25	Operational *(MRSC Kupang)*
KOREA, NORTH				
CHOLSAN (COAST RADIO STATION)	004451016	39°36'·72N 124°32'·50E	25	Operational *(MRCC DPR Korea)*
HONGWON (COAST RADIO STATION)	004451009	39°59'·50N 127°56'·28E	25	Operational *(MRCC DPR Korea)*
HWADAE (COAST RADIO STATION)	004451005	40°48'·21N 129°31'·39E	25	Operational *(MRCC DPR Korea)*
KANGWON PROVINCE MRSC	004451013	39°07'·79N 127°44'·58E	25	Operational *(MRCC DPR Korea)*
KIM CHAEK (COAST RADIO STATION)	004451006	40°39'·25N 129°11'·95E	25	Operational *(MRCC DPR Korea)*
KOSONG (COAST RADIO STATION)	004451014	38°51'·40N 128°03'·34E	25	Operational *(MRCC DPR Korea)*
KUMYA (COAST RADIO STATION)	004451011	39°26'·81N 127°31'·19E	25	Operational *(MRCC DPR Korea)*
KWAKSAN (COAST RADIO STATION)	004451018	39°34'·38N 125°07'·57E	25	Operational *(MRCC DPR Korea)*
MYONGCHON (COAST RADIO STATION)	004451004	41°02'·97N 129°43'·17E	25	Operational *(MRCC DPR Korea)*
NAMPHO MRSC	004451021	38°43'·62N 125°24'·60E	25	Operational *(MRCC DPR Korea)*
NORTH HAMGYONG PROVINCE MRSC	004451029	41°45'·85N 129°50'·93E	25	Operational *(MRCC DPR Korea)*
NORTH PHYONGAN PROVINCE MRSC	004451015	39°54'·36N 124°18'·84E	25	Operational *(MRCC DPR Korea)*
ONCHON (COAST RADIO STATION)	004451020	38°50'·44N 125°11'·83E	25	Operational *(MRCC DPR Korea)*
ONGJIN (COAST RADIO STATION)	004451025	37°55'·56N 124°58'·85E	25	Operational *(MRCC DPR Korea)*
ORANG (COAST RADIO STATION)	004451003	41°22'·79N 129°47'·73E	25	Operational *(MRCC DPR Korea)*
RASON MRSC	004451001	42°18'·85N 130°27'·00E	25	Operational *(MRCC DPR Korea)*
RIWON (COAST RADIO STATION)	004451008	40°11'·04N 128°36'·77E	25	Operational *(MRCC DPR Korea)*
RYONGYON (COAST RADIO STATION)	004451024	38°11'·18N 124°47'·11E	25	Operational *(MRCC DPR Korea)*
SINAM (COAST RADIO STATION)	004451002	41°45'·83N 129°50'·91E	25	Operational *(MRCC DPR Korea)*
SONCHON (COAST RADIO STATION)	004451017	39°31'·95N 124°52'·28E	25	Operational *(MRCC DPR Korea)*
SOUTH HAMGYONG PROVINCE MRSC	004451012	39°49'·38N 127°39'·53E	25	Operational *(MRCC DPR Korea)*
SOUTH HWANGHAE PROVINCE MRSC	004451027	37°47'·66N 125°37'·12E	25	Operational *(MRCC DPR Korea)*
SOUTH PHYONGAN PROVINCE MRSC	004451019	39°12'·18N 125°20'·32E	25	Operational *(MRCC DPR Korea)*
TANCHON (COAST RADIO STATION)	004451007	40°24'·03N 128°53'·95E	25	Operational *(MRCC DPR Korea)*
TUNGAM (COAST RADIO STATION)	004451026	37°40'·82N 125°20'·48E	25	Operational *(MRCC DPR Korea)*
UNRYUL (COAST RADIO STATION)	004451022	38°36'·24N 125°04'·48E	25	Operational *(MRCC DPR Korea)*
KOREA, SOUTH				
CHEJU (JEJU)				
Remotely controlled stations:-				Operational *(MRCC Cheju)*
Cheju (Jeju)	004400701	33°18'·97N 126°20'·82E	25	
Seogwipo	004400702	33°14'·41N 126°33'·72E	25	
CHEJU (JEJU) MRCC	004401005	33°31'·25N 126°32'·50E	25	Operational *(MRCC Cheju)*

(1)	(2)	(3)	(4)	(5)
KOREA, SOUTH				
INCH'ŎN (INCHEON)				
Remotely controlled stations:-				Operational *(MRCC Inch'ŏn)*
Deokjeokdo	004400004	37°13'·50N 126°08'·58E	25	
Yeongjongdo	004400003	37°29'·00N 126°33'·00E	25	
INCH'ŎN (INCHEON) MRCC	004401001	37°27'·33N 126°36'·23E	25	Operational *(MRCC Inch'ŏn)*
KANGNUNG				
Remotely controlled stations:-				Operational *(MRCC Tonghae)*
Jeongdongjin	004400602	37°42'·00N 129°00'·00E	25	
Samcheok	004400603	37°26'·00N 129°10'·00E	25	
Tonghae (Donghae)	004400604	38°11'·00N 128°35'·00E	25	
KUNSAN (GUNSAN)				
Remotely controlled stations:-				Operational *(MRCC Inch'ŏn)*
Boryeong	004400201	36°18'·00N 126°38'·00E	25	
Kunsan (Gunsan)	004400501	35°57'·00N 126°41'·00E	25	
MOKP'O (MOKPO)				
Remotely controlled stations:-				Operational *(MRCC Mokp'o)*
Anjwa Do	004400304	34°44'·00N 126°07'·00E	25	
Daedunsan	004400310	34°27'·00N 126°37'·27E	25	
Heuksando	004400308	34°41'·00N 125°26'·90E	25	
Imja Do	004400307	35°07'·58N 126°06'·25E	25	
Mokp'o (Mokpo)	004400309	34°48'·00N 126°24'·00E	25	
MOKP'O (MOKPO) MRCC	004401003	34°47'·15N 126°39'·37E	25	Operational *(MRCC Mokp'o)*
P'OHANG				
Remotely controlled stations:-				Operational *(MRCC Tonghae)*
Chuksan	004400401	36°30'·00N 129°26'·00E	25	
Hyeonjongsan	004400402	36°51'·00N 129°24'·00E	25	
PUSAN (BUSAN)				
Remotely controlled stations:-				Operational *(MRCC Pusan)*
Jinhae	004400106	35°09'·00N 128°44'·00E	25	
Pusan (Busan)	004400105	35°08'·00N 129°02'·00E	25	
Tongyeong	004400103	34°48'·00N 128°25'·00E	25	
Yŏng Do	004400101	35°05'·06N 129°03'·27E	25	
PUSAN (BUSAN) MRCC	004401004	35°04'·70N 129°04'·68E	25	Operational *(MRCC Pusan)*
TONGHAE (DONGHAE) MRCC	004401002	37°31'·23N 129°06'·82E	25	Operational *(MRCC Tonghae)*
ULLUNG (ULREUNG)				
Remotely controlled stations:-				Operational *(MRCC Tonghae)*
Ullung (Ulreung) North	004400404	37°32'·00N 130°52'·00E	25	
Ullung (Ulreung) South	004400403	37°28'·04N 130°52'·62E	25	
ULSAN	004400102	35°35'·00N 129°24'·00E	25	Operational *(MRCC Pusan)*
YEOSU				
Remotely controlled stations:-				Operational *(MRCC Mokp'o)*
Gwangyang	004400104	34°59'·00N 127°52'·00E	25	
Oenarodo	004400306	34°26'·00N 127°30'·00E	25	
Yeosu	004400305	34°45'·00N 127°44'·00E	25	
MALAYSIA (Sabah)				
KOTA KINABALU	005330013	6°02'·00N 116°12'·00E	75	Operational *(MRCC Putrajaya)*
LABUAN	005330014	5°17'·00N 115°15'·00E	22	Operational *(MRCC Putrajaya)*
Note Network remotely controlled from Penang.				
MALAYSIA (Sarawak)				
BINTULU	005330012	3°13'·00N 113°05'·00E	48	Operational *(MRCC Putrajaya)*
KUCHING	005330011	1°35'·00N 110°11'·00E	85	Operational *(MRCC Port Klang)*
Note Network remotely controlled from Penang.				
MALAYSIA, PENINSULAR				
BUKIT KEMUNING	005330008	4°19'·00N 103°28'·00E	57	Operational *(MRCC Putrajaya)*
GUNUNG BERINCHANG	005330003	4°31'·00N 101°23'·00E	117	Operational *(MRCC Putrajaya)*
GUNUNG JERAI	005330001	5°47'·00N 100°26'·00E	95	Operational *(MRCC Putrajaya)*
GUNUNG LEDANG	005330005	2°03'·08N 102°33'·93E	95	Operational *(MRCC Putrajaya)*
KUALA ROMPIN	005330007	2°48'·00N 103°29'·00E	38	Operational *(MRCC Putrajaya)*
KUALA TERENGGANU	005330009	5°18'·00N 103°08'·00E	55	Operational *(MRCC Putrajaya)*
MACHANG	005330010	5°42'·00N 102°17'·00E	70	Operational *(MRCC Putrajaya)*
PULAU TIOMAN	005330006	2°48'·00N 104°12'·00E	27	Operational *(MRCC Putrajaya)*
ULU KALI	005330004	3°26'·00N 101°47'·00E	114	Operational *(MRCC Putrajaya)*
Note Network remotely controlled from Penang.				

(1)	(2)	(3)	(4)	(5)
PHILIPPINES				
MANILA RESCUE COORDINATION CENTRE - NATIONAL HEADQUARTERS PHILIPPINE COAST GUARD (NHPCG) (MRCC PHILIPPINES)	005480020	14°35'·15N 121°01'·00E	25	Operational
Remotely controlled stations:-				Operational
Aparri		18°21'·58N 121°37'·82E	25	
Bacalod		10°28'·68N 123°25'·33E	25	
Basco		20°26'·88N 121°58'·07E	25	
Bataan		14°38'·50N 120°28'·90E	25	
Batangas		13°45'·00N 121°02'·62E	25	
Bislig		8°12'·90N 126°18'·67E	25	
Brooke's Point		8°46'·33N 117°49'·95E	25	
Butuan		8°57'·00N 125°32'·65E	25	
Cagayan de Oro		8°29'·78N 124°39'·63E	25	
Calapan		13°25'·67N 121°11'·70E	25	
Caticlan		11°56'·28N 121°57'·05E	25	
Cebu		10°16'·30N 123°53'·88E	25	
Coron		11°59'·48N 120°12'·70E	25	
Cotobato		7°12'·28N 124°09'·77E	25	
Currimao		17°59'·20N 120°29'·33E	25	
Cuyo		10°50'·13N 121°00'·40E	25	
Dapitan		8°37'·67N 123°23'·73E	25	
Davao		7°08'·00N 125°40'·00E	25	
General Santos		6°05'·57N 125°09'·27E	25	
Iligan		8°13'·83N 124°13'·98E	25	
Iloilo		10°41'·37N 122°34'·32E	25	
Jolo		6°03'·37N 121°00'·00E	25	
Legaspi		13°08'·58N 123°45'·52E	25	
Liminang Cong		10°49'·62N 119°31'·05E	25	
Lucena		13°54'·00N 121°38'·00E	25	
Maasin		10°07'·90N 124°50'·13E	25	
Mapun		6°58'·35N 118°30'·55E	25	
Masbate		12°22'·20N 123°36'·95E	25	
Mati		6°57'·10N 126°12'·90E	25	
Puerto Real		14°40'·25N 121°36'·78E	25	
Romblon		12°34'·67N 122°16'·13E	25	
Roxas		11°36'·25N 122°42'·57E	25	
San Fernando		16°36'·52N 120°17'·70E	25	
San Jose		12°20'·00N 121°05'·00E	25	
San Jose de Buenavista		10°44'·28N 121°56'·27E	25	
Sarangani		5°24'·75N 125°25'·53E	25	
Sorsogon		12°58'·02N 124°00'·23E	25	
Sual		16°04'·55N 120°29'·33E	25	
Subic		14°52'·57N 120°17'·42E	25	
Tacloban		11°03'·90N 125°01'·40E	25	
Tagbilaran		9°38'·93N 123°50'·83E	25	
Zamboanga		6°54'·22N 122°04'·27E	25	
SINGAPORE				
SINGAPORE PORT OPERATIONS CONTROL MRCC	005630002	1°16'·39N 103°50'·63E	25	Operational *(Port Operations Control Centre)*

(1)	(2)	(3)	(4)	(5)
TAIWAN				
KEELUNG	004162019		N/A	Operational
Remotely controlled stations:-				Operational
Anmashan (North)		24°16′·17N 121°00′·16E	86	
Anmashan (West)		24°16′·17N 121°00′·16E	86	
Baisha		23°40′·00N 119°35′·47E	17	
Caoshan		25°05′·38N 121°52′·27E	51	
Fukueichiao		25°13′·40N 121°31′·23E	40	
Hotien Shan		23°52′·46N 121°34′·52E	42	
Hsichuan Shuan		22°41′·04N 121°01′·07E	40	
Jinmen		24°27′·33N 118°22′·15E	27	
Keelung		25°08′·05N 121°45′·19E	22	
Mazu (Matzu)		26°13′·32N 119°59′·18E	27	
San-I		24°23′·47N 121°44′·05E	43	
Shou Shan		22°38′·37N 120°15′·78E	39	
Taiho Shan		22°14′·27N 120°51′·02E	46	
Taping		23°35′·00N 120°33′·07E	49	
Tapingding		22°01′·18N 120°41′·39E	31	
Yingtzuling (North East)		24°53′·57N 121°47′·39E	65	
Yingtzuling (South East)		24°53′·57N 121°47′·39E	65	
THAILAND				
BANGKOK	005671000		N/A	Operational *(RCC Bangkok)*
Remotely controlled stations:-				
Phetchaburi Station		12°59′·74N 100°03′·30E	27	
Sriracha		13°11′·00N 100°57′·00E	27	Operational *(RCC Bangkok)*
VIETNAM				
BAC LIEU	005743040	9°41′·65N 106°34′·42E	30	Operational *(MRCC Vung Tau)*
BACH LONG VI	005741050	20°07′·98N 107°43′·52E	30	Operational *(MRCC Hai Phong)*
BEN THUY	005741070	18°48′·83N 105°43′·12E	30	Operational *(MRCC Hai Phong)*
CA MAU	005743070	9°11′·38N 105°08′·02E	30	Operational *(MRCC Vung Tau)*
CAM RANH	005742090	12°04′·78N 109°10′·92E	30	Operational *(MRCC Nha Trang)*
CAN THO	005743050	10°04′·30N 105°45′·53E	30	Operational *(MRCC Vung Tau)*
CON DAO	005743060	8°40′·02N 106°34′·77E	30	Operational *(MRCC Vung Tau)*
CUA ONG	005741020	21°01′·57N 107°22′·00E	30	Operational *(MRCC Hai Phong)*
CUA VIET	005742010	16°53′·82N 107°11′·25E	30	Operational *(MRCC Đa Nang)*
ĐA NANG	005742030	16°11′·53N 108°08′·22E	30	Operational *(MRCC Đa Nang)*
DUNG QUAT	005742040	15°13′·05N 108°54′·95E	30	Operational *(MRCC Đa Nang)*
HA TIEN	005743090	10°08′·77N 104°36′·12E	30	Operational *(MRCC Vung Tau)*
HAI PHONG	005741040	20°48′·05N 106°42′·62E	30	Operational *(MRCC Hai Phong)*
HO CHI MINH	005743030	10°42′·20N 106°43′·73E	30	Operational *(MRCC Vung Tau)*
HON GAI	005741030	20°57′·35N 107°04′·12E	30	Operational *(MRCC Hai Phong)*
HON LA	005741080	17°57′·65N 106°29′·87E	30	Operational *(MRCC Hai Phong)*
HUÉ	005742020	16°33′·03N 107°38′·47E	30	Operational *(MRCC Đa Nang)*
KIEN GIANG	005743080	9°59′·48N 105°06′·15E	30	Operational *(MRCC Vung Tau)*
LY SON	005742050	14°16′·35N 109°10′·60E	30	Operational *(MRCC Đa Nang)*
MONG CAI	005741010	21°31′·55N 107°57′·98E	30	Operational *(MRCC Hai Phong)*
NHA TRANG	005742080	12°12′·77N 109°12′·60E	30	Operational *(MRCC Nha Trang)*
PHAN RANG	005742100	11°33′·85N 109°00′·70E	30	Operational *(MRCC Nha Trang)*
PHAN THIET	005743010	10°55′·07N 108°06′·37E	30	Operational *(MRCC Vung Tau)*
PHU QUOC	005743110	10°01′·48N 104°00′·87E	30	Operational *(MRCC Vung Tau)*
PHU YEN	005742070	13°06′·37N 109°18′·68E	30	Operational *(MRCC Nha Trang)*
QUY NHON	005742060	13°46′·67N 109°14′·35E	30	Operational *(MRCC Đa Nang)*
THANH HOA	005741060	19°20′·97N 105°47′·60E	30	Operational *(MRCC Hai Phong)*
THO CHU	005743100	10°22′·98N 104°26′·73E	30	Operational *(MRCC Vung Tau)*
VIETNAM				
VUNG TAU	005743020	10°21′·58N 107°04′·00E	30	Operational *(MRCC Vung Tau)*

NAVAREA XII

Country Station (1)	MMSI (2)	Position (3)	Range (n miles) (4)	Status (*Associated RCCs*) (5)
CANADA (Pacific Coast)				
PRINCE RUPERT (CANADIAN COAST GUARD)	003160013	54°19'·80N 130°16'·70W	N/A	Operational *(JRCC Victoria)* Operational *(JRCC Victoria)*
Remotely controlled stations:-				
Calvert Island		51°35'·35N 128°00'·72W	40	
Cumshewa		53°09'·55N 131°59'·78W	40	
Dundas Island		54°31'·27N 130°54'·92W	40	
Eliza Dome		49°52'·38N 127°07'·38W	40	
Holberg		50°38'·39N 128°08'·22W	40	
Klemtu		52°34'·75N 128°33'·75W	40	
Mount Gil		53°15'·77N 129°11'·70W	40	
Mount Hays		54°17'·20N 130°18'·82W	40	
Mount Ozzard		48°57'·55N 125°29'·58W	40	
Naden Harbour		53°57'·30N 132°56'·50W	40	
Rose Inlet		52°13'·30N 131°12'·90W	40	
VICTORIA (CANADIAN COAST GUARD)	003160011	48°39'·10N 123°26'·80W	N/A	Operational *(JRCC Victoria)* Operational *(JRCC Victoria)*
Remotely controlled stations:-				
Annacis Island		49°11'·58N 122°55'·15W	40	
Bowen Island		49°20'·73N 123°23'·17W	40	
Discovery Mountain		50°19'·42N 125°22'·27W	40	
Mount Helmcken		48°24'·12N 123°34'·28W	40	
Mount Newton		48°36'·80N 123°26'·58W	40	
Mount Parke		48°50'·38N 123°17'·68W	40	
Port Hardy		50°41'·58N 127°41'·88W	40	
Texada Island		49°41'·88N 124°26'·34W	40	
Vancouver		49°17'·08N 123°06'·73W	40	
Watts Point (Howe Sound)		49°38'·90N 123°12'·60W	40	
COLOMBIA (Pacific Coast)				
BUENAVENTURA	007300101	3°54'·37N 77°03'·69W	26	Operational *(MRCC Pacifico)* Operational *(MRCC Pacifico)*
Remotely controlled stations:-				
Malpelo		4°00'·24N 81°36'·45W	37	
TUMACO	007300201	1°49'·32N 78°43'·77W	24	Operational *(MRCC Pacifico)*
ECUADOR				
GUAYAQUIL	007354750	2°11'·50S 79°53'·93W	30	Operational *(Guayaquil Coastguard HQ)*
Remotely controlled stations:-				
Bahía de Caráquez	007354753	0°35'·01S 80°23'·81W	30	
Esmeraldas	007354752	0°57'·20N 79°39'·50W	30	
Manta	007354754	0°57'·50S 80°43'·80W	30	
Puerto Bolivar	007354756	3°15'·71S 79°59'·07W	30	
Salinas	007354755	2°12'·40S 80°52'·00W	30	
GALAPAGOS ISLANDS (Ecuador)				
AYORA (ISLA SANTA CRUZ)	007354757	0°44'·80S 90°19'·00W	30	Operational
CRISTÓBAL (BAQUERIZO MORENO - ISLA SAN CRISTÓBAL)	007354758	0°54'·00S 89°37'·00W	30	Operational
MEXICO (Pacific Coast)				
ACAPULCO	003451810	16°50'·68N 99°54'·82W	80	Operational *(MRSC Acapulco)*
ENSENADA MRCC (Mexican Navy - 2nd Region)	003450210	31°51'·08N 116°37'·07W	80	Operational *(MRCC Ensenada)*
LÁZARO CÁRDENAS	003451610	17°57'·70N 102°11'·80W	80	Operational *(MRSC Lázaro Cárdenas)*
MANZANILLO	003451410	19°01'·20N 104°20'·00W	80	Operational *(MRSC Puerto Vallarta)*
MAZATLÁN	003450810	23°11'·36N 106°25'·51W	80	Operational *(MRCC Mazatlán)*
PUERTO VALLARTA	003451210	20°46'·92N 105°31'·48W	80	Operational *(MRSC Puerto Vallarta)*
SALINA CRUZ MRSC	003452071	16°10'·52N 95°11'·18W	80	Operational *(MRSC Salina Cruz)*
SAN BLAS MRSC	003450174	21°32'·00N 105°17'·00W	20	Operational *(MRSC San Blas)*
UNITED STATES (Hawaii)				
HONOLULU SECTOR (US COAST GUARD)	003669939	21°18'·39N 157°52'·41W	20	Operational *(JRCC Honolulu)*

Note The site shown represents a U. S. Coast Guard Sector Command Center. Sector Command Centers, among other equipment and functions, utilize and control equipment at the site indicated as well as at several remote radio communication facilities that comprise a segment of a VHF FM Communications system that provides voice on Channel 16 (156·8 MHz) and Digital Selective Calling on Channel 70 (156·525 MHz) coverage to a minimum of 20 miles off shore throughout the continental United States, the Great Lakes (not included in this entry), the State of Hawaii, Puerto Rico and selected other U.S. Territories. Construction is ongoing to provide similar coverage to selected portions of the State of Alaska's coastline.

(1)	(2)	(3)	(4)	(5)
UNITED STATES (Pacific Coast)				
COLUMBIA RIVER SECTOR (US COAST GUARD)	003669937	46°09'·25N 123°53'·10W	20	Operational (JRCC Seattle)
HUMBOLDT BAY SECTOR (US COAST GUARD)	003669909	40°45'·99N 124°13'·11W	20	Operational (JRCC Alameda)
LOS ANGELES - LONG BEACH SECTOR (US COAST GUARD)	003669912	33°43'·60N 118°16'·10W	20	Operational (JRCC Alameda)
NORTH BEND SECTOR (US COAST GUARD)	003669911	43°24'·66N 124°14'·52W	20	Operational (JRCC Seattle)
SAN DIEGO SECTOR (US COAST GUARD)	003669913	32°43'·59N 117°10'·99W	20	Operational (JRCC Alameda)
SAN FRANCISCO SECTOR (US COAST GUARD)	003669926	37°48'·58N 122°21'·70W	20	Operational (JRCC Alameda)
SEATTLE (PUGET SOUND) SECTOR (US COAST GUARD)	003669938	47°35'·39N 122°20'·30W	20	Operational (JRCC Seattle)

NAVAREA XIII

Country Station	MMSI	Position	Range (n miles)	Status (Associated RCCs)
(1)	(2)	(3)	(4)	(5)
RUSSIA (Pacific Coast)				
MAGADAN (MRSC YUZHNO-SAKHALINSK)	002734416	59°34'·61N 150°43'·97E	19	Operational (MRSC Petropavlovsk-Kamchatskiy)
PETROPAVLOVSK-KAMCHATSKIY MRSC	002734418	52°59'·00N 158°39'·00E	7	Operational (MRSC Petropavlovsk-Kamchatskiy)
VANINO	002734421	48°55'·00N 140°20'·00E	45	Operational (MRSC Yuzhno-Sakhalinsk)
VLADIVOSTOK MRCC	002734412	43°07'·00N 131°53'·00E	55	Operational (MRCC Vladivostok)
Remotely controlled stations:-				Operational (MRCC Vladivostok)
Nakhodka		42°49'·00N 132°52'·98E	45	
Tumannaya (Posiet)		42°34'·66N 131°11'·26E	70	
RUSSIA (Pacific Coast)				
YUZHNO-SAKHALINSK (REGIONAL CENTRE) MRSC	002733733		N/A	Operational (MRSC Yuzhno-Sakhalinsk)
Remotely controlled stations:-				Operational (MRSC Yuzhno-Sakhalinsk)
Cape Svobodniy VHF		46°50'·85N 143°26'·13E	32	
Kholmsk		47°02'·00N 142°03'·00E	31	
Korsakov		46°45'·00N 142°27'·00E	42	
Nevel'sk VHF		46°38'·00N 141°51'·00E	40	

NAVAREA XIV

Country Station	MMSI	Position	Range (n miles)	Status (Associated RCCs)
(1)	(2)	(3)	(4)	(5)
NONE				

NAVAREA XV

Country Station	MMSI	Position	Range (n miles)	Status (Associated RCCs)
(1)	(2)	(3)	(4)	(5)
ARGENTINA				
USHUAIA MRCC (NAVY) & USHUAIA (Prefectura Naval)	007010011	54°47'·63S 68°18'·39W	35	Operational (MRCC Ushuaia)
CHILE				
ANCUD	007250240	41°51'·98S 73°49'·86W	15	Operational (MRCC Castro)
ANTOFAGASTA ZONAL RADIO STATION	007250050	23°38'·93S 70°24'·02W	30	Operational (MRSC Iquique)
ARICA MRSC	007250010	18°28'·58S 70°19'·25W	39	Operational (MRSC Arica)
BAHÍA FÉLIX	007250370	52°57'·72S 74°04'·85W	19	Operational (MRCC Punta Arenas)
CABO RÁPER, LIGHT	007250310	46°49'·09S 75°37'·39W	22	Operational (MRSC Aysen)
CALDERA MRSC	007250080	27°03'·97S 70°49'·38W	15	Operational (MRSC Caldera)
CASTRO	007250250	42°28'·97S 73°46'·06W	15	Operational (MRSC Castro)
CHAITÉN	007250260	42°54'·98S 72°42'·38W	15	Operational (MRSC Castro)
CHAÑARAL	007250070	26°21'·00S 70°38'·33W	15	Operational (MRSC Caldera)
CONSTITUCIÓN	007250150	35°20'·10S 72°25'·13W	15	Operational (MRCC Talcahuano)
COQUIMBO MRSC	007250110	29°56'·97S 71°20'·13W	62	Operational (MRSC Coquimbo)
CORRAL	007250210	39°53'·42S 73°25'·74W	15	Operational (MRSC Valdiva)
HUASCO	007250090	28°27'·66S 71°13'·50W	15	Operational (MRSC Caldera)
IQUIQUE MRCC	007250020	20°12'·65S 70°09'·15W	64	Operational (MRCC Iquique)
ISLA DE PASCUA (EASTER ISLAND) AREA RADIO STATION	007250100	27°10'·97S 109°25'·82W	44	Operational (MRSC Valparaíso)

(1)	(2)	(3)	(4)	(5)
CHILE				
ISLA DIEGO RAMÍREZ	007250440	56°31'·40S 68°42'·60W	28	Operational *(MRSC Puerto Williams)*
Note See Antarctica for Chilean Station details				
ISLA GUAFO, LIGHT	007250290	43°34'·08S 74°49'·97W	33	Operational *(MRCC Puerto Montt)*
ISLA SAN PEDRO	007250320	47°41'·95S 74°51'·92W	18	Operational *(MRCC Punta Arenas)*
ISLOTES EVANGELISTAS, LIGHT	007250350	52°23'·12S 75°05'·90W	21	Operational *(MRCC Punta Arenas)*
ISLOTES FAIRWAY, LIGHT	007250360	52°43'·92S 73°46'·88W	19	Operational *(MRCC Punta Arenas)*
JUAN FERNÁNDEZ	007250130	33°38'·16S 78°49'·98W	15	Operational *(MRCC Valparaíso)*
LOS VILOS	007250120	31°54'·60S 71°30'·85W	15	Operational *(MRSC Coquimbo)*
MAGALLANES ZONAL RADIO STATION	007250380	53°09'·91S 70°54'·27W	64	Operational *(MRCC Punta Arenas)*
MEJILLONES	007250040	23°06'·01S 70°26'·90W	15	Operational *(MRSC Antofagasta)*
MELINKA	007250280	43°53'·90S 73°44'·75W	15	Operational *(MRSC Aysen)*
PUERTO AGUIRRE	007250294	45°09'·75S 73°31'·60W	15	Operational *(MRSC Aysen)*
PUERTO AYSÉN	007250300	45°24'·48S 72°43'·08W	16	Operational *(MRSC Aysen)*
PUERTO CHACABUCO	007250298	45°26'·80S 72°49'·30W	15	Operational *(MRSC Aysen)*
PUERTO EDÉN CAPUERTO		49°48'·00S 74°27'·00W	15	Operational *(MRCC Punta Arenas)*
PUERTO MONTT	007250230	41°28'·90S 72°57'·57W	34	Operational *(MRCC Puerto Montt)*
PUERTO NATALES CAPUERTO	007250340	51°44'·90S 72°32'·17W	15	Operational *(MRCC Punta Arenas)*
PUERTO WILLIAMS CAPUERTO	007250420	54°55'·95S 67°36'·45W	22	Operational *(MRSC Puerto Williams)*
PUNTA CORONA, LIGHT	007250235	41°47'·03S 73°52'·81W	26	Operational *(MRCC Puerto Montt)*
PUNTA DELGADA	007250390	52°27'·35S 69°32'·82W	17	Operational *(MRCC Punta Arenas)*
QUELLÓN	007250270	43°07'·24S 73°37'·30W	15	Operational *(MRSC Castro)*
QUINTERO	007250125	32°46'·58S 71°31'·61W	15	Operational *(MRCC Valparaíso)*
SAN ANTONIO MRSC	007250140	33°34'·31S 71°36'·97W	31	Operational *(MRSC San Antonio)*
TALCAHUANO	007250170	36°41'·50S 73°06'·51W	32	Operational *(MRCC Talcahuano)*
TALTAL	007250060	25°24'·39S 70°28'·76W	15	Operational *(MRSC Antofagasta)*
TOCOPILLA	007250030	22°06'·05S 70°12'·24W	15	Operational *(MRSC Antofagasta)*
VALDIVIA MRSC	007250220	39°53'·36S 73°25'·59W	15	Operational *(MRSC Valdiva)*
VALPARAÍSO (PLAYA ANCHA) PRINCIPAL RADIO STATION	007251860	33°04'·70S 71°36'·80W	63	Operational *(MRCC Valparaíso)*
WOLLASTON	007250430	55°36'·80S 67°25'·80W	28	Operational *(MRSC Puerto Williams)*

NAVAREA XVI

Country Station	MMSI	Position	Range (n miles)	Status *(Associated RCCs)*
(1)	(2)	(3)	(4)	(5)
PERU				
CALLAO MRCC	007600125	12°04'·34S 77°10'·13W	50	Operational *(MRSC Callao)*
CHANCAY MRSC	007600135	11°35'·01S 77°15'·90W	30	Operational *(MRSC Chancay)*
CHIMBOTE MRSC	007600126	9°04'·00S 78°36'·00W	12	Operational *(MRSC Chimbote)*
HUACHO MRSC	007600128	11°07'·00S 77°36'·00W	30	Operational *(MRSC Huacho)*
ILO MRSC	007600132	17°35'·00S 71°20'·00W	53	Operational *(MRSC Ilo)*
MOLLENDO MRSC	007600129	17°00'·60S 72°02'·10W	30	Operational *(MRSC Mollendo)*
PAITA MRSC	007600121	5°05'·29S 81°06'·39W	30	Operational *(MRSC Paita)*
PIMENTEL MRSC	007600123	6°50'·10S 79°56'·14W	25	Operational *(MRSC Pimentel)*
PISCO MRSC	007600130	13°43'·00S 76°13'·00W	17	Operational *(MRSC Pisco)*
SALAVERRY MRSC	007600124	8°13'·42S 78°58'·85W	25	Operational *(MRSC Salaverry)*
SAN JUÁN MRSC	007600131	15°21'·65S 75°10'·23W	30	Operational *(MRSC San Juan)*
SUPE MRSC	007600127	10°47'·00S 77°45'·00W	15	Operational *(MRSC Supe)*
TALARA MRSC	007600122	4°34'·53S 81°15'·41W	30	Operational *(MRSC Talara)*
PERU				
ZORRITOS MRSC	007600120	3°40'·17S 80°39'·54W	30	Operational *(MRSC Zorritos)*

NAVAREA XVII

Country Station (1)	MMSI (2)	Position (3)	Range (n miles) (4)	Status (Associated RCCs) (5)
NONE				

NAVAREA XVIII

Country Station (1)	MMSI (2)	Position (3)	Range (n miles) (4)	Status (Associated RCCs) (5)
NONE				

NAVAREA XIX

Country Station (1)	MMSI (2)	Position (3)	Range (n miles) (4)	Status (Associated RCCs) (5)
BJØRNØYA (Norway)				
BJØRNØYA	002570000	74°30'·23N 18°59'·90E	40	Operational (JRCC North Norway Bodø)
NORWAY				
NORWEGIAN COASTAL RADIO NORTH	002570000	67°16'·48N 14°23'·48E	41	
Remotely controlled stations:-				Operational (JRCC North Norway Bodø)
Central Area (North of 67°30'N)				
Andenes (Ramnan)		69°16'·42N 16°00'·48E	54	
Fredvang		68°05'·67N 13°11'·00E	21	
Hagskaret		68°09'·67N 13°41'·75E	36	
Harstad (Harstadåsen)		68°47'·90N 16°30'·98E	36	
Lenvik (Kistefjell)		69°17'·52N 18°08'·43E	85	
Lødingen (Fenes)		68°24'·08N 15°58'·32E	13	
Raften (Svolvaer)		68°24'·18N 15°07'·03E	18	
Stamnes (Sortland)		68°48'·70N 15°28'·90E	13	
Steigen (Småtindane)		67°49'·95N 15°00'·35E	77	
Storheia (Hadsel)		68°32'·65N 14°52'·23E	61	
Vaerøy		67°39'·83N 12°37'·55E	59	
Veggen (Narvik)		68°27'·80N 17°10'·00E	48	
Vesterålen (Kraakenes)		68°56'·55N 15°01'·43E	30	
Vestvagoy (Kvalnes)		68°20'·55N 13°57'·65E	40	
Northern Area (North of 69°30'N)				
Alta (Helligfjell)		70°06'·80N 22°55'·95E	55	
Båtsfjord (Haminefjell)		70°40'·15N 29°42'·70E	56	
Berlevåg (Berlevaagfjell)		70°51'·70N 29°04'·68E	28	
Bjørnøya		74°30'·16N 18°59'·72E	40	
Hammerfest (Tyven)		70°38'·37N 23°41'·78E	49	
Hasvik (Fuglen)		70°39'·33N 21°57'·90E	47	
Havøysund (Havoygavlen)		71°00'·00N 24°36'·00E	44	
Isfjord/Svalbard		78°03'·70N 13°36'·98E	23	
Karlsoy (Torsvåg)		70°14'·53N 19°30'·10E	14	
Kirkenes		69°45'·04N 30°07'·97E	38	
Lebesby (Oksen)		70°57'·88N 27°21'·05E	44	
Mehamn (Trollhetta)		71°03'·00N 28°07'·00E	42	
Nordkapp (Honningsvågfjell)		70°58'·97N 25°53'·90E	49	
Platåfjellet (Longyearbyen)		78°14'·30N 15°21'·10E	21	
Skjervøy (Stussnesfjell)		70°01'·45N 20°58'·95E	34	
Skjervoy (Trolltind)		70°04'·47N 20°26'·00E	68	
Tana (Algasvarre)		70°28'·08N 28°13'·42E	56	
Tromsø		69°39'·13N 18°56'·83E	80	
Tromsø (Hillesoy)		69°38'·52N 17°58'·40E	63	
Tromsø (Tønsnes)		69°43'·08N 19°07'·83E	47	
Varangerfjord (Torsvade)		70°05'·83N 29°49'·15E	37	
Vardø (Domen)		70°20'·13N 31°02'·00E	35	
Southern Area (North of 65°30'N)				
Leirfjord (Horva)		66°00'·90N 12°49'·20E	57	
Meløy		66°51'·27N 13°38'·87E	50	
Mo i Rana (Vettahaugen)		66°12'·00N 13°44'·00E	71	
Norne		66°01'·63N 8°05'·30E	26	
Rønvikfjell/ Bodø		67°18'·20N 14°26'·80E	41	
Sorfold (Fornesfjell)		67°25'·85N 15°27'·38E	68	
Traenfjord (Hestmannen)		66°31'·87N 12°49'·05E	48	
Vega (Gulsvågfjell)		65°39'·00N 11°49'·72E	75	

(1)	(2)	(3)	(4)	(5)

NAVAREA XX

Country Station	MMSI	Position	Range (n miles)	Status (*Associated RCCs*)
(1)	(2)	(3)	(4)	(5)

RUSSIA (Arctic Coast)

Country Station	MMSI	Position	Range (n miles)	Status (*Associated RCCs*)
ARKHANGEL'SK MRSC	002734414	64°32'·00N 40°32'·00E	25.6	Operational *(MRSC Arkhangel'sk)*
Remotely controlled stations:-				
Mudyug		64°51'·14N 40°16'·50E	24.5	
DIKSON MRCC	002731107	73°30'·23N 80°31'·35E	N/A	Operational *(MRCC Dikson)*
KANDALAKSHA	002733741	67°07'·57N 32°27'·14E	32	Operational *(MRSC Arkhangelsk)*
MURMANSK MRCC	002734420		N/A	Operational *(MRCC Murmansk)*
				Operational *(MRCC Murmansk)*
Remotely controlled stations:-				
Abram-Mys		68°58'·00N 33°01'·00E	16.5	
Krestovy		69°08'·00N 33°32'·00E	45	
Set-Navolok		69°23'·89N 33°29'·84E	30	

NAVAREA XXI

Country Station	MMSI	Position	Range (n miles)	Status (*Associated RCCs*)
(1)	(2)	(3)	(4)	(5)

RUSSIA (Arctic Coast)

Country Station	MMSI	Position	Range (n miles)	Status (*Associated RCCs*)
PEVEK MRSC	002731117	69°42'·03N 170°15'·26E	N/A	Operational *(MRSC Pevek)*
TIKSI MRSC	002731117	71°41'·36N 128°52'·21E	N/A	Operational *(MRSC Tiksi)*

MF DSC, LIST OF COAST STATIONS FOR SEA AREA A2

(See diagrams at end of section)
N/A = Not applicable
TBD = To be decided

NAVAREA I				
Country Station (1)	MMSI (2)	Position (3)	Range (n miles) (4)	Status (*Associated RCCs*) (5)
BELGIUM				
OOSTENDE	002050480			
Remotely controlled stations:-				Operational (*MRCC Oostende*)
Ruiselede (Wingene)		51°04′·44N 3°20′·08E	155	
DENMARK				
LYNGBY	002191000	55°45′·95N 12°28′·50E	N/A	Operational (*JRCC Denmark*)
Remotely controlled stations:-				Operational (*JRCC Denmark*)
Blåvand (Rx)		55°33′·47N 8°05′·00E	153	
Skagen (Tx/Rx)		57°44′·35N 10°34′·55E	148	
Varde (Tx)		55°39′·42N 8°40′·28E	170	
ESTONIA				
KURESSAARE MRSC	002760120	58°15′·00N 22°29′·00E	150	Operational (*JRCC Tallinn*)
TALLINN	002761000	59°27′·84N 24°21′·42E	N/A	Operational (*JRCC Tallinn*)
Remotely controlled stations:-				Operational (*JRCC Tallinn*)
Undva		58°30′·89N 21°55′·29E	150	
TALLINN NORTH	002760100	59°24′·00N 24°40′·00E	150	Operational (*JRCC Tallinn*)
FAROE ISLANDS (Denmark)				
TÓRSHAVN	002311000	62°00′·87N 6°48′·01W	225	Operational (*MRCC Tørshavn*)
FINLAND				
TURKU MRCC	002301000	60°26′·40N 22°13′·60E	N/A	Operational (*MRCC Turku*)
Remotely controlled stations:-				Operational (*MRCC Turku*)
Hailuoto (MF)		65°02′·40N 24°34′·36E	150	
Mariehamn		60°06′·78N 19°56′·98E	150	
Vaasa		63°06′·07N 21°34′·60E	150	
FRANCE (Atlantic and English Channel Coasts)				
CORSEN (CROSS) MRCC	002275300	48°24′·85N 4°47′·28W	N/A	Operational (*MRCC Corsen*)
Remotely controlled stations:-				Operational (*MRCC Corsen*)
Corsen MF Aerial (Rx)		48°24′·85N 4°47′·28W	140	
Ouessant (Tx)		48°28′·00N 5°03′·00W	140	
GRIS-NEZ (CROSS) MRCC	002275100	50°52′·09N 1°34′·96E	N/A	Operational (*MRCC Gris-Nez*)
GERMANY				
BREMEN MRCC	002111240			
Remotely controlled stations:-				Operational (*MRCC Bremen*)
Cuxhaven		53°51′·83N 8°37′·58E	200	
ICELAND				
REYKJAVÍK (COAST GUARD RADIO)	002510100	64°05′·00N 21°50′·00W	216	Operational (*MRCC Reykjavík*)
Remotely controlled stations:-				
Hornafjördur		64°15′·08N 15°12′·66W	194	Operational (*MRCC Reykjavik*)
Ísafjördur		66°05′·93N 23°02′·32W	227	Operational (*MRCC Reykjavik*)
Neskaupstadur		65°09′·00N 13°42′·00W	194	Operational (*MRCC Reykjavik*)
Siglufjördur		66°11′·22N 18°57′·05W	216	Operational (*MRCC Reykjavik*)
Vestmannaeyjar		63°26′·89N 20°17′·23W	194	Operational (*MRCC Reykjavik*)
IRELAND				
MALIN HEAD (COAST GUARD MRSC)	002500100	55°21′·80N 7°20′·39W	150	Operational (*MRSC Malin Head*)
VALENTIA (COAST GUARD MRSC)	002500200	51°55′·80N 10°20′·95W	150	Operational (*MRSC Valentia*)
JAN MAYEN (Norway)				
JAN MAYEN	002570000	70°56′·63N 8°39′·77W	200	Operational (*JRCC North Norway Bodø*)
LATVIA				
RĪGA MRCC & RĪGA RESCUE RADIO	002750100	57°01′·94N 24°05′·29E	150	Operational (*MRCC Rīga*)
Remotely controlled stations:-				
Akmenrags (Rx)		56°50′·00N 21°03′·00E	120	
Užava (Tx)		57°13′·00N 21°26′·00E	120	

(1)	(2)	(3)	(4)	(5)
LITHUANIA				
KLAIPĖDA MRCC	002770330	55°43'·13N 21°06'·05E	100	Operational *(MRCC Klaipėda)*
NETHERLANDS				
NETHERLANDS COASTGUARD (DEN HELDER)	002442000		N/A	Operational *(JRCC Den Helder)*
				Operational *(JRCC Den Helder)*
Remotely controlled stations:-				
Appingedam (Tx)		53°20'·13N 6°51'·55E	150	
Noordwijk (Rx)		52°18'·00N 4°28'·00E	150	
Scheveningen (Tx)		52°05'·68N 4°15'·45E	250	
West Terschelling (Rx)		53°21'·43N 5°12'·83E	150	
NORWAY				
NORWEGIAN COASTAL RADIO SOUTH	002570000		N/A	
Remotely controlled stations:-				Operational *(JRCC South Norway Stavanger)*
Central Area (South of 63°00´N)				
Bergen (MF aerial)		60°42'·72N 4°52'·20E	200	
Florø		61°35'·86N 4°59'·88E	200	
Northern Area (South of 65°30´N)				
Ørlandet		63°39'·70N 9°32'·80E	200	
Southern Area (South of 60°00´N)				
Bergen (Rogaland)		58°39'·50N 5°36'·30E	200	
Farsund		58°04'·32N 6°44'·67E	200	
POLAND				
POLISH RESCUE RADIO	002618102			
Remotely controlled stations:-				*(Gdynia MRCC)*
Ustka		54°35'·28N 16°51'·01E	150	
RUSSIA (Baltic Coast)				
KALININGRAD	002734417	50°43'·00N 20°44'·00E	125	Operational *(MRCC Kaliningrad)*
				Operational *(MRCC Kaliningrad)*
Remotely controlled stations:-				
Kaliningrad (Rx)		54°45'·00N 20°35'·00E	125	
KALININGRAD MRCC	002734417	54°45'·00N 20°35'·00E	125	Operational *(MRCC Kaliningrad)*
				Operational *(MRCC Kaliningrad)*
Remotely controlled stations:-				
Kaliningrad (Tx)		54°43'·00N 20°44'·00E	125	
SANKT PETERBURG	002733700	59°52'·67N 30°13'·01E	150	Operational *(MRCC Sankt Peterburg)*
				Operational *(MRCC Sankt Peterburg)*
Remotely controlled stations:-				
Gorki (Rx)		59°48'·00N 28°30'·00E	N/A	
Karavaldayskiy (Tx)		59°59'·10N 29°07'·63E	150	
SWEDEN				
SWEDEN JRCC	002653000	57°40'·45N 11°51'·89E	210	Operational *(JRCC Sweden)*
				Operational *(JRCC Sweden)*
Remotely controlled stations:-				
Bjuröklubb		64°27'·70N 21°35'·42E	210	
Gislövshammar		55°29'·38N 14°18'·87E	210	
Grimeton		57°06'·33N 12°23'·42E	150	
Härnösand		62°36'·53N 17°57'·70E	210	
Tingstäde		57°43'·85N 18°35'·81E	250	

UNITED KINGDOM

The United Kingdom maritime radio infrastructure is a single network of operations centres, all data and communications being available to every officer on duty. The National Maritime Operations Centre (NMOC) and the 10 Coastguard Operations Centres (CGOCs) carry out a range of coast guard duties. All centres carry out the function of an MRCC.

If operationally required, all operations centres can temporarily extend or contract the area that is normally covered. This might occur during busy periods or because of a major incident.

(1)	(2)	(3)	(4)	(5)
ABERDEEN MRCC	002320004		N/A	Operational *(Aberdeen MRCC)*
				Operational *(Aberdeen MRCC)*
Remotely controlled stations:-				
Cruden Bay		57°25'·00N 1°52'·00W	150	
Gregness		57°07'·65N 2°03'·22W	150	
DOVER MRCC	002320010			
Remotely controlled stations:-				Operational *(Dover MRCC)*
Bawdsey		51°59'·61N 1°24'·49E	150	
FALMOUTH MRCC	002320014		N/A	Operational *(Falmouth MRCC)*
				Operational *(Falmouth MRCC)*
Remotely controlled stations:-				
Scillies		49°55'·73N 6°18'·23W	150	
Treen		50°04'·22N 5°40'·96W	150	
HUMBER MRCC	002320007		N/A	Operational *(Humber MRCC)*
				Operational *(Humber MRCC)*
Remotely controlled stations:-				
Amble		55°21'·99N 1°42'·02W	150	
Cullercoats		55°04'·40N 1°27'·80W	150	
Humber (Bridlington)		54°05'·64N 0°10'·55W	150	
Langham		52°56'·53N 0°57'·24E	150	

(1)	(2)	(3)	(4)	(5)
UNITED KINGDOM				
MILFORD HAVEN MRCC	002320017	51°42'·50N 5°03'·20E	N/A	Operational *(Milford Haven MRCC)*
Remotely controlled stations:-				Operational *(Milford Haven MRCC)*
St Annes Head		51°41'·00N 5°10'·58W	150	
SHETLAND MRCC	002320001	60°08'·92N 1°08'·43W	150	Operational *(Shetland MRCC)*
Remotely controlled stations:-				Operational *(Shetland MRCC)*
Collafirth Hill		60°32'·00N 1°23'·50W	150	
St Margarets Hope		58°49'·26N 2°57'·35W	150	

UNITED KINGDOM

The United Kingdom maritime radio infrastructure is a single network of operations centres, all data and communications being available to every officer on duty. The National Maritime Operations Centre (NMOC) and the 10 Coastguard Operations Centres (CGOCs) carry out a range of coast guard duties. All centres carry out the function of an MRCC.

If operationally required, all operations centres can temporarily extend or contract the area that is normally covered. This might occur during busy periods or because of a major incident.

STORNOWAY MRCC	002320024		N/A	Operational *(Stornoway MRCC)*
Remotely controlled stations:-				Operational *(Stornoway MRCC)*
Butt of Lewis LH		58°30'·90N 6°15'·68W	150	
Ness		58°28'·05N 6°19'·06W	150	
Tiree		56°30'·23N 6°57'·84W	150	
Tiree Airport		56°29'·99N 6°52'·80W	150	

NAVAREA II

Country Station	MMSI	Position	Range (n miles)	Status *(Associated RCCs)*
(1)	(2)	(3)	(4)	(5)
AÇORES (Portugal)				
CENTRO DE COMUNICAÇÕES DOS AÇORES (CENCOMARACORES) & DELGADA MRCC	002040100			
Remotely controlled stations:-				Operational *(MRCC Delgada)*
Albarnaz (Rx)		39°31'·11N 31°14'·06W	150	
Fajã de Cima (Rx)		37°45'·49N 25°39'·55W	200	
Horta (Tx)		38°31'·53N 28°37'·55W	150	
Santana (Tx)		37°48'·40N 25°33'·16W	200	
BENIN				
COTONOU	006100001	6°28'·00N 2°21'·00E	150	Operational

CANARIAS, ISLAS (Spain)

The Las Palmas (CCR) Coast Radio Station remotely controls stations on Islas Canarias and mainland Spain, located in both NAVAREA II and NAVAREA III regions. The whole network is displayed in each NAVAREA section for completeness.

LAS PALMAS	002241026		N/A	Operational *(MRCC Las Palmas)*
Remotely controlled stations:-				
Tenerife (Igueque)		28°18'·40N 16°30'·15W	150	Operational *(MRCC Tenerife)*
Arrecife				
Orzola		29°13'·01N 13°28'·70W	150	Operational *(MRCC Las Palmas)*
LAS PALMAS MRCC	002240995	28°08'·82N 15°25'·12W	150	Operational *(MRCC Las Palmas)*
TENERIFE MRCC	002241007	28°28'·91N 16°14'·39W	150	Operational *(MRCC Tenerife)*

CAPE VERDE

SÃO VICENTE DE CABO VERDE	006170000		N/A	
Remotely controlled stations:-				
Ilha de São Vicente		16°52'·12N 24°56'·02W	200	Operational

FRANCE (Atlantic and English Channel Coasts)

ÉTEL (CROSS) MRCC	002275000			
Remotely controlled stations:-				Operational *(MRCC Étel)*
Cap Ferret		44°37'·83N 1°15'·12W	127	
Saint-Philibert		47°34'·00N 3°00'·00W	128	

IVORY COAST

ABIDJAN	006191000		500	Operational *(MRCC Abidjan)*

MADEIRA (Portugal)

FUNCHAL MRSC	002550100			
Remotely controlled stations:-				Operational *(MRSC Funchal)*
Camacha (Tx)		33°05'·38N 16°20'·22W	200	
Pico das Eiras (Rx)		33°03'·49N 16°22'·18W	200	

(1)	(2)	(3)	(4)	(5)

PORTUGAL

LISBOA MRCC	002630100			
Remotely controlled stations:-				Operational *(MRCC Lisboa)*
Fonte da Telha (Rx)		38°33'·25N 9°10'·52W	200	
Penalva (Tx)		38°36'·20N 9°01'·80W	200	

SENEGAL

DAKAR MRCC	006631008	14°39'·00N 17°28'·00W	200	Operational *(MRCC Dakar)*

SPAIN (North Coast)

The primary responsibility for the receipt of MF DSC distress alerts for Spain (North Coast) is carried out via CORUÑA Remote Stations. The facilities maintained at other MRCCs and MRSCs are only complementary to the Coast Radio Stations network.

BILBAO MRCC	002240996	43°20'·78N 3°01'·90W	150	Operational *(MRCC Bilbao)*
CORUÑA	002241022			
Remotely controlled stations:-				
Cabo Peñas		43°29'·53N 5°56'·49W	150	Operational *(MRCC Gijon)*
Cabo Quejo		43°30'·15N 3°33'·06W	150	Operational *(MRCC Bilbao, MRCC Gijón)*
Coruña				
Ares		43°27'·10N 8°17'·09W	150	Operational *(MRSC Coruña)*
Boal		43°27'·39N 6°49'·23W	150	Operational *(MRSC Coruña)*
Cabo Ortegal		43°43'·03N 7°53'·88W	150	Operational *(MRCC Finisterre)*
Finisterre				
Finisterre (Corcubión)		42°55'·80N 9°11'·88W	150	Operational *(MRCC Finisterre)*
Finisterre (Muxia)		43°04'·63N 9°13'·51W	150	Operational *(MRCC Finisterre)*
Pastoriza		42°20'·30N 8°44'·27W	150	Operational *(MRCC Finisterre)*
Machichaco				
Jaizquibel		43°20'·61N 1°51'·43W	150	Operational *(MRCC Bilbao)*
Rostrio		43°28'·71N 3°51'·02W	150	Operational *(MRCC Bilbao)*
FINISTERRE MRCC	002240993	42°42'·20N 8°59'·03W	150	Operational *(MRCC Finisterre)*
GIJÓN MRCC	002240997	43°33'·56N 5°42'·01W	150	Operational *(MRCC Gijón)*

NAVAREA III

Country Station	MMSI	Position	Range (n miles)	Status *(Associated RCCs)*
(1)	(2)	(3)	(4)	(5)

ALGERIA

ALGER	006052110	36°44'·60N 3°10'·85E	200	Operational *(CNOSS Alger)*
ANNABA	006053814	36°54'·00N 7°46'·00E	200	Operational *(CROSS Jijel)*
ORAN	006054117	35°44'·82N 0°34'·33W	200	Operational *(CROSS Oran)*

AZERBAIJAN

BAKU	004231000	40°21'·21N 49°49'·87E	200	Operational *(Azerbaijan LRIT NC)*
	004232000			
Remotely controlled stations:-				Operational *(Azerbaijan LRIT NC)*
Chilov		40°19'·63N 50°36'·74E	200	

BULGARIA

VARNA	002070810	43°04'·01N 27°47'·19E	200	Operational *(MRCC Varna)*

CANARIAS, ISLAS (Spain)

The Las Palmas (CCR) Coast Radio Station remotely controls stations on Islas Canarias and mainland Spain, located in both NAVAREA II and NAVAREA III regions. The whole network is displayed in each NAVAREA section for completeness.

LAS PALMAS	002241026	28°09'·44N 15°24'·85W	150	Operational *(MRCC Tenerife)*
Remotely controlled stations:-				
Tarifa		36°07'·52N 5°45'·80W	150	Operational *(MRCC Tarifa)*

Note The primary responsibility for the receipt of MF DSC distress alerts for Spain (South Coast) is carried out via Las Palmas. The facility maintained at MRCC Tarifa is only complementary to the Coast Radio Stations network.

Arrecife				
Haria		29°08'·45N 13°31'·04W	150	Operational *(MRCC Las Palmas)*
Los Hoyos		28°02'·92N 15°26'·98W	150	Operational *(MRCC Las Palmas)*
Puerto del Rosario		28°32'·62N 13°52'·68W	150	Operational *(MRCC Las Palmas)*
Las Palmas (Gran Canaria)				
Fuencaliente		28°30'·54N 17°50'·37W	150	Operational *(MRCC Tenerife)*
Las Mesas		28°28'·97N 16°16'·17W	150	Operational *(MRCC Tenerife)*
Pico del Inglés		28°31'·94N 16°15'·77W	150	Operational *(MRCC Tenerife)*
Tarifa (Southern Spain)				
Conil		36°17'·81N 6°08'·31W	150	Operational *(MRCC Tarifa)*
Huelva		37°12'·42N 7°01'·20W	150	Operational *(MRCC Tarifa)*
Vejer		36°15'·97N 6°00'·80W	150	Operational *(MRCC Tarifa)*

(1)	(2)	(3)	(4)	(5)
CROATIA				
RIJEKA MRCC	002387010	45°19′·43N 14°26′·46E	160	Operational (*MRCC Rijeka*)
CYPRUS				
CYPRUS	002091000	34°44′·28N 32°39′·52E	300	Operational (*JRCC Larnaca*)
EGYPT (Mediterranean Coast)				
AL ISKANDARÎYAH (ALEXANDRIA)	006221111	31°11′·96N 29°51′·88E	200	Operational (*RCC Cairo*)
PORT SAID (BŪR SA`ĪD)	006221113	31°14′·59N 32°19′·83E	200	Operational (*RCC Cairo*)
FRANCE (Mediterranean Coast)				
LA GARDE (CROSS) MRCC	002275400		N/A	Operational (*MRCC La Garde*)
Remotely controlled stations:-				Operational (*MRCC La Garde*)
La Garde (Rx)		43°06′·26N 5°59′·48E	110	
Porquerolles (Tx)		42°59′·06N 6°12′·38E	110	
GEORGIA				
GEORGIA MRCC	002130100	41°38′·80N 41°39′·13E	150	Operational (*MRCC Georgia*)
GREECE				

The primary responsibility for the receipt of MF DSC distress alerts for Greece is carried out via Olympia Coast Radio Station and its remotely controlled stations with MF capability. The stations operated by Hellenic Coast Guard keep watch for additional safety only.

ASPROPÝRGOS ATTIKíS (JRCC) (HELLENIC COASTGUARD)	002391000	38°03′·00N 23°35′·00E	130	Operational (*JRCC Piraeus*)

Note   Operational Hours HJ only. Hot standby mode at other times.

OLYMPIA	002371000	37°36′·00N 21°29′·17E	N/A	Operational (*JRCC Piraeus*)
Remotely controlled stations:-				
Irákleion (SVH)		35°20′·33N 25°07′·33E	200	Operational (*JRCC Piraeus*)
Kérkyra (SVK)		39°37′·39N 19°54′·74E	200	Operational (*JRCC Piraeus*)
Límnos (SVL)		39°52′·14N 25°04′·00E	200	Operational (*JRCC Piraeus*)
Ródos		36°16′·25N 27°56′·07E	200	
PEIRAIÁS JRCC (HELLENIC COAST GUARD)	002392000 237673000	37°58′·00N 23°40′·00E	100	Operational (*JRCC Piraeus*)
IRAN (Caspian Sea)				
AMĪRĀBĀD	004225601	36°51′·04N 48°17′·00E	250	Operational
ANZALĪ	004225500	37°28′·06N 49°27′·06E	250	Operational
ISRAEL (Mediterranean Coast)				
HEFA JRCC	004280001	32°49′·00N 35°00′·00E	120	Operational (*JRCC Hefa*)
ISRAEL (Red Sea Coast)				
EILAT	004280003	29°31′·57N 34°56′·06E	120	Operational (*JRCC Hefa*)

Note   Remotely controlled from Ḥefa (Haifa).

ITALY				
PALERMO	002470002			
Remotely controlled stations:-				
Palermo (Punta Raisi)		38°08′·33N 13°22′·07E	200	Operational (*MRSC Palermo*)
Adriatic Coast				
Bari		41°05′·55N 16°55′·04E	200	Operational (*MRSC Bari*)
Sicilia & Isole Pelagie				
Augusta		37°14′·32N 15°14′·40E	200	Operational (*MRSC Catania*)
Mazara del Vallo		37°40′·65N 12°36′·63E	200	Operational (*MRSC Palermo*)
ROMA RADIO	002470001	41°47′·00N 12°27′·00E	200	Operational (*MRSC Roma*)
Remotely controlled stations:-				
Adriatic Coast				
Ancona		43°35′·70N 13°28′·59E	200	Operational (*MRSC Ancona*)
Trieste		45°40′·43N 13°45′·89E	200	Operational (*MRSC Trieste*)
Sardegna				
Margine Rosso		39°13′·62N 9°14′·03E	200	Operational (*MRSC Cagliari*)
West Coast				
Genova		44°25′·78N 8°55′·98E	200	Operational (*MRSC Genova*)
KAZAKHSTAN				
AKTAU		43°36′·15N 51°13′·25E	100	Operational (*MRCC Astrakhan*)
LEBANON				
BEYROUTH	004501000	33°51′·00N 35°32′·00E	150	Operational (*Lebanese Army*)
MALTA				
MALTA RCC	002150100	35°51′·30N 14°29′·30E	370	Operational (*RCC Malta*)
MONTENEGRO				
BAR	002620001	42°03′·13N 19°08′·87E	150	Operational (*MRCC Bar*)

(1)	(2)	(3)	(4)	(5)
ROMANIA				
CONSTANȚA	002640570	44°06'·18N 28°37'·49E	400	Operational *(Constanţa Harbour Master)*
RUSSIA (Black Sea Coast)				
NOVOROSSIYSK MRCC	002734411	44°41'·00N 37°47'·00E	173	Operational *(MRCC Novorossiysk)*
				Operational *(MRCC Novorossiysk)*
Remotely controlled stations:-				
Doob		44°36'·00N 37°58'·00E	173	
TAGANROG	002734487	47°12'·10N 38°56'·80E	86	Operational *(MRSC Taman)*
				Operational *(MRSC Taman)*
Remotely controlled stations:-				
Beglica (Rx)		47°08'·00N 38°30'·00E	86	
Veselo-Voznesenka (Tx)		47°08'·00N 38°18'·00E	86	
TAMAN MRSC	002734446			
Remotely controlled stations:-				Operational *(MRSC Taman)*
Temryuk		45°19'·82N 37°13'·87E	70	
RUSSIA (Caspian Sea)				
ASTRAKHAN MRCC	002734419	46°18'·00N 47°58'·00E	120	Operational *(MRCC Astrakhan)*
				Operational *(MRCC Astrakhan)*
Remotely controlled stations:-				
Iskusstvennyi MF (Rx)		45°23'·00N 47°47'·00E	120	
Ninovka (Tx)		45°51'·00N 47°39'·00E	120	
MAKHACHKALA	002734423	42°59'·00N 47°30'·00E	150	Operational *(MRCC Astrakhan)*
Remotely controlled stations:-				
Makhachkala (Tx)		43°00'·00N 47°28'·00E	150	
Sulak (Rx)		43°15'·00N 47°32'·00E	150	
SPAIN (Mediterranean Coast)				

SPAIN (Mediterranean Coast)

The primary responsibility for the receipt of MF DSC distress alerts for Spain (Mediterranean Coast) is carried out via Valencia (CCR) Coast Radio Station and its remotely controlled stations with MF capability. The facilities maintained at the various MRCCs are only complementary to the Coast Radio Stations network.

(1)	(2)	(3)	(4)	(5)
ALMERÍA MRCC	002241002	36°49'·84N 2°28'·01W	150	Operational *(MRCC Tarifa)*
BARCELONA MRCC	002240991	41°20'·09N 2°08'·54E	150	Operational *(MRCC Barcelona)*
VALENCIA	002241024	39°25'·80N 0°28'·59W	N/A	Operational
Remotely controlled stations:-				
Cabo de La Nao		38°39'·13N 0°16'·33W	150	Operational *(MRCC Valencia)*
Palma		39°44'·07N 2°42'·79E	150	Operational *(MRCC Palma)*
Cabo de Gata				
La Guapa		36°44'·60N 3°18'·55W	150	Operational *(MRCC Almería)*
Roquetas		36°43'·80N 2°38'·49W	150	Operational *(MRCC Almería)*
Sabinar		36°41'·21N 2°42'·08W	150	Operational *(MRCC Almería)*
Cabo la Nao				
Aguilas (Conil) (Cartagena)		37°29'·42N 1°33'·80W	150	Operational *(MRSC Valencia)*
Ibiza (San José)		38°55'·02N 1°16'·72E	150	Operational *(MRCC Palma, MRCC Valencia, MRCC Cartagena)*
La Asomada		37°37'·80N 0°57'·81W	150	Operational *(MRCC Valencia)*
Palma				
Fornells		41°57'·00N 3°13'·80E	150	Operational *(MRCC Palma, MRCC Barcelona)*
Marratxi		39°38'·09N 2°40'·20E	150	Operational *(MRCC Palma)*
VALENCIA MRCC	002241004	39°26'·63N 0°19'·73W	150	Operational *(MRCC Valencia)*
SPAIN (South West Coast)				
TARIFA MRCC	002240994	36°01'·05N 5°34'·90W	150	Operational *(MRCC Tarifa)*
SYRIA				
AL LĀDHIQĪYAH (LATAKIA)	004680011	35°30'·05N 35°46'·50E	400	Operational
TURKEY				
ANTALYA	002713000	36°09'·17N 32°26'·72E	250	Operational *(MSRCC Ankara)*
ISTANBUL	002711000	40°59'·00N 28°49'·00E	250	Operational *(MSRCC Ankara)*
İZMIR	002715000	38°24'·79N 27°08'·80E	250	Operational *(MSRCC Ankara)*
SAMSUN	002712000	41°23'·18N 36°11'·37E	250	Operational *(MSRCC Ankara)*
UKRAINE				
ODESA MRCC	002723660	46°22'·65N 30°44'·87E	200	Operational *(MRCC Odesa)*

NAVAREA IV

Country Station (1)	MMSI (2)	Position (3)	Range (n miles) (4)	Status (*Associated RCCs*) (5)
BERMUDA (UK)				
BERMUDA	003100001	32°22'·82N 64°40'·97W	200	Operational (*RCC / Bermuda Harbour*)
COLOMBIA (Caribbean Coast)				
BARRANQUILLA	007300301	11°01'·30N 74°47'·68W	200	Operational (*MRCC Caribe*)
CARTAGENA	007300501	10°25'·21N 75°33'·01W	200	Operational (*MRCC Caribe*)
COVEÑAS	007300901	9°24'·70N 75°40'·32W	200	Operational (*MRCC Caribe*)
PROVIDENCIA	007301201	13°22'·36N 81°22'·22W	200	Operational (*MRCC San Andrés*)
SAN ANDRÉS	007300701	12°31'·30N 81°43'·51W	200	Operational (*MRCC San Andrés*)
SANTA MARTA	007300401	11°12'·89N 74°13'·95W	200	Operational (*MRCC Caribe*)
TURBO	007300801	8°04'·88N 76°44'·05W	200	Operational (*MRCC Caribe*)
CURAÇAO				
CURAÇAO (JRCC)	003061000		N/A	Operational (*JRCC Curaçao*)
Remotely controlled stations:-				Operational (*JRCC Curaçao*)
Ronde Klip (Tx)	003061000	12°10'·31N 68°51'·82W	400	
Sint Joris (Rx)	003061000	12°08'·65N 68°51'·02W	400	
GREENLAND				
AASIAAT	003313000			
Remotely controlled stations:-				Operational (*MRCC Grønnedal*)
Ikerasassuaq		60°03'·00N 43°09'·00W	220	
Nuuk		64°04'·12N 52°00'·51W	250	
Paamiut		61°59'·75N 49°39'·00W	230	
Qaqortoq (Simiutaq)		60°41'·20N 46°36'·00W	220	
Sisimiut		66°56'·03N 53°41'·90W	270	
Tasiilaq		65°36'·56N 37°38'·17W	280	
MEXICO (Caribbean and Gulf Coast)				
TAMPICO	003450110	22°12'·74N 97°51'·40W	150	Operational (*MRCC Ciudad Madero*)

NAVAREA V

Country Station (1)	MMSI (2)	Position (3)	Range (n miles) (4)	Status (*Associated RCCs*) (5)
NONE				

NAVAREA VI

Country Station (1)	MMSI (2)	Position (3)	Range (n miles) (4)	Status (*Associated RCCs*) (5)
ANTARCTICA				
BAHÍA FILDES (ANTÁRTICA CHILENA MRSC)	007250450	62°12'·09S 58°57'·67W	180	Operational (*MRCC Punta Arenas*)
ARGENTINA				
BUENOS AIRES (Prefectura Naval)	007010001	34°36'·17S 58°22'·03W	150	Operational (*MRCC Rio de La Plata*)
COMODORO RIVADAVIA (Prefectura Naval)	007010008	45°50'·81S 67°28'·99W	150	Operational (*MRSC Comodoro Rivadavia*)
MAR DEL PLATA (Prefectura Naval)	007010003	38°02'·24S 57°32'·29W	150	Operational (*MRSC Mar del Plata*)
RIO GALLEGOS (Prefectura Naval)	007010010	51°37'·39S 69°12'·71W	150	Operational (*MRSC Río Gallegos*)
SAN BLAS (Prefectura Naval)	007010006	40°33'·00S 62°14'·10W	150	Operational (*MRSC Bahía Blanca*)
URUGUAY				
MONTEVIDEO ARMADA	007703870	34°52'·00S 56°19'·00W	100	Operational (*MRCC Uruguay*)

NAVAREA VII

Country Station	MMSI	Position	Range (n miles)	Status (Associated RCCs)
(1)	(2)	(3)	(4)	(5)

MOZAMBIQUE

| MAPUTO MRCC | 006501000 | 25°57'·00S 32°28'·00E | 200 | Operational (MRCC Maputo) |

NAVAREA VIII

Country Station	MMSI	Position	Range (n miles)	Status (Associated RCCs)
(1)	(2)	(3)	(4)	(5)

BURMA

| AYEYARWADY MRCC | 005061411 | 16°45'·98N 96°11'·77E | 200 | Operational (MRCC Ayeyarwady) |
| YANGON | 005060100 | 16°42'·00N 96°17'·00E | 200 | Operational (MRCC Yangon) |

INDIA (Andaman and Nicobar Region)

| PORT BLAIR MRCC | 004194409 | 11°40'·63N 92°45'·89E | 250 | Operational (MRCC Port Blair) |

INDIA (Eastern Region (Including Bay of Bengal))

CHENNAI MRCC	004194401	13°05'·98N 80°17'·89E	250	Operational (MRCC Chennai)
HALDIA MRSC	004194404	22°02'·00N 88°06'·00E	200	Operational (MRCC Chennai)
MANDAPAM MRSSC	004194406	9°17'·00N 79°05'·00E	200	Operational (MRCC Chennai)

INDIA (North Western Region)

| DAMAN CGAS | 004192201 | 20°25'·00N 72°52'·00E | 200 | Operational (MRCC Mumbai) |
| PORBANDAR MRSC | 004192202 | 21°37'·51N 69°37'·22E | 200 | Operational (MRCC Mumbai) |

INDIA (Western Region)

| MUMBAI MRCC | 004192203 | 18°55'·00N 72°49'·80E | 250 | Operational (MRCC Mumbai) |

MAURITIUS

MAURITIUS	006452700		N/A	Operational
Remotely controlled stations:-				
Belle Mare		20°11'·00S 57°46'·00E	150	Operational (MRCC Mauritius)
Cassis		20°09'·00S 57°28'·00E	150	Operational (MRCC Mauritius)

RÉUNION (France)

LA RÉUNION (CROSSRU) MRCC	006601000			
Remotely controlled stations:-				Operational (MRCC Réunion)
Bel-Air (Tx)		20°54'·51S 55°35'·31E	103	
Rivière-des-Pluies (Rx)		20°55'·00S 55°31'·00E	103	

NAVAREA IX

Country Station	MMSI	Position	Range (n miles)	Status (Associated RCCs)
(1)	(2)	(3)	(4)	(5)

EGYPT (Red Sea Coast)

| AL QUŞAYR | 006221112 | 26°06'·00N 34°17'·00E | 200 | Operational (SAR Centre Cairo) |

IRAN

| BANDAR-E EMÃM KHOMEYNÏ | 004225100 | 30°25'·49N 49°03'·87E | 250 | Operational (MRCC Bandar 'Abbās) |
| BANDAR-E SHAHÏD RAJÃ'Ï | 004225300 | 27°06'·15N 56°04'·41E | 250 | Operational (MRCC Bandar 'Abbās) |

IRAQ

| UMM QAŞR | 004250001 | 30°02'·15N 47°57'·16E | 100 | Operational |

KUWAIT

| AL KUWAYT (KUWAIT) | 004472188 | 29°23'·86N 47°38'·80E | N/A | Operational |

Note Nominal MF range of 120 n miles used for diagram.

PAKISTAN

| KARACHI | 004634060 | 24°50'·40N 66°58'·30E | 50 | Operational (MRCC Karachi) |

SAUDI ARABIA

| JEDDAH | 004030000 | 21°14'·00N 39°09'·00E | 500 | Operational (RCC Jeddah) |

NAVAREA X

Country Station (1)	MMSI (2)	Position (3)	Range (n miles) (4)	Status (Associated RCCs) (5)
		NONE		

NAVAREA XI

Country Station (1)	MMSI (2)	Position (3)	Range (n miles) (4)	Status (Associated RCCs) (5)
CHINA				
BASUO	004123600	19°05'·98N 108°36'·83E	100	Operational (MRSC Basuo)
BEIHAI	004123400	21°28'·99N 109°04'·89E	100	Operational (MRSC Beihai)
DALIAN	004121300	38°50'·69N 121°31'·09E	100	Operational (MRCC Liaoning)
FUZHOU	004122600	26°03'·00N 119°18'·00E	100	Operational (MRCC Fujian)
GUANGZHOU	004123100	23°09'·00N 113°29'·00E	100	Operational (MRCC Guangdong)
HONG KONG MARINE RESCUE	004773500	22°12'·57N 114°15'·03E	200	Operational (MRCC Hong Kong)
LIANYUNGANG	004122300	34°44'·00N 119°21'·00E	100	Operational (MRCC Lianyungang)
NINGBO	004122400	30°01'·00N 121°36'·00E	100	Operational (MRSC Ningbo)
QINGDAO	004122200	36°10'·00N 120°28'·00E	100	Operational (MRSC Qingdao)
SANYA	004123700	18°17'·46N 109°21'·67E	100	Operational (MRSC Sanya)
SHANGHAI	004122100	31°06'·00N 121°32'·00E	100	Operational (MRCC Shanghai)
SHANTOU	004123200	23°21'·00N 116°40'·00E	100	Operational (MRSC Shantou)
TIANJIN	004121100	39°03'·00N 117°25'·50E	100	Operational (MRCC Tianjin)
WENZHOU	004122500	28°01'·06N 120°38'·08E	100	Operational
XIAMEN	004122700	24°29'·63N 118°04'·59E	100	Operational (MRSC Xiamen)
YANTAI	004121400	37°25'·00N 121°30'·00E	100	Operational (MRSC Yantai)
ZHANJIANG	004123300	21°11'·00N 110°24'·00E	100	Operational (MRSC Zhanjiang)
EAST TIMOR				
DILI	005250015	8°33'·00S 125°34'·00E	100	Operational (MRSC Kupang)
INDONESIA (Bali)				
BENOA	005250014	8°45'·18S 115°13'·08E	100	Operational (MRSC Denpasar)
Note This station is not H24. Hours of service are 0200-0400 0700-0800 0900-1000 1100-1200.				
GILIMANUK	005251555	8°10'·68S 114°26'·08E	100	Operational (MRSC Denpasar)
INDONESIA (Halmahera)				
NAMLEA	005250096	2°16'·62N 128°11'·88E	100	Operational (MRSC Ambon)
TERNATE	005250020	0°47'·30N 127°21'·13E	100	Operational (MRSC Ternate)
INDONESIA (Jawa)				
CIGADING	005250033	5°56'·08S 106°00'·38E	100	Operational (MRSC Jakarta)
CILACAP	005250030	7°44'·47S 108°59'·80E	100	Operational (MRSC Semarang)
CIREBON	005250032	6°43'·00S 108°34'·33E	100	Operational (MRSC Bandung)
JAKARTA	005250000	6°07'·47S 106°51'·27E	100	Operational (MRSC Jakarta)
SEMARANG	005250008	6°57'·61S 110°23'·55E	100	Operational (MRSC Semarang)
SURABAYA	005250001	7°13'·08S 112°44'·13E	100	Operational (MRSC Surabaya)
INDONESIA (Kalimantan)				
BALIKPAPAN	005250009	1°15'·73S 116°49'·22E	100	Operational (MRSC Balikpapan)
BANJARMASIN	005251520	3°19'·67S 114°35'·58E	100	Operational (MRSC Banjarmasin)
KETAPANG	005251503	1°48'·73S 109°57'·40E	100	Operational (MRSC Pontianak)
PONTIANAK	005250016	0°01'·43S 109°18'·10E	100	Operational (MRSC Pontianak)
SAMARINDA	005251524	0°30'·50S 117°09'·20E	100	Operational (MRSC Balikpapan)
SAMPIT	005251521	2°32'·33S 112°56'·78E	100	Operational (MRSC Banjarmasin)
SINTETE	005251565	1°11'·70N 109°03'·63E	100	Operational (MRSC Pontianak)
TARAKAN	005250017	3°17'·47N 117°35'·42E	100	Operational (MRSC Balikpapan)
INDONESIA (Lombok)				
LEMBAR	005250022	8°43'·68S 116°04'·38E	100	Operational (MRSC Mataram)
INDONESIA (Maluka)				
SAUMLAKI	005251531	7°58'·25S 131°18'·32E	100	Operational (MRSC Ambon)
TUAL	005251530	5°37'·77S 132°44'·77E	100	Operational (MRSC Ambon)
INDONESIA (Nusa Tenggara)				
BIMA	005251516	8°26'·55S 118°42'·52E	100	Operational (MRSC Mataram)
ENDE	005251517	8°50'·80S 121°40'·42E	100	Operational (MRSC Kupang)

(1)	(2)	(3)	(4)	(5)
INDONESIA (Nusa Tenggara)				
WAINGAPU	005251564	9°39'·18S 120°17'·58E	100	Operational *(MRSC Kupang)*
INDONESIA (Papua)				
AGATS	005251532	5°32'·17S 138°07'·67E	100	Operational *(MRSC Timika)*
BIAK	005250031	1°11'·09S 136°04'·67E	100	Operational *(MRSC Biak)*
BINTUNI	005250026	2°07'·18S 133°30'·07E	100	Operational *(MRSC Manokwari)*
FAK-FAK	005250026	2°56'·03S 132°17'·93E	100	Operational *(MRSC Sorong)*
JAYAPURA	005250007	2°31'·11S 140°43'·29E	100	Operational *(MRSC Jayapura)*
MANOKWARI	005250023	0°51'·93S 134°04'·58E	100	Operational *(MRSC Manokwari)*
MERAUKE	005250021	8°28'·78S 140°23'·63E	100	Operational *(MRSC Merauke)*
SERUI	005251567	1°53'·20S 136°14'·45E	100	Operational *(MRSC Biak)*
SORONG	005250011	0°53'·05S 131°16'·48E	100	Operational *(MRSC Sorong)*
INDONESIA (Riau)				
NATUNA	005251505	3°40'·00N 108°07'·73E	100	Operational *(MRSC Tanjung Pinang)*
INDONESIA (Seram)				
AMBOINA	005250006	3°41'·84S 128°11'·06E	100	Operational *(MRSC Ambon)*
INDONESIA (Sulawesi)				
BAUBAU	005251526	5°29'·23S 122°34'·52E	100	Operational *(MRSC Kendan)*
BITUNG	005250005	1°27'·42N 125°11'·19E	100	Operational *(MRSC Menado)*
KENDARI	005250019	3°58'·00S 122°34'·33E	100	Operational *(MRSC Kendari)*
MAKASSAR	005250002	5°06'·57S 119°26'·33E	100	Operational *(MRSC Makassar)*
PANTOLOAN	005250018	0°39'·90S 119°44'·75E	100	Operational *(MRSC Palu)*
POSO	005251527	1°22'·85S 120°45'·32E	100	Operational *(MRSC Palu)*
TOLI-TOLI	005251528	1°03'·13N 120°48'·05E	100	Operational *(MRSC Palu)*
INDONESIA (Sumatera)				
AIR BANGIS	005251558	0°12'·33N 99°22'·33E	100	Operational *(MRSC Padang)*
BATU AMPAR	005250012	1°09'·45N 104°00'·87E	100	Operational *(MRSC Tanjung Pinang)*
BELAWAN	005250003	3°43'·28N 98°40'·13E	100	Operational *(MRSC Medan)*
BENGKALIS	005250034	1°28'·65N 102°06'·57E	100	Operational *(MRSC Pekanbaru)*
BENGKULU	005250062	3°53'·98S 102°18'·53E	100	Operational *(MRSC Bengkulu)*
DABO SINGKEP	005251559	0°30'·17S 104°34'·00E	100	Operational *(MRSC Tanjung Pinang)*
DUMAI	005250004	1°41'·17N 101°27'·33E	100	Operational *(MRSC Pekanbaru)*
GUNUNG SITOLI	005251556	1°16'·88N 97°37'·27E	100	Operational *(MRSC Medan)*
KUALA LANGSA	005251562	4°31'·63N 98°01'·08E	100	Operational *(MRSC Banda Aceh)*
LHOKSEUMAWE	005251503	5°12'·68N 97°02'·35E	100	Operational *(MRSC Banda Aceh)*
PALEMBANG	005251507	2°58'·13S 104°46'·93E	100	Operational *(MRSC Palembang)*
PANGKAL BALAM	005251508	2°06'·12S 106°07'·82E	100	Operational *(MRSC Tanjung Pinang)*
PANGKALAN SUSU	005251563	4°06'·80N 98°12'·35E	100	Operational *(MRSC Medan)*
PANJANG	005250013	5°28'·29S 105°19'·23E	100	Operational *(MRSC Lampung)*
RENGAT	005251560	0°28'·48S 102°41'·17E	100	Operational *(MRSC Pekanbaru)*
SABANG	005251501	5°52'·83N 95°19'·97E	100	Operational *(MRSC Banda Aceh)*
SEI KOLAK KIJANG	005250029	0°51'·07N 104°36'·52E	100	Operational *(MRSC Tanjung Pinang)*
SELAT PANJANG	005251561	1°01'·25N 102°43'·17E	100	Operational *(MRSC Pekanbaru)*
SIBOLGA	005250028	1°44'·48N 98°46'·59E	100	Operational *(MRSC Medan)*
SIPORA	005250047	2°12'·12S 99°41'·28E	100	Operational *(MRSC Padang)*
TANJUNG BALAI ASAHAN	005251552	2°58'·00N 99°48'·40E	100	Operational *(MRSC Medan)*
TANJUNG PANDAN	005251553	2°44'·63S 107°37'·78E	100	Operational *(MRSC Pangkal Pingang)*
TAPAK TUAN	005251502	3°16'·32N 97°09'·80E	100	Operational *(MRSC Banda Aceh)*
TELUK BAYUR	005250075	1°00'·17S 100°21'·92E	100	Operational *(MRSC Padang)*
TELUK DALAM	005251557	0°33'·87N 97°49'·08E	100	Operational *(MRSC Padang, MRSC Medan)*
INDONESIA (Timor)				
KUPANG	005250010	10°12'·82S 123°37'·08E	100	Operational *(MRSC Kupang)*
JAPAN				
HIROSHIMA (HIROSHIMA MRCC)	004310601		N/A	Operational *(MRCC Hiroshima)*
Remotely controlled stations:-				Operational *(MRCC Hiroshima)*
Kanosan (Tx)		33°55'·00N 132°15'·00E	60	
Noro (Rx)		34°15'·00N 132°40'·00E	60	

(1)	(2)	(3)	(4)	(5)
JAPAN				
HOKKAIDO (OTARU MRCC)	004310101		N/A	Operational *(MRCC Otaru)*
Remotely controlled stations:-				Operational *(MRCC Otaru)*
Hakodateyama (Rx)		41°44'·79N 140°42'·58E	150	
Shakotan (Rx)		43°20'·00N 140°32'·00E	150	
Shikotan (Tx)		43°20'·00N 140°27'·00E	150	
Souyamisaki (Rx)		45°31'·00N 141°56'·00E	150	
Tokotan (Rx)		43°00'·00N 144°53'·00E	150	
KAGOSHIMA (KAGOSHIMA MRCC)	004311001		N/A	Operational *(MRCC Kagoshima)*
Remotely controlled stations:-				Operational *(MRCC Kagoshima)*
Aburatsu (Rx)		31°35'·00N 131°25'·00E	150	
Naze (Rx)		28°23'·00N 129°30'·00E	100	
Yoko (Rx)		31°19'·00N 130°49'·00E	150	
Yoshimiyama (Tx)		31°18'·00N 130°32'·00E	150	
KOBE (KOBE MRCC)	004310501		N/A	Operational *(MRCC Kobe)*
Remotely controlled stations:-				Operational *(MRCC Kobe)*
Senzan (Rx)		34°22'·00N 134°49'·00E	60	
Shionomisaki (Rx)		33°26'·00N 135°47'·00E	150	
Tosayama (Rx)		33°37'·00N 133°31'·00E	150	
Tsuna (Tx)		34°29'·00N 134°55'·00E	150	
MAIZURU (MAIZURU MRCC)	004310801		N/A	Operational *(MRCC Maizuru)*
Remotely controlled stations:-				Operational *(MRCC Maizuru)*
Echizen (Tx)		35°52'·70N 136°01'·00E	150	
Nawa (Rx)		35°31'·00N 133°32'·00E	150	
MOJI (KITAKYUSHI MRCC)	004310701		N/A	Operational *(MRCC Moji)*
Remotely controlled stations:-				Operational *(MRCC Moji)*
Mokkoku (Rx)		34°08'·00N 129°12'·00E	150	
Nobuyuki (Tx)		34°01'·00N 130°56'·00E	150	
NAGOYA (NAGOYA MRCC)	004310401		N/A	Operational *(MRCC Nagoya)*
Remotely controlled stations:-				Operational *(MRCC Nagoya)*
Asamagatake (Rx)		34°27'·00N 136°49'·00E	150	
Matsuo (Tx)		34°25'·00N 136°53'·00E	150	
NIIGATA (NIIGATA MRCC)	004310901		N/A	Operational *(MRCC Niigata)*
Remotely controlled stations:-				Operational *(MRCC Niigata)*
Arakawa (Tx)		38°06'·00N 139°28'·00E	150	
Nekogatake (Rx)		37°28'·00N 137°08'·00E	150	
OKINAWA (NAHA MRCC)	004311101		N/A	Operational *(MRCC Naha)*
Remotely controlled stations:-				Operational *(MRCC Naha)*
Kochinda (Tx)		26°08'·00N 127°43'·00E	150	
Miyara (Rx)		24°22'·00N 124°12'·00E	150	
Tamagusuku (Rx)		26°09'·00N 127°46'·00E	150	
SHIOGAMA (SHIOGAMA MRCC)	004310201		N/A	Operational *(MRCC Shiogama)*
Remotely controlled stations:-				Operational *(MRCC Shiogama)*
Kamaishi (Rx)		39°16'·00N 141°54'·00E	150	
Komagamine (Rx)		38°18'·00N 141°32'·00E	150	
Nyudozake (Rx)		40°00'·00N 139°42'·00E	150	
Same (Rx)		40°29'·00N 141°37'·00E	150	
Utazu (Tx)		38°44'·00N 141°33'·00E	150	
YOKOHAMA (YOKOHAMA MRCC)	004310301		N/A	Operational *(MRCC Yokohama)*
Remotely controlled stations:-				Operational *(MRCC Yokohama)*
Chikura (Rx)		34°56'·00N 139°56'·00E	150	
Choshi (Rx)		35°44'·00N 140°52'·00E	150	
Shimoda (Rx)		34°40'·00N 138°57'·00E	150	
Shirahama (Tx)		34°54'·70N 139°49'·93E	150	
KOREA, NORTH				
NAMPHO MRSC	004451021	38°43'·62N 125°24'·60E	150	Operational *(MRCC DPR Korea)*
NORTH HAMGYONG PROVINCE MRSC	004451029	41°45'·85N 129°50'·93E	150	Operational *(MRCC DPR Korea)*
SOUTH HAMGYONG PROVINCE MRSC	004451012	39°49'·38N 127°39'·53E	150	Operational *(MRCC DPR Korea)*
KOREA, SOUTH				
CHEJU (JEJU)				
Remotely controlled stations:-				Operational *(MRCC Cheju)*
Cheju (Jeju)	004400701	33°18'·97N 126°20'·82E	250	
CHEJU (JEJU) MRCC	004401005	33°31'·25N 126°32'·50E	250	Operational *(MRCC Cheju)*
INCH'ŎN (INCHEON)				
Remotely controlled stations:-				Operational *(MRCC Inch'ŏn)*
Deokjeokdo	004400004	37°13'·50N 126°08'·58E	250	

(1)	(2)	(3)	(4)	(5)
KOREA, SOUTH				
INCH'ŎN (INCHEON) MRCC	004401001	37°27'·33N 126°36'·23E	250	Operational *(MRCC Inch'ŏn)*
MOKP'O (MOKPO) MRCC	004401003	34°47'·15N 126°39'·37E	250	Operational *(MRCC Seohae)*
PUSAN (BUSAN)				
Remotely controlled stations:-				Operational *(MRCC Pusan)*
Yŏng Do	004400101	35°05'·06N 129°03'·27E	250	
PUSAN (BUSAN) MRCC	004401004	35°04'·70N 129°04'·68E	250	Operational *(MRCC Namhae)*
SEOUL	004400002	37°31'·00N 127°05'·00E	250	Operational *(MRCC Inch'ŏn)*
TONGHAE (DONGHAE) MRCC	004401002	37°31'·23N 129°06'·82E	250	Operational *(MRCC Tonghae)*
MALAYSIA (Sabah)				
KOTA KINABALU	005330013		N/A	Operational *(MRCC Port Klang)*
Remotely controlled stations:-				Operational *(MRCC Port Klang)*
Kota Kinabalu (MF DSC)		5°57'·00N 116°03'·00E	200	
MALAYSIA (Sarawak)				
KUCHING	005330011	1°35'·00N 110°11'·00E	N/A	Operational *(MRCC Port Klang)*
Remotely controlled stations:-				Operational *(MRCC Port Klang)*
Kuching (MF DSC)		1°49'·00N 109°46'·00E	200	
MALAYSIA, PENINSULAR				
KUANTAN	005330008	4°06'·00N 103°23'·00E	200	Operational *(MRCC Putrajaya)*
PERMATANG PAUH	005330002	5°25'·10N 100°24'·00E	200	Operational *(MRCC Putrajaya)*
PHILIPPINES				
MANILA RESCUE COORDINATION CENTRE - NATIONAL HEADQUARTERS PHILIPPINE COAST GUARD (NHPCG) (MRCC PHILIPPINES)	005480020	14°35'·15N 121°01'·00E	300	Operational
TAIWAN				
KEELUNG	004162019		N/A	Operational
Remotely controlled stations:-				Operational
Hotien Shan (Rx)		23°53'·00N 121°35'·00E	100	
Keelung		25°08'·08N 121°45'·37E	97	
Linyuan		22°29'·00N 120°24'·00E	97	
Sanchih (Rx)		25°16'·00N 121°28'·00E	90	
Tapingding (Rx)		22°01'·27N 120°41'·66E	100	
Yüanli (Rx)		24°26'·00N 120°38'·00E	90	
THAILAND				
BANGKOK	005671000		N/A	Operational *(RCC Bangkok)*
Remotely controlled stations:-				Operational *(RCC Bangkok)*
Sriracha MF Station		13°06'·51N 100°55'·84E	162	
VIETNAM				
BEN THUY	005741070	18°48'·83N 105°43'·12E	200	Operational *(MRCC Hai Phong)*
CA MAU	005743070	9°11'·38N 105°08'·02E	200	Operational *(MRCC Vung Tau)*
CAN THO	005743050	10°04'·30N 105°45'·53E	200	Operational *(MRCC Vung Tau)*
CUA ONG	005741020	21°01'·57N 107°22'·00E	200	Operational *(MRCC Hai Phong)*
ĐA NANG	005742030	16°03'·28N 108°09'·47E	200	Operational *(MRCC Đa Nang)*
HAI PHONG	005741040	20°51'·02N 106°44'·02E	200	Operational *(MRCC Hai Phong)*
HO CHI MINH	005743030	10°23'·68N 107°08'·70E	200	Operational *(MRCC Vung Tau)*
HON GAI	005741030	20°57'·35N 107°04'·12E	200	Operational *(MRCC Hai Phong)*
HUÉ	005742020	16°33'·03N 107°38'·47E	200	Operational *(MRCC Đa Nang)*
KIEN GIANG	005743080	9°59'·48N 105°06'·15E	200	Operational *(MRCC Vung Tau)*
MONG CAI	005741010	21°31'·55N 107°57'·98E	200	Operational *(MRCC Hai Phong)*
NHA TRANG	005742080	12°13'·32N 109°10'·83E	200	Operational *(MRCC Nha Trang)*
PHAN THIET	005743010	10°55'·07N 108°06'·37E	200	Operational *(MRCC Vung Tau)*
PHU YEN	005742070	13°06'·37N 109°18'·68E	200	Operational *(MRCC Nha Trang)*
QUY NHON	005742060	13°46'·67N 109°14'·35E	200	Operational *(MRCC Đa Nang)*
VIETNAM				
VUNG TAU	005743020	10°23'·68N 107°08'·73E	200	Operational *(MRCC Vung Tau)*

NAVAREA XII

Country Station (1)	MMSI (2)	Position (3)	Range (n miles) (4)	Status (Associated RCCs) (5)
COLOMBIA (Pacific Coast)				
BUENAVENTURA	007300101	3°54'·37N 77°03'·69W	200	Operational (MRCC Pacifico)
TUMACO	007300201	1°49'·32N 78°43'·77W	200	Operational (MRCC Pacifico)
GALAPAGOS ISLANDS (Ecuador)				
AYORA (ISLA SANTA CRUZ)	007354757	0°44'·80S 90°19'·00W	250	Operational
MEXICO (Pacific Coast)				
MAZATLÁN	003450810	23°11'·36N 106°25'·51W	150	Operational (MRCC Mazatlán)

NAVAREA XIII

Country Station (1)	MMSI (2)	Position (3)	Range (n miles) (4)	Status (Associated RCCs) (5)
RUSSIA (Pacific Coast)				
PETROPAVLOVSK-KAMCHATSKIY	002733737		N/A	Operational (MRSC Petropavlovsk-Kamchatskiy)
Remotely controlled stations:-				Operational (MRSC Petropavlovsk-Kamchatskiy)
Avacha (Rx)		53°04'·00N 158°32'·00E	150	
Zhelezniy (Tx)		53°15'·00N 158°25'·00E	150	
PLASTUN	002734442	44°46'·31N 136°19'·49E	160	Operational (MRCC Vladivostok)
VANINO	002734421	48°55'·00N 140°20'·00E	72	Operational (MRSC Yuzhno-Sakhalinsk)
VLADIVOSTOK MRCC	002734412	42°45'·86N 133°03'·01E	150	Operational (MRCC Vladivostok)
RUSSIA (Pacific Coast)				
YUZHNO-SAKHALINSK (REGIONAL CENTRE) MRSC	002733733		N/A	Operational (MRSC Yuzhno-Sakhalinsk)
Remotely controlled stations:-				Operational (MRSC Yuzhno-Sakhalinsk)
Cape Svobodniy MF (Rx)		46°50'·85N 143°26'·13E	170	
Nevel'sk (Rx)		46°39'·00N 141°52'·00E	165	
Seleznevo (Tx)		46°38'·00N 141°51'·50E	165	
Vygoda (Tx)		46°52'·00N 143°09'·00E	170	

NAVAREA XIV

Country Station (1)	MMSI (2)	Position (3)	Range (n miles) (4)	Status (Associated RCCs) (5)
FIJI				
FIJI MARITIME SURVEILLANCE RCC	005201100	18°08'·00S 178°26'·00E	200	Operational (RCC Suva)

NAVAREA XV

Country Station (1)	MMSI (2)	Position (3)	Range (n miles) (4)	Status (Associated RCCs) (5)
ARGENTINA				
USHUAIA MRCC (NAVY) & USHUAIA (Prefectura Naval)	007010011	54°47'·63S 68°18'·39W	150	Operational (MRCC Ushuaia)
CHILE				
ANTOFAGASTA ZONAL RADIO STATION	007250050	23°38'·93S 70°24'·02W	180	Operational (MRSC Iquique)
ARICA MRSC	007250010	18°28'·58S 70°19'·25W	180	Operational (MRSC Arica)
BAHÍA FÉLIX	007250370	52°57'·72S 74°04'·85W	180	Operational (MRCC Punta Arenas)
CALDERA MRSC	007250080	27°03'·97S 70°49'·38W	180	Operational (MRSC Caldera)
COQUIMBO MRSC	007250110	29°56'·97S 71°20'·13W	180	Operational (MRSC Coquimbo)
IQUIQUE MRCC	007250020	20°12'·65S 70°09'·15W	180	Operational (MRCC Iquique)
ISLA DE PASCUA (EASTER ISLAND) AREA RADIO STATION	007250100	27°10'·97S 109°25'·82W	180	Operational (MRSC Valparaíso)
ISLA SAN PEDRO	007250320	47°41'·95S 74°51'·92W	180	Operational (MRCC Punta Arenas)
JUAN FERNÁNDEZ	007250130	33°38'·16S 78°49'·98W	180	Operational (MRCC Valparaíso)
MAGALLANES ZONAL RADIO STATION	007250380	53°09'·91S 70°54'·27W	180	Operational (MRCC Punta Arenas)
PUERTO AYSÉN	007250300	45°24'·48S 72°43'·08W	180	Operational (MRSC Aysen)
PUERTO MONTT	007250230	41°28'·90S 72°57'·57W	180	Operational (MRCC Puerto Montt)
PUERTO WILLIAMS CAPUERTO	007250420	54°55'·95S 67°36'·45W	180	Operational (MRSC Puerto Williams)
PUNTA DELGADA	007250390	52°27'·35S 69°32'·82W	180	Operational (MRCC Punta Arenas)

(1)	(2)	(3)	(4)	(5)

CHILE

(1)	(2)	(3)	(4)	(5)
SAN ANTONIO MRSC	007250140	33°34'·31S 71°36'·97W	180	Operational *(MRSC San Antonio)*
TALCAHUANO	007250170	36°41'·50S 73°06'·51W	180	Operational *(MRCC Talcahuano)*
VALPARAÍSO (PLAYA ANCHA) PRINCIPAL RADIO STATION	007251860	33°01'·24S 71°38'·55W	180	Operational *(MRCC Valparaíso)*

NAVAREA XVI

Country Station	MMSI	Position	Range (n miles)	Status *(Associated RCCs)*
(1)	(2)	(3)	(4)	(5)

PERU

CALLAO MRCC	007600125	12°04'·34S 77°10'·13W	200	Operational *(MRSC Callao)*
MOLLENDO MRSC	007600129	17°00'·60S 72°02'·10W	200	Operational *(MRSC Mollendo)*
PAITA MRSC	007600121	5°05'·29S 81°06'·39W	200	Operational *(MRSC Paita)*

NAVAREA XVII

Country Station	MMSI	Position	Range (n miles)	Status *(Associated RCCs)*
(1)	(2)	(3)	(4)	(5)

NONE

NAVAREA XVIII

Country Station	MMSI	Position	Range (n miles)	Status *(Associated RCCs)*
(1)	(2)	(3)	(4)	(5)

GREENLAND

AASIAAT	003313000			
Remotely controlled stations:-				Operational *(MRCC Grønnedal)*
Qeqertarsuaq		69°14'·67N 53°31'·60W	250	
Upernavik		72°46'·98N 56°08'·33W	280	

NAVAREA XIX

Country Station	MMSI	Position	Range (n miles)	Status *(Associated RCCs)*
(1)	(2)	(3)	(4)	(5)

BJØRNØYA (Norway)

BJØRNØYA	002570000	74°30'·23N 18°59'·90E	200	Operational *(JRCC North Norway Bodø)*

NORWAY

NORWEGIAN COASTAL RADIO NORTH	002570000	67°16'·48N 14°23'·48E	200	
Remotely controlled stations:-				Operational *(JRCC North Norway Bodø)*
Northern Area (North of 69°30′N)				
Berlevåg		70°51'·78N 29°04'·57E	200	
Bjørnøya		74°30'·16N 18°59'·72E	200	
Hammerfest (Hammerfjell)		70°41'·50N 23°40'·42E	200	
Isfjord/Svalbard		78°03'·70N 13°36'·98E	200	
Jan Mayen		70°56'·68N 8°40'·02W	200	
Tromsø		69°39'·13N 18°56'·83E	200	
Vardø (Domen) MF Aerial		70°22'·00N 31°06'·00E	200	
Southern Area (North of 65°30′N)				
Andenes (Ramnan)		69°16'·42N 16°00'·48E	200	
Bodøsjøen		67°16'·00N 14°23'·00E	200	
Sandnessjøen		66°01'·17N 12°36'·53E	200	

NAVAREA XX				
Country Station	MMSI	Position	Range (n miles)	Status (*Associated RCCs*)
(1)	(2)	(3)	(4)	(5)

RUSSIA (Arctic Coast)

ARKHANGEL'SK MRSC	002734414	64°21'·00N 40°37'·00E	170	
DIKSON MRCC	002733717	73°30'·23N 80°31'·35E	N/A	Operational (*MRCC Dikson*)
MURMANSK MRCC	002734420	68°52'·00N 33°05'·00E	170	Operational (*MRCC Murmansk*)
Remotely controlled stations:-				Operational (*MRCC Murmansk*)
Murmansk (Tx)		68°46'·00N 32°58'·00E	170	

NAVAREA XXI				
Country Station	MMSI	Position	Range (n miles)	Status (*Associated RCCs*)
(1)	(2)	(3)	(4)	(5)

RUSSIA (Arctic Coast)

PEVEK MRSC	002733730	69°42'·03N 170°15'·26E	N/A	Operational (*MRSC Pevek*)
TIKSI MRSC	002733730	71°41'·36N 128°52'·21E	N/A	Operational (*MRSC Tiksi*)

HF DSC, LIST OF COAST STATIONS FOR SEA AREAS A3/A4

N/A = Not applicable
TBD = To be decided

NAVAREA I			
Country Station	MMSI	Operational Frequency bands	Status (Associated RCCs)
(1)	(2)	(3)	(4)
NONE			

NAVAREA II			
Country Station	MMSI	Operational Frequency bands	Status (Associated RCCs)
(1)	(2)	(3)	(4)
IVORY COAST			
ABIDJAN	006191000	4, 6, 8, 12, 16 MHz	Operational (MRCC Abidjan)
SENEGAL			
DAKAR MRCC	006631008	4, 6, 8, 12, 16 MHz	Operational (MRCC Dakar)
SPAIN			
MADRID	002241022	4, 8, 12 MHz	Operational (MRCC Madrid)
Remotely controlled stations:-			
Arganda (Rx)		4, 8, 12 MHz	
Trijueque (Tx)		4, 8, 12 MHz	
SPAIN (North Coast)			
CORUÑA	002241022		
Remotely controlled stations:-			Operational (MRSC Coruña)
Ares		8, 12 MHz	

NAVAREA III			
Country Station	MMSI	Operational Frequency bands	Status (Associated RCCs)
(1)	(2)	(3)	(4)
AZERBAIJAN			
BAKU	004231000 004232000	4, 6, 8, 12, 16 MHz	Operational (Azerbaijan LRIT NC)
Remotely controlled stations:-			Operational (Azerbaijan LRIT NC)
Chilov		4, 6, 8, 12, 16 MHz	
CYPRUS			
CYPRUS	002091000	4, 8 MHz	Operational (JRCC Larnaca)
EGYPT (Mediterranean Coast)			
AL ISKANDARĪYAH (ALEXANDRIA)	006221111	4, 6, 8, 12, 16 MHz	Operational (RCC Cairo)
GREECE			
The primary responsibility for the receipt of HF DSC distress alerts for Greece is carried out via Olympia Coast Radio Station. Pieraiás (Piraeus) JRCC, operated by Hellenic Coast Guard, keeps H24 watch on HF DSC distress frequencies for additional safety only. Aspropýrgos Attikís remains in a constant state of operational readiness.			
ASPROPÝRGOS ATTIKÍS (JRCC) (HELLENIC COASTGUARD)	002391000	4, 6, 8, 12, 16 MHz	Operational (JRCC Piraeus)
Note Operational Hours HJ only. Hot standby mode at other times.			
OLYMPIA	002371000	4, 6, 8, 12, 16 MHz	Operational (JRCC Piræus)
PEIRAIÁS JRCC (HELLENIC COAST GUARD)	002392000 237673000	4, 6, 8, 12, 16 MHz	Operational (JRCC Piraeus)
IRAN (Caspian Sea)			
AMĪRĀBĀD	004225601	4, 6, 8, 12, 16 MHz	Operational
ANZALĪ	004225500	4, 6, 8, 12, 16 MHz	Operational
ROMANIA			
CONSTANŢA	002640570	4, 8, 12 MHz	Operational (Constanţa Harbour Master)
SYRIA			
AL LĀDHIQĪYAH (LATAKIA)	004680011	4, 6, 8, 12, 16 MHz	Operational
TURKEY			
ISTANBUL	002711000	4, 6, 8, 12, 16 MHz	Operational (MSRCC Ankara)

NAVAREA IV

Country Station (1)	MMSI (2)	Operational Frequency bands (3)	Status (*Associated RCCs*) (4)
CANADA (Arctic Coast, Atlantic Coast and Saint Lawrence River)			
IQALUIT (NUNAVUT) (CANADIAN COAST GUARD)	003160023	4, 6, 8, 12, 16 MHz	Operational (navigation season only) (*RCC Halifax/Trenton*)
Remotely controlled stations:-			
Resolute (Rx)		4, 6, 8, 12, 16 MHz	
Note This station serves both NAVAREA XVII AND XVIII			
COLOMBIA (Caribbean Coast)			
BARRANQUILLA	007300301	4, 6, 8, 12, 16 MHz	Operational (*MRCC Caribe*)
CARTAGENA	007300501	4, 6, 8, 12, 16 MHz	Operational (*MRCC Caribe*)
COVEÑAS	007300901	4, 6, 8, 12, 16 MHz	Operational (*MRCC Caribe*)
PROVIDENCIA	007301201	4, 6, 8, 12, 16 MHz	Operational (*MRCC San Andrés*)
SAN ANDRÉS	007300701	4, 6, 8, 12, 16 MHz	Operational (*MRCC San Andrés*)
SANTA MARTA	007300401	4, 6, 8, 12, 16 MHz	Operational (*MRCC Caribe*)
TURBO	007300801	4, 6, 8, 12, 16 MHz	Operational (*MRCC Caribe*)
PUERTO RICO (USA)			
SAN JUAN SECTOR & RSC (US COAST GUARD)	003669992	4, 6, 8, 12, 16 MHz	Operational (*RSC San Juan*)
Note HF DSC test call facility. To initiate an automatic test call response, the ship will use the MMSI of the station, select 4 MHz DSC frequency and "Test". The USCG will automatically respond to the test request.			
UNITED STATES (Atlantic Coast)			
BOSTON RCF (US COAST GUARD FIRST DISTRICT)	003669991	4, 6, 8, 12, 16 MHz	Operational (*JRCC Boston*)
COMMCOM (COMMUNICATIONS COMMAND) (US COAST GUARD)	003669995		
Remotely controlled stations:-			Operational (*JRCC Norfolk*)
Chesapeake (NMN)	003669995	4, 6, 8, 12, 16 MHz	
MIAMI RCF (US COAST GUARD SEVENTH DISTRICT)	003669997	4, 6, 8, 12, 16 MHz	Operational (*JRCC Miami*)
UNITED STATES (Gulf Coast)			
NEW ORLEANS RCF (US COAST GUARD EIGHTH DISTRICT)	003669998	4, 6, 8, 12, 16 MHz	Operational (*JRCC New Orleans*)
Note HF DSC test call facility. To initiate an automatic test call response, the ship will use the MMSI of the station, select 4 MHz DSC frequency and "Test". The USCG will automatically respond to the test request.			

NAVAREA V

Country Station (1)	MMSI (2)	Operational Frequency bands (3)	Status (*Associated RCCs*) (4)
BRAZIL			
MANAUS	007100003	4, 6, 8, 12, 16 MHz	Operational (*MRCC Brazil*)
RECIFE (Pernambuco)	007100002	4, 6, 8, 12, 16 MHz	Operational (*MRCC Brazil*)
RIO DE JANEIRO (RENEC - EMBRATEL)	007100001	4, 6, 8, 12, 16 MHz	Operational (*MRCC Brazil*)

NAVAREA VI

Country Station	MMSI	Operational Frequency bands	Status (*Associated RCCs*)
(1)	(2)	(3)	(4)
ARGENTINA			
BUENOS AIRES (Prefectura Naval)	007010001	4, 6, 8, 12, 16 MHz	Operational (*MRCC Rio de La Plata*)
COMODORO RIVADAVIA (Prefectura Naval)	007010008	4, 6, 8, 12, 16 MHz	Operational (*MRSC Comodoro Rivadavia*)
MAR DEL PLATA (Prefectura Naval)	007010003	4, 6, 8, 12, 16 MHz	Operational (*MRSC Mar del Plata*)
URUGUAY			
MONTEVIDEO ARMADA	007703870	4, 6, 8, 12, 16 MHz	Operational (*MRCC Uruguay*)

NAVAREA VII

Country Station	MMSI	Operational Frequency bands	Status (*Associated RCCs*)
(1)	(2)	(3)	(4)
SOUTH AFRICA			
CAPE TOWN (Including DURBAN and PORT ELIZABETH)	006010001	4, 6, 8, 12, 16 MHz	Operational (*MRCC Cape Town*)

NAVAREA VIII

Country Station	MMSI	Operational Frequency bands	Status (*Associated RCCs*)
(1)	(2)	(3)	(4)
BANGLADESH			
DHAKA MRCC	405000236	4, 6, 8, 12, 16 MHz	
BURMA			
AYEYARWADY MRCC	005061411	4, 6, 8, 12, 16 MHz	Operational (*MRCC Ayeyarwady*)
YANGON	005060100	4, 6, 8, 12, 16 MHz	Operational (*MRCC Yangon*)
INDIA (Andaman and Nicobar Region)			
PORT BLAIR MRCC	004194409	4, 6, 8, 12, 16 MHz	Operational (*MRCC Port Blair*)
INDIA (Eastern Region (Including Bay of Bengal))			
CHENNAI MRCC	004194401	4, 6, 8, 12, 16 MHz	Operational (*MRCC Chennai*)
HALDIA MRSC	004194404	4, 6, 8, 12, 16 MHz	Operational (*MRCC Chennai*)
MANDAPAM MRSSC	004194406	4, 6, 8, 12, 16 MHz	Operational (*MRCC Chennai*)
INDIA (North Western Region)			
DAMAN CGAS	004192201	4, 6, 8, 12, 16 MHz	Operational (*MRCC Mumbai*)
PORBANDAR MRSC	004192202	4, 6, 8, 12, 16 MHz	Operational (*MRCC Mumbai*)
INDIA (Western Region)			
MUMBAI MRCC	004192203	4, 6, 8, 12, 16 MHz	Operational (*MRCC Mumbai*)
MAURITIUS			
MAURITIUS	006452700	4, 6, 8, 12, 16 MHz	Operational

NAVAREA IX

Country Station	MMSI	Operational Frequency bands	Status (*Associated RCCs*)
(1)	(2)	(3)	(4)
IRAN			
BANDAR-E EMĀM KHOMEYNĪ	004225100	4, 6, 8, 12, 16 MHz	Operational (*MRCC Bandar 'Abbās*)
BANDAR-E SHAHĪD RAJĀ'Ī	004225300	4, 6, 8, 12, 16 MHz	Operational (*MRCC Bandar 'Abbās*)
PAKISTAN			
KARACHI	004634060	4, 6, 8, 12, 16 MHz	Operational (*MRCC Karachi*)

NAVAREA X

Country Station (1)	MMSI (2)	Operational Frequency bands (3)	Status (*Associated RCCs*) (4)
AUSTRALIA			
JRCC AUSTRALIA (CANBERRA)	005030001		
Remotely controlled stations:-			Operational (*RCC Australia*)
Charleville	005030001	4, 6, 8, 12, 16 MHz	
Wiluna	005030001	4, 6, 8, 12, 16 MHz	
SOLOMON ISLANDS			
HONIARA	005570001	4, 6, 8 MHz	Operational (*MRCC Honiara*)

NAVAREA XI

Country Station (1)	MMSI (2)	Operational Frequency bands (3)	Status (*Associated RCCs*) (4)
CHINA			
HONG KONG MARINE RESCUE	004773500	4, 6, 8, 12, 16 MHz	Operational (*MRCC Hong Kong*)
SHANGHAI	004122100	4, 6, 8, 12, 16 MHz	Operational (*MRCC Shanghai*)
GUAM (USA)			
GUAM SECTOR (US COAST GUARD)	003669994	4, 6, 8, 12, 16 MHz	Operational (*RSC Guam, JRCC Honolulu*)
Note HF DSC test call facility. To initiate an automatic test call response, the ship will use the MMSI of the station, select 4 MHz DSC frequency and "Test". The USCG will automatically respond to the test request.			
INDONESIA (Jawa)			
JAKARTA	005250000	4, 6, 8, 12, 16 MHz	Operational (*MRSC Jakarta*)
SEMARANG	005250008	8 MHz	Operational (*MRSC Semarang*)
SURABAYA	005250001	4, 6, 8, 12, 16 MHz	Operational (*MRSC Surabaya*)
INDONESIA (Kalimantan)			
BALIKPAPAN	005250009	8 MHz	Operational (*MRSC Balikpapan*)
INDONESIA (Papua)			
JAYAPURA	005250007	4, 6, 8, 12, 16 MHz	Operational (*MRSC Jayapura*)
SORONG	005250011	8 MHz	Operational (*MRSC Sorong*)
INDONESIA (Seram)			
AMBOINA	005250006	4, 6, 8, 12, 16 MHz	Operational (*MRSC Ambon*)
INDONESIA (Sulawesi)			
BITUNG	005250005	4, 6, 8, 12, 16 MHz	Operational (*MRSC Menado*)
MAKASSAR	005250002	4, 6, 8, 12, 16 MHz	Operational (*MRSC Makassar*)
INDONESIA (Sumatera)			
BELAWAN	005250003	4, 6, 8, 12, 16 MHz	Operational (*MRSC Medan*)
DUMAI	005250004	4, 6, 8, 12, 16 MHz	Operational (*MRSC Pekanbaru*)
INDONESIA (Timor)			
KUPANG	005250010	8 MHz	Operational (*MRSC Kupang*)
JAPAN			
TOKYO (JCG HQ)	004310001	4, 6, 8, 12, 16 MHz	Operational (*Japan Coast Guard MRCCs*)
KOREA, NORTH			
NAMPHO MRSC	004451021	4, 6, 8, 12, 16 MHz	Operational (*MRCC DPR Korea*)
NORTH HAMGYONG PROVINCE MRSC	004451029	4, 6, 8, 12, 16 MHz	Operational (*MRCC DPR Korea*)
SOUTH HAMGYONG PROVINCE MRSC	004451012	4, 6, 8, 12, 16 MHz	Operational (*MRCC DPR Korea*)
KOREA, SOUTH			
CHEJU (JEJU) MRCC	004401005	4, 6, 8, 12, 16 MHz	Operational (*MRCC Cheju*)
INCH'ÖN (INCHEON) MRCC	004401001	4, 6, 8, 12, 16 MHz	Operational (*MRCC Inch'ön*)
MOKP'O (MOKPO) MRCC	004401003	4, 6, 8, 12, 16 MHz	Operational (*MRCC Seohae*)
PUSAN (BUSAN) MRCC	004401004	4, 6, 8, 12, 16 MHz	Operational (*MRCC Namhae*)
SEOUL	004400002	4, 6, 8, 12, 16 MHz	Operational (*MRCC Inch'ön*)
TONGHAE (DONGHAE) MRCC	004401002	4, 6, 8, 12, 16 MHz	Operational (*MRCC Tonghae*)
PHILIPPINES			
MANILA RESCUE COORDINATION CENTRE - NATIONAL HEADQUARTERS PHILIPPINE COAST GUARD (NHPCG) (MRCC PHILIPPINES)	005480020	4, 6, 8, 12, 16 MHz	Operational

(1)	(2)	(3)	(4)
TAIWAN			
KEELUNG	004162019	4, 6, 8, 12, 16 MHz	Operational
THAILAND			
BANGKOK	005671000	4, 6, 8, 12, 16 MHz	Operational *(RCC Bangkok)*
VIETNAM			
ĐA NANG	005742030	4, 6, 8 MHz	Operational *(MRCC Đa Nang)*
HAI PHONG	005741040	4, 6, 8, 12, 16 MHz	Operational *(MRCC Hai Phong)*
HO CHI MINH	005743030	4, 6, 8, 12, 16 MHz	Operational *(MRCC Vung Tau)*
NHA TRANG	005742080	4, 6, 8 MHz	Operational *(MRCC Nha Trang)*
VIETNAM			
VUNG TAU	005743020	4, 6, 8 MHz	Operational *(MRCC Vung Tau)*

NAVAREA XII

Country Station	MMSI	Operational Frequency bands	Status *(Associated RCCs)*
(1)	(2)	(3)	(4)
COLOMBIA (Pacific Coast)			
BUENAVENTURA	007300101	4, 6, 8, 12, 16 MHz	Operational *(MRCC Pacifico)*
TUMACO	007300201	4, 6, 8, 12, 16 MHz	Operational *(MRCC Pacifico)*
GALAPAGOS ISLANDS (Ecuador)			
AYORA (ISLA SANTA CRUZ)	007354757	4, 6, 8, 12, 16 MHz	Operational
UNITED STATES (Alaska)			
KODIAK (US COAST GUARD)	003669899	4, 6, 8, 12, 16 MHz	Operational *(JRCC Alameda)*
UNITED STATES (Hawaii)			
HONOLULU RCF (US COAST GUARD FOURTEENTH DISTRICT)	003669993	4, 6, 8, 12, 16 MHz	Operational *(JRCC Honolulu)*
UNITED STATES (Pacific Coast)			
Universal US Coast Guard shore based identity: 003669999			
POINT REYES RCF	003669990	4, 6, 8, 12, 16 MHz	Operational *(JRCC Alameda)*

Note   HF DSC Test call facility. To initiate an automatic test call response, the ship will use the MMSI of the called station, select 4 MHz DSC frequency and "TEST". The USCG will automatically respond to the test request.

NAVAREA XIII

Country Station	MMSI	Operational Frequency bands	Status *(Associated RCCs)*
(1)	(2)	(3)	(4)

NAVAREA XIV

Country Station	MMSI	Operational Frequency bands	Status *(Associated RCCs)*
(1)	(2)	(3)	(4)
FIJI			
FIJI MARITIME SURVEILLANCE RCC	005201100	4, 6, 8, 12, 16 MHz	Operational *(RCC Suva)*
NEW ZEALAND			
TAUPO MARITIME RADIO	005120010	4, 6, 8, 12, 16 MHz	Operational *(RCC New Zealand)*

NAVAREA XV

Country Station	MMSI	Operational Frequency bands	Status (*Associated RCCs*)
(1)	(2)	(3)	(4)

CHILE

ANTOFAGASTA ZONAL RADIO STATION	007250050	4 MHz	Operational (*MRSC Iquique*)
ISLA DE PASCUA (EASTER ISLAND) AREA RADIO STATION	007250100	4 MHz	Operational (*MRSC Valparaíso*)
MAGALLANES ZONAL RADIO STATION	007250380	4, 8 MHz	Operational (*MRCC Punta Arenas*)
PUERTO MONTT	007250230	4 MHz	Operational (*MRCC Puerto Montt*)
TALCAHUANO	007250170	4 MHz	Operational (*MRCC Talcahuano*)
VALPARAÍSO (PLAYA ANCHA) PRINCIPAL RADIO STATION	007251860	4, 6, 8, 12, 16 MHz	Operational (*MRCC Valparaíso*)

NAVAREA XVI

Country Station	MMSI	Operational Frequency bands	Status (*Associated RCCs*)
(1)	(2)	(3)	(4)

PERU

CALLAO MRCC	007600125	8 MHz	Operational (*MRSC Callao*)
MOLLENDO MRSC	007600129	8 MHz	Operational (*MRSC Mollendo*)
PAITA MRSC	007600121	8 MHz	Operational (*MRSC Paita*)

NAVAREA XVII

Country Station	MMSI	Operational Frequency bands	Status (*Associated RCCs*)
(1)	(2)	(3)	(4)

NONE

NAVAREA XVIII

Country Station	MMSI	Operational Frequency bands	Status (*Associated RCCs*)
(1)	(2)	(3)	(4)

NONE

NAVAREA XIX

Country Station	MMSI	Operational Frequency bands	Status (*Associated RCCs*)
(1)	(2)	(3)	(4)

NORWAY

NORWEGIAN COASTAL RADIO NORTH	002570000		
Remotely controlled stations:-			Operational (*JRCC North Norway Bodø*)
Hammerfest (Hammerfjell)		4, 6, 8 MHz	
Note Hammerfest is used as a backup site.			
Isfjord/Svalbard		4, 6, 8 MHz	

NAVAREA XX

Country Station	MMSI	Operational Frequency bands	Status (*Associated RCCs*)
(1)	(2)	(3)	(4)

NONE

NAVAREA XXI

Country Station	MMSI	Operational Frequency bands	Status (*Associated RCCs*)
(1)	(2)	(3)	(4)

NONE

Operational HF DSC Stations for Sea Areas A3 and A4

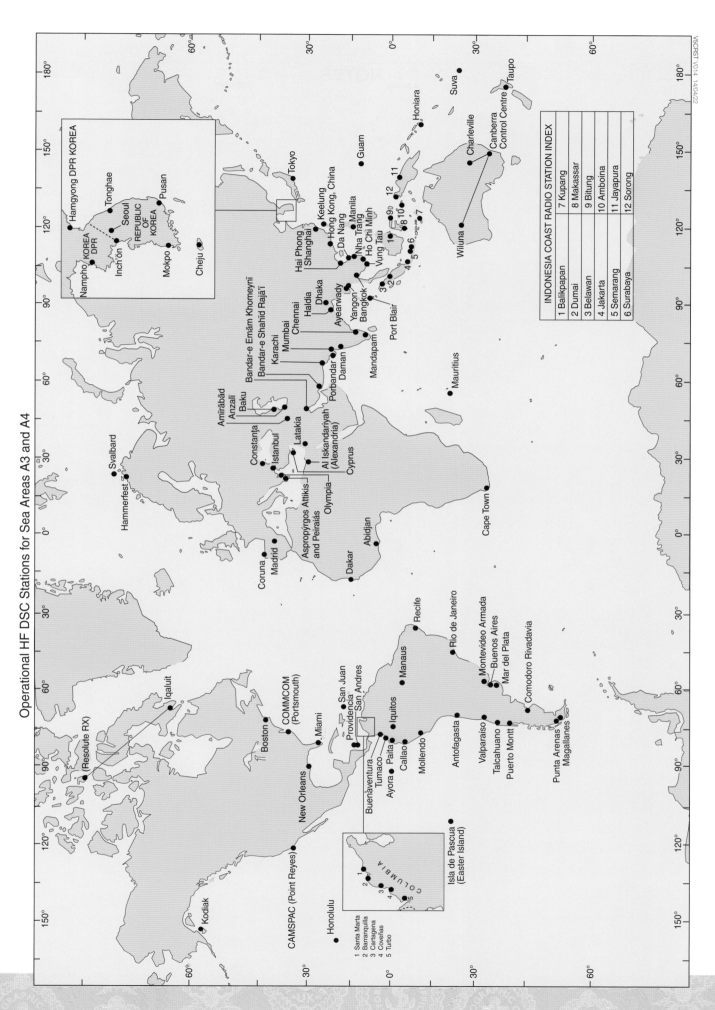

INDONESIA COAST RADIO STATION INDEX

1 Balikpapan	7 Kupang
2 Dumai	8 Makassar
3 Belawan	9 Bitung
4 Jakarta	10 Amboina
5 Semarang	11 Jayapura
6 Surabaya	12 Sorong

V5CRST V014 14/04/22

NOTES

MARITIME SAFETY INFORMATION (MSI) UNDER THE GMDSS

HF NBDP MARITIME SAFETY INFORMATION BROADCAST SERVICE

Annex 9 of the IMO GMDSS Master Plan contains details of the radio stations which transmit MSI via HF NBDP.

Operational details and broadcast times of these stations are held in ADMIRALTY List of Radio Signals Volume 3, Parts 1 and 2 (NP283(1) and NP283(2)) or digital equivalent ADRS1345.

PROMULGATION OF MARITIME SAFETY INFORMATION

The Maritime Safety Information service of the GMDSS is the internationally and nationally coordinated network of broadcasts containing information which is necessary for safe navigation, received by vessels equipment which automatically monitors the appropriate transmissions, displays information which is relevant to the ship and provides a print capability. This concept is illustrated in the diagram below.

Resolution A.706(17), as amended on the World-Wide Navigational Warning Service (MSC.1/Circ.1288) requires that "All NAVAREA, Sub-Area and coastal warnings shall be broadcast only in English in the International NAVTEX and SafetyNET services".

Maritime Safety Information is of vital concern to all ships. It is therefore essential that common standards are applied to the collection, editing and dissemination of this information. Only by doing so will the mariner be assured of receiving the information required, in a form which is understandable and at the earliest possible time.

The International Maritime Safety Information Service

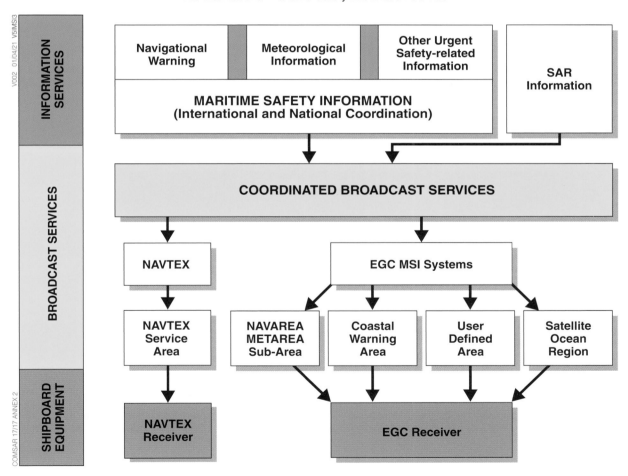

Broadcast methods

Three principal methods are used for broadcasting Maritime Safety Information in accordance with the provisions of the International Convention for the Safety of Life at Sea, 1974, as amended, in the areas covered by these methods, as follows:

1 NAVTEX: broadcasts to coastal waters; and
2 SafetyNET: broadcasts which cover all the waters of the globe except for Sea Area A4, as defined by IMO resolution A.801(19), Annex 3, as amended and SafetyNET II.
3 SafetyCast: broadcasts which are via the Iridium system, (please refer to the EGC Services section of this publication for the Iridium SafetyCast operational status by NAVAREA/METAREA).

Information should be provided for unique and precisely defined sea areas, each being served only by the most appropriate of the above methods. Although there will be some duplication to allow a vessel to change from one method to another, the majority of messages will be broadcast either on NAVTEX or by and EGC MSI Broadcast System .

NAVTEX broadcasts shall be made in accordance with the standards and procedures set out in the NAVTEX Manual.

SafetyNET broadcasts shall be made in accordance with the standards and procedures set out in the International SafetyNET Manual.
SafetyCast broadcasts shall be made in accordance with the standards and procedures set out in the International SafetyCast Manual.

SafetyNET II is the new generation international broadcast and automatic reception service for Maritime Safety Information. SafetyNET II is an enhancement to the current SafetyNET system and provides a user-friendly, interactive web interface for Maritime Safety Information Providers to create their Maritime Safety Information messages and deliver them simultaneously over multiple Inmarsat networks, including Inmarsat C, Mini C and Fleet Safety.

HF NBDP may be used to promulgate Maritime Safety Information in areas outside Inmarsat or NAVTEX coverage (SOLAS regulation IV/7.1.5).

In addition, administrations may also provide Maritime Safety Information by other means.

In the event of failure of normal transmission facilities, an alternative means of transmission should be utilized. A NAVAREA Warning and a coastal Warning, if possible, should be issued detailing the failure, its duration and, if known, the alternative route for the dissemination of MSI.

Scheduling

Automated methods (NAVTEX / EGC MSI Broadcast Systems)

Navigational warnings shall be broadcast as soon as possible or as dictated by the nature and timing of the event. Normally, the initial broadcast should be made as follows:

1 for NAVTEX, at the next scheduled broadcast, unless circumstances indicate the use of procedures for VITAL or IMPORTANT warnings; and
2 for EGC, within 30 minutes of receipt of original information, or at the next scheduled broadcast.

Navigational warnings shall be repeated in scheduled broadcasts in accordance with the guidelines promulgated in the NAVTEX Manual, International SafetyNET Manual, SafetyCast Manual or other Manual relating to a recognised IMO GMDSS service provider.

At least two scheduled daily broadcast times are necessary to provide adequate promulgation of NAVAREA warnings. When NAVAREAs extend across more than six time zones, more than two broadcasts should be considered to ensure that warnings can be received. When using SafetyNET in lieu of NAVTEX for coastal warnings, administrations may need to consider an increase in the number of scheduled daily broadcasts compared with the requirement for NAVAREA warnings. Please refer to the Iridium SafetyCast manual for details on coastal warnings.

Schedule changes

Broadcast times for NAVTEX are defined by the B_1 character of the station, allocated by the IMO NAVTEX Coordinating Panel.

Times of scheduled broadcasts under the International SafetyNET service are coordinated through the International EGC Coordinating Panel. The SafetyCast EGC broadcast service is also coordinated by the International EGC Coordinating Panel.

Shipboard equipment

Ships are required to be capable of receiving Maritime Safety Information broadcasts for the area in which they operate in accordance with the provisions of the International Convention for the Safety of Life at Sea, 1974, as amended.

The NAVTEX receiver should operate in accordance with the technical specifications set out in Recommendation ITU-R M.540, as amended, and should meet the performance standards adopted by the IMO resolution MSC.148(77), as amended.

The EGC MSI receiver should conform to the Maritime Design and Installation Guidelines (DIGs) published by Inmarsat, and should meet the performance standards adopted by the IMO resolution A.664(16).

In Sea Area A4, outside of the coverage of NAVTEX, where MSI is received using HF NBDP, the HF NBDP receiver should operate in accordance with the technical specifications set out in Recommendation ITU-R M.688, as amended, and should meet the performance standards adopted by the IMO resolution A.700(17), as amended.

Provision of information

Navigational warnings shall be provided in accordance with the standards, organisation and procedures of the WWNWS under the functional guidelines of the IHO through its Sub-Committee on Promulgation of Radio Navigational Warnings. Details of NAVAREA coordinators are maintained on the IHO Web site https://iho.int/en/navigation-warnings-on-the-web and are also published by an IMO COMSAR Circular.

Meteorological information shall be provided in accordance with the WMO technical regulations and recommendations, monitored and reviewed by the Expert Team on Maritime Safety Services of the Joint WMO/IOC Commission for Oceanography and Marine Meteorology (JCOMM).

SAR information shall be provided by the various authorities responsible for coordinating maritime search and rescue operations in accordance with the standards and procedures established by the IMO.

Other urgent safety-related information shall be provided by the relevant national or international authority responsible for managing the system or scheme.

Relevant national or international authorities shall take into account the need for contingency planning.

Coordination procedures

In order to make the best use of automated reception facilities and to ensure that the mariner receives at least the minimum information necessary for safe navigation, careful coordination is required.

In general, this requirement for coordination will be met by the standard operational procedures of IMO, IHO, WMO, International Telecommunication Union (ITU) and International Mobile Satellite Organization (IMSO). Cases of difficulty should be referred, in the first instance, to the most appropriate parent body.

Administrations broadcasting maritime safety information should provide details of services to the IMO, which will maintain and publish this as part of the GMDSS Master Plan.

Administrations should design their broadcasts to suit specific service areas. The designation of service areas is an important part of the coordination process since it is intended that a ship should be able to obtain all the information relevant to a given area from a single source. The Maritime Safety Committee approves NAVAREAs / METAREAs and service areas for the International NAVTEX and EGC service as advised by IHO and WMO.

General EGC System Capabilities

EGC (Enhanced Group Call) is a satellite communication system which enables Information Providers to send messages for *selective reception* by EGC receivers located anywhere in the Ocean Regions.

Based on this selective capability, the EGC system supports:

- **The SafetyNET Service**, (Inmarsat system) allows information providers to broadcast Maritime Safety Information to all Inmarsat GMDSS vessels, addressed either to fixed geographical areas such as the IMO defined NAVAREAs or METAREAs, or user defined circular, rectangular or coastal areas.

- **The SafetyCast Service**, (Iridium system) allows information providers to broadcast Maritime Safety Information to all Iridium GMDSS vessels, addressed either to fixed geographical areas such as the IMO defined NAVAREAs or METAREAs, or user defined circular, rectangular or coastal areas.

General EGC System capabilities

Graphic courtesy of Inmarsat

For further details of promulgation of MSI, it is recommended that the following publications are consulted:

- JOINT IMO / IHO / WMO MANUAL ON MARITIME SAFETY INFORMATION
  Special Publication S-53-Appendix 1
  Published by:
  The IHB
  4 quai Antoine 1er
  MC 98011 MONACO

- The "IMO International SafetyNET Manual" and the "Manual on Maritime Safety"

NAVIGATIONAL WARNINGS FOR THE WORLD-WIDE NAVIGATIONAL WARNING SERVICE (WWNWS)

General

Navigational Warnings are issued in response to SOLAS regulation V/4 and carry information which may have a direct bearing on the safety of life at sea. It is the fundamental nature of Navigational Warnings that they will often be based on incomplete or unconfirmed information and mariners will need to take this into account when deciding what reliance to place on the information contained therein.

In order to achieve necessary impact on the mariner it is essential to present timely and relevant information in a consistent format that is CLEAR, UNAMBIGUOUS and BRIEF. This is ensured by using structured messages in standard formats.

The resources employed by administrations and the mariner are extremely limited. Thus only information which is vital to the safe conduct of vessels should be transmitted. Notices to Mariners and other means exist for passing less urgent information to ships after they have reached port. Information of a purely administrative nature should never be broadcast on the regular international Navigational Warning schedules.

There are four types of Navigational Warnings: NAVAREA warnings, Sub-Area warnings, coastal warnings and local warnings. The WWNWS guidance and coordination are involved with only three of them:

1 NAVAREA warnings
2 Sub-Area warnings; and:
3 Coastal warnings

Navigational Warnings shall remain in force until cancelled by the originating coordinator. Navigational Warnings should be broadcast for as long as the information is valid; however, if they are readily available to mariners by official means, for example in Notices to Mariners, then after a period of six weeks they may no longer be broadcast.

The minimum information in a Navigational Warning which a mariner requires is "hazard" and "position". It is usual, however, to include sufficient extra detail to allow some freedom of action in the vicinity of the hazard. This means that the message should give enough extra data for the mariner to be able to recognize the hazard and assess its effect upon his navigation.

If known, the duration of the event causing a Navigational Warning should be given in the text.

Some of the subjects for Navigational Warnings may also be suitable for promulgation as METAREA forecasts or warnings.

NAVAREA warnings

NAVAREA warnings are concerned with the information detailed below which ocean-going mariners require for their safe navigation. This includes, in particular, new navigational hazards and failures of important aids to navigation as well as information which may require changes to planned navigational routes.

The following subject areas are considered suitable for broadcast as NAVAREA warnings. This list is not exhaustive and should be regarded only as a guideline. Furthermore, it pre-supposes that sufficiently precise information about the item has not previously been disseminated in a Notice to Mariners:

1. Casualties to lights, fog signals, buoys and other aids to navigation affecting main shipping lanes;
2. The presence of dangerous wrecks in or near main shipping lanes and if relevant, their marking;
3. Establishment of major new aids to navigation or significant changes to existing ones when such establishment or change, might be misleading to shipping;
4. The presence of large unwieldy tows in congested waters;
5. Drifting hazards (including derelict vessels, ice, mines, containers, other large items etc.);
6. Areas where search and rescue (SAR) and anti-pollution operations are being carried out (for avoidance of such areas);
7. The presence of newly-discovered rocks, shoals, reefs and wrecks likely to constitute a danger to shipping and if relevant, their marking;
8. Unexpected alteration or suspension of established routes;
9. Cable or pipe-laying activities, the towing of large submerged objects for research or exploration purposes, the employment of manned or unmanned submersibles, or other underwater operations constituting potential dangers in or near shipping lanes;
10. The establishment of research or scientific instruments in or near shipping lanes;
11. The establishment of offshore structures in or near shipping lanes;
12. Significant malfunctioning of radio-navigation services and shore-based maritime safety information radio or satellite services;
13. Information concerning special operations which might affect the safety of shipping, sometimes over wide areas, e.g. naval exercises, missile firings, space missions, nuclear tests, ordnance dumping zones etc. It is important that where the degree of hazard is known, this information is included in the relevant warning. Whenever possible, such warnings should be originated not less than five days in advance of the scheduled event and reference may be made to relevant national publications in the warning.
14. Acts of piracy and armed robbery against ships.
15. Tsunamis and other natural phenomena, such as abnormal changes to sea level;
16. World Health Organization (WHO) health advisory information; and:
17. Security related requirements.

Sub-area warnings

Sub-area warnings broadcast information which is necessary for safe navigation within a Sub-area. They will normally include all subjects listed above, but will usually affect only the Sub-area.

Coastal warnings

Coastal warnings broadcast information which is necessary for safe navigation within areas seaward of the fairway buoy or pilot station and should not be restricted to main shipping lanes. Where the area is served by NAVTEX, it should provide Navigational Warnings for the entire NAVTEX service area. Where the area is not served by NAVTEX, it is necessary to include all warnings relevant to the coastal waters up to 250 n miles from the coast in the EGC Satellite Service broadcast.

Coastal warnings should include at least the subjects above.

Local warnings

Local warnings broadcast information which cover inshore waters often within the limits of jurisdiction of a harbour or port authority. They are broadcast by means other than NAVTEX or EGC Satellite Services and supplement coastal warnings by giving detailed information within inshore waters.

WEB PORTAL FOR IMO/WMO WORLDWIDE MET-OCEAN INFORMATION AND WARNING SERVICE (WWMIWS)

A web portal is available to fleet managers and ship operations providing all meteorological forecast and warning bulletins that are issued for METAREAs using SafetyNET, as part of the IMO/WMO Worldwide Met-Ocean Information and Warning Service (WWMIWS). In addition, bulletins issued through NAVTEX are also available.

Due to the geographic limitation of SafetyNET broadcast coverage at high latitudes, the web portal provides an important means for ships operating in polar waters to access meteorological MSI and ice information:

http://weather.gmdss.org/index.html

The internet is not part of the Maritime Safety Information system and should never be relied upon as the only means to obtain the latest forecast and warning information. Access to the service may be interrupted or delayed from time to time, updates may also be delayed. Please refer to GMDSS services, EGC Satellite Services, international NAVTEX or the national meteorological service concerned for the latest information.

(Baltic Sea Sub-Area Coordinator)
Swedish Maritime Administration
BALTICO
SE-601 78 NORRKÖPING
Sweden
Telephone: +46 711 630605
email: ufs@sjofartsverket.se
Website: www.sjofartsverket.se/en/services/ntm---notices-to-mariners/navigational-warnings
Warning Url: www.sjofartsverket.se/en/services/ntm---notices-to-mariners/navigational-warnings

National Coordinators

COUNTRY	TELEPHONE	FACSIMILE	EMAIL/OTHER
Denmark	+45 72850370		mas@sok.dk vagts@dma.dk https://dma.dk/safety-at-sea/navigational-information/nautical-information
Estonia	+372 6205665		navinfo@transpordiamet.ee www.transpordiamet.ee https://transpordiamet.ee/NTM (Estonian Notices to Mariners) https://gis.vta.ee/navhoiatustehaldus/et.html#warnings (Navigational Warnings)
Finland	+358 204 486400		turku.radio@fta.fi https://extranet.liikennevirasto.fi/pooki_www/merivaroitukset/list_en.html
Germany	+49 4927 1877283		seewarndienst.wsa-emd@t-online.de https://www.bsh.de/EN/TOPICS/Shipping/Navigational_information/Warnings_and_notices/warnings_and_notices_node.html
Latvia	+371 67062101	+371 67860082	navarea@lhd.lv sar@mrcc.lv lja@lja.lv www.navtex.lv www.lhd.lv
Lithuania	+370 52785601	+370 52132270	ltsa@ltsa.lrv.lt mardep@ltsa.lrv.lt hydrography@ltsa.lrv.lt https://hydro.eltsa.lt/portal/apps/sites/#/hidrografine-veikla-1
Poland	+48 261 266208 (H24) +48 723 651713 (H24)	+48 261 266203 (H24)	bhmw.msi@ron.mil.pl https://bhmw.gov.pl/en/
Russian Federation	+7 812 7175900	+7 812 7175900	unio_main@mil.ru (General contact address) unio_navarea@mil.ru (naviagation warning providing purpose only)
Sweden	+46 771 630685 (H24)		swedentraffic@sjofartsverket.se www.sjofartsverket.se/en/services/ntm---notices-to-mariners/navigational-warnings

NAVAREA I (United Kingdom)

United Kingdom National Hydrographer
United Kingdom Hydrographic Office
Admiralty Way
TAUNTON Somerset TA1 2DN
United Kingdom
Telephone: +44(0)1823 353448
Fax: +44(0)1823 322352
email: navwarnings@ukho.gov.uk
Warning Url: https://www.admiralty.co.uk/maritime-safety-information/radio-navigational-warnings

National Coordinators

COUNTRY	TELEPHONE	FACSIMILE	EMAIL/OTHER
Belgium	+32 59 255493	+32 59 255467	rmd@mil.be
Denmark	+45 72850370	+45 72850384	mas@sok.dk
Faroe Islands	+298 351302	+298 351301	mrcc@vorn.fo
France	+33 2 98221667 +33 2 56312424	+33 2 56312584	coord.navarea2@shom.fr
Germany	+49 4927 1877283	+49 4927 1877288	seewarndienst.wsa-emd@t-online.de
Iceland	+354 5452120	+354 5452001	sjomis@lhg.is
Ireland	+353 16620922	+353 16620795	mrccdublin@irishcoastguard.ie
Netherlands	+31 2 23542300	+31 2 23658358	ccc@kustwacht.nl
Norway	+47 22422331	+47 22410491	navco@kystverket.no www.kystverket.no
United Kingdom	+44 1823 353448	+44 1823 322352	navwarnings@ukho.gov.uk

NAVAREA II (France)

Department Information et Ouvrages Nautiques
Service Hydrographique et Océanographique de la Marine
13 Rue du Chatellier
CS 92803
29228 BREST CEDEX 2
France
Telephone: +33 (0)2 56312424 (H24) (Duty Officer)
    +33 (0)2 98221667 (H24) (Duty Officer)
    +33 6 24800892 (Mobile)
Fax: +33 (0)2 56312584
email: coord.navarea2@shom.fr (H24)
    coord.navarea2@gmail.com (HX)
Website: https://diffusion.shom.fr/pro/informations_nautiques
Warning Url: http://diffusion.shom.fr/navarea-en-vigueur

National Coordinators

COUNTRY	TELEPHONE	FACSIMILE	EMAIL/OTHER
Benin	+229 21315280	+229 21312891	forces.navales.benin@gmail.com vetbos@yahoo.fr
Cameroon	+237 33420133	+237 33426797	georgescracite.menye@pad.cm
Cape Verde	+238 2324342	+238 2324271	armindo.graca@imp.cv
Congo	+242 940052	+242 942042	info@papn-cg.org
Congo (Dem Rep)	+243 815193396 +243 813663357		coord.nat.rsmrdc@gmail.com patrickmusitumbu2@gmail.com
France (Atlantic Coast)	+33 298220619	+33 298377658	combrest.infonaut@premar-atlantique.gouv.fr www.premar-atlantique.gouv.fr
Gabon	+241 764833		
Gambia, The	+220 4229940 +220 9977038	+220 4227268	info@gambiaports.gm kmanneh@gambiaports.gm www.gambiaports.gm

Ghana	+233 0302663506 +233 0303968564 +233 0303204153		tema@ghanaports.net www.ghanaports.gov.gh
Guinea	+224 622621889 +224 622210702 +224 622125186 +224 622481014	+224 30413577	dnmm.guinee@gmail.com mrsc.guinee@gmail.com dnmmgn@yahoo.fr
Guinea Bissau	+245 201984	+245 201984	capitania_bissau@yahoo.com
Ivory Coast	+225 241762315	+225 21238115	cor.navareaci@gmail.com
Liberia	+231 777092229 +231 777290158 +231 886889738 +231 770323474		mrmrcc@lima-liberia.com mrcc.monrovia@yahoo.fr
Mauritania	+222 45256104 +222 36361300		dmm.dir@peches.gov.mr tolmamoctar@yahoo.fr tolba@mauritanie.mr
Morocco	+212 06 50890829 +212 05 22294028		dhoc-cdiv-mr@far.ma www.equipement.gov.ma/publications/portuaireetmaritime/pages/publications.aspx
Nigeria	+234 809 5039888 (H24)		msi@nnho.ng info@nnho.ng www.nnho.ng
Portugal	+351 21 4401950 +351 21 0984454	+351 214401954 +351 211938442	avisos.navegacao@marinha.pt
Senegal	+221 338265001	+221 338265000	marinenat@orange.sn
Sierra Leone	+232 22 226480	+232 22 226443	sierraleoneports@yahoo.com
Spain	+34 917559191	+34 917559192	radioavisos.cncs@sasemar.es www.salvamentomaritimo.es
Togo	+228 22270517 +228 22237080	+228 22710110	base.marine@yahoo.com

NAVAREA III (Spain)
Representative of NAVAREA III Coordinator
Director del Instituto Hidrográfico de la Marina
Head of the Navigational Section
Instituto Hidrográfico de la Marina
Plaza San Severiano No 3
11007 CADIZ
Spain

Telephone:	+34 956 599399 (Head of Navigation Section)
	+34 956 599409
	+34 956 599414
Fax:	+34 956 599396
	+34 956 545347
email:	avisosihm@fn.mde.es
	ihmesp@fn.mde.es
Website:	http://www.armada.mde.es/ihm
Warning Url:	https://armada.defensa.gob.es/ihm/Aplicaciones/Navareas/Index_Navareas_xml_eng.htm

National Coordinators

COUNTRY	TELEPHONE	FACSIMILE	EMAIL/OTHER
Albania	+355 52 260955	+355 52 60243	hydroal@gmail.com
Algeria	+213 23 951204 +213 23 951128	+213 23 951132 +213 23 951127	shfn@mdn.dz www.mdn.dz
Bulgaria	+359 52 684922 +359 29 300910	+359 52 602378 +359 29 930092	bma@marad.bg mrcc.varna@gmail.com mrcc_vn@marad.bg www.marad.bg
Croatia	+385 21 308800 +385 21 308845 +385 915051621 (Mobile)	+385 21 347208 +385 21 347242	naut@hhi.hr office@hhi.hr https://www.hhi.hr/en/e-services/radio-navigational-warnings
Cyprus	+357 2 4304723 +357 2 4304737 +357 2 4643005	+357 2 4643254	cyprus.radio@cyta.com.cy cartogr@dis.moi.gov.cy jrcc_cyp@cytanet.com.cy jrcc.cyprus@cyta.com.cy www.mod.gov.cy
Egypt	+20 3 4801006	+20 3 4802233	hydro@enhd.gov.eg maritime@eams.gov.eg https://www.eams.gov.eg
France	+33 2 98221559	+33 2 98221432	coord.navarea2@shom.fr www.shom.fr http://diffusion.shom.fr/navarea-en-vigueur
Georgia	+995 493 278405	+995 493 221772	info@hydrography.ge www.hydrography.ge
Greece	+30 210 6551750 +30 210 6551806	+30 210 6517811 +30 210 6557139	nasf_hnhs@navy.mil.gr navtex_hnhs@navy.mil.gr www.hnhs.gr
Israel	+972 4 8632080 +972 4 8632145	+972 4 8632118	techni@mot.gov.il rcc@mot.gov.il lahavs@mot.gov.il bennyr@mot.gov.il http://asp.mot.gov.il/en/shipping/notice2mariners
Italy	+39 065 9083493 +39 065 9084527 +39 01 024431	+39 065 9084440 +39 065 9084793 +39 010 261400	navtex@mit.gov.it itmrcc@mit.gov.it www.guardiacostiera.gov.it
Lebanon	+961 1 371644 +961 1 983470 +961 1 371645 +961 3 371647	+961 1 371647 +961 1 983460	shmal.navy@army.gov.lb ministry@transportation.gov.lb www.transportation.gov.lb
Libya	+218 213 619912 +218 213 603068 +218 214 891415	+218 213 603061 +218 214 893435	m.tabeaa@tripoliseaport.ly hassan_zawia@lttnet.net h.i.zawia@gptc.ly

Malta	+356 22 494202 +356 22 494206 +356 21 222203	+356 21 809860 +356 21 250365 +356 21 222208	opsroom.afm@gov.mt info.tm@transport.gov.mt rccmalta@gov.mt https://www.transport.gov.mt/maritime/notices-to-mariners-coastal-93
Montenegro	+382 3 2686120	+382 3 2686120	office@meteo.co.me hidrografija@meteo.co.me branislav.gloginja@meteo.co.me www.meteo.co.me
Morocco	+212 537 688174 +212 537 704790 +212 660192659 (Mobile) +212 661730190 (Mobile)	+212 537 704607 +212 537 688112	mrcc.rabat@mpm.gov.ma drissi@mpm.gov.ma doghmi@mtpnet.gov.ma dgmf@dmm.gov.ma www.mtpnet.gov.ma
Romania	+40 241 651040 +40 241 616411 +40 241 602706	+40 241 513065 +40 241 616411 +40 241 737103	horia.popa@radionav.ro office@radionav.ro hidro@dhmfn.ro
Russia	+7 812 7175900	+7 812 7175900	unionavarea@mil.ru navtex@rmpnovo.ru www.structure.mil.ru/structure/forces/hydrographic/info/notices.htm
Slovenia	+386 5 6632100 +386 5 6632102	+386 5 6632102	ursp.box@gov.si koper.mrcc@gov.si primoz.bajec1@gov.si https://www.gov.si/drzavni-organi/ministrstva/ministrstvo-za-infrastrukturo/o-ministrstvu/direktorat-za-letalski-in-pomorski-promet/sektor-za-pomorstvo/obvestila-za-pomorscake/
Spain	+34 91 7559191	+34 91 7559192	radioavisos.cncs@sasemar.es www.salvamentomaritimo.es
Syria	+963 41 473876 +963 41 473333 +963 41 472593	+963 41 475805	danco@net.sy info@gdp-sy.com
Tunisia	+216 72 510267	+216 72 510777	sho@defence.tn www.defense.tn
Turkey	+90 212 4259728 +90 216 3222580	+90 212 5410338 +90 216 3310525	info@shodb.gov.tr teletext@shodb.gov.tr trmrcc@denizcilik.gov.tr telsiz@kiyiemniyeti.gov.tr http://www.shodb.gov.tr/shodb_esas/index.php/en/
Ukraine	+380 44 2924120 +380 44 2966040 +380 50 4118473 (Mobile)	+380 44 2924120 +380 44 2966040	navtex@ukr.net navtexukr@gmail.com navigation@hydro.gov.ua http://charts.gov.ua/pm_arhive_en.htm

NAVAREA IV (United States)
Maritime Watch
National Geospatial-Intelligence Agency
MAIL STOP N65-SH
7500 GEOINT Drive
Springfield, VA 22150-7500
United States of America

Telephone:	+1 571 557 5455
	+1 571 557 6746
Fax:	+1 571 558 3261
email:	navsafety@nga.mil
Website:	https://www.nga.mil/resources/Maritime_Safety_Products_and_Services.html
Warning Url:	http://msi.nga.mil/NGAPortal/MSI.portal (Select Broadcast Warnings)

National Coordinators within the United States

COUNTRY	TELEPHONE	FACSIMILE	EMAIL/OTHER
COMCOMM (OSCS Butierries)	+1 757 421 6240		daniel.g.butierries@uscg.mil
Coast Guard District 1	+1 617 223 8555	+1 617 223 8117	d01-smb-d1cmdcenter@uscg.mil
Coast Guard District 5	+1 757 398 6231	+1 757 398 6392	d05-smb-d5cg@uscg.mil
Coast Guard District 7	+1 305 415 6800	+1 305 415 6809	d07-smb-cmdcenter@uscg.mil
Coast Guard District 8	+1 504 589 6225	+1 504 589 2148	d08-comandcenter@uscg.mil
Coast Guard District 11	+1 510 437 3701	+1 510 437 3017	rccalameda@uscg.mil
Coast Guard District 13	+1 206 220 7001	+1 206 220 7009	d13cc@uscg.mil
Coast Guard District 14	+1 808 535 3333	+1 808 535 3338	jrcchonolulu@uscg.mil
Coast Guard District 17	+1 907 463 2000	+1 907 463 2023	jrccjuneau@uscg.mil
International Ice Patrol	+1 860 271 2626	+1 860 271 2773	iipcoms@uscg.mil

National Coordinators

COUNTRY	TELEPHONE	FACSIMILE	EMAIL/OTHER
Anguilla	+1 264 497 2651		rawle.hazell@gov.ai
Antigua & Barbuda	+1 268 462 1273 +1 268 779 8799	+1 268 462 2510 +1 268 460 6024	dlake@abregistry.ag
Barbados	+1 246 434 6100		kfergusson@barbadosport.com
Belize	+501 223 0714		mmcord@portauthority.bz
Bermuda	+1 441 2971010		
Canada MCTS Iqaluit	+1 867 979 5724	+1 867 979 4264	iqanordreg@innav.gc.ca www.marinfo.gc.ca/e-nav
Canada JRCC Halifax	+1 902 427 8200	+1 902 427 2144	jrcchalifax@sarnet.dnd.ca www.marinfo.gc.ca/e-nav
Canada MCTS Prescott	+1 613 925 4471	+1 613 925 4519	www.marinfo.gc.ca/e-nav
Colombia	+57 5 6694465 ext 5142 +57 5 6694465 ext 5121		jortizbuitrago@dimar.mil.co
Costa Rica	+506 2255 3854 +506 2233 5022	+506 2223 2697	dlealoba@mopt.go.cr atebyanc@mopt.go.cr
Cuba	+53 72090926	+53 77940409	hg@unicom.co.cu avisosshg@emarinos.geocuba.cu
Curacao	+599 9 463 7747		gjg.felida@mindef.nl
Curacao RCC Curacao	+599 9 463 7700		rcc.curacao@mindef.nl
Dominica	+1 767 449 2185	+1767 449 2020	metoffice@cwdom.dm
Dominican Republic	+1 809 593 5900		primitivo.lopez@live.com

Ecuador	+593 232 0400		avisos.navegantes@inocar.mil.ec sec-aln@inocar.mil.ec
El Salvador	+503 259 35497		jesus.villalta@cnr.gob.sv
French Antilles **(Adjoint Mer Antilles** **"C")**	+596 596 395059 +596 696 284082	+596 596 395165	emia-antilles.ccmoh24.fct@def.gouv.fr
French Guiana **(Adjoint Mer Guyane** **"A")**	+594 594 395669	+594 594 395585	info-nautique.charge-com.fct@def.gouv.fr
Greenland **Aasiaat Radio**	+299 130000 +299 386993	+299 892777	oyr@telepost.gl
Greenland JRCC **Greenland**	+299 364010 +299 364000		jrcc@jrcc.gl
Grenada	+1 473 440 7678 +1 473 420 6376	+1 868 730 6454	grenport@spiceisle.com
Guatemala	+502 4497 4254	+502 2334 4775	hidrografia@dgam.gob.gt
Guyana	+592 226 0860		sos@marad.gov.gy mikel_figueria@hotmail.com
Haiti	+509 2816 1630		frenoldcheristin@yahoo.fr
Honduras	+504 8990 0520		malcab1430@gmail.com
Jamaica	+1 876 379 7169 +1 876 967 1060	+1 876 922 5765	htomlinson@jamaicaships.com
Martinique **MRCC Fort de France**	+596 596 709292	+596 596 735730	
Mexico	+52 55 56246500 ext 7230	+52 55 56246500	depto.ayudas.nav@gmail.com
Nicaragua	+505 2222 3738		leinael.0983@gmail.com
Panama	+507 501 5150		operaport@amp.gob.pa fpitty@amp.gob.pa
Puerto Rico	+1 787 2892041	+1 787 7296706	ssjcc@uscg.mil
Saint Kitts	+1 869 465 5451 +1 869 466 7032 ext 243	+1 869 466 7256	harveylharvey@yahoo.com maritimeaffairs@yahoo.com
Saint Lucia	+1 758 457 6152		christopher.alexander@slapsa.com
Saint-Pierre and **Miquelon**	+508 411530 (Primary) +508 551616 (Alternative)	+508 414834	uam.samp.dtam-975@equipement-agriculture.gouv.fr
Saint Vincent & The **Grenadines**	+1 784 456 1378	+1 784 451 2245	svgmarad@gmail.com
Suriname	+597 476 733 ext 242		ossedo@mas.sr
Trinidad	+1 868 625 3804 ext 409	+1 868 624 5884	solmso@gov.tt
Virgin Islands (UK)	+1 284 468 2902 +1 284 468 2903		rfrett@gov.vg

NAVAREA V (Brazil)

Brazilian Navy Hydrographic Centre

Telephone:	+55 21 21893023
	+55 21 21893210
Fax:	+55 21 21893210
email:	rafaela.castro@marinha.mil.br
	avradio@marinha.mil.br
Website:	http://www.marinha.mil.br/dhn/
Warning Url:	https://www.marinha.mil.br/chm/dados-do-segnav-aviso-radio-nautico-tela/radio-navigational-warnings-and-sar-warnings

National Coordinators

COUNTRY	TELEPHONE	FACSIMILE	EMAIL/OTHER
Brazil	+55 21 21893023 +55 21 21893210	+55 21 21893210	rafaela.castro@marinha.mil.br avradio@marinha.mil.br

NAVAREA VI (Argentina)

Head Maritime Safety Department
Naval Hydrographic Service
Montes de Oca 2124
Buenos Aires C1270 ABV
Argentina

Telephone:	+54 11 43012249
	+54 11 43010061-67 (ext 4028)
Fax:	+54 11 43012249
email:	snautica@hidro.gov.ar
	shn_orgint@hidro.gov.ar
Website:	http://www.hidro.gob.ar/Nautica/radioav.asp
Warning Url:	http://www.hidro.gob.ar/Nautica/CNV.asp

National Coordinators

COUNTRY	TELEPHONE	FACSIMILE	EMAIL/OTHER
Argentina	+54 11 43012249 +54 11 4301 0061-67 ext 4028	+54 11 43012249	snautica@hidro.gov.ar shn_orgint@hidro.gov.ar www.hidro.gob.ar
Uruguay	+59 82 3093775 +59 82 3093861 +59 82 3071777	+59 82 3099220	sohma@armada.mil.uy www.armada.mil.uy

NAVAREA VII (South Africa)

The Hydrographer, S.A. Navy
Hydrographic Office
Private Bag X1, Tokai
7966 Cape Town
South Africa

Telephone: +27 21 7872408 (0730 - 1600 Mon - Fri)
Fax: +27 21 7872228 (H24 for Urgent navigational information)
email: hydrosan@iafrica.com (0730 - 1600 Mon - Fri)
　　　　 ncc@sanavy.co.za (H24 for Urgent navigational information)
Website: www.sanho.co.za

National Coordinators

COUNTRY	TELEPHONE	FACSIMILE	EMAIL/OTHER
South Africa	+27 21 7872445 +27 21 7872444 +27 21 7872408	+27 21 7872233	hydrosan@iafrica.com
Mozambique	+258 21 430186 +258 21 430188	+258 21 430185 +258 21 428670	hidro@inahina.uem.mz

NAVAREA VIII (India)

The Chief Hydrographer to the Govt of India for Joint Director of Hydrography (Maritime Safety Information Services)
National Hydrographic Office
107A Rajpur Road
Dehradun, Uttaranchal
India 248001

Telephone: +91 135 2746290-95
Fax: +91 135 2748373
email: inho@navy.gov.in
　　　　 msis-inho@navy.gov.in
　　　　 ncdm-inho@navy.gov.in
　　　　 navarea8@gmail.com
Website: www.hydrobharat.gov.in
Warning Url: https://hydrobharat.gov.in/navarea-warnings/

National Coordinators

COUNTRY	TELEPHONE	FACSIMILE	EMAIL/OTHER
Bangladesh	+880 2 9553584	+880 2 9587301	cns@dos.gov.bd
Burma	+95 31 31669	+95 31 31669	mintheintint.hydro2010@gmail.com cdryelwin@gmail.com ityehtuntoo.mnhc@gmail.com zawlat33410@gmail.com snowyflower2893@gmail.com slt.hsumonoo@gmail.com soenyuntthaw52@gmail.com naingphyomaung52@gmail.com kyawzaya570@gmail.com
Kenya	+254 737719414 +254 721368313 +870 764626657 (Inmarsat)	+254 208007776	rmrcc@kma.go.ke
Maldives	+960 3395981 +960 3398898	+960 3391665	mrcc@mndf.gov.mv
Mauritius	+230 2085950 +230 2110839	+230 2110838	3bm.mrs@mauritiustelecom.com 3bm.mrs@telecom.mu
Réunion	+262 262 907932	+262 262 907931	cellmer.emia@fazsoi.defense.gouv.fr
Seychelles	+248 4224866	+248 4224829	dg@smsa.sc hydroffr.seycoast@email.sc
Somalia			

Sri Lanka	+94 11 2385401 +94 11 2435896 +94 11 2482121 +94 11 2435127	+94 11 2327160 +94 11 2435160 +94 11 2434055	ravi@slpa.lk dmsmos@sltnet.lk
Tanzania	+255 222 129325 +255 222 129326 +255 222 129327	+255 222 129326	mrccdar@sumatra.or.tz ken.chimwejo@sumatra.or.tz

NAVAREA IX (Pakistan)

Hydrographer of Pakistan Navy
PN Hydrographic Department
11, Liaquat Barracks
Karachi 75530
Pakistan

Telephone:	+92 21 48506819 +92 21 48506821 +92 21 48506151
Fax:	+92 21 99201623 +92 21 35867737
email:	hydropk@paknavy.gov.pk hydrpk@gmail.com
Website:	hydrography.paknavy.gov.pk

National Coordinators

COUNTRY	TELEPHONE	FACSIMILE	EMAIL/OTHER
Bahrain	+973 17810021	+973 17725591	khalidaas@sirb.gov.bh
Djibouti	+253 353475 +253 353208	+253 3561538	
Egypt	+20 3 4802233	+20 3 4875633	e.n.h.d@hotmail.com
Eritrea			
Ethiopia	+251 1 154915 +251 1 159013		
Iran	+9821 88651116 +9821 84932143 +9821 84932152	+9821 84932675	aparhizi@pmo.ir parizi@pmo.ir
Iraq			
Jordan	+962 32014031 +962 32016320	+962 32016204	info@aqabaports.gov.jo
Kuwait	+965 24990333	+965 24990333	mazidi@moc.kw.or
Oman	+968 24312350 +968 24322831	+968 24312460	nhooman@omantel.net.om hydromo@mod.gov.om
Pakistan	+92 21 48506151	+92 21 99201623	hydropk@paknavy.gov.pk hydrpk@gmail.com
Qatar	+974 44955947	+974 44955947	vladan@up.org.qa
Saudi Arabia	+966 14 532161	+966 14 532161	hydro@gdms.gov.sa
Somalia			
Sudan	+249 1171659		
United Arab Emirates	+971 2 651900	+971 2 651691	msd2000@emirates.net.ae
Yemen	+967 2 203521	+967 2 205805	ypa@y.net.ye

NAVAREA X (Australia)

Senior Search & Rescue Officer
JRCC Australia
Emergency Response Division
Australian Maritime Safety Authority
82 Northbourne Avenue, Braddon ACT 2612
GPO Box 2181
Canberra, ACT 2601
Australia

Telephone:	+61 2 62306811 (H24) (Maritime)
	+61 2 62306899 (H24) (Aviation)
email:	rccaus@amsa.gov.au
Website:	http://www.amsa.gov.au
Warning Url:	www.amsa.gov.au/search-and-rescue/about-the-gmdss/msi-information/msi-email/index.asp

National Coordinators

COUNTRY	TELEPHONE	FACSIMILE	EMAIL/OTHER
New Caledonia	+687 292332	+687 292303	operations@mrcc.nc
Papua New Guinea	+675 3212969 +675 73517017	+675 3210873	pngmrcc@nmsa.gov.pg
Solomon Islands	+677 21609	+677 23798	mrcc@solomon.com.sb
Vanuatu	+678 33600 +678 22475		trobson@vanuatu.gov.vu

NAVAREA XI (Japan)

Notice to Mariners Office
Hydrographic and Oceanographic Department
Japan Coast Guard
3-1-1, Kasumigaseki, Chiyoda-ku
TOKYO 100-8932
Japan

Telephone:	+81 3 35953645 (0930 JST to 1815 JST Mon to Fri)
	+81 3 35953647 (Sat, Sun, national holidays and times other than above)
Fax:	+81 3 35953571
email:	tuho@jodc.go.jp
	jcg-tuho@navarea11.go.jp
Website:	http://www1.kaiho.mlit.go.jp
Warning Url:	www1.kaiho.mlit.go.jp/TUHO/tuho/nm_en.html

National Coordinators

COUNTRY	TELEPHONE	FACSIMILE	EMAIL/OTHER
China	+86 10 65292325	+86 10 65292465	warning@msa.gov.cn
Indonesia	+62 21 64714809 +62 21 64714810 +62 21 64714819	+62 21 64714809 +62 21 64714819	infohid@pushidrosal.id
Japan	+81 3 35953647	+81 3 35953571	tuho@jodc.go.jp jcg-tuho@navarea11.go.jp
Korea, North	+850 2 3818888	+850 2 3814692	mrcc.dprk@ssalink.net
Korea, South (Republic of)	+82 51 4004331-4004334	+82 51 4004194	ntmkhoa@korea.kr www.khoa.go.kr
Malaysia	+60 33 1694545 +60 33 1695211	+60 33 1671334	hairizam@marine.gov.my
Philippines	+63 282413494 +63 282450295	+63 282422090	maritime.affairs@namria.gov.ph
Singapore	+65 63751562 +65 63751600	+65 62759247 +65 62787646	hydrographic@mpa.gov.sg
Thailand	+66 2 613369 +66 2 4753369	+66 2 1736570	hydronav@navy.mi.th
United States (Guam)	+1 301 2273147	+1 705 3396210	navsafety@nga.mil
Vietnam	+84 31 3551817 +84 31 3550685	+84 31 3550797	bangleminh@vms-north.vn

Details for Navarea XII are identical to the listing for Navarea IV.

NAVAREA XIII (Russian Federation)
Notices to Mariners Division
Department of Navigation and Oceanography
Ministry of Defence,
2, Atamanskaya st.
St. Petersburg 191167,
Russian Federation

Telephone:	+7 812 7175900
Fax:	+7 812 7175900
email:	unio_navarea@mil.ru
Website:	http://mil.ru/navigation.htm
Warning Url:	http://structure.mil.ru/structure/forces/hydrographic/info/navwar.htm

National Coordinators

COUNTRY	TELEPHONE	FACSIMILE	EMAIL/OTHER
Russian Federation	+7 812 7175900	+7 812 7175900	unio_main@mil.ru (General contact address)
			unio_navarea@mil.ru (naviagation warning providing purpose only)

NAVAREA XIV (New Zealand)
Maritime New Zealand
RCCNZ
41 Percy Cameron Street, Avalon Studios Level 1
PO Box 30050
LOWER HUTT 5040
New Zealand

Telephone:	+64 4 577 8030 (H24)
Fax:	+64 4 577 8038 (H24)
email:	rccnz@maritimenz.govt.nz (H24)
Website:	http://www.maritimenz.govt.nz
Warning Url:	http://www.maritimenz.govt.nz/navarea

National Coordinators

COUNTRY	TELEPHONE	FACSIMILE	EMAIL/OTHER
Cook Islands	+682 74530		saungaki.rasmussen@cookislands.gov.ck
Fiji	+679 3315266	+679 3313127	msi@msaf.com.fj
			skumar@msaf.com.fj
French Polynesia JRCC Tahiti	+689 40541616	+689 40423915	contact@jrcc.pf
Kingdom of Tonga	+676 22555	+676 42467	sioeli.fifita@moi.gov.to
	+676 7786157 (Mobile)		marineport@moi.gov.to
Kiribati	+686 74026003 (Extension 232)		eritaia.tauro@mcttd.gov.ki
	+686 73022727 (Mobile)		
New Caledonia (MRCC)	+687 292121	+687 292303	operations@mrcc.nc
New Zealand RCCNZ	+64 45778030	+64 45778038	rccnz@maritimenz.govt.nz
Niue	+683 8886983		lynsey.talagi@mail.gov.nu
Samoa	+685 22141	+685 22671	hoe.viali@mwti.gov.ws
	+685 7707794 (Mobile)		anastacia.amoa@mwti.gov.ws
			makerita.antonio@mwti.gov.ws
			tapaga.collins@mwti.gov.ws
Tuvalu	+688 20055		taasi.pitoi@gmail.com
Wallis & Futuna Islands MRCC New Caledonia	+687 292121	+687 292303	operations@mrcc.nc

NAVAREA XV (Chile)

South Pacific (East of 120°W)
Director,
Hydrographic and Oceanographic Service of the Chilean Navy
Errazuriz 254
Playa Ancha
VALPARAISO
Chile

Telephone:	+56 32 2266666
Fax:	+56 32 2266542
email:	navareaxv@shoa.cl
Website:	www.shoa.cl
Warning Url:	www.shoa.mil.cl/php/radioavisos.php

National Coordinators

COUNTRY	TELEPHONE	FACSIMILE	EMAIL/OTHER
Chile - Valparaiso	+56 32 2266612 +56 32 2266541	+56 32 2266542	navareaxv@shoa.cl

NAVAREA XVI (Peru)

South Pacific (East of 120°W, 3°24'S-18°21'S)
Dirección de Hidrografía y Navegación
Calle Roca No. 118
Chucuito
CALLAO 1
Peru

Telephone:	+51 1 2078160
Fax:	+51 1 4658312
email:	dihidronav@dhn.mil.pe
Website:	http://www.dhn.mil.pe
Warning Url:	www.dhn.mil.pe/radioavisos

National Coordinators

COUNTRY	TELEPHONE	FACSIMILE	EMAIL/OTHER
Peru - Head of Navigation Department	+51 1 2078160 ext 6480	+51 1 6136759	rmera@dhn.mil.pe
Operator of Navarea XVI	+51 1 2078160 ext 6401/6463	+51 1 2078178	navareaxvi@dhn.mil.pe dportilla@dhn.mil.pe

NAVAREA XVII (Canada)

National Strategies, Preparedness and Response
Canadian Coast Guard
Centennial Towers
200 Kent Street
Ottawa, Ontario K1A 0E6
Canada

Telephone:	+1 613 925 0666 (Preferred contact number)
	+1 613 925 4471 (Operations and General)
Fax:	+1 613 925 4519
email:	navarea17.18@innav.gc.ca
Warning Url:	https://www.ccg-gcc.gc.ca/navigation/index-eng.html

National Coordinators

COUNTRY	TELEPHONE	FACSIMILE	EMAIL/OTHER
Canada	+1 613 9254471	+1 613 9254519	navarea17.18@innav.gc.ca

Details for Navarea XVIII are identical to the listing for Navarea XVII.

NAVAREA XIX (Norway)

NAVAREA XIX Coordinator
Department of Maritime Safety
Norwegian Coastal Administration
P.O. Box 1502
6025 Ålesund
Norway

Telephone:	+47 78 989898
	+47 78 943000 (Direct)
Fax:	+47 78 989899
email:	navarea19@kystverket.no
Website:	http://www.navarea-xix.no/
Warning Url:	www.navarea-xix.no/

National Coordinators

COUNTRY	TELEPHONE	FACSIMILE	EMAIL/OTHER
Norway	+47 22422331	+47 22410491	navco@kystverket.no

NAVAREA XX (Russian Federation)

NAVAREA XX/XXI Coordinator
MSI Service
Federal State Unitary Enterprise "Rosmorport"
Bld.7, 19 Suschevskaya Street
Moscow, 127055
Russian Federation

Telephone:	+7 495 6261425 (Extensions 1060, 1702, 1707 & 1710)
Fax:	+7 495 6261239
email:	navarea@rosmorport.ru
Warning Url:	Details not available

National Coordinators

COUNTRY	TELEPHONE	FACSIMILE	EMAIL/OTHER
Russian Federation	+7 495 6261425 (Extensions 1060, 1702, 1707 & 1710)	+7 495 6261239	navarea@rosmorport.ru

NAVAREA XXI (Russian Federation)

Warning Url:	Details not available

EGC SERVICES

The International SafetyNET system

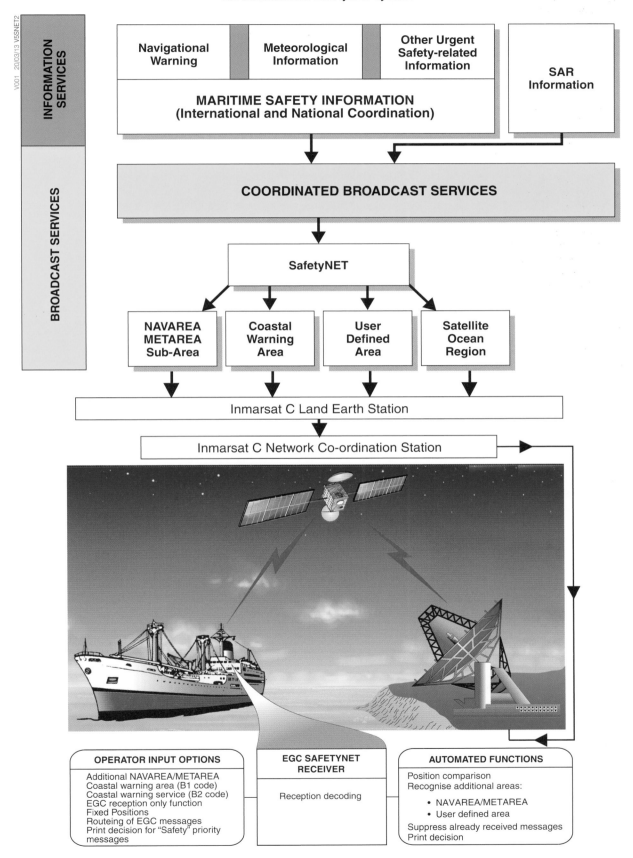

INFORMATION SERVICES

| Navigational Warning | Meteorological Information | Other Urgent Safety-related Information |

MARITIME SAFETY INFORMATION
(International and National Coordination)

SAR Information

BROADCAST SERVICES

COORDINATED BROADCAST SERVICES

SafetyNET

| NAVAREA METAREA Sub-Area | Coastal Warning Area | User Defined Area | Satellite Ocean Region |

Inmarsat C Land Earth Station

Inmarsat C Network Co-ordination Station

OPERATOR INPUT OPTIONS
Additional NAVAREA/METAREA
Coastal warning area (B1 code)
Coastal warning service (B2 code)
EGC reception only function
Fixed Positions
Routeing of EGC messages
Print decision for "Safety" priority messages

EGC SAFETYNET RECEIVER
Reception decoding

AUTOMATED FUNCTIONS
Position comparison
Recognise additional areas:
• NAVAREA/METAREA
• User defined area
Suppress already received messages
Print decision

Operation of the SafetyNET Service - An Overview

Operation of the SafetyNET service, involves a sequence of events:

1. A registered Information Provider, such as a national Hydrographic Office, Rescue Coordination Centre (RCC), Meteorological Office or other receives information from its specialized sources.

2. Each Information Provider prepares an MSI message in a standardized format and submits it to the appropriate coordinator (Navigational Warning Coordinator, SAR Coordinator or Meteorological Issuing Service).

3. The coordinator checks the message with any other information received, and edits it accordingly, then submits the finalized text to a selected Inmarsat C LES.

Included with the message are the following codes (known as the "C" codes), to instruct the LES and MES on how to process the message automatically:

- C_0 - **Ocean Region Code** (Optional) - Atlantic Ocean Region East (1), Atlantic Ocean Region West (0), Indian Ocean Region (3), Pacific Ocean Region (2) or all Ocean Regions (9) supported by the selected LES; check with LES operator or service provider.
- C_1 - **Priority Code** (distress, urgency or safety); 1 digit code.
- C_2 - **Service Code** to identify the message type, for example a shore-to-ship distress alert or meteorological forecast; 2 digit code.
- C_3 - **Address Code** to identify the geographical area for which the MSI is applicable - this may be a fixed geographical area, such as one of the 21 NAVAREAs/METAREAs, a temporary area determined by the originator, such as a circular or rectangular area or a coastal area. 2, 4, 10 or 12 alphanumeric code.
- C_4 - **Repetition Code** to indicate the number of times the message should be broadcast; 2 digit code.
- C_5 - **Presentation Code** to indicate the character set in which the message will be transmitted. (The character set used is always the International Alphabet Number 5, which is also known as 7-bit ASCII). 2 digit code.

4. The information provider submits scheduled MSI for broadcast via a nominated satellite at time(s) shown on the transmission schedule.

5. The LES receives the message with its instructions, and queues it with any other messages received, according to priority and time of submission.

6. At the required time for transmission, if it is indicated, the LES forwards the message over the Interstation Signalling Link (ISL) to the NCS for the Ocean Region.

7. The Network Coordination Station (NCS) automatically broadcasts the message on the NCS Common Signalling Channel over the entire Ocean Region.

8. All EGC receivers (that meet the requirements specified at the end of this chapter) will receive the MSI message addressed to the area where the ship is navigating, unless the operator has chosen to reject messages of a certain type, or the message has already been received by that terminal. EGC messages with Distress and Urgency priority will also be printed out automatically while Safety priority messages will be stored and may be printed later.

MSI broadcast over the SafetyNET service

Coastal Warnings (see note 1)

- Navigational Warnings;
- Meteorological warnings;
- Ice reports;
- Search and rescue information, acts of piracy warnings, tsunami and other natural phenomena;
- Meteorological forecasts;
- Pilot and VTS service messages;
- AIS service messages;
- LORAN system messages;
- GNSS messages;
- Other electronic navaid messages;
- Other Navigational Warnings.
- No messages on hand;

Meteorological and NAVAREA warnings and meteorological forecasts to ships within specified NAVAREAs / METAREAs.

Search and rescue coordination to ships within specified circular or rectangular areas.

Urgency messages, meteorological and Navigational Warnings to ships within specified circular areas.

Shore-to-ship distress alerts to ships within specified circular areas.

Urgency messages and navigational warnings to ships within specified rectangular areas.

Updates for official electronic chart databases may be broadcast via SafetyNET in future. However, the standards for this service have not yet been developed.

Other safety-related information (e.g. tsunami warnings, piracy warnings).

Notes:
1. The SafetyNET coastal warning broadcast facility is made available for the transmission of coastal information to areas where NAVTEX MSI is not provided.
2. MSI messages are generally broadcast with a keyword in their header indicating the priority of the message - for example DISTRESS or MAYDAY for priority
3. URGENT or PAN PAN for priority 2 and SAFETY or SÉCURITÉ for priority 1.

Availability of MSI in different areas

To avoid excessive duplication of broadcasts, the IMO has authorised the following arrangements:

For a given NAVAREA/METAREA which is covered by more than one Ocean Region satellite, scheduled broadcasts of MSI, such as Navigational Warnings and meteorological information, are made only via a single nominated satellite/Ocean Region.

For a NAVAREA/METAREA which is covered by more than one Ocean Region satellite, unscheduled broadcasts of MSI, such as gale warnings and distress alert relays, are made via all satellites/Ocean Regions which cover the area concerned.

SafetyNET message addressed to a circular area

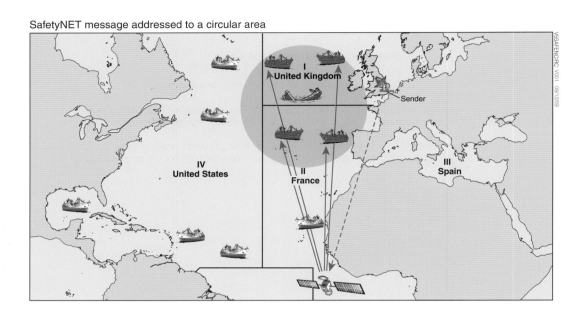

SafetyNET message addressed to a rectangular area

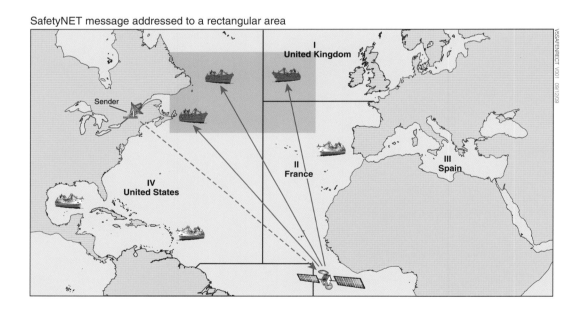

Requirements for receiving SafetyNET MSI broadcasts

For a ship to be able to receive SafetyNET MSI broadcasts, certain technical and legal requirements must be met:

- The ship must be equipped with a type-approved MES with EGC receiver.
- For optimal performance and GMDSS certification, the MES should be installed in the vessel in accordance with the Design and Installation Guidelines available from Inmarsat.
- For the ship to be certificated in the GMDSS, the installation must comply with the GMDSS requirements of the national administration for the country in which the vessel is registered.
- The MES with EGC receive capability must be activated by Inmarsat which involves completing and submitting a Service Activation Request Form to the Point of Service Activation for the country of registration of the vessel;
- The MES must be set-up as indicated in the manufacturer's instructions - this includes ensuring that the Inmarsat MES is tuned (synchronized) to the Inmarsat NCS Common Signalling Channel.
- The printer and any other peripherals connected to the MES must be made ready as indicated in their manufacturer's instructions.

EGC Receiver set up procedure

Although reception of SafetyNET traffic is automatic, the shipboard operator must set up the receiver properly before the start of the voyage as follows:

- Select the appropriate satellite/Ocean Region
- Select one or more of the following (as appropriate)
  a) NAVAREA/METAREA [or Sub-Area] number(s)
  b) Relevant coastal warning area identification letter and subject indicator characters (if any)
  c) Fixed position(s)

Repeat broadcasts of MSI

Some classes of EGC receivers/MESs may not provide uninterrupted monitoring of the channel used for MSI broadcasts and may switch to a different channel for normal commercial traffic. To improve the probability of these receivers receiving MSI broadcasts, Information Providers re-broadcast some messages: Unscheduled messages, such as distress alerts and gale warnings are re-broadcast 6 minutes after the initial broadcast; Scheduled broadcasts, such as Navigational Warnings and other longer-term information are repeated at every scheduled time, for as long as they remain in force.

Typical MSI broadcasts

Typical MSI broadcasts which you may receive on your terminal are shown overpage. Note that the time in the message is in UTC.

The term PosOK, which some terminals/models include with EGC messages, indicates to the operator that the ships position in the terminal has been updated within the last 12 hours.

The term NoPos indicates that the position has not been updated within the last 12 hours or is unknown. It means that the terminal will receive all geographically addressed EGC messages broadcast via selected satellite instead of limited reception of SafetyNET messages to specified areas. If your terminal gives this indication, you should make arrangements for regular position update.

Managing your EGC receiver

The section should be read in conjunction with the manufacturer's instructions, for specific information on how to do the following:

Select a satellite/Ocean Region;

Program the receiver for additional NAVAREAs / METAREAs for which to receive messages;

Update the receiver regularly with the ship's position if it is not done automatically;

Specify the additional types of MSI message required; e.g. coastal warnings and

Tune in (log in) to the appropriate Ocean Region at the scheduled times of MSI broadcasts if the terminal logs in to another satellite.

Selective message reception

Although an EGC receiver will receive and can print all SafetyNET broadcasts made throughout an entire Ocean Region, many messages may not be useful to the ship - for example those applicable to NAVAREAs/METAREAs beyond the ship's planned voyage, or those on subjects not relevant to the ships circumstances. To avoid a receiver printing a large number of unnecessary messages, it can be programmed to receive and print only essential messages and to reject all other messages (Note, however, that the receiver cannot be programmed to reject messages, such as shore-to-ship distress alerts and Met/Nav warnings addressed to areas where the ship is navigating). The receiver examines the message handling instructions (the "C" codes) included with each message and uses this information to decide which messages to print. Similarly, the receiver stores the unique number included with each message and uses this to avoid printing extra copies of those messages already received and printed correctly.

Coastal SafetyNET

Coastal SafetyNET broadcasts are used very effectively by Australia and New Zealand as they have no NAVTEX service. Confusion may arise if the Inmarsat C instruction manual states "Set Coastal Warning Areas (Navtex areas)" for EGC reception. This should read "Set Coastal Warning Areas (Coastal SafetyNET areas)" for EGC reception. Coastal Warning Areas are identified by A - Z characters as are Navtex areas but they are distinctly different in their delivery.

Effective use of Coastal SafetyNET broadcasts is administered for example by Navarea X (Australia) and Navarea XIV (New Zealand). See Figures SN-10N and SN-14. An explanation of the set up required to receive is included on both of these diagrams. Mariners may want to practise setting up their Inmarsat C equipment to receive coastal broadcasts as part of their routine GMDSS test program and make appropriate log entries.

Navarea III Safety priority

NAVAREA III 1200/20

EASTERN MEDITERRANEAN SEA

1.- Gunnery exercise will take place, 10 SEP20 from 0600UTC to 1300UTC in
area bounded by: 33-19.467N 032-31.817E33-29.250N 032-47.083E33-29.417N
033-13.567E33-10.417N 033-17.083E33-20.467N 033-28.717E33-19.617N 033-47.000E
33-03.150N 033-47.417E
33-03.083N 033-41.917E
32-45.733N 033-24.717E
32-45.650N 033-04.983E
32-59.517N 032-32.100E
The area is dangerous for navigation
Advised not to enter the area.
2.- Cancel this message on 101400UTC SEP20

Navarea III Safety priority

LES 340 - MSG 2612 - NAV/METAREA Safety Call to Area: 3 - PosOk

NAVAREA III 1208/20
EASTERN MEDITERRANEAN SEA - CYPRUS
1.- Multinational SAR exercise, on 12 SEP20, from 0400 UTC to 0700 UTC, in
area bounded by: 34-36N 033-16E34-36N 033-22E34-31N 033-22E34-31N 033-16E
3.- Cancel this message on 120800 UTC SEP20

Navarea III Safety priority

LES 340 - MSG 2626 - NAV/METAREA Safety Call to Area: 3 - PosOk

NAVAREA III 1213/20
KRITIKO SEA

1.- Scientific research by O/V "AIGAIO" as follows:
Day 11 SEP20 from 0001 UTC to 0500 UTC, in position: 35-50.70N 023-09.76E
Day 11 SEP20 from 1300 UTC to 1800 UTC, in position: 34-42.10N 024-07.39E
wide berth requested.
2.- Cancel this message on 111900 UTC SEP20.

Navarea III Safety priority

LES 340 - MSG 2633 - NAV/MET Safety Call to Area: 3 - PosOk

NAVAREA III 1214/20
LIGURIAN SEA
1.- Savona VTS is limited operational capability, provides only information
service on Channel 71 VHF/FM.
All transiting ship beware.
2.- Cancel this message on 130100 UTC SEP2O.

Navarea I Safety priority

LES 340 - MSG 2685 - NAV/METAREA Safety Call to Area: 1 - PosOk

NAVAREA I 136

1.   NAVAREA I WARNINGS IN FORCE AT 111000 UTC SEP 20:
        2020 SERIES: 103, 112, 120, 122, 125, 130, 135, 136

NOTES:
A.   Texts of NAVAREA I Warnings issued each week are published in weekly
        editions of the ADMIRALTY Notices to Mariners bulletin (ANMB).
B.   NAVAREA I Warnings less than 42 days old (103/20 onward) are
        promulgated via SafetyNET and/or relevant NAVTEX transmitters.
C.   The complete texts of all in-force NAVAREA I warnings, including those
        which are no longer being broadcast, are reprinted in Section III of ANMB in
        weeks I, 13, 26 and 39 and are also available from the UKHO website at:
        www.admiralty.co.uk/RNW.
Alternatively, these may be requested by e-mail from NAVAREA I Co-ordinator
at: navwarnings(at)ukho.gov.uk
2.   Cancel NAVAREA I 133/20.

Navarea II Safety priority

LES 340 - MSG 2605 - NAV/METAREA Safety Call to Area: 2 - PosOk

NAVAREA II 260/20
GULF OF GUINEA
NIGERIA
PIRACY
1.   M/V ATTACKED IN 05-53N 003-17E AT 080550 UTC SEPT 20.
        VESSELS ARE ADVISED TO KEEP CLEAR OF THIS
        POSITION AND TO EXERCISE EXTREME CAUTION.
        REPORT TO MDAT-GOG,
        PHONE: +33 2 98 22 88 88
        E-MAIL: WATCHKEEPERS@MDAT-GOG.ORG
2.   CANCEL THIS MSG 110630 UTC SEP 20.

Navarea II Safety priority

LES 340 - MSG 2629 - NAV/METAREA Safety Call to Area: 2 - PosOk

NAVAREA II 261/20
SIERRA LEONE.
SENEGAL.
1.   GUNNERY EXERCISE FROM 120800 UTC TO 121100 UTC SEP 20
        IN AREA WITHIN 8 MILES OF 14-28N 017-52W.
2.   CANCEL THIS MSG 121200 UTC SEP 20.

Navarea II Safety priority

LES 340 - MSG 2649 - NAV/METAREA Safety Call to Area: 2 - PosOk

NAVAREA II 263/20
PAZENN.
1.   CABLE LAYING OPERATIONS IN PROGRESS UNTIL 13 SEPT 20
        BY CABLESHIP DEPENDABLE IN AREA BOUNDED BY:
        A. 45-56.7N 008-48.9W
        B. 45-54.7N 006-49.2W
        C. 45-40.0N 007-02.0W
        D. 45-49.6N 008-39.5W
        ONE MILE BERTH REQUESTED.
2.   CANCEL NAVAREA II 262/20.
3.   CANCEL THIS MSG 140100 UTC SEP20.

Regular position updates

Your EGC receiver MUST be updated regularly with the ship's position either automatically or manually. The reasons for updating your EGC receiver regularly with the ship's position include: To receive and print only messages for the required areas - if the ship's position has not been updated for more than 12 hours, the receiver will automatically receive (and may print) all geographically addressed messages within the entire Ocean Region. Another important reason for updating the terminal regularly with the ship's position, while not directly related to the SafetyNET service, is to ensure that the correct position is given if a distress alert has to be sent.

Two ways are available to update a terminal with the ship's position:

Automatically, using an electronic navigational device; the use of a GPS (Global Positioning System) receiver to provide position updates is highly recommended because of its accuracy and reliability. The latest SES models are available with an integral GPS receiver, whilst some can be interconnected with a separate on-board GPS receiver. (If, however, your terminal does not support GPS inter-connection, contact the manufacturer/agent about having it upgraded);

Manually, by keying the position coordinates directly into the terminal; IMO recommends this be done every 4 hours. It is strongly recommended that automatic position updating is used whenever available.

Reducing the number of alarms

Your receiver activates an audible/visual alarm on receiving MSI with Distress or Urgency priority, to which you should respond immediately. To make sure that you do not get any unnecessary alarms, however, you should do the following: Keep the ship's position updated, to ensure that the receiver rejects messages for any geographic areas which do not include the ship's position.

Good operating practice

The following advice is given to help you obtain the best possible use of the SafetyNET service:

Make sure all equipment associated with the EGC receiver is working properly, as indicated in the manufacturer's instructions, and that the printer is loaded with paper/ribbon.

Make sure that the terminal is not storing unwanted messages and has storage space for new messages.

If your printer has an option for printing in a small font, consider selecting this option to reduce the amount of paper used for messages.

Make sure that your current position is entered into the terminal, and that it is regularly updated, to ensure that you only receive appropriate MSI throughout your voyage.

On the terminal, enter additional NAVAREAs/METAREAs and coastal areas for which you want to receive MSI, considering your intended voyage, and message types you want to receive, rejecting any unwanted types.

While in port, keep the EGC receiver in operation, to ensure that you have received all necessary MSI before sailing.

Make sure your Inmarsat C MES monitors the appropriate satellite/Ocean Region at the time of a scheduled broadcast.

Note that if you wish to continue to receive MSI information from a particular Ocean Region, you must select the Ocean Region on your Inmarsat C MES by making it the **preferred Ocean Region.** For details please refer to the **Inmarsat Maritime Communications Handbook,** and to your Inmarsat C manufacturer's operating handbook.

Throughout your voyage, ensure that a written log is kept of the identities of all received messages, and a printed copy is kept of all distress traffic.

What to do about missed messages

If you think you have missed any messages, for example at a scheduled broadcast time, you can:

Switch the terminal off and on again - this will clear the internal memory of all stored message IDs, so that if the message is re-broadcast, your receiver will not reject it as a repeated message, and will print/store it.

The full version of the SafetyNET User's Handbook published by Inmarsat Ltd is available at www.inmarsat.com/safety then follow the link.

EGC SERVICES

For general information on the International EGC services, and the GMDSS, contact:

The Chairman
International EGC Coordinating Panel
International Maritime Organization (IMO)
4 Albert Embankment
London SE1 7SR
United Kingdom

Telephone: +44(0)207 7357611
Fax: +44(0)207 5873210

For general information on Inmarsat satellite system and services, you can contact the Inmarsat Customer Services:

Customer Services
Inmarsat Global Ltd.
99 City Road
London EC1Y 1AX
United Kingdom
Telephone: +44(0)207 7281020
Fax: +44(0)207 7281142
email: custom
Website: www.inmarsat.com/service-group/safety

IRIDIUM

Maritime Safety Information – The International SafetyCast System

The Iridium SafetyCast service is an enhanced group call service.
This Iridium EGC service for the promulgation of Maritime Safety Information (MSI) includes navigational and meteorological warnings, meteorological forecasts, Search and Rescue (SAR) related information and other urgent safety-related messages to ships.

MSI or SAR related information is promulgated by registered information providers whose Certificates of Authorization to promulgate via Iridium SafetyCast are issued by IMO in accordance with the procedures of the IMO EGC Coordinating Panel. Please refer to the Iridium SafetyCast manual for full details of this service.

Maritime Safety Information and Distress Alert Relays – Iridium SafetyCast

The Iridium SafetyCast service is an enhanced group call service. This is a satellite-based service for the promulgation of Maritime Safety Information (MSI), including navigational and meteorological warnings, meteorological forecasts, Search and Rescue (SAR) related information and other urgent safety-related messages to ships.

Format of messages composed for transmission:

All messages composed are in the format required by IMO Resolutions A.705(17), A.706(17) and A.1051(27), as amended.

Receiving Iridium SafetyCast messages

When a message has been received, a record is made of the message identification associated with that message. The unique sequence number is used to suppress the display and printing of repeated transmissions of the same message. The Iridium SafetyCast system tracks the transmission and receipt of MSI broadcasts for each ship in the targeted area. The Iridium SafetyCast system filters messages that have already been received by the Iridium ship earth stations in the area targeted by the registered information provider.

The "Echo and "Repeat" functions of the Inmarsat system are not used by the Iridium system in same the way that the Inmarsat system uses them. Instead they are replaced by the "expiry" function. The "expiry" of a message transmission period is set by the message sender (such as a NAVAREA or METAREA Coordinator), and Iridium SafetyCast uses the system control functions to constantly contact each ship earth station in the addressed area to ensure that it receives a message during the period. All received messages remain available in the terminal's memory after the SafetyCast transmission's expiry time.

It is not possible to reject mandatory "all ship" messages such as shore-to-ship distress alert relays for the area within which the ship is located. When a distress or urgency message is received, an audio and visual alarm will be given.

It is recommended that, in order to ensure that all necessary MSI is available before sailing, the ship earth station should remain in operation while the ship is in port. When the ship earth station is switched ON and logged onto the Iridium SafetyCast system it will automatically receive in-force messages.

Detail of MSI message-log, on Ship Earth Station

Although reception of MSI and SAR related information is automatic, the shipboard operator must set up the ship earth station properly before the start of the voyage, in accordance with the manufacturer's instructions.

The position information in a ship earth station is updated automatically from integrated navigational receivers and these are fitted on all ship earth stations or may be updated from a separate electronic position-fixing system.

Details of Ship Earth Station Screen for Received MSI; NAVAREA and METAREA messages:

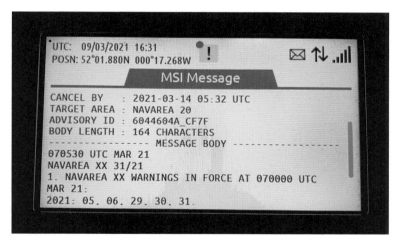

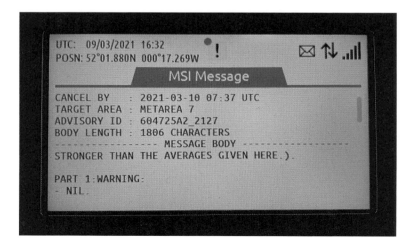

Iridium SafetyCast Transmission:

The Iridium SafetyCast service monitors and transmits messages to receiving terminals, ensuring all those terminals which should receive a message do so, indicating by reply that they have received it correctly and completely. This process continues until the message "expires" according to the expiry time and date set by the registered information provider, or until the registered information provider sends a message to cancel that previous message. Once a terminal has received a message, that message will be stored in the terminal's local memory.

The IMO performance standards for ship earth stations for use in the GMDSS require that facilities should be provided for the ship earth stations to receive MSI for the NAVAREA/METAREA and the coastal warning areas and different classes of messages where the ship is sailing and 300 nautical miles beyond the limits of the NAVAREA/METAREA. Therefore, the delivery area for each NAVAREA/METAREA extends from the boundary of each of the areas to 300 nautical miles beyond the line of demarcation with an adjacent NAVAREA/METAREA. This permits a ship earth station outside of a NAVAREA/METAREA to receive a message in that adjacent NAVAREA/METAREA if the ship earth station is within 300 nautical miles of that NAVAREA/METAREA boundary.

At the end of the expiry period, the system will stop automatically broadcasting a message to ships entering the area or activating their terminals within the area. It is also possible for a registered information provider to cancel the automatic broadcast of their messages before the end of the expiry period. According to the IMO performance standard MSC.434(98), and the IEC testing standard IEC 61097-16, the terminal must be attached to either a printer, or to a dedicated display unit and a memory unit. The terminal must include a non-volatile memory to record transmitted messages, but in any and all cases, the terminal enables the mariner to meet requirements of SOLAS regulation IV/17, on keeping the Radio Log of transmissions which are relevant to the safety of navigation.

Transmission scheduling

The Iridium MSI transmission schedule for EGC SafetyCast is the same as the Inmarsat EGC SafetyNET schedule. These transmission schedules are agreed between the NAVAREA and METAREA Coordinators and the IMO EGC Coordinating Panel.

Further Information and Contact Details

Questions concerning promulgation of MSI and SAR related information through the Iridium SafetyCast service can be addressed to the IMO EGC Coordinating Panel:
The Chair, IMO Enhanced Group Call Coordinating Panel
International Maritime Organization
4 Albert Embankment
London SE1 7SR
United Kingdom
email: ncsr@imo.org (in subject line add: for Chair, IMO Enhanced Group Call Coordinating Panel)

Questions concerning the operation of the Iridium GMDSS system, including the Distress and SafetyCast services, should be addressed to:
Maritime Safety Services
Iridium Satellite LLC
1750 Tysons Boulevard, Suite 1400
McLean, VA
22102 USA

Area of Responsibility for High Seas (GMDSS)

MetArea	Issuing Service	Preparation Service	Area LES for a) Scheduled broadcasts b) Unscheduled broadcasts	Notes
I	United Kingdom	United Kingdom, Norway	a) Burum AOR-E b) Burum AOR-E	1,2,3
II	France	France	a) Aussaguel AOR-E Aussaguel AOR-E b) Aussaguel AOR-E Aussaguel AOR-E	1,2,3
III	Greece	Greece, France	a) Burum (IOR) b) Burum (IOR)	1,2,3
IV	USA	USA	a) Eik (AOR-E) b) Eik (AOR-E) Eik (AOR-E)	1,2,3
V	Brazil	Brazil	a) Burum (AOR-E) b) Burum (AOR-E)	1,2,3,4
VI	Argentina	Argentina	a) Eik (AOR-E) b) Eik (AOR-E)	1,2,3
VII	South Africa	South Africa	a) Burum (AOR-E, IOR) b) Burum (AOR-E, IOR)	1,2,3
VII	South Africa	South Africa, Réunion	a) Burum (AOR-E, IOR) b) Burum (AOR-E, IOR)	1,2,3
VIII(N)	India	India	a) Pune (IOR) b) Pune (IOR)	1,2,3
VIII(S)	Mauritius / Réunion	Mauritius / Réunion / Kenya	a) Aussaguel (IOR) b) Aussaguel (IOR)	3,5
VIII(S)	Australia	Australia	b) Burum (IOR, POR)	3,5
IX	Pakistan	Pakistan	a) Burum (IOR, POR) b) Burum (IOR, POR)	3,5
X	Australia	Australia, Mauritius / Réunion	a) Burum (For IOR) b) Burum (For IOR and POR)	5
X	Australia	Australia, Fiji, New Zealand	a) Burum (For POR) b) Burum (For POR and IOR)	5
XI	China	China, Hong Kong SAR	a) Beijing (POR) b) Beijing (POR)	1,2,3
XI	Japan	Japan, Hong Kong SAR, Australia	a) Yamaguchi (POR) b) Yamaguchi (POR)	1,2,3
XII	USA	USA	a) Eik (AOR-W, POR) Eik (AOR-W, POR) b) Eik (AOR-W, POR) Eik (AOR-W, POR) Eik (AOR-W, POR)	1,2,3
XIII	Russian Federation	Russian Federation	a) Nudol (POR) b) Nudol (POR)	2,3
XIV	New Zealand	Fiji, New Zealand	a) Stratos Burum (For POR) b) Stratos Burum (For POR)	5
XV	Chile	Chile	a) Eik (AOR-W) b) Eik (AOR-W)	1,2,3
XVI	Peru	Peru	a) Eik (AOR-W) b) Eik (AOR-W)	3,4
XVII	Canada	Canada	Eik (AOR-W, POR)	3
XVIII	Canada	Canada	Eik (AOR-W, AOR-E)	3
XIX	Norway	Norway	Eik (IOR)	3
XX	Russian Federation	Russian Federation	Nudol (IOR)	3
XXI	Russian Federation	Russian Federation	Nudol (POR)	3

1 Full coverage via SafetyNET for areas not covered by NAVTEX
2 Partial NAVTEX coverage

3 See EGC MSI SYSTEM NEW SCHEDULE TABLE (ADP main menu - reference section).
4 Full coastal coverage via SafetyNET
5 No NAVTEX coverage

Inmarsat C and Mini C coverage NAVAREAs

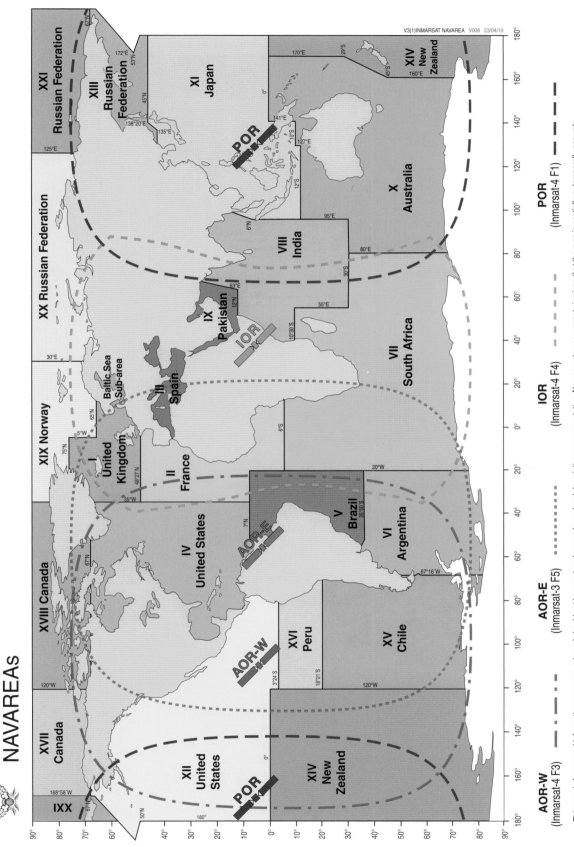

V3(1)INMARSAT NAVAREA V008 23/04/19

AOR-W (Inmarsat-4 F3)	**AOR-E** (Inmarsat-3 F5)
IOR (Inmarsat-4 F4)	**POR** (Inmarsat-4 F1)

This map is for general information purposes only and should not be construed or used as a legal description or representation. No guarantee or warranty is given that the map is spatially or temporally accurate or fit for a particular use. Coverage is subject to change at any time. Inmarsat shall have no liability for decisions made or actions taken/not taken in reliance upon the map or for any resulting losses suffered.

Inmarsat C and Mini C coverage
METAREAs

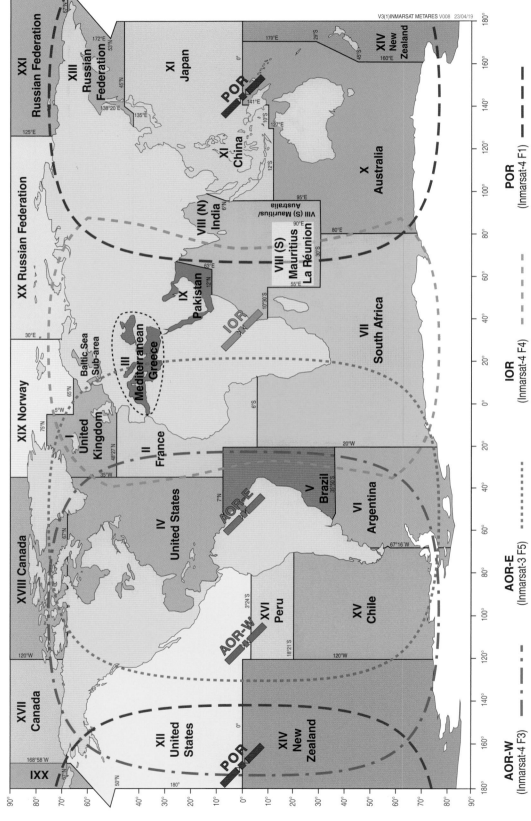

V3(1)INMARSAT METARES V008 23/04/19

AOR-W
(Inmarsat-4 F3) — · — · —

AOR-E
(Inmarsat-3 F5) — — — —

IOR
(Inmarsat-4 F4) · · · · · ·

POR
(Inmarsat-4 F1) — — — —

This map is for general information purposes only and should not be construed or used as a legal description or representation. No guarantee or warranty is given that the map is spatially or temporally accurate or fit for a particular use. Coverage is subject to change at any time. Inmarsat shall have no liability for decisions made or actions taken/not taken in reliance upon the map or for any resulting losses suffered.

Inmarsat FleetBroadband coverage
NAVAREAs

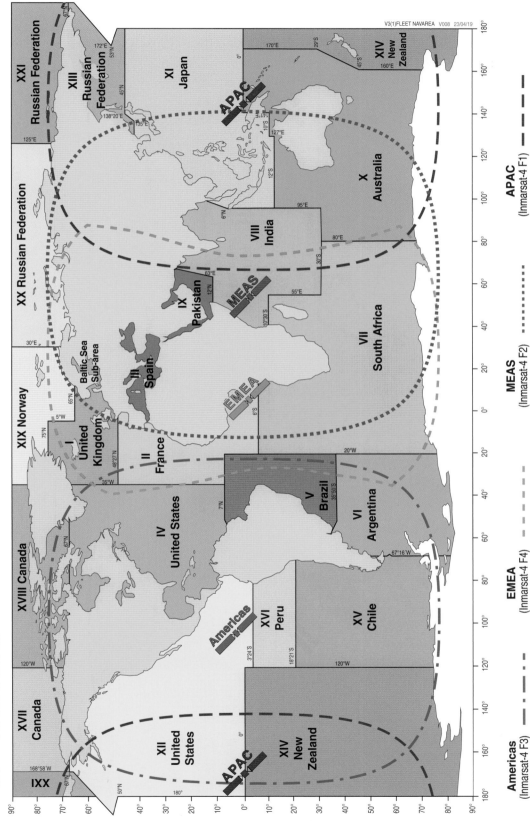

V3(1)FLEET NAVAREA V008 23/04/19

Americas
(Inmarsat-4 F3) — · — · —

EMEA
(Inmarsat-4 F4) — — — —

MEAS
(Inmarsat-4 F2) · · · · · ·

APAC
(Inmarsat-4 F1) — — — —

This map is for general information purposes only and should not be construed or used as a legal description or representation. No guarantee or warranty is given that the map is spatially or temporally accurate or fit for a particular use. Coverage is subject to change at any time. Inmarsat shall have no liability for decisions made or actions taken/not taken in reliance upon the map or for any resulting losses suffered.

Inmarsat FleetBroadband coverage
METAREAs

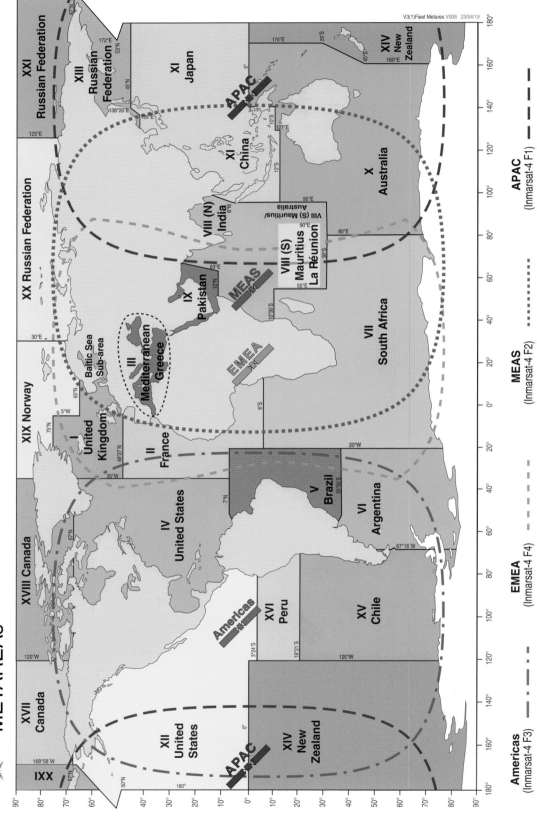

Americas
(Inmarsat-4 F3)

EMEA
(Inmarsat-4 F4)

MEAS
(Inmarsat-4 F2)

APAC
(Inmarsat-4 F1)

V3(1)Fleet Metares V008   23/04/19

EGC MSI Broadcast Systems
Operational Information

Please Note:

1. This is the latest information made available to the UKHO by the EGC Coordinating Panel of the IMO. If you have any queries regarding Inmarsat C Ocean Region satellite coverage, please contact the IMO EGC Coordinating Panel Chairman at: info@imo.org ensuring that the subject line includes *'for Chairman IMO EGC Coordinating Panel'*.

2. Inmarsat **Fleet Safety** Ship Earth Stations receive EGC broadcasts on all satellites covering the NAV/MET Areas and as such there is no requirement to choose specific satellites to receive EGC broadcasts.

NAVAREA	NAVIGATIONAL INFORMATION			
	COORDINATOR	EGC Services Broadcast Times (UTC)	INMARSAT C Ocean Region	IRIDIUM Operational Status
I	United Kingdom	0530, 1730	AOR-E, IOR	On Trial
II	France	0430 1630	AOR-E	Planned
III	Spain	1200, 2400 & on receipt	IOR	On Trial
IV	United States	1000, 2200 (2200 Ice reports N Atlantic) 0900 2100 French West Indies 0900 2100 French Guyana	AOR-E	Operational
V	Brazil	0030, 1230		Planned
VI	Argentina	0200, 1400		Planned
VII	South Africa	0940 1940 0040, 1240 Réunion 0140, 1340 Kerguelen Islands 0330, 1530 Mayotte	AOR-E, IOR	On Trial
VIII	India	1000 2200 0040, 1240 Réunion 0330, 1530 Mayotte	POR, IOR	On Trial
IX	Pakistan	0300, 1500	IOR	Operational
X	Australia	0700, 1900 & on receipt 0140 1340 New Caledonia (Area N)	POR, IOR	On Trial
		Coastal Warnings 0700, 1900 & on receipt (POR only)[7]		
XI	Japan	0005, 1205[9]	POR	Planned
XII	United States	1030, 2230	AOR-W, POR	Operational
XIII	Russian Federation	0930, 2130	POR	On Trial
XIV	New Zealand	0900, 2100 New Zealand 0140, 1340 New Caledonia 0030, 1230 Wallis & Futuna 0250, 1450 French Polynesia	AOR-W/POR[8]	Operational
XV	Chile	0210, 1410	AOR-W	On Trial
XVI	Peru	0500, 1700	AOR-W	On Trial
XVII	Canada	1130, 2330	AOR-W, POR	Operational
XVIII	Canada	1100, 2300	AOR-W, AOR-E	Operational
XIX	Norway	0630, 1830	IOR	Operational
XX	Russian Federation	0530, 1730	IOR	On Trial
XXI	Russian Federation	0630, 1830	POR	On Trial

METAREA	METEOROLOGICAL INFORMATION			
	COORDINATOR	EGC Services Broadcast Times (UTC)	INMARSAT C Ocean Region	IRIDIUM Operational Status
I	United Kingdom	0930, 2130 On receipt, warnings only	AOR-E	On Trial
II	France	1015 2215	AOR-E	Planned
III	Greece[1]	1000, 2200	IOR	Operational
IV	Canada (Hudson Bay & Approaches)	0300 1500[5]	AOR-E	On Trial
	United States	0430, 1030, 1630, 2230		On Trial
V	Brazil	0730, 1930		Planned
		Coastal Warnings for Amazon Basin and additional coastal areas		Planned
VI	Argentina	0230 1730		Planned
VII	South Africa	0940, 1940[2]	AOR-E, IOR	On Trial
VIII(N)	India	0900, 1800 for N of 0°	POR, IOR	Planned
VIII(S)	Mauritius / Réunion	0130, 1330 for S of 0° 0000[3], 0600[3], 1200[3], 1800[3] for S of 0°		Planned
	Australia	Warnings only for S of 0° and E of 90°E, issued as unscheduled broadcasts		Planned
IX	Pakistan	0700, 1900[6]	IOR, POR	On Trial
X	Australia	1100, 2300	IOR/POR	On Trial
		Coastal Warnings (POR)[7] – see Figure SN-10N and EGC Annex		On Trial
XI	China	0330, 1015, 1530, 2215	POR	Planned
	Japan	0230, 0830, 1430, 2030 for N of 0° 0815, 2015[4] for S of 0°		Planned
XII	United States	0545, 1145, 1745, 2345	AOR-W, POR	On Trial
XIII	Russian Federation	0930, 2130	POR	Planned
XIV	New Zealand	Warnings for High Seas areas: 0330, 0930, 1530, 2130 Synopses and forecasts for High Seas areas: 0930, 2130 Situation and forecast for NZ coast only: 0130, 1330[8]	AOR-W/POR	Operational
XV	Chile	0100, 1330 for Sea Areas 1–8 1450 for Sea Area 9 0345, 1845 for Sea Area 10	AOR-W	Operational
XVI	Peru	1115, 2315	AOR-W	Planned
XVII	Canada	0300, 1500[5]	AOR-W, POR	Operational
XVIII	Canada	0300, 1500[5]	AOR-W, AOR-E	Operational
XIX	Norway	1100, 2300	IOR	Operational
XX	Russian Federation	0600, 1800	IOR	On Trial
XXI	Russian Federation	0600, 1800	POR	Planned

[1] Scheduled bulletins and warnings for Western Mediterranean Sea are prepared by France.

[2] Forecasts for areas 30°S - 50°E / 50°S - 80°E and tropical cyclone warnings are prepared by Réunion.

[3] Tropical cyclone warnings (if any) issued by Réunion as an unscheduled broadcast.

[4] Scheduled bulletins and warnings for south of the equator prepared by Australia.

[5] For areas South of 75°N and only during the shipping season.

[6] Only if cyclone/depression development.

[7] AUSCOAST SafetyNET warnings are ONLY broadcast via POR satellite - see Figure SN-10N and EGC Annex.

[8] For Coastal Area designators and further information, please see diagram FIGURES SN-10/14 and SN-14.

[9] In force warnings issued during the last 6 weeks are broadcast at 1205 UTC every Saturday.

Broadcast times for MET information published in the table above are for routine Weather Messages. Storm Warnings are also broadcast on receipt. Routine broadcasts of Navigational Warnings and meteorological forecasts are made at scheduled times over a single nominated satellite for each NAVAREA/METAREA. Unscheduled broadcasts of SAR alert relays and severe weather warnings will be made over all satellites which serve the area concerned.

EGC ANNEX

Table 1:

AUSTRALIA COASTAL WATERS FORECAST BULLETINS						
METAREA	**COORDINATOR**	**Coastal Waters Bulletin Region**	**Nav Area see Figure SN-10N**	**INMARSAT C Ocean Region**	**INMARSAT EGC Services Broadcast Times (Local)**	**INMARSAT EGC Services Broadcast Times (UTC)**
X	Australia	Bass Strait	D	POR	0530 1715 AEST	0715[1] 1930[1]
		Northern Territory	H		0445 1600 ACST	0630 1915
		Torres Strait	Uses EGC rectangular area		0445 1600 AEST	0600 1845
		Western Australia	F and G		0430 1630 AWST	0830 2030
[1] 1 hour earlier during Australian Eastern Daylight Saving Time KEY: LST – Local Standard Time; ACST – Australian Central standard Time; AWST – Australian Western Standard Time See also Figure SN-10N						

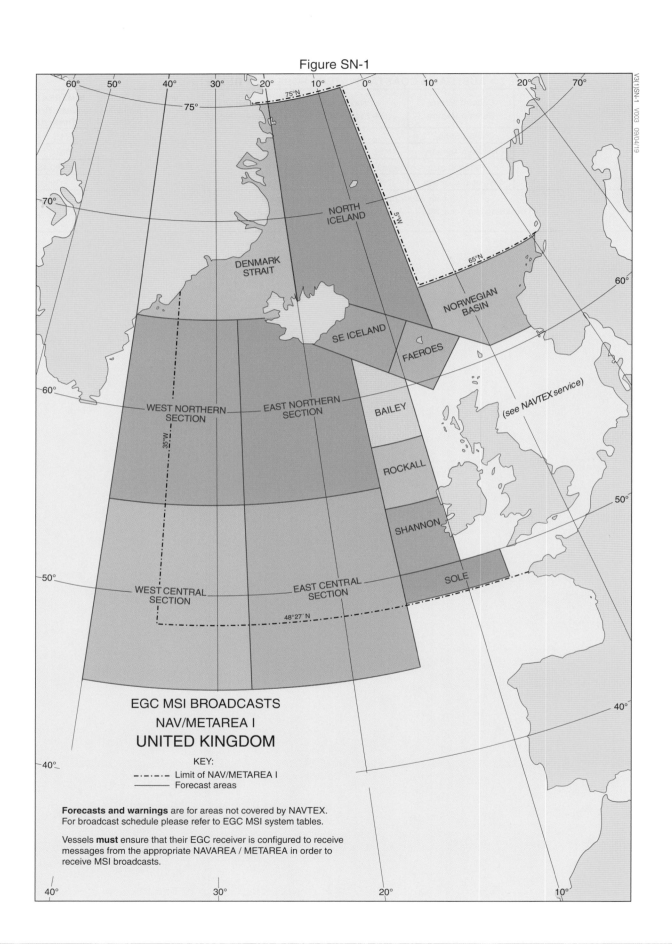

EGC MSI BROADCASTS
NAV/METAREA I
UNITED KINGDOM

KEY:
–·–·–·– Limit of NAV/METAREA I
——— Forecast areas

Forecasts and warnings are for areas not covered by NAVTEX.
For broadcast schedule please refer to EGC MSI system tables.

Vessels **must** ensure that their EGC receiver is configured to receive
messages from the appropriate NAVAREA / METAREA in order to
receive MSI broadcasts.

Figure SN-2

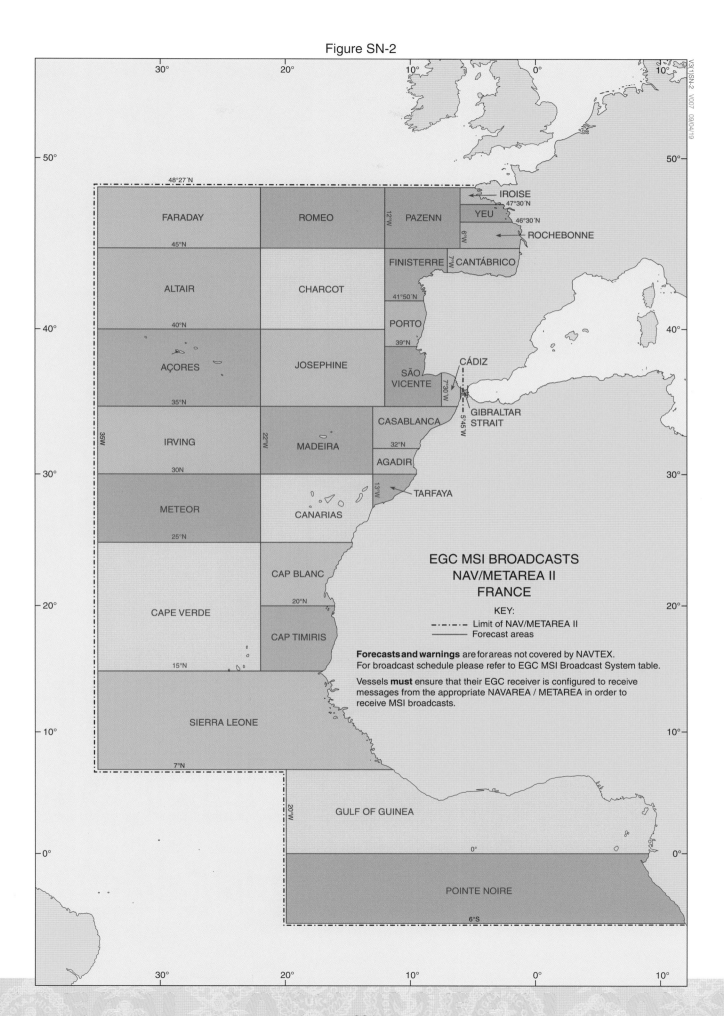

FARADAY
ROMEO
PAZENN
IROISE
47°30′N
YEU
46°30′N
ROCHEBONNE
48°27′N
45°N
12°W
9°W

ALTAIR
CHARCOT
FINISTERRE
CANTÁBRICO
40°N
41°50′N
7°W

PORTO
39°N

AÇORES
JOSEPHINE
SÃO VICENTE
CÁDIZ
35°N
7°30′W

CASABLANCA
GIBRALTAR STRAIT
5°45′W

IRVING
MADEIRA
32°N
AGADIR
30N
35W
22°W

TARFAYA
13°W

METEOR
CANARIAS
25°N

CAP BLANC
20°N

CAPE VERDE
CAP TIMIRIS
15°N

SIERRA LEONE
7°N

EGC MSI BROADCASTS
NAV/METAREA II
FRANCE

KEY:
–·–·–·– Limit of NAV/METAREA II
———— Forecast areas

Forecasts and warnings are for areas not covered by NAVTEX.
For broadcast schedule please refer to EGC MSI Broadcast System table.

Vessels **must** ensure that their EGC receiver is configured to receive
messages from the appropriate NAVAREA / METAREA in order to
receive MSI broadcasts.

GULF OF GUINEA
20°W
0°

POINTE NOIRE
6°S

V3(1)SN-2   V007   09/04/19

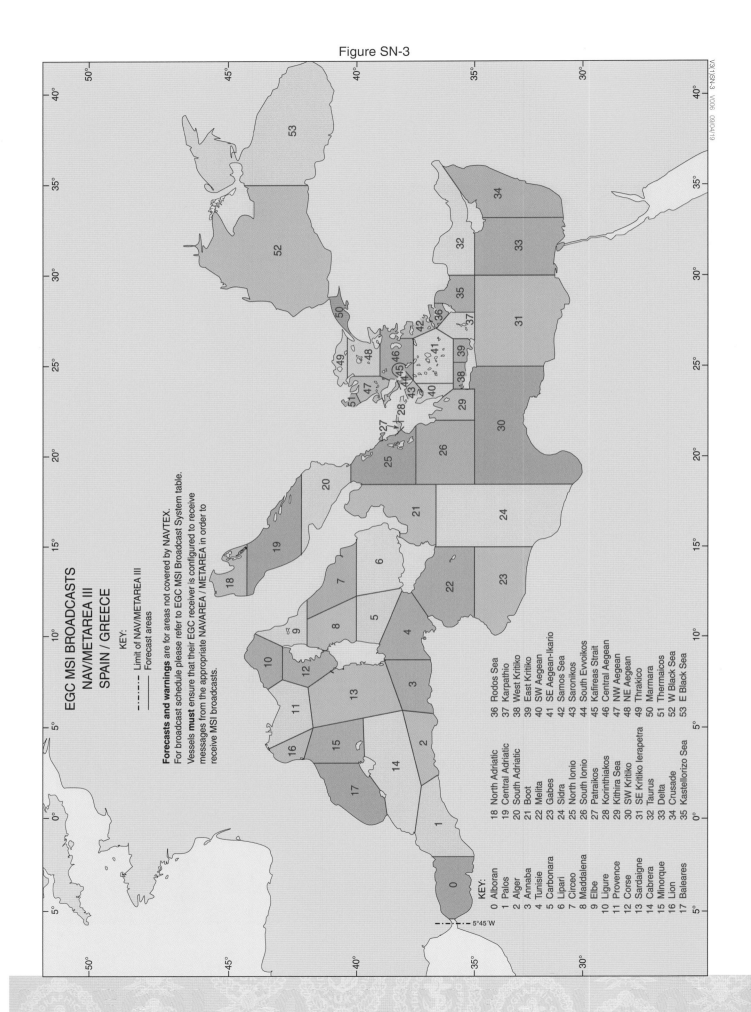

Figure SN-3

EGC MSI BROADCASTS
NAV/METAREA III
SPAIN / GREECE

KEY:
–·–·–·– Limit of NAV/METAREA III
——— Forecast areas

Forecasts and warnings are for areas not covered by NAVTEX.
For broadcast schedule please refer to EGC MSI Broadcast System table.
Vessels **must** ensure that their EGC receiver is configured to receive
messages from the appropriate NAVAREA / METAREA in order to
receive MSI broadcasts.

KEY:
0 Alboran	18 North Adriatic	36 Rodos Sea
1 Palos	19 Central Adriatic	37 Karpathio
2 Alger	20 South Adriatic	38 West Kritiko
3 Annaba	21 Boot	39 East Kritiko
4 Tunisie	22 Melita	40 SW Aegean
5 Carbonara	23 Gabes	41 SE Aegean-Ikario
6 Lipari	24 Sidra	42 Samos Sea
7 Circeo	25 North Ionio	43 Saronikos
8 Maddalena	26 South Ionio	44 South Evvoikos
9 Elbe	27 Patraikos	45 Kafireas Strait
10 Ligure	28 Korinthiakos	46 Central Aegean
11 Provence	29 Kithira Sea	47 NW Aegean
12 Corse	30 SW Kritiko	48 NE Aegean
13 Sardaigne	31 SE Kritiko Ierapetra	49 Thrakico
14 Cabrera	32 Taurus	50 Marmara
15 Minorque	33 Delta	51 Thermaicos
16 Lion	34 Crusade	52 W Black Sea
17 Baleares	35 Kastellorizo Sea	53 E Black Sea

V3(1)SN-3   V006   09/04/19

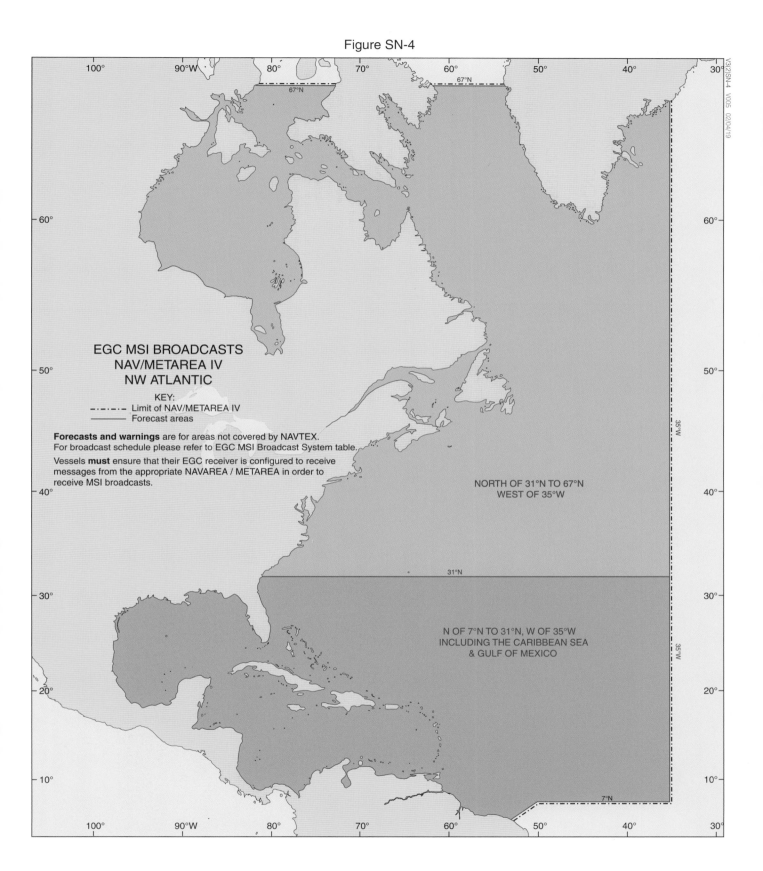

EGC MSI BROADCASTS
NAV/METAREA IV
NW ATLANTIC

KEY:
—·—·—·— Limit of NAV/METAREA IV
———— Forecast areas

Forecasts and warnings are for areas not covered by NAVTEX.
For broadcast schedule please refer to EGC MSI Broadcast System table.

Vessels **must** ensure that their EGC receiver is configured to receive messages from the appropriate NAVAREA / METAREA in order to receive MSI broadcasts.

NORTH OF 31°N TO 67°N
WEST OF 35°W

N OF 7°N TO 31°N, W OF 35°W
INCLUDING THE CARIBBEAN SEA
& GULF OF MEXICO

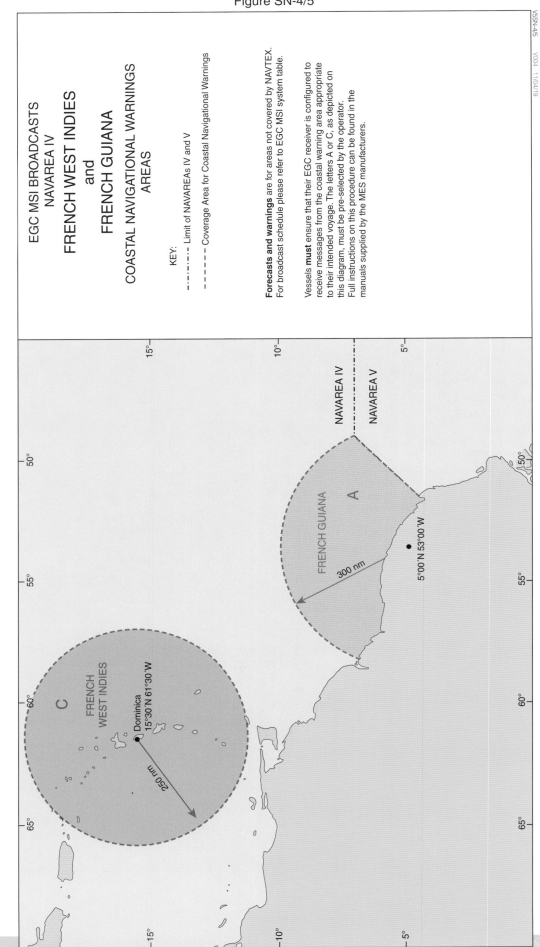

EGC MSI BROADCASTS
NAVAREA IV
FRENCH WEST INDIES
and
FRENCH GUIANA

COASTAL NAVIGATIONAL WARNINGS
AREAS

KEY:

–··–··– Limit of NAVAREAs IV and V

– – – – – Coverage Area for Coastal Navigational Warnings

Forecasts and warnings are for areas not covered by NAVTEX.
For broadcast schedule please refer to EGC MSI system table.

Vessels **must** ensure that their EGC receiver is configured to
receive messages from the coastal warning area appropriate
to their intended voyage. The letters A or C, as depicted on
this diagram, must be pre-selected by the operator.
Full instructions on this procedure can be found in the
manuals supplied by the MES manufacturers.

Figure SN-5M

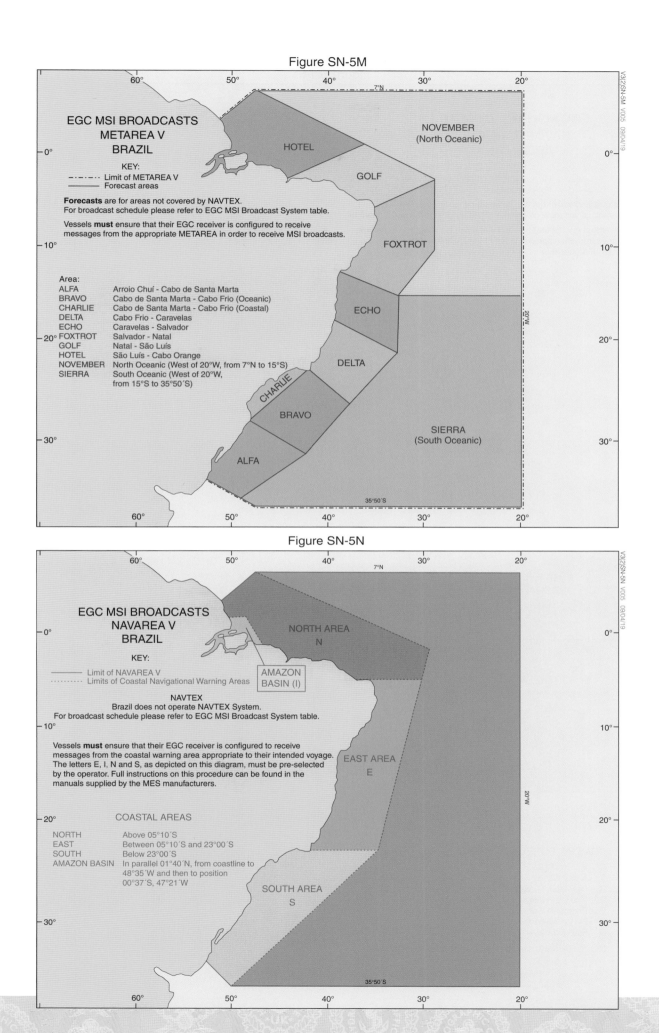

EGC MSI BROADCASTS
METAREA V
BRAZIL

KEY:
—·—·— Limit of METAREA V
———— Forecast areas

Forecasts are for areas not covered by NAVTEX.
For broadcast schedule please refer to EGC MSI Broadcast System table.

Vessels **must** ensure that their EGC receiver is configured to receive
messages from the appropriate METAREA in order to receive MSI broadcasts.

Area:
ALFA	Arroio Chuí - Cabo de Santa Marta
BRAVO	Cabo de Santa Marta - Cabo Frio (Oceanic)
CHARLIE	Cabo de Santa Marta - Cabo Frio (Coastal)
DELTA	Cabo Frio - Caravelas
ECHO	Caravelas - Salvador
FOXTROT	Salvador - Natal
GOLF	Natal - São Luís
HOTEL	São Luís - Cabo Orange
NOVEMBER	North Oceanic (West of 20°W, from 7°N to 15°S)
SIERRA	South Oceanic (West of 20°W, from 15°S to 35°50′S)

NOVEMBER
(North Oceanic)

HOTEL

GOLF

FOXTROT

ECHO

DELTA

CHARLIE

BRAVO

ALFA

SIERRA
(South Oceanic)

7°N

20°W

35°50′S

Figure SN-5N

EGC MSI BROADCASTS
NAVAREA V
BRAZIL

KEY:
———— Limit of NAVAREA V
·········· Limits of Coastal Navigational Warning Areas

NORTH AREA
N

AMAZON
BASIN (I)

NAVTEX
Brazil does not operate NAVTEX System.
For broadcast schedule please refer to EGC MSI Broadcast System table.

Vessels **must** ensure that their EGC receiver is configured to receive
messages from the coastal warning area appropriate to their intended voyage.
The letters E, I, N and S, as depicted on this diagram, must be pre-selected
by the operator. Full instructions on this procedure can be found in the
manuals supplied by the MES manufacturers.

COASTAL AREAS

NORTH	Above 05°10′S
EAST	Between 05°10′S and 23°00′S
SOUTH	Below 23°00′S
AMAZON BASIN	In parallel 01°40′N, from coastline to 48°35′W and then to position 00°37′S, 47°21′W

EAST AREA
E

SOUTH AREA
S

7°N

20°W

35°50′S

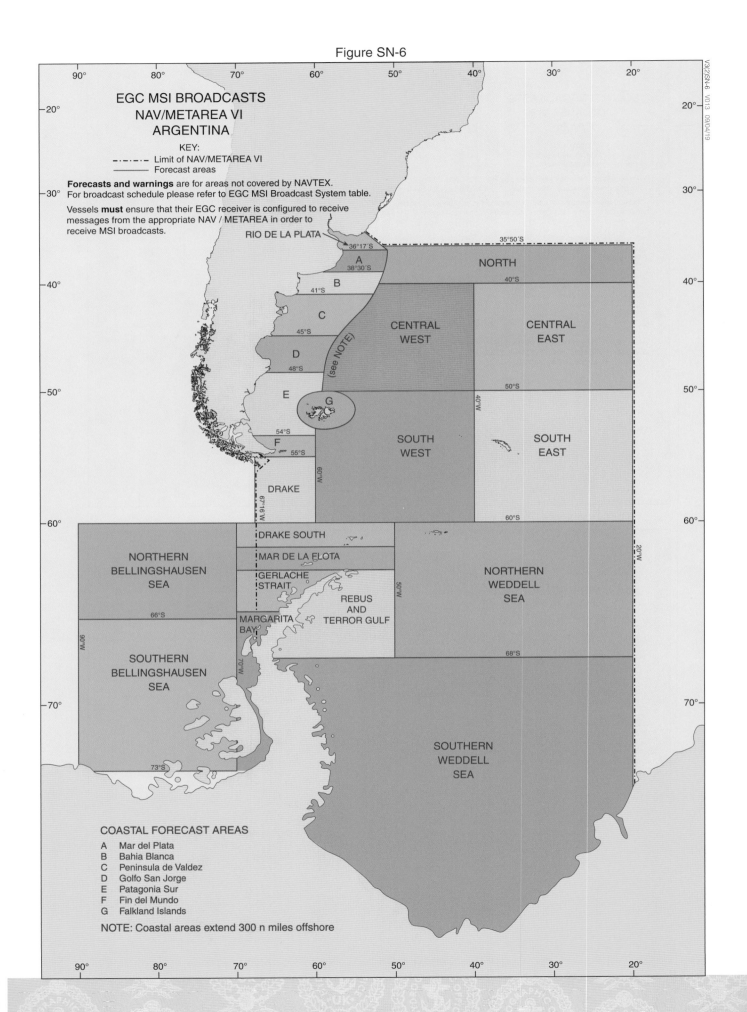

EGC MSI BROADCASTS
NAV/METAREA VI
ARGENTINA

KEY:
–·–·–·– Limit of NAV/METAREA VI
———— Forecast areas

Forecasts and warnings are for areas not covered by NAVTEX.
For broadcast schedule please refer to EGC MSI Broadcast System table.

Vessels **must** ensure that their EGC receiver is configured to receive
messages from the appropriate NAV / METAREA in order to
receive MSI broadcasts.

RIO DE LA PLATA

COASTAL FORECAST AREAS

A   Mar del Plata
B   Bahia Blanca
C   Peninsula de Valdez
D   Golfo San Jorge
E   Patagonia Sur
F   Fin del Mundo
G   Falkland Islands

NOTE: Coastal areas extend 300 n miles offshore

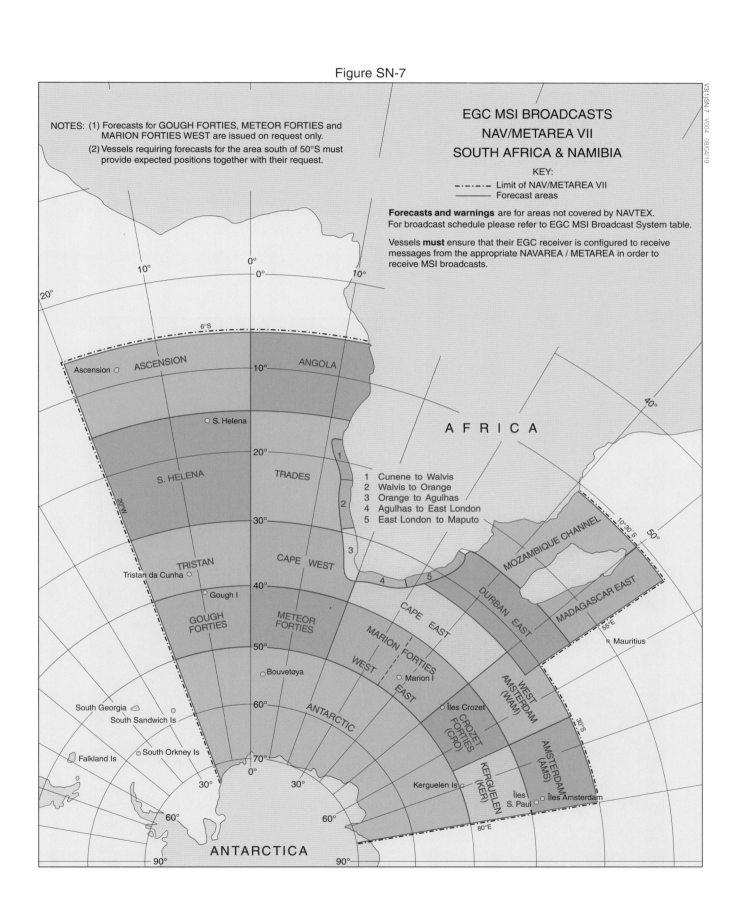

NOTES: (1) Forecasts for GOUGH FORTIES, METEOR FORTIES and
MARION FORTIES WEST are issued on request only.

(2) Vessels requiring forecasts for the area south of 50°S must
provide expected positions together with their request.

EGC MSI BROADCASTS
NAV/METAREA VII
SOUTH AFRICA & NAMIBIA

KEY:
–·–·–·– Limit of NAV/METAREA VII
———— Forecast areas

Forecasts and warnings are for areas not covered by NAVTEX.
For broadcast schedule please refer to EGC MSI Broadcast System table.

Vessels **must** ensure that their EGC receiver is configured to receive
messages from the appropriate NAVAREA / METAREA in order to
receive MSI broadcasts.

1 Cunene to Walvis
2 Walvis to Orange
3 Orange to Agulhas
4 Agulhas to East London
5 East London to Maputo

EGC MSI BROADCASTS
NAVAREAS VII and VIII
RÉUNION, MAYOTTE and KERGUELEN ISLANDS
COASTAL NAVIGATIONAL WARNING AREAS

KEY:

–·–·–·– Limit of NAVAREAs VII and VIII

– – – – – Coverage Area for Coastal Navigational Warnings

Forecasts and warnings are for areas not covered by NAVTEX. For broadcast schedule please refer to EGC MSI Broadcast System table.

Vessels **must** ensure that their EGC receiver is configured to receive messages from the coastal warning area appropriate to their intended voyage. The letters D, K or V, as depicted on this diagram, must be pre-selected by the operator. Full instructions on this procedure can be found in the manuals supplied by the MES manufacturers.

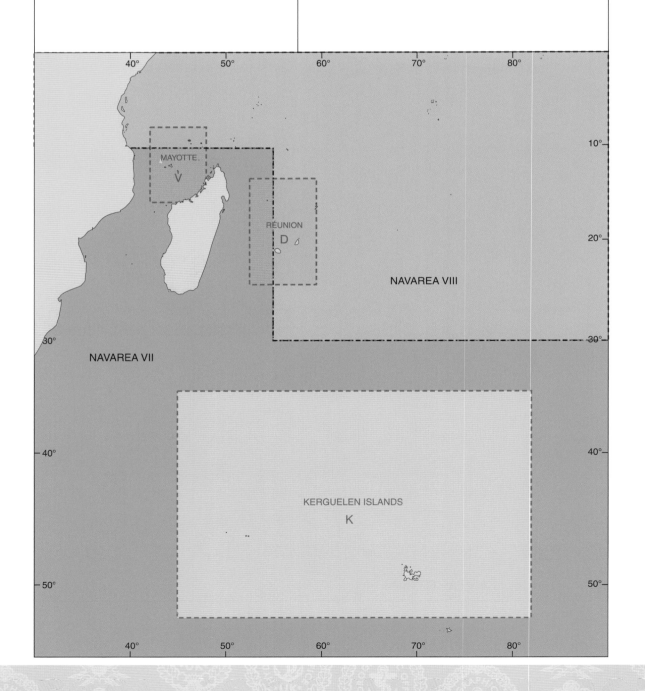

EGC MSI BROADCASTS
NAV/METAREA VIII
INDIA & MAURITIUS / RÉUNION

KEY:
–·–·–·– Limit of METAREA VIII
——— Forecast areas
——— Cyclone warnings area (Prepared and issued by Réunion)

MET information:

INDIA (North of 0°)

AUSTRALIA (South of 0° and East of 90°)
Tropical cyclone warnings, if any, prepared and issued by Australia as unscheduled broadcasts

MAURITIUS / RÉUNION (South of 0°)
Tropical cyclone warnings, if any, prepared and issued by Réunion as unscheduled broadcasts

Forecasts and warnings are for areas not covered by NAVTEX.
For broadcast schedule please refer to EGC MSI Broadcast System table.

Vessels **must** ensure that their EGC receiver is configured to receive messages from the appropriate NAVAREA / METAREA in order to receive MSI broadcasts.

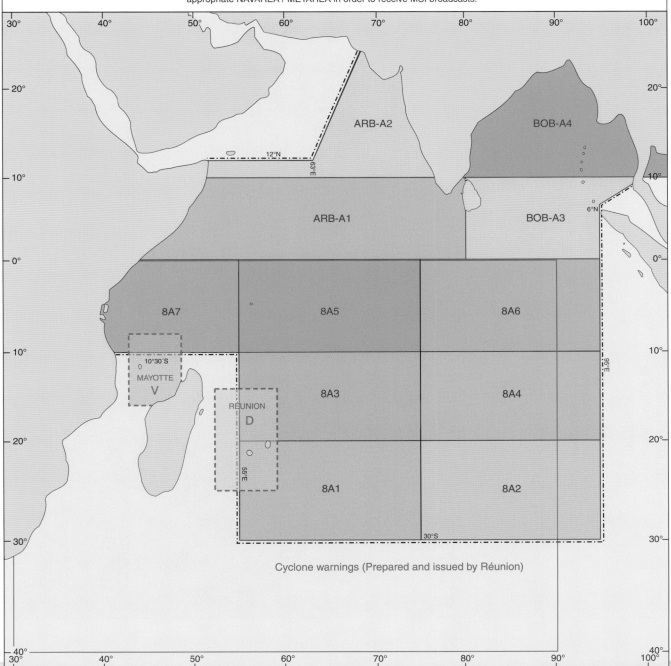

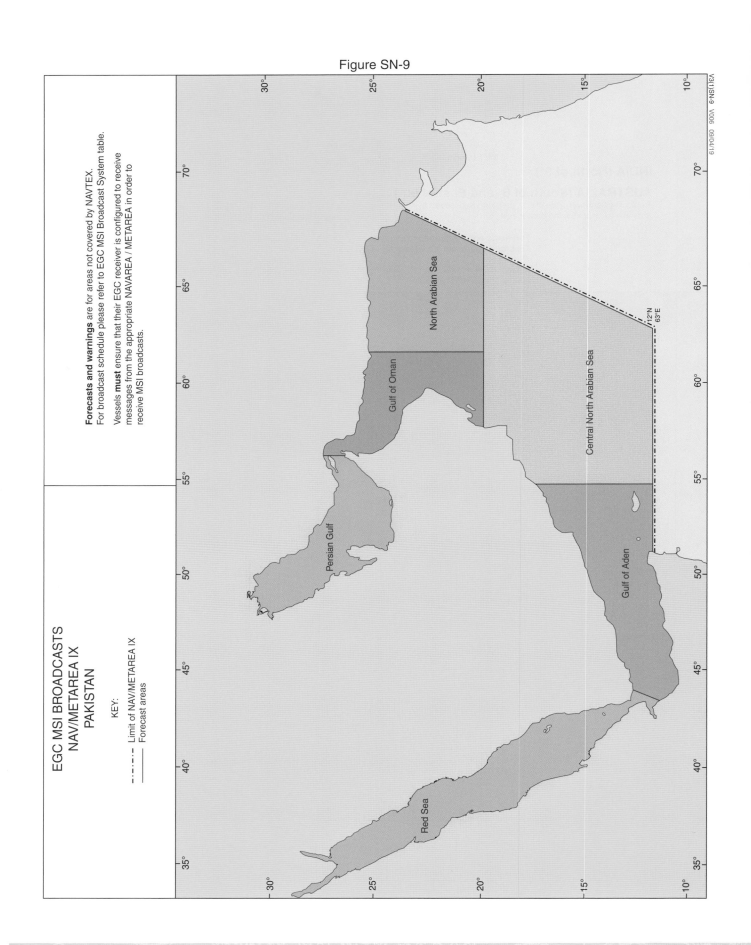

EGC MSI BROADCASTS
NAV/METAREA IX
PAKISTAN

KEY:

-··-··-··- Limit of NAV/METAREA IX
———— Forecast areas

Forecasts and warnings are for areas not covered by NAVTEX.
For broadcast schedule please refer to EGC MSI Broadcast System table.

Vessels **must** ensure that their EGC receiver is configured to receive messages from the appropriate NAVAREA / METAREA in order to receive MSI broadcasts.

Persian Gulf

Gulf of Oman

North Arabian Sea

Central North Arabian Sea

Gulf of Aden

Red Sea

12°N
63°E

Figure SN-10M

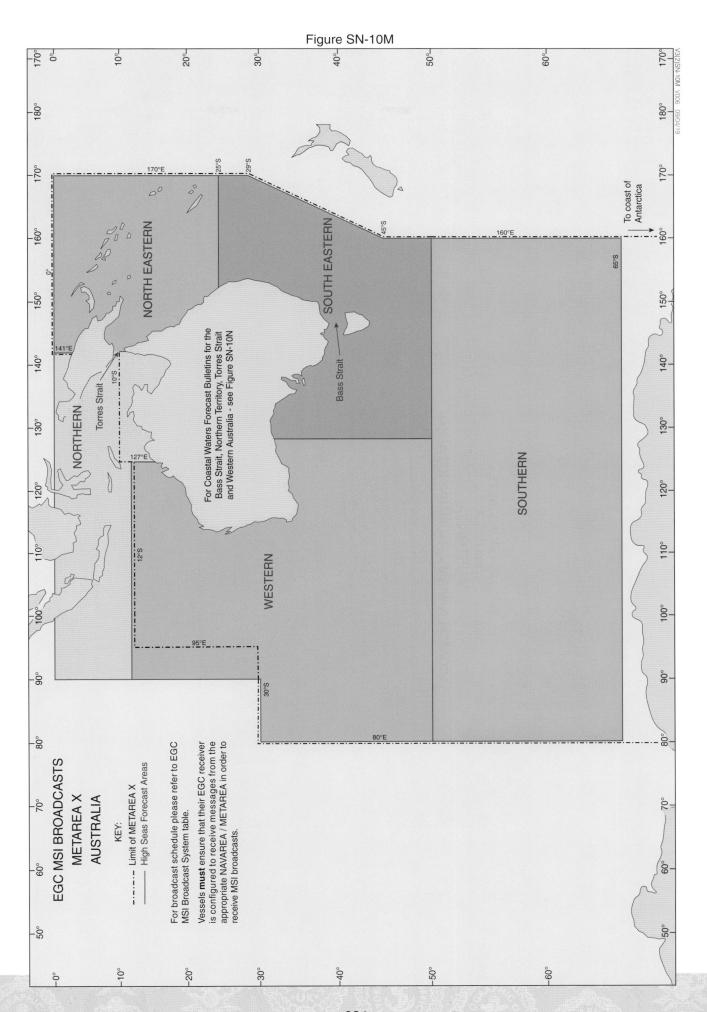

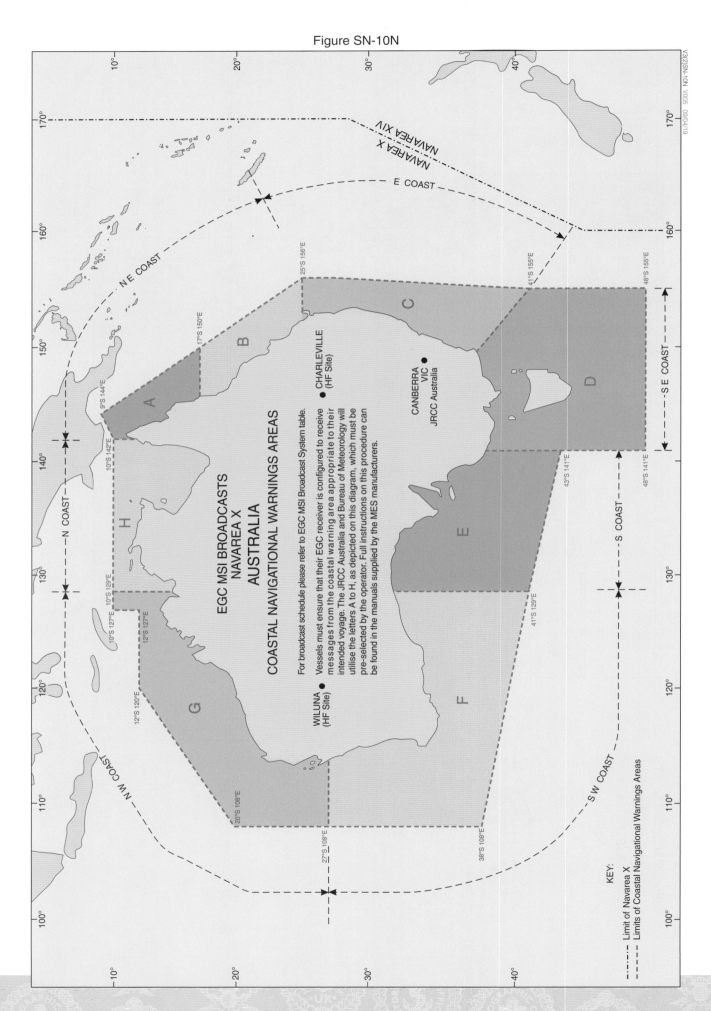

EGC MSI BROADCASTS
NAVAREA X
AUSTRALIA
COASTAL NAVIGATIONAL WARNINGS AREAS

For broadcast schedule please refer to EGC MSI Broadcast System table.

Vessels must ensure that their EGC receiver is configured to receive messages from the coastal warning area appropriate to their intended voyage. The JRCC Australia and Bureau of Meteorology will utilise the letters A to H, as depicted on this diagram, which must be pre-selected by the operator. Full instructions on this procedure can be found in the manuals supplied by the MES manufacturers.

● CHARLEVILLE
(HF Site)

● WILUNA
(HF Site)

CANBERRA
VIC ●
JRCC Australia

NAVAREA X
NAVAREA XIV

KEY:
—··—··— Limit of Navarea X
———— Limits of Coastal Navigational Warnings Areas

V3(2)SN-10N V005 09/04/19

Figure SN-10/14

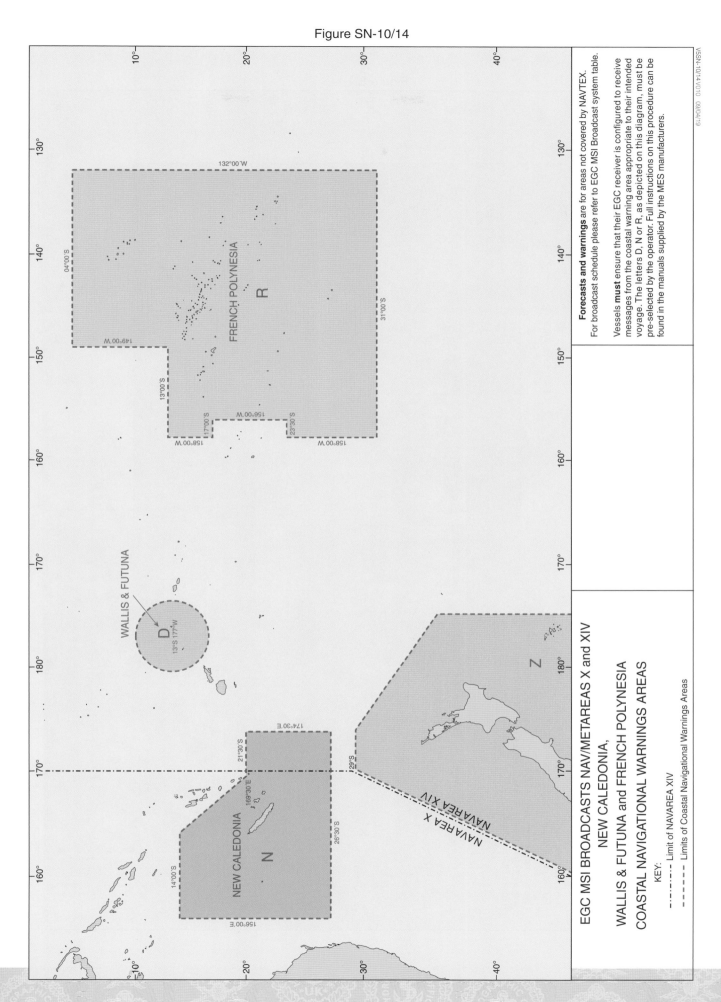

EGC MSI BROADCASTS NAV/METAREAS X and XIV
NEW CALEDONIA,
WALLIS & FUTUNA and FRENCH POLYNESIA
COASTAL NAVIGATIONAL WARNINGS AREAS

KEY:
-··-··-··- Limit of NAVAREA XIV
- - - - - Limits of Coastal Navigational Warnings Areas

Forecasts and warnings are for areas not covered by NAVTEX. For broadcast schedule please refer to EGC MSI Broadcast system table.

Vessels **must** ensure that their EGC receiver is configured to receive messages from the coastal warning area appropriate to their intended voyage. The letters D, N or R, as depicted on this diagram, must be pre-selected by the operator. Full instructions on this procedure can be found in the manuals supplied by the MES manufacturers.

V5SN-10/14 V010 09/04/19

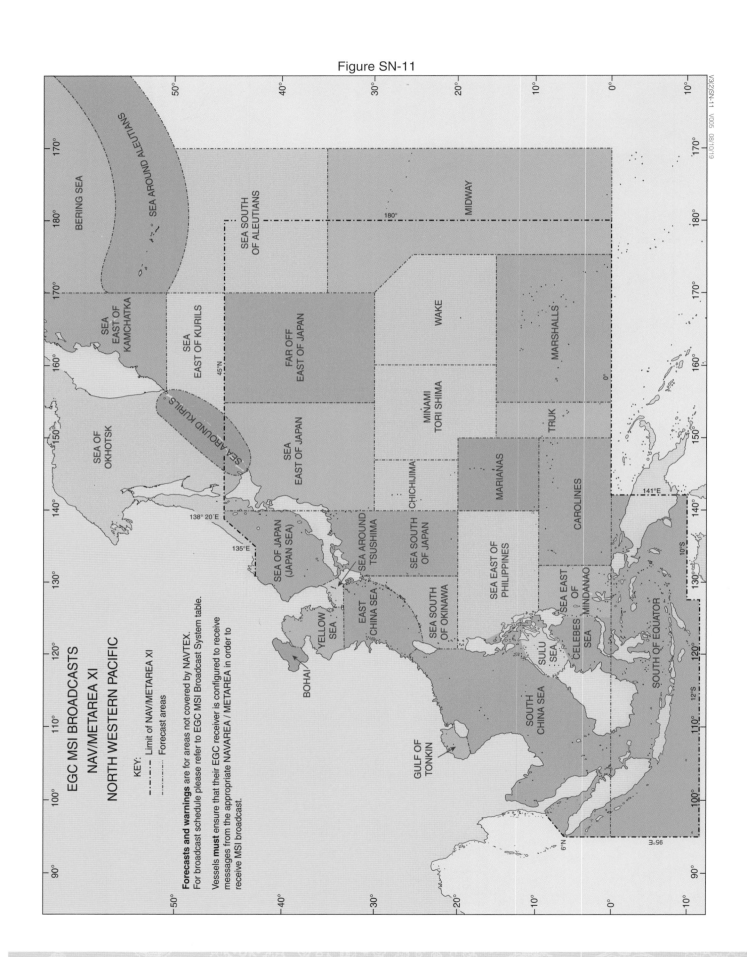

EGC MSI BROADCASTS
NAV/METAREA XI
NORTH WESTERN PACIFIC

KEY:
—··—··— Limit of NAV/METAREA XI
·········· Forecast areas

Forecasts and warnings are for areas not covered by NAVTEX.
For broadcast schedule please refer to EGC MSI Broadcast System table.

Vessels **must** ensure that their EGC receiver is configured to receive messages from the appropriate NAVAREA / METAREA in order to receive MSI broadcast.

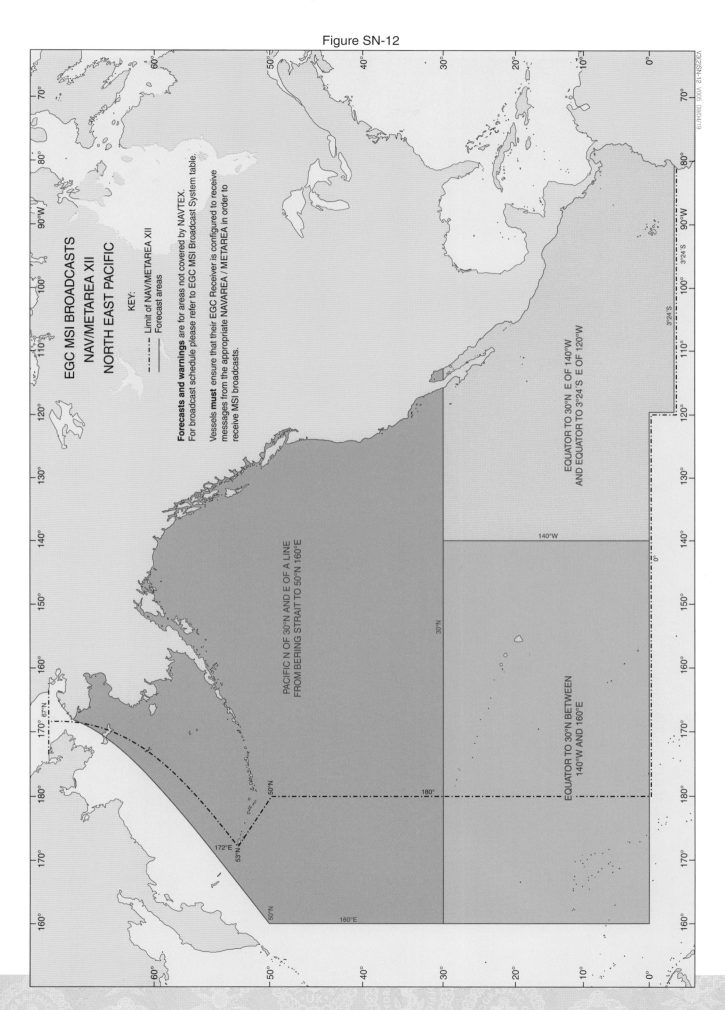

EGC MSI BROADCASTS
NAV/METAREA XII
NORTH EAST PACIFIC

KEY:

—··—··— Limit of NAV/METAREA XII
———— Forecast areas

Forecasts and warnings are for areas not covered by NAVTEX.
For broadcast schedule please refer to EGC MSI Broadcast System table.

Vessels **must** ensure that their EGC Receiver is configured to receive
messages from the appropriate NAVAREA / METAREA in order to
receive MSI broadcasts.

PACIFIC N OF 30°N AND E OF A LINE
FROM BERING STRAIT TO 50°N 160°E

EQUATOR TO 30°N E OF 140°W
AND EQUATOR TO 3°24'S E OF 120°W

EQUATOR TO 30°N BETWEEN
140°W AND 160°E

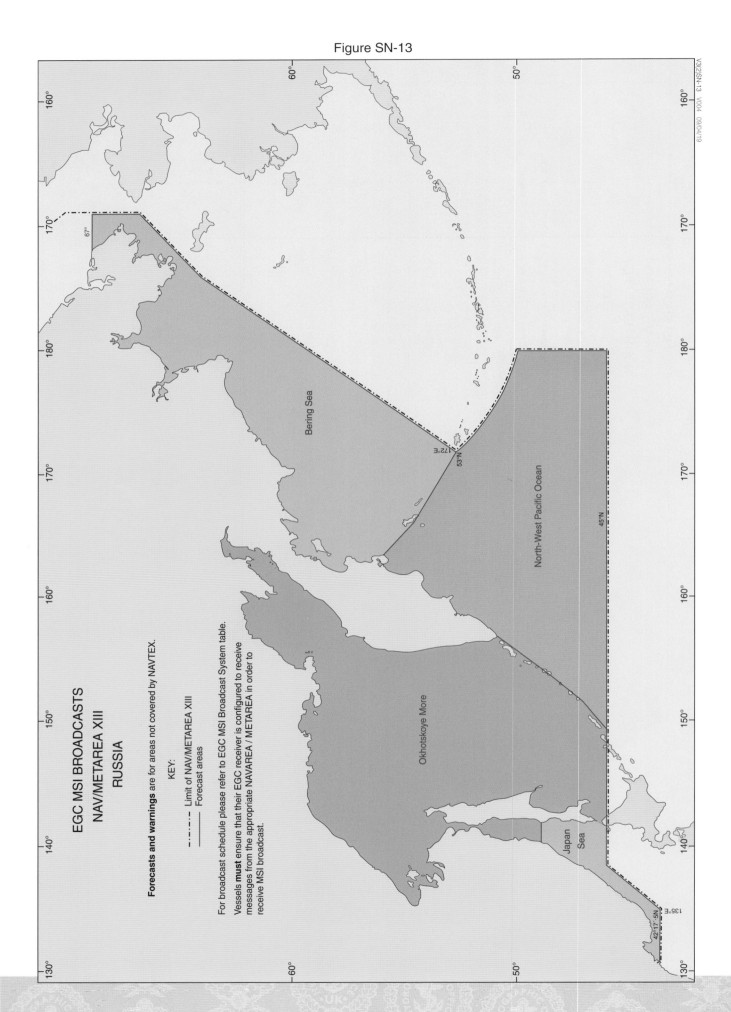

EGC MSI BROADCASTS
NAV/METAREA XIII
RUSSIA

Forecasts and warnings are for areas not covered by NAVTEX.

KEY:

–··–··– Limit of NAV/METAREA XIII
———— Forecast areas

For broadcast schedule please refer to EGC MSI Broadcast System table.

Vessels **must** ensure that their EGC receiver is configured to receive messages from the appropriate NAVAREA / METAREA in order to receive MSI broadcast.

Bering Sea

North-West Pacific Ocean

Okhotskoye More

Japan Sea

EGC MSI BROADCASTS
NAV/METAREA XIV
NEW ZEALAND

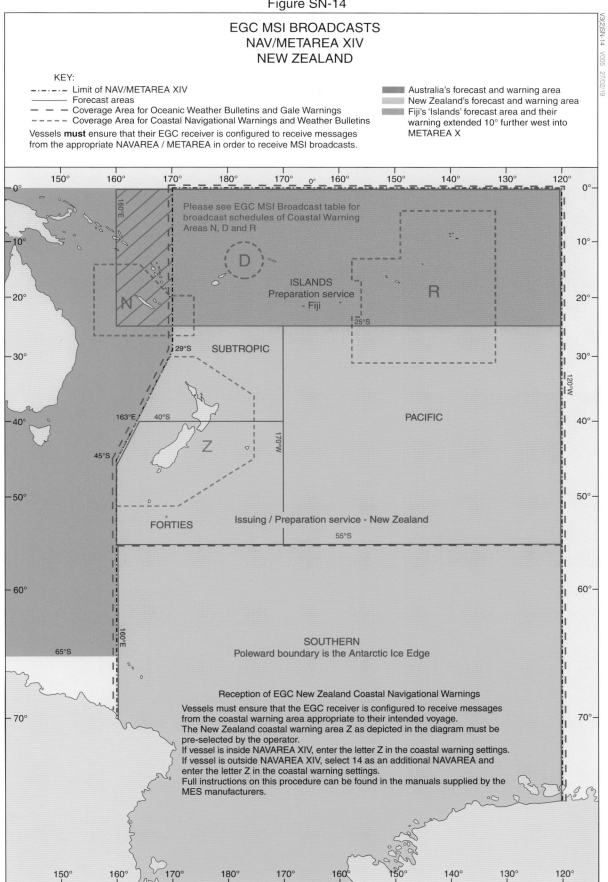

KEY:
- –·–·–·– Limit of NAV/METAREA XIV
- ———— Forecast areas
- – – – Coverage Area for Oceanic Weather Bulletins and Gale Warnings
- - - - - Coverage Area for Coastal Navigational Warnings and Weather Bulletins

Vessels **must** ensure that their EGC receiver is configured to receive messages from the appropriate NAVAREA / METAREA in order to receive MSI broadcasts.

- ▮ Australia's forecast and warning area
- ▮ New Zealand's forecast and warning area
- ▮ Fiji's 'Islands' forecast area and their warning extended 10° further west into METAREA X

Please see EGC MSI Broadcast table for broadcast schedules of Coastal Warning Areas N, D and R

D

ISLANDS
Preparation service
- Fiji

N

R

SUBTROPIC

Z

PACIFIC

FORTIES

Issuing / Preparation service - New Zealand

SOUTHERN
Poleward boundary is the Antarctic Ice Edge

Reception of EGC New Zealand Coastal Navigational Warnings

Vessels must ensure that the EGC receiver is configured to receive messages from the coastal warning area appropriate to their intended voyage.
The New Zealand coastal warning area Z as depicted in the diagram must be pre-selected by the operator.
If vessel is inside NAVAREA XIV, enter the letter Z in the coastal warning settings.
If vessel is outside NAVAREA XIV, select 14 as an additional NAVAREA and enter the letter Z in the coastal warning settings.
Full instructions on this procedure can be found in the manuals supplied by the MES manufacturers.

V3(2)SN-14   V005   27/02/19

Figure SN-15

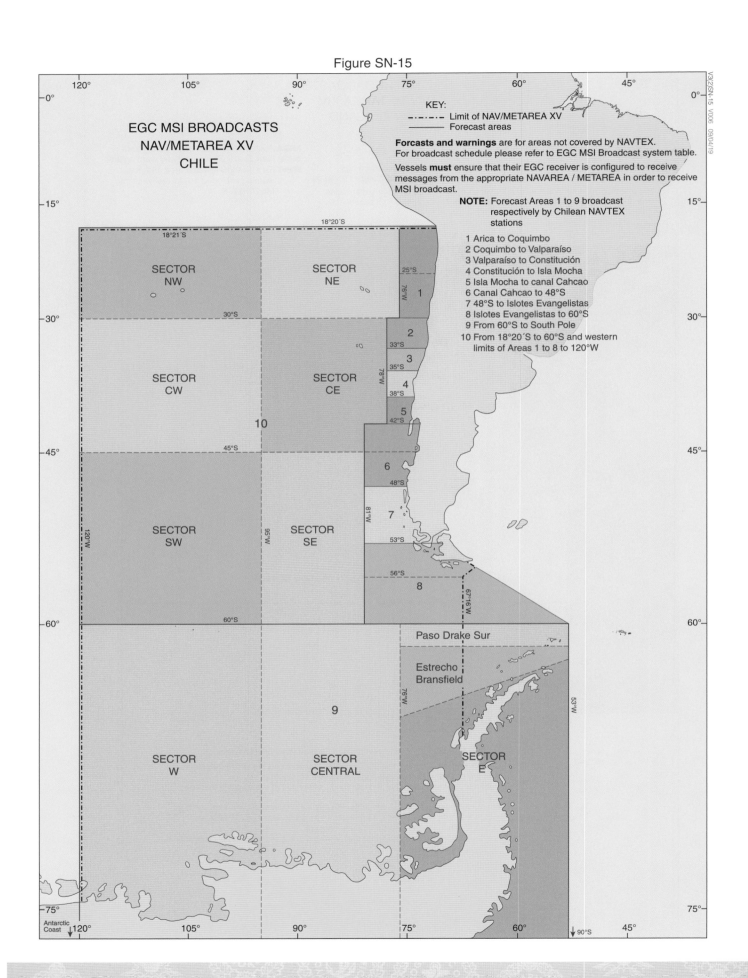

EGC MSI BROADCASTS
NAV/METAREA XV
CHILE

KEY:
— · — · — Limit of NAV/METAREA XV
————— Forecast areas

Forcasts and warnings are for areas not covered by NAVTEX.
For broadcast schedule please refer to EGC MSI Broadcast system table.

Vessels **must** ensure that their EGC receiver is configured to receive
messages from the appropriate NAVAREA / METAREA in order to receive
MSI broadcast.

NOTE: Forecast Areas 1 to 9 broadcast
respectively by Chilean NAVTEX
stations

1 Arica to Coquimbo
2 Coquimbo to Valparaíso
3 Valparaíso to Constitución
4 Constitución to Isla Mocha
5 Isla Mocha to canal Cahcao
6 Canal Cahcao to 48°S
7 48°S to Islotes Evangelistas
8 Islotes Evangelistas to 60°S
9 From 60°S to South Pole
10 From 18°20´S to 60°S and western
limits of Areas 1 to 8 to 120°W

SECTOR NW
SECTOR NE
SECTOR CW
SECTOR CE
SECTOR SW
SECTOR SE
10

Paso Drake Sur
Estrecho Bransfield

SECTOR W
SECTOR CENTRAL
SECTOR E
9

Antarctic Coast

Figure SN-16

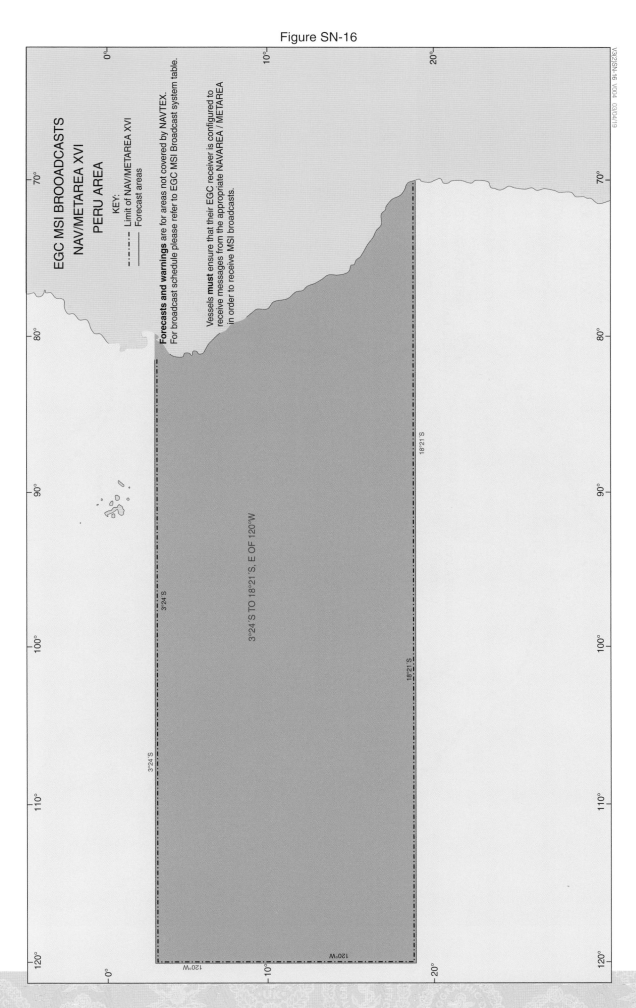

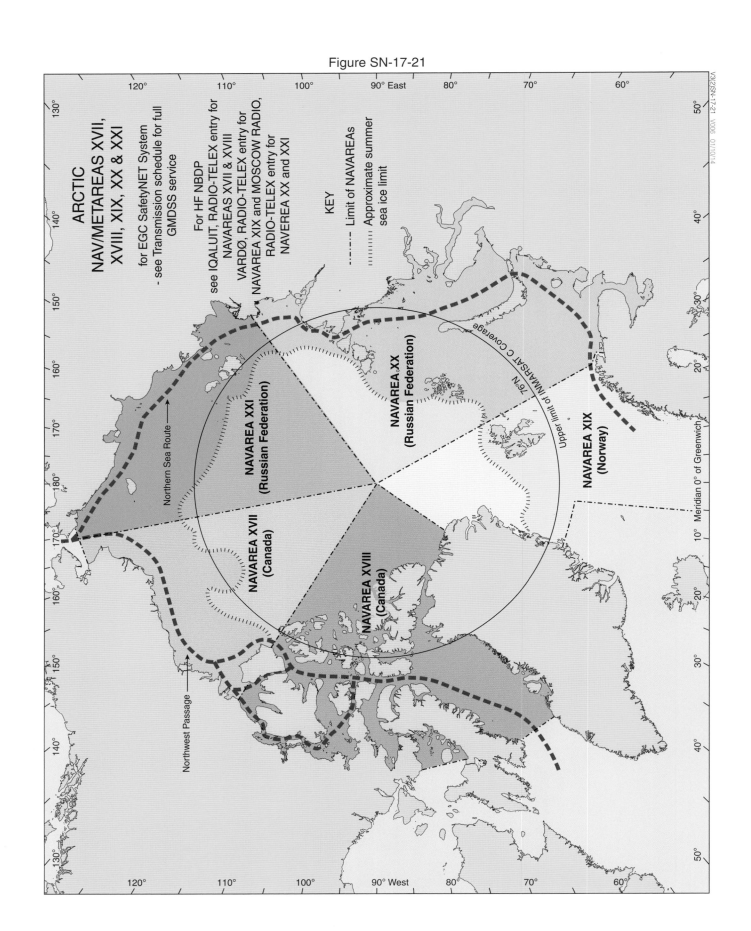

ARCTIC
NAV/METAREAS XVII,
XVIII, XIX, XX & XXI

for EGC SafetyNET System
- see Transmission schedule for full
GMDSS service

For HF NBDP
see IQALUIT, RADIO-TELEX entry for
NAVAREAS XVII & XVIII
VARDØ, RADIO-TELEX entry for
NAVAREA XIX and MOSCOW RADIO,
RADIO-TELEX entry for
NAVAREA XX and XXI

KEY
—·—·— Limit of NAVAREAs
·········· Approximate summer
sea ice limit

NAVAREA XXI
(Russian Federation)

NAVAREA XX
(Russian Federation)

NAVAREA XIX
(Norway)

NAVAREA XVII
(Canada)

NAVAREA XVIII
(Canada)

Northern Sea Route

Northwest Passage

Upper limit of INMARSAT C Coverage

Meridian 0° of Greenwich

76°N

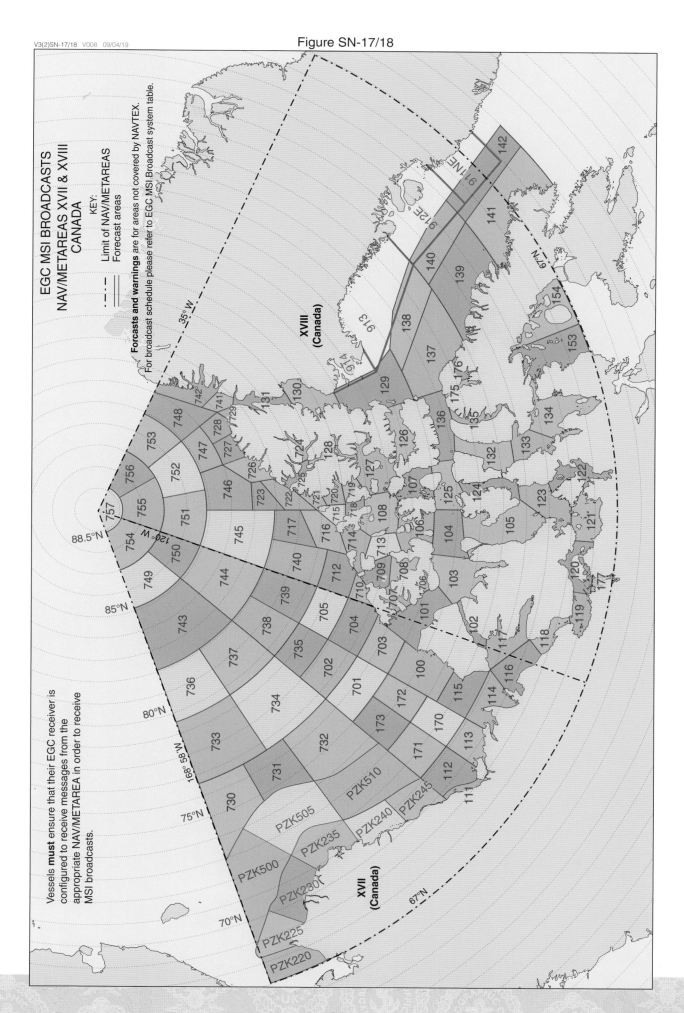

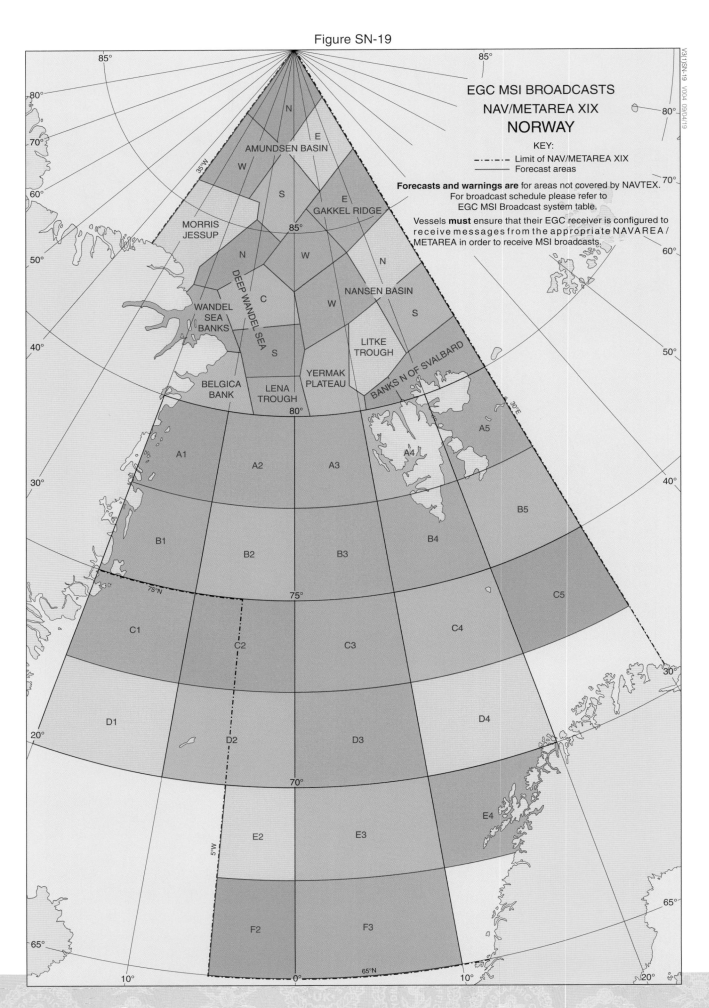

EGC MSI BROADCASTS
NAV/METAREA XIX
NORWAY

KEY:
–·–·–·– Limit of NAV/METAREA XIX
——— Forecast areas

Forecasts and warnings are for areas not covered by NAVTEX.
For broadcast schedule please refer to
EGC MSI Broadcast system table.

Vessels **must** ensure that their EGC receiver is configured to
receive messages from the appropriate NAVAREA /
METAREA in order to receive MSI broadcasts.

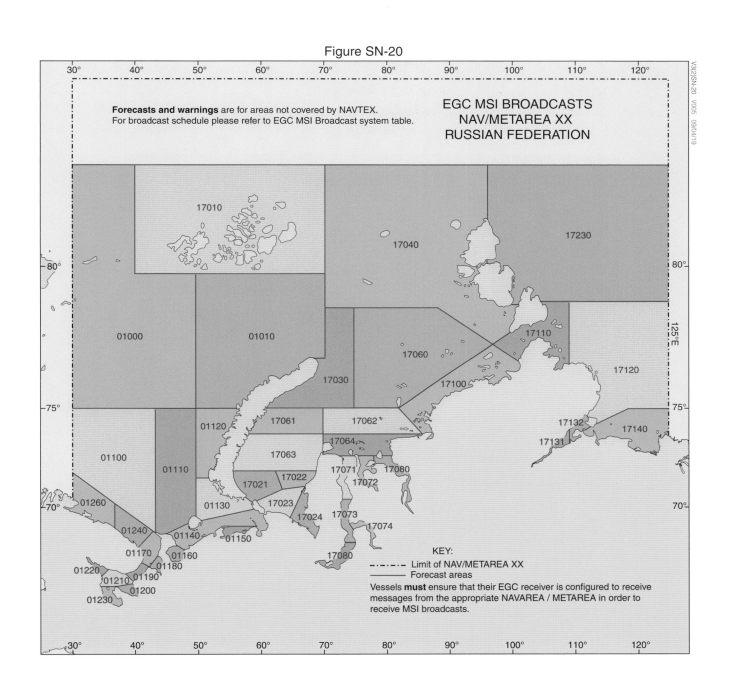

EGC MSI BROADCASTS
NAV/METAREA XX
RUSSIAN FEDERATION

Forecasts and warnings are for areas not covered by NAVTEX.
For broadcast schedule please refer to EGC MSI Broadcast system table.

KEY:
–·–·–·– Limit of NAV/METAREA XX
———— Forecast areas
Vessels **must** ensure that their EGC receiver is configured to receive messages from the appropriate NAVAREA / METAREA in order to receive MSI broadcasts.

Figure SN-21

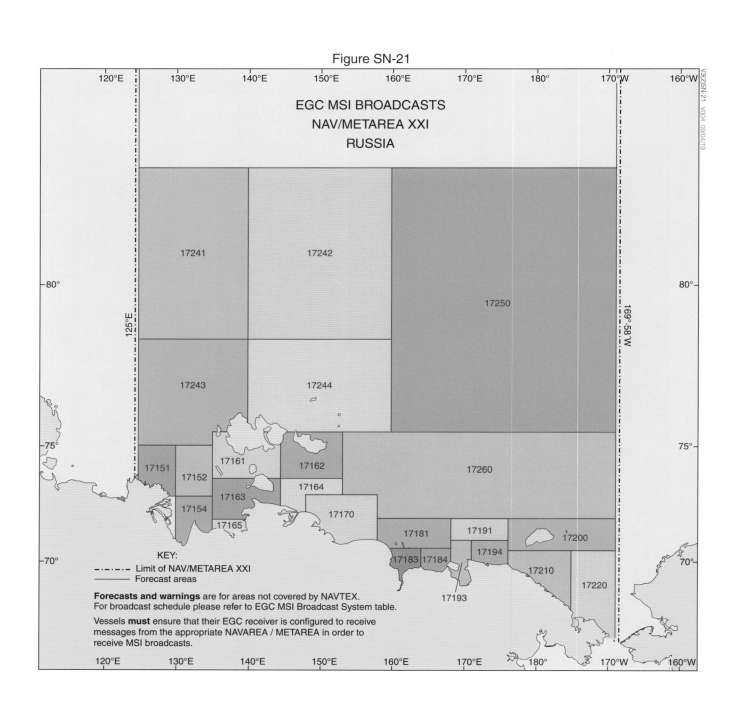

EGC MSI BROADCASTS
NAV/METAREA XXI
RUSSIA

KEY:
–·–·–·– Limit of NAV/METAREA XXI
——— Forecast areas

Forecasts and warnings are for areas not covered by NAVTEX.
For broadcast schedule please refer to EGC MSI Broadcast System table.

Vessels **must** ensure that their EGC receiver is configured to receive
messages from the appropriate NAVAREA / METAREA in order to
receive MSI broadcasts.

NAVTEX

INTRODUCTION

NAVTEX is an international automated direct-printing service for promulgation of Maritime Safety Information (MSI), navigational and meteorological warnings, meteorological forecasts and other urgent information to ships. It was developed to provide a low cost, simple and automated means of receiving MSI on board ships at sea in coastal waters. The information transmitted may be relevant to all sizes and types of vessel and the selective message-rejection feature ensures that every mariner can receive MSI broadcasts which are tailored to their particular needs.

NAVTEX fulfils an integral role in the Global Maritime Distress and Safety System (GMDSS) developed by the International Maritime Organization (IMO) and incorporated into the 1988 amendments to the International Convention for the Safety of Life at Sea (SOLAS), 1974, as amended, as a requirement for ships to which the Convention applies.

The operational and technical characteristics of the NAVTEX system are contained in Recommendation ITU-R M. 540-2. Performance standards for shipborne narrow-band direct-printing (NBDP) equipment are laid down in IMO Assembly resolution A.525(13). For further information it is recommended that the NAVTEX Manual, published by the IMO, should be consulted.

Basic concept of the NAVTEX system

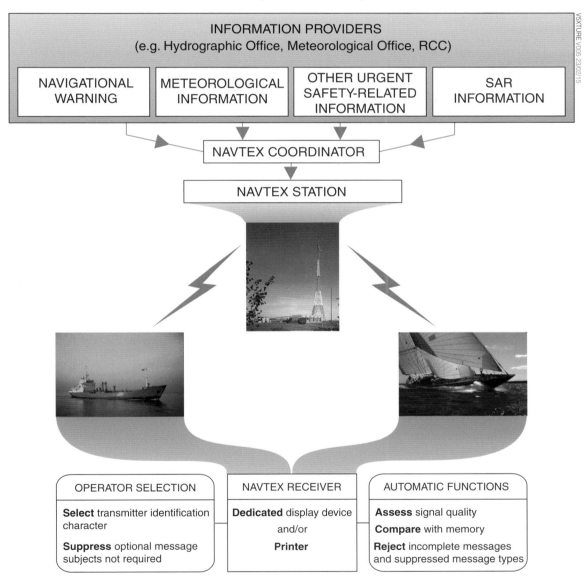

RECEPTION

Users should be aware that where there is a significant overland path between the transmitter site and the user, the strength of the signal will be markedly reduced, as will the range at which that signal may be received. Furthermore the topography of ports, harbours and marinas and the presence of high rise buildings may distort or preclude reception of NAVTEX. Up to date NAVTEX weather information SHOULD be available from all Harbour Masters. However, many still do not provide such a service.

1. Definitions

(a) *NAVTEX* means the system for the broadcast and automatic reception of maritime safety information by means of narrow-band direct-printing telegraphy.

(b) *International NAVTEX service* means the coordinated broadcast and automatic reception on 518 kHz of maritime safety information by means of narrow-band direct-printing telegraphy using the English language.

(c) *National NAVTEX service* means the broadcast and automatic reception of maritime safety information by means of narrow-band direct-printing telegraphy using frequencies other than 518 kHz and languages as decided by the Administrations concerned. These services may simply repeat the messages broadcast over the International NAVTEX service but in the national language, or they may be tailored to meet particular national requirements, for example by providing different or additional information to that broadcast on the International NAVTEX service targeted at recreational vessels or fishing fleets. These navigational NAVTEX services may be broadcast on 490 kHz or 4209·5 kHz (frequencies coordinated by IMO through the NAVTEX Coordinating Panel) or on nationally assigned frequencies.

(d) *NAVTEX coverage area* means an area defined by an arc of a circle having a radius from the transmitter calculated according to the method and criteria given in resolution A.801(19), as amended.

(e) *NAVTEX service area* means a unique and precisely defined sea area, wholly contained within the NAVTEX coverage area, for which maritime safety information is provided from a particular NAVTEX transmitter. It is normally defined by a line that takes full account of local propagation conditions and the character and volume of information and maritime traffic patterns in the region, as given in resolution A.801(19), as amended.

2. Principal features of NAVTEX

The International NAVTEX service uses a single frequency with transmissions from nominated stations within each NAVAREA/METAREA being arranged on a time-sharing basis to reduce the risk of mutual interference. All necessary information is contained in each transmission. Similarly, broadcasts on other IMO coordinated frequencies are operated on a time-sharing basis.

The power of each transmitter is regulated so as to reduce the risk of interference between transmitters with the same B_1 character in different parts of the world.

A dedicated NAVTEX receiver which has the ability to select messages to be printed, according to:

(a) a technical code ($B_1B_2B_3B_4$), which appears in the preamble of each message; and

(b) whether or not the particular message has already been printed.

Certain essential classes of safety information such as navigational and meteorological warnings and search and rescue information are non-rejectable to ensure that ships using NAVTEX always receive the most vital information.

NAVTEX coordinators exercise control of messages transmitted by each station according to the information contained in each message and the geographical coverage required. Thus a user may choose to accept messages either from the single transmitter which serves the sea area around his position, or from a number of transmitters as appropriate. Ideally, the user should select the station within whose coverage his vessel is currently operating and the station into whose coverage area his vessel will transit next.

3. Language and National Broadcast Options

There is often a requirement for broadcasts to be made in national languages, in addition to English, and for subject matter other than that on standard SUBJECT INDICATOR CHARACTERS (B_2). Methods of achieving these objectives are outlined below:

3.1. Provision of national NAVTEX services on the internationally adopted frequency for such services (490 kHz or 4209·5 kHz) or on a nationally allocated frequency, as defined in paragraph 1(c).

3.2. Use of additional subject indicator characters (B_2) V, W, X and Y on 518 kHz. (Subject to allocation by the NAVTEX Panel).

MESSAGE PRIORITIES

3 message priorities are used to dictate the timing of the first broadcast of a new warning in the NAVTEX service. In descending order of urgency they are:

VITAL — for immediate broadcast, subject to avoiding interference to ongoing transmissions. Such messages should also be passed to the appropriate NAVAREA Coordinator for possible transmission as a NAVAREA warning via SafetyNET;

IMPORTANT — for broadcast at the next available period when the frequency is unused;

ROUTINE — for broadcast at the next scheduled transmission period.

Note: Both VITAL and IMPORTANT warnings will normally be repeated, if still valid, at the next scheduled transmission period.

Meteorological NAVTEX messages

The following priorities are to be assigned to meteorological NAVTEX messages:

Tsunami warnings — VITAL

Meteorological warnings — IMPORTANT

Meteorological forecasts — ROUTINE

Note: For other natural phenomena warnings, either VITAL or IMPORTANT may be used.

The standard format of NAVTEX messages

ZCZC
(Phasing signals > 10sec)
(End of the phasing period)

$B_1 B_2 B_3 B_4$
(B_1: Transmitter Identity)
(B_2: Message type)
($B_3 B_4$: NAVTEX number)

TIME OF ORIGIN
(Optional)

SERIES IDENTITY + CONSECUTIVE NUMBER

MESSAGE TEXT

NNNN
(End of message)
(Idle signals aa.....a > 2sec)
(End of emission)

TRANSMITTER IDENTIFICATION CHARACTER (B_1)

The transmitter identification character B_1 is a single unique letter which is allocated to each transmitter. It is used to identify the broadcasts which are to be accepted by the receiver, and those which are to be rejected, and also the time slot for the transmission.

In order to avoid erroneous reception of transmissions from two stations having the same B_1 character, it is necessary to ensure that such stations have a large geographical separation. Originally, this was achieved by allocating B_1 characters in line with the general global scheme. Experience has shown that when traffic levels increase significantly, some NAVTEX Coordinators are unable to control the data volumes broadcast from their stations and transmissions may overrun their allocated timeslots. The impact of this is that if adjacent stations have adjacent B_1 characters, and the first station overruns, its signal masks the phasing signal of the second station. To the receiver, this seems as if the second station is off the air and vital safety information can be missed. Hence B_1 characters are now allocated in a more random manner with consecutive letters not allocated to adjacent stations, but still achieving the required separation between stations having the same B_1 character.

NAVTEX transmissions have a designed maximum range of about 400 n miles. The minimum distance between two transmitters with the same B_1 identifier is usually sufficient to ensure that a receiver cannot be within range of both at the same time.

The table below shows the transmitter identification characters and their associated transmission start times used by the IMO NAVTEX Coordinating Panel to evaluate and allocate transmitter identification characters A to X, regardless of the geographical position of the station anywhere in the world. Each transmitter identification character is allocated a maximum transmission time of 10 minutes every 4 hours. Because the NAVTEX system always utilises a single frequency, it is **fundamental** to its successful operation that the following time slots are strictly adhered to, and that broadcasts do not overrun their allotted 10 minutes.

Transmitter identification character (B_1)	Transmission start times (UTC)					
A	0000	0400	0800	1200	1600	2000
B	0010	0410	0810	1210	1610	2010
C	0020	0420	0820	1220	1620	2020
D	0030	0430	0830	1230	1630	2030
E	0040	0440	0840	1240	1640	2040
F	0050	0450	0850	1250	1650	2050
G	0100	0500	0900	1300	1700	2100
H	0110	0510	0910	1310	1710	2110
I	0120	0520	0920	1320	1720	2120
J	0130	0530	0930	1330	1730	2130
K	0140	0540	0940	1340	1740	2140

Continued overleaf

L	0150	0550	0950	1350	1750	2150
M	0200	0600	1000	1400	1800	2200
N	0210	0610	1010	1410	1810	2210
O	0220	0620	1020	1420	1820	2220
P	0230	0630	1030	1430	1830	2230
Q	0240	0640	1040	1440	1840	2240
R	0250	0650	1050	1450	1850	2250
S	0300	0700	1100	1500	1900	2300
T	0310	0710	1110	1510	1910	2310
U	0320	0720	1120	1520	1920	2320
V	0330	0730	1130	1530	1930	2330
W	0340	0740	1140	1540	1940	2340
X	0350	0750	1150	1550	1950	2350

SUBJECT INDICATOR CHARACTER (B_2)

Information is grouped by subject on the NAVTEX broadcast, and each subject group is allocated a subject indicator character, B_2.

The subject indicator character is used by the receiver to identify different classes of messages as listed below. The indicator is also used to reject messages concerning certain optional subjects which are not required by the vessel. For example, LORAN messages might be rejected in a ship which is not fitted with an LORAN receiver. Receivers also use the B_2 character to identify messages which, because of their importance, may not be rejected. The following subject indicator characters are in use:

A = Navigational warnings (cannot be rejected by the receiver)
B = Meteorological warnings (cannot be rejected by the receiver)
C = Ice reports
D = Search and rescue information, acts of piracy warnings, tsunamis and other natural phenomena (cannot be rejected by the receiver)
E = Meteorological forecasts
F = Pilot and VTS service messages
G = AIS service messages
H = LORAN Messages
I = Spare
J = GNSS system messages regarding PRN status
K = Other electronic navigational aid system messages
L = Other navigational warnings - additional to B_2 character A (should not be rejected at the receiver)
M-U = Spare
V = Special services- allocation by the NAVTEX Panel
W = Special services- allocation by the NAVTEX Panel
X = Special services- allocation by the NAVTEX Panel
Y = Special services- allocation by the NAVTEX Panel
Z = No messages on hand

MESSAGE NUMBERING ($B_3 B_4$)

Each message within a subject group is allocated a serial number, $B_3 B_4$, between 01 and 99. This number will not necessarily relate to series numbering in other Radio Navigational Warning systems. On reaching 99, numbering will re-commence at 01 but avoiding the use of message numbers still in force.

A shortage of numbers will, where possible, be alleviated by the allocation of messages to other, relevant subject groups. It has been found that 99 messages are not always enough for some subject groups, and B_2 = L may be used for additional Navigational Warnings, to receive the overflow from B_2 = A when necessary.

COMMON ABBREVIATIONS FOR THE INTERNATIONAL NAVTEX SERVICE

Terminology in full	NAVTEX abbreviation
North or Northerly	N
Northeast or Northeasterly	NE
East or Easterly	E
Southeast or Southeasterly	SE
South or Southerly	S
Southwest or Southwesterly	SW
West or Westerly	W
Northwest or Northwesterly	NW
Decreasing	DECR

Continued on next page

Increasing	INCR
Variable	VRB
Becoming	BECMG
Locally	LOC
Moderate	MOD
Occasionally	OCNL
Scattered	SCT
Temporarily / Temporary	TEMPO
Isolated	ISOL
Frequent / Frequency	FRQ
Showers	SHWRS or SH
Cold Front	C-FRONT or CFNT
Warm Front	W-FRONT or WFNT
Occlusion Front	O-FRONT or OFNT
Weakening	WKN
Building	BLDN
Filling	FLN
Deepening	DPN
Intensifiying / Intensify	INTSF
Improving / Improve	IMPR
Stationary	STNR
Quasi-Stationary	QSTNR
Moving / Move	MOV or MVG
Veering	VEER
Backing	BACK
Slowly	SLWY
Quickly	QCKY
Rapidly	RPDY
Knots	KT
Km/h	KMH
Nautical miles	NM
Metres	M
HectoPascal	HPA
Meteo...	MET
Forecast	FCST
Further outlooks	TEND
Visibility	VIS
Slight	SLGT or SLT
Quadrant	QUAD
Possible	POSS
Probability / Probable	PROB
Significant	SIG
No change	NC
No significant change	NOSIG
Following	FLW
Next	NXT
Heavy	HVY
Severe	SEV or SVR
Strong	STRG
From	FM
Expected	EXP
Latitude / Longitude	LAT/LONG

REVISED PERFORMANCE STANDARDS FOR NAVTEX RECEIVERS (MSC.148(77) ADOPTED 3rd JUNE 2003)

The equipment should comprise radio receivers, a signal processor and:
either;

1. An integrated printing device; or
2. A dedicated display device[1], printer output port and a non-volatile message memory; or
3. A connection to an integrated navigation system and a non-volatile message memory.

[1] Where there is no printer, the dedicated display should be located in the position from which the ship is normally navigated.

Display Device and Printer

The display device and/or printer should be able to display a minimum of 32 characters per line.

If a dedicated display device is used, the following should be met:

1. An indication of newly received unsuppressed messages should be immediately displayed until acknowledgement or until 24 hours after receipt; and
2. Newly received unsuppressed messages should also be displayed.

The display device should be able to display at least 16 lines of message text.

Where the printer is not integrated, it should be possible to select the following data to be output to a printer:

1. All messages as they are received;
2. All messages stored in the message memory;
3. All messages received on specified frequencies, from specified locations or having specified message designators;
4. All messages currently displayed; and
5. Individual messages selected from those appearing on the display.

PRACTICAL INSTRUCTIONS FOR THE USE OF A NAVTEX RECEIVER

The NAVTEX receiver is a Narrow-Band Direct-Printing (NBDP) device operating on the frequency 518 kHz (some equipment can also operate on 490 and 4209.5 kHz), and is a vital part of the Global Maritime Distress and Safety System (GMDSS).

It automatically receives Maritime Safety Information such as Radio Navigational Warnings, Storm/Gale Warnings, Meteorological Forecasts, Piracy Warnings & Distress Alerts etc (full details of the system can be found in IMO Publication IMO-951E - The NAVTEX Manual).

The information received is printed on the receiver's own paper recorder roll. Each message begins with a start of message function (ZCZC) followed by a space then four B characters.

The first, (B_1), identifies the station being received, the second, (B_2), identifies the subject ie Navigational Warning, Met Forecasts etc, and the third and fourth, ($B_3 + B_4$), form the consecutive number of the message from that station. This is followed by the text of the message and ends with an end of message function (NNNN).

The NAVTEX system broadcasts COASTAL WARNINGS which cover the area from the Fairway Buoy out to 250 nautical miles from the transmitter; the transmissions from some transmitters can be received out to 400 nautical miles and even further in unusual propagational conditions.

The practical advice on the obverse of this card will help to ensure that you make the most efficient use of your NAVTEX receiver, guaranteeing the reception of Maritime Safety Information within the respective coverage areas of the NAVTEX stations being used.

NAVTEX RECEIVER CHECK-OFF LIST

For a NAVTEX receiver to function effectively, it is essential that the operator should have a sound knowledge of how to programme and operate his particular receiver. This is not difficult provided the following practical steps are followed:

1. Make sure that there are sufficient rolls of NAVTEX paper on board.

2. Check that there is paper in the receiver.

3. Turn the NAVTEX receiver on at least 4 hours before sailing or, better still, leave it turned on permanently. This avoids the chance of losing vital information which could affect the vessel during its voyage.

4. Make sure that the **Equipment Operating Manual** is available close to the equipment, paying particular attention to the fact that your equipment may be programmed differently from other makes and models.

5. Using the Equipment Operating Manual, make a handy guide for **programming, status and autotesting procedures** for your vessel's equipment, place it in a plastic cover and keep it with the equipment.

6. Have available next to the equipment a plasticised copy of the **Navareas / Metareas** in which the vessel is likely to sail, **showing the NAVTEX stations, their coverage ranges, their respective time schedules and B_1 characters.**

7. Programme your receiver to accept only those messages identified with the B_1 character of the NAVTEX station which covers the area in which your vessel is currently sailing and the one covering the area into which you are about to sail. This will avoid the equipment printing information which has no relevance to your voyage and will avoid unnecessary waste of paper.

8. Programme your receiver to accept only those messages identified with the B_2 characters (type of message) you wish to receive. It is recommended that most B_2 characters (A to Z) be programmed, but you may exclude those for navaid equipments (Loran C for example) with which your vessel is **NOT** fitted. Be aware that the characters A, B and D, **MUST** be included as they are mandatory.

9. Take extra care not to confuse the programming of B_1 characters (station designators) with those of B_2 characters (type of messages). It is very easy for an operator to believe that he/she is programming B_1 characters when in fact they are programming B_2 characters. After programming **ALWAYS CHECK** the programme status to ensure that it is correct.

10. If information is received incomplete/garbled, inform the relevant NAVTEX station, giving the UTC and your vessel's position. By so doing, not only will you obtain the information you require, but you will also help to improve the system. In the same way, any navigationally significant occurences observed during the voyage should be passed immediately to the nearest (or most convenient) Coast Radio Station and addressed to the relevant NAVAREA/METAREA or National Coordinator responsible for the area in which you are sailing.

STATIONS WITH OPERATIONAL NAVTEX FACILITIES
(See diagrams X0 to X13 at the end of this section)

GENERAL NOTES
Facilities of stations which have commenced OPERATIONAL **NAVTEX**, are listed below. Planned stations are not listed.
Throughout the following tables, NAVTEX messages are broadcast in English and on 518 kHz unless otherwise stated.
Meteorological Warnings (where a weather bulletin service is provided) and Urgent Navigational Information (including SAR information) will additionally be broadcast on receipt and at the next scheduled broadcast time whilst still in force.
The approximate NAVTEX operational range is shown in nautical miles for each station.

NAVAREA I

BELGIUM

Oostende [T] [V] [B] 51°04'·44N 3°20'·08E
TELEPHONE: +32 59 342493 X2
FAX: +32 59 342467 55 n miles
E-MAIL: rmd@mil.be
MMSI: 002050480

NAVTEX [T]

TIME UT(GMT)	WEATHER BULLETINS	NAVIGATIONAL WARNINGS	ICE WARNINGS AND REPORTS
0310		•	•
0710	•	•	•
1110		•	•
1510		•	•
1910	•	•	•
2310		•	•

NAVTEX [V] Range is 150 n miles

TIME UT(GMT)	NAVIGATIONAL WARNINGS
0330	•
0730	•
1130	•
1530	•
1930	•
2330	•

NAVTEX [B] Range is 55 n miles
Frequency: 490 kHz Language: Dutch and sometimes in English

TIME UT(GMT)	WEATHER BULLETINS	NAVIGATIONAL WARNINGS
0010		•
0410		•
0810	•	•
1210	•	•
1610	•	•
2010	•	•

ESTONIA

Tallinn [F] 59°27'·84N 24°21'·42E
NOTE: Broadcasts relayed by Sweden X2
Traffic/Stockholm Radio.
TELEPHONE: +372 699 1170 250 n miles
FAX: +372 699 1171
E-MAIL: tallinnradio@riks.ee

NAVTEX [F]

TIME UT(GMT)	WEATHER BULLETINS	NAVIGATIONAL WARNINGS
0050		•
0450	•	•
0850		•
1250		•
1650	•	•
2050		•

FAROE ISLANDS (Denmark)

Tórshavn [D] 62°00'·87N 6°48'·01W
TELEPHONE: +298 312965 X1, X2
FAX: +298 315546 300 n miles
E-MAIL: telegramm@vorn.fo
MMSI: 002311000

NAVTEX [D]

TIME UT(GMT)	WEATHER BULLETINS	NAVIGATIONAL WARNINGS
0030	•	•
0430		•
0830		•
1230	•	•
1630		•
2030		•

FRANCE (Atlantic and English Channel Coasts)

Corsen (CROSS (MRCC)) [A] [E] 48°28'·56N 5°03'·17W
TELEPHONE: +33 2 98893131 X2, X3
FAX: +33 2 98896575 300 n miles
TELEX: +42 940 086 CROCO A
E-MAIL: corsen@mrccfr.eu
MMSI: 002275300

NAVTEX [A]

TIME UT(GMT)	WEATHER BULLETINS	NAVIGATIONAL WARNINGS
0000	•	•
0400		•
0800		•
1200	•	•
1600		•
2000		•

FRANCE (Atlantic and English Channel Coasts)
NAVTEX [E]
Frequency: 490 kHz Language: French (local bcst)

TIME UT(GMT)	WEATHER BULLETINS	NAVIGATIONAL WARNINGS
0040		●
0440		●
0840	●	●
1240		●
1640		●
2040	●	●

Niton (UK) [K] [T]   50°35'·18N 1°15'·28W

NOTE: Broadcasts are remotely controlled by   X2, X3
Falmouth and Humber Coastguards. There may be
a delay in broadcast action if there is Search and
Rescue in progress.

TELEPHONE:	+44(0)1262 672317
FAX:	+44(0)1262 400779
E-MAIL:	humbercoastguard@mcga.gov.uk

NAVTEX [K]

TIME UT(GMT)	NAVIGATIONAL WARNINGS
0140	●
0540	●
0940	●
1340	●
1740	●
2140	●

NAVTEX [T]
Frequency: 490 kHz

TIME UT(GMT)	WEATHER BULLETINS	NAVIGATIONAL WARNINGS
0710	●	●
1910	●	●

GERMANY

Pinneberg [S] [L]   53°40'·50N 9°48'·50E

TELEPHONE:	+49 69 8062 6160	X2
FAX:	+49 69 8062 6103	250 n miles
E-MAIL:	ncc.navtex@dwd.de	

NAVTEX [S]
Weather and Navigational Warnings Broadcasts also contain wind/gale warnings.
Ice Warnings and Reports are broadcast when required.

TIME UT(GMT)	WEATHER BULLETINS	NAVIGATIONAL WARNINGS	ICE WARNINGS AND REPORTS
0300		●	
0700	●		
1100	●		●
1500	●		
1900		●	
2300		●	

GERMANY
NAVTEX [L]
Weather and Navigational Warnings Broadcasts also contain wind/gale warnings.
Ice Warnings and Reports are broadcast when required.
Frequency: 490 kHz Language: German (local bcst)

TIME UT(GMT)	WEATHER BULLETINS	NAVIGATIONAL WARNINGS	ICE WARNINGS AND REPORTS
0150	●	●	
0550	●	●	
0950	●	●	●
1350	●	●	●
1750	●	●	
2150	●	●	

GREENLAND

Grindavik (Iceland) [X]   63°49'·99N 22°27'·04W

NOTE: Weather and Navigational Warnings for the   X12, X13
east coast of Greenland are broadcast by Iceland
where necessary - see relevant entry.

TELEPHONE:	+354 5452100	450 n miles
FAX:	+354 5452001	
E-MAIL:	reyrad@lhg.is	
MMSI:	002510100	

NAVTEX [X]

TIME UT(GMT)	WEATHER BULLETINS	NAVIGATIONAL WARNINGS
0350	●	●
0750	●	●
1150	●	●
1550	●	●
1950	●	●
2350	●	●

Saudanes (Iceland) [R]   66°11'·17N 18°57'·12W

NOTE: Weather and Navigational Warnings for the   X12, X13
east coast of Greenland are broadcast by Iceland
where necessary - see relevant entry.

TELEPHONE:	+354 5452100	450 n miles
FAX:	+354 5452001	
E-MAIL:	reyrad@lhg.is	

NAVTEX [R]

TIME UT(GMT)	WEATHER BULLETINS	NAVIGATIONAL WARNINGS
0250	●	●
0650	●	●
1050	●	●
1450	●	●
1850	●	●
2250	●	●

ICELAND

Grindavik [X] [K]   63°49'·99N 22°27'·04W
TELEPHONE: +354 5452100   X1, X2, X13
FAX: +354 5452001   450 n miles
E-MAIL: reyrad@lhg.is
MMSI: 002510100

NAVTEX [X]
Weather and Navigational Warnings to include ice reports for east coast of
Greenland where necessary

TIME UT(GMT)	WEATHER BULLETINS	NAVIGATIONAL WARNINGS
0350	●	●
0750	●	●
1150	●	●
1550	●	●
1950	●	●
2350	●	●

NAVTEX [K]
Weather and Navigational Warnings to include ice reports where necessary
Frequency: 490 kHz Language: Icelandic

TIME UT(GMT)	WEATHER BULLETINS	NAVIGATIONAL WARNINGS
0140	●	●
0540	●	●
0940	●	●
1340	●	●
1740	●	●
2140	●	●

Saudanes [R] [E]   66°11'·17N 18°57'·12W
TELEPHONE: +354 5452100   X1, X2, X13
FAX: +354 5452001   450 n miles
E-MAIL: reyrad@lhg.is

NAVTEX [R]

TIME UT(GMT)	WEATHER BULLETINS	NAVIGATIONAL WARNINGS
0250	●	●
0650	●	●
1050	●	●
1450	●	●
1850	●	●
2250	●	●

NAVTEX [E]
Frequency: 490 kHz Language: Icelandic

TIME UT(GMT)	WEATHER BULLETINS	NAVIGATIONAL WARNINGS
0040	●	●
0440	●	●
0840	●	●
1240	●	●
1640	●	●
2040	●	●

IRELAND

Malin Head (Coast Guard MRSC) [Q] [A]   55°21'·80N 7°20'·39W
TELEPHONE: +353(0)74 9370103   X2
FAX: +353(0)74 9370221   400 n miles
E-MAIL: mrscmalin@transport.gov.ie
MMSI: 002500100

NAVTEX [Q]

TIME UT(GMT)	WEATHER BULLETINS	NAVIGATIONAL WARNINGS
0240		●
0640	●	●
1040	●	●
1440		●
1840	●	●
2240	●	●

NAVTEX [A]
Frequency: 490 kHz Language: English

TIME UT(GMT)	WEATHER BULLETINS[1]
0000	●
0400	●
0800	●
1200	●
1600	●
2000	●

[1] Inshore waters forecast for Sea Areas 13–17.

Valentia (Coast Guard MRSC) [W]   51°55'·80N 10°20'·95W
TELEPHONE: +353(0)66 9476109   X2
FAX: +353(0)66 9476289   400 n miles
E-MAIL: mrscvalentia@transport.gov.ie
MMSI: 002500200

NAVTEX [W]

TIME UT(GMT)	WEATHER BULLETINS	NAVIGATIONAL WARNINGS
0340		●
0740	●	●
1140	●	●
1540		●
1940	●	●
2340	●	●

NETHERLANDS

Netherlands Coastguard [P]   52°55'·00N 4°44'·00E
TELEPHONE: +31 223 542300 (H24   X2
             Operational)
FAX: +31 223 658358   250 n miles
TELEX: +44 71088 KUSTW NL
E-MAIL: ccc@kustwacht.nl
MMSI: 002442000

NAVTEX [P]

TIME UT(GMT)	WEATHER BULLETINS	NAVIGATIONAL WARNINGS	ICE WARNINGS AND REPORTS
0230	●	●	
0630		●	
1030		●	●
1430	●	●	
1830		●	
2230		●	

NORWAY

Jeløya [M]
		59°26'·21N 10°35'·66E
TELEPHONE:	+47 51642480	X1, X2, X13
E-MAIL:	kystradio.sor@telenor.com	150 n miles
MMSI:	002570000	

NAVTEX [M]

TIME UT(GMT)	WEATHER BULLETINS	NAVIGATIONAL WARNINGS
0200	●	●
0600		●
1000		●
1400	●	●
1800		●
2200		●

Ørlandet [N]
Remotely controlled from Rogaland

		63°39'·70N 9°32'·80E
		X1, X2, X13
TELEPHONE:	+47 51642480	450 n miles
E-MAIL:	kystradio.sor@telenor.com	
MMSI:	002570000	

NAVTEX [N]

TIME UT(GMT)	WEATHER BULLETINS	NAVIGATIONAL WARNINGS
0210	●	●
0610		●
1010		●
1410	●	●
1810		●
2210		●

Rogaland [L]
		58°39'·48N 5°36'·23E
TELEPHONE:	+47 51642480	X1, X2, X13
E-MAIL:	kystradio.sor@telenor.com	450 n miles
MMSI:	002570000	

NAVTEX [L]

TIME UT(GMT)	WEATHER BULLETINS	NAVIGATIONAL WARNINGS
0150	●	●
0550		●
0950		●
1350	●	●
1750		●
2150		●

SWEDEN

Bjuröklubb (Sweden Traffic-Baltic) [H]
		64°27'·70N 21°35'·42E
NOTE: Broadcasts relayed by Sweden Traffic/Stockholm Radio. Ice reports are no longer made on VHF, MF or NAVTEX – see Ice Reports section in ALRS Vol.3 for alternative ways of obtaining this information.		X2
TELEPHONE:	+46 711 630685	300 n miles
E-MAIL:	swedentraffic@sjofartsverket.se	
WEBSITE:	www.sjofartsverket.se/baltico	
MMSI:	002653500	

NAVTEX [H]

TIME UT(GMT)	WEATHER BULLETINS	NAVIGATIONAL WARNINGS
0110		●
0510	●	●
0910		●
1310		●
1710	●	●
2110		●

Gislövshammar (Sweden Traffic-Baltic) [J]
		55°29'·38N 14°18'·87E
NOTE: Broadcasts relayed by Sweden Traffic/Stockholm Radio. Ice reports are no longer made on VHF, MF or NAVTEX – see Ice Reports section in ALRS Vol.3 for alternative ways of obtaining this information.		X2
TELEPHONE:	+46 711 630685	300 n miles
E-MAIL:	swedentraffic@sjofartsverket.se	
WEBSITE:	www.sjofartsverket.se/baltico	

NAVTEX [J]

TIME UT(GMT)	WEATHER BULLETINS	NAVIGATIONAL WARNINGS
0130		●
0530	●	●
0930		●
1330		●
1730	●	●
2130		●

Grimeton (Sweden Traffic-Baltic) [I]
		57°06'·33N 12°23'·42E
NOTE: Broadcasts relayed by Sweden Traffic/Stockholm Radio. Ice reports are no longer made on VHF, MF or NAVTEX – see Ice Reports section in ALRS Vol.3 for alternative ways of obtaining this information.		X2
TELEPHONE:	+46 711 630685	300 n miles
E-MAIL:	swedentraffic@sjofartsverket.se	
WEBSITE:	www.sjofartsverket.se/baltico	

NAVTEX [I]

TIME UT(GMT)	WEATHER BULLETINS	NAVIGATIONAL WARNINGS
0120		●
0520	●	●
0920		●
1320		●
1720	●	●
2120		●

NAVTEX

UNITED KINGDOM

Cullercoats [G] [U]

55°04'·48N 1°27'·78W

X2

NOTE: Broadcasts are remotely controlled by Humber and Shetland Coastguards. There may be a delay in broadcast action if there is Search and Rescue in progress.

TELEPHONE: +44(0)1262 672317 270 n miles

FAX: +44(0)1262 400779

E-MAIL: humbercoastguard@mcga.gov.uk

NAVTEX [G]

TIME UT(GMT)	WEATHER BULLETINS	NAVIGATIONAL WARNINGS
0100	●	●
0500		●
0900	●	●
1300		●
1700		●
2100	●	●

NAVTEX [U]

Strong wind warnings and coastal observations on receipt.

Frequency: 490 kHz Language: English

TIME UT(GMT)	WEATHER BULLETINS	NAVIGATIONAL WARNINGS
0720	●	
1120	●	
1920	●	
2320	●	
On receipt	●	

Niton [E] [K] [I] [T]

50°35'·18N 1°15'·28W

X2

NOTE: Broadcasts are remotely controlled by Humber and Shetland Coastguards. There may be a delay in broadcast action if there is Search and Rescue in progress.

TELEPHONE: +44(0)1262 672317 270 n miles

FAX: +44(0)1262 400779

E-MAIL: humbercoastguard@mcga.gov.uk

NAVTEX [E]

TIME UT(GMT)	WEATHER BULLETINS	NAVIGATIONAL WARNINGS
0040	●	●
0440		●
0840	●	●
1240		●
1640		●
2040	●	●

NAVTEX [K]

TIME UT(GMT)	NAVIGATIONAL WARNINGS
0140	●
0540	●
0940	●
1340	●
1740	●
2140	●

UNITED KINGDOM

NAVTEX [I]

Strong wind warnings and coastal observations on receipt.

Frequency: 490 kHz Language: English

TIME UT(GMT)	WEATHER BULLETINS	NAVIGATIONAL WARNINGS
0120	●	
0520	●	
1320	●	
1720	●	
On receipt	●	

NAVTEX [T]

Frequency: 490 kHz Language: French (local bcst)

TIME UT(GMT)	WEATHER BULLETINS	NAVIGATIONAL WARNINGS
0710	●	●
1910	●	●

Portpatrick [O] [C]

54°50'·65N 5°07'·47W

X2

NOTE: Broadcasts are remotely controlled by Humber and Shetland Coastguards. There may be a delay in broadcast action if there is Search and Rescue in progress.

TELEPHONE: +44(0)1262 672317 270 n miles

FAX: +44(0)1262 400779

E-MAIL: humbercoastguard@mcga.gov.uk

NAVTEX [O]

TIME UT(GMT)	WEATHER BULLETINS	NAVIGATIONAL WARNINGS
0220	●	●
0620	●	●
1020		●
1420		●
1820	●	●
2220		●
On receipt		●

NAVTEX [C]

Strong wind warnings and coastal observations on receipt.

Frequency: 490 kHz Language: English

TIME UT(GMT)	WEATHER BULLETINS	NAVIGATIONAL WARNINGS
0020	●	
0820	●	
1220	●	
2020	●	
On receipt	●	

NAVAREA II

AÇORES (Portugal)

CENCOMARACORES (São Miguel) [F] [J]   37°48'·50N 25°33'·20W
TELEPHONE: +351 296 205230   X3
FAX: +351 296 205239   300 n miles
E-MAIL: comar.dir@marinha.pt

NAVTEX [F]

TIME UT(GMT)	WEATHER BULLETINS	NAVIGATIONAL WARNINGS
0050	•	•
0450	•	•
0850	•	•
1250	•	•
1650	•	•
2050	•	•

NAVTEX [J]
Frequency: 490 kHz Language: Portuguese

TIME UT(GMT)	WEATHER BULLETINS	NAVIGATIONAL WARNINGS
0130	•	•
0530	•	•
0930	•	•
1330	•	•
1730	•	•
2130	•	•

CANARIAS, ISLAS (Spain)

Las Palmas (MRCC) [I] [A]   28°25'·97N 16°20'·17W
TELEPHONE: +34 928 467757   X3
FAX: +34 928 467760   450 n miles
E-MAIL: laspalmas@sasemar.es
MMSI: 002240995

NAVTEX [I]

TIME UT(GMT)	WEATHER BULLETINS	NAVIGATIONAL WARNINGS
0120		•
0520		•
0920	•	•
1320	•	•
1720		•
2120	•	•

NAVTEX [A]
Frequency: 490 kHz Language: Spanish

TIME UT(GMT)	WEATHER BULLETINS	NAVIGATIONAL WARNINGS
0000	•	•
0400		•
0800		•
1200	•	•
1600	•	•
2000		•

CAPE VERDE

São Vicente [U] [P]   16°51'·47N 25°00'·04W
NOTE: Temporarily inoperative   X3, X11
TELEPHONE: +238 2322158   250 n miles
   +238 2322263
FAX: +238 2321882
E-MAIL: s.movelmaritimo@cvtelecom.cv
MMSI: 006170000

NAVTEX [U]

TIME UT(GMT)	WEATHER BULLETINS	NAVIGATIONAL WARNINGS
0320	•	•
0720	•	•
1120	•	•
1520	•	•
1920	•	•
2320	•	•

NAVTEX [P]
Frequency: 490 kHz Language: Portuguese

TIME UT(GMT)	WEATHER BULLETINS	NAVIGATIONAL WARNINGS
0230	•	•
0630	•	•
1030	•	•
1430	•	•
1830	•	•
2230	•	•

MADEIRA (Portugal)

CENCOMARMADEIRA (Porto Santo) [P] [M]   33°05'·65N 16°20'·29W
TELEPHONE: +351 291 213110   X3
FAX: +351 291 228232   300 n miles
E-MAIL: comar.dir@marinha.pt

NAVTEX [P]

TIME UT(GMT)	WEATHER BULLETINS	NAVIGATIONAL WARNINGS
0230	•	•
0630	•	•
1030	•	•
1430	•	•
1830	•	•
2230	•	•

NAVTEX [M]
Frequency: 490 kHz Language: Portuguese

TIME UT(GMT)	WEATHER BULLETINS	NAVIGATIONAL WARNINGS
0200	•	•
0600	•	•
1000	•	•
1400	•	•
1800	•	•
2200	•	•

NAVTEX

PORTUGAL

CENCOMAR (Penalva) [R] [G]　　　　　38°36'·20N 9°01'·80W

TELEPHONE:	+351 210 919419	X3
FAX:	+351 210 954492	300 n miles
E-MAIL:	comar.dir@marinha.pt	

NAVTEX [R]

TIME UT(GMT)	WEATHER BULLETINS	NAVIGATIONAL WARNINGS
0250	•	•
0650	•	•
1050	•	•
1450	•	•
1850	•	•
2250	•	•

NAVTEX [G]
Frequency: 490 kHz Language: Portuguese

TIME UT(GMT)	WEATHER BULLETINS	NAVIGATIONAL WARNINGS
0100	•	•
0500	•	•
0900	•	•
1300	•	•
1700	•	•
2100	•	•

SENEGAL

Dakar [C] [M]　　　　　14°46'·25N 17°20'·40W

TELEPHONE:	+221 338 692326	X3, X11
FAX:	+221 338 200600	200 n miles
	+221 338 265000	
E-MAIL:	marinenat@orange.sn	
MMSI:	006630005	

NAVTEX [C]

TIME UT(GMT)	WEATHER BULLETINS	NAVIGATIONAL WARNINGS
0020	•	•
0420	•	•
0820	•	•
1220	•	•
1620	•	•
2020	•	•

NAVTEX [M]
Frequency: 490 kHz Language: French

TIME UT(GMT)	WEATHER BULLETINS	NAVIGATIONAL WARNINGS
0200	•	•
0600	•	•
1000	•	•
1400	•	•
1800	•	•
2200	•	•

SPAIN

Coruña (MRSC) [D] [W]　　　　　43°22'·03N 8°27'·13W

TELEPHONE:	+34 981 209548	X3, X4
FAX:	+34 981 209518	300 n miles
E-MAIL:	radioavisos.cncs@sasemar.es	
MMSI:	002240992	

NAVTEX [D]

TIME UT(GMT)	WEATHER BULLETINS	NAVIGATIONAL WARNINGS
0030		•
0430		•
0830	•	
1230		•
1630		•
2030	•	

NAVTEX [W]
Frequency: 490 kHz Language: Spanish

TIME UT(GMT)	WEATHER BULLETINS	NAVIGATIONAL WARNINGS
0340		•
0740		•
1140	•	
1540		•
1940		•
2340	•	

NAVAREA III

ALGERIA

Bordj-el-Kiffan [B] [V] 36°46'·89N 3°15'·61E
TELEPHONE: +213 21203184 X4
 +213 21203193 200 n miles
FAX: +213 21203193
E-MAIL: mrccalgiers@mdn.dz
MMSI: 006052110

NAVTEX [B]

TIME UT(GMT)	WEATHER BULLETINS	NAVIGATIONAL WARNINGS
0010	•	•
0410	•	•
0810	•	•
1210	•	•
1610	•	•
2010	•	•

NAVTEX [V]
Frequency: 490 kHz Language: French

TIME UT(GMT)	WEATHER BULLETINS	NAVIGATIONAL WARNINGS
0330	•	•
0730	•	•
1130	•	•
1530	•	•
1930	•	•
2330	•	•

AZERBAIJAN

Baku (Chilov) [R] [M] 40°19'·63N 50°36'·74E
TELEPHONE: +994 12 4920606 X5
FAX: +994 12 4920642 200 n miles
E-MAIL: lrit@ardda.gov.az

NAVTEX [R]

TIME UT(GMT)	WEATHER BULLETINS	NAVIGATIONAL WARNINGS
0250	•	•
0650	•	•
1050	•	•
1450	•	•
1850	•	•
2250	•	•

NAVTEX [M]
Frequency: 490 kHz Language: Azerbaijani

TIME UT(GMT)	WEATHER BULLETINS	NAVIGATIONAL WARNINGS
0200	•	•
0600	•	•
1000	•	•
1400	•	•
1800	•	•
2200	•	•

BULGARIA

Varna [J] 43°04'·01N 27°47'·19E
TELEPHONE: +359 52 687973 X5
FAX: +359 52 687984 350 n miles
E-MAIL: varnaradio@bgports.bg
MMSI: 002070810

NAVTEX [J]
Varna also broadcasts information on behalf of Romania, received from Constanța.

TIME UT(GMT)	WEATHER BULLETINS	NAVIGATIONAL WARNINGS
0130		•
0530	•	•
0930	•	•
1330		•
1730	•	•
2130	•	•

CROATIA

Split (Hvar I.) [Q] [F] 43°10'·91N 16°25'·34E
TELEPHONE: +385 21 389190 X4
FAX: +385 21 389185 200 n miles
E-MAIL: office@hhi.hr
MMSI: 002380100

NAVTEX [Q]

TIME UT(GMT)	WEATHER BULLETINS	NAVIGATIONAL WARNINGS
0240	•	•
0640	•	•
1040	•	•
1440	•	•
1840	•	•
2240	•	•

NAVTEX [F]
Frequency: 490 kHz Language: Croatian

TIME UT(GMT)	WEATHER BULLETINS	NAVIGATIONAL WARNINGS
0050	•	•
0450	•	•
0850	•	•
1250	•	•
1650	•	•
2050	•	•

CYPRUS

Cyprus [M] 35°02'·95N 33°17'·07E
TELEPHONE: +357 22 702286 X5
FAX: +357 22 702392 200 n miles
E-MAIL: cyprus.radio@cyta.com.cy
MMSI: 002091000

NAVTEX [M]

TIME UT(GMT)	WEATHER BULLETINS	NAVIGATIONAL WARNINGS
0200	•	•
0600	•	•
1000	•	•
1400	•	•
1800	•	•
2200	•	•

EGYPT

Al Iskanderîyah (Alexandria) [N]

TELEPHONE: +20 3 4801226
+20 3 4809500
+20 3 4810202
FAX: +20 3 4810201
E-MAIL: maritime@eams.gov.eg
eams@eams.gov.eg
MMSI: 006221111

31°11'·96N 29°51'·88E
X5, X6
350 n miles

NAVTEX [N]

TIME UT(GMT)	WEATHER BULLETINS	NAVIGATIONAL WARNINGS
0210		•
0610		•
1010	•	•
1410		•
1810		•
2210	•	•

Ismailia (Al Ismā`īlīyah) [X]

TELEPHONE: +20 64 322299
+20 64 334869
FAX: +20 64 334869

30°28'·00N 32°22'·00E
X5, X6
400 n miles

NAVTEX [X]
Includes rig movements

TIME UT(GMT)	WEATHER BULLETINS	NAVIGATIONAL WARNINGS
0350		•
0750	•	•
1150		•
1550		•
1950	•	•
2350		•

NAVTEX [X]
Includes rig movements
Frequency: 4209·5 kHz

TIME UT(GMT)	WEATHER BULLETINS	NAVIGATIONAL WARNINGS
0750	•	•
1150		•

FRANCE (Mediterranean Coast)

La Garde (CROSS (MRCC)) [W] [S]

NOTE: Temporarily inoperative until further notice
TELEPHONE: +33 4 94617110
FAX: +33 4 94271149
TELEX: +42 430 024 CROMD B
E-MAIL: lagarde@mrccfr.eu
MMSI: 002275400

43°06'·26N 5°59'·48E
X4
250 n miles

NAVTEX [W]

TIME UT(GMT)	WEATHER BULLETINS	NAVIGATIONAL WARNINGS
0340		•
0740		•
1140	•	•
1540		•
1940		•
2340	•	•

FRANCE (Mediterranean Coast)

NAVTEX [S]
Frequency: 490 kHz Language: French (local bcst)

TIME UT(GMT)	WEATHER BULLETINS	NAVIGATIONAL WARNINGS
0300		•
0700		•
1100	•	•
1500		•
1900		•
2300	•	•

GEORGIA

P'ot'i [G]

TELEPHONE: +995 493 278405
E-MAIL: g.kalandadze@hydrography.ge

42°07'·97N 41°39'·66E
X5
250 n miles

NAVTEX [G]
Frequency: 490 kHz Language: English

TIME UT(GMT)	WEATHER BULLETINS	NAVIGATIONAL WARNINGS
0100	•	•[1]
0500	•	•[1]
0900	•	•[1]
1300	•	•[1]
1700	•	•[1]
2100	•	•[1]

[1] As necessary

GREECE

Irákleion [H] [Q] [S]

TELEPHONE: +30 2106060120
FAX: +30 2106002599
E-MAIL: navtex@hnhs.gr

35°19'·33N 25°44'·92E
X4, X5
400 n miles

NAVTEX [H]

TIME UT(GMT)	WEATHER BULLETINS	NAVIGATIONAL WARNINGS
0110		•
0510	•	•
0910	•	•
1310		•
1710	•	•
2110	•	•

NAVTEX [Q]
Frequency: 490 kHz Language: Greek

TIME UT(GMT)	WEATHER BULLETINS	NAVIGATIONAL WARNINGS
0240		•
0640		•
1040	•	•
1440		•
1840	•	•
2240		•

GREECE

NAVTEX [S]
Frequency: 4209·5 kHz Language: Greek

TIME UT(GMT)	WEATHER BULLETINS	NAVIGATIONAL WARNINGS
0300		•
0700		•
1100	•	•
1500		•
1900	•	•
2300		•

Kérkyra [K] [P]   39°36'·43N 19°53'·47E
TELEPHONE: +30 2106060120   X4, X5
FAX: +30 2106002599   400 n miles
E-MAIL: navtex@hnhs.gr

NAVTEX [K]

TIME UT(GMT)	WEATHER BULLETINS	NAVIGATIONAL WARNINGS
0140		•
0540	•	•
0940	•	•
1340		•
1740	•	•
2140	•	•

NAVTEX [P]
Frequency: 490 kHz Language: Greek

TIME UT(GMT)	WEATHER BULLETINS	NAVIGATIONAL WARNINGS
0230		•
0630		•
1030	•	•
1430		•
1830	•	•
2230		•

Límnos [L] [R]   39°54'·41N 25°10'·84E
TELEPHONE: +30 2106060120   X4, X5
FAX: +30 2106002599   400 n miles
E-MAIL: navtex@hnhs.gr

NAVTEX [L]

TIME UT(GMT)	WEATHER BULLETINS	NAVIGATIONAL WARNINGS
0150		•
0550	•	•
0950	•	•
1350		•
1750	•	•
2150	•	•

NAVTEX [R]
Frequency: 490 kHz Language: Greek

TIME UT(GMT)	WEATHER BULLETINS	NAVIGATIONAL WARNINGS
0250		•
0650		•
1050	•	•
1450		•
1850	•	•
2250		•

IRAN (Caspian Sea)

Fereydūn Kenār [G] [J]   36°41'·70N 52°33'·70E
TELEPHONE: +98 112 5664504   X5
FAX: +98 112 5664503   250 n miles
E-MAIL: ferrydoonkenarradio@pmo.ir

NAVTEX [G]

TIME UT(GMT)	WEATHER BULLETINS	NAVIGATIONAL WARNINGS
0100		•
0500	•	•
0900		•
1300	•	•
1700		•
2100		•

NAVTEX [J]
Frequency: 490 kHz Language: Farsi

TIME UT(GMT)	WEATHER BULLETINS	NAVIGATIONAL WARNINGS
0130		•
0530	•	•
0930		•
1330	•	•
1730		•
2130		•

ISRAEL

Ḥefa (Haifa) [P]   32°54'·90N 35°07'·10E
TELEPHONE: +972 4 8632145   X5
               +972 4 8632073   200 n miles
               +972 4 8632075
FAX: +972 4 8699017
               +972 4 8590919
E-MAIL: rcc@mot.gov.il
MMSI: 004280001

NAVTEX [P]

TIME UT(GMT)	WEATHER BULLETINS	NAVIGATIONAL WARNINGS
0230	•	•
0630	•	•
1030	•	•
1430	•	•
1830	•	•
2230	•	•

ITALY

La Maddalena (Roma) [R] [I]   41°13'·45N 9°23'·98E
TELEPHONE: +39 06 59083226   X4
               +39 06 5924145   320 n miles
FAX: +39 06 5922737
               +39 06 59084793
E-MAIL: navtex@guardiacostiera.it

NAVTEX [R]

TIME UT(GMT)	WEATHER BULLETINS	NAVIGATIONAL WARNINGS
0250		•
0650	•	
1050		•
1450		•
1850	•	
2250		•

NAVTEX

ITALY

NAVTEX [I]
Frequency: 490 kHz Language: Italian

TIME UT(GMT)	WEATHER BULLETINS	NAVIGATIONAL WARNINGS
0120		●
0520		●
0920	●	
1320		●
1720		●
2120	●	

Mondolfo (Roma) [U] [E] 43°44'·85N 13°08'·55E

TELEPHONE:	+39 06 59083226	X4
	+39 06 5924145	320 n miles
FAX:	+39 06 5922737	
	+39 06 59084793	
E-MAIL:	navtex@guardiacostiera.it	

NAVTEX [U]

TIME UT(GMT)	WEATHER BULLETINS	NAVIGATIONAL WARNINGS
0320		●
0720	●	
1120		●
1520		●
1920	●	
2320		●

NAVTEX [E]
Frequency: 490 kHz Language: Italian

TIME UT(GMT)	WEATHER BULLETINS	NAVIGATIONAL WARNINGS
0040		●
0440		●
0840	●	
1240		●
1640		●
2040	●	

Piombino (Roma) [N] 42°55'·32N 10°32'·60E

TELEPHONE:	+39 06 59083226	X4
	+39 06 5924145	320 n miles
FAX:	+39 06 5922737	
	+39 06 59084793	
E-MAIL:	navtex@guardiacostiera.it	

NAVTEX [N]
Frequency: 490 kHz

TIME UT(GMT)	WEATHER BULLETINS	NAVIGATIONAL WARNINGS
0210		●
0610		●
1010	●	
1410		●
1810		●
2210	●	

ITALY

Sellia Marina (Roma) [V] [W] 38°52'·35N 16°43'·01E

TELEPHONE:	+39 06 59083226	X4
	+39 06 5924145	320 n miles
FAX:	+39 06 5922737	
	+39 06 59084793	
E-MAIL:	navtex@guardiacostiera.it	

NAVTEX [V]

TIME UT(GMT)	WEATHER BULLETINS	NAVIGATIONAL WARNINGS
0330		●
0730	●	
1130		●
1530		●
1930	●	
2330		●

NAVTEX [W]
Frequency: 490 kHz Language: Italian

TIME UT(GMT)	WEATHER BULLETINS	NAVIGATIONAL WARNINGS
0340		●
0740	●	
1140		●
1540		●
1940	●	
2340		●

MALTA

Malta [O] 35°51'·30N 14°29'·30E

NOTE: Tunisian NAVTEX broadcasts from Kelibia are temporarily inoperative. Malta NAVTEX broadcasts MSI for the Sicilian channel and the east coast of Tunisia in the [T] timeslot – see Tunisian NAVTEX entry.

TELEPHONE:	+356 22 494202	400 n miles
	+356 22 494203	
FAX:	+356 21 809860	
E-MAIL:	rccmalta@gov.mt	

X4

NAVTEX [O]

TIME UT(GMT)	WEATHER BULLETINS	NAVIGATIONAL WARNINGS
0220		●
0620	●	●
1020		●
1420		●
1820	●	●
2220		●

ROMANIA

Constanţa [L]   44°06'·18N 28°37'·49E
TELEPHONE: +40 241 737102   X5
FAX: +40 241 737103   400 n miles
E-MAIL: arrivalro@radionav.ro
MMSI: 002640570

NAVTEX [L]
Frequency: 490 kHz Language: Romanian

TIME UT(GMT)	WEATHER BULLETINS	NAVIGATIONAL WARNINGS
0150	●	●
0550	●	●
0950	●	●
1350	●	●
1750	●	●
2150	●	●

RUSSIA (Black Sea Coast)

Novorossiysk [A]   44°35'·81N 37°57'·69E
TELEPHONE: +7 861 7676421   X5
FAX: +7 861 7676420   270 n miles
TELEX: +64 279194 GMDSS RU
E-MAIL: navtex@mapn.morflot.ru

NAVTEX [A]

TIME UT(GMT)	WEATHER BULLETINS	NAVIGATIONAL WARNINGS
0000	●	●
0400	●	●
0800	●	●
1200	●	●
1600	●	●
2000	●	●

Taganrog [O]   47°08'·44N 38°19'·65E
TELEPHONE: +7 863 4317514   X5
E-MAIL: radio1@abf-rmp.ru   250 n miles

NAVTEX [O]
Frequency: 490 kHz Language: English

TIME UT(GMT)	WEATHER BULLETINS	NAVIGATIONAL WARNINGS
0220	●	●
0620	●	●
1020	●	●
1420	●	●
1820	●	●
2220	●	●

RUSSIA (Caspian Sea)

Astrakhan [W]   45°47'·00N 47°33'·00E
TELEPHONE: +7 8512 584808   X5
FAX: +7 8512 585981   250 n miles

NAVTEX [W]

TIME UT(GMT)	WEATHER BULLETINS	NAVIGATIONAL WARNINGS
0340	●	●
0740	●	●
1140	●	●
1540	●	●
1940	●	●
2340	●	●

SPAIN

Cabo de la Nao (Valencia) (MRCC) [X] [M]   38°43'·01N 0°10'·61E
TELEPHONE: +34 96 3679302   X3, X4
FAX: +34 96 3679403   220 n miles
E-MAIL: radioavisos.valencia@sasemar.es
             valencia@sasemar.es
MMSI: 002241004

NAVTEX [X]

TIME UT(GMT)	WEATHER BULLETINS	NAVIGATIONAL WARNINGS
0350		●
0750	●	
1150		●
1550		●
1950	●	
2350		●

NAVTEX [M]
Frequency: 490 kHz Language: Spanish

TIME UT(GMT)	WEATHER BULLETINS	NAVIGATIONAL WARNINGS
0200		●
0600		●
1000	●	
1400		●
1800		●
2200	●	

Tarifa (MRCC) [G] [T]   36°02'·30N 5°33'·34W
TELEPHONE: +34 956 684740 (Emergency)   X3, X4
FAX: +34 956 680606   300 n miles
E-MAIL: tarifa@sasemar.es
MMSI: 002240994

NAVTEX [G]

TIME UT(GMT)	WEATHER BULLETINS	NAVIGATIONAL WARNINGS
0100		●
0500		●
0900	●	
1300		●
1700		●
2100	●	

NAVTEX [T]
Frequency: 490 kHz Language: Spanish

TIME UT(GMT)	WEATHER BULLETINS	NAVIGATIONAL WARNINGS
0310		●
0710		●
1110	●	
1510		●
1910		●
2310	●	

NAVTEX

TUNISIA

Kelibia [T]
36°48'·08N 11°02'·29E
X4

NOTE: Tunisian NAVTEX broadcasts from Kelibia are temporarily inoperative. Malta NAVTEX broadcasts MSI for the Sicilian channel and the east coast of Tunisia in the [T] timeslot – see Malta NAVTEX entry.

270 n miles

NAVTEX [T]

TIME UT(GMT)	WEATHER BULLETINS	NAVIGATIONAL WARNINGS
0310		•
0710	•	•
1110		•
1510		•
1910	•	•
2310		•

TURKEY

Antalya (Mediterranean Coast) [F] [D]
Remotely controlled from İstanbul
36°09'·17N 32°26'·72E
X5
400 n miles

TELEPHONE: +90 212 4259728
+90 212 5989534
FAX: +90 212 5410338
E-MAIL: turkradyo@kegm.gov.tr
MMSI: 002713000

NAVTEX [F]

TIME UT(GMT)	WEATHER BULLETINS	NAVIGATIONAL WARNINGS
0050	•	•
0450	•	•
0850	•	•
1250	•	•
1650	•	•
2050	•	•

NAVTEX [D]
Frequency: 490 kHz Language: Turkish

TIME UT(GMT)	WEATHER BULLETINS	NAVIGATIONAL WARNINGS
0030	•	•
0430	•	•
0830	•	•
1230	•	•
1630	•	•
2030	•	•

TURKEY

İstanbul (Marmara Denizi) [D] [B] [M]
41°04'·00N 28°57'·00E
X5
400 n miles

TELEPHONE: +90 212 4259728
+90 212 5989534
FAX: +90 212 5410338
E-MAIL: turkradyo@kegm.gov.tr
MMSI: 002711000

NAVTEX [D]

TIME UT(GMT)	WEATHER BULLETINS	NAVIGATIONAL WARNINGS
0030	•	•
0430	•	•
0830	•	•
1230	•	•
1630	•	•
2030	•	•

NAVTEX [B]
Frequency: 490 kHz Language: Turkish

TIME UT(GMT)	WEATHER BULLETINS	NAVIGATIONAL WARNINGS
0010	•	•
0410	•	•
0810	•	•
1210	•	•
1610	•	•
2010	•	•

NAVTEX [M]
Frequency: 4209·5 kHz Language: Turkish

TIME UT(GMT)	WEATHER BULLETINS	NAVIGATIONAL WARNINGS
0200	•	•
0600	•	•
1000	•	•
1400	•	•
1800	•	•
2200	•	•

İzmır (Aegean Coast) [I] [C]
Remotely controlled from İstanbul
38°16'·88N 26°16'·05E
X5
400 n miles

TELEPHONE: +90 212 4259728
+90 212 5989534
FAX: +90 212 5410338
E-MAIL: turkradyo@kegm.gov.tr
MMSI: 002715000

NAVTEX [I]

TIME UT(GMT)	WEATHER BULLETINS	NAVIGATIONAL WARNINGS
0120	•	•
0520	•	•
0920	•	•
1320	•	•
1720	•	•
2120	•	•

TURKEY
NAVTEX [C]
Frequency: 490 kHz Language: Turkish

TIME UT(GMT)	WEATHER BULLETINS	NAVIGATIONAL WARNINGS
0020	●	●
0420	●	●
0820	●	●
1220	●	●
1620	●	●
2020	●	●

Samsun (Black Sea Coast) [E] [A]   41°23′·18N 36°11′·37E
Remotely controlled from İstanbul   X5
TELEPHONE: +90 212 4259728   400 n miles
                       +90 212 5989534
FAX: +90 212 5410338
E-MAIL: turkradyo@kegm.gov.tr
MMSI: 002712000

NAVTEX [E]

TIME UT(GMT)	WEATHER BULLETINS	NAVIGATIONAL WARNINGS
0040	●	●
0440	●	●
0840	●	●
1240	●	●
1640	●	●
2040	●	●

NAVTEX [A]
Frequency: 490 kHz Language: Turkish

TIME UT(GMT)	WEATHER BULLETINS	NAVIGATIONAL WARNINGS
0000	●	●
0400	●	●
0800	●	●
1200	●	●
1600	●	●
2000	●	●

UKRAINE

Berdyans'k [G] [U]   46°38′·18N 36°45′·71E
TELEPHONE: +380 50 4112013   X5
                       +380 61 5337229   250 n miles
FAX: +380 06 29407858
E-MAIL: mayak1878@gmail.com
MMSI: 002723659

NAVTEX [G]

TIME UT(GMT)	WEATHER BULLETINS	NAVIGATIONAL WARNINGS	ICE WARNINGS AND REPORTS
0100		●	
0500		●	
0900	●	●	
1300		●	●
1700	●	●	
2100		●	

UKRAINE
NAVTEX [U]
Frequency: 490 kHz Language: English

TIME UT(GMT)	WEATHER BULLETINS	NAVIGATIONAL WARNINGS	ICE WARNINGS AND REPORTS
0320		●	
0720		●	
1120	●	●	
1520		●	●
1920	●	●	
2320		●	

Odesa [C] [X]   46°22′·54N 30°45′·01E
TELEPHONE: +380 48 7468481   X5
                       +380 48 7468087   250 n miles
                       +380 50 4901547
FAX: +380 48 7731872
E-MAIL: cngi@hydro.od.ua
MMSI: 002725613

NAVTEX [C]

TIME UT(GMT)	WEATHER BULLETINS	NAVIGATIONAL WARNINGS	ICE WARNINGS AND REPORTS
0020		●	
0420		●	
0820	●	●	
1220		●	●
1620	●	●	
2020		●	

NAVTEX [X]
Frequency: 490 kHz Language: English

TIME UT(GMT)	WEATHER BULLETINS	NAVIGATIONAL WARNINGS	ICE WARNINGS AND REPORTS
0350		●	
0750		●	
1150	●	●	
1550		●	●
1950	●	●	
2350		●	

NAVTEX

NAVAREA IV

BERMUDA (UK)

Bermuda [B]   32°21'·07N 64°39'·48W
TELEPHONE: +1 441 2971010   X9
FAX: +1 441 2971530   280 n miles
TELEX: +581 431010110 (Inmarsat C)
              +581 431010120 (Inmarsat C)
MMSI: 003100001

NAVTEX [B]

TIME UT(GMT)	WEATHER BULLETINS	NAVIGATIONAL WARNINGS
0010	●	●
0410	●	●
0810	●	●
1210	●	●
1610	●	●
2010	●	●

CANADA (Arctic Coast, Atlantic Coast and Saint Lawrence River)

Cartwright (Canadian CG) [X]   53°42'·50N 57°01'·28W
TELEPHONE: +1 709 8962252   X9
FAX: +1 709 8968455   300 n miles
E-MAIL: ecaregsnf@innav.gc.ca
MMSI: 003160022

NAVTEX [X]
The Navigational Warnings at 2350 are replaced by Ice Warnings and Reports during the season.

TIME UT(GMT)	WEATHER BULLETINS	NAVIGATIONAL WARNINGS	ICE WARNINGS AND REPORTS
0350	●		
0750	●		
1150		●	
1550	●		
1950	●		
2350		●	●

Chebogue (Canadian CG) [U] [V]   43°44'·67N 66°07'·29W
TELEPHONE: +1 902 4269750   X9
FAX: +1 506 6365000   300 n miles
TELEX: +21 1922510 CCG MRHQ DRT
E-MAIL: ccgops@elsmail.net
MMSI: 003160015

NAVTEX [U]

TIME UT(GMT)	WEATHER BULLETINS	NAVIGATIONAL WARNINGS
0320		●
0720	●	
1120	●	
1520		●
1920	●	
2320	●	

CANADA (Arctic Coast, Atlantic Coast and Saint Lawrence River)
NAVTEX [V]
Frequency: 490 kHz Language: French

TIME UT(GMT)	WEATHER BULLETINS	NAVIGATIONAL WARNINGS
0330		●
0730	●	
1130	●	
1530		●
1930	●	
2330	●	

Iqaluit (Canadian CG) [T] [S]   63°43'·79N 68°32'·73W
NOTE: Operational between mid June to late Dec   X9
approx.
TELEPHONE: +1 867 9790310   300 n miles
FAX: +1 867 9794264
TELEX: +63 15529 NORDREG CDA
E-MAIL: iqanordreg@innav.gc.ca
MMSI: 003160023

NAVTEX [T]

TIME UT(GMT)	WEATHER BULLETINS	NAVIGATIONAL WARNINGS	ICE WARNINGS AND REPORTS
0310	●		
0710		●	●
1110	●		
1510	●		
1910		●	●
2310	●		

NAVTEX [S]
Frequency: 490 kHz Language: French

TIME UT(GMT)	WEATHER BULLETINS	NAVIGATIONAL WARNINGS	ICE WARNINGS AND REPORTS
0300	●		
0700		●	●
1100	●		
1500	●		
1900		●	●
2300	●		

Moisie (Canadian CG) [C] [D]   50°11'·76N 66°06'·70W
TELEPHONE: +1 418 2332194   X9
FAX: +1 418 2695514   300 n miles
E-MAIL: rarecareg@innav.gc.ca
MMSI: 003160025

NAVTEX [C]
The 0020 Weather Bulletins are replaced by Ice Warnings and Reports during the season.

TIME UT(GMT)	WEATHER BULLETINS	NAVIGATIONAL WARNINGS	ICE WARNINGS AND REPORTS
0020	●		●
0420		●	
0820	●		
1220	●		
1620		●	
2020	●		

CANADA (Arctic Coast, Atlantic Coast and Saint Lawrence River)

NAVTEX [D]
The 0030 Weather Bulletins are replaced by Ice Warnings and Reports during the season.
Frequency: 490 kHz Language: French

TIME UT(GMT)	WEATHER BULLETINS	NAVIGATIONAL WARNINGS	ICE WARNINGS AND REPORTS
0030	●		●
0430		●	
0830	●		
1230	●		
1630		●	
2030	●		

Port Caledonia (Canadian CG) [Q] [J]   46°11'·16N 59°53'·64W

TELEPHONE:	+1 902 5647751	X9
FAX:	+1 902 5647662	300 n miles
E-MAIL:	ccgops@elsmail.net	
	hlxecareg1@innav.gc.ca	
MMSI:	003160017	

NAVTEX [Q]
The 2240 Weather Bulletins are replaced by Ice Warnings and Reports during the season.

TIME UT(GMT)	WEATHER BULLETINS	NAVIGATIONAL WARNINGS	ICE WARNINGS AND REPORTS
0240		●	
0640	●		
1040	●		
1440		●	
1840	●		
2240	●		●

NAVTEX [J]
The 0130 Weather Bulletins are replaced by Ice Warnings and Reports during the season.
Frequency: 490 kHz Language: French

TIME UT(GMT)	WEATHER BULLETINS	NAVIGATIONAL WARNINGS	ICE WARNINGS AND REPORTS
0130	●		●
0530	●		
0930	●		
1330		●	
1730	●		
2130		●	

Robin Hood Bay (Canadian CG) [O]   47°36'·65N 52°40'·18W

TELEPHONE:	+1 709 7722182	X9
FAX:	+1 709 7725369	300 n miles
E-MAIL:	ecaregsnf@innav.gc.ca	
MMSI:	003160020	

NAVTEX [O]
0620 and 1820 Weather Bulletins replaced by Ice/Nav Warnings in winter. 1020 Nav Warnings replaced by Weather Bulletins in winter. 2220 Nav/Ice Warnings replaced by Weather Bulletins in winter.

TIME UT(GMT)	WEATHER BULLETINS	NAVIGATIONAL WARNINGS	ICE WARNINGS AND REPORTS
0220	●		
0620	●		●
1020	●	●	
1420	●		
1820	●	●	
2220	●	●	●

CANADA (Great Lakes)

Ferndale (Canadian CG) [H]   44°56'·22N 81°14'·00W

TELEPHONE:	+1 613 9254471	X9
FAX:	+1 613 9254519	300 n miles
MMSI:	003160029	

NAVTEX [H]
During ice season marine forecasts are replaced by ice information

TIME UT(GMT)	WEATHER BULLETINS	NAVIGATIONAL WARNINGS	ICE WARNINGS AND REPORTS
0110		●	●
0510	●		
0910	●		
1310		●	●
1710	●		
2110	●		

Pass Lake (Canadian CG) [P]   48°33'·80N 88°39'·37W

TELEPHONE:	+1 519 3364003	X9
FAX:	+1 807 3452688	300 n miles
MMSI:	003160031	

NAVTEX [P]
During ice season marine forecasts are replaced by ice information

TIME UT(GMT)	WEATHER BULLETINS	NAVIGATIONAL WARNINGS	ICE WARNINGS AND REPORTS
0230	●		
0630		●	●
1030	●		
1430	●		
1830		●	●
2230	●		

COLOMBIA (Caribbean Coast)

Santa Marta [C] [K]   11°03'·34N 74°13'·10W
X9
400 n miles

NAVTEX [C]

TIME UT(GMT)	WEATHER BULLETINS	NAVIGATIONAL WARNINGS
0020	●	●
0420	●	●
0820	●	●
1220	●	●
1620	●	●
2020	●	●

NAVTEX [K]
Frequency: 490 kHz Language: Spanish

TIME UT(GMT)	WEATHER BULLETINS	NAVIGATIONAL WARNINGS
0140	●	●
0540	●	●
0940	●	●
1340	●	●
1740	●	●
2140	●	●

NAVTEX

CURAÇAO

Curaçao [H] 12°10′·31N 68°51′·82W
TELEPHONE: +599 (9)4637733 X9, X11
FAX: +599 (9)4637950 400 n miles
MMSI: 003061000

NAVTEX [H]

TIME UT(GMT)	WEATHER BULLETINS	NAVIGATIONAL WARNINGS
0110		●
0510		●
0910		●
1310	●	●
1710		●
2110		●

GREENLAND

Kook Island (Nuuk) [W] 64°04′·12N 52°00′·51W
NOTE: Weather and Navigational Warnings for the X12, X13
east coast of Greenland are broadcast by Iceland
where necessary - see relevant entry.
TELEPHONE: +299 691911 300 n miles
FAX: +299 691949
Inmarsat C: 433116710

NAVTEX [W]

TIME UT(GMT)	WEATHER BULLETINS	NAVIGATIONAL WARNINGS
0340	●	●
0740	●	●
1140	●	●
1540	●	●
1940	●	●
2340	●	●

Simiutaq [M] 60°41′·20N 46°35′·00W
NOTE: Weather and Navigational Warnings for the X12, X13
east coast of Greenland are broadcast by Iceland
where necessary - see relevant entry.
TELEPHONE: +299 364010 (JRCC Greenland) 300 n miles

NAVTEX [M]

TIME UT(GMT)	WEATHER BULLETINS	NAVIGATIONAL WARNINGS
0200	●	●
0600	●	●
1000	●	●
1400	●	●
1800	●	●
2200	●	●

PUERTO RICO (USA)

Isabella (U.S. Coast Guard) [R] 18°28′·00N 67°04′·32W
TELEPHONE: +1 787 2892041 X9, X11
FAX: +1 787 7296706 200 n miles
MMSI: 003669992

NAVTEX [R]

TIME UT(GMT)	WEATHER BULLETINS	NAVIGATIONAL WARNINGS
0250		●[1]
0650	●	●
1050	●	●
1450		●[1]
1850	●	●
2250	●	●

[1] Repeated navigational warnings

UNITED STATES (Atlantic Coast)

Boston (US Coast Guard) [F] 41°42′·82N 70°30′·27W
Remotely controlled from COMMCOM (NMN) X9
TELEPHONE: +1 757 4216240 200 n miles
FAX: +1 757 4216225
TELEX: +230 127775 USCG RCC NYK
MMSI: 003669991

NAVTEX [F]
Ice Warnings and Reports from February to July approx.
Existing Navigational Warnings are repeated at 0850 and 2050.

TIME UT(GMT)	WEATHER BULLETINS	NAVIGATIONAL WARNINGS	ICE WARNINGS AND REPORTS[1]
0050	●	●	●
0450	●	●	●
0850		●	●
1250	●	●	●
1650	●	●	●
2050		●	●

[1] Feb-July approx

Charleston (US Coast Guard) [E] 32°50′·67N 79°57′·00W
Remotely controlled from COMMCOM (NMN) X9
TELEPHONE: +1 757 4216240 200 n miles
FAX: +1 757 4216225
TELEX: +230 127775 USCG RCC NYK

NAVTEX [E]
Right Whale Warnings on receipt.
Existing Navigational Warnings are repeated at 0840 and 2040.

TIME UT(GMT)	WEATHER BULLETINS	NAVIGATIONAL WARNINGS
0040	●	●
0440	●	●
0840		●
1240	●	●
1640	●	●
2040		●

UNITED STATES (Atlantic Coast)

Miami (US Coast Guard) [A] 25°37'·40N 80°23'·37W
Remotely controlled from COMMCOM (NMN) X9
TELEPHONE: +1 757 4216240 240 n miles
FAX: +1 757 4216225
TELEX: +230 127775 USCG RCC NYK
MMSI: 003669997

NAVTEX [A]
Existing Navigational Warnings are repeated at 0800 and 2000.

TIME UT(GMT)	WEATHER BULLETINS	NAVIGATIONAL WARNINGS
0000	●	●
0400	●	●
0800		●
1200	●	●
1600	●	●
2000		●

Portsmouth (COMMCOM) (US Coast Guard) [N] 36°43'·72N 76°00'·60W
TELEPHONE: +1 757 4216240 X9
FAX: +1 757 4216225 280 n miles
TELEX: +230 127775 USCG RCC NYK
MMSI: 003669995

NAVTEX [N]
Existing Navigational Warnings are repeated at 1010 and 2210.

TIME UT(GMT)	WEATHER BULLETINS	NAVIGATIONAL WARNINGS
0210		●
0610	●	●
1010	●	●
1410		●
1810	●	●
2210	●	●

UNITED STATES (Gulf Coast)

New Orleans (US Coast Guard) [G] 29°53'·08N 89°56'·74W
Remotely controlled from COMMCOM (NMN) X9
TELEPHONE: +1 757 4216240 200 n miles
FAX: +1 757 4216225
TELEX: +230 127775 USCG RCC NYK
MMSI: 003669998

NAVTEX [G]

TIME UT(GMT)	WEATHER BULLETINS	NAVIGATIONAL WARNINGS
0100	●	●[1]
0500	●	●
0900		●
1300	●	●[1]
1700	●	●
2100		●

[1] Repeated Navigational Warnings

NAVAREA V

NO NAVTEX STATIONS WITHIN THIS NAVAREA

NAVAREA VI

ARGENTINA

Bahía Blanca (RSC) [P] [D] 38°52'·00S 62°06'·00W
TELEPHONE: +54 91 4573355 X11
FAX: +54 91 4573555 280 n miles
E-MAIL: bbla@prefecturanaval.gov.ar
  bbla-contrase@prefecturanaval.gov.ar
MMSI: 007100005

NAVTEX [P]

TIME UT(GMT)	WEATHER BULLETINS	NAVIGATIONAL WARNINGS
0230	●	●
0630	●	●
1030	●	●
1430	●	●
1830	●	●
2230	●	●

ARGENTINA
NAVTEX [D]
Frequency: 490 kHz Language: Spanish

TIME UT(GMT)	WEATHER BULLETINS	NAVIGATIONAL WARNINGS
0030	●	●
0430	●	●
0830	●	●
1230	●	●
1630	●	●
2030	●	●

ARGENTINA

Buenos Aires [R] [F] 35°23'·00S 57°10'·00W
TELEPHONE: +54 1 45767657 X11
FAX: +54 1 45767657 280 n miles
E-MAIL: info@prefecturanaval.gov.ar
MMSI: 007010001

NAVTEX [R]

TIME UT(GMT)	WEATHER BULLETINS	NAVIGATIONAL WARNINGS
0250	●	●
0650	●	●
1050	●	●
1450	●	●
1850	●	●
2250	●	●

NAVTEX [F]
Frequency: 490 kHz Language: Spanish

TIME UT(GMT)	WEATHER BULLETINS	NAVIGATIONAL WARNINGS
0050	●	●
0450	●	●
0850	●	●
1250	●	●
1650	●	●
2050	●	●

Comodoro Rivadavia (RSC) [O] [C] 45°50'·53S 67°28'·41W
TELEPHONE: +54 297 4473863 X11
  +54 297 4476800 280 n miles
FAX: +54 297 4462167
E-MAIL: jecriv@prefecturanaval.gov.ar
MMSI: 007010008

NAVTEX [O]

TIME UT(GMT)	WEATHER BULLETINS	NAVIGATIONAL WARNINGS
0220	●	●
0620	●	●
1020	●	●
1420	●	●
1820	●	●
2220	●	●

NAVTEX [C]
Frequency: 490 kHz Language: Spanish

TIME UT(GMT)	WEATHER BULLETINS	NAVIGATIONAL WARNINGS
0020	●	●
0420	●	●
0820	●	●
1220	●	●
1620	●	●
2020	●	●

ARGENTINA

Mar del Plata (RSC) [Q] [E] 38°03'·00S 57°32'·00W
TELEPHONE: +54 223 4803006 X11
FAX: +54 223 4803100 280 n miles
E-MAIL: jempla@prefecturanaval.gov.ar
MMSI: 007010003

NAVTEX [Q]

TIME UT(GMT)	WEATHER BULLETINS	NAVIGATIONAL WARNINGS
0240	●	●
0640	●	●
1040	●	●
1440	●	●
1840	●	●
2240	●	●

NAVTEX [E]
Frequency: 490 kHz Language: Spanish

TIME UT(GMT)	WEATHER BULLETINS	NAVIGATIONAL WARNINGS
0040	●	●
0440	●	●
0840	●	●
1240	●	●
1640	●	●
2040	●	●

Río Gallegos (RSC) [N] [B] 51°37'·39S 69°12'·71W
TELEPHONE: +54 2966 435494 X11
FAX: +54 2966 435494 280 n miles
E-MAIL: rgal-
  costera@prefecturanaval.gov.ar
MMSI: 007010010

NAVTEX [N]

TIME UT(GMT)	WEATHER BULLETINS	NAVIGATIONAL WARNINGS
0210	●	●
0610	●	●
1010	●	●
1410	●	●
1810	●	●
2210	●	●

NAVTEX [B]
Frequency: 490 kHz Language: Spanish

TIME UT(GMT)	WEATHER BULLETINS	NAVIGATIONAL WARNINGS
0010	●	●
0410	●	●
0810	●	●
1210	●	●
1610	●	●
2010	●	●

ARGENTINA

Ushuaia (RSC) [M] [A]
TELEPHONE: +54 2901 422382
FAX: +54 2901 421425
E-MAIL: jeushu@prefecturanaval.gov.ar
MMSI: 007010011

54°48'·00S 68°18'·00W
X10, X11
280 n miles

NAVTEX [M]

TIME UT(GMT)	WEATHER BULLETINS	NAVIGATIONAL WARNINGS
0200	●	●
0600	●	●
1000	●	●
1400	●	●
1800	●	●
2200	●	●

NAVTEX [A]
Frequency: 490 kHz Language: Spanish

TIME UT(GMT)	WEATHER BULLETINS	NAVIGATIONAL WARNINGS
0000	●	●
0400	●	●
0800	●	●
1200	●	●
1600	●	●
2000	●	●

URUGUAY

La Paloma [F] [A]
NOTE: Temporarily inoperative until further notice.
TELEPHONE: +598 2 3093775
+598 2 3093861
FAX: +598 2 3099220
E-MAIL: prela_radio@armada.mil.uy

34°39'·26S 54°08'·56W
X11
280 n miles

NAVTEX [F]

TIME UT(GMT)	WEATHER BULLETINS	NAVIGATIONAL WARNINGS
0050	●	●
0450	●	●
0850	●	●
1250	●	●
1650	●	●
2050	●	●

NAVTEX [A]
Frequency: 490 kHz Language: Spanish

TIME UT(GMT)	WEATHER BULLETINS	NAVIGATIONAL WARNINGS
0000	●	●
0400	●	●
0800	●	●
1200	●	●
1600	●	●
2000	●	●

NAVAREA VII

NAMIBIA

Walvis Bay [B]
TELEPHONE: +264 64203581
FAX: +264 64207497
E-MAIL: wvsradio@telecom.na

23°03'·25S 14°37'·50E
X6
380 n miles

NAVTEX [B]

TIME UT(GMT)	WEATHER BULLETINS	NAVIGATIONAL WARNINGS
0010		●
0410		●
0810		●
1210	●	●
1610	●	●
2010		●

SOUTH AFRICA

Cape Columbine [U]
NOTE: Areas of responsibility for Navigational Warnings covered by adjacent NAVTEX stations have been defined with overlaps in each case. The overlap is expanded in cases of emergency.
Remotely controlled from Cape Town
TELEPHONE: +27 21 5510700
FAX: +27 21 5513760

32°49'·55S 17°50'·97E
X6

250 n miles

NAVTEX [U]

TIME UT(GMT)	WEATHER BULLETINS	NAVIGATIONAL WARNINGS
0320		●
0720		●
1120	●	●
1520		●
1920	●	●
2320		●

SOUTH AFRICA

Cape Town [C]   33°40'·97S 18°43'·09E
NOTE: Areas of responsibility for Navigational   X6
Warnings covered by adjacent NAVTEX stations
have been defined with overlaps in each case. The
overlap is expanded in cases of emergency.
TELEPHONE: +27 21 5510700   250 n miles

NAVTEX [C]

TIME UT(GMT)	WEATHER BULLETINS	NAVIGATIONAL WARNINGS
0020		●
0420		●
0820		●
1220	●	●
1620	●	●
2020		●

Durban [O]   29°48'·35S 30°48'·95E
NOTE: Areas of responsibility for Navigational   X6
Warnings covered by adjacent NAVTEX stations
have been defined with overlaps in each case. The
overlap is expanded in cases of emergency.
Remotely controlled from Cape Town   250 n miles
TELEPHONE: +27 21 5510700

NAVTEX [O]

TIME UT(GMT)	WEATHER BULLETINS	NAVIGATIONAL WARNINGS
0220		●
0620		●
1020	●	●
1420		●
1820	●	●
2220		●

Port Elizabeth [I]   34°02'·20S 25°33'·37E
NOTE: Areas of responsibility for Navigational   X6
Warnings covered by adjacent NAVTEX stations
have been defined with overlaps in each case. The
overlap is expanded in cases of emergency.
Remotely controlled from Cape Town   250 n miles
TELEPHONE: +27 21 5510700

NAVTEX [I]

TIME UT(GMT)	WEATHER BULLETINS	NAVIGATIONAL WARNINGS
0120		●
0520		●
0920	●	●
1320		●
1720	●	●
2120		●

NAVAREA VIII

BURMA

Kyaukpyu [I]   19°17'·03N 93°31'·54E
TELEPHONE: +956 73407712   X6
                                                            200 n miles

NAVTEX [I]

TIME UT(GMT)	WEATHER BULLETINS	NAVIGATIONAL WARNINGS
0120	●	●
0520	●	●
0920	●	●
1320	●	●
1720	●	●
2120	●	●

BURMA

Myeik [G] [R]   12°25'·54N 98°35'·95E
TELEPHONE: +956 73407712   X6
                                                            200 n miles

NAVTEX [G]

TIME UT(GMT)	WEATHER BULLETINS	NAVIGATIONAL WARNINGS
0100	●	●
0500	●	●
0900	●	●
1300	●	●
1700	●	●
2100	●	●

NAVTEX [R]
Frequency: 490 kHz

TIME UT(GMT)	WEATHER BULLETINS	NAVIGATIONAL WARNINGS
0250	●	●
0650	●	●
1050	●	●
1450	●	●
1850	●	●
2250	●	●

BURMA

Yangon [Q]   16°42'·65N 96°17'·28E
TELEPHONE: +956 73407712   X6
200 n miles

NAVTEX [Q]
Frequency: 490 kHz

TIME UT(GMT)	WEATHER BULLETINS	NAVIGATIONAL WARNINGS
0240	●	●
0640	●	●
1040	●	●
1440	●	●
1840	●	●
2240	●	●

INDIA

Balasore [S]   21°29'·18N 86°55'·01E
TELEPHONE: +91 22 25069983   X6
+91 22 22751049   250 n miles

NAVTEX [S]

TIME UT(GMT)	WEATHER BULLETINS	NAVIGATIONAL WARNINGS
0300	●	●
0700	●	●
1100	●	●
1500	●	●
1900	●	●
2300	●	●

Keating Point [V]   9°15'·34N 92°46'·51E
TELEPHONE: +91 22 25069983   X6
+91 22 22751049   250 n miles

NAVTEX [V]

TIME UT(GMT)	WEATHER BULLETINS	NAVIGATIONAL WARNINGS
0330	●	●
0730	●	●
1130	●	●
1530	●	●
1930	●	●
2330	●	●

Muttam Point [L]   8°07'·46N 77°19'·00E
TELEPHONE: +91 22 25069983   X6
+91 22 22751049   250 n miles

NAVTEX [L]

TIME UT(GMT)	WEATHER BULLETINS	NAVIGATIONAL WARNINGS
0150	●	●
0550	●	●
0950	●	●
1350	●	●
1750	●	●
2150	●	●

INDIA

Porto Novo [O]   11°30'·26N 79°46'·23E
TELEPHONE: +91 22 25069983   X6
+91 22 22751049   250 n miles

NAVTEX [O]

TIME UT(GMT)	WEATHER BULLETINS	NAVIGATIONAL WARNINGS
0220	●	●
0620	●	●
1020	●	●
1420	●	●
1820	●	●
2220	●	●

Vakalpudi [Q]   17°00'·87N 82°16'·96E
TELEPHONE: +91 22 25069983   X6
+91 22 22751049   250 n miles

NAVTEX [Q]

TIME UT(GMT)	WEATHER BULLETINS	NAVIGATIONAL WARNINGS
0240	●	●
0640	●	●
1040	●	●
1440	●	●
1840	●	●
2240	●	●

Vengurla Point [J]   15°51'·38N 73°36'·87E
TELEPHONE: +91 22 25069983   X6
+91 22 22751049   250 n miles

NAVTEX [J]

TIME UT(GMT)	WEATHER BULLETINS	NAVIGATIONAL WARNINGS
0130	●	●
0530	●	●
0930	●	●
1330	●	●
1730	●	●
2130	●	●

Veraval [H]   20°54'·77N 70°21'·60E
TELEPHONE: +91 22 25069983   X6
+91 22 22751049   250 n miles

NAVTEX [H]

TIME UT(GMT)	WEATHER BULLETINS	NAVIGATIONAL WARNINGS
0110	●	●
0510	●	●
0910	●	●
1310	●	●
1710	●	●
2110	●	●

MAURITIUS

Mauritius [C]   20°10'·05S 57°28'·69E
TELEPHONE: +230 2085950   X6
FAX: +230 2110838   400 n miles
E-MAIL: 3bm.mrs@mauritiustelecom.com

NAVTEX [C]

TIME UT(GMT)	WEATHER BULLETINS	NAVIGATIONAL WARNINGS
0020	●	●
0420	●	●
0820	●	●
1220	●	●
1620	●	●
2020	●	●

SEYCHELLES

Mahé [T] [M]   4°39'·32S 55°28'·38E
TELEPHONE: +248 4290900   X6
              +248 4224616   400 n miles
FAX: +248 4323288
E-MAIL: mrcc.seycoast@email.sc

NAVTEX [T]

TIME UT(GMT)	WEATHER BULLETINS	NAVIGATIONAL WARNINGS
0310	●	●
0710	●	●
1110	●	●
1510	●	●
1910	●	●
2310	●	●

NAVTEX [M]
Frequency: 490 kHz Language: Creole

TIME UT(GMT)	WEATHER BULLETINS	NAVIGATIONAL WARNINGS
0200	●	●
0600	●	●
1000	●	●
1400	●	●
1800	●	●
2200	●	●

NAVAREA IX

BAHRAIN

Hamala [B]   26°09'·40N 50°28'·61E
TELEPHONE: +973 883939   X6
              +973 883543   300 n miles
FAX: +973 242676

NAVTEX [B]

TIME UT(GMT)	WEATHER BULLETINS	NAVIGATIONAL WARNINGS
0010		●
0410	●	●
0810		●
1210		●
1610	●	●
2010		●

EGYPT

Al Quṣayr [V]   26°06'·40N 34°17'·04E
TELEPHONE: +20 65 330001   X5, X6
FAX: +20 65 330001   400 n miles
TELEX: +91 92350 OWEPT SUK UN
MMSI: 006221112

NAVTEX [V]

TIME UT(GMT)	WEATHER BULLETINS	NAVIGATIONAL WARNINGS
0330	●	●
0730		●
1130		●
1530	●	●
1930		●
2330		●

IRAN

Bandar-e Shahīd Rajā'ī [F] [I]   27°06'·15N 56°04'·41E
TELEPHONE: +98 761 4514032   X6
FAX: +98 761 4514036   300 n miles
E-MAIL: abbasradio@pmo.ir

NAVTEX [F]

TIME UT(GMT)	WEATHER BULLETINS	NAVIGATIONAL WARNINGS
0050		●
0450	●	●
0850		●
1250	●	●
1650		●
2050		●

NAVTEX [I]
Frequency: 490 kHz Language: Farsi

TIME UT(GMT)	WEATHER BULLETINS	NAVIGATIONAL WARNINGS
0120		●
0520	●	●
0920		●
1320	●	●
1720		●
2120		●

IRAN

Būshehr [A] [D]   28°59'·02N 50°50'·03E
TELEPHONE: +98 771 2530074   X6
FAX: +98 771 2530077   300 n miles
E-MAIL: bushenradio@pmo.ir

NAVTEX [A]

TIME UT(GMT)	WEATHER BULLETINS	NAVIGATIONAL WARNINGS
0000		●
0400		●
0800	●	●
1200	●	●
1600		●
2000		●

NAVTEX [D]
Frequency: 490 kHz Language: Farsi

TIME UT(GMT)	WEATHER BULLETINS	NAVIGATIONAL WARNINGS
0030		●
0430		●
0830	●	●
1230	●	●
1630		●
2030		●

IRAQ

Umm Qaşr [W]   30°01'·89N 47°56'·88E
TELEPHONE: +964 7801440543   X6
FAX: +964 40 412377   200 n miles
E-MAIL: aqilsarah@yahoo.com

NAVTEX [W]
Frequency: 490 kHz Language: English

TIME UT(GMT)	WEATHER BULLETINS	NAVIGATIONAL WARNINGS
0340	●	●
0740	●	●
1140	●	●
1540	●	●
1940	●	●
2340	●	●

OMAN

Masqaţ (Muscat) (Wattaya) (Wattaya Radio Station) [M]   23°36'·67N 58°30'·20E
NOTE: Temporarily inoperative.   X6
TELEPHONE: +968 24571400   270 n miles
FAX: +968 24562995

NAVTEX [M]

TIME UT(GMT)	WEATHER BULLETINS	NAVIGATIONAL WARNINGS
0200	●	●
0600	●	●
1000	●	●
1400	●	●
1800	●	●
2200	●	●

PAKISTAN

Karachi [P]   24°52'·78N 67°09'·94E
NOTE: Temporarily inoperative.   X6
TELEPHONE: +92 21 34591161   400 n miles
FAX: +92 21 34591285
MMSI: 004634060

NAVTEX [P]

TIME UT(GMT)	WEATHER BULLETINS	NAVIGATIONAL WARNINGS
0230		●
0630	●	●
1030		●
1430		●
1830	●	●
2230		●

SAUDI ARABIA

JEDDAH [H] [O]   20°39'·33N 39°32'·98E
TELEPHONE: +966 124 237376   X6
FAX: +966 126 530379   390 n miles
E-MAIL: navtex@gamep.gov.sa

NAVTEX [H]

TIME UT(GMT)	WEATHER BULLETINS	NAVIGATIONAL WARNINGS
0110	●	●
0510	●	●
0910	●	●
1310	●	●
1710	●	●
2110	●	●

NAVTEX [O]
Frequency: 490 kHz Language: English

TIME UT(GMT)	WEATHER BULLETINS	NAVIGATIONAL WARNINGS
0220	●	●
0620	●	●
1020	●	●
1420	●	●
1820	●	●
2220	●	●

NAVAREA X

NO NAVTEX STATIONS WITHIN THIS NAVAREA

NAVAREA XI

CHINA

Dalian [R] 38°50'·69N 121°31'·09E
TELEPHONE:	+86 411 82623096	X7, X8
FAX:	+86 411 82626051	250 n miles
MMSI:	004121300	

NAVTEX [R]

TIME UT(GMT)	WEATHER BULLETINS	NAVIGATIONAL WARNINGS
0250	●	
0650		●
1050	●	
1450		●
1850		●
2250		●

Fuzhou [O] 25°59'·96N 119°26'·50E
TELEPHONE:	+86 591 83680690	X7, X8
FAX:	+86 591 83680690	250 n miles
MMSI:	004122600	

NAVTEX [O]

TIME UT(GMT)	NAVIGATIONAL WARNINGS
0220	●
0620	●
1020	●
1420	●
1820	●
2220	●

Guangzhou [N] 23°09'·56N 113°30'·80E
TELEPHONE:	+86 20 84102403	X7, X8
FAX:	+86 20 84428954	250 n miles
E-MAIL:	gzxsq@163.com	
MMSI:	004123100	

NAVTEX [N]

TIME UT(GMT)	WEATHER BULLETINS	NAVIGATIONAL WARNINGS
0210	●	
0610		●
1010	●	
1410	●	●
1810		●
2210	●	●

CHINA

Hong Kong [L] 22°12'·57N 114°15'·03E
TELEPHONE:	+852 22337999	X7, X8
FAX:	+852 25417714	250 n miles
MMSI:	004773500	

NAVTEX [L]
Navigational Warnings are to be vetted by Hong Kong MRCC before broadcasting in NAVTEX.

TIME UT(GMT)	WEATHER BULLETINS	NAVIGATIONAL WARNINGS
0150	●	●
0550	●	●
0950	●	●
1350	●	●
1750	●	●
2150	●	●

Sanya [M] 18°17'·49N 109°21'·80E
TELEPHONE:	+86 898 88272063	X7, X8
FAX:	+86 898 88257841	250 n miles
MMSI:	004123700	

NAVTEX [M]

TIME UT(GMT)	NAVIGATIONAL WARNINGS
0200	●
0600	●
1000	●
1400	●
1800	●
2200	●

Shanghai [Q] 31°06'·79N 121°32'·79E
TELEPHONE:	+86 21 58555840	X7, X8
FAX:	+86 21 58556478	250 n miles
E-MAIL:	wangbc@shmsa.gov.cn	
MMSI:	004122100	

NAVTEX [Q]

TIME UT(GMT)	WEATHER BULLETINS	NAVIGATIONAL WARNINGS
0640		●
1040	●	
1440		●
1840	●	
2240		●

GUAM (USA)

Guam (US Coast Guard) [V]　13°28'·71N 144°50'·26E
NOTE: 518 kHz temporarily inoperative until further notice.　X7

Remotely controlled from COMMCOM.　230 n miles

TELEPHONE:	+1 671 355 4828
FAX:	+1 671 355 4831
MMSI:	003669994

NAVTEX [V]

TIME UT(GMT)	WEATHER BULLETINS	NAVIGATIONAL WARNINGS
0330	●	●
0730	●	●
1130	●	●
1530	●	●
1930	●	●
2330	●	●

NAVTEX [V]
Frequency: 4209·5 kHz Language: English

TIME UT(GMT)	WEATHER BULLETINS	NAVIGATIONAL WARNINGS
0330	●	●
0730	●	●
1130	●	●
1530	●	●
1930	●	●
2330	●	●

INDONESIA

Amboina (Ambon) [B]　3°41'·68S 128°11'·88E
X7
300 n miles

TELEPHONE:	+62 911 352011
FAX:	+62 911 341571
E-MAIL:	disnavambon@outlook.com

NAVTEX [B]

TIME UT(GMT)	WEATHER BULLETINS	NAVIGATIONAL WARNINGS
0010	●	●
0410	●	●
0810	●	●
1210	●	●
1610	●	●
2010	●	●

Jakarta [E]　6°07'·15S 106°51'·78E
X7
300 n miles

TELEPHONE:	+62 21 8812287
FAX:	+62 21 43930070
E-MAIL:	disnav~tgpriok@gmail.com

NAVTEX [E]

TIME UT(GMT)	WEATHER BULLETINS	NAVIGATIONAL WARNINGS
0040	●	●
0440	●	●
0840	●	●
1240	●	●
1640	●	●
2040	●	●

INDONESIA

Jayapura [A]　2°31'·11S 140°43'·29E
X7
300 n miles

TELEPHONE:	+62 967 541122
FAX:	+62 967 541630
E-MAIL:	disnavjayapura@yahoo.co.id

NAVTEX [A]

TIME UT(GMT)	WEATHER BULLETINS	NAVIGATIONAL WARNINGS
0000	●	●
0400	●	●
0800	●	●
1200	●	●
1600	●	●
2000	●	●

Ujungpandang (Makassar) [D]　5°04'·89S 119°29'·83E
X7
300 n miles

TELEPHONE:	+62 411 319282
FAX:	+62 411 322886
E-MAIL:	disnav_kelas1_mks@yahoo.co.id

NAVTEX [D]

TIME UT(GMT)	WEATHER BULLETINS	NAVIGATIONAL WARNINGS
0030	●	●
0430	●	●
0830	●	●
1230	●	●
1630	●	●
2030	●	●

JAPAN

Kushiro (JCG MRCC) [K]　42°57'·35N 144°35'·37E
NOTE: All 424 kHz broadcasts are transmitted on low power for local coverage.　X7, X8

400 n miles

TELEPHONE:	+81 3 35919000
FAX:	+81 3 35918701
E-MAIL:	jcg-navtex@mlit.go.jp
MMSI:	004310102

NAVTEX [K]
Tsunami Warnings on receipt

TIME UT(GMT)	WEATHER BULLETINS	NAVIGATIONAL WARNINGS
0140	●	●
0540	●	●
0940	●	●
1340	●	●
1740	●	●
2140	●	●

NAVTEX [K]
Tsunami Warnings on receipt
Frequency: 424 kHz Language: Japanese

TIME UT(GMT)	WEATHER BULLETINS	NAVIGATIONAL WARNINGS
0108	●	●
0508	●	●
0908	●	●
1308	●	●
1708	●	●
2108	●	●

JAPAN

Moji (JCG MRCC) [H]   34°00'·90N 130°56'·10E
NOTE: All 424 kHz broadcasts are transmitted on   X7, X8
low power for local coverage.
TELEPHONE: +81 3 35919000   400 n miles
FAX: +81 3 35918701
E-MAIL: jcg-navtex@mlit.go.jp
MMSI: 004310701

NAVTEX [H]
Tsunami Warnings on receipt

TIME UT(GMT)	WEATHER BULLETINS	NAVIGATIONAL WARNINGS
0110	●	●
0510	●	●
0910	●	●
1310	●	●
1710	●	●
2110	●	●

NAVTEX [H]
Tsunami Warnings on receipt
Frequency: 424 kHz Language: Japanese

TIME UT(GMT)	WEATHER BULLETINS	NAVIGATIONAL WARNINGS
0017	●	●
0417	●	●
0817	●	●
1217	●	●
1617	●	●
2017	●	●

Naha (JCG MRCC) [G]   26°05'·48N 127°40'·13E
NOTE: All 424 kHz broadcasts are transmitted on   X7, X8
low power for local coverage.
TELEPHONE: +81 3 35919000   400 n miles
FAX: +81 3 35918701
E-MAIL: jcg-navtex@mlit.go.jp
MMSI: 004311101

NAVTEX [G]
Tsunami Warnings on receipt

TIME UT(GMT)	WEATHER BULLETINS	NAVIGATIONAL WARNINGS
0100	●	●
0500	●	●
0900	●	●
1300	●	●
1700	●	●
2100	●	●

NAVTEX [G]
Tsunami Warnings on receipt
Frequency: 424 kHz Language: Japanese

TIME UT(GMT)	WEATHER BULLETINS	NAVIGATIONAL WARNINGS
0000	●	●
0400	●	●
0800	●	●
1200	●	●
1600	●	●
2000	●	●

JAPAN

Otaru (JCG MRCC) [J]   43°19'·53N 140°26'·83E
NOTE: All 424 kHz broadcasts are transmitted on   X7, X8
low power for local coverage.
TELEPHONE: +81 3 35919000   400 n miles
FAX: +81 3 35918701
E-MAIL: jcg-navtex@mlit.go.jp
MMSI: 004310101

NAVTEX [J]
Tsunami Warnings on receipt

TIME UT(GMT)	WEATHER BULLETINS	NAVIGATIONAL WARNINGS
0130	●	●
0530	●	●
0930	●	●
1330	●	●
1730	●	●
2130	●	●

NAVTEX [J]
Tsunami Warnings on receipt
Frequency: 424 kHz Language: Japanese

TIME UT(GMT)	WEATHER BULLETINS	NAVIGATIONAL WARNINGS
0051	●	●
0451	●	●
0851	●	●
1251	●	●
1651	●	●
2051	●	●

Yokohama (JCG MRCC) [I]   35°14'·55N 139°55'·28E
NOTE: All 424 kHz broadcasts are transmitted on   X7, X8
low power for local coverage.
TELEPHONE: +81 3 35919000   400 n miles
FAX: +81 3 35918701
E-MAIL: jcg-navtex@mlit.go.jp
MMSI: 004310301

NAVTEX [I]
Tsunami Warnings on receipt

TIME UT(GMT)	WEATHER BULLETINS	NAVIGATIONAL WARNINGS
0120	●	●
0520	●	●
0920	●	●
1320	●	●
1720	●	●
2120	●	●

NAVTEX [I]
Tsunami Warnings on receipt
Frequency: 424 kHz Language: Japanese

TIME UT(GMT)	WEATHER BULLETINS	NAVIGATIONAL WARNINGS
0034	●	●
0434	●	●
0834	●	●
1234	●	●
1634	●	●
2034	●	●

KOREA, NORTH

Hamhüng [E] [B]

39°50'·00N 127°41'·02E
X8
200 n miles

NAVTEX [E]

TIME UT(GMT)	WEATHER BULLETINS	NAVIGATIONAL WARNINGS
0040	•	•
0440	•	•
0840	•	•
1240	•	•
1640	•	•
2040	•	•

NAVTEX [B]
Frequency: 490 kHz Language: Korean

TIME UT(GMT)	WEATHER BULLETINS	NAVIGATIONAL WARNINGS
0010	•	•
0410	•	•
0810	•	•
1210	•	•
1610	•	•
2010	•	•

Pyongyang [D] [A]

38°59'·58N 125°42'·93E
X8
200 n miles

NAVTEX [D]

TIME UT(GMT)	WEATHER BULLETINS	NAVIGATIONAL WARNINGS
0030	•	•
0430	•	•
0830	•	•
1230	•	•
1630	•	•
2030	•	•

NAVTEX [A]
Frequency: 490 kHz Language: Korean

TIME UT(GMT)	WEATHER BULLETINS	NAVIGATIONAL WARNINGS
0000	•	•
0400	•	•
0800	•	•
1200	•	•
1600	•	•
2000	•	•

KOREA, SOUTH

Jukbyeon [V] [J]

37°03'·49N 129°25'·77E
X8
200 n miles

TELEPHONE: +82 547 502000
FAX: +82 32 8352895
E-MAIL: korea_navtex@kcg.go.kr
WEBSITE: http://navtex.kcg.go.kr

NAVTEX [V]

TIME UT(GMT)	WEATHER BULLETINS	NAVIGATIONAL WARNINGS
0330	•	•
0730	•	•
1130	•	•
1530	•	•
1930	•	•
2330	•	•

NAVTEX [J]
Frequency: 490 kHz Language: Korean

TIME UT(GMT)	WEATHER BULLETINS	NAVIGATIONAL WARNINGS
0130	•	•
0530	•	•
0930	•	•
1330	•	•
1730	•	•
2130	•	•

Pyönsan (Byeonsan) [W] [K]

35°35'·81N 126°29'·17E
X8
200 n miles

TELEPHONE: +82 639 282000
MMSI: 004401004

NAVTEX [W]

TIME UT(GMT)	WEATHER BULLETINS	NAVIGATIONAL WARNINGS
0340	•	•
0740		•
1140	•	•
1540	•	•
1940		•
2340	•	•

NAVTEX [K]
Frequency: 490 kHz Language: Korean

TIME UT(GMT)	WEATHER BULLETINS	NAVIGATIONAL WARNINGS
0140		•
0540	•	•
0940	•	•
1340		•
1740	•	•
2140	•	•

MALAYSIA

Miri (Sarawak) [T] 4°26'·42N 114°01'·51E
TELEPHONE: +60 82 484018 X7
E-MAIL: wz@jls.gov.my 350 n miles

NAVTEX [T]

TIME UT(GMT)	WEATHER BULLETINS	NAVIGATIONAL WARNINGS
0310	●	●
0710		●
1110		●
1510	●	●
1910		●
2310		●

Penang [U] 5°25'·58N 100°24'·40E
TELEPHONE: +60 3 31695211 X7
FAX: +60 3 31671334 350 n miles
E-MAIL: hairizam@marine.gov.my

NAVTEX [U]

TIME UT(GMT)	WEATHER BULLETINS	NAVIGATIONAL WARNINGS
0320	●	●
0720		●
1120		●
1520	●	●
1920		●
2320		●

Sandakan (Sabah) [S] 5°53'·85N 118°00'·24E
TELEPHONE: +60 88 401110 X7
E-MAIL: azman.latif@marine.gov.my 350 n miles

NAVTEX [S]

TIME UT(GMT)	WEATHER BULLETINS	NAVIGATIONAL WARNINGS
0300	●	●
0700		●
1100		●
1500	●	●
1900		●
2300		●

PHILIPPINES

Manila [J] 14°30'·33N 121°03'·90E
E-MAIL: pcgcomcen@coastguard.gov.ph X7
200 n miles

NAVTEX [J]

TIME UT(GMT)	WEATHER BULLETINS	NAVIGATIONAL WARNINGS
0130	●	●
0530	●	●
0930	●	●
1330	●	●
1730	●	●
2130	●	●

SINGAPORE

Singapore (Changi) [C] 1°20'·65N 103°58'·35E
TELEPHONE: +65 62265539 X7
FAX: +65 62279971 400 n miles
TELEX: +87 20021 MARTEL RS
E-MAIL: pocc@mpa.gov.sg
MMSI: 005630002

NAVTEX [C]

TIME UT(GMT)	WEATHER BULLETINS	NAVIGATIONAL WARNINGS
0020	●	●
0420		●
0820		●
1220	●	●
1620		●
2020		●

TAIWAN

Chi-lung [P] 25°08'·09N 121°45'·29E
NOTE: Broadcasts are remotely controlled from X7
Chi-Lung. The [P] time-slots broadcasts are
transmitted alternately between the Chi-lung and
Linyuan aerial sites.

540 n miles

NAVTEX [P]

TIME UT(GMT)	WEATHER BULLETINS	NAVIGATIONAL WARNINGS
0630	●	●
1430	●	●
2230	●	●

Linyuan [P] 22°29'·00N 120°25'·00E
NOTE: Broadcasts are remotely controlled from X7
Chi-Lung. The [P] time-slots broadcasts are
transmitted alternately between the Chi-lung and
Linyuan aerial sites.
Remotely controlled from Chi-lung (Keelung) 540 n miles

NAVTEX [P]

TIME UT(GMT)	WEATHER BULLETINS	NAVIGATIONAL WARNINGS
0230	●	●
1030	●	●
1830	●	●

THAILAND

Bangkok (Nonthaburi) [F] 13°01'·47N 100°01'·20E
TELEPHONE: +66 2 4757077 X7
FAX: +66 2 1736570 400 n miles
E-MAIL: navinfo.hydro@gmail.com
MMSI: 005671000

NAVTEX [F]

TIME UT(GMT)	WEATHER BULLETINS	NAVIGATIONAL WARNINGS
0050	●	●
0450		●
0850	●	●
1250		●
1650		●
2050		●

VIETNAM

Đa Nang [K] [F] 16°03'·33N 108°09'·42E
TELEPHONE:	+84 225 3822332	X7
	+84 225 3746464	400 n miles
FAX:	+84 225 3747062	
E-MAIL:	vncrsnet_total@vishipel.com.vn	
	tienhoang@vishipel.com.vn	
MMSI:	005742030	

NAVTEX [K]

TIME UT(GMT)	WEATHER BULLETINS	NAVIGATIONAL WARNINGS
0140	•	
0540		•
0940		•
1340	•	
1740		•
2140		•

NAVTEX [F]
Frequency: 490 kHz Language: Vietnamese

TIME UT(GMT)	WEATHER BULLETINS	NAVIGATIONAL WARNINGS
0050	•	
0450		•
0850		•
1250	•	
1650		•
2050		•

Hai Phong [M] 20°51'·02N 106°44'·02E
TELEPHONE:	+84 31 3842066	X7
FAX:	+84 31 3842979	
MMSI:	005741040	

NAVTEX [M]
Frequency: 4209·5 kHz Language: Vietnamese

TIME UT(GMT)	WEATHER BULLETINS	NAVIGATIONAL WARNINGS
0200		•
0600		•
1000	•	
1400		•
1800		•
2200	•	

Ho Chi Minh [X] 10°23'·70N 107°08'·65E
TELEPHONE:	+84 225 3822332	X7
	+84 225 3746464	400 n miles
FAX:	+84 225 3747062	
E-MAIL:	vncrsnet_total@vishipel.com.vn	
	tienhoang@vishipel.com.vn	
MMSI:	005743030	

NAVTEX [X]

TIME UT(GMT)	WEATHER BULLETINS	NAVIGATIONAL WARNINGS
0350		•
0750		•
1150	•	
1550		•
1950		•
2350	•	

VIETNAM

Nha Trang [C] 12°13'·35N 109°10'·87E
TELEPHONE:	+84 8 3590098	X7
	+84 8 3590099	
FAX:	+84 8 3590098	
MMSI:	005742080	

NAVTEX [C]
Frequency: 4209·5 kHz Language: Vietnamese

TIME UT(GMT)	WEATHER BULLETINS	NAVIGATIONAL WARNINGS
0020	•	
0420		•
0820		•
1220	•	
1620		•
2020		•

Vung Tau [V] 10°23'·70N 107°08'·72E
TELEPHONE:	+84 8 3811596	X7
	+84 8 3852890	400 n miles
FAX:	+84 8 3811596	
MMSI:	005743020	

NAVTEX [V]
Frequency: 490 kHz Language: Vietnamese

TIME UT(GMT)	WEATHER BULLETINS	NAVIGATIONAL WARNINGS
0330		•
0730		•
1130	•	
1530		•
1930		•
2330	•	

NAVAREA XII

CANADA (Pacific Coast)

Amphitrite Point (Prince Rupert MCTS)
(Canadian CG) [H]   48°55'·51N 125°32'·50W
TELEPHONE: +1 250 6273074   X9
FAX: +1 250 6249075   300 n miles
E-MAIL: mctsprincerupert@dfo-mpo.gc.ca
MMSI: 003160013

NAVTEX [H]

TIME UT(GMT)	WEATHER BULLETINS	NAVIGATIONAL WARNINGS
0110		•
0510	•	
0910	•	
1310		•
1710	•	
2110	•	

Digby Island (Prince Rupert MCTS) (Canadian
CG) [D]   54°17'·91N 130°25'·06W
TELEPHONE: +1 250 6273074   X9
FAX: +1 250 6249075   300 n miles
E-MAIL: mctsprincerupert@dfo-mpo.gc.ca
MMSI: 003160013

NAVTEX [D]

TIME UT(GMT)	WEATHER BULLETINS	NAVIGATIONAL WARNINGS
0030	•	
0430	•	
0830		•
1230	•	
1630	•	
2030		•

COLOMBIA (Pacific Coast)

Buenaventura [O] [C]   3°54'·19N 77°03'·76W
                                          X9, X10
                                      400 n miles

NAVTEX [O]

TIME UT(GMT)	WEATHER BULLETINS	NAVIGATIONAL WARNINGS
0220	•	•
0620	•	•
1020	•	•
1420	•	•
1820	•	•
2220	•	•

NAVTEX [C]
Frequency: 490 kHz Language: Spanish

TIME UT(GMT)	WEATHER BULLETINS	NAVIGATIONAL WARNINGS
0020	•	•
0420	•	•
0820	•	•
1220	•	•
1620	•	•
2020	•	•

ECUADOR

Ayora [L] [A]   0°43'·03S 90°19'·63W
NOTE: Temporarily inoperative.   X9, X10
MMSI: 007354757   400 n miles

NAVTEX [L]

TIME UT(GMT)	NAVIGATIONAL WARNINGS
0150	•
0550	•
0950	•
1350	•
1750	•
2150	•

NAVTEX [A]
Frequency: 490 kHz Language: Spanish

TIME UT(GMT)	NAVIGATIONAL WARNINGS
0000	•
0400	•
0800	•
1200	•
1600	•
2000	•

UNITED STATES (Alaska)

Kodiak (US Coast Guard) [J] [X]   57°46'·63N 152°31'·72W
TELEPHONE: +1 907 4875778   X9
FAX: +1 907 4875430   200 n miles
MMSI: 003669899

NAVTEX [J]

TIME UT(GMT)	WEATHER BULLETINS	NAVIGATIONAL WARNINGS
0130	•	•
0530	•	•
0930		•[1]
1330	•	•
1730	•	•
2130		•[1]

[1] Repeated Navigational Warnings

NAVTEX [X]

TIME UT(GMT)	WEATHER BULLETINS	NAVIGATIONAL WARNINGS
0350	•	•
0750	•	•
1150		•[1]
1550	•	•
1950	•	•
2350		•[1]

[1] Repeated Navigational Warnings

UNITED STATES (Hawaii)

Honolulu (US Coast Guard) [O] 21°25′·25N 158°09′·07W
Remotely controlled from CAMSPAC (NMC) X9
TELEPHONE: +1 415 6692047 350 n miles
FAX: +1 415 6692096
TELEX: +230 172343 AAB CG ALDA
MMSI: 003669993

NAVTEX [O]

TIME UT(GMT)	WEATHER BULLETINS	NAVIGATIONAL WARNINGS
0220	●	●
0620	●	●
1020		●[1]
1420	●	●
1820	●	●
2220		●[1]

[1] Repeated Navigational Warnings

UNITED STATES (Pacific Coast)

Astoria (US Coast Guard) [W] 46°12′·00N 123°56′·79W
Remotely controlled from CAMSPAC (NMC) X9
TELEPHONE: +1 415 6692047 216 n miles
FAX: +1 415 6692096
TELEX: +230 172343 CG ALDA
MMSI: 003669910

NAVTEX [W]

TIME UT(GMT)	WEATHER BULLETINS	NAVIGATIONAL WARNINGS
0340		●
0740	●	●
1140	●	●[1]
1540		●
1940	●	●
2340	●	●[1]

[1] Repeated Navigational Warnings

Long Beach (Cambria) (US Coast Guard) [Q] 35°31′·12N 121°03′·60W
Remotely controlled from CAMSPAC (NMC) X9
TELEPHONE: +1 415 6692047 350 n miles
FAX: +1 415 6692096
TELEX: +230 172343 CG ALDA
MMSI: 003669912

NAVTEX [Q]

TIME UT(GMT)	WEATHER BULLETINS	NAVIGATIONAL WARNINGS
0240		●
0640	●	●[1]
1040	●	●
1440		●
1840	●	●[1]
2240	●	●

[1] Repeated Navigational Warnings

Point Reyes RCF (San Francisco) (US Coast Guard) [C] 37°55′·53N 122°43′·87W
TELEPHONE: +1 415 6692047 X9
FAX: +1 415 6692096 350 n miles
TELEX: +230 172343 CG ALDA
MMSI: 003669990

NAVTEX [C]

TIME UT(GMT)	WEATHER BULLETINS	NAVIGATIONAL WARNINGS
0020	●	●
0420		●[1]
0820	●	●
1220	●	●
1620		●[1]
2020	●	●

[1] Repeated Navigational Warnings

NAVAREA XIII

RUSSIA (Pacific Coast)

Kholmsk [B]   47°02'·00N 142°03'·00E
TELEPHONE: +7 4243 366285   X8
FAX: +7 4243 366020   300 n miles
E-MAIL: marcoms@snc.ru

NAVTEX [B]

TIME UT(GMT)	WEATHER BULLETINS	NAVIGATIONAL WARNINGS
0010	●	●
0410	●	●
0810	●	●
1210	●	●
1610	●	●
2010	●	●

Magadan [D]   59°41'·00N 150°09'·00E
TELEPHONE: +7 4242 785700   X8
FAX: +7 4242 785805   120 n miles
E-MAIL: magadan-radio@mail.ru
MMSI: 002733728

NAVTEX [D]

TIME UT(GMT)	WEATHER BULLETINS	NAVIGATIONAL WARNINGS
0030	●	●
0430	●	●
0830	●	●
1230	●	●
1630	●	●
2030	●	●

Okhotsk [G]   59°21'·50N 143°12'·50E
TELEPHONE: +7 4242 785700   X8
FAX: +7 4242 785805   300 n miles
E-MAIL: navteks@oxt.kht.ru

NAVTEX [G]

TIME UT(GMT)	WEATHER BULLETINS	NAVIGATIONAL WARNINGS
0100	●	●
0500	●	●
0900	●	●
1300	●	●
1700	●	●
2100	●	●

RUSSIA (Pacific Coast)

Petropavlovsk - Kamchatskiy [C]   53°00'·00N 158°25'·40E
TELEPHONE: +7 4152 411341   X8
FAX: +7 4152 412641   300 n miles
E-MAIL: info@krcm.ru
MMSI: 002734418

NAVTEX [C]

TIME UT(GMT)	WEATHER BULLETINS	NAVIGATIONAL WARNINGS
0020	●	●
0420	●	●
0820	●	●
1220	●	●
1620	●	●
2020	●	●

Vladivostok [A]   43°23'·00N 131°55'·00E
TELEPHONE: +7 423 2450300   X8
FAX: +7 423 2450300   230 n miles
E-MAIL: robot_prs@ccdcm.ru
MMSI: 002734412

NAVTEX [A]

TIME UT(GMT)	WEATHER BULLETINS	NAVIGATIONAL WARNINGS
0000	●	●
0400	●	●
0800	●	●
1200	●	●
1600	●	●
2000	●	●

NAVAREA XIV

NO NAVTEX STATIONS WITHIN THIS NAVAREA

NAVAREA XV

CHILE

Antofagasta (MRSC) [A] [G]
23°29'·54S 70°25'·46W
TELEPHONE:	+56 55 2630072
	+56 55 2630000
FAX:	+56 55 2224464
E-MAIL:	cbaradio@directemar.cl
MMSI:	007250050

X10
400 n miles

NAVTEX [A]

TIME UT(GMT)	WEATHER BULLETINS	NAVIGATIONAL WARNINGS
0000	●	
0400		●
0800		●
1200	●	
1600		●
2000		●

NAVTEX [G]
Frequency: 490 kHz Language: Spanish

TIME UT(GMT)	WEATHER BULLETINS	NAVIGATIONAL WARNINGS
0100	●	
0500		●
0900		●
1300	●	
1700		●
2100		●

Isla de Pascua (Easter Island) (MRSC) [F] [L]
27°09'·11S 109°25'·49W
NOTE: Temporarily inoperative.
TELEPHONE:	+56 32 2100222
E-MAIL:	cbyradio@directemar.cl
MMSI:	007250100

X10
400 n miles

NAVTEX [F]

TIME UT(GMT)	WEATHER BULLETINS	NAVIGATIONAL WARNINGS
0050	●	
0450		●
0850		●
1250	●	
1650		●
2050		●

NAVTEX [L]
Frequency: 490 kHz Language: Spanish

TIME UT(GMT)	WEATHER BULLETINS	NAVIGATIONAL WARNINGS
0150	●	
0550		●
0950		●
1350	●	
1750		●
2150		●

CHILE

Puerto Montt (MRCC) [D] [J]
41°28'·90S 72°57'·57W
TELEPHONE:	+56 65 2256828
FAX:	+56 65 2256827
E-MAIL:	cbpradio@directemar.cl
MMSI:	007250230

X10
400 n miles

NAVTEX [D]

TIME UT(GMT)	WEATHER BULLETINS	NAVIGATIONAL WARNINGS
0030	●	
0430		●
0830		●
1230	●	
1630		●
2030		●

NAVTEX [J]
Frequency: 490 kHz Language: Spanish

TIME UT(GMT)	WEATHER BULLETINS	NAVIGATIONAL WARNINGS
0130	●	
0530		●
0930		●
1330	●	
1730		●
2130		●

Punta Arenas (Magallanes) [E] [K]
53°09'·91S 70°54'·27W
TELEPHONE:	+56 61 2201100
	+56 61 2201170
FAX:	+56 61 2201196
E-MAIL:	cbmradio@directemar.cl
MMSI:	007250380

X10
400 n miles

NAVTEX [E]

TIME UT(GMT)	WEATHER BULLETINS	NAVIGATIONAL WARNINGS	ICE WARNINGS AND REPORTS
0040	●		●
0440		●	
0840		●	
1240	●		●
1640		●	
2040		●	

NAVTEX [K]
Frequency: 490 kHz Language: Spanish

TIME UT(GMT)	WEATHER BULLETINS	NAVIGATIONAL WARNINGS	ICE WARNINGS AND REPORTS
0140	●		●
0540		●	
0940		●	
1340	●		●
1740		●	
2140		●	

NAVTEX

CHILE

Talcahuano (MRCC) [C] [I] 36°41'·50S 73°06'·51W
TELEPHONE: +56 41 2541645   X10
            +56 41 2541100   400 n miles
FAX: +56 41 2541634
E-MAIL: cbtradio@directemar.cl
MMSI: 007250170

NAVTEX [C]

TIME UT(GMT)	WEATHER BULLETINS	NAVIGATIONAL WARNINGS
0020	●	
0420		●
0820		●
1220	●	
1620		●
2020		●

NAVTEX [I]
Frequency: 490 kHz Language: Spanish

TIME UT(GMT)	WEATHER BULLETINS	NAVIGATIONAL WARNINGS
0120	●	
0520		●
0920		●
1320	●	
1720		●
2120		●

Valparaíso Playa Ancha (MRCC) [B] [H] 33°04'·70S 71°36'·80W
TELEPHONE: +56 32 2208974   X10
            +56 32 2208961   300 n miles
FAX: +56 32 2281099
E-MAIL: cbvradio@directemar.cl
MMSI: 007251860

NAVTEX [B]

TIME UT(GMT)	WEATHER BULLETINS	NAVIGATIONAL WARNINGS
0010	●	
0410		●
0810		●
1210	●	
1610		●
2010		●

NAVTEX [H]
Frequency: 490 kHz Language: Spanish

TIME UT(GMT)	WEATHER BULLETINS	NAVIGATIONAL WARNINGS
0110	●	
0510		●
0910		●
1310	●	
1710		●
2110		●

NAVAREA XVI

PERU

Callao [U] 12°04'·34S 77°10'·13W
TELEPHONE: +51 1 4299798   X10
            +51 998849812 (Mobile) 250 n miles
E-MAIL: costeracallao@dicapi.mil.pe
MMSI: 007600125

NAVTEX [U]

TIME UT(GMT)	WEATHER BULLETINS	NAVIGATIONAL WARNINGS
0320		●
0720	●	
1120		●
1520		●
1920	●	
2320		●

Mollendo (Matarani) [W] 17°00'·60S 72°02'·10W
TELEPHONE: +51 1 54534383   X10
            +51 959036759 (Mobile) 250 n miles
E-MAIL: costeramollendo@dicapi.mil.pe
MMSI: 007600129

NAVTEX [W]

TIME UT(GMT)	WEATHER BULLETINS	NAVIGATIONAL WARNINGS
0340		●
0740		●
1140	●	
1540		●
1940		●
2340	●	

Paita [S] 5°05'·54S 81°07'·41W
TELEPHONE: +51 1 73211670   X10
            +51 969520961 (Mobile) 250 n miles
E-MAIL: costerapaita@dicapi.mil.pe
MMSI: 007600121

NAVTEX [S]

TIME UT(GMT)	WEATHER BULLETINS	NAVIGATIONAL WARNINGS
0300	●	
0700		●
1100		●
1500	●	
1900		●
2300		●

NAVAREA XVII

NO NAVTEX STATIONS WITHIN THIS NAVAREA

NAVAREA XVIII

GREENLAND

Upernavik [I]   72°46′·98N 56°08′·33W
NOTE: Weather and Navigational Warnings for the   X12, X13
east coast of Greenland are broadcast by Iceland
where necessary - see relevant entry.

                                                              300 n miles

NAVTEX [I]

TIME UT(GMT)	WEATHER BULLETINS	NAVIGATIONAL WARNINGS
0120	●	●
0520	●	●
0920	●	●
1320	●	●
1720	●	●
2120	●	●

NAVAREA XIX

NORWAY

Bodø [B]   67°16′·15N 14°25′·37E
TELEPHONE: +47 75528925   X1, X2, X13
FAX: +47 75525896   450 n miles
E-MAIL: kystradio.nord@telenor.com
MMSI: 002570000

NAVTEX [B]

TIME UT(GMT)	WEATHER BULLETINS	NAVIGATIONAL WARNINGS
0010	●	●
0410		●
0810		●
1210	●	●
1610		●
2010		●

Svalbard [A]   78°03′·70N 13°37′·26E
TELEPHONE: +47 75528925   X1, X2, X13
FAX: +47 75525896   450 n miles
E-MAIL: kystradio.nord@telenor.com
MMSI: 002570000

NAVTEX [A]
Ice Warnings and Reports at 1600 Tues only.

TIME UT(GMT)	WEATHER BULLETINS	NAVIGATIONAL WARNINGS	ICE WARNINGS AND REPORTS
0000	●	●	
0400		●	
0800		●	●
1200	●	●	
1600		●	●
2000		●	

Vardø [C]   70°22′·25N 31°05′·85E
Remotely controlled from Bodø   X1, X2, X13
TELEPHONE: +47 75528925   450 n miles
FAX: +47 75525896
E-MAIL: kystradio.nord@telenor.com
MMSI: 002570000

NAVTEX [C]
Ice Warnings and Reports every Tuesday

TIME UT(GMT)	WEATHER BULLETINS	NAVIGATIONAL WARNINGS	ICE WARNINGS AND REPORTS
0020	●	●	
0420		●	
0820		●	
1220	●	●	
1620		●	●
2020		●	

NAVAREA XX

RUSSIA (Arctic Coast)

Arkhangel'sk [L]   64°51'·14N 40°16'·50E
TELEPHONE: +7 8182 208882   X1, X13
E-MAIL: navtex1@arhrmp.ru   300 n miles
              navtex2@arhrmp.ru
MMSI: 002734414

NAVTEX [L]
Weather Bulletins broadcast when details are available.

TIME UT(GMT)	WEATHER BULLETINS	NAVIGATIONAL WARNINGS
0150	●	●
0550	●	●
0950	●	●
1350	●	●
1750	●	●
2150	●	●

Murmansk [K]   68°46'·00N 32°58'·00E
TELEPHONE: +7 8152 288202   X1, X13
FAX: +7 8152 288202   300 n miles
E-MAIL: rshrs@karat-holding.com
MMSI: 002734420

NAVTEX [K]

TIME UT(GMT)	NAVIGATIONAL WARNINGS	ICE WARNINGS AND REPORTS[1]
0140	●	●
0540	●	●
0940	●	●
1340	●	●
1740	●	●
2140	●	●

[1] When details are available

Sabetta [M]   71°17'·08N 72°01'·77E
TELEPHONE: +7(8)931 4172647   250 n miles
E-MAIL: sabettagmssb@ark.rosmorport.ru

NAVTEX [M]
Range is 184 n miles between 42°-255° azimuth to the S, and 281 n miles between 255° and 42° azimuth to the N.

TIME UT(GMT)	WEATHER BULLETINS	NAVIGATIONAL WARNINGS
0200		●
0600	●	●
1000		●
1400		●
1800	●	●
2200		●

NAVAREA XXI

RUSSIA (Arctic Coast)

Tiksi [Q]   71°38'·00N 128°50'·00E
NOTE: Tiksi is operational 1 Jul–30 Oct.   X1, X13
TELEPHONE: +7 8125 703466   300 n miles
FAX: +7 8125 703466
E-MAIL: ibm@hydrograph.spb.su

NAVTEX [Q]

TIME UT(GMT)	WEATHER BULLETINS	NAVIGATIONAL WARNINGS
0240		●
0640	●	●
1040		●
1440		●
1840	●	●
2240		●

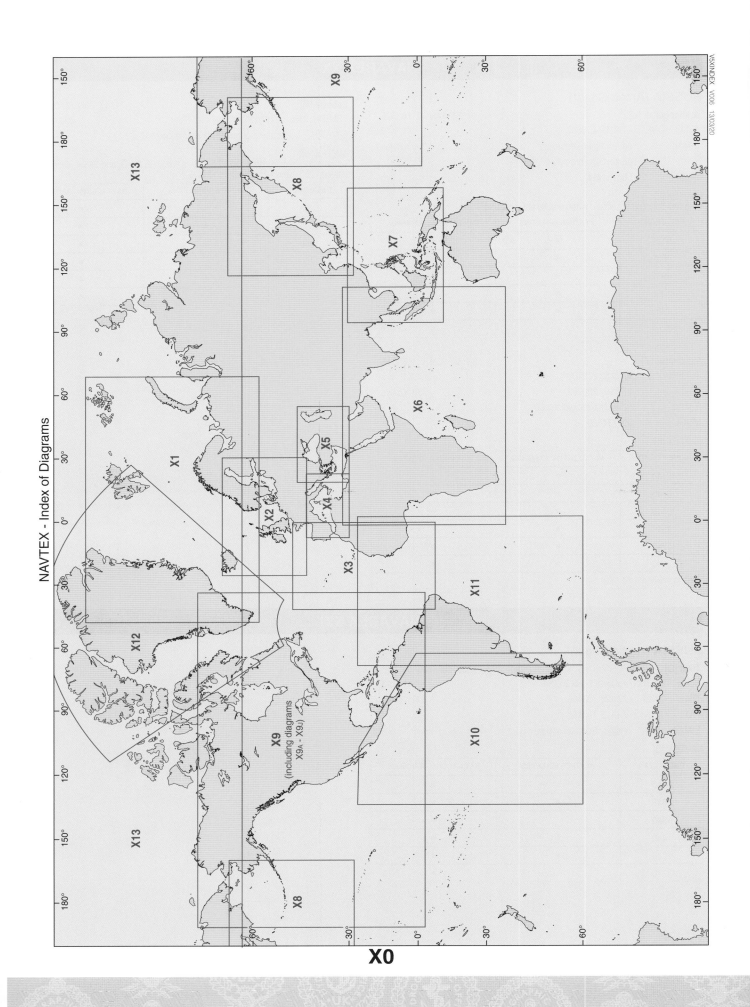

NAVTEX - Index of Diagrams

X0

X13

X9

X8

X7

X6

X5

X4

X3

X2

X1

X12

X11

X10

X9
(including diagrams
X9A - X9J)

X8

X13

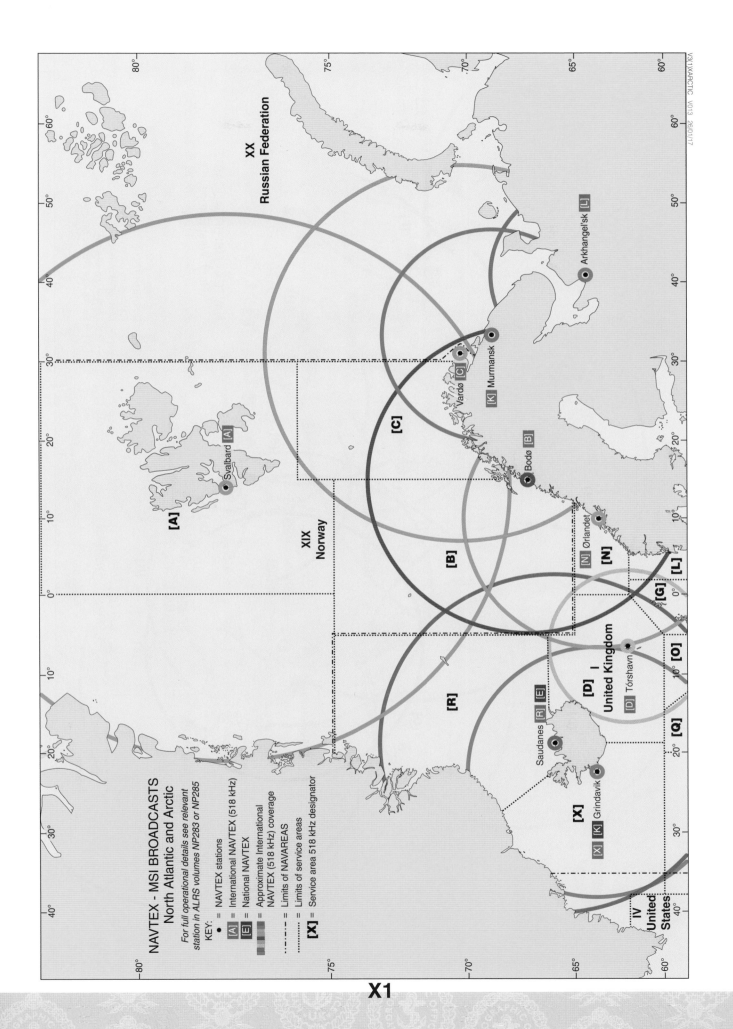

NAVTEX - MSI BROADCASTS
North Atlantic and Arctic

For full operational details see relevant station in ALRS volumes NP283 or NP285

KEY:
• = NAVTEX stations
[A] = International NAVTEX (518 kHz)
[E] = National NAVTEX
= Approximate International NAVTEX (518 kHz) coverage
-··-··- = Limits of NAVAREAS
········ = Limits of service areas
[X] = Service area 518 kHz designator

XX
Russian Federation

XIX
Norway

[A]
Svalbard [A]

[C]
Vardø [C]
[K] Murmansk

Arkhangel'sk [L]

[B]
Bodø [B]

[N] Ørlandet
[N]

[G]

[L]

[O]

[R]

United Kingdom
[D]
[D] Tórshavn

Saudanes [R] [E]

[X]
[X] [K] Grindavík

[Q]

IV
United States

X1

291

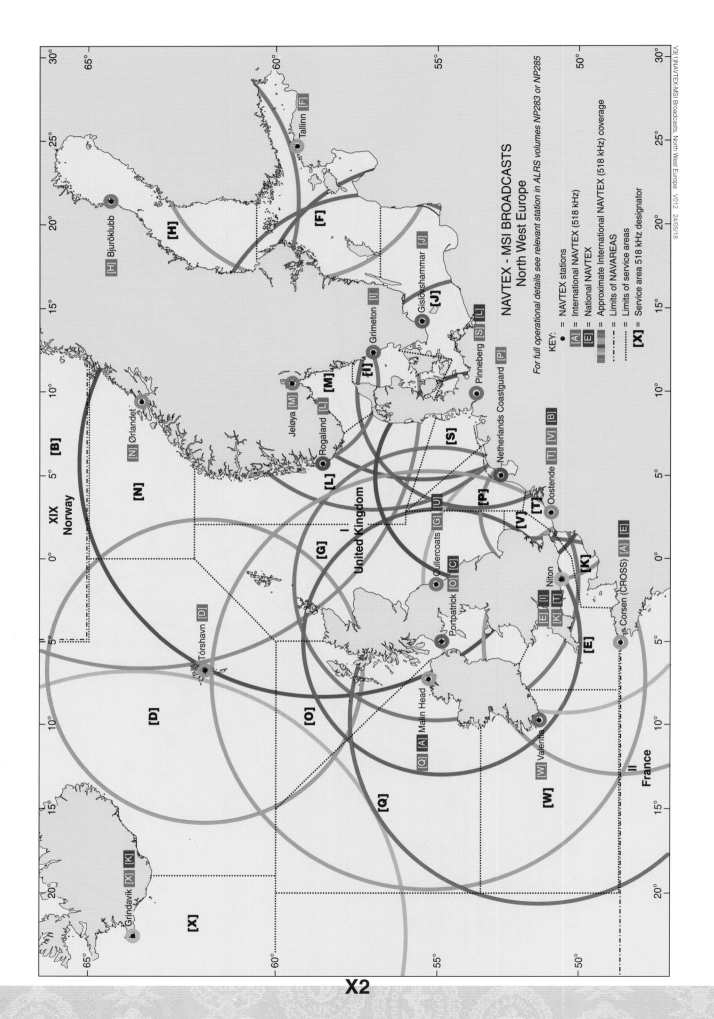

NAVTEX - MSI BROADCASTS
North West Europe

For full operational details see relevant station in ALRS volumes NP283 or NP285

KEY:
- = NAVTEX stations
- [A] = International NAVTEX (518 kHz)
- [E] = National NAVTEX
- = Approximate International NAVTEX (518 kHz) coverage
- = Limits of NAVAREAS
- = Limits of service areas
- [X] = Service area 518 kHz designator

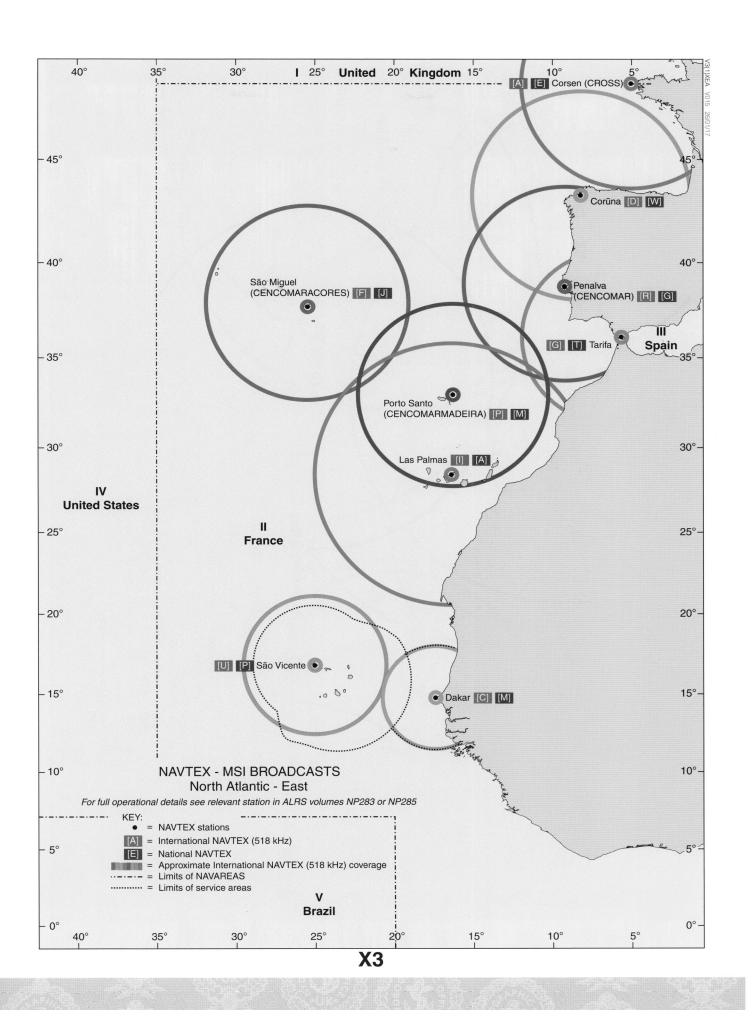

X3

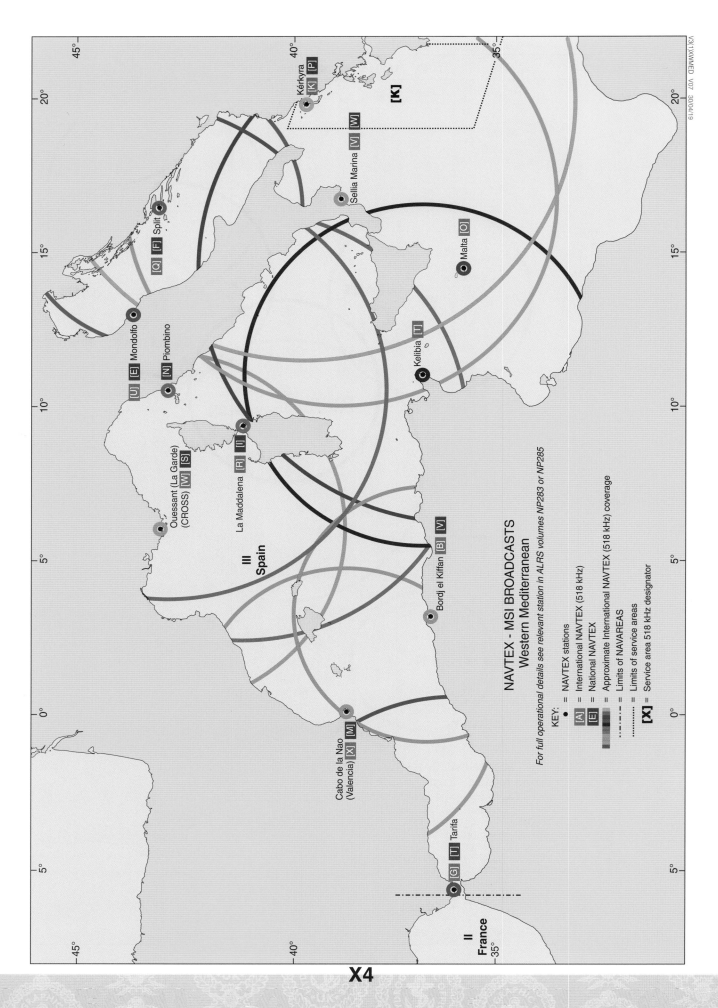

NAVTEX - MSI BROADCASTS
Western Mediterranean

For full operational details see relevant station in ALRS volumes NP283 or NP285

KEY:
● = NAVTEX stations
[A] = International NAVTEX (518 kHz)
[E] = National NAVTEX
▬ = Approximate International NAVTEX (518 kHz) coverage
▬·▬·▬ = Limits of NAVAREAS
······· = Limits of service areas
[X] = Service area 518 kHz designator

Kérkyra [K] [P]
Sellia Marina [V] [W]
[K]
Malta [O]
Split [F]
Mondolfo [E]
Piombino [N]
Ouessant (La Garde) (CROSS) [W] [S]
La Maddalena [R] [I]
Kelibia [T]
III
Spain
Bordj el Kiffan [B] [V]
Cabo de la Nao (Valencia) [X] [M]
Tarifa [T] [T]
[G] [T]
II
France

X4

V3(1)XWMED V07 30/04/19

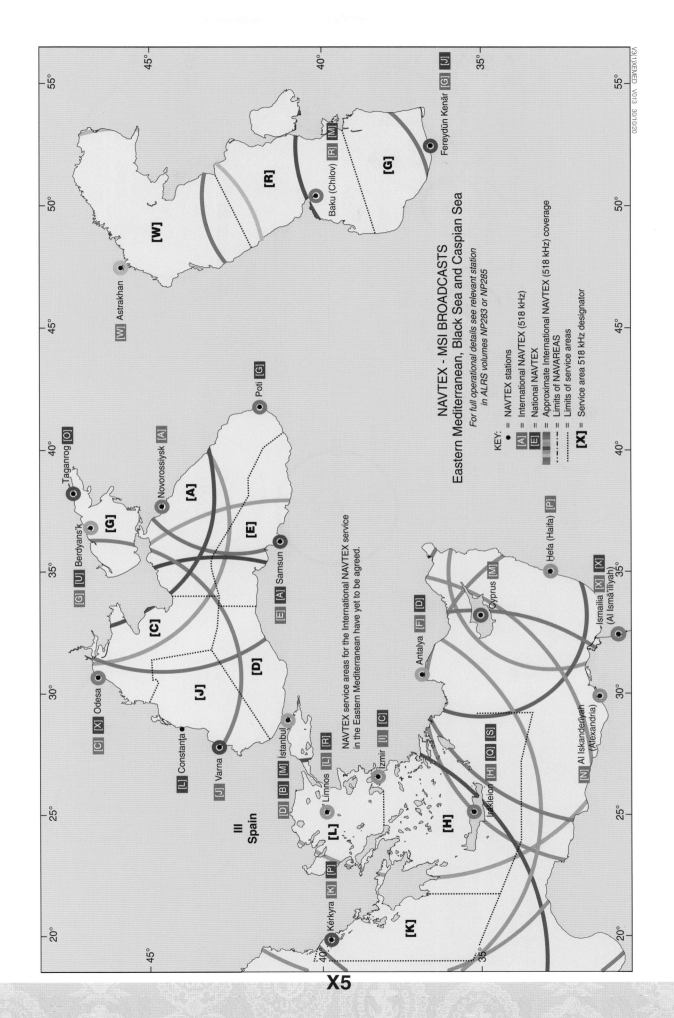

NAVTEX - MSI BROADCASTS
Eastern Mediterranean, Black Sea and Caspian Sea
For full operational details see relevant station
in ALRS volumes NP283 or NP285

KEY:
• = NAVTEX stations
[A] = International NAVTEX (518 kHz)
[E] = National NAVTEX
 = Approximate International NAVTEX (518 kHz) coverage
−·−·− = Limits of NAVAREAS
········· = Limits of service areas
[X] = Service area 518 kHz designator

NAVTEX service areas for the International NAVTEX service
in the Eastern Mediterranean have yet to be agreed.

V3(1)XEMED V013 30/10/20

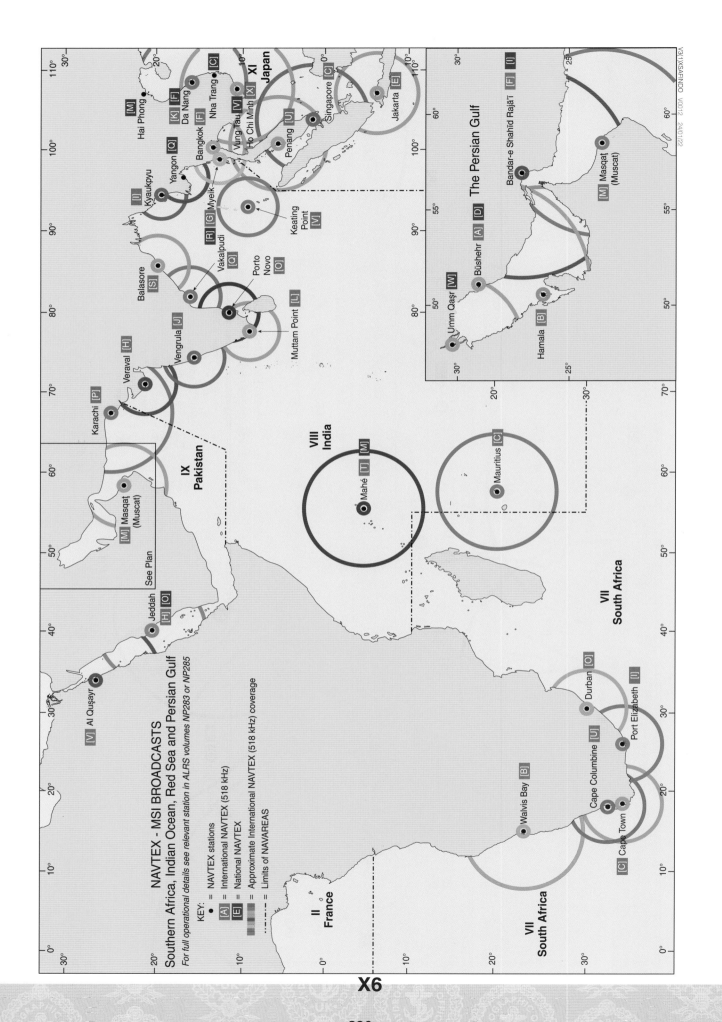

NAVTEX - MSI BROADCASTS
Southern Africa, Indian Ocean, Red Sea and Persian Gulf
For full operational details see relevant station in ALRS volumes NP283 or NP285

KEY:
● = NAVTEX stations
[A] = International NAVTEX (518 kHz)
[E] = National NAVTEX
= Approximate International NAVTEX (518 kHz) coverage
= Limits of NAVAREAS

The Persian Gulf

Umm Qaşr [W]
Büshehr [A] [D]
Bandar-e Shahīd Rajā'ī [F] [I]
Hamala [B]
Masqat (Muscat) [M]

VII
South Africa

Mauritius [C]

VIII
India
Mahé [T] [M]

IX
Pakistan
Karachi [P]
Masqat (Muscat) [M]
See Plan

Al Quşayr [V]
Jeddah [H] [O]

II
France

VII
South Africa

Walvis Bay [B]
Cape Columbine [U]
Cape Town [C]
Port Elizabeth [I]
Durban [O]

XI
Japan

Hai Phong [M]
Da Nang [K] [F]
Nha Trang [C]
Vung Tau [V]
Ho Chi Minh [X]
Bangkok [Q]
Yangon [Q]
Kyaukpyu [U]
Myeik [R] [G]
Vakalpudi [Q]
Porto Novo [O]
Muttam Point [L]
Keating Point [V]
Balasore [S]
Vengrula [J]
Veraval [H]
Masqat (Muscat) [M]
Penang [U]
Singapore [C]
Jakarta [E]

X6

296

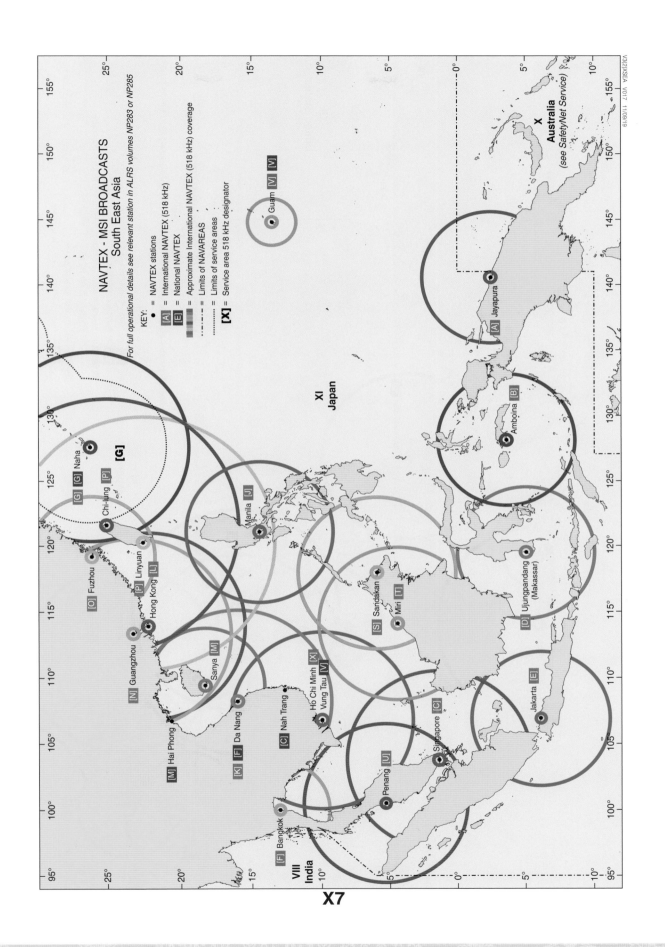

NAVTEX - MSI BROADCASTS
South East Asia

For full operational details see relevant station in ALRS volumes NP283 or NP285

KEY:
● = NAVTEX stations
[A] = International NAVTEX (518 kHz)
[E] = National NAVTEX
▬ = Approximate International NAVTEX (518 kHz) coverage
········· = Limits of NAVAREAS
▬▬ = Limits of service areas
—·—·— = Service area 518 kHz designator
[X] = Service area 518 kHz designator

XI
Japan

[G] [G] Naha
[G]
Chi-lung [P]
[P]
[O] Fuzhou
Linyuan [P]
Hong Kong [L]
[N] Guangzhou
Sanya [M]
Manila [J]
[M] Hai Phong
[K] [F] Da Nang
[C] Nah Trang
Hô Chi Minh [X]
Vung Tau [V]
[S] Sandakan
Miri [U]
[F] Bangkok
VIII
India
Penang [U]
Singapore [C]
[D] Ujungpandang
(Makassar)
Jakarta [E]

Guam [V] [V]

X
Australia
(see SafetyNet Service)

[A] Jayapura

Ambonia [B]
[B]

X7

297

V3(2)XSEA V017 11/09/19

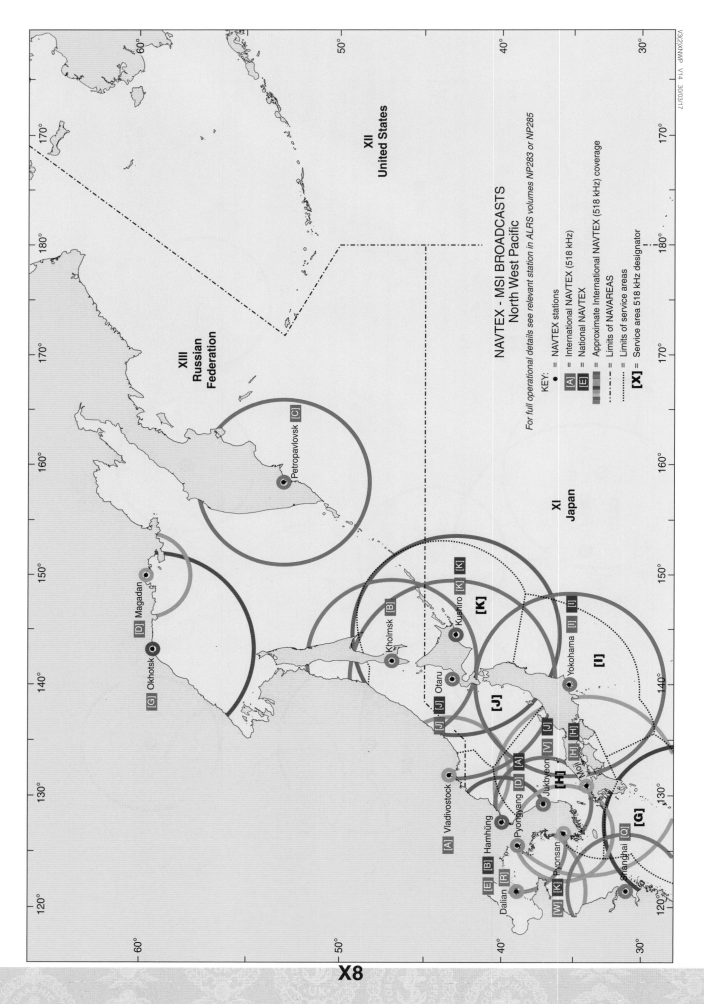

NAVTEX - MSI BROADCASTS
North West Pacific

For full operational details see relevant station in ALRS volumes NP283 or NP285

KEY:
● = NAVTEX stations
[A] = International NAVTEX (518 kHz)
[E] = National NAVTEX
= Approximate International NAVTEX (518 kHz) coverage
= Limits of NAVAREAS
= Limits of service areas
[X] = Service area 518 kHz designator

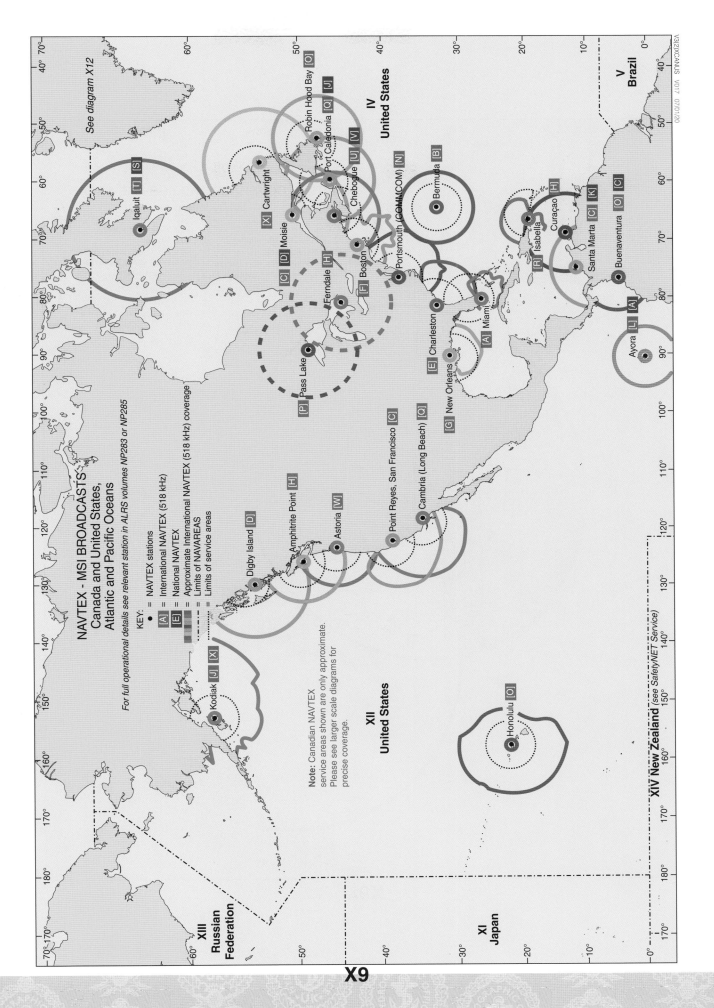

NAVTEX - MSI BROADCASTS
Canada and United States,
Atlantic and Pacific Oceans

For full operational details see relevant station in ALRS volumes NP283 or NP285

KEY:
- ● = NAVTEX stations
- [A] = International NAVTEX (518 kHz)
- [E] = National NAVTEX
- = Approximate International NAVTEX (518 kHz) coverage
- = Limits of NAVAREAS
- = Limits of service areas

Note: Canadian NAVTEX service areas shown are only approximate. Please see larger scale diagrams for precise coverage.

See diagram X12

Iqaluit [T] [S]

Robin Hood Bay [O]

Port Caledonia [Q] [J]

Chebogue [U] [V]

Cartwright [X]

Moisie [C] [D]

Ferndale [H]

Boston [F]

Portsmouth (COMMCOM) [N]

Pass Lake [P]

Bermuda [B]

Charleston [E]

Miami [A]

New Orleans [G]

Curaçao [C]

Isabella [R]

Santa Marta [C]

Buenaventura [O] [C]

Ayora [L] [A]

IV United States

V Brazil

Amphitrite Point [H]

Digby Island [D]

Astoria [W]

Point Reyes, San Francisco [C]

Cambria (Long Beach) [Q]

Kodiak [J] [X]

XII United States

Honolulu [O]

XIII Russian Federation

XI Japan

XIV New Zealand (*see SafetyNET Service*)

V3(2)XCANUS V017 07/01/20

X9

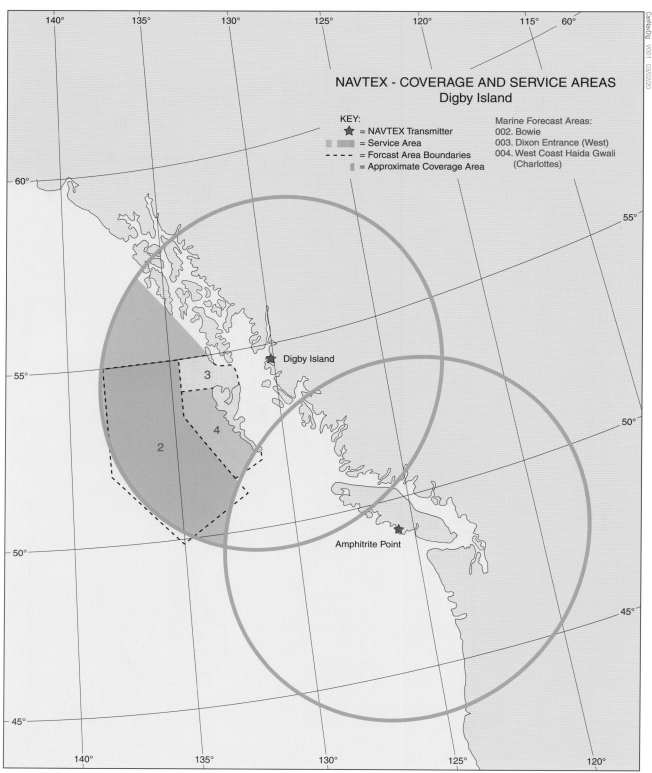

NAVTEX - COVERAGE AND SERVICE AREAS
Digby Island

KEY:
★ = NAVTEX Transmitter
▮▮ = Service Area
- - - = Forcast Area Boundaries
▮ = Approximate Coverage Area

Marine Forecast Areas:
002. Bowie
003. Dixon Entrance (West)
004. West Coast Haida Gwali
     (Charlottes)

Digby Island

Amphitrite Point

X9A

300

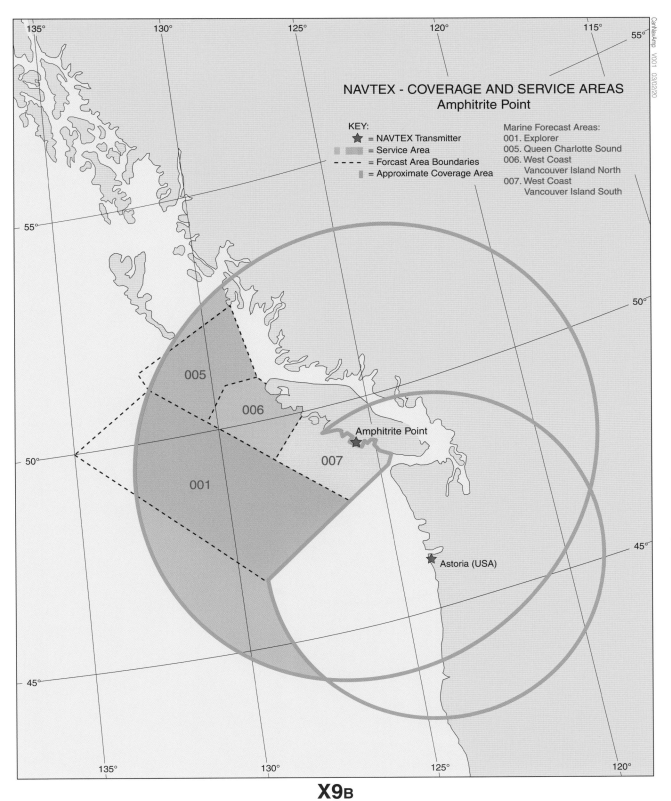

NAVTEX - COVERAGE AND SERVICE AREAS
Amphitrite Point

KEY:
★ = NAVTEX Transmitter
▮ ▮▮ = Service Area
- - - = Forcast Area Boundaries
▮ = Approximate Coverage Area

Marine Forecast Areas:
001. Explorer
005. Queen Charlotte Sound
006. West Coast
    Vancouver Island North
007. West Coast
    Vancouver Island South

005

006

Amphitrite Point

007

001

Astoria (USA)

CanNavAmp V001 03/02/20

X9ʙ

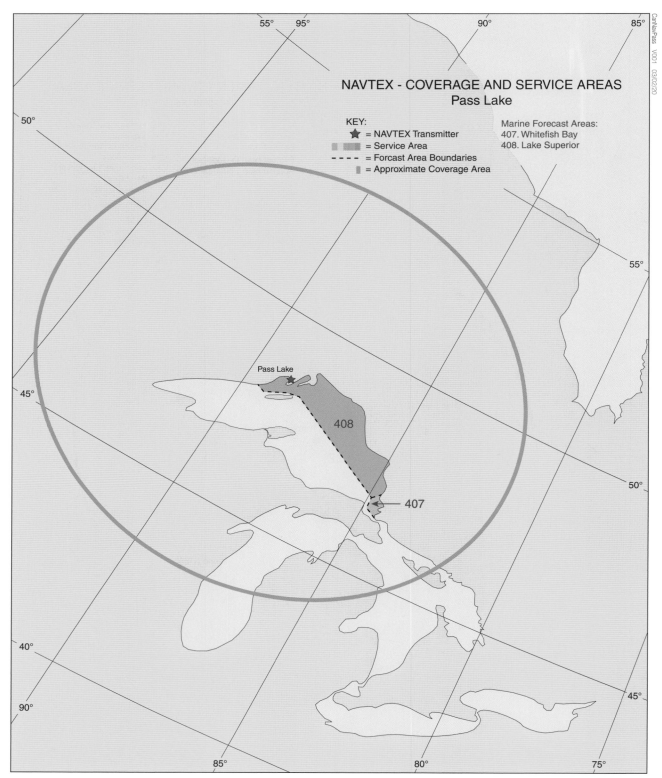

NAVTEX - COVERAGE AND SERVICE AREAS
Pass Lake

KEY:
★ = NAVTEX Transmitter
▨ ▨▨ = Service Area
- - - - = Forcast Area Boundaries
▌ = Approximate Coverage Area

Marine Forecast Areas:
407. Whitefish Bay
408. Lake Superior

Pass Lake

408

407

X9c

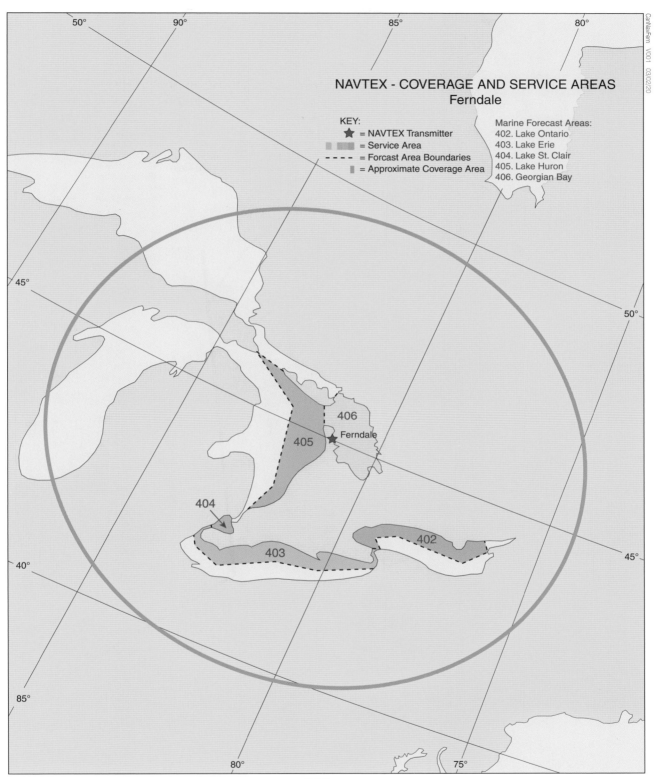

NAVTEX - COVERAGE AND SERVICE AREAS
Ferndale

KEY:
★ = NAVTEX Transmitter
▨ ▨▨▨ = Service Area
- - - - = Forcast Area Boundaries
▌ = Approximate Coverage Area

Marine Forecast Areas:
402. Lake Ontario
403. Lake Erie
404. Lake St. Clair
405. Lake Huron
406. Georgian Bay

406

Ferndale

405

404

403

402

CanNavFern V001 03/02/20

X9ᴅ

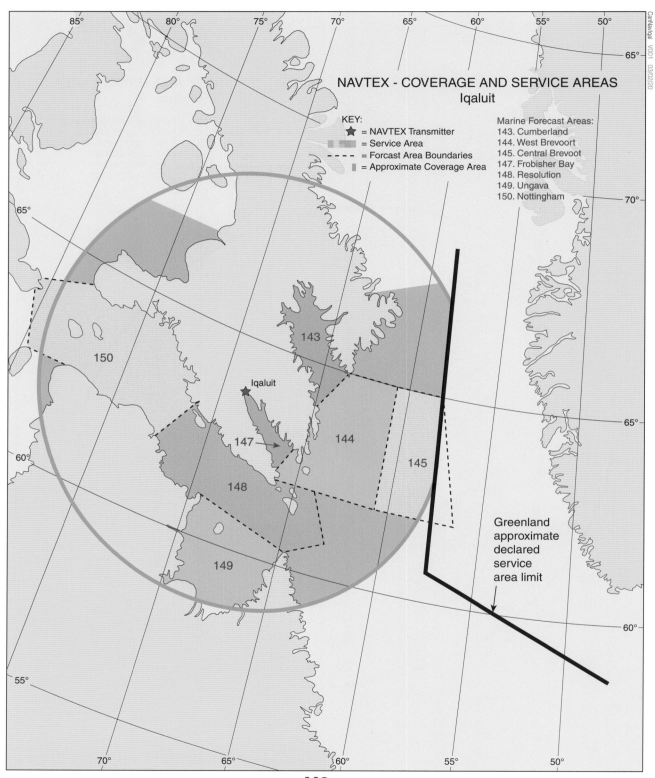

NAVTEX - COVERAGE AND SERVICE AREAS
Iqaluit

KEY:
★ = NAVTEX Transmitter
= Service Area
---- = Forcast Area Boundaries
= Approximate Coverage Area

Marine Forecast Areas:
143. Cumberland
144. West Brevoort
145. Central Brevoot
147. Frobisher Bay
148. Resolution
149. Ungava
150. Nottingham

Iqaluit

143

150

147

144

145

148

149

Greenland
approximate
declared
service
area limit

X9E

CanNavIqal V001   03/02/20

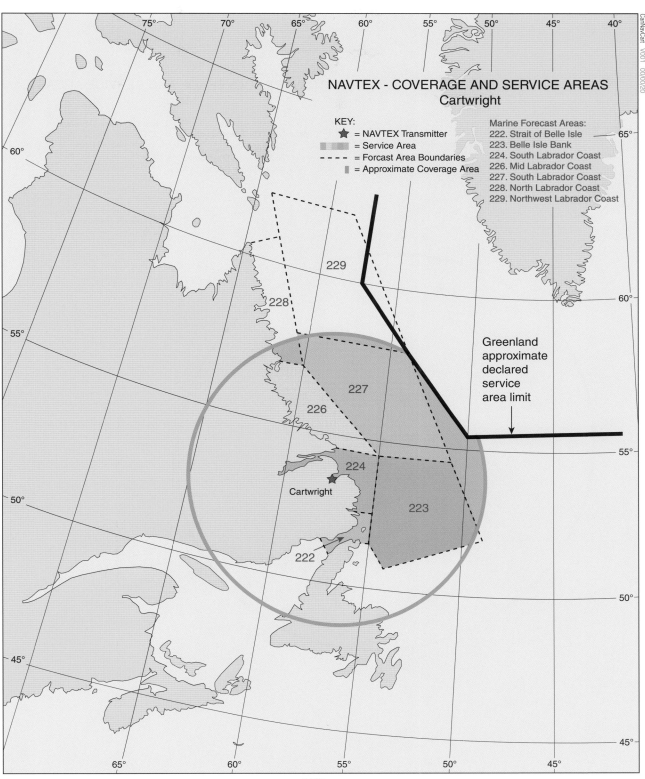

NAVTEX - COVERAGE AND SERVICE AREAS
Cartwright

KEY:
★ = NAVTEX Transmitter
▨ = Service Area
- - - = Forcast Area Boundaries
▮ = Approximate Coverage Area

Marine Forecast Areas:
222. Strait of Belle Isle
223. Belle Isle Bank
224. South Labrador Coast
226. Mid Labrador Coast
227. South Labrador Coast
228. North Labrador Coast
229. Northwest Labrador Coast

Greenland
approximate
declared
service
area limit

Cartwright

X9F

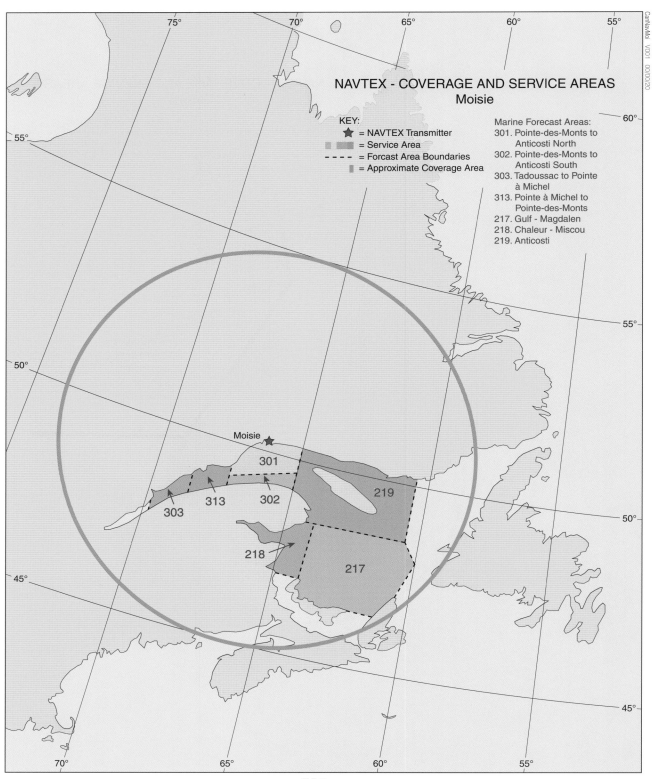

NAVTEX - COVERAGE AND SERVICE AREAS
Moisie

KEY:
★ = NAVTEX Transmitter
▦ = Service Area
- - - = Forcast Area Boundaries
▌ = Approximate Coverage Area

Marine Forecast Areas:
301. Pointe-des-Monts to
     Anticosti North
302. Pointe-des-Monts to
     Anticosti South
303. Tadoussac to Pointe
     à Michel
313. Pointe à Michel to
     Pointe-des-Monts
217. Gulf - Magdalen
218. Chaleur - Miscou
219. Anticosti

Moisie

301
313   302
303
218
219
217

CanNavMoi V001 00/00/20

X9G

306

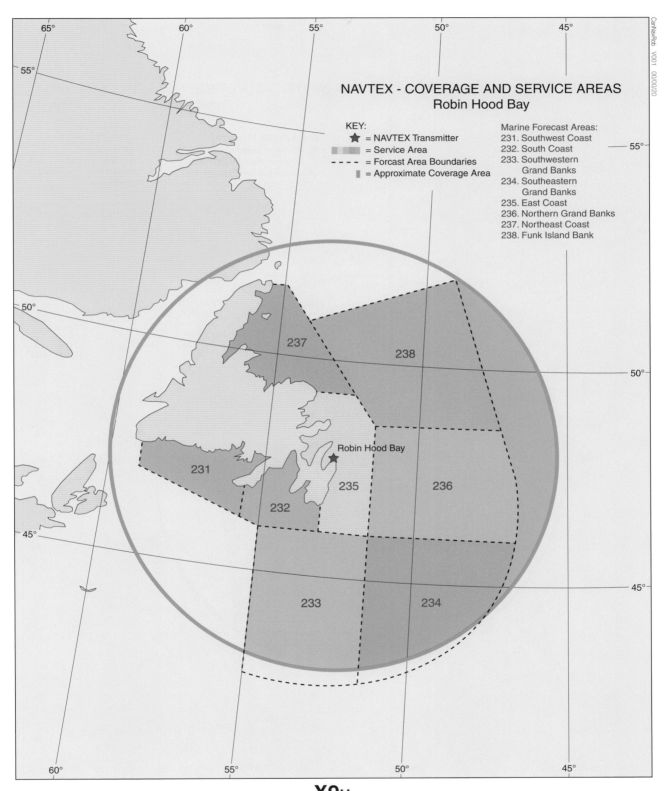

NAVTEX - COVERAGE AND SERVICE AREAS
Robin Hood Bay

KEY:
★ = NAVTEX Transmitter
▓ = Service Area
- - - = Forcast Area Boundaries
▌ = Approximate Coverage Area

Marine Forecast Areas:
231. Southwest Coast
232. South Coast
233. Southwestern
     Grand Banks
234. Southeastern
     Grand Banks
235. East Coast
236. Northern Grand Banks
237. Northeast Coast
238. Funk Island Bank

Robin Hood Bay

237
238
231
235
236
232
233
234

CanNavRob V001 00/00/20

X9н

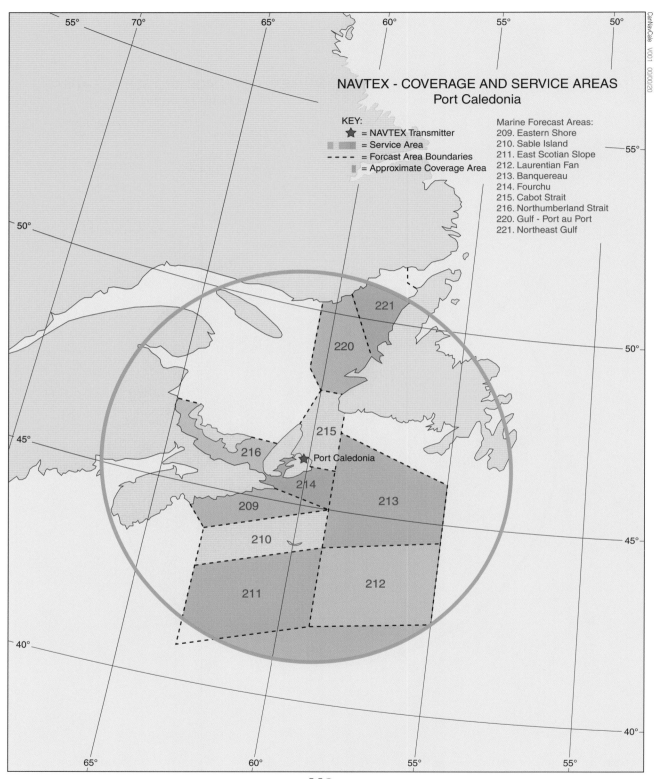

NAVTEX - COVERAGE AND SERVICE AREAS
Port Caledonia

KEY:
★ = NAVTEX Transmitter
▨ = Service Area
- - - - = Forcast Area Boundaries
▨ = Approximate Coverage Area

Marine Forecast Areas:
209. Eastern Shore
210. Sable Island
211. East Scotian Slope
212. Laurentian Fan
213. Banquereau
214. Fourchu
215. Cabot Strait
216. Northumberland Strait
220. Gulf - Port au Port
221. Northeast Gulf

X9ı

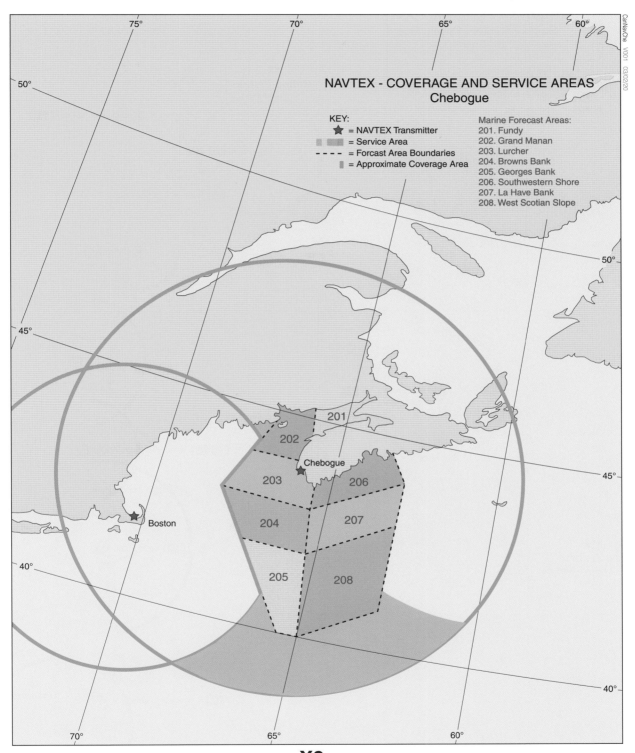

NAVTEX - COVERAGE AND SERVICE AREAS
Chebogue

KEY:
★ = NAVTEX Transmitter
▮ = Service Area
- - - = Forcast Area Boundaries
▮ = Approximate Coverage Area

Marine Forecast Areas:
201. Fundy
202. Grand Manan
203. Lurcher
204. Browns Bank
205. Georges Bank
206. Southwestern Shore
207. La Have Bank
208. West Scotian Slope

X9J

CarNavChe V001 03/02/20

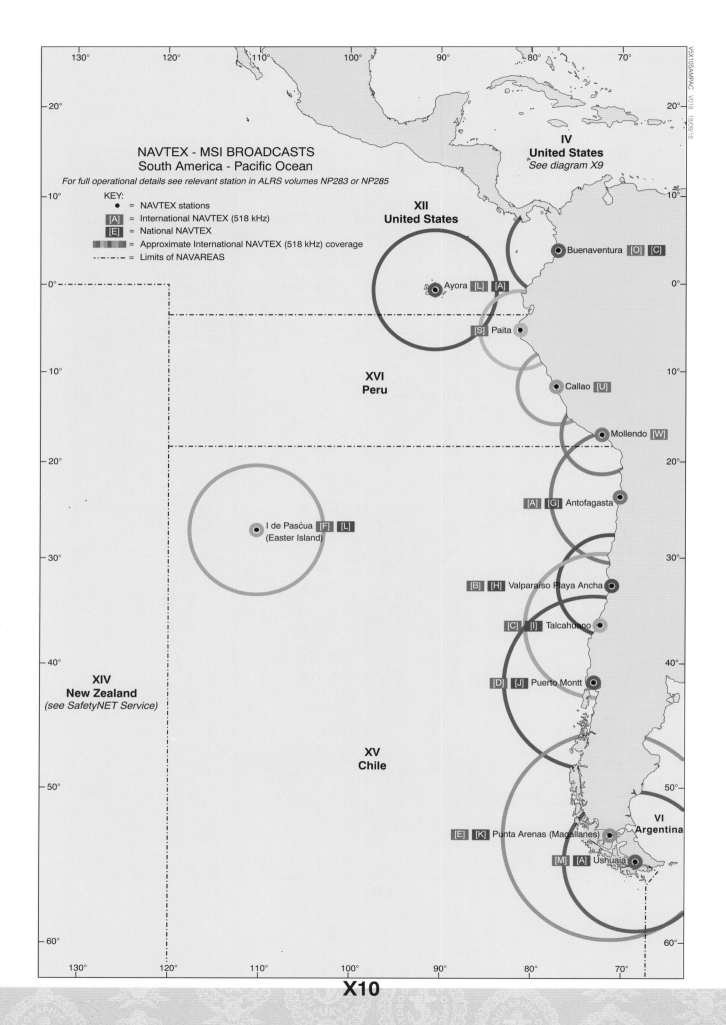

NAVTEX - MSI BROADCASTS
South America - Pacific Ocean

For full operational details see relevant station in ALRS volumes NP283 or NP285

KEY:
● = NAVTEX stations
[A] = International NAVTEX (518 kHz)
[E] = National NAVTEX
▓▓▓▓ = Approximate International NAVTEX (518 kHz) coverage
–·–·– = Limits of NAVAREAS

IV
United States
See diagram X9

XII
United States

Buenaventura [O] [C]

Ayora [L] [A]

[S] Paita

XVI
Peru

Callao [U]

Mollendo [W]

[A] [G] Antofagasta

I de Pascua [F] [L]
(Easter Island)

[B] [H] Valparaíso Playa Ancha

[C] [I] Talcahuano

XIV
New Zealand
(see SafetyNET Service)

[D] [J] Puerto Montt

XV
Chile

VI
Argentina

[E] [K] Punta Arenas (Magallanes)

[M] [A] Ushuaia

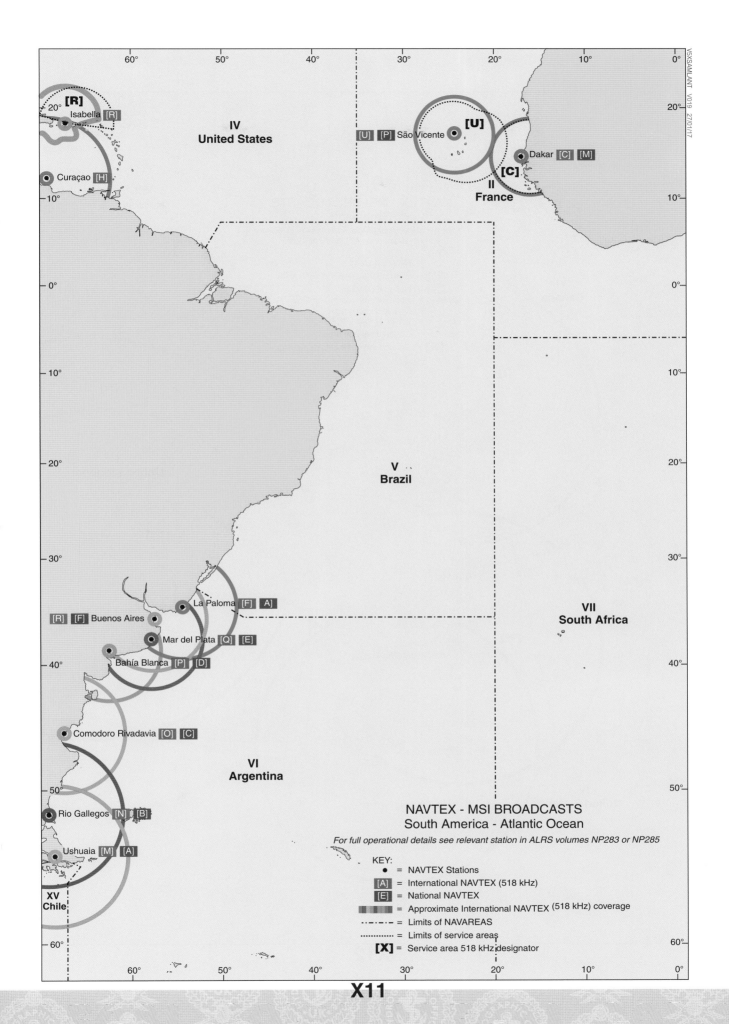

NAVTEX - MSI BROADCASTS
South America - Atlantic Ocean

For full operational details see relevant station in ALRS volumes NP283 or NP285

KEY:
● = NAVTEX Stations
[A] = International NAVTEX (518 kHz)
[E] = National NAVTEX
▦ = Approximate International NAVTEX (518 kHz) coverage
—·—·— = Limits of NAVAREAS
·········· = Limits of service areas
[X] = Service area 518 kHz designator

X11

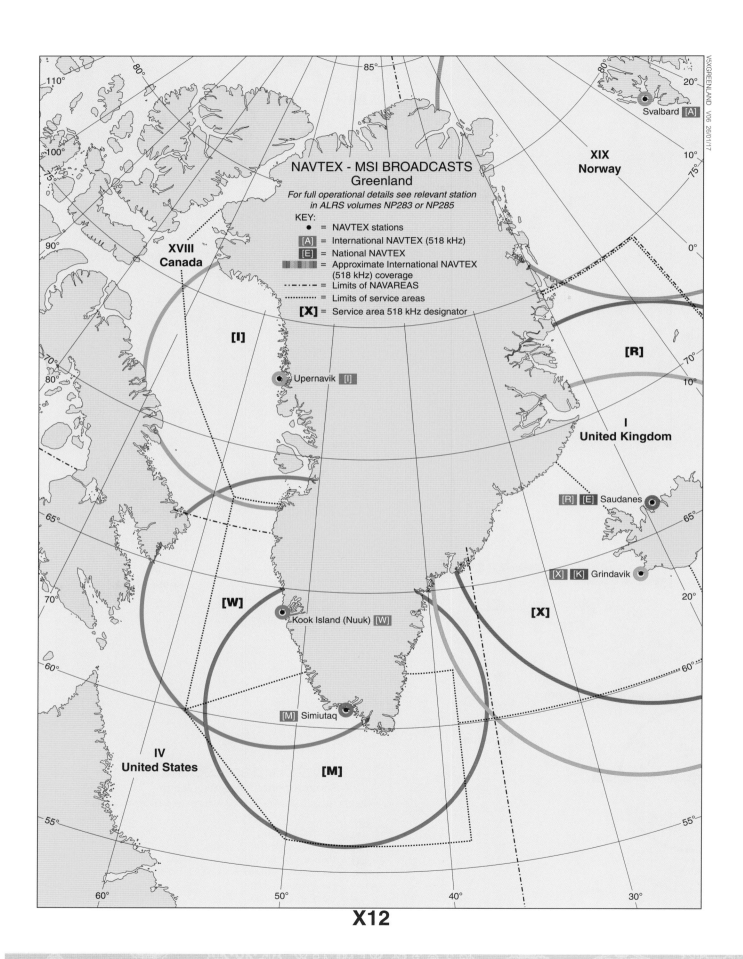

NAVTEX - MSI BROADCASTS
Greenland
*For full operational details see relevant station
in ALRS volumes NP283 or NP285*

KEY:
● = NAVTEX stations
[A] = International NAVTEX (518 kHz)
[E] = National NAVTEX
▮▮▮ = Approximate International NAVTEX
(518 kHz) coverage
─·─· = Limits of NAVAREAS
········ = Limits of service areas
[X] = Service area 518 kHz designator

Svalbard [A]

XIX
Norway

XVIII
Canada

[I]

[R]

Upernavik [I]

I
United Kingdom

[R] [E] Saudanes

[X] [K] Grindavik

[W]

[X]

Kook Island (Nuuk) [W]

IV
United States

[M] Simiutaq

[M]

X12

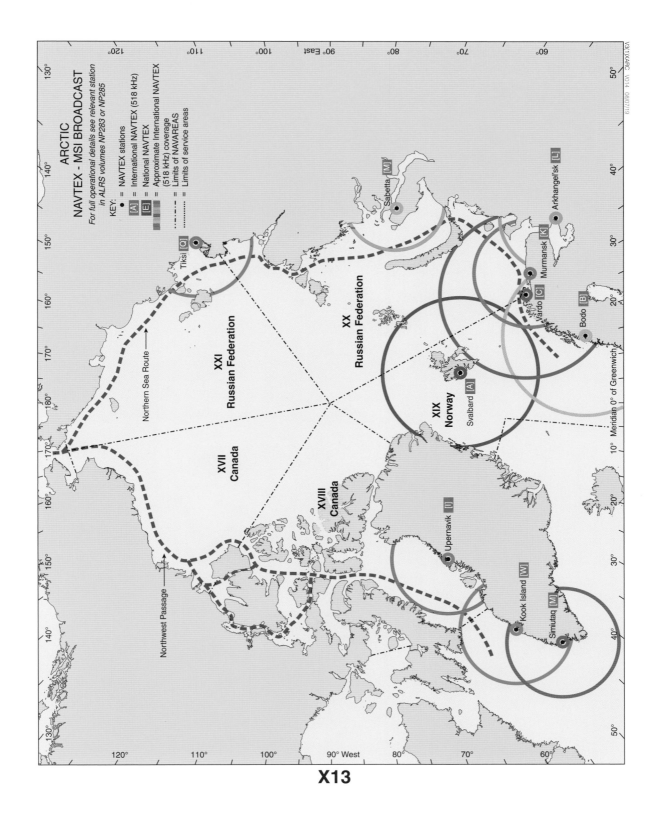

ARCTIC
NAVTEX - MSI BROADCAST
For full operational details see relevant station
in ALRS volumes NP283 or NP285
KEY: ● = NAVTEX stations
[A] = International NAVTEX (518 kHz)
[E] = National NAVTEX
= Approximate International NAVTEX
(518 kHz) coverage
= Limits of NAVAREAS
= Limits of service areas

Sabetta [M]

Arkhangel'sk [L]

Murmansk [K]

Vardo [C]

Bodo [B]

Tiksi [Q]

XXI
Russian Federation

XX
Russian Federation

Northern Sea Route

XIX
Norway

Svalbard [A]

XVII
Canada

XVIII
Canada

Northwest Passage

Upernavik [I]

Kook Island [W]

Simiutaq [M]

Meridian 0° of Greenwich

X13

V3(1)XARC V014 08/07/19

130° 120° 110° 100° 90° East 80° 70° 60° 50°

140°

150°

160°

170°

180°

170°

160°

150°

140°

130°

120° 110° 100° 90° West 80° 70° 60° 50°

50°

40°

30°

20°

10°

20°

30°

40°

50°

NOTES

DISTRESS, SEARCH AND RESCUE

Annex 1 refers to UK Distress and Rescue at Sea - Vessels and Aircraft.

INTERNATIONAL AERONAUTICAL AND MARITIME SEARCH AND RESCUE (IAMSAR) MANUAL

ICAO and IMO have jointly developed a Manual to foster co-operation between themselves, between neighbouring States, and between aeronautical and maritime authorities on SAR. The primary purpose of the 3 volumes of the International Aeronautical and Maritime Search and Rescue (IAMSAR) Manual is to assist States in meeting their own search and rescue (SAR) needs, and the obligations they accepted under the Convention on International Civil Aviation, the International Convention on Maritime Search and Rescue and the International Convention for the Safety of Life at Sea (SOLAS). These 3 volumes provide guidelines for a common aviation and maritime approach to organising and providing SAR services. States are encouraged to develop and improve their SAR services, co-operate with neighbouring States and to consider their SAR services to be part of a global system.

Each volume of the IAMSAR Manual is written with specific SAR system duties in mind, and can be used as a standalone document or in conjunction with the other 2 Manuals, as a means to attain a full view of the SAR system.

This Manual will assist those responsible for establishing, managing, and supporting SAR services to understand the:

- Functions and importance of SAR services;
- Relationships between global, regional, and national aspects of SAR;
- Components and support infrastructure essential for SAR;
- Training needed to coordinate, conduct, and support SAR operations;
- Communications functions and requirements for SAR; and
- Basic principles of managing and improving SAR services to ensure success.

The Manual consists of:

Volume I: ORGANIZATION AND MANAGEMENT.
The Organization and Management volume discusses the global SAR system concept, establishment and improvement of national and regional SAR systems and co-operation with neighbouring States to provide effective and economical SAR services;

Volume II: MISSION CO-ORDINATION.
The Mission Coordination volume assists personnel who plan and coordinate SAR operations and exercises; and

Volume III: MOBILE FACILITIES.
The carriage of this volume is intended to help with performance of a search, rescue or on-scene coordinator function and with aspects of SAR that pertain to emergencies. The current 2016 edition contains "Action Cards" which provide quick access to important information.

SOLAS, Chapter V, Safety of Navigation, Regulation 21:-
Regulation 21
International Code of Signals and IAMSAR Manual

1   All ships which, in accordance with the present Convention, are required to carry a radio installation shall carry the International Code of Signals as may be amended by the Organization. The code shall also be carried by any other ship which, in the opinion of the Administration, has a need to use it.

2   All ships shall carry an up to date copy of Volume III of the International Aeronautical and Maritime Search and Rescue (IAMSAR) Manual.

The Manual is published every three years and can be purchased direct from IMO and ICAO, or from selected book sellers around the world as provided under PUBLICATIONS/Distributors on IMO web page: www.imo.org. It is available in the English, French, Russian and Spanish languages.

International Maritime Organization
4 Albert Embankment
London
SE1 7SR
United Kingdom

International Civil Aviation Organization
999 University Street
Montréal
Québec
Canada H3C 5H7

The following extracts are taken from the various Volumes of the IAMSAR Manual:

The Search and Rescue System
System Organisation

Global SAR System Organisation

The International Civil Aviation Organisation (ICAO) and the International Maritime Organisation (IMO) coordinate, on a global basis, member States' efforts to provide search and rescue (SAR) services. Briefly, the goal of ICAO and IMO is to provide an effective world-wide system, so that wherever people sail or fly, SAR services will be available if needed. The overall approach a State takes in establishing, providing, and improving SAR services is affected by the fact that these efforts are an integral part of a global SAR system.

A basic, practical, and humanitarian effect of having a global SAR system is that it eliminates the need for each State to provide SAR services for its own citizens wherever they travel world-wide. Instead, the globe is divided into Search and Rescue Regions (SRRs), each with a Rescue Coordination Centre (RCC) and associated SAR services, which assist anyone in distress within the SRR without regard to nationality or circumstances.

National and Regional SAR System Organisation

States, by being party to the Safety of Life at Sea (SOLAS) Convention, the International Convention on Maritime Search and Rescue, and the Convention on International Civil Aviation, have accepted the obligation to provide aeronautical and maritime SAR Coordination and services for their territories, territorial seas and, where appropriate, the high seas. SAR services are to be available on a 24 hour basis.

To carry out these responsibilities, a State either should establish a national SAR organisation, or join one or more other States to form a regional SAR organisation. In some areas an effective and practical way to achieve this goal is to develop a regional system associated with a major ocean area and continent.

ICAO Regional Air Navigation Plans (RANPS) depict aeronautical SRRs for most of the world. Many States are given an area of responsibility which is usually composed of one aeronautical SRR. Maritime SRRs are published in the IMO SAR Plan, and are similar, but not necessarily identical, to aeronautical SRRs. The purpose of having SRRs is to clearly define who has primary responsibility for coordinating responses to distress situations in every area of the world, which is especially important for automatic routeing of distress alerts to responsible RCCs.

System Components

SAR as a system

The SAR system, like any other system, has individual components that must work together to provide the overall service. Development of a SAR system typically involves establishment of one or more SRRs, along with capabilities to receive alerts and to coordinate and provide SAR services within each SRR. Each SRR is associated with an RCC. For aeronautical purposes, SRR, often coincide with Flight Information Regions (FIRs). The goal of ICAO and IMO conventions relating to SAR is to establish a global SAR system. Operationally, the global SAR system relies upon States to establish their national SAR systems and then integrate provision of their services with other States for world-wide coverage.

Every SRR has unique transportation, climate, topography and physical characteristics. These factors create a different set of problems for SAR operations in each SRR. Such factors influence the choice and composition of the services, facilities, equipment and staffing required by each SAR service. The primary system components are:

- Communications throughout the SRR and with external SAR services;
- An RCC for the coordination of SAR services;
- If necessary, one or more RSCs to support an RCC within its SRR;
- SAR facilities, including SRUs with specialised equipment and trained personnel, as well as other resources which can be used to conduct SAR operations;
- On-Scene Coordinator (OSC) assigned, as necessary, for coordinating the on-scene activities of all participating facilities; and
- Support facilities that provide services in support of SAR operations.

Communications

Good communications are essential. They should promptly provide the RCC with alerting information permitting the RCC to dispatch SRUs and other resources to search areas without delay and to maintain two-way contact with the persons in distress. The SAR organisation is alerted to an actual of potential distress situation directly or by means of alerting posts. Alerting posts are facilities that relay distress alerts to RCCs or RSCs. The information collected by alerting posts and other reporting sources should be forwarded immediately to the RCC or RSC, which decides on the type of response. The RCC or RSC may have the communications capability itself or may rely upon other facilities to forward alerts and to carry out SAR response communications.

The main functions of a SAR communications system are:
- Receipt of alerts from equipment used by persons in distress;
- Exchange of information with persons in distress, and among the SAR Mission Coordinator (SMC), OSC and SAR facilities for coordination of responses to SAR incidents; and
- Direction Finding (DF) and homing which allow SRUs to be dispatched to the vicinity of the distress and to home on signals from equipment used by survivors.

Alerting Posts

Alerting posts include any facility involved in receiving information about an apparent distress situation and relaying it to an RCC or RSC. They include facilities such as Air Traffic Services (ATS) units or Coast Radio Stations (CRSs). Communications may or may not be the primary purpose for these alerting post, but the post must be able to forward the distress information to the RCC.

The ability of an RCC to act quickly and effectively when an emergency occurs depends largely on the information forwarded to it by alerting posts, it is essential that communications between an alerting post and the RCC, RSC or local SRU are by fast and reliable means. Such channels should be checked regularly and could be established by voice or data communications via direct or public telephone, radiotelephone, radiotelegraph or other means. Ideally, data alerts should be automatically routed to the responsible RCC or RSC over communication links which help preserve the distress priority.

Locating

Locating capabilities enable the responding SAR facilities to minimise the search time and to get to the actual position of distress for rescue. There are basic international requirements for the types of equipment that must be carried by ships and aircraft.

(a) Most civil aircraft operating over ocean areas and remote land areas, and many other aircraft, are required to carry an Emergency Locator Transmitter (ELT). Designated SAR aircraft must be able to home onto ELT 121·5 MHz signals from ELTs used for locating a distress scene and survivors.

(b) Ships and some other craft are required to carry Emergency Position-Indicating Radio Beacons (EPIRBs). The purpose of the EPIRB signals is to indicate that a distress exists and to facilitate the location of survivors in SAR operations. Merchant vessels and survival craft have additional requirements.

Having a very precise search object position is useful but does not eliminate the need for SRU homing capabilities. This is especially true if the SRU does not have precise navigation equipment or if operations take place at night or in other low visibility conditions.

Due to the importance of position information for SAR operations, various suitable means should be provided within an SRR to determine positions. These may include DF stations, surveillance systems for aircraft and vessel traffic service systems. If there is any way to confirm the position reported in an alert, it would be prudent to do so, especially with initial EPIRB and ELT alerts via Cospas-Sarsat which provide both a true and an image position.

SAR and the 1949 Geneva Conventions and their Additional Protocols

In times of armed conflict, SAR services will normally continue to be provided in accordance with the Second Geneva Convention of 1949 (Geneva Convention for the Amelioration of the Condition of Wounded, Sick and Shipwrecked Members of Armed Forces at Sea, of 12 August 1949) and Additional Protocol 1 to the Conventions.

(a) The SAR services recognised by their administrations are afforded protection for their humanitarian missions so far as operational requirements permit. Such protection applies to coastal rescue craft, their personnel and fixed coastal SAR installations. SAR personnel should be informed about their Administration's status regarding, and views on, implementation of the Second Geneva Convention and its Additional Protocol 1.

(b) Chapter XIV of the International Code of Signals illustrates the different means of identification which shall be used to provide effective protection for rescue craft.

SAR Coordination

The SAR system has three levels of coordination associated with **SAR Coordinators (SCs)**, **SAR Mission Coordinators (SMCs)**, and **On-Scene Coordinators (OSCs)**.

SAR Coordinators. SCs have the overall responsibility for establishing, staffing, equipping, and managing the SAR system, including providing appropriate legal and funding support, establishing RCCs and Rescue Sub-Centres (RSCs), providing or arranging for SAR facilities, coordinating SAR training, and developing SAR policies. SCs are the top level SAR managers; each State normally will have one or more persons or agencies for whom this designation may be appropriate. SCs are not normally involved in the conduct of SAR operations.

SAR Mission Coordinator. Each SAR operation is carried out under the guidance of an SMC. This function exists only for the duration of a specific SAR incident and is normally performed by the RCC chief or a designee. For complex cases or those of long duration, the SMC usually has an assisting team.

- The SMC is in charge of a SAR operation until a rescue has been effected or until it has become apparent that further efforts would be of no avail, or until responsibility is accepted by another RCC. The SMC should be able to use readily available facilities and to request additional ones during the operation. The SMC plans the search and coordinates the transit of SAR facilities to the scene.

- The SMC should be well trained in all SAR processes and be thoroughly familiar with the applicable SAR plans. The SMC must competently gather information about distress situations, develop accurate and workable action plans, and dispatch and coordinate the resources which will carry out SAR missions. The plans of operation maintained by the RCC provide information to assist in these efforts. Guidelines for SMC duties include:

  ○ Obtain and evaluate all data on the emergency;
  ○ Ascertain the type of emergency equipment carried by the missing or distressed craft; remain informed of prevailing environmental conditions;
  ○ If necessary, ascertain movements and location of vessels and alert shipping in likely search areas for rescue, lookout and/or radio watch on appropriate frequencies to facilitate communications with SAR facilities;
  ○ Plot the area to be searched and decide on the methods and facilities to be used;
  ○ Develop the search action plan (and rescue action plan as appropriate), i.e., allocate search areas,
  ○ Designate the OSC, dispatch SAR facilities and designate on-scene communications frequencies;

- ○ Inform the RCC chief of the search action plan;
- ○ Coordinate the operation with adjacent RCCs when appropriate; arrange briefing and debriefing of SAR personnel; evaluate all reports from any source and modify the search action plan as necessary;
- ○ Arrange for the fuelling of aircraft and, for prolonged search, make arrangements for the accommodation of SAR personnel;
- ○ Arrange for delivery of supplies to sustain survivors;
- ○ Maintain in chronological order an accurate and up to date record with a plot, where necessary, of all proceedings;
- ○ Issue progress reports;
- ○ Recommend to the RCC chief the abandoning or suspending of the search; release SAR facilities when assistance is no longer required; notify accident investigation authorities;
- ○ If applicable, notify the State of registry of the aircraft in accordance with established arrangements; and
- ○ Prepare a final report on the results of the operation.

On-Scene Coordinator. When two or more SAR units are working together on the same mission, there is sometimes an advantage if one person is assigned to coordinate the activities of all participating units. The SMC designates this On-Scene Coordinator (OSC), who may be the person in charge of a search and rescue unit (SRU), ship or aircraft participating in a search, or someone at another nearby facility in a position to handle OSC duties. The person in charge of the first SAR facility to arrive at the scene will normally assume the function of OSC until the SMC directs that the person be relieved. Conceivably, the OSC may have to assume SMC duties and actually plan the search if the OSC becomes aware of a distress situation directly and communications cannot be established with an RCC. The OSC should be the most capable person available, taking into consideration SAR training, communications capabilities, and the length of time that the unit the OSC is aboard can stay in the search area. Frequent changes in the OSC should be avoided. Duties which the SMC may assign to the OSC, depending on needs and qualification, include any of the following:

- Assume operational coordination of all SAR facilities on-scene;
- Receive the search action plan from the SMC;
- Modify the search action plan based on prevailing environmental conditions and keeping the SMC advised of any changes to the plan (do in consultation with the SMC when practicable);
- Provide relevant information to the other SAR facilities; implement the search action plan; monitor the performance of other units participating in the search; coordinate safety of flight issues for SAR aircraft; develop and implement the rescue plan (when needed); and make consolidated reports (SITREPS) back to the SMC.

Aircraft Co-Ordinator.

The Aircraft Co-Ordinator (ACO) should normally be designated by the SMC, or if that is not practicable, by the OSC. The ACO is a facility that has the most appropriate mix of radios, radar and trained personnel to effectively coordinate the involvement of multiple aircraft in SAR operations while maintaining flight safety. Generally the ACO is responsible to the SMC; however, the ACO work on-scene must be coordinated closely with the OSC, and if no SMC is involved, the ACO and OSC must work in close consultation with each other. Typically, the SMC or OSC, as the case may be, would remain in overall charge of operations. Duties of the ACO can be carried out by a fixed-wing aircraft, helicopter, ship, a fixed structure such as an oil rig, or an appropriate land unit. Depending on needs and qualification, the ACO may be assigned duties that include the following:

- Maintain flight safety;
- Prioritise and allocate tasks;
- Coordinate the coverage of search areas;
- Make consolidated situation reports (SITREPS) to the SMC and the OSC, as appropriate; and
- Work closely with the OSC.

Situation Report Formats and Examples

Situation Reports (SITREPs) are used to pass information about a particular SAR incident. RCCs use them to keep other RCCs, RSCs, and appropriate agencies informed of cases which are of immediate or potential interest. The OSC uses SITREPs to keep the SMC aware of mission events. Search facilities use SITREPs to keep the OSC informed of mission progress. The OSC addresses SITREPs only to the SMC unless otherwise directed. The SMC may address SITREPs to as many agencies as necessary, including other RCCs and RSCs, to keep them informed. SITREPs prepared by an SMC usually include a summary of information received from OSCs. Often a short SITREP is used to provide the earliest notice of a casualty or to pass urgent details when requesting assistance. A more complete SITREP is used to pass amplifying information during SAR operations. Initial SITREPs should be transmitted as soon as some details of an incident become clear and should not be delayed unnecessarily for confirmation of all details.

For SAR incidents where pollution or threat of pollution exists as a result of a casualty, the appropriate agency tasked with environmental protection should be an information addressee on SITREPs.

International SITREP Format

A SITREP format has been adopted internationally which is intended for use, along with the standard codes for international communications between RCCs.

Short form - To pass urgent essential details when requesting assistance, or to provide the earliest notice of casualty, the following information should be provided:

TRANSMISSION	(Distress/urgency)
DATE AND TIME	(UTC or Local date Time Group)
FROM:	(Originating RCC)
TO:	
SAR SITREP (NUMBER)	(To indicate nature of message and completeness of sequence of SITREPs concerning the casualty)
A. IDENTITY OF CASUALTY	(Name/call sign, flag state)
B. POSITION	(Latitude/Longitude)
C. SITUATION	(Type of message, e.g., distress/urgency; date/time; nature of distress/urgency; fire, collision, medico)
D. NUMBER OF PERSONS	
E. ASSISTANCE REQUIRED	
F. COORDINATING RCC	

Full form - To pass amplifying or updating information during SAR operations, the following additional sections should be used as necessary:

G. DESCRIPTION OF CASUALTY	(Physical description, owner/charterer, cargo carried, passage from/to, life-saving equipment carried)
H. WEATHER ON SCENE	(Wind, sea/swell state, air/sea temperature, visibility, cloud cover/ceiling, barometric pressure)
J. INITIAL ACTIONS TAKEN	(By casualty and RCC)
K. SEARCH AREA	(As planned by RCC)
L. COORDINATING INSTRUCTIONS	(OSC designated, units participating, communications)
M. FUTURE PLANS	
N. ADDITIONAL INFORMATION	(Include time SAR operation terminated)

Notes:

1. Each SITREP concerning the same casualty should be numbered sequentially.
2. If help is required from the addressee, the first SITREP should be issued in short form if remaining information is not readily available.
3. When time permits, the full form may be used for the first SITREP, or to amplify it.
4. Further SITREPs should be issued as soon as other relevant information has been obtained. Information already passed should not be repeated.
5. During prolonged operations, "no change" SITREPs, when appropriate, should be issued at intervals of about 3 hours to reassure recipients that nothing has been missed.
6. When the incident is concluded, a final SITREP is to be issued as confirmation.

Example SITREP - International Format

DISTRESS

152230Z SEP 96

FROM RCC LA GUIRIA VENEZUELA

TO SANJUANSARCOORD SAN JUAN PUERTO RICO

BT

SAR SITREP ONE

A.   N999EJ (US)

B   14-20N 064-20W

C.   DISTRESS/152200Z/AIRCRAFT DITCHING

D.   4

E.   REQUEST SANJUANSARCOORD ASSUME SMC AND CONDUCT SEARCH

F.   RCC LA GUIRIA VENEZUELA

G. CESSNA CITATION III/EXECUTIVE JETS, INC, MIAMI, FL/ORIGINATOR VERIFIED AIRCRAFT ON VFR FLIGHT PLAN DEPARTED PORT OF SPAIN TRINIDAD 152100Z EN ROUTE AGUADILLA, PUERTO RICO/8 PERSON LIFERAFT WITH CANOPY AND SURVIVAL SUPPLIES/FLARES

H. WEATHER ON SCENE UNKNOWN

J. AIRCRAFT ISSUED MAYDAY BROADCAST 121·5 MHZ WHICH WAS HEARD BY AIR FRANCE 747. PILOT OF DISTRESS AIRCRAFT GAVE POSITION, STATED BOTH ENGINES FLAMED OUT AND DESCENDING THROUGH 5000 FEET WITH INTENTIONS TO DITCH.

K. NO SEARCH ASSETS AVAILABLE
BT

Alternate SITREP Format

Another SITREP format, in common use in certain SAR regions, is presented below. This format uses 4 main paragraphs and a subject line to convey all essential information:

Identification	The subject line contains the phase of the emergency, SITREP number, a one- or two-word description of the emergency, and identification of the unit sending the SITREP. SITREPs are numbered sequentially throughout the entire case. When an OSC is relieved on-scene, the new OSC continues the SITREP numbering sequence.
Situation	A description of the case, the conditions that affect the case, and any amplifying information that will clarify the problem. After the first SITREP, only changes to the original reported situation need be included.
Bintulu (remotely controlled by Penang/9MG)Action Taken	A report of all action taken since the last report, including results of such action. When an unsuccessful search has been conducted, the report includes the areas searched, a measure of effort such as sorties flown and hours searched, and the track spacing actually achieved.
Future Plans	A description of actions planned for future execution, including any recommendations and, if necessary, a request for additional assistance.
Status of Case	This is used only on the final SITREP to indicate that the case is closed or that the search is suspended pending further developments.

Example SITREP - Alternate Format

160730z SEP 96

FROM COGUARD AIRSTA BORINQUEN PUERTO RICO

TO SANJUANSARCOORD SAN JUAN PUERTO RICO

BT

SUBJ: DISTRESS,SITREP ONE, N999EJ DITCHED, AIRSTA BQN

A. SANJUANSARCOORD SAN JUAN 160010Z SEP 96

1 SITUATION: CGNR 1740 COMPLETED FLARE SEARCH OF AREA A-1 WITH NEGATIVE RESULTS. O/S WX: CEILING 200 OVC, NUMEROUS RAIN SHOWERS, VISIBILATY 3NM, SEAS 200T/6-8FT, WINDS 180T/30 KTS.

2. ACTION TAKEN:

A. 151905Q INFORMED BY RCC OF DITCHED AIRCRAFT IN POSIT 14-20N 064-20W. DIRECTED TO LAUNCH READY C-130.

B. 1955Q CGNR 1740 AIRBORNE, CDR PETERMAN

C. 2120Q CGNR 1740 O/S POSIT 13-50N 064-20W. COMMENCED VECTOR SEARCH, 30NM LEGS, FIRST LEG 180T, ALTITUDE 1500 FEET, TAS 150 KTS.

D. 2135Q CGNR 1740 INSERTED DATUM MARKER BUOY IN POSIT 14-20N 064-20W.

E. 2310Q CGNR 1740 COMPLETED FIRST VS PATTERN, COMMENCED SECOND VECTOR SEARCH FIRST LEG 150T

F. 160100Q CGNR 1740 COMPLETED SECOND SEARCH.

G. 0120Q CGNR 1740 RELOCATED DMB IN POSIT 14-22N 064-17W. DEPARTED SCENE.

H. 0230Q CGNR 1740 LANDED BORINQUEN.

3. FUTURE PLANS: LAUNCH CGNR 1742 AT 0645Q FOR SEARCH OF AREA B-1.
BT

SAR Resources

The SAR organisation includes all of those agencies which perform distress monitoring, communications, coordination, and response functions. This includes providing or arranging for medical advice, initial medical assistance, or medical evacuation, if necessary.

SAR facilities consist of all of the public and private facilities, including co-operating aircraft, vessels, other craft and installations operating under coordination of an RCC. In establishing a SAR service, States should use existing facilities to the fullest extent possible. A successful SAR organisation usually can be created without having designated, full-time SRUs.

A list of potential SAR resources is contained in the *International Aeronautical and Maritime Search and Rescue Manual on Organisation and Management.*

International Resources. Several resources exist internationally which can be used by RCCs while coordinating a specific SAR mission. Examples of such resources available for use by all RCCs are discussed in the following paragraphs.

Ship Reporting Systems
Vessels at sea, although not always available to participate in extended search operations, are potential aeronautical and maritime SAR assets. Masters of vessels have a duty to assist others whenever it can be done without endangering the assisting vessel or crew. Various States have implemented ship reporting systems. A ship reporting system enables the SMC to quickly know the approximate positions, courses, and speeds of vessels in the vicinity of a distress situation by means of a SURface PICture (SURPIC), and other information about the vessels which may be valuable, e.g., whether a doctor is aboard. Masters of vessels should be encouraged to send regular reports to the authority operating a ship reporting system for SAR. Ships are a key SAR resource for RCCs, but requests for them to assist must be weighed against the considerable cost to shipping companies when they do divert to assist. Ship reporting systems enable RCCs to quickly identify the capable vessel which will be least harmed by a diversion, enabling other vessels in the vicinity to be unaffected.

The Automated Mutual-assistance VEssel Rescue (AMVER) system, the only world-wide system operated exclusively to support SAR, makes information available to all RCCs. Any United States RCC can be contacted for this type of SAR information.

Automatic Identification System (AIS)
Although not an element of the GMDSS, AIS may play a part in the management of a SAR incident. AIS using VHF frequencies, transmits the Maritime Mobile Service Identity (MMSI) of the AIS fitted vessel along with additional information e.g. position, course, speed, navigational status and other safety information to AIS receiving shore stations and other AIS equipped vessels.

AIS Class A is currently a carriage requirement and is mandated under Chapter V of SOLAS.

A Class A AIS unit broadcasts the following information every 2 to 10 seconds while underway, and every 3 minutes while at anchor (at a power level of 12·5 watts). The information broadcast includes:

MMSI number - unique identification; Navigation status; Rate of turn; Speed over ground; Position accuracy - differential GPS or other; Longitude and Latitude; Course over ground; True Heading; Time stamp.

Class B differs from Class A. Class B is a voluntary fit on small vessels / workboats, yachts etc. It has a reporting rate less than Class A (e.g. every 30 seconds when under 14 knots, as opposed to every 10 seconds for Class A). Class B does not transmit the vessel's IMO number / call sign, ETA or destination nor the vessel's navigational status and is only required to receive, not transmit, text safety messages. No rate of turn information or draft details are transmitted. In summary it is a very basic system which gives an automatic transmission of vessels own position, speed and heading to other vessels within VHF range.

Use of AIS Safety-related broadcast messages in distress situations
AIS standards include safety-related text messaging functionality in Class A devices as a requirement and as an option in Class B devices. If safety related messaging is provided in Class B devices, it shall be only through the use of pre-configured messages. Certain models of AIS have provided pre-configured safety-related messages which include distress alert information.

IMO has noted several limitations and concerns regarding the ability of these safety-related messages to mitigate distress situations and is of the view that AIS devices should be designed such that they cannot broadcast a pre-configured safety-related message (distress or otherwise).

It is recommended that AIS manufacturers and/or users should delete any pre-configured AIS safety-related messages that could be used to indicate distress.

Furthermore, IMO is of the view that, while the GMDSS is forseen to be subject to continuing improvements and perhaps the use of technologies such as AIS may be considered in future, AIS can not be considered to be a part of GMDSS at the present time.

Automatic Identification System (AIS) Search and Rescue Transmitter (AIS-SART)
AIS-SART, Search and Rescue Transmitter as distinct from a conventional 9 GHz X Band SART (Search and Rescue Transponder). The AIS-SART is used to locate a survival craft or distressed vessel by sending updated position reports using a standard AIS Class A position report. The position and time synchronization of the AIS-SART is derived from a built in GNSS receiver.

Ship Security Alert System (SSAS)
Ship Security Alert System (SSAS) sits outside of the GMDSS system. SSAS is, however, often associated with the GMDSS equipment installed on a vessel, usually the Inmarsat C equipment. SSAS is a requirement under SOLAS Chapter XI-2 for the transmission of an alert, reporting to shore a threat to ship security, e.g. piracy.

Long Range Identification and Tracking (LRIT)
Like AIS and SSAS, Long Range Identification and Tracking (LRIT) is not part of GMDSS but may prove to be a valuable source of information to Rescue Coordination Centres during a SAR incident.

Designation of the RCC or RSC Responsible for Initiating SAR Action
Typically, an RCC will receive a distress alert and assume responsibility for SAR operations for that incident. However, there may be times when the first RCC to receive the distress alert will not be the responsible RCC, such as when the distress is in another SRR. The diagram below depicts the recommended actions of the "First RCC" that receives the distress alert. The following text provides guidance on the responsibilities of that RCC. There should be no undue delay in initiating action while determining the responsible RCC.

Actions by the first Rescue Coordination Centre (RCC) on receipt of distress alert

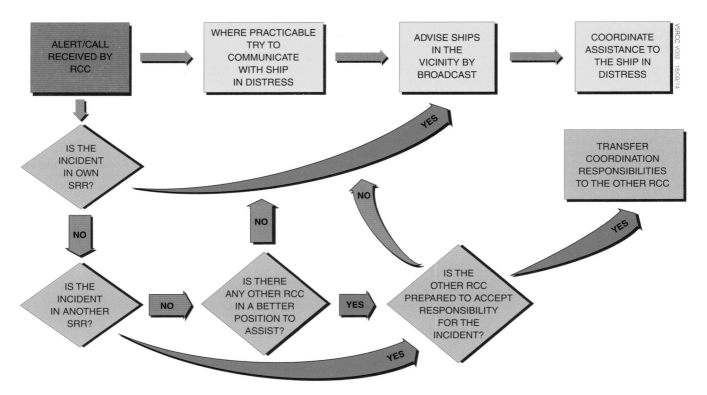

Position of Aircraft, Ship or Craft is known

When it is likely that other RCCs have also received alerts from the distressed craft, any RCC receiving an alert should assume responsibility until coordination with the other RCCs can take place and the appropriate RCC assumes responsibility.

When the position of the distressed craft is known, the responsibility for initiation of a SAR operation will be that of the RCC or RSC in whose area the craft is located.

When the RCC or RSC recognises that the distressed craft is continuing its flight or voyage and may leave the SRR for which it is responsible, it should take the following actions.

(a) Alert the RCCs associated with the planned or intended route of the distressed craft, and pass on all information.

(b) Continue coordination of the SAR operation until it has been notified by an adjacent RCC or RSC that the distressed craft has entered its SRR and that it is assuming responsibility. When transferring the SAR operation to another RCC or RSC, the transfer should be documented in the RCC or RSC log.

(c) Remain ready to assist until informed that this is no longer required.

When an RCC or RSC receives information indicating a distress outside of its SRR, it should immediately notify the appropriate RCC or RSC and should take all necessary action to coordinate the response until the appropriate RCC or RSC has assumed responsibility. When transferring the coordination of a SAR operation to another RCC or RSC, the transfer should be documented in the RCC or RSC log. Procedures to transfer SMC responsibility to another RCC should include:

- Personal discussion between the SMCs of both RCCs concerned;
- The initiating RCC may invite the other RCC to take over responsibility or the other RCC may offer to take over responsibility;
- Responsibility retained by the initiating RCC until the other RCC formally accepts responsibility;
- Full details of action taken passed between the RCCs and,
- Transfer of SMC responsibility recorded by both SMCs in the RCC log and all involved SAR facilities advised of the transfer.

Position of Aircraft, Ship or other Craft is Unknown

When the position of the distressed craft is unknown, the RCC or RSC should assume responsibility for the SAR operation and consult adjacent RCCs along the route of the craft concerned which centre will assume primary responsibility and designate an SMC. Unless otherwise agreed among the RCCs or RSCs concerned, the RCC or RSC assuming responsibility should be determined as follows:

(a) If the last reported position of the distressed craft falls within an SRR, the RCC or RSC responsible for that SRR should assume responsibility for coordinating the response.

(b) If the last known position falls on the line separating two adjacent SRRs, the RCC or RSC responsible for the SRR towards which the distressed craft was proceeding should assume coordination responsibilities.

(c) If the craft was not equipped with suitable two-way radio communications or not under obligation to maintain radio communication, the RCC or RSC responsible for the SRR containing the distressed craft's intended destination should assume coordination responsibilities.

Search and Rescue Regions (SRR)

An SRR is an area of defined dimensions associated with an RCC within which SAR services are provided. ICAO RANPs depict aeronautical SRRs for most of the world. States have agreed to accept SAR responsibility for an area which is composed of one or more aeronautical SRRs. Maritime SRRs are published in the IMO SAR Plan and could be similar, or different, to aeronautical SRRs. The purpose of having an SRR is to clearly define who has primary responsibility for coordinating responses to distress situations in every area of the world and to enable rapid distribution of distress alerts to the proper RCC. A State may have separate aeronautical and maritime SRRs, or separate SRRs in different ocean/sea areas, otherwise, a single SRR (with SRSs, if necessary) will usually suffice.

- Factors Affecting SRR size and shape. When establishing or amending an SRR, States should try to create the most efficient system possible bearing in mind that each SRR is part of a global system. Leading factors to consider should include:
    - Size and shape of the area of responsibility;
    - Availability, distribution, readiness and mobility of SAR resources;
    - Reliability of the communications network; and
    - Which State is fully capable, qualified, and willing to assume responsibility.
- Aeronautical SRRs often are aligned with FIRs for specific reasons.
    - The ATS unit providing flight information service for an FIR is the central point for collecting and forwarding information about aircraft emergencies and coordinates SAR aircraft and other air traffic operating within the FIR.
    - Simplified notification, coordination and liaison between the RCC and the ATS unit.
    - Savings often result from sharing RCC and ATS staff, facilities, and communications networks.
- Upper flight Information Regions (UIRs) sometimes exist above a system of FIRs. UIRs generally are NOT used to define aeronautical SRRs for three reasons.
    - Searches are generally conducted at low altitudes and must be coordinated with other traffic in the FIR.
    - ATS communications facilities useful for SAR, particularly air-ground facilities, are adapted to the FIR rather than to the UIR.
    - Territorial divisions of authority for local agencies used in SAR operations generally correspond to those of the FIRs.
- Experience shows that in most areas there are operational advantages in harmonizing aeronautical and maritime SRRs. Doing so minimizes confusion over which authority is to be alerted when a distress situation arises at and over a specific geographic position. In order to enhance the efficiency of SAR services, neighbouring States should seek to agree on the limits of their SRRs which could enhance coordination and avoid duplication of efforts. To make them easier to use, SRR limits should, if possible, be straight line running north to south or east to west between well-defined geographic points. Such regions should be contiguous and as far as practicable not overlap.
- The delimitation of SRRs is not related to and shall not prejudice the delimitation of any boundary between States. An SRR is established solely to ensure that primary responsibility for coordinating SAR services for that geographic area is assumed by some State. SRR limits should not be viewed as barriers to assisting persons in distress. Any facility within a SAR organisation should respond to all distress situations whenever and wherever it is capable of doing so. In this respect, co-operation between States, their RCCs and their SAR services should be as close as possible.
- An SRR is established by agreement among States. States should propose establishing or amending SRR limits when this would result in the provision of more efficient or effective SAR services. The States concerned should agree among themselves, formally or informally, on the lines separating their SRRs and then inform IMO or the applicable ICAO regional office, depending on whether the SRRs are maritime or aeronautical. After due process, the information will then be published in the IMO SAR plan or the applicable ICAO RANP. Sometimes SRR limits can be tentatively decided at an IMO SAR workshop or an ICAO regional air navigation meeting, subject to later approval.

Operating guidance for Masters of ships observing another vessel apparently in danger

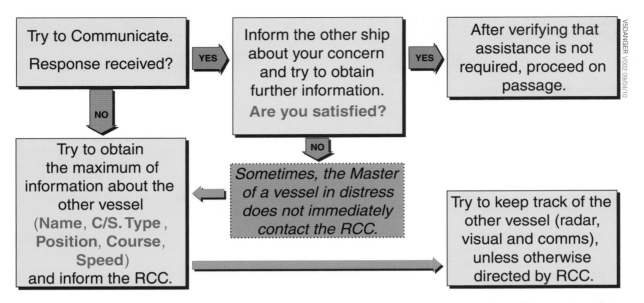

The following diagram shows standard procedures for distress/urgency message routeing. It is for guidance only, and does not preclude the use of any and all available means of distress alerting.

Operating guidance for Masters of ships in distress or urgency situations.

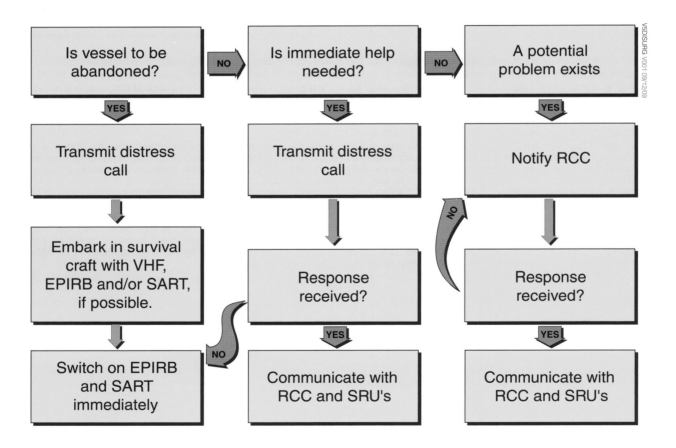

SEARCH AND RESCUE (SAR)

NAVAREA I

BELGIUM
See diagram R1

National SAR Agency: Maritieme Dienstverlening & Kust Afdeling Scheepvaartbegeleiding
Address: Maritiem Plein 3, 8400 Oostende, Belgium
Telephone: +32 59 341020
Fax: +32 59 703605
email: mrcc@mrcc.be
Website: www.scheepvaartbegeleiding.be

The Belgian Coastguard Service, "Coastguard Oostende" is responsible for coordinating Search and Rescue operations from MRCC Oostende. A continuous listening watch on international distress frequencies 2182 kHz, VHF Ch 16 and the DSC frequencies 2187·5 kHz and VHF Ch 70 is maintained.

TeleMedical Assistance Service: MRCC Oostende will contact the Military Hospital Brussels on request who will provide medical advice, alternatively contact may be made via MRCC Oostende with French and English consultation languages.

	Telephone +32	Fax +32	Others/Ship Earth Stations (SES)
ARCC BRUSSELS (Cospas-Sarsat SPOC)	2 7514615	2 7524201	**AFTN:** EBMIYCYX **email:** rcc@mil.be
MRCC OOSTENDE	59 701000 59 701100 59 341020	59 703605	**email:** mrcc@mrcc.be

CHANNEL ISLANDS - GUERNSEY (UK)
See diagram R1

National SAR Agency: MRCC Guernsey
Address: JESCC, Police Headquarters, Hospital Lane, St Peter Port, Guernsey, GY1 2QN
Telephone: +44 1481 720672
Fax: +44 1481 256432
Website: www.harbours.gg/guernseycoastguard

The Channel Islands area is wholly enclosed within the French SAR region and is split into two zones for Search and Rescue operations. Jersey controlling the Southern Area (Jersey Territorial Waters), including the Ecrehou and Minquiers reefs and Guernsey controlling the Northern Area, which includes Alderney, Sark and the other small islands. In the Northern Area, in addition to Guernsey, Alderney is a recognised Sub-Station. The Channel Islands area is recognised as extending up to 12 n miles from the coastline or the median line whichever is the nearer. Both Jersey Coastguard and Guernsey Coastguard maintain a continuous listening watch on VHF Ch 16 and DSC Ch 70. Alderney Coastguard maintains watch on VHF Chs 74, 67 and DSC Ch 70 during daylight hours.

Liaison with UK and France is with Falmouth CGOC and CROSS Jobourg.

	Telephone +44	Fax +44	Others/Ship Earth Stations (SES)
ALDERNEY COASTGUARD	1481 822620		**email:** coastguard@alderney.gov.gg
GUERNSEY COASTGUARD	1481 720672	1481 256432	**email:** guernsey.coastguard@gov.gg

CHANNEL ISLANDS - JERSEY (UK)
See diagram R1

National SAR Agency: MRCC JERSEY
Address: Jersey Harbours, Maritime House, S. Helier, Jersey, JE1 1HB, UK
Telephone: +44 1534 447705
Fax: +44 1534 499089
Website: www.ports.je/jerseycoastguard/pages/default.aspx

The Channel Islands area is wholly enclosed within the French SAR region and is split into two zones for Search and Rescue operations. Jersey controlling the Southern Area (Jersey Territorial waters), including the Ecrehou and Minquiers reefs and Guernsey controlling the Northern Area, which includes Alderney, Sark and the other small islands. In the Northern Area, in addition to Guernsey, Alderney is a recognised Sub-Station. The Channel Islands area is recognised as extending up to 12 n miles from the coastline or the median line whichever is the nearer. Both Jersey Radio and S Peter Port Radio maintain a continuous listening watch on VHF Ch 16 and DSC Ch 70. Alderney Coastguard maintains watch on VHF Ch 16 during daylight hours.

Liaison with UK and France is with Falmouth CGOC and CROSS Jobourg.

	Telephone +44	Fax +44	Others/Ship Earth Stations (SES)
JERSEY COASTGUARD	1534 447705	1534 499089	**email:** jerseycoastguard@ports.je

DENMARK

See diagrams R1 & R2

National SAR Agency: JRCC Defence Command Denmark
Address: Defence Command Denmark, NMOC Herningvej 30, 7470 Karup J, Denmark
Telephone: +45 72850505
Fax: +45 72850384
Website: https://www.forsvaret.dk/en/roles-and-responsibilities/national-role/
　　　　　https://www.forsvaret.dk/da/opgaver/nationale-opgaver/eftersogning-og-redning/

The Search and Rescue Coordination Centre for Denmark is JRCC Denmark.

JRCC Denmark has no direct radio communication with vessels in distress, so communication is through LYNGBY RADIO which maintains a continuous listening watch on international distress frequencies, including full DSC facilities.

See also FAROE ISLANDS and GREENLAND.

TeleMedical Assistance Service: Radio Medical in Esbjerg provide advice. Contact is via JRCC Denmark. Possible consultation languages: Danish and English.

	Telephone +45	Fax +45	Others/Ship Earth Stations (SES)
JRCC DENMARK (Cospas-Sarsat SPOC)	72850450	72850384	**email:** jrcc@sok.dk
JRCC Denmark Duty Officer direct	72850505 72850370 (Maritime Assistance Service/MAS)	72850384	**Inmarsat C:** 492380442=MRCC X **email:** jrcc@sok.dk mas@sok.dk (Maritime Assistance Service/MAS)
LYNGBY	72198410		**email:** lyngbyradio@mil.dk
Radio Medical Denmark	75456766	75456750	**email:** rmd@rsyd.dk

ESTONIA

See diagram R2

National SAR Agency: Police and Border Guard Board
Address: Pärnu mnt 139, Tallinn 15060
Telephone: +372 612 3000 (Mon-Sun 0800 - 1900)
　　　　　　112 (H24) (Emergency Call Number)
Fax: +372 612 3009
email: ppa@politsei.ee
Website: https://www.politsei.ee/en/sea-and-air-rescue

JRCC Tallinn is responsible for coordinating Search and Rescue operations and maintains a continuous listening watch on 2182 kHz, VHF Ch 16, DSC 2187·5 kHz and VHF Ch 70. Tallinn Radio (ESA) keeps watch on these international distress frequencies.

TeleMedical Assistance Service: North Estonian Regional Hospital. Contact via Radio Tallinn or MRCC Riga, MRCC Turku, MRCC Goteborg. Possible consultation languages: Estonian, English and Russian.

	Telephone +372	Fax +372	Others/Ship Earth Stations (SES)
JRCC TALLINN (Cospas-Sarsat SPOC) & Maritime Assistance Service (MAS)	6 191224	6 922501	**Inmarsat C:** 492480040 **email:** jrcc@politsei.ee **Website:** www.politsei.ee/en
MARITIME COMMUNICATION CENTRE - MCC	6 991170	6 991171	**email:** tallinnradio@riks.ee **Website:** https://www.riks.ee/maritime-radio-communications

FAROE ISLANDS

See diagram R1

National SAR Agency: Ministry of Fisheries and Marine Affairs
Address: Yviri við Strond 15, 100 Tórshavn, Faroe Islands
Telephone: +298 353030
Fax: +298 353035

The Faroe Islands Search and Rescue Centre (MRCC Tórshavn), is responsible for coordinating Search and Rescue operations within Faroe Islands regional SRR. Tórshavn Radio (OXJ) maintains a continuous listening watch on VHF Ch 16 and DSC for distress calls.

	Telephone +298	Fax +298	Others/Ship Earth Stations (SES)
MRCC TÓRSHAVN	351300 (SAR) 351302 (Other)	351301	**AFTN:** EKTNYCYX **Inmarsat C:** (AOR-E) 423100010=MRCC X **email:** mrcc@vorn.fo **Website:** https://www.vorn.fo/english

FINLAND

See diagram R2

National SAR Agency: Finnish Border Guard Headquarters, SAR Branch
Address: PL 3, 00131 Helsinki, Finland
Telephone: +358 295 421000
Fax: +358 295 411500
Website: https://raja.fi/en/emergency-notices-and-maritime-radio-traffic

The authority responsible for the Maritime Search and Rescue Service in Finland is the Border Guard.

Organisationally the Search and Rescue Service is identical with the Coast Guard Districts of the Border Guard. The top level is formed by the Border Guard HQ. The Search and Rescue Service is assisted by a national maritime Search and Rescue committee, a body under the Border Guard HQ. MRCC Turku is the central point of contact in operational maritime Search and Rescue matters.

MRCC Turku and MRSC Helsinki maintain a continuous listening watch on international distress frequencies including VHF DSC Ch 70, VHF Ch 16 and MF DSC 2187·5 kHz. The call by radio is "Rescue Centre" Turku or Helsinki.

TeleMedical Assistance Service: Contact via MRCC Turku or MRSC Helsinki. Possible consultation languages: English, Finnish and Swedish. The social and health authorities provide advice.

West Finland Coast Guard District

	Telephone +358	Fax +358	Others/Ship Earth Stations (SES)
MRCC TURKU and Cospas-Sarsat SPOC	294 1000 (alert) 294 1006 (Maritime Assistance Service/MAS)	294 1019 (MRCC, SPOC and MAS)	**Inmarsat C:** 423002211 **email:** mrcc@raja.fi **MMSI:** 002301000

Gulf of Finland Coast Guard District

	Telephone +358	Fax +358	Others/Ship Earth Stations (SES)
MRSC HELSINKI	294 1002 (Alert) 294 1090 (Other)	294 1099	**email:** mrsc.helsinki@raja.fi **MMSI:** 002302000

FRANCE

See diagrams R1 & R5

National SAR Agency: Organisme d'études et de coordination pour la recherche et le sauvetage en mer (SECMAR)
Address: 16 Boulevard Raspail, 75007 Paris, France
Telephone: +33 1 53634159
Fax: +33 1 53634178

Centre Régionaux Operationels de Surveillance et de Sauvetage (CROSS)

France has five MRCCs for its European coasts. CROSS provides a permanent, full time, all weather operational presence along the coast of France and co-operates with foreign MRCCs and MRSCs as required. MRCC Gris-Nez has been designated as the initial point of contact for foreign SAR authorities for any question concerning operational aspects of maritime SAR and when France is involved in an incident where a particular French MRCC is not clearly competent to deal with it.

MRCC Gris-Nez has also been designated as the MRCC associated to the French Cospas-Sarsat Mission Control Centre (FMCC) and the Inmarsat LESs.

TeleMedical Assistance Service: Centre de Consultations Medicales Maritimes provide medical advice. Contact via any foreign Coast Radio Station or any French MRCC or JRCC. Possible consultation languages: French and English. CCMM can receive digital pictures, ECG data files etc and can provide specialized teleconsultation. Any ship can contact the CCMM by Inmarsat using SAC 32 or 38 via a France Telecom LES free of charge.

	Telephone +33	Fax +33	Others/Ship Earth Stations (SES)
FMCC (Cospas-Sarsat SPOC)	5 61254382 5 61254432	5 61274878	**AFTN:** LFIAZSZX **email:** fmcc@cnes.fr

Atlantic Coast

	Telephone +33	Fax +33	Others/Ship Earth Stations (SES)
MRCC GRIS-NEZ	3 21872187	3 21877851	**Telex:** +42 130680 CROSSGN **Inmarsat C:** 422799256 **email:** gris-nez@mrccfr.eu **Website:** www.cross-grisnez.developpement-durable.gouv.fr

Continued overleaf

Atlantic Coast (Continued)

	Telephone +33	Fax +33	Others/Ship Earth Stations (SES)
MRCC JOBOURG	2 33521616	2 33527172	**AFTN:** LFIJYWZQ **email:** jobourg.mrcc@developpement-durable.gouv.fr jobourg@mrccfr.eu jobourgvts@mrcc.fr.eu **Website:** www.cross-jobourg.developpement-durable.gouv.fr
MRCC CORSEN	2 98893131	2 98896575	**AFTN:** LFICYYYX **Telex:** +42 940086 CROCOA **email:** corsen@mrccfr.eu ouessant.traffic@developpement-durable.gouv.fr **Website:** http://www.dirm.nord-atlantique-manche-ouest.develop pement-durable.gouv.fr/cross-corsen-r242.html
MRCC ÉTEL	2 97553535	2 97554934	**AFTN:** LFIEYYYX **Telex:** +42 950519 CROSSB **Inmarsat C:** 422799025 **email:** etel.mrcc@developpement-durable.gouv.fr etel@mrccfr.eu **Website:** http://www.dirm.nord-atlantique-manche-ouest.develop pement-durable.gouv.fr/cross-etel-r239.html

GERMANY   See diagrams R1 & R2

National SAR Agency: German Maritime Search and Rescue Service (Deutsche Gesellschaft zur Rettung Schiffbruechiger - DGzRS) **Address:** Werderstr 2, 28199 Bremen, Germany **Telephone:** +49 421 536870 **Fax:** +49 421 5368714 **Telex:** +41 246466 MRCC D **email:** mail@mrcc-bremen.de
The German Sea Rescue Service (Deutsche Gesellschaft zur Rettung Schiffbruechiger or GSRS) is responsible for coordinating Search and Rescue operations supported by Search and Rescue units of the German Navy. Along the North Sea and Baltic Sea coastlines Bremen Rescue Radio maintains a continuous listening watch on VHF Ch 16, DSC VHF Ch 70 and for the North Sea DSC 2187·5 kHz. In addition MRCC Bremen also guarantees assistance on request to foreign MRCC / RCCs coordinating SAR measures for German vessels in foreign waters. An emergency number 124 124 is available for use by mobile telephone within the coverage of German network providers. Preferred inter RCC language to RCC Munster is English.
TeleMedical Assistance Service: TMAS Germany – Medico Cuxhaven Tel.: +49 4721 785 (Emergency only) Fax: +49 4721 781 520 E-Mail: medico@tmas-germany.de Additionally contact may be made via Bremen Rescue Radio (BRR) or MRCC Bremen. Possible consultation languages: German and English.

	Telephone +49	Fax +49	Others/Ship Earth Stations (SES)
RCC MUNSTER (Cospas-Sarsat SPOC)	251 135757	251 135759	**AFTN:** ETRAYCYX **email:** sarleitstelleland@bundeswehr.org
MRCC BREMEN	421 536870	421 5368714	**AFTN:** EDDWYYYX **Telex:** +41 246466 MRCC D **email:** mail@mrcc-bremen.de (Primary email) mrcc@seenotretter.de (Alternative email) **Website:** www.seenotretter.de

GUERNSEY (UK) - see CHANNEL ISLANDS - GUERNSEY (UK)

ICELAND
See diagrams R1 & R4

National SAR Agency: Icelandic Coast Guard
Address: Skógarhlíð 14, 105 Reykjavik, Iceland
Telephone: +354 545 2000
Fax: +354 545 2001
email: lhg@lhg.is
Website: www.lhg.is

Icelandic Coast Guard (ICG) is responsible for Search and Rescue operations and coordination for the Icelandic maritime Search and Rescue Region, SRR. ICG operates JRCC Iceland at a joint ICG operations, maritime communications and vessel monitoring centre, the Icelandic Maritime Traffic Service, (IMTS). A network of Coastal Radio Stations are remotely controlled from the IMTS and maintain a continuous listening watch on international calling and distress frequencies.

	Telephone +354	Fax +354	Others/Ship Earth Stations (SES)
ICELANDIC COAST GUARD (Cospas-Sarsat SPOC)	545 2100 (Operations) 511 3333 (Emergency)	545 2001	**AFTN:** BIRKICGT **Inmarsat C:** 425101519 492740310 **email:** sar@lhg.is
JRCC Iceland	545 2100 (Operations) 511 3333 (Emergency)	545 2001	**AFTN:** BIRKICGT **Inmarsat C:** 425101519 492740310 **email:** sar@lhg.is

IRELAND
See diagram R1

National SAR Agency: Irish Coast Guard
Address: Department of Transport, Lesson Lane, Dublin 2, Ireland
Telephone: +353 (0)1 6620922
　　　　　　+353 (0)1 6620923
Fax: +353 (0)1 6620795
Website: www.gov.ie/en/organisation/department-of-transport

The Irish Coast Guard has overall executive responsibility for coordinating Search and Rescue operations and is the location of MRCC Dublin. The coordination of Search and Rescue operations is conducted by the Irish Coast Guard centres at MRCC Dublin, MRSC Malin Head and MRSC Valentia, who are each responsible for a designated sub-region of the Ireland SRR. A continuous listening watch is maintained on VHF Ch 16, VHF DSC Ch 70 and MF DSC 2187·5 kHz for distress calls. Prefered inter RCC language is English.

TeleMedical Assistance Service: Medico Cork, Cork University Hospital. Contact via MRCC Dublin MRSC Malin Head or MRSC Valentia. Consultation language is English.

	Telephone +353	Fax +353	Others/Ship Earth Stations (SES)
MRCC DUBLIN (Coast Guard) (Cospas-Sarsat SPOC)	1 6620922 1 6620923	1 6620795	**AFTN:** EIDWIMES **email:** coastguardnmoc@transport.gov.ie mrccdublin@irishcoastguard.ie coastguardNMOC@dttas.gov.ie
MRSC MALIN HEAD (Coast Guard)	74 9370103	74 9370221	**email:** mrscmalin@transport.gov.ie mrscmalin@irishcoastguard.ie mrscmalin@dttas.ie
MRSC VALENTIA (Coast Guard)	66 9476109	66 9476289	**email:** mrscvalentia@transport.gov.ie mrscvalentia@irishcoastguard.ie mrscvalentia@dttas.ie

JERSEY (UK) - see CHANNEL ISLANDS - JERSEY (UK)
LATVIA
See diagram R2

National SAR Agency: Latvian Navy Coast Guard.
Address: Meldru iela 5a, Rīga, LV-1015, Latvia
Telephone: +371 67082070
Fax: +371 67320100
email: sar@mrcc.lv
Website: www.mrcc.lv

MRCC Rīga maintains a continuous watch on MF 2182 kHz and VHF Ch 16, call sign RĪGA RESCUE RADIO. Rīga Rescue Radio, which is co-located with MRCC Rīga, also has DSC facilities on VHF Ch 70 and MF 2187·5 kHz. Radiotelex-ARQ selective number 6060 RMRCC LV. Preferred inter RCC languages are Latvian, English and Russian.

TeleMedical Assistance Service: Specialised Medical Centre provides medical advice via VHF Channels. Contact via MRCC Rīga (Rīga Rescue Radio). Possible consultation languages: Latvian, English and Russian.

LATVIA (Continued)

	Telephone +371	Fax +371	Others/Ship Earth Stations (SES)

MRCC RĪGA (Rīga Rescue)
(Cospas-Sarsat SPOC Latvia)
	67323103 (Emergency)
	67062101 (Office hours)
		67320100 (24/7)
		67860082 (Office hours)
			Inmarsat C: 427502310
			email: sar@mrcc.lv
			    isps1@mrcc.lv (MAS/SafeSeaNet)
			    lja@lja.lv (Office hours)

LITHUANIA   See diagram R2

National SAR Agency: MRCC of the Lithuanian Navy
Address: N. Uosto St. 24, LT 92244 Klaipėda, Lithuania
Telephone: +370 46 391257
            +370 46 391258
Fax: +370 46 391259
email: mrcc@mil.lt

MRCC of the Lithuania Navy (Call sign Klaipeda Rescue) is responsible for coordinating Search and Rescue operations within the Lithuanian SRR. MRCC of the Lithuanian Navy maintains a continuous watch on 2182 kHz, VHF Ch 16 and also has DSC facilities on VHF Ch 70 and 2187·5 kHz.

TeleMedical Assistance Service: Klaipeda Seamen's Hospital Maritime Medical Centre provide assistance. Contact via MRCC of the Lithuanian Navy.

Possible consultation languages: Lithuanian, Russian and English.

	Telephone +370	Fax +370	Others/Ship Earth Stations (SES)
ARCC VILNIUS (Cospas-Sarsat SPOC)	70694588 70694587 610 46024		**AFTN:** EYVCYCYX **email:** arcc@ans.lt
MRCC of the Lithuanian Navy	46 391257 46 391258 698 18275	46 391259	**Inmarsat C:** 427799011 **email:** mrcc@mil.lt **MMSI:** 002770330

NETHERLANDS   See diagram R1

National SAR Agency: SAR Commission Maritime, Ministry of Infrastructure and Watermanagement
Address: PO. Box 5807 2280 HV, The Hague, The Netherlands
Telephone: +31 88 7977100
Fax: +31 70 3951724
email: info@kustwacht.nl
Website: www.kustwacht.nl

The Netherlands Coastguard is responsible for coordinating Search and Rescue operations through JRCC Den Helder. The Netherlands Coastguard Radio (PBK) maintains a continuous listening watch on international VHF distress frequency Ch 16, DSC VHF Ch 70 and MF DSC 2187·5 kHz. Call sign used during Search and Rescue operations is "DEN HELDER RESCUE".

TeleMedical Assistance Service: Radio Medische Dienst (Radio Medical Service) provide assistance. Contact via JRCC Den Helder.

Possible consultation languages: Dutch and English.

	Telephone +31	Fax +31	Others/Ship Earth Stations (SES)
JRCC DEN HELDER (Cospas-Sarsat SPOC)	223 542300 (H24 Emergency and Operational)	223 658358	**email:** ccc@kustwacht.nl

NORWAY   See diagrams R1, R2, R4 & R18

National SAR Agency: Norwegian Ministry of Justice and Public Security
Address: P.O.Box 8005 Dep. N-0030 Oslo, Norway
Telephone: +47 22245429
email: postmottak@jd.dep.no
Website: https://hovedredningssentralen.no/english/

Search and Rescue operations are coordinated from two Joint Rescue Coordination Centres, JRCC Bodø and JRCC Stavanger. The two Rescue Centres are responsible for conducting maritime, aeronautical and land rescue operations within their Search and Rescue Region, North and South of 65° N, respectively. A network of Coast Radio Stations maintains a continuous listening watch on international distress frequencies VHF Ch 16, DSC VHF Ch 70 and DSC MF on 2187·5 kHz. Distress priority calls via satellite communications through Eik LES are routed directly to JRCC Stavanger. Preferred inter RCC language is English.

TeleMedical Assistance Service: National Centre for Maritime Radio Medico provide assistance. Contact via Norwegian Coastal Radio South (LGQ) or JRCC Stavanger and JRCC Bodø.

Possible consultation languages: Norwegian and English.

NORWAY (Continued)

	Telephone	Fax	Others/Ship Earth Stations (SES)
JRCC BODØ (co–located with Norwegian MCC Cospas–Sarsat SPOC)	+47 75559000 +47 75559300	+47 75524200	**AFTN:** ENBOYCYX **Inmarsat C:** 425999999 **Inmarsat Fleet:** 764816062 **email:** operations@jrcc-bodoe.no
JRCC STAVANGER	+47 51517000 +47 51646000 (Admin) +47 51646010 (Press Office)	+47 51652334	**AFTN:** ENZVYCYX **Inmarsat C:** 425899999 **Inmarsat F55:** 764563885 **email:** operations@jrcc-stavanger.no
JAN MAYEN ISLAND MRCC OCEANIC (Iceland)	+354 5113333	+354 5112244 +354 5452001	**Inmarsat C:** 425101519

POLAND   See diagram R2

National SAR Agency: Ministry of Maritime Economy and Inland Waterways, Maritime Economy Department
Address: Nowy Swiat 6/12 Str. Warsaw 00-400, Poland
Telephone: +48 22 5838570
Fax: +48 22 5838571
email: sekretariatdgm@mgm.gov.pl
Website: www.mgm.gov.pl

The Polish Maritime Search and Rescue service is coordinated from MRCC Gdynia. Polish Rescue Radio (SPL) maintains a continuous listening watch on international distress frequencies on MF and VHF DSC.

TeleMedical Assistance Service: Academical Centre for Maritime and Tropical Medicine, Powstania Styczniowego 9B Gdynia 81-519, Poland

Tel: +48 58 6998460

email: tmas@ucmmit.gdynia.pl

Can also be contacted via MRCC Gdynia, Polish Rescue Radio Station or directly.

	Telephone +48	Fax +48	Others/Ship Earth Stations (SES)
ARCC WARSAW (Cospas-Sarsat SPOC)	22 5745190 22 5745191	22 5745199	**Mobile:** +48 885 745 190 **AFTN:** EPWWZQZX EPWWYCYX **email:** arcc@pansa.pl
Polish MAS (Maritime Assistance Service) Centre VTS Gulf of Gdansk	58 6216162 58 6211443	58 6205363 58 6205328	**Mobile:** +48 601 991331 **Inmarsat BGAN:** 772265042 **email:** vtscentrum@umgdy.gov.pl
MRCC GDYNIA	58 6610196 58 6610197 58 6205551 58 6216811	58 6607640	**Mobile:** +48 50 50 50 971 **email:** mrcc@sar.gov.pl polratok.1@sar.gov.pl
MRSC ŚWINOUJŚCIE	91 3214917 91 3215929 91 3216042		**Mobile:** +48 50 50 50 969 **email:** polratok.2@sar.gov.pl mrsc@sar.gov.pl
POLISH RESCUE RADIO (SPL)	58 3553670	58 6205363 58 6205328	**email:** gmdss@umgdy.gov.pl **MMSI:** 002618102
VTS ZATOKA GDAŃSK - VTS CENTRE	58 6216162 58 3553610 58 3553611 58 3553612 60 1991331 (Mobile)	58 6205363 58 6205328	**Inmarsat BGAN:** 772265042 **email:** vts@umgdy.gov.pl gmdss@umgdy.gov.pl **Website:** www.umgdy.gov.pl **MMSI:** 002611400

RUSSIA

See diagrams R2, R6, R15, R16 & R18

National SAR Agency: Ministry of Transport of the Russian Federation
Address: 1/1 U1,Rozhdestvenka Street Moscow, 109112, Russia
Telephone: +7 495 6261000
Fax: +7 495 6269038
      +7 495 6269128
email: info@mintrans.ru
Website: www.mintrans.ru

MRCC Moscow is responsible for coordinating Search and Rescue operations and liaising with Search and Rescue services of neighbouring countries in accordance with intergovernmental agreements. A network of Coast Radio Stations maintains a continuous listening watch on international distress frequencies. Preferred inter RCC language is English.

NORTHERN SEAS (NAVAREAs I, XX and XXI): The following frequencies are reserved for Distress Calls and are not to be used for general communication: 6211 kHz, 4138 kHz & 500 kHz. In all areas (except Beloye More and Barents Sea) a 3 minute watch will be maintained on 500 kHz from 15 minutes past each hour and on 6211 kHz and 4138 kHz from 45 minutes past each hour.

TeleMedical Assistance Service: State Enterprise "Semashko Northern Medical Centre" provides assistance (telemed@atnet.ru). Contact via MRSC Arkhange'lsk. Possible consultation languages: Russian and English.

Additionally, assistance may also be provided by Sakhalin Territorial Centre of the Medicine and Catastrophe (stcmk@mail.ru). Possible consultation language: Russian.

State MRCC

	Telephone +7	Fax +7	Others/Ship Earth Stations (SES)
CMC (Cospas-Sarsat SPOC)	495 2360109 495 2360110	495 2360109 495 9673020	**AFTN:** UUUUYCYX **email:** cmc@marsat.ru
SMRCC MOSCOW	495 6261052 495 6241853 495 6261055	495 6237476	**email:** odsmrcc@morflot.ru od_smrcc@morspas.ru

Baltic Coast

	Telephone +7	Fax +7	Others/Ship Earth Stations (SES)
MRCC KALININGRAD Maritime Assistance Service (MAS)	4012 538470 4012 538153 4012 579471 4012 579473	4012 643199 4012 538470	**Mobile:** +7 909 7905816 **Inmarsat:** 772537019 (BGAN) **email:** mrcckld@pasp.ru
MRCC SANKT PETERBURG Maritime Assistance Service (MAS)	812 3274147 (MAS & Duty Officer) 812 3274145 (Head of MRCC) 812 2451673 (Duty Officer) 812 4958995 (Duty Officer)	812 3274146	**Telex:** +64 121512 RCC RU **Inmarsat C:** 492509012 **email:** mrcc@pasp.ru

SWEDEN

See diagram R2

National SAR Agency: Swedish Maritime Administration (Maritime and Aeronautical SAR)
Address: SE-60178 Norrkoping, Sweden
Telephone: +46 771 63 0000
email: sjofartsverket@sjofartsverket.se
Website: www.sjofartsverket.se

JRCC Sweden is located in Göteborg and maintains continuous monitoring of VHF Ch 16, DSC VHF Ch 70 and DSC MF 2187.5 kHz with coverage of the entire Swedish Search and Rescue Region (SRR). The call by radio is "Sweden Rescue", alternatively contact may be made via the emergency telephone number.

TeleMedical Assistance Service: Contact via JRCC Sweden. Possible consultation languages: Swedish and English.

	Telephone	Fax	Others/Ship Earth Stations (SES)
JRCC SWEDEN (Cospas-Sarsat SPOC)	+46 10 4927780		**AFTN:** ESORYCYX **email:** jrcc@sjofartsverket.se

Continued on next page

SWEDEN (Continued)

	Telephone	Fax	Others/Ship Earth Stations (SES)
JRCC SWEDEN (including Maritime Assistance Service - MAS)	+46 771 409000 (Switchboard) +46 10 4927900 (TMAS) +46 10 4927650 (MAS) +46 10 4927600 (Ice information) 112 (Rescue by telephone only)	+46 31 290134 (All functions at JRCC)	email: jrcc@sjofartsverket.se

UNITED KINGDOM   See diagrams R1, R2 & R4

National SAR Agency: HM Coastguard, Maritime and Coastguard Agency, Department for Transport
Address: Spring Place, 105 Commercial Road, Southampton SO15 1EG, UK
Telephone: +44 (0)203 8172000 (Switchboard / Reception - Office hours only)
email: sar.response@mcga.gov.uk (Routine enquiries - Office hours only)
Website: https://www.gov.uk/government/organisations/maritime-and-coastguard-agency

The general arrangements for search and rescue within the Search and Rescue Region of the United Kingdom are fully described in the Search and Rescue Section, Annex 1.

The voice call sign of a Rescue Coordination Centre (RCC) is the geographical name followed by "Coastguard", e.g. "HUMBER COASTGUARD". However, using the callsign "UK COASTGUARD" the mariner will receive a reply from the station which is responsible for the area they are in.

Note: The United Kingdom maritime radio infrastructure is a single network of operations centres, all data and communications being available to every officer on duty. The Joint Rescue Coordination Centre (JRCC UK), 9 Maritime Rescue Coordination Centres (MRCCs) and one Maritime Rescue Sub-Centre (MRSC) carry out a range of coast guard duties in addition to their Rescue Coordination / Rescue Sub-Centre (RCC/RSC) functions.

If operationally required, all RCCs can temporarily extend or contract the area that is normally covered. This might occur during busy periods or because of a major incident.

TeleMedical Assistance Service: The Aberdeen Royal Infirmary and the Queen Alexandra Hospital at Portsmouth provide assistance. Contact via email: ukmrcc@hmcg.gov.uk or telephone on either Tel: +44 344 3820026 or Tel: +44 208 3127386 requesting Medico assistance.

	Telephone +44	Fax +44	Others/Ship Earth Stations (SES)
SOLENT COASTGUARD	2392 552100	1329 841905	email: zone17@hmcg.gov.uk (FAO JRCC UK)
FALMOUTH COASTGUARD	1326 317575	1329 841905	email: zone23@hmcg.gov.uk (FAO MRCC Falmouth)
MILFORD HAVEN COASTGUARD	1646 690909	1329 841905	email: zone28@hmcg.gov.uk (FAO MRCC Milford Haven)
HOLYHEAD COASTGUARD	1407 762051	1329 841905	email: zone31@hmcg.gov.uk (FAO MRCC Holyhead)
BELFAST COASTGUARD	2891 463933	1329 841905	email: zone34@hmcg.gov.uk (FAO MRCC Belfast)
STORNOWAY COASTGUARD	1851 702013	1329 841905	email: zone36@hmcg.gov.uk (FAO MRCC Stornoway)
SHETLAND COASTGUARD	1595 692976	1329 841905	email: zone1@hmcg.gov.uk (FAO MRCC Shetland)
ABERDEEN COASTGUARD	1224 592334	1329 841905	email: zone3@hmcg.gov.uk (FAO MRCC Aberdeen)
HUMBER COASTGUARD	1262 672317	1329 841905	email: zone8@hmcg.gov.uk (FAO MRCC Humber)
DOVER COASTGUARD	1304 210008	1329 841905	email: zone14@hmcg.gov.uk (FAO MRCC Dover)
LONDON COASTGUARD	208 3127380	1329 841905	email: zone12@hmcg.gov.uk (FAO MRSC London)

Aeronautical SAR

	Telephone +44	Fax +44	Others/Ship Earth Stations (SES)
Joint Rescue Coordination Centre UK (JRCC UK)	344 3820800	1329 244547	email: ukarcc@hmcg.gov.uk

UNITED KINGDOM (Continued)

International SAR

	Telephone +44	Fax +44	Others/Ship Earth Stations (SES)
Joint Rescue Coordination Centre UK (JRCC UK)	344 3820025	1329 841905	**Inmarsat C:** 423200158 423200159 **email:** ukmrcc@hmcg.gov.uk
UK Cospas-Sarsat Mission Control Centre (UK MCC)	344 3820902	1329 841905	**AFTN:** EGQPZSZX **email:** ukmcc@hmcg.gov.uk

NAVAREA II

AÇORES - see PORTUGAL
BENIN   See diagrams R4 & R10

National SAR Agency: Direction de la Marine Marchande
Address: B.P. 1234 Cotonou, Benin
Telephone: +229 21314669
Fax: +229 21315845

	Telephone +229	Fax +229	Others/Ship Earth Stations (SES)
RSC COTONOU (Cospas-Sarsat SPOC)	21 001018 21 304571	21 304571	**AFTN:** DBBBZTZX **email:** anacaero@anac.bj

CAMEROON   See diagrams R4 & R10

National SAR Agency: Director-General, The Port Authority of Douala, Cameroon
Address: BP 4020, 5 Boulevard Leclerc, Douala, Cameroon
Telephone: +237 33455233
+237 33420133
+237 33427322
+237 33425233
Fax: +237 33426797
Website: https://mintransports.net/fr/the-ministry/organisational-chart/divisions/maiw/

Douala (TJC) maintains a continuous listening watch on 2182 kHz for distress calls.

	Telephone +237	Fax +237	Others/Ship Earth Stations (SES)
RSC YAOUNDE (Cospas-Sarsat SPOC)	22305200 22305209	22305203	**AFTN:** FKKYYCYX **email:** rsc-yaounde@ccaa.aero
MRCC DOUALA	690637280		**Inmarsat BGAN:** 772387843 772387844 **Inmarsat C:** 460199033 **email:** camrp1@skysile.com camrp2@skysile.com camrp3@skysile.com camrp4@skysile.com

CANARIAS, ISLAS - see SPAIN

CAPE VERDE
See diagrams R4 & R9

National SAR Agency: Joint Rescue Coordination Centre (JRCC)
Address: Centro VTMS / JRCC Mindelo - São Vicente, PO Box No. 1449, Cabo Verde
Telephone: +238 2325555
   +238 5820125
Fax: +238 2324271
Iridium: +881 631552160
email: jrcc.cv@gmail.com

Centro Conjunto de coordenaçao de Salvamento (JRCC) is the authority responsible for coordinating Search and Rescue operations. A H24/7 Alert Post which relays all calls to JRCC is also stationed at Air Traffic Services - Sal Island.

Operational procedures for vessels in distress:

Activate 406 MHz Distress alert;

Call D4A (São Vicente Radio) which maintains a continuous watch on VHF Ch 16, VHF DSC Ch 70, MF DSC 2187·5 kHz and 2182 kHz MF R/T for distress calls.

	Telephone +238	Fax +238	Others/Ship Earth Stations (SES)
CAPE VERDE JRCC (Cospas-Sarsat SPOC)	2325555 5820125	2324271	**email:** jrcc.cv@gmail.com

CONGO
See diagram R10

National SAR Agency: Direction Generale de la Marine Marchande (DIGEMAR)
Address: B.P. 1107, Pointe Noire, Congo
Telephone: +242 22 2942326
   +242 22 2940107
Website: www.transports.gouv.cg/index.php/maritime/direction-general/direction-generale-maritime

The Direction Generale de la Marine Marchande (DIGEMAR) is the national Search and Rescue agency of the Congo. The Congolese Navy are responsible for coordinating Search and Rescue operations.

	Telephone +242	Fax +242	Others/Ship Earth Stations (SES)
ACC BRAZZAVILLE (Cospas-Sarsat SPOC)	27 753027 27 753028	2820050	**AFTN:** FCCCZRZX FCBBYCYX **email:** micheleouolo@yahoo.fr
RCC NAVY	2 941344	2 940180	

CONGO (DEMOCRATIC REPUBLIC)
See diagram R10

National SAR Agency: Unknown

Banana (9PA) maintains a continuous listening watch on 2182 and VHF Ch 16 for distress calls.

	Telephone	Fax	Others/Ship Earth Stations (SES)
ARCC KINSHASA (Cospas-Sarsat SPOC)	+243 81 0373766 +243 81 2237602	+1 270 8139293	**AFTN:** FZAAYCYX **email:** jeaukitambala2005@yahoo.fr

EQUATORIAL GUINEA
See diagram R10

National SAR Agency: Capitan del Puerto de Malabo
Address: Malabo, Equatorial Guinea
Telephone: +240 09 3564
   +240 09 2669
   +240 09 2459
Fax: +240 09 2210

Capitan del Puerto de Malabo is responsible for coordinating Search and Rescue operations up to 50 n miles from the coastline. Malabo Port Control maintains a continuous listening watch on VHF Ch 16 for distress calls. Procedure for vessels in distress is to call Malabo Port Control on VHF Ch 16, or on (SSB) 8790·2 kHz.

	Telephone +240	Fax +240	Others/Ship Earth Stations (SES)
RSC BATA (Cospas-Sarsat SPOC)	33 31582 22 2276607	33 3093999	**AFTN:** FGBTYCYX FGSLYDYX FGSLYDYT
MALABO PORT CONTROL (and other stations)	09 2648 09 3564 09 3399	09 3313 09 2210	

FRANCE   See diagrams R1 & R5

National SAR Agency: Organisme d'études et de coordination pour la recherche et le sauvetage en mer (SECMAR)
Address: 16 Boulevard Raspail, 75007 Paris, France
Telephone: +33 1 53634159
Fax: +33 1 53634178

Centre Régionaux Operationels de Surveillance et de Sauvetage (CROSS)

France has five MRCCs for its European coasts. CROSS provides a permanent, full time, all weather operational presence along the coast of France and co-operates with foreign MRCCs and MRSCs as required. MRCC Gris-Nez has been designated as the initial point of contact for foreign SAR authorities for any question concerning operational aspects of maritime SAR and when France is involved in an incident where a particular French MRCC is not clearly competent to deal with it.

MRCC Gris-Nez has also been designated as the MRCC associated to the French Cospas-Sarsat Mission Control Centre (FMCC) and the Inmarsat LESs.

TeleMedical Assistance Service: Centre de Consultations Medicales Maritimes provide medical advice. Contact via any foreign Coast Radio Station or any French MRCC or JRCC. Possible consultation languages: French and English. CCMM can receive digital pictures, ECG data files etc and can provide specialized teleconsultation. Any ship can contact the CCMM by Inmarsat using SAC 32 or 38 via a France Telecom LES free of charge.

	Telephone +33	Fax +33	Others/Ship Earth Stations (SES)
FMCC (Cospas-Sarsat SPOC)	5 61254382 5 61254432	5 61274878	**AFTN:** LFIAZSZX **email:** fmcc@cnes.fr

Atlantic Coast

	Telephone +33	Fax +33	Others/Ship Earth Stations (SES)
MRCC GRIS-NEZ	3 21872187	3 21877851	**Telex:** +42 130680 CROSSGN **Inmarsat C:** 422799256 **email:** gris-nez@mrccfr.eu **Website:** www.cross-grisnez.developpement-durable.gouv.fr
MRCC JOBOURG	2 33521616	2 33527172	**AFTN:** LFIJYWZQ **email:** jobourg.mrcc@developpement-durable.gouv.fr jobourg@mrccfr.eu jobourgvts@mrcc.fr.eu **Website:** www.cross-jobourg.developpement-durable.gouv.fr
MRCC CORSEN	2 98893131	2 98896575	**AFTN:** LFICYYYX **Telex:** +42 940086 CROCOA **email:** corsen@mrccfr.eu ouessant.traffic@developpement-durable.gouv.fr **Website:** http://www.dirm.nord-atlantique-manche-ouest.develop pement-durable.gouv.fr/cross-corsen-r242.html
MRCC ÉTEL	2 97553535	2 97554934	**AFTN:** LFIEYYYX **Telex:** +42 950519 CROSSB **Inmarsat C:** 422799025 **email:** etel.mrcc@developpement-durable.gouv.fr etel@mrccfr.eu **Website:** http://www.dirm.nord-atlantique-manche-ouest.develop pement-durable.gouv.fr/cross-etel-r239.html

GABON   See diagram R10

National SAR Agency: Ministere de la Marine Marchande et de la Peche
Address: B.P. 803, Libreville, Gabon
Telephone: +241 01 730267
        +241 01 733207
        +241 01 733210

	Telephone +241	Fax +241	Others/Ship Earth Stations (SES)
RSC LIBREVILLE (Cospas-Sarsat SPOC)	01 732475 01 732100		**AFTN:** FOOLYCYX FOOOZIZX

GAMBIA, THE   See diagrams R4 & R9

National SAR Agency: Harbour Master, Gambia Ports Authority
Address: P.O. Box 617, Banjul, The Gambia
Telephone: +220 4229940
        +220 4227266
Fax: +220 4227266
Website: www.gambiaports.gm

The Ministry of Defence coordinates Search and Rescue operations from RSC Banjul. Banjul (C5G) maintains a continuous listening watch on VHF Ch 16 for distress calls. Preferred inter RCC language is English.

	Telephone +220	Fax +220	Others/Ship Earth Stations (SES)
RSC BANJUL (Cospas-Sarsat SPOC)	9962228 3359905	4472190	**AFTN:** GBYDYCYX GBYDYAYX GBYDYAYT **email:** dggcaa@qannet.gm wwright@gcaa.aero
PORTS AUTHORITY	4229940 4227266	4227268	**email:** info@gamports.com

GHANA   See diagrams R4, R9 & R10

National SAR Agency: Ghana Maritime Authority
Address: P.O. Box M.38, Accra, Ghana
Telephone: +233 30 2662122
        +233 30 2684388
Fax: +233 30 2677702
email: info@ghanamaritime.org

Tema (9GX) maintains a continuous listening watch on all international distress frequencies including full DSC facilities.

MRCC Tema is located at Tema Chemu Lighthouse Yard in the same building as VTMIS East Control Centre (9GP-88) maintains a continuous listening watch on international maritime distress frequencies including DSC facilities on VHF only at the present time.

Preferred language for communication with the MRCC is English.

RCC Accra is located at Air Traffic Services Department of the Ghana Civil Aviation Authority (GCAA).

Preferred language for inter RCC communication is English.

	Telephone +233	Fax +233	Others/Ship Earth Stations (SES)
MRCC TEMA (Call Sign 9GP-88)	30 2953129 30 2953138 30 2953140 30 3211781 20 3820565		**email:** MRCCTEMAGH@ghanamaritime.org **MMSI:** 996271131
GHANA CIVIL AVIATION AUTHORITY (Cospas-Sarsat SPOC)	30 2773283 20 2224073 30 2776171 30 2777320	30 2769401 30 2773293	**AFTN:** DGAAZQZX DGAAZQZT DGAAYFYX **email:** ghana.spoc@gcaa.com.gh
RCC ACCRA	30 2773283 20 8160590	30 2769401	**email:** alometey@gcaa.com.gh
GHANA PORTS AND HARBOUR AUTHORITY - TEMA PORT	30 2904706 30 2906350 30 3202212	30 3202812	**email:** signal_station@ghanaports.gov.gh
GHANA PORTS AND HARBOUT AUTHORITY - TAKORADI PORT	31 2024839 31 2024073 (Ext 4508) 20 4730151	31 2022814	**email:** Signals_tk@ghanaports.gov.gh

GUINEA   See diagrams R4, R9 & R10

National SAR Agency: General Director
Address: A. NA. M. BP: 534, Conakry, Guinea
Telephone: +224 601414029
Fax: +224 601414029

	Telephone +224	Fax +224	Others/Ship Earth Stations (SES)
RSC CONAKRY (Cospas-Sarsat SPOC)	60215314 64201065	30413577	**AFTN:** GUCYYCYX

IVORY COAST
See diagrams R4, R9 & R10

National SAR Agency: Directorate General of Port and Maritime Affairs
Address: B.P.V. 67, Abidjan, Ivory Coast
Telephone: +225 27 23494177

Abidjan (TUA) maintains a continuous listening watch on 2182 kHz and VHF Ch 16 for distress calls.

	Telephone +225	Fax +225	Others/Ship Earth Stations (SES)
Maritime Rescue Coordination Centre (MRCC) (H24 Contact)	27 21 255996 27 21 262998 27 21 266929 07 09770101 (Mobile/WhatsApp) 01 72770101 (Mobile)	27 21 255996	**email:** alertes@mrcc-abidjan.net abidjan.mrcc@gmail.com abidjan.radio@gmail.com **Website:** www.mrcc-abidjan.net
ABIDJAN (TUA)	27 21 255992 (Office) 27 21 255996	27 21 255996	**MMSI:** 006191000
Aeronautical National SAR Agency: National Civil Aviation Authority	27 21 586900 27 21 588169	27 21 276346	
ARCC ABIDJAN (Cospas-Sarsat SPOC)	27 21 580180 27 21 580028 01 01909096 (Mobile)	27 21580028	**AFTN:** DIAPYCYX **email:** rscabidjan@gmail.com

LIBERIA
See diagrams R4, R9 & R10

National SAR Agency: Monrovia Regional Maritime Rescue Coodination Centre
Address: Liberian Coast Guard Headquarters, Bushrod Island, 1000 Monrovia, 10 Liberia
Telephone: +231 777092229
+231 777290158
email: mrmrcc@lima.gov.lr
mrcc.monrovia@yahoo.com

A Marine Rescue Coordination Centre exists at Roberts International Airport.

	Telephone +231	Fax +231	Others/Ship Earth Stations (SES)
RCC ROBERTS (Roberts Int Airport) (Cospas-Sarsat SPOC)	68223776		**AFTN:** GLRBZQZX **email:** robertsfir@yahoo.com
Monrovia Regional MRCC	777092229 777290158 886284317 (Officer in charge)		**Mobile:** +231 777084777 (Officer in charge) **Inmarsat:** 772700138 772700139 **Inmarsat C:** 463728971 463728972 **email:** mrmrcc@lima.gov.lr mrcc.monrovia@yahoo.com omascobotoe@gmail.com (Officer in charge) josiah.botoe@lima.gov.lr (Officer in charge)

MADEIRA - see PORTUGAL
MAURITANIA
See diagrams R4 & R9

National SAR Agency: Centre de Coordination et de Sauvetage Maritime (CCSM)
Address: MRCC Nouakchott, Mauritanian Coast Guard branch in Nouakchott
Telephone: +222 45 242405
+222 25 058981
Fax: +222 45 242403
email: mrccnouakchott@peches.gov.mr

MRCC Nouakchott maintains a continuous listening watch on VHF DSC, VHF Ch 16 and R/T MF 2182 kHz

	Telephone +222	Fax +222	Others/Ship Earth Stations (SES)
RCC NOUAKCHOTT (Cospas-Sarsat SPOC)	45 259673 27 108595	45 259673	**AFTN:** GQNOYCYX **email:** rccnktt@gmail.com

MOROCCO   See diagrams R4 & R5

National SAR Agency: Marine Fisheries Department, National SAR Coordinator **Address:** Rue Mohamed Belhassan El Ouazzani Haut agdal, BP 476, Rabat, Morocco **Telephone:** +212 5 37 688174 **Fax:** +212 5 37 688112 **email:** drissi@mpm.gov.ma **Website:** https://www.itopf.org/knowledge-resources/countries-territories-regions/morocco/	

The Ocean Fisheries Department MRCC Rabat is responsible for coordinating Search and Rescue operations.

MRCC Rabat maintains a continuous listening watch on international distress frequencies.

TeleMedical Assistance Service: Contact MRCC Rabat and send a message for "Radio Medical Assistance" and telemedical advice will be provided from a regional public hospital via MRCC Rabat.

Possible consultation languages: Arabic, French and English.

	Telephone +212	Fax +212	Others/Ship Earth Stations (SES)
MRCC RABAT	5 37 625877	5 37 625017	**Inmarsat C:** 424200893 **email:** mrcc.rabat@mpm.gov.ma mrccrabat@gmail.com **MMSI:** 002424133
MRCC RABAT (Cospas-Sarsat SPOC)	5 37 625877	5 37 625017	**email:** spoc.maritime.maroc@mpm.gov.ma

Atlantic

	Telephone +212	Fax +212	Others/Ship Earth Stations (SES)
MRSC TANGER	5 39 932090	5 37 625017 (Emergency) 5 39 932093	**email:** mrsc.tanger@mpm.gov.ma **MMSI:** 242072000
MRSC AGADIR	5 28 842964 5 28 842984	5 37 625017 (Emergency) 5 28 842820	**email:** mrsc.agadir@mpm.gov.ma **MMSI:** 002424136
MRSC DAKHLA	5 28 897300	5 37 625017 (Emergency) 5 28 898381	**email:** mrsc.dakhla@mpm.gov.ma **MMSI:** 002424137

NIGERIA   See diagrams R4 & R10

National SAR Agency: National Maritime Administration and Safety Agency (NIMASA) **Address:** 4 Burma Road, Apapa - Lagos, Nigeria **Telephone:** +234 1 2713622 +234 1 2713623 +234 1 2713624 +234 1 2713627 **Fax:** +234 1 2713625 **email:** rmrcc.lagos@nimasa.gov.ng **Website:** www.nimasa.gov.ng	

The National Maritime Administration & Safety Agency (NAMASA) is responsible for coordinating Search and Rescue operations.

	Telephone +234	Fax +234	Others/Ship Earth Stations (SES)
NIMCC Cospas–Sarsat SPOC)	806 2684985 805 8245928		**AFTN:** DNAAZXFX **email:** info@kakawamarine.com
RMRCC LAGOS	803 0685167 705 3794383 705 3794380 7000700010 (Mobile) 7000700020 (Mobile) 7000700030 (Mobile)		**Inmarsat BGAN:** 772240598 **Inmarsat C:** 492052551 **email:** rmrccnigeria@yahoo.com rmrcc.lagos@nimasa.gov.ng

PORTUGAL   See diagrams R1 & R4

National SAR Agency: Ministério da Defesa Nacional - Marinha
Address: Estado-Maior da Armada, Rua do Arsenal, Lisboa 1149-001, Portugal
Telephone: +351 213 255498 (0900-1700 LT)
　　　　　　+351 213 217666 (H24)
Fax: +351 214 479591
email: comar.dir@marinha.pt

The Portuguese Navy is responsible for coordinating Search and Rescue operations in two SRR regions, Lisboa and Santa Maria. MRCCs exist at Lisboa and Ponta Delgada. A network of Coast Radio Stations maintain a continuous listening watch on international distress frequencies, 2182 kHz & VHF Ch 16.

MRCC Lisboa (MMSI: 002630100) maintains a continuous mainland listening watch on DSC VHF Ch 70 for DSC A1.

TeleMedical Assistance Service: Centro de Orientação de Doentes no Mar (CODUMAR) provide assistance. Contact via MRCC Lisboa, MRSC Funchal, and MRCC Ponta Delgada.

Possible consultation languages: Portuguese and English.

	Telephone +351	Fax +351	Others/Ship Earth Stations (SES)
MRCC LISBOA (Cospas-Sarsat SPOC)	214 401919 214 401950	214 401954 211 938442	**Inmarsat BGAN:** 776600080 **Inmarsat C:**　　426300032 **email:** mrcc.lisboa@marinha.pt

Açores

	Telephone +351	Fax +351	Others/Ship Earth Stations (SES)
MRCC PONTA DELGADA	296 281777 917 777453	211 938518	**Inmarsat BGAN:** 776600145 **Inmarsat C:**　　426300065 **email:** mrcc.delgada@marinha.pt 　　　　mrcc.delgada@gmail.com

Madeira

	Telephone +351	Fax +351	Others/Ship Earth Stations (SES)
MRSC FUNCHAL	291 213110 919 678140	291 228232	**Inmarsat C:** 426300032 (Shared/relayed by MRCC Lisboa) **email:** mrsc.funchal@marinha.pt

SENEGAL   See diagrams R4 & R9

National SAR Agency: HASSMAR, BP 27074, Dakar, Senegal
Telephone: +221 33 8215801
email: Contact.HASSMAR@hassmar.gouv.sn
Website: https://www.hassmar.gouv.sn/content/mrcc

Dakar MRCC maintains listening watch on VHF DSC, MF DSC and HF DSC for distress calls.

	Telephone +221	Fax +221	Others/Ship Earth Stations (SES)
RCC DAKAR (Cospas-Sarsat SPOC)	33 8603326 33 8604787 77 3338409 77 3330114	33 8603326	**AFTN:** GOOVYCYX **email:** ccsdakarsenegal@gmail.com
MRCC DAKAR	33 8217637 76 3680491 33 8265001 77 7406313	33 8265000	**email:** mrcc.dakar@hassmar.gouv.sn 　　　　marinenat@orange.sn

SIERRA LEONE   See diagrams R4, R9 & R10

National SAR Agency: Harbour Master, Sierra Leone Ports Authority
Address: QEII PMB 386, Cline Town, Freetown, Sierra Leone
Telephone: +232 22 250033
Fax: +232 22 250616

The Sierra Leone Ports Authority is responsible for coordinating Search and Rescue operations. VHF equipment has been designated for Search and Rescue purposes and Sierra Leone has excellent telephone links with RCCs in the developed countries.

	Telephone +232	Fax +232	Others/Ship Earth Stations (SES)
RSC FREETOWN (Cospas-Sarsat SPOC)	33 606061 33 886767	22 224653	**AFTN:** GFLLZPZX **email:** aisgfllbrief@yahoo.com

SPAIN   See diagrams R1, R4 & R5

National SAR Agency: Sociedad de Salvamento y Seguridad Marítima
Address: C / Fruela 3, 28011 Madrid
Telephone: +34 91 7559132
          +34 91 7559133
Fax: +34 91 5261440
Website: www.salvamentomaritimo.es

MRCC Madrid is responsible for coordinating Search and Rescue operations and has twenty one MRCCs and MRSCs (including seasonal MRSC Palamos open from 1 June to 30 Sep), divided into the North Coast, South Coast, Mediterranean Coast and Islas Canarias regions, under its control. All the MRCCs and MRSCs are manned on a 24 hour basis. A network of Coast Radio Stations, connected by intranet and telephone to all Spanish MRCCs, maintains a continuous listening watch on international distress frequencies. Preferred languages for inter RCC are English and Spanish. Please note, email is not to be used for emergency purposes.

	Telephone +34	Fax +34	Others/Ship Earth Stations (SES)
SPMCC (Cospas-Sarsat SPOC)	928 727105	928 727107	**AFTN:** GCMPZSZX **email:** spmcc@inta.es
MRCC MADRID	91 7559132 91 7559133	91 5261440	**Inmarsat C:** 422423124 **email:** cncs@sasemar.es

North Coast

	Telephone +34	Fax +34	Others/Ship Earth Stations (SES)
MRCC BILBAO	944 837053 944 839411 944 839286	944 839161	**email:** bilbao@sasemar.es
MRSC CORUÑA	981 209541 981 209548 981 221005	981 209518	**email:** coruna@sasemar.es
MRCC FINISTERRE	981 767320 981 767738 981 767500	981 767740	**Inmarsat C:** 422423127 **email:** finisterre@sasemar.es
MRCC GIJÓN	985 326050 985 326373	985 320908	**email:** gijon@sasemar.es
MRSC SANTANDER	942 213030 942 213060 942 213157	942 213638	**email:** santander@sasemar.es
MRSC VIGO	986 222230 986 228874 986 227112	986 228957	**email:** vigo@sasemar.es

Islas Canarias

	Telephone +34	Fax +34	Others/Ship Earth Stations (SES)
MRCC LAS PALMAS	928 467757 928 467955	928 467760	**email:** laspalmas@sasemar.es
MRCC TENERIFE	922 597550 922 597551 922 597552	922 597331	**Inmarsat C:** 422423125 **email:** tenerife@sasemar.es

South Coast

	Telephone +34	Fax +34	Others/Ship Earth Stations (SES)
MRSC CÁDIZ	956 214253 956 211621	956 226091	**email:** cadiz@sasemar.es
MRSC HUELVA	959 243000 959 243061 959 243073	959 242103	**email:** huelva@sasemar.es
MRCC TARIFA	956 684740 956 684757	956 680606	**Inmarsat C:** 422423126 **email:** tarifa@sasemar.es

NAVAREA III

ALBANIA

National SAR Agency: Rescue Communication Centre
Address: Rruga "Dibres", Ministry of Defence, General Staff of Armed Forces, Tirana 2324, Albania
Telephone: +355 4 2240081
Fax: +355 4 2270408
email: nsarc@aaf.mil.al
Website: www.aaf.mil.al

	Telephone +355	Fax +355	Others/Ship Earth Stations (SES)
Rescue Communicaton Centre	4 2240081	4 2270408	**email:** nsarc@aaf.mil.al **Website:** www.aaf.mil.al

ALGERIA   See diagram R5

National SAR Agency: Ministère de la Défence Nationale (MDN)
Address: Service Nationale de Garde Côtes, BOP 71, Amirauté, Alger, Algeria
Telephone: +213 21710178
Fax: +213 21714108
email: mcc_algiers@mdn.dz
Website: www.mdn.dz/site_cfn/sommaire/presentation/sngc_an.php

The Coast Guard is responsible for coordinating Search and Rescue maritime operations. A network of Coast Radio Stations maintains a continuous listening watch on international distress frequencies.

	Telephone +213	Fax +213	Others/Ship Earth Stations (SES)
RCC ALGIERS (Cospas-Sarsat SPOC)	23 978538	23 978539	**AFTN:** DAARYCYF **email:** rcc_cfdat@mdn.dz
MRCC (CROSS) ALGIERS	21 203184 23 974147 23 974148	23 974150	**Telex:** +408 55211 **email:** mcc_algiers@mdn.dz
(CROSS) ORAN	41 396701	41 396701	**Telex:** +408 81488 **email:** mcc_algiers@mdn.dz
(CROSS) JIJEL	34 474591	34 474591	**Telex:** +408 84959 **email:** mcc_algiers@mdn.dz

AZERBAIJAN

National SAR Agency: Crisis Management Centre of the Ministry of Emergency Situations of the Republic of Azerbaijan
Telephone: +994 12 5124030
      +994 12 5124031
Fax: +994 12 5124032
email: bvim@fhz.gov.az
Website: www.bvim.fhn.gov.az

	Telephone +994	Fax +994	Others/Ship Earth Stations (SES)
LRIT National Centre of Maritime Safety Centre under the State Maritime Agency of the Republic of Azerbaijan	12 4920606 (H24) 12 4920675	12 4920642	**email:** mrcc@mm.ardda.gov.az security@mm.ardda.gov.az security@ardda.gov.az mm_navtex@mm.ardda.gov.az navtex@mm.ardda.gov.az **MMSI:** 004231000 004232000

BULGARIA
See diagram R6

National SAR Agency: Maritime Administration Executive Agency **Address:** Executive Agency to the Ministry of Transport of the Republic of Bulgaria, 9 Djakon Ignatij Street, Sofia 1000, Bulgaria **Telephone:** +359 2 9300910 **email:** bma@marad.bg **Website:** www.marad.bg			

Varna Radio Coast Station is associated with MRCC Varna.

Varna Radio (LZW) maintains a continuous listening watch on 2182 kHz and VHF Ch.16.

VHF DSC and MF DSC facilities on Ch 70 and 2187.5 kHz are also maintained at Varna Radio."

	Telephone +359	**Fax** +359	**Others/Ship Earth Stations (SES)**
MRCC VARNA (Cospas-Sarsat SPOC)	52 603268 52 633067	52 603265	**Mobile:** +359 888 952113 **Inmarsat:** +870 776724780 (Isat 2 Phone) **Inmarsat C:** 420722210 **email:** mrcc@marad.bg

CORSE - see FRANCE
CROATIA
See diagram R5

National SAR Agency: MRCC Rijeka
Address: 51000 Rijeka, Senjsko Pristanište 3, Croatia
Telephone: +385 195
       +385 51 312301
       +385 51 313266
Fax: +385 51 312254			

The Search and Rescue Coordination Centre for Croatia is located at the Harbour Master's Office at Rijeka, with Sub-Centres in the Harbour Master's Offices at Pula, Senj, Zadar, Šibenik, Split, Ploče and Dubrovnik. The service also includes the branch harbour offices within their authority. A network of Coast Radio Stations maintains a continuous listening watch on international distress frequencies including DSC Ch 70. MRCC Rijeka also maintains a continuous listening watch on GMDSS distress frequencies, VHF DSC Ch 70 and MF DSC 2187·5 kHz.

	Telephone +385	**Fax** +385	**Others/Ship Earth Stations (SES)**
MRCC RIJEKA (Cospas-Sarsat SPOC)	195 51 312301 51 313266	51 312254	**AFTN:** LDZOZGZX (Zagreb) **Inmarsat C:** 423816510=MRCC X **email:** mrcc@pomorstvo.hr
MRSC RIJEKA	51 214031	51 313265	**email:** rijeka.pomorskipromet@pomorstvo.hr
MRSC DUBROVNIK	20 418989	20 419211	**email:** dubrovnik.pomorskipromet@pomorstvo.hr
MRSC PLOČE	20 679008	20 670206	**email:** plpompromet@pomorstvo.hr
MRSC PULA	52 222037	52 222037	**email:** pula.pomorskipromet@pomorstvo.hr
MRSC SENJ	53 881301	53 884128	**email:** senj.pomorskipromet@pomorstvo.hr
MRSC ŠIBENIK	22 217214	22 212626	**email:** sibenik.pomorskipromet@pomorstvo.hr
MRSC SPLIT	21 362436	21 346555	**email:** split.pomorskipromet@pomorstvo.hr
MRSC ZADAR	23 254880	23 254876	**email:** zadar.pomorskipromet@pomorstvo.hr

CYPRUS   See diagram R6

National SAR Agency: Coordinator: Joint Rescue Coordination Centre of Larnaca
Address: 2 Tasou Markou Street, 6029, Larnaca
Telephone: +357 24643005
             +357 24304723
             +357 1441 (Nationwide free call number)
Fax: +357 24643254
AFTN: LCLKYCYX
Inmarsat C: 421099999
email: info@jrcc.org.cy
        rescuecy@gmail.com

The Search and Rescue Coordination Centre of Cyprus is based in the city of Larnaca and is manned on a 24/7 basis and is known as JRCC Larnaca.

All communications concerning Search and Rescue should be addressed to JRCC Larnaca. JRCC Larnaca is the responsible authority for the Search and Rescue system of Cyprus within the Search and Rescue Region (SRR) of the Republic of Cyprus. Maritime SRR coincides with the Aeronautical SRR and with the Nicosia FIR. For any incident within the barracks of the British Forces in Cyprus, the responsible authority to deal with is the Operational Centre at Akrotiri, in cooperation with JRCC Larnaca when necessary.

JRCC Larnaca, Cyprus Radio and CYMCC (Cyprus Mission Control Centre Cospas-Sarsat station are co-located. Cyprus Radio operates a maritime radio service which maintains a continuous listening watch on all the international distress frequencies.

TeleMedical Assistance Service: Provided by Emergency Department, Nicosia General Hospital. Contact through Cyprus Radio MMSI 002091000 on VHF, MF, HF DSC or JRCC Larnaca. Possible consultation languages: Greek and English. Contact telephone +357 22 604006. Please note that email may not be used for an emergency.

	Telephone +357	Fax +357	Others/Ship Earth Stations (SES)
JRCC LARNACA (Cospas-Sarsat SPOC)	24643005 24304723 1441 (Nationwide free call number)	24643254	**AFTN:** LCLKYCYX **Inmarsat C:** 421099999 **Iridium:** +870 772545696 **email:** info@jrcc.org.cy **Website:** http://jrcc-cyprus.mod.gov.cy
JOC AKROTIRI	25276854 25275002 25953449	25276795	**AFTN:** LCRAYWYW **email:** akrotiriops@hotmail.com
CYPRUS RADIO COAST STATION	24304454 24304452	24669950	**email:** cyprus.radio@jrcc.org.cy **Website:** http://jrcc-cyprus.mod.gov.cy
CYMCC (Cyprus Mission Control Centre Cospas-Sarsat station)	24643261		**email:** cymcc@jrcc.org.cy

EGYPT   See diagrams R6 & R11

National SAR Agency: Ministry of Defence
Address: Almaza Airforce Base, Heliopolis, Cairo, Egypt
Telephone: +20 2 24184537
Fax: +20 2 24184531
Telex: +91 21095 RCCCR UN
email: jrcc136@afmic.gov.eg

The authority responsible for coordinating Search and Rescue operations is The Middle East Search and Rescue Centre, JRCC Cairo. The area of responsibility corresponds to the Cairo FIR in the Mediterranean and Red Seas. A network of Coast Radio Stations maintain a continuous listening watch on international distress frequencies.

	Telephone +20	Fax +20	Others/Ship Earth Stations (SES)
JRCC CAIRO (Cospas-Sarsat SPOC)	2 24184537 2 24184531	2 24184531 2 24184537	**AFTN:** HECCYCYS HECAYFYX HECAYTST **Telex:** +91 21095 RCCCR UN **Inmarsat C:** 462299910 (RCCE X) **email:** jrcc136@afmic.gov.eg mcc@saregypt.net
MRCC Al Iskandarīyah (ALEXANDRIA)	3 4842058 3 4842119 3 4878983	3 4832240	
Al Iskandarīyah (ALEXANDRIA) (SUH)	3 4809500 3 4801266 3 4810202	3 4810201	**Telex:** +91 55544 SUH UN
Port Said (Būr Sa`īd) (SUP)	66 3220625 66 3220626	66 3325705 66 3325706	**Telex:** +91 63165 COMPS UN +91 63166 RADPS UN

Continued on next page

EGYPT (Continued)

	Telephone +20	Fax +20	Others/Ship Earth Stations (SES)
SUEZ CANAL (ISMAILIA) (SUQ)	64 3399126 (SAR Operator) 64 3399118 64 3399128	64 3399517 64 3399230	**Telex:** +91 63238 SUCAN UN +91 63528 SUQSC UN **Inmarsat C:** 462299911 462211621 **email:** ismradio@suezcanal.gov.eg
El-Quseir (Al Quşayr) (SUK)	65 3330001	65 3330001	**Telex:** +91 92350
JRSC HURGHADA	65 3330001	65 3330001	**Telex:** +91 92350

FRANCE   See diagrams R1 & R5

National SAR Agency: Organisme d'études et de coordination pour la recherche et le sauvetage en mer (SECMAR)
Address: 16 Boulevard Raspail, 75007 Paris, France
Telephone: +33 1 53634159
Fax: +33 1 53634178

Centre Régionaux Operationels de Surveillance et de Sauvetage (CROSS)

France has five MRCCs for its European coasts. CROSS provides a permanent, full time, all weather operational presence along the coast of France and co-operates with foreign MRCCs and MRSCs as required. MRCC Gris-Nez has been designated as the initial point of contact for foreign SAR authorities for any question concerning operational aspects of maritime SAR and when France is involved in an incident where a particular French MRCC is not clearly competent to deal with it.

MRCC Gris-Nez has also been designated as the MRCC associated to the French Cospas-Sarsat Mission Control Centre (FMCC) and the Inmarsat LESs.

TeleMedical Assistance Service: Centre de Consultations Medicales Maritimes provide medical advice. Contact via any foreign Coast Radio Station or any French MRCC or JRCC. Possible consultation languages: French and English. CCMM can receive digital pictures, ECG data files etc and can provide specialized teleconsultation. Any ship can contact the CCMM by Inmarsat using SAC 32 or 38 via a France Telecom LES free of charge.

	Telephone +33	Fax +33	Others/Ship Earth Stations (SES)
FMCC (Cospas-Sarsat SPOC)	5 61254382 5 61254432	5 61274878	**AFTN:** LFIAZSZX **email:** fmcc@cnes.fr

Mediterranean Coast

	Telephone +33	Fax +33	Others/Ship Earth Stations (SES)
MRCC LA GARDE	4 94611616	4 94271149	**AFTN:** LFJGYYYX **email:** lagarde@mrccfr.eu
MRSC AJACCIO	4 95201363	4 95225191	**email:** ajaccio.mrsc@developpement-durable.gouv.fr ajaccio@mrscfr.eu

GEORGIA   See diagram R6

National SAR Agency: SMRCC Georgia, LEPL Maritime Transport Agency of Georgia, Ministry of Economy and Sustainable Development of Georgia
Address: 50, Baku Street Street, Batumi 6000, Georgia
Telephone: +995 422 273913
Fax: +995 422 273905
email: mrcc@mta.gov.ge
Website: www.mta.gov.ge

The State Coordination Rescue Centre (SMRCC GEORGIA) is based in the Maritime Transport Agency in Batumi and is responsible for the coordination of all maritime distress and safety incidents within the Maritime Search and Rescue Region of Georgia. The Harbour Master's Offices in the ports of Batumi, Poti and Kulevi are designated as Rescue Sub-Centres for the areas up to 12 n miles from the respective ports.

TeleMedical Assistance Service: Maritime Medical Centre provide assistance. Contact via MRCC Georgia.

Possible consultation language is English.

	Telephone +995	Fax +995	Others/Ship Earth Stations (SES)
MRCC GEORGIA (Batumi) (Cospas-Sarsat SPOC)	422 273913 (H24) 599 293736 (H24) (Mobile)	422 273905 (H24)	**Inmarsat C:** 421300183 **email:** mrcc@mta.gov.ge
RSC BATUMI (Harbour Master)	422 276792 (H24) 595 118412 (H24) (Mobile)	422 276792 (H24)	**email:** hmbatumi@mta.gov.ge

Continued overleaf

SAR

GEORGIA (Continued)

	Telephone +995	Fax +995	Others/Ship Earth Stations (SES)
RSC POTI (Harbour Master)	493 277777 ext 7866 (H24) 577 221656 (H24) (Mobile)		email: hmpoti@mta.gov.ge
RSC KULEVI (Harbour Master)	32 2243828 (H24)	32 2243828 (H24)	email: hmkulevi@mta.gov.ge

GIBRALTAR (UK)   See diagram R5

National SAR Agency: Gibraltar VTS
Address: 12 Windmill Hill Road, Gibraltar, GX11 1AA
Telephone: +350 200 61743
        +350 200 46254
Fax: +350 200 77011
email: ops@port.gov.gi
Website: https://www.gibraltarport.com/
MMSI: 002361001

Gibraltar VTS is manned H24 and is responsible for the co-ordination of SAR operations within British Gibraltar Territorial Waters (BGTW)

	Telephone +350	Fax +350	Others/Ship Earth Stations (SES)
GIBRALTAR MARITIME ADMINISTRATION (Cospas-Sarsat SPOC)	569 39000 (H24) 200 73766 (Office Hours 9-5 LT)	20047770	email: maritime.survey@gibraltar.gov.gi
GIBRALTAR VTS	200 61743 200 46254	200 77011	email: ops@port.gov.gi

GREECE   See diagrams R5 & R6

National SAR Agency: Operations Directorate, Ministry of Maritime Affairs and Insular Policy, Hellenic Coast Guard
Address: Akti Vassiliadi, Gate E1-E2, 18510 Peiraiás, Greece
Telephone: +30 213 1371183
        +30 213 1371033
        +30 210 4112500
email: depix.1@hcg.gr
Website: https://www.hcg.gr/en/organization/duties/search-and-rescue/

JRCC Piraeus is responsible for coordinating Search and Rescue operations.

The area for Search and Rescue responsibility is divided into five sub-areas: RSC Thessaloniki (N Aegean Sea), RSC Mytilini (Central Aegean Sea), RSC Ródos (SE Aegean Sea), RSC Chaniá (SW Aegeān Sea) and RSC Pátrai (Ionian Sea). Additionally, all Greek Port Authorities operate as maritime Search and Rescue units and are served by Coast Guard personnel.

A network of Coast Radio Stations maintains a continuous listening watch on international distress frequencies. Contact may also be established with JRCC Pieraiás (Piraeus) through Inmarsat.

TeleMedical Assistance Service: Medical Advice Centre of the Hellenic Red Cross provide assistance. Contact via JRCC Pieraiás (Piraeus). Possible consultation languages: Greek and English

	Telephone +30	Fax +30	Others/Ship Earth Stations (SES)
JRCC PEIRAIÁS (PIRAEUS) (Cospas-Sarsat SPOC)	210 4112500 210 4220772 210 1371325 213 1371126 210 4101116		**AFTN:** LGGGYCYX **Inmarsat C:** 423767310 (RCCG) **email:** jrccpgr@hcg.gr
RSC THESSALONÍKI (N Aegean Sea)	231 3325800 231 3325801		email: thessaloniki@hcg.gr
RSC PÁTRA (Ionian Sea)	261 3615400 261 3615401		email: patra@hcg.gr
RSC CHANIÁ (SW Aegean Sea)	282 1098888 282 1089240 282 1052777		email: chania@hcg.gr
RSC RÓDOS (Rhodes) (SE Aegean Sea)	224 1028666 224 1022203 224 1028888		email: rodos@hcg.gr

Continued on next page

GREECE (Continued)

	Telephone +30	Fax +30	Others/Ship Earth Stations (SES)
RSC MYTILÍNI (Central Aegean Sea)	225 1040827 225 1037447 225 1024115		**email:** mitilini@hcg.gr

IRAN   See diagrams R6 & R11

National SAR Agency: Ports and Maritime Organization, Director General, Maritime Safety and Marine Protection.
Address: No 1. Shahidi St. Shahid Haghani Highway, Vanak Sq. Tehrān Iran. Postal Code: 1518663111
Telephone: +98 21 84932171
           +98 21 84932175
Fax: +98 21 84932190
email: tehran-mrcc@pmo.ir
Website: https://www.pmo.ir/fa/safetyandincidents/searchandrescue

The Ports and Maritime organization is responsible for coordinating maritime Search and Rescue operations. A network of Coast Radio Stations maintain a continuous listening watch on international distress frequencies.

	Telephone +98	Fax +98	Others/Ship Earth Stations (SES)
RCC TEHRĀN Cospas-Sarsat SPOC	21 61022293	21 44525882	**AFTN:** OIIIZRZX
HQ TEHRĀN	21 84932175 21 84932172 21 84932170	21 84932190 21 88651191	
MRCC AMĪRĀBĀD (Caspian Sea)	152 5462019	152 5462019	**Telex:** +88 215124 ENDR IR
MRCC ANZALĪ (Caspian Sea)	181 3225540	181 3223902	**Telex:** +88 232199
MRCC NOW-SHAHR (Caspian Sea)	191 3250984	191 3250982	**Telex:** +88 216643 ENDR IR **email:** nowshahrmrcc@nowshahport.ir
MRCC BANDAR-E SHAHĪD RAJĀ'Ī	763 3514032 763 3514033 763 3514034 763 3514035	763 3514036	**email:** radio@bpa.ir bandarabbas-mrcc@bpa.ir
MRCC BANDAR-E-EMĀM KHOMEYNĪ	651 2226902 652 2522451 652 2522452 652 2522453	651 2226902	**Telex:** +88 612051 ENDR IR
MRCC BŪSHEHR	771 2530075 771 2566449	771 2566400 771 2530077	**Telex:** +88 222208 **email:** radio@pso.ir
MRCC CHĀBAHĀR (Gulf of Oman)	545 2221415 545 2221215	545 2221215	

ISRAEL   See diagram R6

National SAR Agency: JRCC Hefa (Haifa)
Address: POB 806, Hefa 31007 Israel
Telephone: +972 4 8632145
Fax: +972 4 8632117
      +972 3 6849867 (Fax to Mail)
email: rcc@mot.gov.il
      rcchaifa@gmail.com

	Telephone +972	Fax +972	Others/Ship Earth Stations (SES)
RCC BEN GURION AIRPORT (Cospas-Sarsat SPOC)	3 9756215 3 9756216 3 9756217	3 9756219	**AFTN:** LLBGYDYX **email:** fpl@iaa.gov.il
JRCC HEFA (Haifa) (Cospas-Sarsat SPOC)	4 8632145 4 8632072 4 8632073 4 8632074 4 8632075	4 8632117 3 6849867 (Fax to Mail)	**Inmarsat:** 772577926 (Telephone) **Inmarsat C:** 423594249 **Iridium:** +881 623472554 **email:** rcc@mot.gov.il rcchaifa@gmail.com

National SAR Agency: Ministry of Infrastructure and Transport
Address: Comando Generale del Corpo Delle Capitanerie di Porto - Guardia Costiera, Viale dell'Arte, 16 - Rome 00144, Italy
Telephone: +39 06 5923569
+39 06 5924145
+39 06 59084409
+39 06 59084527
+39 06 59084697
Fax: +39 06 5922737
+39 06 59084793
email: itmrcc@mit.gov.it
cgcp3rep4@mit.gov.it
itmrcc@outlook.it
Website: www.guardiacostiera.gov.it

MRCC Rome is responsible for coordinating Search and Rescue operations within Italian waters and liaising with RCCs of other nations.

A network of Coast Radio Stations maintain a continuous listening watch on international distress frequencies.

TeleMedical Assistance Service: Centro Internazionale Radio Medico - (C.I.R.M.)

Via dell'Architettura 41

Rome 00144

Tel: +39 06 59290263

email: telesoccorso@cirm.it

Web: www.cirm.it

C.I.R.M. can also be contacted via any Italian Coast Radio Station or MRCC / MRSC.

Possible consultation languages: Italian, French and English.

	Telephone +39	Fax +39	Others/Ship Earth Stations (SES)
ITMCC Cospas-Sarsat	080 5341571 080 5344033	080 5342145	**AFTN:** LIJCYFYX **email:** itmcc247@cospas-sarsat-italy.it itmccoperator@cospas-sarsat-italy.it **Website:** www.cospas-sarsat-italy.it
MRCC ROME	06 5923569 06 5924145 06 59084409 06 59084527 06 59084697 06 59084793 06 5922737		**AFTN:** LIJIYFYX **Inmarsat C:** 424744220=MRCC X **email:** itmrcc@mit.gov.it cgcp3rep4@mit.gov.it itmrcc@outlook.it
MRSC ANCONA	071 227581 071 502101	071 55393	**email:** so.cpancona@mit.gov.it ancona@guardiacostiera.it
MRSC BARI	080 5281511 080 5281544 080 5281546 080 5216860	080 5211726	**email:** so.cpbari@mit.gov.it cpbari@mit.gov.it dm.bari@pec.mit.gov.it
MRSC CIVITAVECCHIA	06 65617326 06 65617349 06 65617376 06 65617574 06 65617575	07 66679642	**email:** roperativo.dmcivita@mit.gov.it civitacecchia@guardiacostiera.it cpciv@mit.gov.it cproma@mit.gov.it
MRSC GENOVA	010 2777465 010 2777387 010 2777385 010 2777477 010 2777572 010 2777577	010 2777427	**email:** so.cpgenova@mit.gov.it vts.dmgenova@mit.gov.it roperativo.dmgenova@mit.gov.it soperazioni.dmgenova@mit.gov.it
MRSC LIVORNO	0586 826070 0586 826069 0586 894493 0586 826068	0586 826090	**email:** so.cplivorno@mit.gov.it cplivorno@guardiacostiera.gov.it

Continued on next page

SAR

ITALY (Continued)

	Telephone +39	Fax +39	Others/Ship Earth Stations (SES)
MRSC NAPOLI	081 2445308 081 2445431 081 2445432 081 2445433 081 2445434 081 5536017	081 2445347	email: so.cpnapoli@mit.gov.it napoli@guardiacostiera.it
MRSC PESCARA	085 694040 085 9189800 085 4510117	085 4510117	email: so.cppescara@mit.gov.it cppescara@mit.gov.it MMSI: 002470025
MRSC RAVENNA	0544 443013 0544 443011		email: so.cpravenna@mit.gov.it cpravenna@mit.gov.it dm.ravenna@pec.mit.gov.it MMSI: 002470018
MRSC REGGIO CALABRIA	0965 6561 0965 650090 0965 656268	0965 656333 0965 656294	email: reggiocalabria@guardiacostiera.it cpreggio@mit.gov.it MMSI: 002470015
MRSC TRIESTE	040 676611 040 676616 040 676677	040 676665	email: trieste@guardiacostiera.it MMSI: 002470020
MRSC VENEZIA	041 2405711 041 2405745 041 2405706	041 2405730	email: so.cpvenezia@mit.gov.it venezia@guardiacostiera.it cpvenezia@mit.gov.it MMSI: 002470019

Sardegna

	Telephone +39	Fax +39	Others/Ship Earth Stations (SES)
MRSC CAGLIARI	070 659210 070 659225 070 60517240	070 60517218 070 669576	email: cpcagliari@mit.gov.it cagliari@guardiacostiera.gov.it
MRSC OLBIA	0789 21243 0789 26666 0789 26492 0789 56360 0789 26938	0789 563639	email: so.cpolbia@mit.gov.it cpolbia@mit.gov.it

Sicilia

	Telephone +39	Fax +39	Others/Ship Earth Stations (SES)
MRSC CATANIA	095 7474321 095 7474319 095 7474211 095 538888 095 7474111	095 5533962	email: so.cpcatania@mit.gov.it cpcatania@mit.gov.it catania@guardiacostiera.it
CAPITANERIA DI PORTO DI MESSINA	090 344444 090 45830	090 5730832	email: so.cpmessina@mit.gov.it cpmessina@mit.gov.it
MRSC PALERMO	091 331538 091 6043110 091 6043165 091 6043188 091 6043111	091 325519 (RX) 091 327213 (TX)	email: so.cppalermo@mit.gov.it palermo@guardiacostiera.it cppalermo@mit.gov.it MMSI: 002470022

JORDAN   See diagram R11

National SAR Agency: `Aqaba Port Control
Address: P.O. Box 731, 77110 `Aqaba, Jordan
Telephone: +962 32015549
Fax: +962 32016110

`Aqaba Harbour Master is responsible for coordinating Search and Rescue operations and maintains a continuous listening watch on DSC VHF Ch 70 and VHF Ch 16 for distress calls.

	Telephone +962	Fax +962	Others/Ship Earth Stations (SES)
RCC ATC AMMAN (Cospas-Sarsat SPOC)	64451672 65536771	64451667	**AFTN:** OJACZQZX
ACC AMMAN	64451607 64451114 64451160 64451672 64452026	64452033	**AFTN:** OJAIYCYX **email:** sar@carc.gov.jo **Website:** www.carc.jo
HARBOUR MASTER	32015858	32031553	**email:** harbour.comm@nic.net.jo

LEBANON   See diagram R6

National SAR Agency: Lebanese Navy
Address: Naval Base, Beyrouth Port

The Lebanese Navy is responsible for Search and Rescue in Lebanese waters. A continuous listening watch is maintained on VHF Ch 16 and 2182 kHz, through Lebanese Naval Bases.

	Telephone +961	Fax +961	Others/Ship Earth Stations (SES)
RCC BEYROUTH (Cospas-Sarsat SPOC)	1 629026	1 629023	**AFTN:** OLBBZQZX OLDDYAYZ OLBAZPZX **email:** ais@beirutairport.gov.lb
LEBANESE NAVY HQ	1 313478 1 983458	1 983460	**email:** navy@army.gov.lb

LIBYA   See diagram R5

National SAR Agency: RCC Libya
Address: Tripoli 00218, Libya
Telephone: +218 214446799
Fax: +218 213606868
email: sar@ans.caa.gov.ly
Website: https://caa.gov.ly/en/

	Telephone +218	Fax +218	Others/Ship Earth Stations (SES)
RCC LIBYA	214446799 215631578	213606868 214446799	**AFTN:** HLLTYCYX **email:** sar@ans.caa.gov.ly salem.elkabir@caa.gov.ly

MALTA   See diagram R5

National SAR Agency: Rescue Coordination Centre Malta c/o Armed Forces of Malta Operations Centre
Address: Luqa Barracks, Luqa, Malta VLT 2000
Telephone: +356 22 494202
          +356 21 257267
Fax: +356 21 809860
email: rccmalta@gov.mt

The Operations Centre of the Armed Forces of Malta (AFM) doubles as Malta RCC and is responsible for coordinating SAR Operations within the Malta SRR which coincides with the Malta FIR. Transport Malta and Malta Air Traffic Services assist RCC Malta in the conduct of such operations. RCC Malta works closely with neighbouring RCCs, particularly during incidents in remote areas of Malta SRR. Distress information originating from Cospas-Sarsat and Inmarsat is transmitted to Malta RCC or the Malta International Airport plc Air Traffic Control Tower.

	Telephone +356	Fax +356	Others/Ship Earth Stations (SES)
RCC MALTA (Cospas-Sarsat SPOC)	21 257267 22 494202 22 494203	21 809860	**AFTN:** LMMCYCYX (For emergencies only) LMMLYCYC (For emergencies only) **Inmarsat C:** 421599999 **email:** rccmalta@gov.mt

Continued on next page

MALTA (Continued)

	Telephone +356	Fax +356	Others/Ship Earth Stations (SES)
MALTA AIR TRAFFIC SERVICES LTD	23 696520 23 695339	23 695411 23 695432	**AFTN:** LMMMZQZX
TRANSPORT MALTA	22 91 4490 22 91 4491 22 91 4492 21 25 0360	21 222208 21 241460 22 914419	**email:** mershipmalta@transport.gov.mt

MONACO   See diagram R5

National SAR Agency: Monaco Maritime Police
Address: 14 quai Antoine 1er, MC 98000, Monaco
Telephone: +377 93 15 30 16
Fax: +377 93 30 22 45
email: dpma@gouv.mc
Website:
https://en.gouv.mc/Government-Institutions/The-Government/Ministry-of-Interior/Police-Department/Marine-and-Airport-Police-Division

The Monaco Maritime Police Headquarters is equipped with terrestrial maritime radio communication facilities and is the location of the foreign alerting post for MRCC La Garde. An agreement for co-operation in SAR operations has been established with France.

MONTENEGRO   See diagram R5

National SAR Agency: The Maritime Safety Department
Address: Maršala Tita br. 7, PO Box 14, 8500 BAR, Montenegro
Telephone: +382 30313240
        +382 30313241
        +382 69333252
Mobile: +382 67642179
Fax: +382 30313274
email: vladan.radonjic@msd-ups.org

CRS Bar Radio (4OB) maintains a continuous listening watch on international distress frequencies, 2182 kHz, VHF Ch 16, DSC MF 2187·5 kHz and DSC VHF Ch 70. The Maritime Safety Department with the Harbour Master's Offices in Bar and Kotor are responsible for distress and safety communications and action within the coastal waters of Montenegro. Preferred inter RCC language is English.

	Telephone +382	Fax +382	Others/Ship Earth Stations (SES)
MRCC BAR - CRS Bar Radio	30 313088	30 313600	**Mobile:** +382 67 642179 **email:** barradio@pomorstvo.me

MOROCCO   See diagrams R4 & R5

National SAR Agency: Marine Fisheries Department, National SAR Coordinator
Address: Rue Mohamed Belhassan El Ouazzani Haut agdal, BP 476, Rabat, Morocco
Telephone: +212 5 37 688174
Fax: +212 5 37 688112
email: drissi@mpm.gov.ma
Website: https://www.itopf.org/knowledge-resources/countries-territories-regions/morocco/

The Ocean Fisheries Department MRCC Rabat is responsible for coordinating Search and Rescue operations.

MRCC Rabat maintains a continuous listening watch on international distress frequencies.

TeleMedical Assistance Service: Contact MRCC Rabat and send a message for "Radio Medical Assistance" and telemedical advice will be provided from a regional public hospital via MRCC Rabat.

Possible consultation languages: Arabic, French and English.

	Telephone +212	Fax +212	Others/Ship Earth Stations (SES)
MRCC RABAT	5 37 625877	5 37 625017	**Inmarsat C:** 424200893 **email:** mrcc.rabat@mpm.gov.ma mrccrabat@gmail.com **MMSI:** 002424133
MRCC RABAT (Cospas-Sarsat SPOC)	5 37 625877	5 37 625017	**email:** spoc.maritime.maroc@mpm.gov.ma

Mediterranean

	Telephone +212	Fax +212	Others/Ship Earth Stations (SES)
MRSC AL HOCEÏMA	5 39 982730 5 39 982219	5 37 625017 (Emergency) 5 39 982547	**email:** mrsc.alhoceima@mpm.gov.ma **MMSI:** 002424134

ROMANIA   See diagram R6

National SAR Agency: Romanian Naval Authority
Address: Nr. 1 gate of Constanţa port, code 900900, Romania
Telephone: +40 372 419801
Fax: +40 372 416807
email: rna@rna.ro
Website: https://portal.rna.ro/english/Pagini/CMC.aspx

Constanţa Radio (YQI) maintains a continuous listening watch on 500 kHz MF WT, 2182 kHz MF RT and VHF Ch 16 for distress calls. VHF DSC and MF DSC facilities are also fully operational, HF DSC is operational on 4207·5 kHz, 8414·5 kHz and 12577 kHz.

TeleMedical Assistance Service: University Hospital C.F. Constanţa provides assistance. Contact through Constanţa Radio and MRCC Constanţa.

Possible consultation languages: Romanian and English.

	Telephone +40	Fax +40	Others/Ship Earth Stations (SES)
CAA BUCHAREST (Cospas-Sarsat SPOC)	212 083129	212 320099	**AFTN:** LRBBZQZQ
MRCC CONSTANŢA	241 615949 723 634122 740 173032	241 606065	**email:** mrcc@rna.ro
CONSTANŢA (RADIONAV SA)	241 737102 241 602781	241 737103 241 739469 241 602789 241 605140	**Inmarsat C:** 492260041 **email:** isps@constanta-radio.ro arrivalro@constanta-radio.ro
Harbour Master's Office Mangalia (Alerting point)	241 751299	241 751299	**email:** cpmangalia@rna.ro
Harbour Master's Office Midia (Alerting point)	372 742554	372 408424	**email:** cpmidia@rna.ro
Harbour Master's Office Sulina (Alerting point)	240 543510 240 543151	240 543510 240 543151	**email:** cpsulina@rna.ro vtmissl@rna.ro

RUSSIA   See diagrams R2, R6, R15, R16 & R18

National SAR Agency: Ministry of Transport of the Russian Federation
Address: 1/1 U1,Rozhdestvenka Street Moscow, 109112, Russia
Telephone: +7 495 6261000
Fax: +7 495 6269038
     +7 495 6269128
email: info@mintrans.ru
Website: www.mintrans.ru

MRCC Moscow is responsible for coordinating Search and Rescue operations and liaising with Search and Rescue services of neighbouring countries in accordance with intergovernmental agreements. A network of Coast Radio Stations maintains a continuous listening watch on international distress frequencies. Preferred inter RCC language is English.

NORTHERN SEAS (NAVAREAs I, XX and XXI): The following frequencies are reserved for Distress Calls and are not to be used for general communication: 6211 kHz, 4138 kHz & 500 kHz. In all areas (except Beloye More and Barents Sea) a 3 minute watch will be maintained on 500 kHz from 15 minutes past each hour and on 6211 kHz and 4138 kHz from 45 minutes past each hour.

TeleMedical Assistance Service: State Enterprise "Semashko Northern Medical Centre" provides assistance (telemed@atnet.ru). Contact via MRSC Arkhange'lsk. Possible consultation languages: Russian and English.

Additionally, assistance may also be provided by Sakhalin Territorial Centre of the Medicine and Catastrophe (stcmk@mail.ru). Possible consultation language: Russian.

State MRCC

	Telephone +7	Fax +7	Others/Ship Earth Stations (SES)
CMC (Cospas-Sarsat SPOC)	495 2360109 495 2360110	495 2360109 495 9673020	**AFTN:** UUUUYCYX **email:** cmc@marsat.ru
SMRCC MOSCOW	495 6261052 495 6241853 495 6261055	495 6237476	**email:** odsmrcc@morflot.ru od_smrcc@morspas.ru

Black Sea Coast

	Telephone +7	Fax +7	Others/Ship Earth Stations (SES)
MRCC NOVOROSSIYSK	8617 676417 8617 676418 8617 675543	8617 676420 8617 619424	**email:** mrcc3@ampnovo.ru

Continued on next page

Black Sea Coast (Continued)

	Telephone +7	Fax +7	Others/Ship Earth Stations (SES)
MRSC TAMAN	929 8467886 928 2607240 928 8478144	861 4841722	email: mrsc3@amptaman.ru mrsc1@amptaman.ru

Caspian Sea Coast

	Telephone +7	Fax +7	Others/Ship Earth Stations (SES)
MRCC ASTRAKHAN	8512 584808	8512 585981	Telex: +64 254173 POMOR RU Inmarsat C: 427310985 email: odmrcc@ampastra.ru

SARDEGNA - see ITALY

SICILIA - see ITALY
SLOVENIA   See diagram R5

National SAR Agency: Ministry of Infrastructure Address: Slovenian Maritime Administration, MRCC Koper, Kopališko nabrežje 9, 6000 Koper, Slovenia Telephone: +386 5 6632100 Fax: +386 5 6632102 email: ursp.box@gov.si

The Search and Rescue Coordination Centre keeps watch on VHF Ch 16 and DSC Ch 70.

	Telephone +386	Fax +386	Others/Ship Earth Stations (SES)
MRCC KOPER	5 6632106 5 6632107 5 6632108	5 6632110	email: koper.mrcc@gov.si

SPAIN   See diagrams R1, R4 & R5

National SAR Agency: Sociedad de Salvamento y Seguridad Marítima Address: C / Fruela 3, 28011 Madrid Telephone: +34 91 7559132   +34 91 7559133 Fax: +34 91 5261440 Website: www.salvamentomaritimo.es

MRCC Madrid is responsible for coordinating Search and Rescue operations and has twenty one MRCCs and MRSCs (including seasonal MRSC Palamos open from 1 June to 30 Sep), divided into the North Coast, South Coast, Mediterranean Coast and Islas Canarias regions, under its control. All the MRCCs and MRSCs are manned on a 24 hour basis. A network of Coast Radio Stations, connected by intranet and telephone to all Spanish MRCCs, maintains a continuous listening watch on international distress frequencies. Preferred languages for inter RCC are English and Spanish. Please note, email is not to be used for emergency purposes.

	Telephone +34	Fax +34	Others/Ship Earth Stations (SES)
SPMCC (Cospas-Sarsat SPOC)	928 727105	928 727107	AFTN: GCMPZSZX email: spmcc@inta.es
MRCC MADRID	91 7559132 91 7559133	91 5261440	Inmarsat C: 422423124 email: cncs@sasemar.es

Mediterranean Coast

	Telephone +34	Fax +34	Others/Ship Earth Stations (SES)
MRSC ALGECIRAS	956 580035	956 581951	email: algeciras@sasemar.es
MRCC ALMERÍA	950 271726 950 275477 950 270715	950 270402	email: almeria@sasemar.es
MRCC BARCELONA	93 2234733 93 2234748 93 2234759	93 2234613	email: barcelona@sasemar.es
MRSC CARTAGENA	968 529817 968 529594	968 529748	email: cartagena@sasemar.es
MRSC CASTELLÓN	964 737202	964 737105	email: castellon@sasemar.es

Continued overleaf

Mediterranean Coast (Continued)

	Telephone +34	Fax +34	Others/Ship Earth Stations (SES)
MRCC PALMA (Mallorca)	971 724562	971 728352	**email:** palma@sasemar.es
MRSC TARRAGONA	977 216203 977 216215	977 216209	**email:** tarragona@sasemar.es
MRCC VALENCIA	96 3679302 96 3679204	96 3679403	**email:** valencia@sasemar.es

SWITZERLAND   See diagram R1

National SAR Agency: Swiss Maritime Navigation Office
Address: Elisabethenstrasse 33, P.O.Box 4010, Basel.
Telephone: +41 58 4671120
Fax: +41 58 4671129
email: dv-ssa@eda.admin.ch
Website: www.eda.admin.ch

Switzerland has an MRCC and an ARCC located at Zurich Airport. Preferred inter RCC languages are English, German and French.

	Telephone +41	Fax +41	Others/Ship Earth Stations (SES)
MRCC ZURICH (Cospas-Sarsat SPOC - Maritime)	58 6543938	58 6543987	**AFTN:** LSARYCYM **email:** ops@rega.ch
ARCC Zurich (Cospas-Sarsat SPOC - Aero)	58 4841000	58 4842005	**AFTN:** LSARYCYX **email:** rcc.lw@vtg.admin.ch

SYRIA   See diagram R6

National SAR Agency: General Directorate of Ports
Address: P.O. Box 505, Lattakia, Syria
Telephone: +963 41 472593
          +963 41 471416
Fax: +963 41 475805
Website: http://www.gdp.gov.sy/en/about/coast-guards-department

The General Director of Ports in Al Lādhiqīyah (Lattakia) is responsible for coordinating Search and Rescue operations. A network of Coast Radio Stations maintains a continuous listening watch on international distress frequencies.

	Telephone +963	Fax +963	Others/Ship Earth Stations (SES)
RCC ATC DAMASCUS (Cospas-Sarsat SPOC)	11 5400540	11 5400312	**AFTN:** OSDIZAZX
MRCC SYRIA	41 233333 41 233876 41 235890		
AL LĀDHIQĪYAH (Lattakia) SHIPPING AGENCIES CO.	41 233163 41 234263		
BĀNIYĀS (YKM5)	43 711300	43 710418	
BĀNIYĀS SHIPPING AGENCIES CO.	43 711403	43 711403	
ṬARṬŪS (Tartous) PILOT	43 220562 43 220566		
ṬARṬŪS (Tartous) (YKO)	43 221615		
ṬARṬŪS (Tartous) (YKI)	43 315841		

TUNISIA   See diagram R5

National SAR Agency: Service National de Surveillance Côtière
Address: Base navale de La Goulette, 2080 La Goulette, Tunisie
Telephone: +216 71 736300
          +216 71 736360
Fax: +216 71 736180

The Tunisian Navy are responsible for coordinating Search and Rescue operations. A network of Coast Radio Stations maintains a continuous listening watch on international distress frequencies. Preferred inter RCC languages are English, French and Arabic.

	Telephone +216	Fax +216	Others/Ship Earth Stations (SES)
TUNIS ACC (Cospas-Sarsat SPOC)	71 755000	71 783126	**AFTN:** DTTCZRZS
MRCC TUNIS	71 560240 71 560244	71 561804	**email:** defnat@defense.tn

TURKEY

See diagram R6

National SAR Agency: General Directorate of Maritime and Inland Waters Regulation (Republic of Turkey, Ministry of Transport and Infrastructure).
Address: Gazi Mustafa Kemal Bulvari No. 128A, Maltepe, Ankara, Turkey
Telephone: +90 312 2319105
         +90 312 2324783
Fax: +90 312 2320823
Telex: +607 44144 DZMS TR
email: trmrcc@uab.gov.tr
    sar@uab.gov.tr

The Directorate General of Maritime and Inland Waters Regulation (Republic of Turkey, Ministry of Transport and Infrastructure), in conjunction with regional Turkish Coast Guard centres, are responsible for the coordination of all maritime distress and safety incidents within the Maritime Search and Rescue Region of Turkey. A network of Coast Radio Stations maintains a continuous listening watch on international distress frequencies, including VHF, MF and HF DSC. Preferred inter RCC language is English.

TeleMedical Assistance Service: Only one TMAS agency provides assistance. Contact shoud be made through RCC's Istanbul, Izmir, Mersin, and Samsun, and RSC's Amasra, Antalya, Canakkale, Iskenderun, Marmaris, Mudanya and Trabzon.

Possible consultation language: English and Turkish.

	Telephone +90	Fax +90	Others/Ship Earth Stations (SES)
TRMCC	312 2313374 552 7270727 (SAR)	312 2312902	**AFTN:** LTACZSZX **email:** trmcc@uab.gov.tr
MSRCC ANKARA (Main SAR Coordination Centre)	312 2319105 312 2324783	312 2320823	**email:** trmrcc@uab.gov.tr
MRCC ANKARA (Turkish Coast Guard Command)	312 4164801	312 4253337	**email:** ihbar@sg.gov.tr
RCC İSTANBUL (Coast Guard Marmara and the Turkish Straits Regional Command)	212 2424000	212 2424252	
RCC SAMSUN (Coast Guard Black Sea Regional Command)	362 4452908	362 4452908	
RCC İZMİR (Coast Guard Aegean Sea Regional Command)	232 3656825	232 3825226	
RCC MERSİN (Coast Guard Mediterranean Sea Regional Command)	324 2388790	324 2388691	
RSC ÇANAKKALE (Coast Guard Çanakkale Group Command)	286 2177656	286 2127202	
RSC TRABZON (Coast Guard Eastern Black Sea Group Command)	462 3280793	462 3250118	
RSC AMASRA (Coast Guard Western Black Sea Group Command)	378 3151037	378 3153925 378 3153923	
RSC MARMARİS (Coast Guard Southern Aegean Sea Group Command)	252 4121807	252 4127777	
RSC ANTALYA (Coast Guard Antalya Group Command)	242 2592406	242 2592407	
RSC İSKENDERUN (Coast Guard Iskenderun Group Command)	326 6130765	326 6132054	
RSC MUDANYA (Coast Guard Southern Marmara Group Command)	224 5441589	224 5440076	

UKRAINE
See diagram R6

National SAR Agency: Ministry of Infrastructure of Ukraine, Department of State Policy on Maritime and Inland Water **Address:** 14 Peremogy Avenue, Kiev, 01135 Ukraine **Telephone:** +380 44 3514916 **Fax:** +380 44 3514964	

For general coordination of SAR at sea, safety of life at open sea in the SAR area of Ukraine, a Maritime Search and Rescue Service (MSRS) has been established under the Ministry of Infrastructure of Ukraine in accordance with international treaties, to which Ukraine is a party.

The Maritime Search and Rescue Service keeps constant communication with respective organizations and institutions of Ukraine, with all Ukrainian ports, with the nearest maritime coordination and rescue centres and subcentres of the Global Maritime Distress and Safety System of neighbouring countries.

The State Maritime Rescue Coordination Centre (SMRCC) in Odesa and Maritime Rescue Subcentre (MRSC) in Berdyansk operate on the Ukrainian coast of the Black Sea and the Sea of Azov.

	Telephone +380	Fax +380	Others/Ship Earth Stations (SES)
STATE MARITIME RESCUE COORDINATION CENTRE (SMRCC) ODESA (Cospas-Sarsat SPOC)	48 7776609	48 7776610	**Inmarsat C:** 427288812 **email:** mrcc.ode@sar.gov.ua
MARITIME SEARCH AND RESCUE SERVICE (MSRS), ODESA	48 7850717	48 7850718	**email:** semsrs@sar.gov.ua
MRCSC MARIUPOL'	629 402989	629 402854	**email:** mrsc.mar@sar.gov.ua
MSRC BERDYANSK	6153 46865	6153 46866	**email:** mrsc.ber@sar.gov.ua

NAVAREA IV

ANGUILLA (UK)
See diagram R7

National SAR Agency: Marine Police Unit **Address:** Sandy Ground Police Station, Anguilla, (BWI) **Telephone:** +1 264 4972354 **Fax:** +1 264 4975112	

Anguilla Marine Police Unit is responsible for coordinating Search and Rescue operations in association with MRCC Fort-de-France.

	Telephone +596	Fax +596	Others/Ship Earth Stations (SES)
MRCC FORT-DE-FRANCE (CROSSAG) (Cospas-Sarsat SPOC)	596 709292 596 731616	596 632450	**Inmarsat C:** 422799024 422799244 **email:** fortdefrance.mrcc@mer.gouv.fr antilles@mrccfr.eu

ANTIGUA AND BARBUDA
See diagram R7

National SAR Agency: Antigua and Barbuda Defence Force Coast Guards **Address:** Deep Water Harbour, P.O. Box 1572, S. John, Antigua **Telephone:** +1 268 4620671 **Fax:** +1 268 4622842 **email:** abdfcg@candw.ag cgopsmail@gmail.com **Website:** http://abdf.gov.ag/units/antigua-and-barbuda-coast-guard/	

MRCC Fort-de-France is responsible for coordinating Search and Rescue operations in association with Antigua and Barbuda Defence Force Coast Guards.

	Telephone	Fax	Others/Ship Earth Stations (SES)
MRCC FORT-DE-FRANCE (CROSSAG) (Cospas-Sarsat SPOC)	+596 596 709292	+596 596 632450	**Inmarsat C:** 422799024 (AOR-W) 422799244 (AOR-E) **email:** antilles@mrccfr.eu fortdefrance.mrcc@mer.gouv.fr
ANTIGUA AND BARBUDA SAR ASSOCIATION (ABSAR)	+1 268 5621234		**email:** info@absar.org

BAHAMAS See diagram R7

National SAR Agency: Bahamas Air Sea Rescue Association (BASRA)
Address: East Bay Street, P.O. Box SS 6247, Nassau, Bahamas
Telephone: +1 242 3258864 (HJ)
Fax: +1 242 3252737
email: admin@basra.org

The Bahamas Air Sea Rescue Association (BASRA) is a voluntary organisation working in co-operation with the US Coast Guard and Royal Bahamas Defence Force. A continuous listening watch on VHF Ch 16 is NOT maintained.

	Telephone +1	Fax +1	Others/Ship Earth Stations (SES)
ROYAL BAHAMAS DEFENCE FORCE (RBDF)	242 8263117 242 3263815 242 3623700		**email:** operations@rbdf.gov.bs
	The RBDF are assisted with SAR in the Bahamas by the USCG and BASRA.		
RCC BAHAMAS	242 3594888	242 3252737	
H24 POLICE ANSWERING SERVICE	242 3522628		
NASSAU HARBOUR MASTER	242 3233191	242 3225545	

BARBADOS See diagram R7

National SAR Agency: Barbados Coast Guard
Address: HMBS Pelican, Spring Garden, S. Michael, Bridgetown, Barbados
Telephone: +1 246 5362948
+1 246 5362949
Fax: +1 246 5362953
Website: https://www.bdfbarbados.com/the-barbados-coast-guard/

Barbados Defence Force (Coast Guard) is responsible for coordinating Search and Rescue operations. Barbados Coast Guard and Barbados External Communications (BET) maintain a continuous listening watch on 2182 kHz and VHF Ch 16 for distress calls. BET monitors calls through Barbados (8PO) maintaining a continuous listening watch on 2182 kHz and VHF Ch 16 for distress calls.

	Telephone +1	Fax +1	Others/Ship Earth Stations (SES)
MRSC BARBADOS COAST GUARD	246 5362948 246 5362949	246 5362953	**email:** bcg@bdf.gov.bb
BARBADOS DEFENCE FORCE	246 4366185	246 4350516	

BELIZE See diagram R7

National SAR Agency: Officer Commanding Belize Defence Force (CBDF)
Address: Price Barracks, Ladyville, Belize City, Belize, P.O. Box 141
Telephone: +501 225 2174
Fax: +501 225 2175
email: fhq@belizedefenceforce.net

The Maritime Wing of the Belize Defence Force is responsible for the coordination of Search and Rescue operations. A continuous distress watch is maintained on international distress frequencies 2182 kHz and VHF Ch 16, as well as the aeronautical distress frequency 121.5 MHz.

	Telephone +501	Fax +501	Others/Ship Earth Stations (SES)
COMMANDER BELIZE DEFENCE FORCE (CBDF) H24 BDF Search and Rescue	225 2174 205 2098	225 2175	**email:** cbdf@belizedefenceforce.net
DEFENCE FORCE MARITIME WING	225 2171 (Not H24)	225 3334 (Not H24)	
DEFENCE FORCE AIR WING	225 2172 (Not H24)	225 2094 (Not H24)	
SRC BELIZE (COCESNA)	225 2014	225 2533	**email:** ricodecom@yahoo.com

BERMUDA (UK)   See diagram R7

National SAR Agency: Bermuda Government, Department of Marine and Ports
Address: 19 Fort George Hill, S. George's GE02, Bermuda
Telephone: +1 441 2971010
Fax: +1 441 2971530
Inmarsat C: 431010110
           431010120
email: operations@rccbermuda.bm
       dutyofficer@marops.bm
Website: www.marops.bm

Bermuda Radio maintains a continuous listening watch on 2182 kHz, 4125 kHz and VHF Ch 16 for distress calls and the DSC frequencies 2187·5 kHz and VHF Ch 70 for distress calls. It is also the location of RCC BERMUDA.

	Telephone +1	Fax +1	Others/Ship Earth Stations (SES)
JRCC BERMUDA (Cospas-Sarsat SPOC)	441 2971010 441 2970686	441 2971530	**AFTN:** TXKFYCYX **Inmarsat C:** 431010110 431010120 **email:** operations@rccbermuda.bm

CANADA   See diagrams R3/4, R16 & R18

National SAR Agency: Canadian Coast Guard Headquarters
Address: 5th Floor, 200 Kent Street, Director Search and Rescue, Ottawa, Ontario, Canada, K1A 0E6
email: dfo.nationalsarmanager-gestionnairenationalres.mpo@dfo-mpo.gc.ca
Website: www.ccg-gcc.gc.ca

The Canadian Armed Forces (CAF) have overall responsibility for coordination of Search and Rescue (SAR) activities in Canada, including Canadian waters and adjacent seas off the coast of Canada, and for the provision of dedicated SAR aircraft in support of maritime SAR incidents. The Canadian Coast Guard (CCG) coordinates maritime SAR activities within this SAR zone, in co-operation with CAF, and provides dedicated maritime SAR vessels in strategic locations. Joint Rescue Coordination Centres (JRCC) are maintained at Victoria, B.C., Trenton, Ont. and Halifax, N.S. These centres are manned H24 by CAF and CCG personnel. Two Marine Rescue Sub-Centres (MRSC) are also located in Québec and St.John's Newfoundland to coordinate local SAR operations. Contact is established through the Canadian Coast Guard Radio Stations which provide coverage on all marine distress frequencies or through Inmarsat.

TeleMedical Assistance Service: Contact any Canadian CRS, JRC / MRSC -Prefix the message "Radio Medico" medical advice will be provided by TMAS or any regional hospital. Possible consultation languages: English and French. Interpreters may be provided for other languages.

	Telephone +1	Fax +1	Others/Ship Earth Stations (SES)
CMCC (Cospas-Sarsat) SPOC	613 9657265 800 211 8107	613 9657494	**AFTN:** CYTRYCYT **email:** cmcc2@sarnet.dnd.ca

Atlantic Coast

	Telephone +1	Fax +1	Others/Ship Earth Stations (SES)
JRCC HALIFAX	800 5651582 (Maritimes Region, toll free) 902 4278200	902 4272114	**email:** jrcchalifax@sarnet.dnd.ca

Newfoundland & Labrador

	Telephone +1	Fax +1	Others/Ship Earth Stations (SES)
MRSC ST.JOHN'S	800 5632444 (In Canada, toll free) 709 7725151	709 7722224	**email:** mrscsj@sarnet.dnd.ca

S. Lawrence River

	Telephone +1	Fax +1	Others/Ship Earth Stations (SES)
MRSC QUÉBEC	800 4634393 (Québec Region, toll free) 418 6483599	418 6483614	**email:** mrscqbc@dfo-mpo.gc.ca

CANADA (Continued)

Great Lakes

	Telephone +1	Fax +1	Others/Ship Earth Stations (SES)
JRCC TRENTON	800 2677270 (In Canada, toll free) 613 9653870	613 9657190	**email:** jrcctrenton@sarnet.dnd.ca

CAYMAN ISLANDS (UK)   See diagram R7

National SAR Agency: Royal Cayman Islands Police (Marine Unit)
Address: P.O. Box 909, GT, Grand Cayman, Cayman Islands
Telephone: +1 345 945 2432 (HJ / Marine Division)
Fax: +1 345 945 9133 (HJ)
Website: https://www.rcips.ky/about

The Marine Unit of the Cayman Islands Police is responsible for the coordination of Search and Rescue operations.

	Telephone +1	Fax +1	Others/Ship Earth Stations (SES)
POLICE Marine Office	345 9499009 345 9497710	345 9499133	
PORT SECURITY	345 9492055		**email:** security@caymanport.com

COLOMBIA   See diagrams R7 & R8

National SAR Agency: MRCC COPA
Address: Bahía Málaga, Buenaventura - Valle, Colombia
Telephone: +57 2 2460630
Fax: +57 2 2460630

Coastguard stations maintain a continuous listening watch on VHF Chs 16 and 11 on Atlantic Coast and VHF Chs 16 and 68 on Pacific Coast.

	Telephone +57	Fax +57	Others/Ship Earth Stations (SES)
Oficino Grupo Busqueda Rescate (Cospas-Sarsat SPOC)	1 2962700 1 2962554	1 2962825	**AFTN:** SKBOYCYX **Telex:** +396 44620 DAAC CO +396 44840 DAAC CO

Caribbean Coast

	Telephone +57	Fax +57	Others/Ship Earth Stations (SES)
BALLENAS COAST GUARD STATION	5 6550316	5 6550316	**Iridium:** +8816 31720013 **email:** ceguc@fnc.armada.mil.co
BARRANQUILLA COAST GUARD STATION	5 3441428 ext 206	5 6550316	**Iridium:** +8816 31720013 **email:** cegbar@fnc.armada.mil.co
CARTAGENA COAST GUARD STATION	5 6550316	5 6550316	**Iridium:** +8816 31720013 **email:** ceguc@fnc.armada.mil.co
COVEÑAS COAST GUARD STATION	5 6550316	5 6550316	**Iridium:** +8816 31720013 **email:** ceguc@fnc.armada.mil.co
PUERTO BOLIVAR COAST GUARD STATION	5 6550316 5 3506690 5 3506631	5 6550316	**Iridium:** +8816 31720013 **email:** ceguc@fnc.armada.mil.co
SAN ANDRES COAST GUARD STATION	8 5132153	8 5132153	**Iridium:** +8816 31710711 **email:** cegsai@fnc.armada.mil.co
SANTA MARTA COAST GUARD STATION	5 4231666	5 4231608	**Iridium:** +8816 31710710 +8816 31710397 **email:** cegsam@fnc.armada.mil.co
TURBO COAST GUARD STATION	4 8275379	4 8275380	**Iridium:** +8816 31710708 **email:** cegut@fnc.armada.mil.co

COSTA RICA   See diagram R7

National SAR Agency: DGAC Costa Rica Air Navigation Department Address: PO Box 5026-1000, San Jose, Costa Rica Telephone: +506 2443 8965			
Puntarenas (TEC) maintains a continuous listening watch on VHF Ch 16 for distress calls.			
	Telephone +506	Fax +506	Others/Ship Earth Stations (SES)
MRCC COSTA RICA (Coastguard)	2600 5630 2286 5813 2286 4418 8913 7432 (WhatsApp)		email: operaciones.sng.cr@gmail.com ariasm@msp.go.cr jhernandez@msp.go.cr

CUBA   See diagram R7

National SAR Agency: Maritime Safety and Survey Directorate, Ministry of Transport
Address: Avenida Boyeros y Tulipán, Plaza, Ciudad de la Habana, Cuba
Telephone: +53 7 8816607
          +53 7 8819498
          +53 7 8818177
Fax: +53 7 8811514
email: dsim@mitrans.transnet.cu			

The Ministry of Transport is responsible for coordinating Search and Rescue operations. A network of Coast Radio Stations maintains a continuous listening watch on international distress frequencies			
	Telephone +53	Fax +53	Others/Ship Earth Stations (SES)
MRCC CUBA CUBAN BORDER GUARD	7 330364		

CURAÇAO   See diagram R7

National SAR Agency: Dutch Caribbean Coast Guard Address: NAPO 399, 3509 VS Utrecht, Netherlands (Marine base Parera, Nightingale weg 22, Willemstad, Curaçao) Telephone: +599 9 4637700 Fax: +599 9 4637700			
Dutch Caribbean Coast Guard is responsible for coordinating Search and Rescue operations. RCC Curaçao (PJC) maintains a continuous listening watch on international distress frequencies. Call sign used during Search and Rescue operations is "Curaçao Rescue".			
TeleMedical Assistance Service: Contact via RCC Curaçao, telemedical assistance will be provided by regional doctors. Possible consultation languages are Dutch, English and Spanish.			
	Telephone +599	Fax +599	Others/Ship Earth Stations (SES)
JRCC CURAÇAO (PJC) (Cospas-Sarsat SPOC)	9 4637700	9 4637950	Mobile: +599 95100913 (Also WhatsApp) Inmarsat C: 424402072 email: rcc.curacao@mindef.nl MMSI: 003061000
CURAÇAO PORTS AUTHORITY (FORT NASSAU)	9 4614581 9 4345953		
COASTGUARD AIRSTATION HATO (PJX)	9 4637945 9 4637907		Mobile: +599 9 5102724 email: hatooperaties@mindef.nl
CITRO CURAÇAO (CIVIL RESCUE ORGANISATION)	9 4637700 (RCC) 9 7471600 (CITRO)		

SAR

DOMINICA See diagram R7

National SAR Agency: Commonwealth of Dominica Marine Police Unit Address: Woodbridge Bay, Dominica Telephone: +1 767 448 22 22 +1 767 448 88 50 Fax: +1 767 448 71 58			
MRCC Fort-de-France is responsible for coordinating Search and Rescue operations in association with Dominica Marine Police Unit. The headquarters of the Dominica Coast Guard is based at Roseau from where a distress watch is maintained on VHF Ch 16 and also HF 7850 kHz.			
	Telephone +596	Fax +596	Others/Ship Earth Stations (SES)

MRCC FORT-DE-FRANCE (CROSSAG) (Cospas-Sarsat SPOC)	596 709292	596 632450	Inmarsat C: 422799024 (AOR-W)
			             422799244 (AOR-E)
			email: fortdefrance.mrcc@mer.gouv.fr
			             antilles@mrccfr.eu

DOMINICAN REPUBLIC See diagram R7

National SAR Agency: Marina de Guerra, Centro De Operaciones Navales (M-3) Address: Base Naval 27 de Febrero De La Marina De Guerra Dominicana, Sans Souci, D.N. Dominican Republic Telephone: +1 809 592 0707			
The Operations Centre of the Dominican Republic Navy is responsible for the coordination of Search and Rescue operations. A continuous listening watch is maintained on the international distress frequencies VHF Ch 16 and 2182 kHz.			
	Telephone +1	Fax +1	Others/Ship Earth Stations (SES)
RCC SAN DOMINGO (Cospas-Sarsat SPOC)	809 549 0137 809 274 4322 (ext 2039)	809 549 2734	AFTN: MDSDYCYX email: rccsantodomingo@gmail.com
DOMINICAN NAVY	809 604 6506 809 592 0707		email: com@marina.mil.do

EL SALVADOR See diagram R7

National SAR Agency: National Civil Defence Committee Address: 5th Floor, Ministry of Interior, Centro de Gobierno, San Salvador, El Salvador, C.A. Telephone: +503 22711280			
The El Salvador Air Force is responsible for coordinating Search and Rescue operations.			
	Telephone +503	Fax +503	Others/Ship Earth Stations (SES)
MRCC COMMANDER OF THE NAVY	22762605	22762605 22761930	
FUERZA AEREA (Air Force)	22500070	22500389	
PORT COMMANDER OF ACAJUTLA	24053201	24053390	
SRC EL SALVADOR (COCESNA)	22950264	22950264	email: rhernandez@aac.gob.sv

FRENCH GUIANA - see MARTINIQUE AND FRENCH GUIANA
GREENLAND See diagrams R3/4 & R18

National SAR Agency: JRCC Greenland Address: Joint Arctic Command (JACO), Post Box 1072, Aalisartut Aqqutaa 47, 3900 Nuuk, Greenland Telephone: +299 364000 (Joint Arctic Command) Inmarsat C: 433116710 Iridium: +881 677754507 email: jrcc@jrcc.gl
The responsibility for Search and Rescue services in Greenland is with JRCC Greenland and The Commissioner of Police in Greenland. A mandatory reporting system GREENPOS for SAR purposes is established for all ships cruising within the waters of the Greenland continental shelf or the EEZ. Procedures for GREENPOS can be received through JRCC Greenland. All SAR agencies in Greenland are fully GMDSS equipped. Preferred languages at JRCC Greenland are English and Danish.
TeleMedical Assistance Service: Contact via MRCC Nuuk. Possible consultation languages: Greenlandic, Danish and English

GREENLAND (Continued)

	Telephone +299	Fax +299	Others/Ship Earth Stations (SES)
JRCC GREENLAND	364010 (Duty Officer) 364012 (Duty Officer) 364022 (Commcentre) 364023 (Commcentre)		**Inmarsat C:** 433116710 **Iridium:** +881 677754507 **email:** jrcc@jrcc.gl greenpos@jrcc.gl (GREENPOS only)
NAVAIR (Part of JRCC Greenland)	363304	363309	**AFTN:** BGGHYCYC **Iridium:** +881 631417431 (Backup) +881 623457247 (Backup) **email:** fic@naviair.dk
Commissioner of Police in Greenland	701448 (Ext 200)	323348	**email:** grl-politi@politi.dk

GRENADA   See diagram R7

National SAR Agency: Grenada Coast Guard
Address: True Blue, S. George's, Grenada
Telephone: +1 473 4441931
Fax: +1 473 4442839

The Grenada Coast Guard is responsible for the coordination of Search and Rescue operations. MRSC Grenada is also the centre for the National Emergency Relief Organisation whose duties include the control of communications for any local major disaster.

	Telephone +1	Fax +1	Others/Ship Earth Stations (SES)
MRSC GRENADA (Grenada Coast Guard)	473 4441931 473 4441932	473 4442839	

GUATEMALA   See diagram R7

National SAR Agency: Sistema de Busqueda y Salvamento Estado Mayor de la Defensa Nacional
Address: 2 Av. 4-63 Zona 10, Guatemala City, Guatemala
Telephone: +502 4497411

A Marine Rescue Coordination Centre exists at the Centro de Operaciones Conjuntas, del estado Mayor de la Defensa Nacional in Guatemala City for both the Pacific and Atlantic Coasts.

	Telephone +502	Fax +502	Others/Ship Earth Stations (SES)
CENTRO DE OPERACIONES DEL ESTADO MAYOR DE LA DEFENSA NACIONAL	44974116 31285507		**email:** cocemdn@gmail.com
DIRECCIÓN GENERAL DE ASUNTOS MARITIMOS DEL MINISTERIO DE LA DEFENSA NACIONAL	44974255		**email:** seguridadmaritima@dgam.gob.gt
CENTRO DE OPERACIONES AÉREAS DE LA FUERZA AÉREA	31285767 22913436		**email:** secretariauda@gmail.com

Atlantic Coast

	Telephone +502	Fax +502	Others/Ship Earth Stations (SES)
COMANDO NAVAL DEL CARIBE	44974267 44974269 44974270		
PUERTO BARRIOS, IZABAL (GUATEMALA PORT TRAFFIC CONTROL)	79317058		
PUERTO SANTO TOMAS DE CASTILLA (GUATEMALA PORT TRAFFIC CONTROL)	77204160		

SAR

GUYANA
See diagram R7

National SAR Agency: Headquarters Maritime Corps, Guyana Defence Force, Georgetown
Address: Ruimvldt, Georgetown, Guyana
Telephone: +592 22 68410
+592 22 60570
+592 22 60579
Fax: +592 225 9090
email: ocsigs@gdf-gy.org

The Maritime Corps of the Guyana Defence Force is responsible for coordinating Search and Rescue operations. Demerara (8RB) maintains a continuous listening watch on 2182 kHz for distress calls. Preferred inter RCC language is English.

	Telephone +592	Fax +592	Others/Ship Earth Stations (SES)
Civil Aviation Department (Cospas-Sarsat SPOC)	26 12573 26 13012	26 12279	AFTN: SYCJYFYX email: director-general@gcaa-gy.org
MRCC GEORGETOWN	22 68410 22 60570 22 60579		
GEORGETOWN LIGHTHOUSE	22 69871		

HAITI
See diagram R7

National SAR Agency: Service Maritime et du Navigation d'Haiti (Semanah)
Address: Blvd. la Saline, P.O. Box 1563, Port-au-Prince, Haiti
Telephone: +509 28 161629
+509 28 161630
email: semanahaiti@gmail.com
carlcerome@gmail.com
Website: www.semanah.gouv.ht

The Service Maritime et du Navigation d'Haiti is responsible for coordinating Search and Rescue operations.

	Telephone +509	Fax +509	Others/Ship Earth Stations (SES)
MRCC SEMANAH	2810 8720 2810 8721 2810 8722		Mobile: +509 48937810 +509 36856810 email: semanahaiti@gmail.com carlcerome@gmail.com
HAITIAN COAST GUARD			Mobile: +509 36581111
JRCC	2922 1616		Mobile: +509 39166722 +509 40177939

HONDURAS
See diagram R7

National SAR Agency: Centro de Coordinacion de Rescate
Address: Direccion General de Aeronautical Civil, Apartado Postal No. 30145, Aeropuerto International Toncontin, Teguicigalpa DC, Honduras
Telephone: +5042 2331115
Fax: +5042 2333683

The Aeronautical SAR agency responsible for all Central American countries is RCC Centro America.

The following countries are part of the Central American Aeronautical SAR network, Corporación Centroamericana de Servicios de Navegación Aérea (COCESNA): Belize, Costa Rica, El Salvador, Guatemala, Honduras and Nicaragua. Each country has a Rescue Sub-Centre (RSC) working into RCC Centro America.

Preferred languages for inter RCC communication are English and Spanish.

	Telephone +504	Fax +504	Others/Ship Earth Stations (SES)
RCC CENTRO AMERICA & SPOC (CORPORACIÓN CENTROAMERICANA DE SERVICIOS DE NAVEGACIÓN AEREA) & RSC HONDURAS SAR COORDINATOR	22342507 22834750	22342488	AFTN: MHTGYCYX email: rcc_sar@cocesna.org Website: www.cocesna.org
GENERAL STAFF, HONDURAN NAVY	22334020		email: naval@honduras.com

JAMAICA   See diagram R7

National SAR Agency: Jamaica Defence Force Coast Guard
Address: HMJS Cagway, Port Royal, Kingston 1, Jamaica
Telephone: +1 876 9678193
             +1 876 9678031
             +1 876 3226602
             +1 876 3495728
Fax: +1 876 9678278
email: jdfcgradioroom@yahoo.com
           odojdfcg@gmail.com
           jdfcgopso@gmail.com
Website: https://www.jdfweb.com/1st-dist-jdf-coast-guard/

The Jamaica Defence Force Coast Guard (JDF CG) is responsible for the coordination of Search and Rescue operations. An H24 watch is maintained on 2182 kHz and VHF Ch 16 at Coast Guard Headquarters, located at Port Royal. The call sign is COAST GUARD RADIO KINGSTON (6YX).

There are also five Rescue Sub-Centre locations at St. Ann, (Discovery Bay); St. Elizabeth, (Black River); St. Thomas, (Port Morant); Portland, (Port Antonio) and Pedro, (Pedro Cays).

TeleMedical Assistance Service: RCC Jamaica provides assistance. Contact via Coast Guard Radio Kingston (6YX) or MRCC Kingston.

Possible consultation language is English.

	Telephone +1	Fax +1	Others/Ship Earth Stations (SES)
MRCC KINGSTON AGENCY CG	876 9678193 876 9678031 876 3226602 876 2199781	876 9678278	
MRSC ST. ANN (Discovery Bay)	876 3226599 876 9901307		
MRSC ST. ELIZABETH (Black River)	876 3437100		
MRSC ST. THOMAS (Port Morant)	876 3495767		
MRSC PORTLAND (Port Antonio)	876 8092984		
MRSC PEDRO (Pedro Cays)	876 5518913 (No cellphone coverage in this area, all calls to be made through MRCC Kingson)		
MRSC MONTEGO BAY (St. James)	876 8165400		
MRSC ST. CATHERINE (Old Harbour Bay)	876 8100183		

MARTINIQUE AND FRENCH GUIANA   See diagram R7

National SAR Agency: Organisme d'études et de coordination pour la recherche et le sauvetage en mer (SECMAR)
Address: 16 Boulevard Raspail, 75007 Paris, France
Telephone: +33 1 53634159

MRCC Fort-de-France is located on Martinique and is the Centre Régionaux Opérationel de Surveillance et de Sauvetage aux Antilles-Guyane (CROSSAG). CROSSAG is responsible for coordination of Search and Rescue cases within its SRR in the West Indies, French Guyana and the North Atlantic.

On Martinique and Guadeloupe, CROSSAG maintains a continuous listening watch on VHF Ch 16 and 2182 kHz for distress communications.

	Telephone	Fax	Others/Ship Earth Stations (SES)
MRCC FORT-DE-FRANCE (CROSSAG) (Cospas-Sarsat SPOC)	+596 596 709292 196	+596 596 632450	**Inmarsat C:** 422799024 (AOR-W) 422799244 (AOR-E) **email:** fortdefrance.mrcc@mer.gouv.fr antilles@mrccfr.eu
MRSC CAYENNE (FRENCH GUIANA)	+594 594 304444	+594 594 395589	**email:** cayenne@mrscfr.eu mrsc@netfag.fr

MEXICO
See diagrams R7, R8/9, R16 & R17

National SAR Agency: Mexican Navy MRCC Mexico
Address: Secretaria de Marina, Jefatura del Estado Mayor General, De la Armada de Mexico, Eje 2 Oriente Tramo. Heroica Escuela Naval, Militar No 861, Edificio "B" Primer Nivel, Col. Los Cipreses, Deleg. Coyoacán, México D.F., C.P. 04830
Telephone: +52 55 56246500
+52 55 56246200 ext 1000 (For SAR Office use ext 7242 or 7843)
+52 55 56246200 ext 2000
Fax: +52 55 56849642
email: sarmarina@semar.gob.mx
s3jemg@semar.gob.mx

The Mexican Navy is responsible for coordinating Search and Rescue operations within the limits of the Exclusive Economic Zone of Mexico in the Gulf of Mexico, Caribbean Sea and Pacific Ocean. All sections of the Mexican Navy are linked by radio and telephone with TELECOMM. The following Coast Radio Stations maintain a continuous listening watch on international distress frequencies. Preferred inter RCC languages are English and Spanish:

Caribbean Sea (NAVAREA IV) - Cancún (XFO), Isla Cozumel (XFC), Chetumal (XFP)

Gulf of Mexico (NAVAREA IV) - Tampico (XFS), Veracruz (XFU) Coatzacoalcos (XFF) CD.del Carmen (XFB) and Radiomex (XDA)

Pacific Ocean (NAVAREA XII) - Ensenada (XFE), La Paz (XFK), Guaymas (XFY), Mazatlán (XFL), Manzanillo (XFM), Acapulco (XFA), Salina Cruz (XFQ).

	Telephone +52	Fax +52	Others/Ship Earth Stations (SES)
Cospas-Sarsat SPOC		55 56132214	**email:** cegg@telecomm.net.mx

Regional Control Centre

	Telephone +52	Fax +52	Others/Ship Earth Stations (SES)
GULF OF MEXICO MRCC TAMPICO	833 2107205 833 2107206 833 2107207 833 2107209 833 2107210	833 2107208	**email:** radiotam@telecomm.net.mx
PACIFIC OCEAN MRCC MAZATLÁN	669 9852411	669 9852428	**email:** maritm@telecomm.net.mx

Gulf of Mexico and Caribbean Coasts

	Telephone +52	Fax +52	Others/Ship Earth Stations (SES)
MRCC TUXPAN (1st Region)	783 8370720 783 8370709 783 8370810 783 8370713 938 3814777		**email:** rn1@csi.sedemar.mil.mx
MRCC CARMEN (3rd Region)	938 3814777 938 3821931 938 3820424 938 3821945		**email:** rn3@csi.sedemar.mil.mx
MRCC MUJERES (5th Region)	998 8771306 998 8770196 998 8770186	998 8770194	**email:** rn5@csi.sedemar.mil.mx

MONTSERRAT (UK)
See diagram R7

National SAR Agency: Police Headquarters
Address: Woodlands, Montserrat
Telephone: +1 664 4912555
+1 664 4912791 (Port Authority)
Fax: +1 664 4918013

MRCC Fort-de-France is responsible for coordinating Search and Rescue operations in association with Montserrat Marine Police Unit.

Continuous listening watch is maintained on VHF Ch 16 and HF 7850 kHz. Preferred inter RCC language is English.

	Telephone +596	Fax +596	Others/Ship Earth Stations (SES)
MRCC FORT-DE-FRANCE (CROSSAG) (Cospas-Sarsat SPOC)	596 709292	596 632450	**Inmarsat C:** 422799024 (AOR-W) 422799244 (AOR-E) **email:** fortdefrance.mrcc@mer.gouv.fr antilles@mrccfr.eu

NICARAGUA   See diagram R7

National SAR Agency: El Instituto Nicaragüense de Aeronáutica Civil (INAC)
Address: Km 11.5 Carretera, Norte Apodo, 4936 Nicaragua.
Telephone: +505 2276 8580
            +505 2276 8586 ext 1550
Fax: +505 2276 8588
email: sarjulio@gmail.com
        sar@inac.gob.ni
Website: www.inac.gob.ni

The Fuerza Aérea y Defensa Anti Aerea (FASDAA) is responsible for coordinating Search and Rescue operations.

	Telephone +505	**Fax** +505	**Others/Ship Earth Stations (SES)**
SRC NICARAGUA (COCESNA)	276 2507 233 1602	276 8580 233 1602	**email:** cap-j.pinell@hotmail.com oguevara@hotmail.com

PANAMA   See diagram R7

National SAR Agency: National Maritime Service (Servicio Maritimo Nacional)
Address: Cocoli Naval Base, Panama, Republic of Panama
Telephone: +507 211 6004
Fax: +507 211 1943
email: comandoarmada@smn.gob.pa

	Telephone +507	**Fax** +507	**Others/Ship Earth Stations (SES)**
AIR NAVIGATION SAR UNIT (Cospas-Sarsat SPOC)	501 9847 (Office hours only) 501 9807 (H24)	501 9849	**AFTN:** MPLBYCYX **email:** naerea@aeronautica.gob.pa
PANAMA CANAL CONTROL	272 4220		
PANAMA REGISTRY	2070166		

PUERTO RICO (USA)   See diagram R7

National SAR Agency: Commander US Coast Guard
Address: Greater Antilles Section, P.O. Box 2029, Old San Juan Station, San Juan, Pr 00903 2029
Telephone: +1 787 7296770
Fax: +1 787 7296706
email: gantopswatch@gantsec.uscg.mil

Other contact details: EasyLink Mailbox (via CGHQ): 62845879, International EasyLink: 3450430

United States Coast Guard Section Office, Greater Antilles maintains a watch on 2182 kHz and VHF Ch 16 through a series of local and remotely controlled sites providing coverage throughout Puerto Rico and the US Virgin Islands.

	Telephone +1	**Fax** +1	**Others/Ship Earth Stations (SES)**
RSC SAN JUAN (USCG) (Cospas-Sarsat SPOC)	787 2892041 787 7296770 787 2892040	787 7296706	**email:** gantopswatch@gantsec.uscg.mil

SAINT KITTS & NEVIS   See diagram R7

National SAR Agency: Saint Kitts & Nevis Defence Force Coast Guard
Address: P.O. Box 189, Coast Guard Base, Basseterre, Saint Kitts
Telephone: +1 869 4658384
Fax: +1 869 4658406
      +1 869 4667312

MRCC Fort-de-France is responsible for coordinating Search and Rescue operations in association with Saint Kitts & Nevis Defence Force Coast Guard. Preferred inter RCC language is English.

	Telephone +596	**Fax** +596	**Others/Ship Earth Stations (SES)**
MRCC FORT-DE-FRANCE (CROSSAG) (Cospas-Sarsat SPOC)	596 709292	596 632450	**Inmarsat C:** 422799024 (AOR-W) 422799244 (AOR-E) **email:** fortdefrance.mrcc@mer.gouv.fr antilles@mrccfr.eu

SAINT LUCIA   See diagram R7

National SAR Agency: Royal Saint Lucia Police Force **Address:** Marine Police Unit, P.O. Box 109, Castries, Saint Lucia **Telephone:** +1 758 456 3870 **Fax:** +1 758 45 22261		

MRCC Fort-de-France is responsible for coordinating Search and Rescue operations in association with Royal Saint Lucia Police Force.

On Saint Lucia, Castries Port Authority Radio is used for vessels in distress and requiring assistance, and maintains a continuous listening watch on VHF Ch 16 and 2182 kHz for distress calls.

	Telephone +596	**Fax** +596	**Others/Ship Earth Stations (SES)**
MRCC FORT-DE-FRANCE (CROSSAG) (Cospas-Sarsat SPOC)	596 709292	596 632450	**Inmarsat C:** 422799024 (AOR-W) 422799244 (AOR-E) **email:** fortdefrance.mrcc@mer.gouv.fr antilles@mrccfr.eu

SAINT VINCENT AND THE GRENADINES   See diagram R7

National SAR Agency: Saint Vincent and The Grenadines Coast Guard Service **Address:** c/o Royal Saint Vincent Police Force, P.O. Box 835, Kingstown, Saint Vincent and The Grenadines **Telephone:** +1 784 457 1211 **Fax:** +1 784 456 2816		

The Saint Vincent and The Grenadines Coast Guard is responsible for all Maritime Distress, Search and Rescue Operations. An H24 radio watch is maintained on 2182 kHz & VHF Ch 16. The Coast Guard Base is located at Calliagua, Saint Vincent.

Fort Charlotte Coast Guard Radio Station located at the North Western headland of capital Kingstown also maintains an H24 radio watch on 2182 kHz and VHF Ch 16.

Saint Vincent and the Grenadines fall within the SRR of Trinidad and Tobago with MRCC Port of Spain providing SAR support.

	Telephone +1	**Fax** +1	**Others/Ship Earth Stations (SES)**
SAINT VINCENT AND THE GRENADINES COAST GUARD BASE	784 457 4568 784 457 4578 784 457 4554	784 457 4586	
RSC SAN JUAN (USCG) Puerto Rico (Cospas-Sarsat SPOC)	784 7296770 784 2892040 784 2892041	784 7296706	**email:** gantopswatch@gantsec.uscg.mil
MRCC PORT OF SPAIN (Trinidad and Tobago Coast Guard)	784 6348824 784 6342717 784 6342727 784 6341476 (SAR direct line)	784 6344944	

SAINT PIERRE AND MIQUELON (FRANCE)   See diagram R3

National SAR Agency: Organisme d'études et de coordination pour la recherche et le sauvetage en mer (SECMAR) **Address:** 16 Boulevard Raspail, 75007 Paris, France **Telephone:** +33 1 53 634159 **Fax:** +33 1 53 634178		

The Quartier des Affaires Maritimes (AFMAR Saint Pierre et Miquelon) is responsible for coordinating Search and Rescue operations and is also a foreign central alerting post in link with MRSC S. John's, Newfoundland, Canada.

	Telephone +508	**Fax** +508	**Others/Ship Earth Stations (SES)**
AFMAR SAINT PIERRE ET MIQUELON	411530 (Primary) 551616 (Alternative)	414834	
E-mails can be sent to: uam.samp.dtam-975@equipement-agriculture.gouv.fr			

SURINAME
See diagram R7

National SAR Agency: Ministry of Transport, Communication and Tourism
Address: Department of Civil Aviation, P.O. Box 2956 Paramaribo, Suriname
Telephone: +597 498898
          +597 497914
          +597 499561
Fax: +597 498901
email: dca@cadsur.sr
      atssur@cadsur.sr
      sar@cadsur.sr
Website: https://cadsur.sr/index.html

MRCC Paramaribo maintains a continuous listening watch on VHF Ch 16 for distress calls. VHF Ch 12 is also monitored.

	Telephone +597	Fax +597	Others/Ship Earth Stations (SES)
DEPARTMENT OF CIVIL AVIATION (Cospas-Sarsat SPOC)	498898 497914 0325203 0325176	498901 0325453	**AFTN:** SMPBYAYX **email:** dca@cadsur.sr atssur@cadsur.sr
SEARCH AND RESCUE COORDINATOR	491728	491728	**AFTN:** SMPBYCYX **email:** sar@cadsur.sr
MRCC PARAMARIBO	474575	472845	

TRINIDAD AND TOBAGO
See diagram R7

National SAR Agency: Trinidad and Tobago Coast Guard (TTCG)
Address: Staubles Bay, Chaguaramas, c/o Carenage Post Office, Trinidad
Telephone: +1 868 6342717
          +1 868 6342727
Fax: +1 868 6344944
email: 1ttcg@ttdf.mil.tt

The TTCG is responsible for coordinating SAR operations. Vessels in distress should call or radio either the Coast Guard or North Post Radio (Trinidad) (9YL) for assistance. North Post Radio maintains a continuous listening watch on 2182 kHz and VHF Ch 16 for distress calls. Preferred inter RCC language is English.

	Telephone +1	Fax +1	Others/Ship Earth Stations (SES)
ARCC PIARCO (ATC)	868 6694852	868 6694259	**email:** atcivp_e@caa.gov.tt
MRCC PORT OF SPAIN (Trinidad and Tobago Coast Guard)	868 6254939 868 6342718 868 6344439 868 6344440 (SAR direct line) 868 6341476 (SAR direct line)	868 6344944	**email:** 1ttcg@ttdf.mil.tt ttcgops@gmail.com
NORTH POST (9YL)	868 6374474 868 6330059 868 6379104 868 6325879	868 6379104	**email:** npradio-9yl@tstt.net.tt

TURKS AND CAICOS ISLANDS (UK)
See diagram R7

National SAR Agency: Turks and Caicos Islands Rescue Association
Address: Police Headquarters, Airport Road, Grand Turk, Turks and Caicos Islands
Telephone: +1 649 9415007

The Turks and Caicos Islands Rescue Association is responsible for coordinating Search and Rescue operations. The USCG in Miami maintains a continuous listening watch on VHF Ch 16 for distress calls, and on international distress frequencies 2182 and 4125 kHz. The Turks and Caicos Islands Rescue Association is assisted by the Police aeroplane, VHF callsign "Skyhawk" and 50ft patrol vessel, VHF callsign "Seaquest" for fast response.

	Telephone +1	Fax +1	Others/Ship Earth Stations (SES)
MRCC GRAND TURK	649 9462299 649 9462399 649 9462499		

UNITED STATES OF AMERICA   See diagrams R3, R7, R8, R16, R17 & R18

National SAR Agency: US Coast Guard.
Address: Commandant (CG-534), 2100 2nd Street, S.W. Washington D.C. 20593-7363, USA
Telephone: +1 202 3722075
Fax: +1 202 3722912
Website: https://www.uscg.mil/

The US Coast Guard National VHF Distress System provides continuous coastal coverage outwards to 20 n miles on VHF Ch 16. After contact on Ch 16, communications with the Coast Guard should be on VHF Ch 22A. Vessels not equipped with VHF Ch 22A should use VHF Ch 12. Selected Coast Radio Stations and Coast Guard Stations maintain continuous watch on 2182 kHz.

	Telephone +1	Fax +1	Others/Ship Earth Stations (SES)
USMCC (Cospas-Sarsat SPOC)	301 8174576	301 8174568	**AFTN:** KZDCZSZA **email:** usmcc@noaa.gov
AMVER surface picture (SURPIC)	Contact any US Coast Guard RCC or www.amver.com/surpicrequest.asp		

Atlantic Coast

	Telephone +1	Fax +1	Others/Ship Earth Stations (SES)
COMMUNICATION AREA MASTER STATION ATLANTIC (CAMSLANT)	757 4216240	757 4216225	**Telex:** +230 127775 USCG RCC NYK **email:** camslantcwo@uscg.mil
ATLANTIC SAR COORDINATOR	757 3986700	757 3986775	**email:** lantwatch@uscg.mil
JRCC BOSTON (1st District)	617 2238555	617 2238117	**email:** rccboston@uscg.mil
JRCC NORFOLK (5th District)	757 3986231	757 3986392	**Telex:** +230 127775 USCG RCC NYK **Inmarsat C:** (AOR-E) 430370670 (AOR-W) 430370680 **email:** d05-smb-caa-lant30cc@uscg.mil d05-smb-d5cc@uscg.mil rccnorfolk@uscg.mil
JRCC MIAMI (7th District)	305 4156800	305 4156809	**email:** rccmiami@uscg.mil

Great Lakes

	Telephone +1	Fax +1	Others/Ship Earth Stations (SES)
JRCC CLEVELAND (9th District)	216 9026117	216 9026121	**email:** d9cc@uscg.mil

Gulf Coast

	Telephone +1	Fax +1	Others/Ship Earth Stations (SES)
JRCC NEW ORLEANS (8th District)	504 5896225	504 5892148	**Telex:** +230 701801 **email:** d8commandcenter@uscg.mil

VENEZUELA   See diagram R7

National SAR Agency: Instituto Nacional de los Espacios Acuáticos (INEA) National Authority
Address: Av. Orinoco, entre Perijá y Mucuchies. Edif. INEA, Las Mercedes, Dtto. Capital, Venezuela
Telephone: +58 212 9091429
Website: www.inea.gob.ve

Port Authorities maintain a continuous listening watch on VHF Ch 16 only during working hours.

	Telephone +58	Fax +58	Others/Ship Earth Stations (SES)
MRCC VENEZUELA	212 3034511	212 3551518	**AFTN:** SVMIZSZX **email:** sar@inac.gob.ve
RCC MAIQUETÍA	212 3551920	212 3551518	**email:** sar@inac.gob.ve
MRSC MARACAIBO (military)	261 721188	261 7226480	**email:** epgmatel@gmail.com
MRSC PUERTO CABELLO (military)	242 3618448	212 3616353	**email:** epgcpc11@gmail.com
MRSC LA GUAIRA (military)	212 3323115	212 3326148	**email:** epgiradiocom555@gmail.com
MRSC CARENERO	234 3230117	234 3230950	**email:** carenero@inea.gob.ve
MRSC PUERTO LA CRUZ	281 2677932	281 2677452	**email:** capitaniaplc@gmail.com
MRSC PAMPATAR (military)	295 2621454	295 2626377	**email:** guardacostaspampatar1@gmail.com
MRSC CIUDAD GUAYANA	286 9303549	286 9237228	**email:** cpciudadguayana@gmail.com
COAST GUARD (military)	212 3038800	212 3322891	**email:** guardiacguard@gmail.com

Continued overleaf

VENEZUELA (Continued)

	Telephone +58	Fax +58	Others/Ship Earth Stations (SES)
CG PUERTO CABELLO (military)	242 3601230	212 3601245	**email:** epgpc@hotmail.com
CG PUNTO FIJO (military)	269 2502373	269 2502372	**email:** guardacostaspf@hotmail.com
ONSA VENEZUELA	212 7157105 424 1808189	212 2375572	**email:** sar@onsa.org.ve **Website:** www.onsa.org.ve
RESCATE HUMBOLDT (aeronautical)	416 7090239	212 2375572	**email:** rescatehumboldt@hotmail.com **Website:** www.rescate.com

VIRGIN ISLANDS, BRITISH (UK)   See diagram R7

National SAR Agency: Virgin Islands Search And Rescue (VISAR)
Address: P.O. Box 3042, Road Town, Tortola, British Virgin Islands (BVI)
Telephone: +1 284 4944357
Fax: +1 284 4946613
email: admin@visar.org
　　　visarbvi@gmail.com
Website: www.visar.org

A National Emergency Committee is responsible for coordinating National Distress and Mass Casualties operations. Virgin Islands Search And Rescue (VISAR) is a self-tasking SAR provider that operates its own rescue coordination suite. VISAR works closely with the US Coast Guard. VISAR has limited capability for RDF on 121·5 or 243 MHz. There is currently no H24 listening watch on VHF Ch 16 in the BVI. This is covered by the US Coast Guard Greater Antilles Section in San Juan, Puerto Rico. VISAR is a volunteer force and is not manned H24, however, rescue coordinators and lifeboat crews are on-call H24.

	Telephone +1	Fax +1	Others/Ship Earth Stations (SES)
SRCC VISAR	284 4990911	284 4946613	**email:** admin@visar.org

NAVAREA V

BRAZIL   See diagram R9

National SAR Agency: MRCC Brazil
Address: Praça Barao de Ladário S / N, Edificio Almirante Tamandaré, CEP; 20.091-000, Rio de Janeiro, RJ - Brazil
Telephone: +55 21 21046056
　　　　　+55 21 21046863
　　　　　+55 21 22538824
Fax: +55 21 22538824
AFTN: SBRJYCYM
Inmarsat C: 471013483
email: mrccbrazil@marinha.mil.br
　　　mrccbrazil@gmail.com

A network of Coast Radio Stations maintain a continuous listening watch on international distress frequencies.

	Telephone +55	Fax +55	Others/Ship Earth Stations (SES)
ARCC BRAZILIA (Cospas-Sarsat SPOC)	61 33648394 61 33651212	61 33652964	**Mobile:** +55 61 99681632 　　　+55 61 99713769 **AFTN:** SBBRYCYX **email:** arccbs.cindacta1@fab.mil.br 　　　arcc.cindacta1@fab.mil.br 　　　salvaerobrasilia@gmail.com
BRMCC (Cospas-Sarsat SPOC)	61 33652964 61 33648395	61 33652964	**AFTN:** SBBRZSZX **email:** brmcc.cindacta1@fab.mil.br 　　　brmccsarsat@gmail.com (Secondary email)
SALVAERO BRASÍLIA	61 33651212 61 33648394 61 33648392 61 33648419	61 33651212	**Mobile:** +55 61 99681632 　　　+55 61 99713769 **email:** arcc.cindacta1@fab.mil.br 　　　salvaerobrasilia@gmail.com
SALVAMAR BRASIL (MRCC Brazil)	21 21046056 21 21046863 21 22538824	21 22538824	**AFTN:** SBRJYCYM **Inmarsat C:** 471013483 **email:** mrccbrazil@marinha.mil.br 　　　mrccbrazil@gmail.com
SALVAMAR SOUTHEAST (MRCC Rio de Janeiro)	21 21046119 21 21046120	21 21046104 21 21046196	**email:** mrccrio@marinha.mil.br

Continued on next page

BRAZIL (Continued)

	Telephone +55	Fax +55	Others/Ship Earth Stations (SES)
SALVAMAR EAST (MRCC Salvador)	71 35073730 71 35073772		**email:** mrccsalvador@marinha.mil.br
SALVAMAR NORTHEAST (MRCC Natal)	84 32163009 84 32163018		**email:** mrccnatal@marinha.mil.br
SALVAMAR NORTH (MRCC Belém)	91 32164030 91 32164031	91 32164030	**email:** mrccbelem@marinha.mil.br
SALVAMAR SOUTH (MRCC Rio Grande)	53 32336130 53 32336131 53 32336139	53 32311519	**email:** mrrccriogrande@marinha.mil.br
SALVAMAR WEST (MRCC Ladário)	67 32341030 67 32341031 67 32341032	67 32341069	**email:** rccladario@marinha.mil.br
SALVAMAR CENTRAL-WEST (RCC Brasília)	61 34291186 61 34291149		**email:** rccbrasilia@marinha.mil.br
SALVAMAR SOUTH SOUTHEAST (MRCC São Paulo)	11 50804733 11 50804734	11 50804736	**email:** mrccsaopaulo@marinha.mil.br
SALVAMAR NORTHWEST (MRCC Manaus)	92 21232237 92 21232238 92 21232239	92 21232238	**email:** rccmanaus@marinha.mil.br
CISMAR (Centro Integrado de Seguança Maritima)	21 21046353 21 21046337	21 21046341 21 21046346	**email:** cismar.cctram@marinha.mil.br

NAVAREA VI

ARGENTINA   See diagrams R8/9 & R19

National SAR Agency: Agencia Nacional SAR (ACSM)/Argentina National SAR Agency Armada Argentina / Argentine Navy
Address: Puerto Belgrano (8111), Buenos Aires, Argentina
Telephone: +54 2932 487162
            +54 2932 487150
            0800 6667727 (within Argentina)
Fax: +54 2932 487163
Inmarsat C: 470100125
email: acsm@armada.mil.ar

The authority responsible for National Maritime SAR is the Argentine Navy. The Maritime SAR organization joins the Argentine Navy and Prefectura Naval SAR capabilities and facilities. The Argentine Navy acts as the National Maritime SAR Agency for operation of all MRCCs, and Prefectura is responsible for the operation of all RSCs. The Prefectura Naval Argentina provides the Safety of Navigation Communication Service (SECOSENA) through Argentine Naval Authority Coast Radio Stations.

The SECOSENA stations maintain a continuous watch on international distress frequencies. Whenever possible vessels should maintain a permanent watch on VHF Ch 16 when within range of a SECOSENA station. If watch cannot be kept on VHF Ch 16, then Ch 12 or Ch 14 should be used giving notice to the nearest SECOSENA station.

TeleMedical Assistance Service: Contact via any of the MRCCs/MRSCs. Possible consultation languages: Spanish and English.

	Telephone +54	Fax +54	Others/Ship Earth Stations (SES)
ARMCC (Cospas-Sarsat SPOC)	1144 802486 1147 512935	1147 512935	**AFTN:** SAEZZSZX **email:** armcc@sass.gov.ar
MRCC BUENOS AIRES	1143 172300	1143 132889	**email:** mrccbuenosaires@armada.mil.ar
MRCC PUERTO BELGRANO	2932 487162 1143 172038	2932 487163	**Inmarsat C:** 470100125 470101167 **email:** mrccpuertobelgrano@armada.mil.ar
MRCC USHUAIA	2901 431098	2901 431098	**email:** mrccushuaia@armada.mil.ar armada_emanau@armada.mil.ar
	Antarctic Summer (Mid Nov - Mid Mar): R/T on 2182 kHz and 4660 kHz		
RSC RIO DE LA PLATA (L2A)	1145 767646	1145 767646	**email:** contrasebsas@prefecturanaval.gov.ar
RSC TIGRE	1145 124902	1145 124902	**email:** pzde-operaciones@prefecturanaval.gov.ar
RSC ROSARIO	3414 720340	3414 720348	**email:** pzbp-divoper@prefecturanaval.gov.ar
RSC CORRIENTES	3794 423318	3794 423318	**email:** pzonapzpp@prefecturanaval.gov.ar

Continued overleaf

ARGENTINA (Continued)

	Telephone +54	Fax +54	Others/Ship Earth Stations (SES)
RSC POSADAS	3764 460946	3764 402231	**email:** pzonapzap@prefecturanaval.gov.ar
RSC CONCEPCION DEL URUGUAY	3442 422044	3442 423377	**email:** pzbu-radio@prefecturanaval.gov.ar
RSC PASO DE LOS LIBRES	3772 422000	3772 424326	**email:** pzonapzau@prefecturanaval.gov.ar
RSC MAR DEL PLATA	2234 803006	2234 803006	**email:** mpla@prefecturanaval.gov.ar
RSC BAHÍA BLANCA	2914 573036	2914 571720	**email:** bbla-contrase@prefecturanaval.gov.ar
RSC COMODORO RIVADAVIA	2974 476800	2974 476800	**email:** criv@prefecturanaval.gov.ar
RSC PUERTO DESEADO	2974 872200	2974 872322	**email:** dese-ecostera@prefecturanaval.gov.ar
RSC PUERTO MADRYN	2804 451603	2804 451263	**email:** madr@prefecturanaval.gov.ar
RSC SAN ANTONIO OESTE	2934 421480	2934 421202	**email:** sant@prefecturanaval.gov.ar
RSC SAN CARLOS DE BARILOCHE	2944 422798	2944 425522	**email:** scba@prefecturanaval.gov.ar
RSC NEUQUEN	2991 5634 2569	2991 5634 2569	**email:** chue@prefecturanaval.gov.ar
RSC RIO GALLEGOS	2966 435494	2966 435494	**email:** rgal-costera@prefecturanaval.gov.ar
RSC LAGO ARGENTINO	2902 497653	2902 497653	**email:** larg@prefecturanaval.gov.ar
RSC USHUAIA	2901 422296	2901 421425	**email:** ushu-contrase@prefecturanaval.gov.ar
RSC ISLAS ORCADAS	Communication via MRCC USHUAIA		

FALKLAND ISLANDS (UK)   See diagram R9

URUGUAY   See diagram R9

National SAR Agency: MRCC URUGUAY

Address: Rambla, 25 de Agosto de 1825 S/N, Hangar B, CP 11.000, Montevideo, Uruguay
Telephone: +598 2 9161389
Fax: +598 2 9161389
        +598 2 9167922
email: mrccuruguay@gmail.com
        mrccuy@armada.mil.uy
        comflo_radio@armada.mil.uy

MRCC Uruguay is responsible for coordinating Search and Rescue operations. A network of Coast Radio Stations maintains a continuous listening watch on international distress frequencies.
TeleMedical Assistance Service: Contact via MRCC Uruguay. Possible consultation language: Spanish.

	Telephone +598	Fax +598	Others/Ship Earth Stations (SES)
RCC CARRASCO (Cospas-Sarsat SPOC)	2 6040297	2 6040112	**AFTN:** SUMUYCYX **email:** ccrfau@adinet.com.uy ccr@fau.mil.uy

MRCC URUGUAY	2 9161389	2 9161389
		2 9167922
			Inmarsat C: 497480210
			email: mrccuruguay@gmail.com
			        mrccuy@armada.mil.uy
			        comflo_radio@armada.mil.uy

Asociación Honoraria de Salvamentos Marítimos y Fluviales (ADES) (ILF)	2 1767	2 6280999	**email:** sosades@adinet.com.uy

NAVAREA VII

ANGOLA
See diagram R10

National SAR Agency: Departamento de Seguranca Maritima
Address: Av. Rainha Girga 74-4th Floor, Luanda, Angola
Telephone: +244 2 22394478
+244 2 22396478
Fax: +244 2 22339848
Telex: +991 3352

MRCC ANGOLA maintains a continuous listening watch on 2182 and 4125 kHz and VHF Ch 16 for distress calls.			
	Telephone +244	**Fax** +244	**Others/Ship Earth Stations (SES)**
RCC LUANDA (Cospas-Sarsat SPOC)	2 2372819 912506739		**AFTN:** FNLUYFYX **email:** arquimedes.ferreira@inavic.gv.ao
MRCC ANGOLA	923439336		**email:** sarmar.angola_c@hotmail.com mamueiro_s@hotmail.com

ASCENSION ISLAND (UK)
See diagram R9

Ascension Island has no formal Maritime Rescue Coordination Centre. The RAF coordinates rescue through ARCC Kinloss, UK and the USAF through the US Coast Guard in New York. Ascension Island (ZBI), with a range of up to 200 n miles around Ascension Island, maintains a continuous listening watch on 2182 kHz and will relay relevant messages by request. Fire and Security (operated for the USAF) and Turtle Radio (operated by the RAF) maintain a continuous listening watch on VHF Ch 16 for distress calls. Other organisations on the island offer help wherever possible. Coast Radio Station, S. Helena (ZHH), on the island of S. Helena about 700 n miles SSE of Ascension Island, can also offer assistance in this area but does not maintain a continuous listening watch on international distress frequencies.			
	Telephone	**Fax**	**Others/Ship Earth Stations (SES)**
TURTLE RADIO (RAF ASCENSION) Air Operations (Cospas-Sarsat SPOC)	+247 6338 +247 3315 +247 2515	+247 6780	**AFTN:** FHAWYWYO **email:** ops.ascension@atlantis.co.uk
ARCC KINLOSS (UK)	+44 1309 678301	+44 1309 678308	
ASCENSION I (ZBI)	+247 6721	+247 6464 +247 6783	
H.H. THE ADMINISTRATOR	+247 6311 +247 4525 (Police)	+247 6152	**Telex:** +939 3214 GOVT AV

MADAGASCAR
See diagrams R10 & R12

National SAR Agency: Joint Rescue Coordination Centre (JRCC) Antananarivo
Address: B.P. "D" - Ivato Aeroport Antananarivo 105 - Madagascar
Telephone: +261 32 1125743
+261 34 1374247
Fax: +261 20 2253934
email: jrccmad@moov.mg

A network of Coast Radio Stations maintains a continuous listening watch on international distress frequencies.			
	Telephone +261	**Fax** +261	**Others/Ship Earth Stations (SES)**
JRCC MADAGASCAR (Cospas-Sarsat SPOC)	32 1125743 34 1374247		**AFTN:** FMMIYCYX **email:** jrccmad@moov.mg **Website:** www.acm.mg

MOZAMBIQUE
See diagrams R10 & R12

National SAR Agency: SAFMAR
Address: INAMAR - National Maritime Authority, Av. Marquês do Pombal, No. 279, Caixa Postal 4317, Maputo, Mozambique
Telephone: +258 21 301963
         +258 21 420552
Fax: +258 21 424007
email: safmar@zebra.uem.mz

The National Maritime Administration and Safety Authority (SAFMAR) is an autonomous section of the Ministry of Transport and Communications. One of the main objectives of SAFMAR is to ensure safety of life at sea and it is therefore responsible for the coordination of maritime Search and Rescue operations within the maritime Search and Rescue Region of Mozambique. MRCC Maputo currently maintains a continuous listening watch on 2182 kHz and VHF Ch 16 for distress calls.

	Telephone +258	Fax +258	Others/Ship Earth Stations (SES)
MRCC MAPUTO (C9L234)	21 494396	21 494396	**email:** safmar@zebra.uem.mz
ARCC BEIRA	23 302330 (Direct RCC) 23 301626 (ACC)	23 302330	**AFTN:** FQBEZIZX (ACC)

NAMIBIA
See diagram R10

National SAR Agency: Namibian Search and Rescue (NAMSAR) Organisation
Address: Ministry of Works Transport and Communication, Directorate of Maritime Affairs, Windhoek, Namibia
Telephone: +264 61 2088025
         +264 61 2088026
         +264 61 2088027
Fax: +264 61 240024
email: mmnangolo@mwtc.gov.na

Namibian Search and Rescue (NAMSAR) coordinates all Search and Rescue efforts in Namibia and works in close co-operation with the South African Search and Rescue organisation (SASAR). Walvis Bay Port control acts as an MRSC under the control of the MRCC of SASAR. Lüderitz acts under the control of Walvis Bay MRSC. Inshore rescue craft stationed at Walvis Bay and Swakopmund are called out with the authority of the Port Captain in Walvis Bay.

Walvis Bay (V5W) maintains a continuous listening watch on 2182 and 4125 kHz and VHF Ch 16, and Lüderitz (V5L) on 2182 kHz for distress calls. Preferred inter RCC language is English.

	Telephone	Fax	Others/Ship Earth Stations (SES)
NAMSAR via WALVIS BAY (V5W) (Cospas-Sarsat SPOC)	+264 64 203581 (Ops. H24)	+264 64 207497 (Ops. H24)	**email:** wvsradio@telecom.na
WALVIS BAY PORT CONTROL	+264 64 2082265	+264 64 2082325	**email:** portc@namport.com.na
MRCC SOUTH AFRICA (CAPE TOWN)	+27 21 9383300	+27 21 9383309	**email:** mrcc.ct@samsa.org.za

SOUTH AFRICA
See diagrams R10, R12 & R19

National SAR Agency: The South African Search and Rescue Organization (SASAR) Secretariat
Address: Department of Transport, Private Bag X193, Pretoria 0001, South Africa
Telephone: +27 12 3093520
Fax: +27 12 3093109
Website: https://www.transport.gov.za/web/search-and-rescue

The South African Department of Transport is responsible for coordinating Search and Rescue operations. The national MRCC exists at Plattekloof, near Cape Town and the port control offices at Saldanha Bay, Cape Town, Mossel Bay, Port Elizabeth, East London, Durban and Richards Bay act as MRSCs under its control. The MRCC and MRSCs are manned on a 24 hour basis. Any police station or manned lighthouse will pass a distress signal on to the nearest port control office. South Africa does not have an Inmarsat Land Earth Station (LES) in the GMDSS. Vessels making a distress call through a LES can dial direct through a LES to MRCC South Africa. A network of Coast Radio Stations maintains a continuous listening watch on international distress frequencies. NAVTEX and SafetyNET MSI broadcasts, DSC, and the Cospas-Sarsat Africa South Mission Control Centre (ASMCC) and Local User Terminal are controlled from one single point at Cape Town Radio. Preferred inter RCC language is English.

	Telephone +27	Fax +27	Others/Ship Earth Stations (SES)
ASMCC (Cospas-Sarsat SPOC)	21 5529752	21 5513760	**AFTN:** FACTYCYX **email:** maritimeradio@telkom.co.za
	No attachments accepted for any e-mail messages.		
MRCC CAPE TOWN	21 9383300	21 9383309	**email:** mrcc.ct@samsa.org.za

NAVAREA VIII

ANDAMAN ISLANDS - see INDIA
BANGLADESH

See diagrams R13 & R14

National SAR Agency: Director General, Department of Shipping
Address: 141-143, Motijheel C/A (8th floor), Dhaka 1000, Bangladesh
Telephone: +880 2 9555128
　　　　　　 +880 2 9553584
Fax: +880 2 7168363

The Department of Shipping is responsible for coordinating Search and Rescue operations. Coast Radio Stations maintain a continuous listening watch on international distress frequencies.

	Telephone +880	Fax +880	Others/Ship Earth Stations (SES)
CAAB HQ	2 8901241	2 8901411	**AFTN:** VGHQYAYS
Dhaka ACC (Cospas-Sarsat SPOC)	2 8901462 2 8901463 2 8901464	2 8901924	**AFTN:** VGFRZQZX 　　　 VGHSZQZX **email:** rcc_dhaka@caab.gov.bd
MRCC DHAKA (NHQ Ops Room Naval HQ) - Primary	2 9836314 (Direct) 2 8871247 (Direct) 2 9836141-9 ext 2116 (PABX)	2 8871254	**Mobile:** +880 1 769701111 (Duty Officer) 　　　　 +880 1 769702113 (Staff Officer) 　　　　 +880 1 769702116 (Duty Staff) **Inmarsat C:** 440500362 **email:** mrccdhk@navy.mil.bd **Website:** www.navy.mil.bd
MRCC DHAKA (COMCEN Naval HQ) - Secondary	2 8711439 (Direct) 2 9836141-9 ext 2821 (PABX) 2 9836141-9 ext 2822 (PABX)	2 9836270 2 8712243	**Mobile:** +880 1 769702820 (Staff Officer) 　　　　 +880 1 769702822 (Duty Staff) **email:** cmcndhk@navy.mil.bd
MRSC CHITTAGONG (Naval area Ops Room) - Primary	31 740655 (Direct) 31 740391-9 ext 4108 4109 (PABX)	31 741162	**Mobile:** +880 1 769721111 (Duty Officer) 　　　　 +880 1 769724107 (Staff Officer) 　　　　 +880 1 769724140 (Duty Staff) **email:** mrscctg@navy.mil.bd
MRSC CHITTAGONG (COMCEN) - Secondary	31 741642 (Direct) 31 740391-9 ext 4137 (PABX) 31 740400-9 ext 6137 (PABX) 31 740400-9 ext 4137 (PABX)	31 741162 31 740426	**Mobile:** +880 1 769724131 (Staff Officer) **email:** mrscctg@navy.mil.bd
MRSC KHULNA (COMKHUL) - Primary	2 55059279 (Direct) 2 55059200 - 23 ext 4108 (PABX)	2 55059281 2 55059282	**Mobile:** +880 1 769781111 (Duty Officer) 　　　　 +880 1 769784107 (Staff Officer) **email:** mrsckln@navy.mil.bd
MRSC KHULNA (COMCEN) - Secondary	2 55059280 (Direct) 2 55059200-23 ext 4133 (PABX)	2 55059281 2 55059282	**Mobile:** +880 1 769784131 (Staff Officer) **email:** cmcnkln@navy.mil.bd

DIEGO GARCIA (BRITISH INDIAN OCEAN TERRITORY)

See diagram R12/13

National SAR Agency: Police / British Representative
Address: BFPO 485, United Kingdom
Telephone: +246 370 2938
　　　　　　 +246 370 2939 (Police H24)
　　　　　　 +246 370 3503 (HQ Admin/BritSec not H24)
Fax: +246 370 3943
email: biotrmdetadmin@a.dii.mod.uk

Continuous listening watch is maintained on the following frequencies 282.8 MHz, 243.0 MHz, 121.5 MHz and VHF Ch 16 (Port Control)

	Telephone +246	Fax +246	Others/Ship Earth Stations (SES)
AIRPORT CONTROL (NKW)	370 3322		
BRITISH REPRESENTATIVE (BritRep)	370 3500		**email:** christopher.moorey.uk@fe.navy.mil
PORT CONTROL (Diego Garcia)	370 4301	370 3028	

INDIA   **See diagrams R12/13 & R14**

National SAR Agency: Indian Coast Guard
Address: Coast Guard Headquarters, National Stadium Complex, Purana Quila Road, New Delhi - 110 001, India
Telephone: +91 11 23384934
                        +91 11 23383999
Fax: +91 11 23383196
email: dte-ops@indiancoastguard.nic.in
Website: https://indiancoastguard.gov.in/

The Indian Coast Guard is responsible for coordinating SAR operations in the Indian Maritime SRR. The Indian SRR is divided into five sub-regions.

The MRCCs are co-located with Coast Guard Regional Headquarters (RHQs) and coordinate missions with other agencies via a network of MRSCs.

Merchant vessels plying through the Indian SRR may participate in a Computerised Vessel Reporting System for SAR known as "INDSAR". Position reporting by using two digit Inmarsat service code 43 via LES Arvi is voluntary and free of charge. The INDSAR system is coordinated by MRCC Mumbai, MMSI 004192203, email: mrcc-west@indiancoastguard.nic.in. Preferred inter RCC language is English.

North Western Region

	Telephone +91	**Fax** +91	**Others/Ship Earth Stations (SES)**
MRSSC VĀDĪNĀR	2833 256560 M-SAR call 1554 (Toll free)	2833 256560	**Inmarsat C:** 441900448=CGVD X **email:** cgs-vdr@indiancoastguard.nic.in cgsvadinar@yahoo.co.in
MRSSC OKHA	2892 262261 2892 262259 M-SAR call 1554 (Toll free)	2892 263421 2892 263435	**Inmarsat C:** 441923271 **email:** cgs-okha@indiancoastguard.nic.in
MRSC PORBANDAR	286 2242451 286 2244056 M-SAR call 1554 (Toll free)	286 2210559	**Inmarsat C:** 441908210 **email:** dhq1@indiancoastguard.nic.in opsdhq1@yahoo.co.in

Western Region

	Telephone +91	**Fax** +91	**Others/Ship Earth Stations (SES)**
MRCC MUMBAI (Cospas-Sarsat SPOC)	22 24388065 22 24316558 22 24383592 M-SAR call 1554 (Toll free)	22 24388065 22 24316558 22 24383592	**AFTN:** VABBYXYC **Inmarsat C:** 441907210=BMCG X **email:** mrcc-west@indiancoastguard.nic.in
MRSC GOA	832 2521718 832 2521607 M-SAR call 1554 (Toll free)	832 2520584	**Inmarsat C:** 441900445 **email:** dhq11@indiancoastguard.nic.in
MRSC NEW MANGALORE	824 2405278 M-SAR call 1554 (Toll free)	824 2405267	**Inmarsat C:** 441844822 **Inmarsat Fleet:** 773213830 (Voice) 783238659 (Fax) **email:** dhq3@indiancoastguard.nic.in
MRSC KOCHI (Cochin)	484 2218969 M-SAR call 1554 (Toll free)	484 2218460 484 2217164	**email:** dhq4@indiancoastguard.nic.in dhq4opsroom@gmail.com
MRSSC BEYPORE	495 2417995 M-SAR call 1554 (Toll free)	495 2417994	**email:** cgs-bpe@indiancoastguard.nic.in
MRSSC VIZHINJAM	471 2481855 M-SAR call 1554 (Toll free)	471 2486484	**Inmarsat C:** 441900449 **email:** cgs-vzm@indiancoastguard.nic.in

INDIA (Continued)

Eastern Region

	Telephone +91	Fax +91	Others/Ship Earth Stations (SES)

MRCC CHENNAI	44 25395018	44 23460405	**AFTN:** VOMMYXCG
			Inmarsat C: 441922669=MSCG X
			Inmarsat Fleet: 773154749 (Voice)
			                783246626 (Fax)
			email: mrcc-east@indiancoastguard.nic.in
			      mrccchennai@gmail.com

MRSC VISHĀKHAPATNAM	891 2547266 M-SAR call 1554 (Toll free)	891 2741130 891 2703487 891 2768879	**Inmarsat C:** 441907010=CEDD X **email:** dhq6@indiancoastguard.nic.in ops-dhq6@indiancoastguard.nic.in
MRSC TUTICORIN	461 2352046 M-SAR call 1554 (Toll free)	461 2353503	**Inmarsat C:** 441900447=CTUT X **email:** cgs-tut@indiancoastguard.nic.in
MRSSC MANDAPAM	4573 241634 4573 242020 M-SAR call 1554 (Toll free)	4573 241142 4573 241634	**Inmarsat C:** 441907810=CGSM X **Inmarsat Fleet:** 773213566 (Voice) **email:** cgsmdp@indiancoastguard.nic.in cgsmdpindiancoastguard@gmail.com

North Eastern Region

	Telephone +91	Fax +91	Others/Ship Earth Stations (SES)
MRSC HALDIA	3224 267755 M-SAR call 1554 (Toll free)	3224 264541	**Inmarsat C:** 441907110 **email:** dhq8@indiancoastguard.nic.in coastguardhaldia@gmail.com

MRSC PĀRĀDIP	6722 223359
	M-SAR call 1554
	(Toll free)
		6722 220174	**Inmarsat C:** 441907710=DHQP X
			Inmarsat Fleet: 773213679 (Voice)
			                783232805 (Fax)
			                783238448 (Data)
			email: dhq7@indiancoastguard.nic.in

Andaman & Nicobar Region

	Telephone +91	Fax +91	Others/Ship Earth Stations (SES)

MRCC PORT BLAIR	3192 245530
	3192 246081
	M-SAR call 1554
	(Toll free)
		3192 242948	**Inmarsat C:** 441922666
			      441908010=CGPB X
			email: mrcc-ptb@indiancoastguard.nic.in
			      com_cs@dataone.in

MRSC CAMPBELL BAY	3192 264666 3192 264235 M-SAR call 1554 (Toll free)	3192 264215	**Inmarsat C:** 441907910=CPCB X **email:** dhq10@indiancoastguard.nic.in
MRSC DIGLIPUR	3192 272332 M-SAR call 1554 (Toll free)	3192 272345	**Inmarsat C:** 441908110=DGPR X **email:** cgdhq9diglipur@gmail.com dhq9@indiancoastguard.nic.in

KENYA   See diagrams R10 & R12

National SAR Agency: This agency is in the process of formation, no information available.

	Telephone +254	Fax +254	Others/Ship Earth Stations (SES)
RCC NAIROBI (Cospas-Sarsat SPOC)	20 6827027 20 6827026 20 6827802		**Iridium:** +881 632714255 **email:** kenyasar@kcaa.or.ke sar@kcaa.or.ke

MRCC MOMBASA	73 7719414
	72 1368313
			Inmarsat C: 463400071
			Inmarsat Fleet: 764626655 (Voice)
			                764626656 (Fax)
			                764626657 (Voice)
			                764626658
			email: rmrcc@kma.go.ke

MALDIVES   See diagram R12/13

National SAR Agency: Maldives Coast Guard
Address: Coastguard Headquarters, Coast Guard Building, Male', Republic of Maldives
Telephone: +960 3325981
          +960 3338898
Fax: +960 3310054
Website: https://mndf.gov.mv

Maldives Coastguard is responsible for coordinating Search and Rescue operations within the Maldives Search and Rescue Region. GMDSS Operation Centre maintains a continuous listening watch on international distress frequencies VHF Ch 16 and 2182 kHz.

	Telephone +960	Fax +960	Others/Ship Earth Stations (SES)
MALDIVES AIRPORTS COMPANY LTD (Cospas-Sarsat SPOC)	3322071 3317202	3309905	**AFTN:** VRMMYCYX **Telex:** +896 66034 CIVAV **email:** sup_macc@macl.aero
COAST GUARD HEADQUARTERS (Operations Centre)	3398898 3395981	3391665	**email:** maldivescoastguard@defence.gov.mv
MALE' Harbour Control	3327883	3328624	**email:** maldport@dhivenet.net.mv

MAURITIUS   See diagram R12

National SAR Agency: MRCC Mauritius / National Coast Guard
Address: Headquarters, Fort William, Les Salines, Port Louis, Mauritius
Telephone: +230 2083935
          +230 2088317
Fax: +230 2122757
email: ncgops.mpf@govmu.org
       opsncghq@intnet.mu

Search and Rescue operations within the waters around Mauritius are coordinated by the National Coast Guard. They can be contacted through Mauritius (3BM) which maintains a continuous listening watch on international distress frequencies VHF Ch 16, 2182 kHz and DSC VHF Ch 70 and MF 2187·5 kHz. Preferred inter RCC languages are English and French.

	Telephone +230	Fax +230	Others/Ship Earth Stations (SES)
MRCC MAURITIUS (COAST GUARD OPERATIONS ROOM) (Cospas-Sarsat SPOC)	2083935 2088317	2122757	**AFTN:** FIMPYCYX **Inmarsat C:** 464500096 464500097 **Iridium:** +8816 31427287 **email:** ncgops.mpf@govmu.org opsncghq@intnet.mu
MAURITIUS RADIO (3BM)	2085950 2110839 (SAR)	2110838	**Inmarsat BGAN:** 772391532 **email:** 3bm.mrs@telecom.mu

RÉUNION (FRANCE)   See diagrams R10 & R12

National SAR Agency: Organisme d'études et de coordination pour la recherche et le sauvetage en mer (SECMAR)
Address: 20 Avenue de de Ségur 75007 Paris, France
Telephone: +33 1 53634159
Fax: +33 1 53634178

Centre Régional Opérationnel de Surveillance et de Sauvetage Sud Océan Indien [CROSS SOI = MRCC La Réunion + VTM (Vessel Traffic Monitoring)]

Watch 24/7 on 2187.5 kHz (DSC) / CH 16 VHF (La Réunion Island - Mayotte Island) - SPOC COSPAS SARSAT

	Telephone	Fax	Others/Ship Earth Stations (SES)
MRCC RÉUNION (CROSSRU) Officer of the Watch (Cospas-Sarsat SPOC)	196 (Emergency Number) +262 262 434343 +262 692 880433 (SMS) +262 692 610108 (Voice/SMS/MMS/ WhatsApp)	+262 262 711595	**Telex:** +961 916140 CROSSRU **Inmarsat C:** 422799193 **Iridium:** +8816 31448080 **email:** reunion@mrccfr.eu lareunion.mrcc@developpement-durable.gouv.fr

SEYCHELLES
See diagram R12

National SAR Agency: Seychelles Coast Guard with assistance of Port and Marine Services Division
Address: Seychelles Coast Guard, P.O. Box 257 Victoria, Mahe, Seychelles
Telephone: +248 4290900
　　　　　　+248 4224616
Fax: +248 4323288
email: mrcc.seycoast@email.sc

The Seychelles Coast Guard coordinates Search and Rescue Operations.

The MRCC at Seychelles Coast Guard and Control Tower at Port and Marine Services Division maintains a continuous listening watch on VHF Ch 16. Seychelles Radio (S7Q) maintains continuous listening watch on international distress frequencies. Preferred inter RCC language is English.

	Telephone +248	Fax +248	Others/Ship Earth Stations (SES)
JRCC SEYCHELLES (Cospas-Sarsat SPOC)	4290900 4290080 4224411	4323288 4224665	**AFTN:** FSIAYNYX 　　　　FSSSZQZX **email:** mrcc.seycoast@email.sc
SEYCHELLES (S7Q)	2375733	2376291	
TOWER CONTROL PORT AND MARINE SERVICES DIVISION	2224701	2224004	

SRI LANKA
See diagrams R12/13 & R14

National SAR Agency: Sri Lanka Navy
Address: Naval Head Quarters, Colombo, Sri Lanka
Telephone: +94 11 2423645
Fax: +94 11 2424651
Website: https://www.navy.lk/

Maritime Search and Rescue operations are coordinated by the Sri Lankan Navy.

MRCC Colombo is manned 24 hours by a duty Staff Officer of the Sri Lankan Navy. Colombo Radio (4PB) maintains a continuous listening watch on 2182 kHz and VHF Ch 16 for distress calls. Galle (4PG), a remote controlled station operated from Colombo Radio maintains a continuous listening watch on VHF Ch 16 for distress calls.

	Telephone +94	Fax +94	Others/Ship Earth Stations (SES)
MRCC COLOMBO	11 2445368 11 2212230 11 2212231	11 2441454	**email:** mrcccolombo@gmail.com 　　　　nhqdno@yahoo.com
COLOMBO (4PB)	11 2423644 11 2423645 11 2423646	11 2424651	

TANZANIA
See diagrams R10 & R12

National SAR Agency: Surface and Marine Transport Regulatory Authority (SUMATRA)
Address: P.O. Box 3093, Dar es Salaam, Tanzania
Telephone: +255 22 2197516
Fax: +255 22 2116697
email: dg@sumatra.or.tz
　　　　info@sumatra.or.tz
Website: www.sumatra.or.tz

Tanzania Harbour Authority is responsible for Search and Rescue operations within coastal waters of Tanzania. Dar es Salaam Port Control maintains a listening watch on VHF Ch 16 for distress calls.

	Telephone +255	Fax +255	Others/Ship Earth Stations (SES)
DAR ES SALAAM RCC (Cospas-Sarsat SPOC)	222 110223 222 110224 222 110254	222 110264 222 124914	**AFTN:** HTDCYCYX **email:** tcaadia@tcaa.go.tz
MRSC DAR ES SALAAM	222 129325 222 129326 222 129327	222 129326	**Mobile:** +255 225 501731 　　　　+255 715 886295 　　　　+255 767 886295 　　　　+255 783 886295 **Inmarsat C:** 420500028 **email:** mrccdar@sumatra.or.tz

NAVAREA IX

BAHRAIN   See diagram R11

National SAR Agency: Directorate of Ports, Ministry of Finance and National Economy
Address: P.O. Box 15, Manama, Bahrain
Telephone: +973 17 725555
Website: https://www.mtt.gov.bh/directorates/ports-and-maritime

Bahrain (A9M) maintains a continuous listening watch on international distress frequencies. The Directorate of Ports is responsible for coordinating maritime Search and Rescue operations within the Bahraini territorial sea.

	Telephone +973	Fax +973	Others/Ship Earth Stations (SES)
RCC / ATC BAHRAIN (Cospas -Sarsat SPOC)	17 329969 17 329959 17 321158	17 321029	**AFTN:** OBBBYCYX **email:** bahatc@caa.gov.bh
RCC BAHRAIN	17 719404 17 727447	17 727985	
BAHRAIN Radio (A9M) (Maritime Ops Centre)	17 883939 17 883543	17 242676	**email:** moc@btc.com.bh
MENAS (Bahrain Operations Centre)	17 828541 17 727912 (Emergency)	17 727765	**email:** info@menas.com.bh **Website:** www.menas.org

DJIBOUTI   See diagram R11

National SAR Agency: Unknown

Djibouti (J2A) maintains a continuous listening watch on VHF Ch 16 for distress calls.

	Telephone +253	Fax +253	Others/Ship Earth Stations (SES)
RSC DJIBOUTI (Cospas-Sarsat SPOC)	21340350 21340977	21340723	**AFTN:** HDAMYDYD **Telex:** +979 5889
DJIBOUTI (J2A)	21351501 21350489 21350498	21355900	**email:** djiboutiradio@intnet.dj

ERITREA   See diagram R11

National SAR Agency: Unknown

Eritrea has a Search and Rescue organisation under the Department of the Civil Aviation tasked with the coordination of aeronautical, land and maritime Search and Rescue. Port Harbour Master offices are responsible for coordinating maritime Search and Rescue.

	Telephone +291	Fax +291	Others/Ship Earth Stations (SES)
JRCC Asmara (Cospas-Sarsat SPOC)	1 181424 1 182729 1 189121	1 181520	**AFTN:** HHAAYCYX **email:** ercaahq@gmail.com
CAA	1 189121 (Director General) 1 180187 (Director, Air Navigation) 1 181424 (Air Navigation)	1 181520 (Director General)	**email:** pauloscaadg@tse.com.er (Director General) ghebreab@tse.com.er (Director, Air Navigation)
PORT HARBOUR MASTER OFFICE ASSAB	1 660710 1 660192 1 660687	1 661249 1 661226	
PORT HARBOUR MASTER OFFICE MASSAWA	8 534272		**email:** harbourmaster@masawaport.com

IRAN   See diagrams R6 & R11

National SAR Agency: Ports and Maritime Organization, Director General, Maritime Safety and Marine Protection.
Address: No 1. Shahidi St. Shahid Haghani Highway, Vanak Sq. Tehrān Iran. Postal Code: 1518663111
Telephone: +98 21 84932171
　　　　　　+98 21 84932175
Fax: +98 21 84932190
email: tehran-mrcc@pmo.ir
Website: https://www.pmo.ir/fa/safetyandincidents/searchandrescue

The Ports and Maritime organization is responsible for coordinating maritime Search and Rescue operations. A network of Coast Radio Stations maintain a continuous listening watch on international distress frequencies.

	Telephone +98	Fax +98	Others/Ship Earth Stations (SES)
RCC TEHRĀN Cospas-Sarsat SPOC	21 61022293	21 44525882	**AFTN:** OIIIZRZX
HQ TEHRĀN	21 84932175 21 84932172 21 84932170	21 84932190 21 88651191	
MRCC AMĪRĀBĀD (Caspian Sea)	152 5462019	152 5462019	**Telex:** +88 215124 ENDR IR
MRCC ANZALĪ (Caspian Sea)	181 3225540	181 3223902	**Telex:** +88 232199
MRCC NOW-SHAHR (Caspian Sea)	191 3250984	191 3250982	**Telex:** +88 216643 ENDR IR **email:** nowshahrmrcc@nowshahport.ir
MRCC BANDAR-E SHAHĪD RAJĀ'Ī	763 3514032 763 3514033 763 3514034 763 3514035	763 3514036	**email:** radio@bpa.ir 　　　bandarabbas-mrcc@bpa.ir
MRCC BANDAR-E-EMĀM KHOMEYNĪ	651 2226902 652 2522451 652 2522452 652 2522453	651 2226902	**Telex:** +88 612051 ENDR IR
MRCC BŪSHEHR	771 2530075 771 2566449	771 2566400 771 2530077	**Telex:** +88 222208 **email:** radio@pso.ir
MRCC CHĀBAHĀR (Gulf of Oman)	545 2221415 545 2221215	545 2221215	

IRAQ   See diagram R11

National SAR Agency: Unknown

Başrah Control (YIR) and Umm Qaşr (YIU) maintain a continuous listening watch on VHF Ch 16 for distress calls.

	Telephone +964	Fax +964	Others/Ship Earth Stations (SES)
BAŞRAH CONTROL (YIR)	40 413211		

KUWAIT   See diagram R11

National SAR Agency: Maritime Affairs Department
Address: Transport Sector, Ministry of Communications, P.O. Box 33845, Al Rawdah, Code 73458, Kuwait
Telephone: +965 24814371
　　　　　　+965 24844102
Fax: +965 24814372
email: marine-dept@mockw.net

The Maritime Affairs Department is responsible for coordinating Search and Rescue operations.

	Telephone +965	Fax +965	Others/Ship Earth Stations (SES)
RCC ATC KUWAIT (Cospas-Sarsat SPOC)	24360463 24762994 24346221	24746515 24315349	**AFTN:** OKBKZOZX
ARCC KUWAIT	24742774		

OMAN   See diagrams R11 & R12

National SAR Agency: Royal Air Force of Oman
Address: Headquarters, Royal Air Force of Oman, P.O. Box 722, PC 111, Oman
Telephone: +968 24334211
                   +968 24334212
                   +968 24334305
                   +968 24334244
Fax: +968 24334776
          +968 24334743
Telex: +498 5592 RAFO OMAN ON

The Royal Air Force of Oman is responsible for coordinating Search and Rescue operations. Masqaṭ (Muscat) (A4M) maintains a continuous listening watch on international distress frequencies.

	Telephone +968	Fax +968	Others/Ship Earth Stations (SES)
RCC MASQAṬ (MUSCAT) OMAN AIR FORCE (Cospas-Sarsat SPOC)	24338211 24332212	24334776 24334743	**AFTN:** OOMSYCYX OOMMZRZX **Telex:** +498 5592 RAFO OMAN ON
ROYAL NAVY OF OMAN	24338805	24334730	**Telex:** +498 5593 RNO OMAN ON
ROYAL OMAN POLICE COAST GUARD	24714888 24711399	24714937	**Telex:** +498 5178 POLMAR **email:** coastguard@rop.gov.om
MASQAṬ (MUSCAT) (A4M)	24571400 24571500 24571300	24562995	**Telex:** +498 5310 MUSRAD ON

PAKISTAN   See diagrams R11 & R12

National SAR Agency: Pakistan Maritime Security Agency
Address: Headquarters, Pakistan Maritime Security Agency, Plot No 34-A, West Wharf Road, Karachi - 74200, Pakistan
Telephone: +92 21 99214624
                   +92 21 99214964
                   +92 21 99214965
                   +92 21 99214966
                   +92 21 99214967
                   +92 21 99214865
Fax: +92 21 99214625
Website: https://pmsa.gov.pk

Pakistan Maritime Security Agency under the Ministry of Defence is responsible for manning the Maritime Rescue Coordination Centre of Pakistan for the coordination of Search and Rescue operations within the Pakistan SAR region. Karachi Radio (ASK) is responsible for maintaining a continuous listening watch on all international distress frequencies.

The Joint Maritime Information and Coordination Centre (JMICC) will coordinate and harmonize efforts for maritime security within Pakistan's maritime jurisdiction to facilitate shipping transiting through the North Arabian Sea (NAS)

	Telephone +92	Fax +92	Others/Ship Earth Stations (SES)
RCC KARACHI (Airport)	21 99242401	21 92242404	**email:** rcckarfir@caapakistan.com.pk
MRCC PAKISTAN (MARITIME SECURITY AGENCY)	21 99214624 21 99214964 21 99214965 21 99214966 21 99214967 21 99214865	21 99214625	**Inmarsat C:** 446300048 **Inmarsat mini-C:** 446300033 **email:** mrccpmsa@cyber.net.pk hqmsa@cyber.net.pk
JOINT MARITIME INFORMATION AND COORDINATION CENTRE (JMICC)	21 48505275	21 99232195 21 99232196	**email:** jmio@paknavy.gov.pk jmio24@hotmail.com **Website:** www.jmicc.gov.pk
KARACHI (ASK)	21 34591161	21 34591285	

QATAR

See diagram R11

National SAR Agency: Doha Joint Rescue Coordination Centre (DJRCC), Ministry of Defence
Address: Near Ooredoo Maritime Coastal Station, Al Daayan Lusail Circuit Al Khor Coastal Road Lusail, State of Qatar
Telephone: +974 44218877
+974 44218649
Fax: +974 44218989
+974 44218538
email: info.pr@customs.gov.qa
Website: https://www.djrcc.com.qa

The Department of Customs & Ports General Authority is responsible for coordinating Search and Rescue operations. Doha (A7D) maintains a continuous listening watch on 2182 kHz and VHF Ch 16 for distress calls.

	Telephone +974	Fax +974	Others/Ship Earth Stations (SES)
JRCC DOHA (Cospas-Sarsat SPOC)	44218877 44218649	44218989	**AFTN:** OTBDYFYX **email:** djrccqatar@gmail.com
DOHA PORT (SAR)	44434377 44042735	44042738	**email:** marine.services@mwani.com.qa (SAR)
DOHA (A7D)	44404088 44864444	44980360	**email:** a7d@ooredoo.qa

SAUDI ARABIA

See diagram R11

National SAR Agency: Marine Department

A network of Coastal Radio Stations on the Persian Gulf and Red Sea coasts maintain a continuous listening watch on international distress frequencies.

	Telephone +966	Fax +966	Others/Ship Earth Stations (SES)
SAMCC JEDDAH (Cospas-Sarsat SPOC)	12 6150170 12 6855812 12 6717717 (ext 1840)	12 6150171 12 6402855	**AFTN:** OEJNJSAR OEJDYCYX (Back up link to Jeddah RCC)

Red Sea

	Telephone +966	Fax +966	Others/Ship Earth Stations (SES)
JEDDAH (HZH)	12 6481357	12 6474675	**email:** jeddahradio@stc.com.sa

UNITED ARAB EMIRATES

See diagram R11

National SAR Agency: Dubai Police G.H.Q.
Address: General Department of Administration's Affairs, Dubai Police HQ, Dubai. United Arab Emirates
Telephone: +971 4 6095040
Fax: +971 4 2215158

Dubai Ports and Emirates (A6L) maintain a continuous listening watch on VHF DSC and Ch 16 for distress calls. Preferred inter RCC language is English.

	Telephone +971	Fax +971	Others/Ship Earth Stations (SES)
RCC ABŪ ẒABY (Abu Dhabi) (Cospas-Sarsat SPOC)	2 4054590 2 5851323 2 5996969	2 5996852 2 4443735	**AFTN:** OMAEYCYX
ABŪ ẒABY (Abu Dhabi) POLICE	4 6095555 (Rescue Desk) 4 6095040 (Duty Officer)	4 2215158	**email:** mail@dubaipolice.gov.ae

YEMEN

See diagrams R10, R11 & R12

National SAR Agency: Maritime Search and Rescue
Address: PO Box 1316, Aden Port Authority, Steamer Point, Aden, Yemen
Telephone: +967 2 203521
Fax: +967 2 203521

Preferred inter RCC languages are English and Arabic.

YEMEN (Continued)

	Telephone +967	Fax +967	Others/Ship Earth Stations (SES)
RCC SANA'A	1 344671 1 344672 1 344673 1 345402 (Morning period)	1 345916 1 344047 (Morning period)	**Mobile:** +967 777 214088 **AFTN:** OYSYNCYX **email:** moh.ali001@yahoo.com
ADEN HARBOUR CONTROL TOWER	2 202238 2 202676		

NAVAREA X

AUSTRALIA
See diagrams R12/13, R14, R17 & R19

National SAR Agency: JRCC Australia, Australian Maritime Safety Authority (AMSA)
Address: GPO Box 2181, Canberra 2601, Australia
Telephone: +61 2 62306811
email: rccaus@amsa.gov.au
Website: www.amsa.gov.au/safety-navigation/search-and-rescue

JRCC Australia is situated in Canberra and is the national agency for Maritime & Aviation SAR in the Australian SRR. JRCC Australia is also responsible for MAS (Maritime Assistance Services) & the Australian Ship Reporting System (MASTREP) (see ALRS Volume 6 Part 4 (NP286(4)) for details).

Messages are received either directly through Inmarsat or through the HF DSC network.

TeleMedical Assistance Service: CareFlight provides medical advice. Contact via JRCC Australia, HF DSC. Inmarsat SAC 32 via LES 212 or 312. Consultation language: English

	Telephone +61	Fax +61	Others/Ship Earth Stations (SES)
JRCC AUSTRALIA (Cospas - Sarsat) SPOC	2 62306811 2 62306820		**AFTN:** YSARYCYX **email:** rccaus@amsa.gov.au
MASTREP	2 62306880		
HF DSC NETWORK CONTROL CENTRE (NCC)	2 62795771 (Main Number) 2 62795772 (Secondary Number) 2 61516688 (Non-emergency Number)	2 61516695	

NEW CALEDONIA (FRANCE)
See diagram R17

National SAR Agency: Organisme d'études et de coordination pour la recherche et le sauvetage en mer (SECMAR)
Address: 16 Boulevard Raspail, 75007 Paris, France
Telephone: +33 1 53634159

Locally, Nouméa Radio (FJP) maintains a continuous watch on VHF Ch 16. Preferred inter RCC languages are English and French.

	Telephone +687	Fax +687	Others/Ship Earth Stations (SES)
MRCC NOUMÉA (Cospas-Sarsat SPOC)	292121	292303	**Inmarsat C:** 422799194 **email:** operations@mrcc.nc noumea.traffic@mrcc.nc **Website:** www.mrcc.nc
RSC TONTOUTA (Cospas-Sarsat SPOC)	352422		**AFTN:** NWWWYCYX
TONTOUTA AIRPORT	352400		

PAPUA NEW GUINEA

See diagram R17

National SAR Agency: National Maritime Safety Authority
Address: P.O. Box 668, Port Moresby NCD, Papua New Guinea
Telephone: +675 3211244
Fax: +675 3210484
email: nmsa@nmsa.gov.pg
Website: www.nmsa.gov.pg/search-and-rescue

PNG Air Services Ltd also provide National SAR Agency services.

Address: P.O.Box 684, Boroko, NCD, Papua New Guinea

Telephone: +675 3121500

Fax: +675 3254094

email: sar@pngairservices.com.pg & cc@pngairservices.com.pg

	Telephone +675	Fax +675	Others/Ship Earth Stations (SES)
RCC PORT MORESBY (Cospas-Sarsat SPOC)	3121532 3121531 71176400	3254094 3259658	**AFTN:** AYPYYCYX **email:** sar@pngairservices.com.pg cc@pngairservices.com.pg
MRCC PAPUA NEW GUINEA	3212969 3213033	3210484	**Mobile:** +675 73517017 **email:** pngnmrcc@nmsa.gov.pg
PORT MORESBY (P2M)	3255005 3259658	3259658	**email:** etirip@nmsa.gov.pg nmsa@nmsa.gov.pg

PITCAIRN ISLANDS

See diagram R17

National SAR Agency: Pitcairn Police

	Telephone +870	Fax +870	Others/Ship Earth Stations (SES)
Pitcairn Police	762854699 (Inmarsat)	762941161 (Inmarsat)	**email:** mop.pitcairn@gtnet.gov.uk

SOLOMON ISLANDS

See diagram R17

National SAR Agency: Solomon Islands Maritime Safety Authority (SIMA)
Address: P.O. Box 1932, Honiara, Solomon Islands
Telephone: +677 21609
+677 27685
+677 21535 ext 217
email: mrcc@solomon.com.sb
Website: www.sima.gov.sb/environmental-protection-marine-pollution/search-rescue-coordination

The Solomon Islands Maritime Authority (SIMA) is the Solomon Islands Government Agency responsible for coordinating Search and Rescue operations. Honiara (H4H) maintains a continuous listening watch on 2182 kHz for distress calls.

	Telephone +677	Fax +677	Others/Ship Earth Stations (SES)
MRCC HONIARA	21609 27685		**email:** mrcc@solomon.com.sb
HONIARA (H4H)	21609 27685		

TUVALU

See diagram R17

National SAR Agency: Fishery Officer, Tuvalu Government
Address: Funafuti, Tuvalu
Telephone: +688 20344

A Search and Rescue Committee has been established under the Tuvalu Government. Funafuti Radio provides limited HF radio telephone service with vessels and neighbouring islands and operates a radiotelegraph AFTN circuit with Fiji, RCC Nadi.

	Telephone +688	Fax +688	Others/Ship Earth Stations (SES)
ARCC FUNAFUTI (Cospas-Sarsat SPOC)	20726 20187	20159	**AFTN:** NGFUYFYX **email:** talaloi@yahoo.com.au

VANUATU
See diagram R17

National SAR Agency: Vanuatu Maritime Authority
Address: P.O. Box 320, Port Vila, Efate Vanuatu
Telephone: +678 23128
           +678 23768
Fax: +678 22949

Port-Vila (YJM) maintains a listening watch on 2182 kHz and VHF Ch 16, but it is not continuous. All distress alerts are relayed to Fiji, RCC Nadi.

	Telephone +678	Fax +678	Others/Ship Earth Stations (SES)
VANUATU MARITIME AUTHORITY (Cospas-Sarsat SPOC)	23128 23768		AFTN: NVVVYMYX
METEOROLOGICAL SERVICES (Bauerfield Airport)	22433 22550		AFTN: NVVVYMYX

NAVAREA XI

BRUNEI
See diagram R14

National SAR Agency: National SAR Centre (NSARCC)
Address: Royal Brunei Armed Forces Headquarters, Berakas Camp, Negara Brunei Darussalam
Telephone: +673 2 332777

The Royal Brunei Armed Forces are responsible for coordinating Search and Rescue operations.

	Telephone +673	Fax +673	Others/Ship Earth Stations (SES)
BRUNEI INTERNATIONAL AIRPORT SAR CONTROL: BERAKAS	2 332600 2 334189 2 334763 2 330454	2 344191 2 344201	AFTN: WBSBYCYX
MUARA HARBOUR STATION VSL3	2 770270 2 332600	2 770293	
MRCC MALAYSIA	See MALAYSIA		

BURMA
See diagram R14

National SAR Agency: Maritime Rescue Coordination Centre (Ayeyarwady)
Address: Ayeyarwady Naval Region Command, Monkey Point Street, Botahtaung Township, Yangon, Burma.
Telephone: +95 31 31651
           +95 9 795279576

Search and Rescue operations are coordinated between the Burmese Navy and Airforce and the Department of Civil and Aviation and Maritime Administration.

MRCC (Ayeyarwady) and Coastal Radio Stations maintain a continuous listening watch on international distress frequencies.

	Telephone +95	Fax +95	Others/Ship Earth Stations (SES)
MRCC (AYEYARWADY) (XYY)	31 31651 9 795279576	1 202417	**Inmarsat C:** 450614011 **email:** mrcc.yangon@mptmail.com.mm mrcc.myanmar2012@gmail.com
COASTAL RADIO STATION YANGON (RANGOON) (XYR)	56 21507		**email:** myanmar.crs.hq@gmail.com
COASTAL RADIO STATION MYEIK (XYM)	59 41180		**email:** myanmar.crs.hq@gmail.com

CAMBODIA
See diagram R14

National SAR Agency: Unknown

A Rescue Central Committee, which is operational H24 is based at Pochentong Air Traffic Control Centre. The Cambodian Ministry of Defence Navy is responsible for marine SAR Coordination.

	Telephone +855	Fax +855	Others/Ship Earth Stations (SES)
ARCC PHNOM PENH (Cospas-Sarsat SPOC)	23 890193 12994878 (Mobile)	23 890192	AFTN: VDPPYCYX **email:** sieng.sar@gmail.com
KOMPONG SAOM-VILLE (XUK)	N/A		

CHINA

See diagrams R14 & R15

National SAR Agency: China Maritime Search and Rescue Centre
Address: 11 Jianguomennei Street, Beijing, China 100736
Telephone: +86 10 65292221
　　　　　　+86 10 65292218
Fax: +86 10 65292245
email: cnmrcc@mot.gov.cn

The China Maritime Search and Rescue Centre exists in Beijing and coordinates Search and Rescue operations. A network of coastal radio stations maintains a continuous listening watch on international distress frequencies.

	Telephone +86	Fax +86	Others/Ship Earth Stations (SES)
MRCC CHINA (SAR Centre-Beijing)	10 65292221 10 65292218	10 65292245	**email:** cnmrcc@mot.gov.cn
CNMCC (Cospas-Sarsat SPOC)	10 65293294 10 65293298	10 65293296	**AFTN:** ZBBBZSZX **email:** cnmrcc@cttic.cn
MRCC LIAONING PROVINCE (SAR Centre-Dalian)	411 82635487	411 82622230	**email:** liaoningmrcc@lnmsa.gov.cn
MRCC TIANJIN (SAR Centre-Tianjin)	22 58806991	22 58876990	**email:** 02212395@163.com
MRCC HEBEI PROVINCE (SAR Centre-Qinhuangdao)	335 5366806	335 5366809	**email:** hebeizhzx@163.com
MRCC SHANDONG PROVINCE (SAR Centre-Qingdao)	532 82654437	532 82654497	**email:** sdmsa12395@126.com
MRCC JIANGSU PROVINCE (SAR Centre-Nanjing)	25 83279620	25 83279663	
MRCC SHANGHAI (SAR Centre-Shanghai)	21 53931419	21 53931420	**email:** jzhzx@shmsa.gov.cn
MRCC ZHEJIANG PROVINCE (SAR Centre-Hangzhou)	571 85454372	571 85454810	**email:** zjmsa12395@163.com
MRCC FUJIAN PROVINCE (SAR Centre-Fuzhou)	591 83838801	591 83838820	**email:** 1499457067@qq.com
MRCC GUANGDONG PROVINCE (SAR Centre-Guangzhou)	20 34283886	20 34281854	**email:** gdmrcc@163.com
MRCC GUANGXI (SAR Centre-Nanning)	771 5531110	771 5537517	**email:** gxmrcc@163.com
MRCC HAINAN PROVINCE (SAR Centre-Haikou)	898 68653899	898 68666231	**email:** hnrcc@hainan.gov.cn
MRCC YANGTSE RIVER (SAR Centre-Wuhan)	27 82765555	27 82418021	**email:** 2894012482@qq.com
MRCC HEILONGJIANG PROVINCE (SAR Centre-Harbin)	451 88912331	451 88912337	**email:** hlj12395@163.com
MRCC LIANYUNGANG (SAR Centre-Lianyungang)	518 82310309	518 82236977	**email:** lygmsazhzx@163.com
MRCC HONG KONG	Hong Kong has its own SAR entry; refer to CHINA HONG KONG.		

CHINA HONG KONG

See diagrams R14 & R15

National SAR Agency: Hong Kong MRCC
Address: G.P.O. Box 4155, Hong Kong, China
Telephone: +852 22337999
Fax: +852 25417714
email: hkmrcc@mardep.gov.hk
Website: www.mardep.gov.hk

Hong Kong Marine Rescue Radio (VRC) maintains a continuous listening watch on GMDSS frequencies only and is also the location of MRCC HONG KONG. Preferred languages for inter RCC communication are Chinese and English.

	Telephone +852	Fax +852	Others/Ship Earth Stations (SES)
MRCC HONG KONG (Cospas-Sarsat SPOC)	22337999	25417714	**AFTN:** VHHHYKYX **Inmarsat C:** 447735011 (MRCC X) 　　　　　　447735012 (MRCC X) **email:** hkmrcc@mardep.gov.hk

EAST TIMOR   See diagram R17

National SAR Agency: Unknown

	Telephone +670	Fax +670	Others/Ship Earth Stations (SES)
RCC TIMOR-LESTE	3317110 3313821	3317111	**AFTN:** WPDLZTZX WPDLYNYX **email:** comroatsc@hotmail.com

GUAM (Northern Mariana Islands) - see UNITED STATES OF AMERICA
INDONESIA   See diagram R14

National SAR Agency: Baden SAR National (BASARNAS)
Address: Jl. Angkasa Blok B 15 Kav 2-3 Kemayoran, Jakarta pusat - Indonesia 10720
Telephone: +62 21 65701116
          +62 21 65867510
Fax: +62 21 65857512
email: basarnas@basarnas.go.id
       kagahar@basarnas.go.id
       kagahar@yahoo.com
       kagahar@gmail.com
Website: www.basarnas.go.id

	Telephone +62	Fax +62	Others/Ship Earth Stations (SES)
IDMCC JAKARTA	21 65701172 21 65867510	21 65867512	**AFTN:** WIIIYCYL **email:** indonesia_mrcc@yahoo.com
RCC JAKARTA (Soekarno-Hatta Airport	21 5501512	21 55915697 21 5501513	**AFTN:** WIIIYCYX **email:** kansar.jkt@gmail.com
RSC BANDA ACEH	651 33876 651 21324	651 33876	**AFTN:** WITTYCYX **email:** kansaraceh@gmail.com
RCC MEDAN	61 8225111	61 8225111	**AFTN:** WIMMYCYX **email:** sarmedan@gmail.com
RCC PADANG	751 484534	751 484534	**email:** sarcom_padang@yahoo.co.id
RSC PEKANBARU	761 674821 761 679991	761 676758	**AFTN:** WIBBYCYX **email:** sar.pekanbaru@yahoo.co.id
RSC PONTIANAK	561 721234	561 721234	**AFTN:** WIOOYCYX **email:** ops_kom105ptk@yahoo.com
RSC TANJUNG PINANG	771 319300	771 319309	**AFTN:** WIDNYCYX **email:** sar.x.tanjungpinang@gmail.com
RSC SEMARANG	24 7628345 24 7629192	24 7629189	**AFTN:** WARSYCYX **email:** sar_semarang@yahoo.co.id
RSC BANDUNG	22 7780414 22 7780413 22 7780416	22 7780437	**email:** kansarbandung@gmail.com
RSC PANGKAL PINANG	717 4261338 717 9100389	717 9100389	**email:** kansar_pangkalpinang@yahoo.com
RSC JAMBI	741 571111	741 571111	**email:** kansarjambi@yahoo.com
RSC BENGKULU	736 5500666	736 5500666	
RSC LAMPUNG	721 7697026	721 769026	**email:** sarlampung@gmail.com
RSC SURABAYA	31 8666611 31 8669611	31 8667111	**AFTN:** WAGGYCYX **email:** surabayarescue@yahoo.co.id
RSC BANJARMASIN	511 4707911	511 4707856	**AFTN:** WRBBYCYX **email:** basarnas_202@yahoo.co.id
RCC DENPASAR	361 703300 361 705536	361 705579 361 705536	**AFTN:** WADDYCYX **email:** sar.denpasar@yahoo.com
RSC BALIKPAPAN	542 762111	542 760366	**AFTN:** WALLYCYX **email:** sar203balikpapan@gmail.com
RSC MATARAM	370 633253	370 639785	**email:** sar_mataram@yahoo.co.id
RCC MAKASSAR	411 550024 411 555515	411 554852	**email:** kansar_makassar@yahoo.co.id

Continued on next page

INDONESIA (Continued)

	Telephone +62	Fax +62	Others/Ship Earth Stations (SES)
RSC AMBON	911 323774 911 3302860	911 323782	**email:** sar.ambon@basarnas.go.id
RSC MANADO	438 51995	438 52189	**email:** sar_manado@gmail.com
RSC KUPANG	380 881573	380 881573	**email:** kantorsarkupang@yahoo.com
RSC KENDARI	401 3196557	401 3196558	**email:** sar_kdi@yahoo.co.id
RSC PALU	451 481110	451 481009	
RSC TERNATE	931 3120069	931 3120068	**email:** sarternate@yahoo.co.id
RSC GORONTALO	435 828469	435 828469	
RCC BIAK	981 21111 981 25911	981 23330	**email:** sar.biak@yahoo.co.id
RSC JAYAPURA	967 591093 967 593785	967 591956	**email:** sar_jayapura@yahoo.com
RSC SORONG	951 3102316	951 329220	**email:** kantor.sar.sorong@gmail.com
RSC MERAUKE	971 321158 971 321108 971 321015	971 321158	**email:** kansarmrk@yahoo.com
RSC TIMIKA	901 3125190	901 3125189	**email:** sar_timika1@yahoo.co.id
RSC MANOKWARI	986 213263	986 213263	**email:** sar.manokwari@gmail.com

JAPAN   See diagrams R15 & R16

National SAR Agency: Japan Coast Guard (JCG)
Address: 2-1-3 Kasumigaseki, Chiyoda-ku, Tokyo 100-8918, Japan
Telephone: +81 3 35919000 (Operations Centre)
        +81 3 35919812 (Operations Centre)
Fax: +81 3 35918701 (Operations Centre)
    +81 3 35812853 (Operations Centre)
Telex: +72 2225193 JMSAHQ J
email: jcg-op@mlit.go.jp
Website: https://www.kaiho.mlit.go.jp/

Operations Centre of Japan Coast Guard HQ will receive SAR information and disseminate to the relevant domestic and foreign RCCs. Coast Radio Stations of the Japan Coast Guard maintain a continuous watch on international distress frequencies VHF Ch 16 and DSC 2187·5 kHz. Tokyo Coast Guard Radio maintains a watch on HF DSC frequencies 4, 6, 8, 12 & 16 MHz. Eleven Coast Guard Radio stations are assigned to the eleven Regional Coast Guard Headquarters.

TeleMedical Assistance Service: There are a number of Japanese hospitals providing assistance. Contact via all Japanese RCC's.

Possible consultation languages: Japanese and English.

	Telephone +81	Fax +81	Others/Ship Earth Stations (SES)
JCG HQ - TOKYO (Operations Centre) JAMCC (Cospas-Sarsat SPOC)	3 35919812	3 35812853	**AFTN:** RJTTYKYY **email:** jcg-op@mlit.go.jp jcg-jamcc@mlit.go.jp
1st Regional HQ - OTARU	134 276172	134 212835	**email:** jcg01op@mlit.go.jp
2nd Regional HQ - SHIOGAMA	22 3654999	22 3679098	**email:** jcg02op@mlit.go.jp
3rd Regional HQ - YOKOHAMA	45 6634999	45 2122010	**email:** jcg03op@mlit.go.jp
4th Regional HQ - NAGOYA	52 6514999	52 6611640	**email:** jcg04op@mlit.go.jp
5th Regional HQ - KOBE	78 3914999	78 3916609	**email:** jcg05op@mlit.go.jp
6th Regional HQ - HIROSHIMA	82 2515115	82 2515185	**email:** jcg06op@mlit.go.jp
7th Regional HQ - KITAKYUSHU	93 3210556	93 3218611	**email:** jcg07op@mlit.go.jp
8th Regional HQ - MAIZURU	773 754999	773 782375	**email:** jcg08op@mlit.go.jp
9th Regional HQ - NIIGATA	25 2850122	25 2882613	**email:** jcg09op@mlit.go.jp
10th Regional HQ - KAGOSHIMA	99 2554999	99 2526878	**email:** jcg10op@mlit.go.jp
11th Regional HQ - NAHA	98 8664999	98 8691167	**email:** jcg11op@mlit.go.jp

KIRIBATI   See diagrams R16 & R17

National SAR Agency: Marine Superintendent, Marine Division, Ministry of Communication
Address: P.O. Box 506, Betio, Tarawa, Kiribati

The Marine Division of the Ministry of Communication is responsible for co-ordinating Search and Rescue operations.

	Telephone +686	Fax +686	Others/Ship Earth Stations (SES)
MARINE GUARD (Cospas-Sarsat SPOC)	26523 26469 26468		
MARINE OFFICER	26474		

KOREA, NORTH   See diagram R15

National SAR Agency: Maritime Rescue Coordination Centre (MRCC) of DPR Korea
Address: Mirae-Dong, Phyongchon District, Pyongyang, DPR Korea
Telephone: +850 2 18111 (ext 381 8047)
Fax: +850 2 381 2100
email: mrcc.dprk@sealink.net
Website: www.ma.gov.kp

The competent authority responsible for the national maritime Search and Rescue (SAR) in the DPR Korea is the Maritime Rescue Coordination Centre (MRCC) of the DPR Korea.

MRCC, DPR Korea serves as the specialised agency for the national maritime SAR. It is responsible for operations of all the Maritime Rescue Sub-Centres (MRSCs) and the Coast Radio Stations (CRSs) in the DPR Korea and undertakes to coordinate any maritime SAR operation in the DPR Korea Maritime Search and Rescue Region (SRR).

A network of all MRSCs and Coast Radio Stations maintain a continuous listening watch on international distress frequencies VHF Ch. 16 and VHF DSC Ch. 70. Also MRSC of North Hamgyong Province, MRSC of South Hamgyong Province and Nampho MRSC maintain a continuous listening watch on international distress frequencies MF/HF DSC.

TeleMedical Assistance Service: Provided by Pyongyang Friendship Hospital. Contact is established via MRCC, DPR Korea.

Possible consultation languages: Korean and English.

	Telephone +850	Fax +850	Others/Ship Earth Stations (SES)
MRCC DPR KOREA (Cospas-Sarsat SPOC)	2 18111 (ext. 381 8047)	2 381 2100	**AFTN:** ZKKKYCYX **Inmarsat C:** 444540010 **email:** mrcc.dprk@sealink.net **Website:** www.ma.gov.kp
MRSC North Hamgyong Province	2 18111 (ext. 381 8614)		
MRSC South Hamgyong Province	2 18111 (ext.381 8424)		
MRSC Kangwon Province	2 18111 (ext. 381 8074)		
MRSC North Phyongan Province	2 18111 (ext. 381 8401)		
MRSC South Phyongan Province	2 18111 (ext. 381 8104)		
MRSC South Hwanghae Province	2 18111 (ext. 381 8405)		
Nampho MRSC	2 18111 (ext. 381 8144)		
Rason MRSC	2 18111 (ext. 381 8704)		
Cholsan Coast Radio Station	2 18111 (ext. 381 8402)		
Hwadae Coast Radio Station	2 18111 (ext. 381 8684)		
Hongwon Coast Radio Station	2 18111 (ext. 381 8464)		
Kim Chaek Coast Radio Station	2 18111 (ext. 381 8694)		
Kosong Coast Radio Station	2 18111 (ext. 381 8494)		

Continued on next page

KOREA, NORTH (Continued)

	Telephone +850	Fax +850	Others/Ship Earth Stations (SES)
Kumya Coast Radio Station	2 18111 (ext. 381 8434)		
Kwaksan Coast Radio Station	2 18111 (ext. 381 8404)		
Myongchon Coast Radio Station	2 18111 (ext. 381 8674)		
Onchon Coast Radio Station	2 18111 (ext. 381 8154)		
Ongjin Coast Radio Station	2 18111 (ext. 381 8409)		
Orang Coast Radio Station	2 18111 (ext. 381 8654)		
Riwon Coast Radio Station	2 18111 (ext. 381 8747)		
Ryongyon Coast Radio Station	2 18111 (ext. 8408)		
Sinam Coast Radio Station	2 18111 (ext. 8624)		
Sonchon Coast Radio Station	2 18111 (ext. 381 8403)		
Tanchon Coast Radio Station	2 18111 (ext. 381 8484)		
Tungam Coast Radio Station	2 18111 (ext. 381 8407)		
Unryul Coast Radio Station	2 18111 (ext. 381 8406)		

KOREA, SOUTH   See diagram R15

National SAR Agency: Korea Coast Guard (KCG)
Address: 130, Haedoji-ro, Yeonsu-gu, Incheon, South Korea
Telephone: +82 32 8588184
Fax: +82 32 8588182
email: mcckorea@korea.kr
Website: www.kcg.go.kr/english/main.do

Korea Coast Guard (KCG) coordinates Search and Rescue operations. The KCG operates SAR command centres on a 24 hour basis. A continuous listening watch is maintained on international distress frequencies on VHF, MF and DSC. Preferred inter RCC languages are Korean, English, Japanese, Russian and Chinese.

TeleMedical Assistance Service: There are several Korean hospitals, affiliated with KCG and Emergency medical technicians belonging to KCG, providing assistance. Contact via all Korean RCC's. Possible consultation languages: Korean and English.

	Telephone +82	Fax +82	Others/Ship Earth Stations (SES)
KCG HQ - KOMCC	32 8588184	32 8588182	**Telex:** +801 24920 KOMCC **email:** mcckorea@korea.kr
CENTRAL REGIONAL CG	32 7288342	32 7288942	**Telex:** +801 35522 **email:** rcccentral@korea.kr
INCHEON CG Station	32 6502342	32 6502924	
PYEONGTAEK CG Station	31 80462242	31 80462900	
TAEAN CG Station	41 9502342	41 9502941	
BORYEONG CG Station	41 4022342	41 4022942	
WEST SEA SPECIAL SECURITY UNIT	32 8353142	32 8353900	
WESTERN REGIONAL CG	61 2882342	61 2882942	**Telex:** +801 67116 **email:** rccwest@korea.kr
GUNSAN CG Station	63 5392342	63 5392900	
BUAN CG Station	63 9282342	63 9282900	
MOKPO CG Station	61 2412342	61 2412942	
WANDO CG Station	61 5502342	61 5502942	

Continued overleaf

KOREA, SOUTH (Continued)

	Telephone +82	Fax +82	Others/Ship Earth Stations (SES)
YEOSU CG Station	61 8402342	61 8402942	
SOUTHERN REGIONAL CG	51 6632442	51 6393513	**Telex:** +801 53343 **email:** rccsouth@korea.kr
TONGYŎNG CG Station	55 6472442	55 6472942	
CHANGWON CG Station	55 9812542	55 9812942	
BUSAN CG Station	51 6642442	51 6642900	
ULSAN CG Station	52 2302442	52 2302942	
EASTERN REGIONAL CG	33 6802242	33 6802942	**Telex:** +801 35521 **email:** rcceast@korea.kr
POHANG CG Station	54 7502342	54 7502942	
ULJIN CG Sstation	54 5022342	54 5022900	
EAST SEA CG Station	33 7412342	33 5319595	
SOKCHO CG Station	33 6342342	33 6342942	
JEJU REGIONAL CG	64 8012342	64 8012900	**Telex:** +801 67117 **email:** rccjeju@korea.kr
JEJU CG Station	64 7662342	64 7662900	
SEOGWIPO CG Station	64 7932342	64 7932900	

MALAYSIA   See diagram R14

National SAR Agency: Malaysian Maritime Enforcement Agency (Malaysia Coast Guard)
Address: Prime Minister's Department, 4-11th Floor, One IOI Square, IOI Resort, 62502 Putrajaya, Malaysia
Telephone: +60 3 89413140
Fax: +60 3 89413129
email: mrccputrajaya@mmea.gov.my
Website: https://www.mmea.gov.my/eng/index.php/ms/

The Malaysian Maritime Enforcement Agency (Malaysia Coast Guard) is responsible for coordinating Search and Rescue operations. A network of stations monitor VHF and MF DSC and 2182 kHz and VHF Ch 16. Preferred inter RCC languages are English and Malay.

	Telephone +60	Fax +60	Others/Ship Earth Stations (SES)
KUALA LUMPUR ARCC (Cospas-Sarsat SPOC)	3 78473573	3 78473572	**AFTN:** WMKKZQZX **email:** klatcc@caam.gov.my **Website:** www.caam.gov.my
Malaysian Maritime Communications Centre (MMCC)	3 31670530	3 31664332	**email:** mmcc@marine.gov.my
Malaysian Mission Control Centre (MyMCC)	9 5807175	9 5807176	**email:** mymcc@mmea.gov.my
MRCC PUTRAJAYA	3 89413140	3 89413129	**email:** mrccputrajaya@mmea.gov.my

Peninsular Malaysia

	Telephone +60	Fax +60	Others/Ship Earth Stations (SES)
MRSC JOHOR BAHRU	7 2219231	7 2279285	**email:** mrscjohorbharu@mmea.gov.my
MRSC KUANTAN	9 5717345	9 5738476	**email:** mrsckuantan@mmea.gov.my
MRSC LANGKAWI	4 9665307	4 9662768	**email:** mrsclangkawi@mmea.gov.my

Sabah and Sarawak

	Telephone +60	Fax +60	Others/Ship Earth Stations (SES)
MRSC KOTA KINABALU	88 387774	88 387444	**email:** mrsckotakinabalu@mmea.gov.my
MRSC KUCHING	82 432544	82 432554	**email:** mrsckuching@mmea.gov.my

MARSHALL ISLANDS

See diagrams R16 & R17

National SAR Agency: Majuro SAR Coordinator
Address: P.O. Box 15, Majuro, Marshall Islands RMI 96960
Telephone: +692 1 808541
Fax: +692 1 808541

Search and Rescue operations are coordinated at Majuro and by MRCC Honolulu. Majuro (KUP65) maintains a continuous listening watch on 2182 kHz for distress calls.

	Telephone	Fax	Others/Ship Earth Stations (SES)
JRCC HONOLULU (Cospas-Sarsat SPOC)	+1 808 5353333 +1 808 3316176	+1 808 5353338	**email:** jrcchonolulu@uscg.mil
MARSHALL ISLANDS OPERATIONS CENTRE	+692 625 7232 (Office)		
RMI POLICE COMMISSIONER SAR MANAGER	+692 625 4049 (Office)	+692 625 5134	**Mobile:** +692 455 1032
CHIEF OF SURVEILLANCE - SEA PATROL			**Mobile:** +692 625 8666 **email:** hkaiko2010@gmail.com

MICRONESIA

See diagrams R14, R16 & R17

National SAR Agency: National Police Headquarters
Address: P.O. Box PS 11, Palikir, Pohnpei, Federated States of Micronesia, 96941
Telephone: +691 320 2628
+691 320 2058
Fax: +691 320 3243
email: nphq@mail.fm

The Federated States of Micronesia National Police are responsible for the coordination of Search and Rescue operations. The Office of National Disaster is assisted by a designated SAR Coordinator and 4 regional Disaster Control Officers. A continuous listening watch is maintained on HF 5205 and 7876·5 kHz and VHF Ch 16 for Distress calls. JRCC Honolulu will provide SAR support.

	Telephone	Fax	Others/Ship Earth Stations (SES)
JRCC HONOLULU (Cospas-Sarsat SPOC)	+1 808 5353333 +1 800 3316176	+1 808 5353338	**email:** jrcchonolulu@uscg.mil
SAR COORDINATION	+691 320 2628 +691 320 2058	+691 320 3243	
KOSRAE SAR LIAISON	+691 370 3009	+691 370 3162	**Mobile:** +691 9970 1145 **email:** kosraedco@gmail.com
POHNPEI SAR LIAISON	+691 320 2384	+691 320 3895	**Mobile:** +691 926 1094 **email:** fsmnpvms@gmail.com
CHUUK STATE SAR LIAISON	+691 330 5520		**email:** fritzjustin5@gmail.com
YAP SAR LIAISON	+691 350 2182		**Mobile:** +691 950 1842 **email:** yapdco@gmail.com

PALAU

See diagram R17

National SAR Agency: National Emergency Management Office (NEMO), Office of the Vice President, Ministry of Justice
Address: P.O. Box 100, Koror, Republic of Palau 96940
Telephone: +680 488 2249
+680 488 2422
Mobile: +680 775 6898
Fax: +680 488 3312

The National Emergency Management Office (NEMO) is responsible for coordinating Search and Rescue operations. Preferred inter RCC language is English. JRCC Honolulu will provide Palau with SAR Services.

PHILIPPINES   **See diagram R14**

National SAR Agency: Manila Rescue Coordination Centre, National Headquarters, Philippine Coast Guard (NHPCG)
Address: 139 25th Street, Port Area, Manila, Philippines
Telephone: +63 2 85278481 (Local 6136/6137)
           +63 917 7243682
           +63 998 5855327
Fax: +63 2 85273877
AFTN: RPMMYCYX
email: pcgcomcen@coastguard.gov.ph
Website: https://coastguard.gov.ph

The Manila Rescue Coordination Centre at the Headquarters of the Philippine Coast Guard is responsible for coordinating Search and Rescue operations. There are MRSC's situated at the thirteen Coast Guard Districts: Manila, Cebu, Zamboanga, Palawan, Batangas, Iloilo, La Union, Dava, Bicol, Cagayan de Oro, Tacloban, Aparri and Negros Occidental. A network of Coast Radio Stations maintains a continuous listening watch on international distress frequencies.

	Telephone +63	Fax +63	Others/Ship Earth Stations (SES)
CAAP ORCC (Operations and Rescue Coordination Centre)	2 9442032 2 9442031		**AFTN:** RPLLYCYX **email:** opcencaap@gmail.com
MRCC PHILIPPINES - PCG Command Centre	2 85278481 (Local 6136/6137) 917 7243682 998 5855327	2 85273877	**email:** pcgcomcen@coastguard.gov.ph
MRSC MANILA - Coastguard District National Capital Region - Central Luzon	2 5273882 917 8218124 998 5858198		**email:** ncrcl@coastguard.gov.ph ncrcld3@gmail.com
MRSC CEBU - Coast Guard District Central Visayas	32 2685274 917 8427102 998 5858301		**email:** cgd.cv@coastguard.gov.ph viscom_opns@yahoo.com
MRSC ZAMBOANGA - Coastguard District Southwestern Mindanao	62 9931004 917 8428446 998 5857972		**email:** cgdswm@coastguard.gov.ph hcgdswm@yahoo.com
MRSC PALAWAN - Coastguard District Palawan	48 4332974 917 8161072 998 5858465		**email:** cgpal@coastguard.gov.ph
MRSC BATANGAS - Coastguard District Southern Tagalog	43 7235624 917 8426633 909 8587956		**email:** cgdstl@coastguard.gov.ph cgdstl.actioncenter@coastguard.gov.ph hcgdstl_opn@yahoo.com
MRSC ILOILO - Coastguard District Western Visayas	33 3354594 917 8428447 998 5858301		**email:** cgdwv@coastguard.gov.ph
MRSC LA UNION (SAN FERNANDO) - Coastguard District Northwestern Luzon	72 7004474 917 8088412 998 5858578	72 7004474	**email:** cgdnwlzn@coastguard.gov.ph
MRSC DAVAO - Coastguard District Southeastern Mindanao	82 2350002 917 8313197 998 5858479	82 2350002	**email:** cgdsem@coastguard.gov.ph coastguardsem@yahoo.com
MRSC BICOL (LEGASPI) - Coastguard District Bicol	52 8206364 998 5856438 917 8426820		**email:** cgd.bicol@coastguard.gov.ph
MRSC CAGAYAN DE ORO - Coastguard District Northern Mindanao	88 8805956 917 8428196 998 5856239		**email:** cgdnm@coastguard.gov.ph
MRSC TACLOBAN - Coastguard District Eastern Visayas	53 5612890 917 8427656 998 5858320		**email:** cgdev@coastguard.gov.ph
MRSC APARRI - Coastguard District Northeastern Luzon	78 8880320 917 8012545 998 5856229		**email:** cgdnelzn.operation@coastguard.gov.ph cgdnortheasternluzon@gmail.com
MRSC NEGROS OCCIDENTAL - Coast Guard District Southern Visayas	998 5858103		**email:** cgd.sv@coastguard.gov.ph

SABAH & SARAWAK - see MALAYSIA
SINGAPORE
See diagram R14

National SAR Agency: Maritime and Port Authority of Singapore (MPA) **Address:** 08-00, PSA Vista, 20 Harbour Drive, Singapore 117612, Republic of Singapore **Telephone:** +65 62265539 +65 63252493 **Fax:** +65 62279971 **Website:** www.mpa.gov.sg			

The Maritime and Port Authority of Singapore (MPA) is responsible for coordinating Search and Rescue operations. Singapore Port Operations Control Centre (POCC) maintains a continuous listening watch on VHF Ch 16 and DSC VHF Ch 70. POCC also receives distress messages from the Cospas-Sarsat system and Inmarsat services.

TeleMedical Assistance Service: Contact MRCC for connection to a hospital. Consultation language will be English.

	Telephone +65	Fax +65	Others/Ship Earth Stations (SES)
MCC Singapore (Cospas-Sarsat SPOC)	65425024 65412668	65422548	**AFTN:** WSSSZSZX **email:** caas_rcc@caas.gov.sg
SINGAPORE PORT OPERATIONS CONTROL (MRCC)	62265539 63252493 63252494	62279971 62245776	**Telex:** +87 20021 MARTEL RS **email:** pocc@mpa.gov.sg

TAIWAN
See diagrams R14 & R15

National SAR Agency: The National Rescue Command Centre of the Executive Yuan **Address:** 3F, No. 200, Sec. 3, Beixin Rd, Xindian Dist., New Taipei City 231, Taiwan **Telephone:** +886 2 81966119 +886 2 89127119 **Fax:** +886 2 81966736 +886 2 81966737 **email:** taipeircc@gmail.com j08@nfa.gov.tw **Website:** www.cga.gov.tw			

The National Rescue Command Centre of the Executive Yuan (NRCC) is responsible for coordinating Search and Rescue operations. KEELUNG (XSX) is a network of Coast Radio Stations which maintain a continuous listening watch on international distress frequencies.

	Telephone +886	Fax +886	Others/Ship Earth Stations (SES)
KEELUNG (XSX)	2 24241913 2 24241914	2 24241923 2 24243524	**email:** klgmdss@ms1.hinet.net

THAILAND
See diagram R14

National SAR Agency: Department of Civil Aviation **Address:** 71 Soi Ngamduplee, Rama IV Road, Krung Thep (Bangkok) 10120, Thailand **Telephone:** +66 2 2860506 +66 2 2890594 +66 2 2869353 **Fax:** +66 2 2873186 **AFTN:** VTBAYCYX **Website:** www.caat.or.th			

Search and Rescue operations in Thailand are coordinated by the Department of Civil Aviation at the Krung Thep (Bangkok) RCC, with the Royal Thai Navy, the Thai Marine Police Division and the Marine Department. RCC Bangkok can be contacted through Krung Thep (Bangkok) Radio . A network of Coast Radio Stations maintain a continuous listening watch on international distress frequencies.

	Telephone +66	Fax +66	Others/Ship Earth Stations (SES)
RCC Bangkok (Cospas-Sarsat SPOC)	2 2860506 2 2860594 2 2869353	2 2873186	**AFTN:** VTBAYCYX **email:** bkkrcc@aviation.go.th
BANGKOK (Nonthaburi)	2 4022001 2 4022002 2 4022003 2 4022004	2 4022000	
MARINE DEPARTMENT	2 2331311 2 2333780	2 2330437	
ROYAL THAI NAVY	2 4655356 2 4653511	2 4661697	

Continued overleaf

SAR

THAILAND (Continued)

	Telephone +66	Fax +66	Others/Ship Earth Stations (SES)
THAI MARINE POLICE DIVISION	2 3941962	2 3941962	
MRSC SONGKHLA (Royal Thai Navy)		74 325805	
MRSC PHUKET (Royal Thai Navy)		76 391598	

UNITED STATES OF AMERICA   See diagrams R3, R7, R8, R16, R17 & R18

National SAR Agency: US Coast Guard.
Address: Commandant (CG-534), 2100 2nd Street, S.W. Washington D.C. 20593-7363, USA
Telephone: +1 202 3722075
Fax: +1 202 3722912
Website: https://www.uscg.mil/

The US Coast Guard National VHF Distress System provides continuous coastal coverage outwards to 20 n miles on VHF Ch 16. After contact on Ch 16, communications with the Coast Guard should be on VHF Ch 22A. Vessels not equipped with VHF Ch 22A should use VHF Ch 12. Selected Coast Radio Stations and Coast Guard Stations maintain continuous watch on 2182 kHz.

	Telephone +1	Fax +1	Others/Ship Earth Stations (SES)
USMCC (Cospas-Sarsat SPOC)	301 8174576	301 8174568	**AFTN:** KZDCZSZA **email:** usmcc@noaa.gov
AMVER surface picture (SURPIC)	Contact any US Coast Guard RCC or www.amver.com/surpicrequest.asp		

Pacific Ocean

	Telephone +1	Fax +1	Others/Ship Earth Stations (SES)
PACIFIC SAR COORDINATOR	510 4373701	510 4373017	**email:** rccalameda@uscg.mil

Northern Mariana Islands - GUAM

	Telephone +1	Fax +1	Others/Ship Earth Stations (SES)
JRSC GUAM	671 3554824	671 3554831	**email:** rccguam@uscg.mil

VIETNAM   See diagram R14

National SAR Agency: Vietnam Maritime Search and Rescue Coordinataion Centre
Address: 11A Lang Ha Street Thanh Cong ward, Ba Dinh district, Ha Noi, Vietnam
Telephone: +84 2437683050
Fax: +84 2437683048
email: rescuevietnam@yahoo.com.vn

Vietnam National Search and Rescue Committee is responsible for conducting and coordinating Search and Rescue operations. Vietnam Maritime Search and Rescue Coordination Centre (VIETNAM MRCC) is responsible for coordinating maritime Search and Rescue operations. A network of Coast Radio Stations maintain continuous listening watch on international distress frequencies.

	Telephone +84	Fax +84	Others/Ship Earth Stations (SES)
VIETNAM MRCC	24 37683050	24 37683048	**email:** rescuevietnam@yahoo.com.vn
HAI PHONG MRCC (Regional MRCC No I)	22 53759508	22 53759507	**email:** rescuehaiphong@gmail.com
DA NANG MRCC (Regional MRCC No II)	23 63924957	23 63924956	**email:** phcn2.mrcc@gmail.com
VUNG TAU MRCC (Regional MRCC No III)	25 43850950	25 43810353	**email:** vtmrcc@gmail.com
NHA TRANG MRCC (Regional Centre No IV)	25 83880373	25 83880517	**email:** phcnnhatrangmrcc@gmail.com

NAVAREA XII

ALASKA - see UNITED STATES OF AMERICA
CANADA   See diagrams R3/4, R16 & R18

National SAR Agency: Canadian Coast Guard Headquarters **Address:** 5th Floor, 200 Kent Street, Director Search and Rescue, Ottawa, Ontario, Canada, K1A 0E6 **email:** dfo.nationalsarmanager-gestionnairenationalres.mpo@dfo-mpo.gc.ca **Website:** www.ccg-gcc.gc.ca			

The Canadian Armed Forces (CAF) have overall responsibility for coordination of Search and Rescue (SAR) activities in Canada, including Canadian waters and adjacent seas off the coast of Canada, and for the provision of dedicated SAR aircraft in support of maritime SAR incidents. The Canadian Coast Guard (CCG) coordinates maritime SAR activities within this SAR zone, in co-operation with CAF, and provides dedicated maritime SAR vessels in strategic locations. Joint Rescue Coordination Centres (JRCC) are maintained at Victoria, B.C., Trenton, Ont. and Halifax, N.S. These centres are manned H24 by CAF and CCG personnel. Two Marine Rescue Sub-Centres (MRSC) are also located in Québec and St.John's Newfoundland to coordinate local SAR operations. Contact is established through the Canadian Coast Guard Radio Stations which provide coverage on all marine distress frequencies or through Inmarsat.

TeleMedical Assistance Service: Contact any Canadian CRS, JRC / MRSC -Prefix the message "Radio Medico" medical advice will be provided by TMAS or any regional hospital. Possible consultation languages: English and French. Interpreters may be provided for other languages.

	Telephone +1	Fax +1	Others/Ship Earth Stations (SES)
CMCC (Cospas-Sarsat) SPOC	613 9657265 800 211 8107	613 9657494	**AFTN:** CYTRYCYT **email:** cmcc2@sarnet.dnd.ca

Pacific Coast

	Telephone +1	Fax +1	Others/Ship Earth Stations (SES)
JRCC VICTORIA	800 5675111 (British Columbia and Yukon, toll free) 250 4138933	250 4138932	**email:** jrccvictoria@sarnet.dnd.ca

COLOMBIA   See diagrams R7 & R8

National SAR Agency: MRCC COPA **Address:** Bahía Málaga, Buenaventura - Valle, Colombia **Telephone:** +57 2 2460630 **Fax:** +57 2 2460630			

Coastguard stations maintain a continuous listening watch on VHF Chs 16 and 11 on Atlantic Coast and VHF Chs 16 and 68 on Pacific Coast.

	Telephone +57	Fax +57	Others/Ship Earth Stations (SES)
Oficino Grupo Busqueda Rescate (Cospas-Sarsat SPOC)	1 2962700 1 2962554	1 2962825	**AFTN:** SKBOYCYX **Telex:** +396 44620 DAAC CO +396 44840 DAAC CO

Pacific Coast

	Telephone +57	Fax +57	Others/Ship Earth Stations (SES)
CENTRO DE OPERACIONES DEL PACIFICO (COPA)	2 2460585	2 2460630	**email:** copafnp@armada.mil.co

ECUADOR   See diagram R8

National SAR Agency: Direccion General de la Marina Mercante y del Litoral
Address: Elialde 101 y, Malecon, Simon Bolivar, Guayaquil, Ecuador
Telephone: +593 42 320400 ext 212
　　　　　+593 42 324768 (Watchkeeping H24)
Fax: +593 42 324714
　　+593 42 324768
　　+593 42 480176 (Comando De GuardaCostas Radio Headquarters)
email: coguaroperaciones@armada.mil.ec
　　　guayaquil_radio@digmer.org

Coastguard Headquarters is responsible for coordinating Search and Rescue. Guayaquil (HCG) maintains a continuous listening watch on 2182 kHz and VHF Chs 16, 26 & Ch 70 DSC. Preferred inter RCC languages are English and Spanish.

TeleMedical Assistance Service: Hospital Naval Guayaquil provide advice. Contact is via HCG Guayaquil Radio, HCY Ayora Radio or Comando De GuardaCostas (CCSM) Aviacion Naval (SCSC). Possible consultation languages: Spanish and English.

	Telephone +593	Fax +593	Others/Ship Earth Stations (SES)
COASTGUARD HEADQUARTERS	4 2483530	4 2480812 4 2480176	**email:** coguar-operations@digmer.org 　　　coguar-operations@armada.mil.ec
ARSC GUAYAQUIL (Cospas-Sarsat SPOC)	4 2925466 4 2947400 (Ext 2180)		**AFTN:** SEQUYCYX
GUAYAQUIL (HCG)	4 2505302	4 2505294	**email:** guayaquil_radio@dirneg.org
FUERZA AÉREA ECUATORIANA Ala de Combate No 22 Grupo de Combate No 221	4 2281002 4 2294519	4 2281002 4 2281002	**email:** gruposarecuador@gmail.com 　　　coaala22@fae.ffaa.mil.ec

GUATEMALA   See diagram R7

National SAR Agency: Sistema de Busqueda y Salvamento Estado Mayor de la Defensa Nacional
Address: 2 Av. 4-63 Zona 10, Guatemala City, Guatemala
Telephone: +502 4497411

A Marine Rescue Coordination Centre exists at the Centro de Operaciones Conjuntas, del estado Mayor de la Defensa Nacional in Guatemala City for both the Pacific and Atlantic Coasts.

	Telephone +502	Fax +502	Others/Ship Earth Stations (SES)
CENTRO DE OPERACIONES DEL ESTADO MAYOR DE LA DEFENSA NACIONAL	44974116 31285507		**email:** cocemdn@gmail.com
DIRECCIÓN GENERAL DE ASUNTOS MARITIMOS DEL MINISTERIO DE LA DEFENSA NACIONAL	44974255		**email:** seguridadmaritima@dgam.gob.gt
CENTRO DE OPERACIONES AÉREAS DE LA FUERZA AÉREA	31285767 22913436		**email:** secretariauda@gmail.com

Pacific Coast

	Telephone +502	Fax +502	Others/Ship Earth Stations (SES)
COMANDO NAVAL DEL PACIFICO	44974084 44974085		
PUERTO QUETZAL, ESCUINTLA (GUATEMALA PORT TRAFFIC CONTROL)	78283500 ext 516		
COMANDO AÉREO DEL SUR	44974274		

MEXICO   See diagrams R7, R8/9, R16 & R17

National SAR Agency: Mexican Navy MRCC Mexico
Address: Secretaria de Marina, Jefatura del Estado Mayor General, De la Armada de Mexico, Eje 2 Oriente Tramo. Heroica Escuela Naval, Militar No 861, Edificio "B" Primer Nivel, Col. Los Cipreses, Deleg. Coyoacán, México D.F., C.P. 04830
Telephone: +52 55 56246500
                +52 55 56246200 ext 1000 (For SAR Office use ext 7242 or 7843)
                +52 55 56246200 ext 2000
Fax: +52 55 56849642
email: sarmarina@semar.gob.mx
          s3jemg@semar.gob.mx

The Mexican Navy is responsible for coordinating Search and Rescue operations within the limits of the Exclusive Economic Zone of Mexico in the Gulf of Mexico, Caribbean Sea and Pacific Ocean. All sections of the Mexican Navy are linked by radio and telephone with TELECOMM. The following Coast Radio Stations maintain a continuous listening watch on international distress frequencies. Preferred inter RCC languages are English and Spanish:

Caribbean Sea (NAVAREA IV) - Cancún (XFO), Isla Cozumel (XFC), Chetumal (XFP)

Gulf of Mexico (NAVAREA IV) - Tampico (XFS), Veracruz (XFU) Coatzacoalcos (XFF) CD.del Carmen (XFB) and Radiomex (XDA)

Pacific Ocean (NAVAREA XII) - Ensenada (XFE), La Paz (XFK), Guaymas (XFY), Mazatlán (XFL), Manzanillo (XFM), Acapulco (XFA), Salina Cruz (XFQ).

	Telephone +52	Fax +52	Others/Ship Earth Stations (SES)
Cospas-Sarsat SPOC		55 56132214	**email:** cegg@telecomm.net.mx

Regional Control Centre

	Telephone +52	Fax +52	Others/Ship Earth Stations (SES)
GULF OF MEXICO MRCC TAMPICO	833 2107205 833 2107206 833 2107207 833 2107209 833 2107210	833 2107208	**email:** radiotam@telecomm.net.mx
PACIFIC OCEAN MRCC MAZATLÁN	669 9852411	669 9852428	**email:** maritm@telecomm.net.mx

Pacific Coast

	Telephone +52	Fax +52	Others/Ship Earth Stations (SES)
MRCC ENSENADA (2nd Region)	646 1725009 (Primary 24/7) 646 1734748 (Commanding Officer) 646 1734854 (Chief of Staff)	646 1773835 646 1773935	**email:** ensarensenada@semar.gob.mx
MRCC GUAYMAS (4th Region)	622 2243830 622 2222178 622 2229588 622 2226228	622 2243830	**email:** rn4@csi.sedemar.mil.mx
MRCC MANZANILLO (6th Region)	314 3320497 314 3320568 314 3320634 314 3320367		**email:** rn6@csi.sedemar.mil.mx
MRCC ACAPULCO (8th Region)	744 4847554 744 4842766 744 4844375		**email:** rn8@csi.sedemar.mil.mx

NICARAGUA   See diagram R7

National SAR Agency: El Instituto Nicaragüense de Aeronáutica Civil (INAC)
Address: Km 11.5 Carretera, Norte Apodo, 4936 Nicaragua.
Telephone: +505 2276 8580
              +505 2276 8586 ext 1550
Fax: +505 2276 8588
email: sarjulio@gmail.com
          sar@inac.gob.ni
Website: www.inac.gob.ni

The Fuerza Aérea y Defensa Anti Aerea (FASDAA) is responsible for coordinating Search and Rescue operations.

	Telephone +505	Fax +505	Others/Ship Earth Stations (SES)
SRC NICARAGUA (COCESNA)	276 2507 233 1602	276 8580 233 1602	**email:** cap-j.pinell@hotmail.com oguevara@hotmail.com

Pacific Coast

	Telephone +505	Fax +505	Others/Ship Earth Stations (SES)
RCC MANAGUA	223 31428	223 31981	**AFTN:** MYMGYOYR **email:** fzaaerea@tmx.com.ni

UNITED STATES OF AMERICA   See diagrams R3, R7, R8, R16, R17 & R18

National SAR Agency: US Coast Guard.
Address: Commandant (CG-534), 2100 2nd Street, S.W. Washington D.C. 20593-7363, USA
Telephone: +1 202 3722075
Fax: +1 202 3722912
Website: https://www.uscg.mil/

The US Coast Guard National VHF Distress System provides continuous coastal coverage outwards to 20 n miles on VHF Ch 16. After contact on Ch 16, communications with the Coast Guard should be on VHF Ch 22A. Vessels not equipped with VHF Ch 22A should use VHF Ch 12. Selected Coast Radio Stations and Coast Guard Stations maintain continuous watch on 2182 kHz.

	Telephone +1	Fax +1	Others/Ship Earth Stations (SES)
USMCC (Cospas-Sarsat SPOC)	301 8174576	301 8174568	**AFTN:** KZDCZSZA **email:** usmcc@noaa.gov
AMVER surface picture (SURPIC)	Contact any US Coast Guard RCC or www.amver.com/surpicrequest.asp		

Alaska

	Telephone +1	Fax +1	Others/Ship Earth Stations (SES)
AKRCC ELMENDORF AFB (Cospas-Sarsat SPOC)	907 5517230 800 4207230	907 5517245	**AFTN:** PAEDYCYX **email:** rccmessages@elmendorf.af.mil
COMMSTA (Kodiak)	907 4875778	907 4875430	**email:** d17-dg-m-k-commstakodiak-cwo@uscg.mil
JRCC JUNEAU (17th District)	907 4632000	907 4632023	**Telex:** +023 49615066 US CG JUNEAU **email:** jrccjuneau@uscg.mil

Pacific Coast

	Telephone +1	Fax +1	Others/Ship Earth Stations (SES)
COMMUNICATION AREA MASTER STATION PACIFIC (CAMSPAC) (Alameda)	415 6692047	415 6692096	**Telex:** +230 172343 **email:** d11-dg-m-camspac-cwos@uscg.mil
JRCC ALAMEDA (11th District)	510 4373701	510 4373017	**Telex:** +230 172343 CG ALDA **email:** rccalameda1@uscg.mil
JRCC SEATTLE (13th District)	206 2207001	206 2207009	**email:** jrccseattle@uscg.mil

Hawaii

	Telephone +1	Fax +1	Others/Ship Earth Stations (SES)
JRCC HONOLULU (14th District)	808 5353333	808 5353338	**Telex:** +230 392401 CG14 UD **email:** jrcchonolulu@uscg.mil

NAVAREA XIII

RUSSIA

See diagrams R2, R6, R15, R16 & R18

National SAR Agency: Ministry of Transport of the Russian Federation
Address: 1/1 U1,Rozhdestvenka Street Moscow, 109112, Russia
Telephone: +7 495 6261000
Fax: +7 495 6269038
　　　+7 495 6269128
email: info@mintrans.ru
Website: www.mintrans.ru

MRCC Moscow is responsible for coordinating Search and Rescue operations and liaising with Search and Rescue services of neighbouring countries in accordance with intergovernmental agreements. A network of Coast Radio Stations maintains a continuous listening watch on international distress frequencies. Preferred inter RCC language is English.

NORTHERN SEAS (NAVAREAs I, XX and XXI): The following frequencies are reserved for Distress Calls and are not to be used for general communication: 6211 kHz, 4138 kHz & 500 kHz. In all areas (except Beloye More and Barents Sea) a 3 minute watch will be maintained on 500 kHz from 15 minutes past each hour and on 6211 kHz and 4138 kHz from 45 minutes past each hour.

TeleMedical Assistance Service: State Enterprise "Semashko Northern Medical Centre" provides assistance (telemed@atnet.ru). Contact via MRSC Arkhange'lsk. Possible consultation languages: Russian and English.

Additionally, assistance may also be provided by Sakhalin Territorial Centre of the Medicine and Catastrophe (stcmk@mail.ru). Possible consultation language: Russian.

State MRCC

	Telephone +7	Fax +7	Others/Ship Earth Stations (SES)
CMC (Cospas-Sarsat SPOC)	495 2360109 495 2360110	495 2360109 495 9673020	**AFTN:** UUUUYCYX **email:** cmc@marsat.ru
SMRCC MOSCOW	495 6261052 495 6241853 495 6261055	495 6237476	**email:** odsmrcc@morflot.ru 　　　od_smrcc@morspas.ru

Pacific Coast

	Telephone +7	Fax +7	Others/Ship Earth Stations (SES)
MRCC VLADIVOSTOK	4232 495522 4232 227782 4232 497401	4232 495895	**Telex:** +64 213115 MRF RU **Inmarsat C:** 427312137 **email:** vldvmrcc@pma.ru
MRSC PETROPAVLOVSK-KAMCHATSKIY	4152 434180 914 7839583	4152 434180	**Telex:** +64 244138 PSC PK RU **email:** pkspc@ampskk.ru **MMSI:** 002734418
MRSC YUZHNO-SAKHALINSK	4242 785704	4242 722341	**Telex:** +64 152068 GMDSS RU **Inmarsat C:** 427311122 **email:** mspc@sakhalin.ru

NAVAREA XIV

COOK ISLANDS (NEW ZEALAND)

See diagram R17

National SAR Agency: Commissioner of Police, Cook Islands Police Services
Address: National Headquarters, P.O. Box 101, Rarotonga, Cook Islands
Telephone: +682 22499
Website: https://www.facebook.com/CookIslandsPolice

The Cook Islands Police are responsible for coordinating Search and Rescue operations. Rarotonga (ZKR) maintains a continuous listening watch on 2182 kHz and VHF Ch 16.

	Telephone +682	Fax +682	Others/Ship Earth Stations (SES)
RCC RAROTONGA	22499		**email:** enquiries@police.gov.ck
POLICE NCCC RAROTONGA	22941 (Direct)		**email:** ccc.operations@police.gov.ck 　　　areumu.ingaua@police.gov.ck 　　　solomon.tuaati@police.gov.ck 　　　tepaki.bacter@police.gov.ck

FIJI
See diagram R17

National SAR Agency: Maritime Surveillance Centre
Address: HQ Fiji Navy, Box 12387, Suva, Fiji
Telephone: +679 3315380
Fax: +679 3306295

Search and Rescue operations within the waters around Fiji are coordinated by a National Search and Rescue Committee. RCCs are located at Suva and Nadi. Rescue Sub-Centres (RSCs) may be temporarily established in other areas as demanded by the situation. Suva (3DP) maintains a continuous listening watch on 2182 kHz and VHF Ch 16 for distress calls. The station is also equipped with 6215·5 kHz for Search and Rescue operations.

	Telephone +679	Fax +679	Others/Ship Earth Stations (SES)
RCC NADI Nadi International Airport (Cospas-Sarsat SPOC)	6725777 ext 4183/4446/4811 (Nadi Area Control Centre)	6722470 (2000-0430 UTC Mon - Fri)	**AFTN:** NFFNYCYX **email:** nadircc1@afl.com.fj (SAR Controller)
FMSRCC (Fiji Maritime Surveillance Rescue Coordination Centre)	3315380 3316204 3316205 3316206	3306295	**email:** operations@rccfiji.org (RCC Fiji) operations@mrscfiji.org (Maritime Surveillance)
SUVA RADIO (3DP)	4502771	3381585	**email:** suvaradio@yahoo.com

FRENCH POLYNESIA
See diagrams R8 & R17

National SAR Agency: Organisme d'études et de coordination pour la recherche et le sauvetage en mer (SECMAR)
Address: 16 Boulevard Raspail, 75007 Paris, France
Telephone: +33 1 53634159

Local coordination is provided by JRCC Tahiti, which maintains a continuous listening watch on VHF Ch 16 (Society Archipelagos only), MF on 2182 kHz, HF on 8291 kHz and MF DSC on 2187.5 kHz.

	Telephone +689	Fax +689	Others/Ship Earth Stations (SES)
JRCC TAHITI (Cospas-Sarsat SPOC)	40 541616 (Emergency) 40 541617 (Office) 40 541615 (Information)	40 423915 (H24)	**Mobile:** +689 87757547 **AFTN:** NTAAYCYX **Inmarsat C:** 422799192 **email:** contact@jrcc.pf jrcctahiti@gmail.com (Rescue) **Website:** www.jrcc.pf

NEW ZEALAND
See diagrams R17 & R19

National SAR Agency: Maritime New Zealand
Address: Level 11, Optimation House, 1 Grey Street, Wellington, PO Box 72006, New Zealand
Telephone: +64 4 4730111 (MNZ Head Office)
         +64 4 5778034 (RCCNZ Office Administration)
Fax: +64 4 4941263 (MNZ Head Office)
      +64 4 5778041 (RCCNZ Office Administration)
Website: https://maritimenz.govt.nz/

The Rescue Coordination Centre New Zealand RCCNZ is a joint coordination centre based at Lower Hutt. RCCNZ is responsible for the coordination of sea, air and land SAR in the NZSRR. Language is English although interpreting may be available for other languages. The Maritime Operations Centre, co-located with RCCNZ, provides New Zealand's maritime radio distress and safety service. It remotely controls 30 coastal VHF stations and operates the MF and HF Coast Radio Station, Taupo Maritime Radio (ZLM), in the central North Island provides a 24/7 listening watch on international distress frequencies.

TeleMedical Assistance Service: The Life Flight Trust provide assistance. Contact via RCCNZ. Preferred consultation language: English.

	Telephone +64	Fax +64	Others/Ship Earth Stations (SES)
RCC NEW ZEALAND (RCCNZ) (Cospas-Sarsat SPOC)	4 577 8030	4 577 8038 4 577 8041	**Inmarsat C:** 451200067=MRNZ X **email:** rccnz@maritimenz.govt.nz
MARITIME OPERATIONS CENTRE	4 550 5280 (H24)	4 550 4001 (H24)	**Inmarsat C:** 451200067=MRNZ X **email:** maritime@kordia.co.nz

PITCAIRN ISLANDS
See diagram R17

National SAR Agency: Pitcairn Police

	Telephone +870	Fax +870	Others/Ship Earth Stations (SES)
Pitcairn Police	762854699 (Inmarsat)	762941161 (Inmarsat)	**email:** mop.pitcairn@gtnet.gov.uk

SAMOA
See diagram R17

National SAR Agency: Ministry of Transport
Address: P.O. Box 1607, Apia, Western Samoa
Telephone: +685 23700
+685 23701
+685 23702

Apia (5WA) maintains a continuous listening watch on 2182 kHz.

	Telephone +685	Fax +685	Others/Ship Earth Stations (SES)
NATIONAL SURVEILLANCE CENTRE (Cospas-Sarsat SPOC)	22222 24957		**AFTN:** NSFAZTZX

TONGA
See diagram R17

National SAR Agency: Ministry of Police
Address: Tonga
Telephone: +676 23222

Search and Rescue operations are coordinated from RCC Tonga Defence Services (TDS) and ARCC Fua'amotu International Airport. Nukualofa (A3A) maintains a continuous listening watch on 2182 kHz for distress calls.

	Telephone +676	Fax +676	Others/Ship Earth Stations (SES)
RCC TONGA DEFENCE SERVICES (TDS) (Cospas-Sarsat SPOC)	23099 23119	23934 23190	**AFTN:** NFTFYSYX
ARCC FUA'AMOTU INTERNATIONAL AIRPORT	35393	35395	**AFTN:** NFTFZTZX
NUKUALOFA (A3A)	23350		

NAVAREA XV

CHILE
See diagrams R8/9, R17 & R19

National SAR Agency: Directorate General of the Maritime Territory and Merchant Marine
Address: Errázuriz 537, Valparaíso, Chile
Telephone: +56 32 2208637
+56 32 2208638
+56 32 2208639
Fax: +56 32 2208662
email: mrccchile@directemar.cl
Website: https://www.directemar.cl/directemar/seguridad-maritima/mrcc-chile/servicio-de-busqueda-y-salvamento-maritimo-mrcc-chile

The Chilean Maritime Rescue Coordination Centre - MRCC Chile, is located in Valparaíso, and is sub-divided into 5 districts. Chile has an extensive coastline where five Maritime Rescue Coordination Centres (MRCCs) and eleven Maritime Rescue Coordination Sub-Centres (MRSCs) are located. They are fitted with modern maritime communication systems and facilities to carry out Search and Rescue operations. The responsibility area also covers the Drake Passage and an area which extends to the Antarctic, where weather conditions are generally adverse. A network of Coast Radio Stations maintains continuous listening watch on international distress frequencies, which are monitored by MRCC Chile.

TeleMedical Assistance Service: In association with MRCC Chile, TMAS is operated by "Salud Responde" on telephone +56 600 360 7777. Possible consultation languages: Spanish and English.

	Telephone +56	Fax +56	Others/Ship Earth Stations (SES)
CHMCC (Cospas-Sarsat SPOC)	2 29764042 2 29764041		**AFTN:** SCTIZSZX **email:** sarchmcc@gmail.com sarchmcc.meosar@gmail.com
MRCC CHILE	32 2208637 32 2208638 32 2208639		**email:** mrccchile@directemar.cl cbvradio@directemar.cl
MRSC ARICA	58 2206470 58 2206486		**email:** mrscarica@directemar.cl comafari@dgtm.cl

Continued overleaf

CHILE (Continued)

	Telephone +56	Fax +56	Others/Ship Earth Stations (SES)
MRCC IQUIQUE	57 2401945		**email:** mrcciquique@directemar.cl
MRSC ANTOFAGASTA	55 2630000 55 2630037		**email:** mrscantofagasta@directemar.cl cbaradio@directemar.cl
MRSC CALDERA	52 2315276		**email:** mrsccaldera@directemar.cl
MRSC COQUIMBO	51 2558134		**email:** mrsccoquimbo@directemar.cl
MRCC VALPARAÍSO	32 2528909		**email:** mrccvalparaiso@directemar.cl cbvradio@directemar.cl
MRSC HANGA ROA, ISLA DE PASCUA (EASTER ISLAND)	32 2100567 32 2100222		**email:** mrschangaroa@directemar.cl cbyradio@directemar.cl
MRSC SAN ANTONIO	35 2584886 35 2584846		**email:** mrscsanantonio@directemar.cl
MRCC TALCAHUANO	41 2266162		**email:** mrcctalcahuano@directemar.cl cbtradio@directemar.cl
MRSC VALDIVIA	63 2361370 63 2361386		**email:** mrscvaldivia@directemar.cl
MRCC PUERTO MONTT	65 2561190		**email:** mrccpuertomontt@directemar.cl cbpradio@directemar.cl
MRSC CASTRO	65 2561204		**email:** mrsccastro@directemar.cl
MRSC AYSÉN	67 2331461		**email:** mrscaysen@directemar.cl
MRCC PUNTA ARENAS	61 2201161		**email:** mrccpuntaarenas@directemar.cl cbmradio@directemar.cl
MRSC PUERTO WILLIAMS	61 2621090		**email:** mrscpuertowilliams@directemar.cl
MRSC ANTARCTICA CHILENA	32 2208557 32 2208556 32 2203381		**email:** mrscantarctica@directemar.cl odmcpfildes@directemar.cl

NAVAREA XVI

PERU   See diagram R8

National SAR Agency: Comandancia de Operaciones Guardacostas (COMOPERGUARD)
Address: Avenida Contralmirante Mora sin Número, Base Naval del Callao, Callao 01 Perú
Telephone: +51 1 4202020
             +51 1 4291547
             +51 4 4121085
Fax: +51 1 4291547
      +51 1 4299798
email: pemcc@dicapi.mil.pe
Website: https://www.dicapi.mil.pe/direcciones/comoperguard

The Coast Guard Operations Command (COMOPERGUARD) is responsible for coordinating Maritime Search and Rescue operations. MRCC PERÚ covers the Navarea XVI. A network of Coast Radio Stations maintain a continuous listening watch on international distress frequencies. COMOPERGUARD is also responsible for PEMCC and PELUT which receive and distribute alert messages as a ground segment provider in the Cospas-Sarsat system

TeleMedical Assistance Service: Centro Medico Naval (Cirujano Mayor Santiago Tavara) provide assistance. Contact via Callao Radio (CBC3) MMSI 007600125 on VHF, MF or HF DSC (8MHz), MRCC Peru or any MRSC.

Possible consultation languages: Spanish and English.

	Telephone +51	Fax +51	Others/Ship Earth Stations (SES)
PEMCC (Cospas-Sarsat SPOC)	1 4202020 1 4121085	1 4291547 1 4299798	**email:** pemcc@dicapi.mil.pe
MRCC CALLAO (PERU)	1 4202020	1 4291547	**email:** pemcc@dicapi.mil.pe
MRSC PAITA	1 73211670	1 73211670	**email:** costerapaita@dicapi.mil.pe
MRSC MOLLENDO	1 54534383	1 54534383	**Telex:** +36 59655 PE DICAPI **email:** costera.mollendo@dicapi.mil.pe

NAVAREA XVII & XVIII

GREENLAND
See diagrams R3/4 & R18

National SAR Agency: JRCC Greenland
Address: Joint Arctic Command (JACO), Post Box 1072, Aalisartut Aqqutaa 47, 3900 Nuuk, Greenland
Telephone: +299 364000 (Joint Arctic Command)
Inmarsat C: 433116710
Iridium: +881 677754507
email: jrcc@jrcc.gl

The responsibility for Search and Rescue services in Greenland is with JRCC Greenland and The Commissioner of Police in Greenland.

A mandatory reporting system GREENPOS for SAR purposes is established for all ships cruising within the waters of the Greenland continental shelf or the EEZ. Procedures for GREENPOS can be received through JRCC Greenland.

All SAR agencies in Greenland are fully GMDSS equipped. Preferred languages at JRCC Greenland are English and Danish.

TeleMedical Assistance Service: Contact via MRCC Nuuk. Possible consultation languages: Greenlandic, Danish and English

	Telephone +299	Fax +299	Others/Ship Earth Stations (SES)
JRCC GREENLAND	364010 (Duty Officer) 364012 (Duty Officer) 364022 (Commcentre) 364023 (Commcentre)		**Inmarsat C:** 433116710 **Iridium:** +881 677754507 **email:** jrcc@jrcc.gl greenpos@jrcc.gl (GREENPOS only)
NAVAIR (Part of JRCC Greenland)	363304	363309	**AFTN:** BGGHYCYC **Iridium:** +881 631417431 (Backup) +881 623457247 (Backup) **email:** fic@naviair.dk
Commissioner of Police in Greenland	701448 (Ext 200)	323348	**email:** grl-politi@politi.dk

NAVAREA XIX

NORWAY (BJØRNØYA)
See diagram R18

National SAR Agency: Ministry of Justice and Police, SAR Division
Address: P.O.Box 8005 Dep. 0030 Oslo, Norway
Telephone: +47 22249090
Fax: +47 22249533
email: postmottak@jd.dep.no

The Coast Radio Station monitors all the maritime emergency channels: VHF DSC (Ch 70) VHF voice (Ch 16) MF DSC distress (2187,5 kHz) follow up on voice channel 2182 kHz

In addition the Coast Radio Station monitor the following channels 24-7: MF DSC international (2189,5 kHz) All VHF working channels

Ships are encouraged to contact the Norwegian Coast Radio Station using digital selective Call (DSC). Using MMSI 002570000 in the call, the system automatically selects the nearest Norwegian Coast Radio Station.

Coastal Radio ended listening to all MF voice channels from March 1 2018. From this date only DSC will be monitored.

All voice channels will still be in operation, but only after callback using DSC.

	Telephone +47	Fax +47	Others/Ship Earth Stations (SES)
JRCC BODØ	75559000 (Alarm/Operations) 75559300	75524200	**AFTN:** ENBOYCYX **Inmarsat C:** 425999999 **Inmarsat Fleet:** 764816062 **email:** mailto@jrcc-bodoe.no (Admin) operations@jrcc-bodoe.no (Operations)
NORWEGIAN COASTAL RADIO NORTH	75528925	78988331	**email:** kystradio.nord@telenor.com

NORWAY (SVALBARD)

See diagram R18

National SAR Agency: Ministry of Justice and Police, SAR Division **Address:** P.O.Box 8005 Dep. 0030 Oslo, Norway **Telephone:** +47 22249090 **Fax:** +47 22249533 **email:** postmottak@jd.dep.no

The Coast Radio Station monitors all the maritime emergency channels: VHF DSC (Ch 70) VHF voice (Ch 16) MF DSC distress (2187,5 kHz) follow up on voice channel 2182 kHz

In addition the Coast Radio Station monitor the following channels 24-7: MF DSC international (2189,5 kHz) All VHF working channels

Ships are encouraged to contact the Norwegian Coast Radio Station using digital selective Call (DSC). Using MMSI 002570000 in the call, the system automatically selects the nearest Norwegian Coast Radio Station.

Coastal Radio ended listening to all MF voice channels from March 1 2018. From this date only DSC will be monitored.

All voice channels will still be in operation, but only after callback using DSC.

The responsibility for all other incidents is assumed by MRCC Reykjavik, Iceland.

	Telephone +47	Fax +47	Others/Ship Earth Stations (SES)
JRCC BODØ	75559000	75524200	**AFTN:** ENBOYCYX **Inmarsat C:** 425999999 **Inmarsat Fleet:** 764816062 **email:** operations@jrcc-bodoe.no
NORWEGIAN COASTAL RADIO NORTH	75528925	78988331	**email:** kystradio.nord@telenor.com

NAVAREA XX & XXI

RUSSIA

See diagrams R2, R6, R15, R16 & R18

National SAR Agency: Ministry of Transport of the Russian Federation **Address:** 1/1 U1,Rozhdestvenka Street Moscow, 109112, Russia **Telephone:** +7 495 6261000 **Fax:** +7 495 6269038   +7 495 6269128 **email:** info@mintrans.ru **Website:** www.mintrans.ru

MRCC Moscow is responsible for coordinating Search and Rescue operations and liaising with Search and Rescue services of neighbouring countries in accordance with intergovernmental agreements. A network of Coast Radio Stations maintains a continuous listening watch on international distress frequencies. Preferred inter RCC language is English.

NORTHERN SEAS (NAVAREAs I, XX and XXI): The following frequencies are reserved for Distress Calls and are not to be used for general communication: 6211 kHz, 4138 kHz & 500 kHz. In all areas (except Beloye More and Barents Sea) a 3 minute watch will be maintained on 500 kHz from 15 minutes past each hour and on 6211 kHz and 4138 kHz from 45 minutes past each hour.

TeleMedical Assistance Service: State Enterprise "Semashko Northern Medical Centre" provides assistance (telemed@atnet.ru). Contact via MRSC Arkhange'lsk. Possible consultation languages: Russian and English.

Additionally, assistance may also be provided by Sakhalin Territorial Centre of the Medicine and Catastrophe (stcmk@mail.ru). Possible consultation language: Russian.

State MRCC

	Telephone +7	Fax +7	Others/Ship Earth Stations (SES)
CMC (Cospas-Sarsat SPOC)	495 2360109 495 2360110	495 2360109 495 9673020	**AFTN:** UUUUYCYX **email:** cmc@marsat.ru
SMRCC MOSCOW	495 6261052 495 6241853 495 6261055	495 6237476	**email:** odsmrcc@morflot.ru od_smrcc@morspas.ru

Arctic Coast

	Telephone +7	Fax +7	Others/Ship Earth Stations (SES)
MRCC MURMANSK	8152 428307 8152 480220	8152 423256	**Inmarsat BGAN:** 772236879 **Iridium:** +79541063065 **email:** rcc_murmansk@morspas.com

Continued on next page

Arctic Coast (Continued)

	Telephone +7	Fax +7	Others/Ship Earth Stations (SES)
MRSC ARKHANGEL'SK	8182 208921 8182 200358	8182 200359	**Telex:** +64 242278 +64 242225 **Inmarsat C:** 492509110 **email:** rcc_arkhangelsk@morspas.com
MRCC DIKSON	39152 24100 906 9030657	39152 24200	**Mobile:** +7 9069030657 **Telex:** +64 788790 **Inmarsat BGAN:** 772536162 **Iridium:** +79541122830 **email:** rcc_dikson@morspas.com **MMSI:** 002731107
	Overall control of the Russian Eastern Arctic Sector. Coordination of search and rescue and oil spill elimination in the Arctic Zone of the Russian Federation (Kara Gate Strait to the Bering Strait).		

Northern Sea Route

These Control Centres are in service during the summer navigation period (approximately July to November). Operational times of MRSC Pevek and MRSC Tiksi will be rotated.

Coordination of Search and Rescue and oil spill elimination in the Eastern sector of the Arctic Zone of the Russian Federation to include the East Siberian Sea and the Chukchi Sea.

	Telephone +7	Fax +7	Others/Ship Earth Stations (SES)
MRSC PEVEK	42737 42113		**Inmarsat BGAN:** 772397870 **email:** mspcpevek@pma.ru
MRSC TIKSI	41167 28549 41167 28424		**Mobile:** +7 9246658864 **Inmarsat BGAN:** 772397397 **email:** mspctiksi@pma.ru

GENERAL ARRANGEMENTS FOR SEARCH AND RESCUE (SAR)
United Kingdom related content updated by the Maritied Kingdome and Coastguard Agency.

1. General information

The radio watch on the international distress frequencies, which certain classes of vessels are required to keep when at sea, is one of the most important factors in the arrangements for the rescue of people in distress at sea. Every vessel should make its contribution to safety by listening to one or more of these distress frequencies for as long as is practicable whether or not they are required to do so by regulation.

To supplement the efforts of vessels at sea, most maritime countries maintain a life saving service for the rescue of people in distress around their coasts. The organisation of SAR measures varies from country to country, but effective terrestrial radio communications over short to medium ranges always play an important part in the operation of the service.
Masters and owners of all vessels governed by the regulations contained in SOLAS Chapter IV (vessels over 300 GT, passenger vessels on international voyages and certain other craft such as particular classes of high speed vessels and rigs etc) should be fully aware of the requirements of the Global Maritime Distress and Safety System (GMDSS) which entered into force on 1 February 1999. The GMDSS is a largely, but not fully, automated system which, among other things, requires vessels to have a range of equipment capable of performing nine radio-communication functions, viz:

- Transmission of ship-to-shore distress alerts by at least two separate and independent means, each using a different radiocommunication service;
- Reception of shore-to-ship distress alerts;
- Transmission and reception of ship-to-ship distress alerts;
- Transmission and reception of search and rescue coordinating communications;
- Transmission and reception of on-scene communications;
- Transmission and reception of signals for locating;
- Transmission and reception of maritime safety information;
- Transmission and reception of general radio-communications to and from shore-based radio systems or networks; and:
- Transmission and reception of bridge-to-bridge communications.

Special attention should also be given to IMO Resolution MSC.131(75) (adopted on 21 May 2002), which urged that all vessels should be fitted with facilities capable of transmitting and receiving distress alerts by Digital Selective Calling (DSC) on VHF Ch 70. The 78th Session of the IMO Maritime Safety Committee (May 2004) decided that a listening watch will, when practicable, also be maintained on VHF Ch 16, as a mandatory requirement, in order to provide a common means of communication between all classes of vessels for distress and safety purposes.

In the United Kingdom, the JRCC UK is supported by 9 MRCC's and 1 MRSC around the UK coastline.

2. GMDSS implementation

Distress and safety communications in support of SAR activities use the systems and procedures of the GMDSS. All vessels built after 1 February 1995 must comply with the applicable GMDSS requirements. Descriptions of the operational procedures to be observed by vessels fitted with GMDSS equipment are contained in the manual for use by the Maritime Mobile and Maritime Mobile Satellite Services published by the ITU, Geneva. When referring to ITU publications, the latest versions of the Recommendations on the use of Marine Radio Communications equipment must be consulted.

Under the GMDSS there are four sea areas. Sea Area A1 is an area within VHF range of coast stations equipped with DSC. Sea Area A2 is an area within MF range of coast stations equipped with DSC. Sea Area A3 is an area, excluding Sea Areas A1 and A2 within the coverage of an Inmarsat geostationary satellite in which continuous alerting is available (N.B.: Inmarsat network coverage is effective up to about latitudes 76°, North and South). Sea Area A4 comprises those areas outside Sea Areas A1, A2 and A3 - this is essentially the polar regions, above about 76°of latitude, but excludes any other areas. Details of these sea areas, together within formation on the GMDSS communication systems, are shown elsewhere in this Volume.
Vessels equipped for DSC shall, while at sea, maintain an automatic DSC watch on the appropriate distress and safety calling frequencies in the frequency bands appropriate for the sea area in which they are operating. Vessels, where so equipped, should also maintain watch on the appropriate frequencies for the automatic reception of transmissions of Meteorological and Navigational Warnings and other urgent information. Ship Earth Stations (SES) in use for the reception of shore-to-ship distress alert relay should maintain a listening watch.

The importance of maintaining some of the Radio Telephony (RT) procedures used prior to the introduction of the GMDSS has been recognised for many of those vessels around the world that are not subject to SOLAS, in particular small commercial and leisure craft. This includes participation in responding to distress incidents and ensuring that coast stations and SOLAS vessels can communicate effectively with such vessels in order to coordinate SAR operations. To this end, the ITU World Radiocommunication Conference held in 2007 (WRC-07) incorporated the VHF Ch 16 RT procedures into the terrestrial distress, urgency and safety procedures of the GMDSS (see below). In addition, administrations may continue the use of RT procedures on the MF distress frequency 2182 kHz on a national basis, as an adjunct to the GMDSS. The United Kingdom no longer maintains a Distress watch on 2182 kHz.

TERRESTRIAL DISTRESS, URGENCY AND SAFETY COMMUNICATIONS

3. Distress communications in the GMDSS

Ship-to-shore distress alerts in the GMDSS are used to alert (Maritime) Rescue Coordination Centres (MRCC's), either directly or via a Coast Radio Station (CRS) or Coast Earth Station (CES), that a vessel is in distress. These alerts are based on the use of transmissions through satellites (from an SES, a satellite Emergency Position Indicating Radio Beacon (EPIRB)) and/or terrestrial services using DSC assigned calling frequencies.

Ship-to-ship distress alerts are used to alert other vessels in the vicinity of the vessel in distress and are based on the use of DSC or RT in the VHF band and DSC in the MF band. When in distress, vessels not equipped with DSC should immediately try to initiate distress communications by transmitting a distress call and message by RT on the frequency 156·8 MHz (VHF Ch 16) (see section 5 below).

In order to attract attention from as many vessels as possible and to supplement the basic information given in a DSC distress alert, a vessel that has sent a distress alert by DSC should, immediately afterwards, also send a distress call and distress message by RT.

Vessels at sea may report a distress situation on behalf of another vessel or aircraft or person, e.g. sighting of a distress situation.

4. DSC distress alerts

The DSC distress alert indicates that a vessel, aircraft or other vehicle, or a person, is threatened by grave and imminent danger and requires immediate assistance. The DSC distress alert consists of one or more distress call attempts in which a DSC alert message is transmitted identifying the station in distress, giving its last recorded position and, if entered, the nature of the distress. The identity of the vessel making the DSC alert can only be derived from the MMSI number which is included as part of the alert message. This fulfils the requirement that distress alerts in the GMDSS must provide the identification and position of the station in distress. FOR FULL DETAILS ON DSC ALERTING SEE "Operational procedures for the use of DSC equipment in the Maritime Mobile Service" section.

The following frequencies are used for DSC Distress, Urgency and Safety alerts:

TABLE 1	
VHF	156·525 MHz (Ch 70)
MF	2187·5 kHz
HF	4207·5 kHz
	6312 kHz
	8414·5 kHz
	12577 kHz
	16804·5 kHz

Every vessel equipped for DSC shall, while at sea, maintain a continuous DSC watch on the distress and safety calling frequencies in the frequency bands in which they are operating listed in TABLE 1. The following frequencies are used for subsequent communications by RT following the transmission of a DSC distress alert:

TABLE 2	
VHF	156·800 MHz (Ch 16)
MF	2182 kHz
HF	4125 kHz
	6215 kHz
	8291 kHz
	12290 kHz
	16420 kHz

Note: 2182 kHz and VHF Ch 16 are the two frequencies most likely to be used for subsequent communications and on-scene communications during SAR operations.

Vessels at sea may report a distress situation on behalf of another vessel or aircraft or person e.g. sighting of a distress situation.

5. Radio telephony (RT) distress calls

The VHF Ch 16 Distress, Urgency and Safety RT procedures used prior to the introduction of the GMDSS have now been added to the GMDSS procedures following the decision requiring SOLAS vessels to maintain a listening watch on VHF Ch 16, when practicable, and the subsequent action by WRC-07 to amend the ITU Radio Regulations. National administrations may also authorise the continued use of 2182 kHz for such purposes within the coastal regions under their authority. RT procedures will therefore continue to provide an essential means of communication between SOLAS and non-SOLAS vessels, particularly for distress, urgency and safety communications. However, VHF Ch 16 is the only frequency from those listed in TABLE 2 above where there is a worldwide requirement to maintain a listening watch. Vessels that are not equipped for DSC should, therefore, initiate distress communications by transmitting a RT distress call and message on VHF Ch 16, as well as using any other means available, such as an EPIRB or a Personal Locator Beacon (PLB), for sending a distress alert.

The VHF Ch 16 RT distress procedure consists of a distress call and a distress message, which shall be sent in accordance with the following procedure

Distress Call

The distress call sent by RT consists of:

- The distress signal "MAYDAY" (spoken 3 times);
- The words "THIS IS";
- The NAME of the vessel in distress (spoken 3 times);
- The CALL SIGN or other identification;
- The MMSI (if the initial alert has been sent by DSC)

n.b.: The distress signal "MAYDAY" indicates that the vessel, aircraft or any other vehicle or person is threatened by grave and imminent danger and requires immediate assistance.

Distress Message

The message which follows the distress call, consists of:

- The distress signal "MAYDAY"
- The NAME of the vessel in distress;
- The CALL SIGN or other identification;
- The MMSI 123456789 (where a vessel has sent a DSC alert first);
- The position, given as the latitude and longitude, or if the latitude and longitude are not known or if time is insufficient, in relation to a known geographical location;
- The nature of the distress;
- The kind of assistance required;
- Any other useful information.

An example of a complete sequence of a distress transmission from vessel "Wanderer", call sign "MMVR":

Distress Call

> *MAYDAY MAYDAY MAYDAY*
> *THIS IS*
> *WANDERER WANDERER WANDERER*
> *MIKE MIKE VICTOR ROMEO*

followed by

Distress Message

> *MAYDAY*
> *WANDERER MIKE MIKE VICTOR ROMEO*
> *I AM 3 MILES SOUTH OF CHICKEN ROCK*
> *FIRE AND EXPLOSION IN ENGINE ROOM*
> *REQUIRE IMMEDIATE ASSISTANCE*
> *FIFTEEN PERSONS ON BOARD*
> *OVER*

Further Information

"Any other useful information" (some of which may be sent later if conditions permit) includes:
- Master's intentions
- Type of cargo (if dangerous)
- Weather, visibility and sea condition
- Time of abandonment
- Number and type of survival craft
- Number of persons abandoning/staying on board
- Details of location aids in survival craft or sea.

Continued on next page

6. Receipt and acknowledgement of a DSC distress alert or RT distress call
(See Section 5, Annex 3, Figures 10a and 10b)

1.	On receipt of a distress alert or a distress call, all stations shall prepare for subsequent distress communications by setting watch on the radio telephone distress and safety traffic frequency used or associated with the DSC distress and safety calling frequency on which the distress alert was received (i.e. 2182 kHz on MF, VHF Ch 16). Ship or SES in receipt of a distress alert or distress call shall, as soon as possible, make the Master or person responsible for the vessel aware of the information received.
2.	**Role of Coast Radio Stations (CRS), Coast Earth Stations (CES) and Rescue Coordination Centres (RCC)** The primary role of the shore based rescue coordination infrastructure in the GMDSS requires that, where direct alerting to an MRCC/RCC does not exist, a CRS or appropriate CES that receives a distress alert or distress call shall ensure that the information is routed as soon as possible to an MRCC/RCC. The receipt of a distress alert or a distress call on shore must be acknowledged as soon as possible by a CRS, or by an MRCC/RCC via a coast station or an appropriate CES. When making the acknowledgement by DSC, the CRS shall use the same frequency on which the DSC distress alert was received, address it to "All Ships" and include the identification of the vessel in distress.
3.	The CRS or MRCC/RCC that receives a distress alert or distress call shall also initiate the transmission of a shore-to-ship distress relay when the method of receipt warrants a broadcast to shipping or when the circumstances of the distress incident indicate that further help is necessary. Shore-to-ship distress relays must contain the identification of the vessel in distress, its position and all other information that might assist rescue operations.
4.	Because of the essential role of the shore-based authorities in managing distress incidents in the GMDSS, and the consequent need to avoid confusion with well-intentioned DSC acknowledgements by ship stations, acknowledgement of a DSC distress alert by use of DSC should normally only be made by an MRCC/RCC or CRS. **n.b. The first acknowledgement by DSC will cancel any further automated repetition of the DSC distress alert from the vessel in distress.**
5.	**Role of ship stations** If a vessel is in an area covered by one or more MRCC/RCCs or CRS and receives a DSC distress alert or a RT distress call from another vessel, they should not make any acknowledgement for a short interval in order to give the MRCC/RCC or CRS time to acknowledge the distress alert or distress call and then provide further instructions, usually by means of a shore-to-ship distress alert relay by DSC or distress call relay by RT.
6.	A vessel in receipt of a shore-to-ship distress alert relay or distress call relay should establish communication as directed and render such assistance as required and appropriate.
7.	A vessel acknowledging receipt of a distress alert sent from another vessel by DSC should: (a) In the first instance, acknowledge receipt of the distress alert by using RT on the distress and safety traffic frequency in the band used for the alert, taking into account any instructions which may be issued by a responding MRCC/RCC or CRS; (b) Only send an acknowledgement by DSC if instructed to do so by a MRCC/RCC or CRS, or in the case that: - No acknowledgement by DSC from a coast station has been observed; and - No other communication involving the vessel in distress has been observed; and - At least five minutes have elapsed and the distress alert by DSC has been repeated.
8.	If it becomes necessary for a vessel to send a DSC acknowledgement to another vessel, it shall be done on the same distress frequency on which the distress alert was received. The nearest coast station should then be informed by any suitable communication means.
9.	A vessel acknowledging receipt of a distress call sent from another vessel by RT should: (a) In the first instance, listen for any instructions which may be issued by a responding MRCC/RCC or CRS; (b) If the call is not acknowledged by an MRCC/RCC or CRS or another vessel within five minutes, acknowledge receipt to the vessel in distress and then use any means available to relay the distress call to an appropriate RCC, CRS or CES.
10.	The form of acknowledgement by RT of the receipt of a distress alert or a distress call from another vessel consists of: — The distress signal "MAYDAY"; — The NAME followed by the CALL SIGN or the MMSI or other identification of the station sending the distress message; — The words "THIS IS"; — The name and call sign or other identification of the station acknowledging receipt; — The word "RECEIVED"; — The distress signal "MAYDAY".
11.	Vessels operating in areas where reliable communications with a MRCC/RCC or CRS are not practicable and which receive a distress alert or call from a vessel which is, beyond doubt, in their vicinity, shall, as soon as possible and if appropriately equipped, acknowledge receipt to the vessel in distress and inform a coordinating MRCC/RCC directly or, if necessary, through a CRS or CES. However, in order to avoid making unnecessary or confusing responses to DSC distress alerts received on HF, vessels that may be at a considerable distance from the incident, shall not acknowledge but shall monitor the distress frequencies concerned and shall, if no acknowledgement by an MRCC/RCC or CRS is observed within five minutes, make a DSC distress alert relay, but only to an appropriate MRCC/RCC, CRS or CES.

7. Transmission of a distress alert relay or a distress call relay by a station not itself in distress

1.	The distress alert relay and the distress call relay shall contain the identification of the vessel, aircraft or other mobile unit in distress, its position and all other information which might facilitate rescue operations.
2.	**Role of Coast Radio Stations (CRS), Coast Earth Stations (CES) and Maritime Rescue Coordination Centres (MRCC/RCC)** A CRS or an RCC that receives a distress alert or distress call shall initiate the transmission of a shore-to-ship distress alert relay addressed, as appropriate, to all vessels, to a selected group of vessels, or to a specific vessel, by satellite and/or terrestrial means.
3.	**Role of ship stations** Vessels able to assist should acknowledge the shore-to-ship relay as instructed by an MRCC/RCC or CRS and, if appropriate, make an acknowledgement directly to the vessel in distress (see paragraph 6). Where an RCC or CRS is aware of the distress incident, there should be no need for a vessel to consider sending a distress alert relay by DSC or a distress relay call by RT on its own authority.
4.	**Distress Calls By Vessels on Behalf of Other Aircraft, Vessels or Persons** Only in the specific circumstances below should a vessel, that learns of a mobile unit in distress (e.g. by a radio call or by observation), consider initiating and transmitting a distress alert relay or a distress call relay on behalf of the mobile unit in distress: — On receiving a distress alert or distress call which is not acknowledged by an MRCC/RCC or CRS or another vessel within five minutes; *or* — On learning or observing that the mobile unit in distress is unable or incapable of participating in distress communications, and if the Master or other person responsible for the mobile unit not in distress considers that further help is necessary.
5.	A vessel is most likely to consider making a relay on its own authority when in receipt of a VHF RT distress call and message. This is because there may be no MRCC/RCC or CRS in range. Moreover, if there is no indication other than the distress call on VHF, then it may have originated from a non-SOLAS vessel with only basic communication facilities or, a larger vessel where all other means to make a distress call have failed or are unavailable. If no RCC or CRS or vessel is heard to acknowledge then, in addition to acknowledging receipt of the distress call (see paragraph 6), any means available should be used to make a distress relay call to the nearest MRCC/RCC or CRS. *Note:* Unless an administration has published information on the use of other frequencies such as 2182 kHz, distress calls and messages using RT should be sent on the frequency 156·8 MHz (VHF Ch 16) in order to maximise the likelihood of reception.
6.	The distress relay on behalf of a mobile unit in distress shall be sent in a form appropriate to the circumstances, using either a distress call relay by RT, an individually addressed distress alert relay by DSC, or a distress priority (level 3) message through a SES. The priorities for a vessel making a distress alert relay or a distress call relay are to ensure that an appropriate MRCC/RCC or CRS is informed of any distress communications previously exchanged and to indicate clearly that it is not itself in distress.
7.	When it is known that an aural watch is being maintained on shore and reliable ship-to-shore communications can be established by RT, the preferred course of action is to send distress call relay by RT, addressed to the relevant MRCC/RCC or CRS on the appropriate frequency. The distress relay call sent by RT consists of: — The distress signal "MAYDAY RELAY" (spoken 3 times); — ALL STATIONS or coast station name, as appropriate (spoken 3 times); — The words "THIS IS" — The name of the relaying station (spoken 3 times); — The call sign or other identification of the relaying station; — The MMSI e.g. "this is the MMSI number" (if the initial alert has been sent by DSC) of the relaying station (the vessel not in distress); — Complete repetition of the ORIGINAL DISTRESS ALERT INFORMATION OR DISTRESS MESSAGE. *Note:* If the station in distress could not be identified, and you therefore have to originate the distress message as well, then you must not use the name of your own station, i.e. you would say 'Unidentified Trawler' or 'Unidentified Helicopter'.
8.	When no aural watch is being maintained on shore, or there are other difficulties in establishing reliable ship-to-shore communications by RT, an appropriate RCC or CRS may be contacted by sending an individual distress alert relay by DSC, addressed solely to that station and using the appropriate call formats. FOR FULL DETAILS ON DSC PROCEDURES SEE SECTION 5. *Note:* In no circumstances, may a vessel transmit a DSC distress alert relay addressed to "All Ships" on the VHF or MF distress frequencies following receipt of a DSC distress alert sent by another vessel.
9.	In the event of continued failure to contact an RCC or CRS directly, it may be appropriate to send a distress call relay by RT addressed to all vessels, or to all vessels in a certain geographical area.

Continued on next page

8. Cancellation of an inadvertent distress transmission

1.	In the event that a distress alert or distress call is sent inadvertently, the station responsible must immediately cancel the distress transmission.
2.	An inadvertent distress alert sent by DSC must be cancelled by DSC using the self-cancellation procedure (essentially acknowledging one's own alert) as set out in Recommendation ITU-RM.493, followed upon RT with a voice cancellation call. Likewise, an inadvertent distress call sent by RT must be cancelled by means of a voice call.
3.	The voice cancellation call must be sent on the RT distress and safety frequency in the same band on which the distress transmission was sent. Note that any MMSI number, referred to in the distress cancellation voice message, must be that of the DSC device that transmitted the alert. This is because some DSC devices use a serial number MMSI that is not related to the parent vessel MMSI, using the following procedure: — The call "ALL STATIONS" *(spoken 3 times)*; — The words "THIS IS"; — The NAME of the vessel *(spoken 3 times)*; — The CALL SIGN and MMSI or other identification; — PLEASE CANCEL MY DISTRESS ALERT OF *(time in UTC)*.
4.	Then monitor the same band on which the inadvertent distress transmission was sent and respond to any communications concerning that distress transmission as appropriate.
5.	If the inadvertent distress transmission was made in several bands then the above procedure must be repeated for all the bands in which the inadvertent transmission was made.

9. Distress/SAR communications

1.	Distress communications indicate that a vessel, aircraft or person is in distress and therefore in grave and imminent danger and requires immediate assistance. Distress traffic consists of all messages relating to SAR communications and on-scene communications. The essential common elements of these communications, irrespective of whether DSC or RT distress procedures were used to alert other stations, are summarised below.
2.	The control of traffic is initially the responsibility of the station in distress but is usually transferred, when appropriate, to a properly equipped station such as an MRCC/RCC (this is normally the MRCC/RCC designated in the GMDSS Master Plan) or CRS. A vessel in receipt of a shore-to-ship distress alert should establish communication as directed and render such assistance as required and appropriate.
3.	**Subsequent communications:** Subsequent communications between the vessel in distress, assisting vessels and coordinating MRCC/RCC may be directly to an MRCC/RCC or, where this is not available, via a CRS, the vessel in distress or, for example, during a lengthy or complex SAR operation by an On-Scene Coordinator (OSC). All stations will observe the procedures for maintaining radio discipline and organising SAR operations set out in the ITU Radio Regulations and the IMO/ICAO International Aeronautical and Maritime Search and Rescue (IAMSAR)Manual throughout the duration of the distress incident. The spoken distress signal "MAYDAY" should precede all distress/SAR communications using RT. Every vessel which acknowledges receipt of a distress message shall comply with Regulation 10 of SOLAS Chapter V, as amplified by the IAMSAR Manual. The Master of a vessel proceeding to the scene of a distress incident shall transmit, as soon as possible, the following information: — MAYDAY — ALL STATIONS — NAME, call sign — Own vessel's current position, course and speed — ETA at the distress position *Note:* Before transmission, the operator must ensure that no interference can be caused to stations that are in a better position to render assistance to the station in distress. The transmitting vessel's MMSI number should be included in the voice message so that other stations can link that with the previously received DSC signal.
4.	**On-scene coordination** In a distress or SAR situation it may be necessary for one of the participating stations to be assigned or to assume the role of On-Scene Coordinator(OSC). If specialised SAR units (lifeboats, aircraft or warships) are proceeding or at the scene then one of those units may be assigned the role of On Scene Coordinator (OSC) if so directed by the coordinating MRCC/RCC. If there is no coordinating RCC then a suitable vessel might need to assume the role of OSC to ensure a well-coordinated response by assisting vessels. The duties of the OSC are many and varied; vessel Masters, mates and radio operators should therefore familiarise themselves with the IAMSAR Manual Volume III.

Continued overleaf

5.	**On-scene communications** (a) On-scene communications are those between the mobile unit in distress and assisting mobile units, and between the mobile units and the unit coordinating SAR operations. (b) The control of on-scene communications is the responsibility of the MRCC/RCC, or may be delegated to the OSC if one is appointed; and these units will nominate in discussion with the coordinating MRCC/RCC, the frequencies to be used. Simplex transmissions shall be used so that all on-scene mobile stations may share relevant information concerning the distress incident. The preferred frequencies in RT for on-scene communications are VHF Ch 16 (156·8 MHz) and, on MF, 2182 kHz, but other frequencies may be designated. (c) Vessel stations may also need to communicate with aircraft stations for distress and safety purposes. Both VHF Ch 16 (156·8 MHz) and VHF Ch 06 (156·3 MHz) may be used for on-scene communications between vessels and SAR aircraft. If the appropriate aeronautical VHF band equipment is available, the frequencies 121·5 MHz and 123·1 MHz may also be used in mode of emission A3E; the former for the purposes of distress and urgency only, the latter for SAR operations between aircraft and ships. Note that not all aircraft have marine band communications. (d) During distress working, the MRCC/RCC coordinating distress traffic, the OSC, MRCC/RCC or CRS involved may impose silence on any interfering stations by using the term: "SEELONCE MAYDAY"
6.	**End of Distress Traffic** (a) Until they receive the message indicating that normal working may be resumed, all stations which are aware of the distress traffic, and which are not taking part in it and which are not in distress, are forbidden to transmit on the frequencies on which the distress traffic is taking place. (b) Vessels which, while following distress traffic, are able to continue normal service under these conditions, may do so when the distress traffic is well established provided that, noting (a) above, they do not interfere with distress traffic. (c When distress traffic has ceased on frequencies which have been used for distress traffic, the MRCC/RCC coordinating a SAR operation shall initiate a message for transmission on these frequencies indicating that distress traffic has finished, as follows: — The distress signal "MAYDAY"; — The call "ALL STATIONS" (spoken 3 times); — The words "THIS IS"; — The name of the station sending that message (spoken 3 times) ; — The call sign or other identification of the station sending that message; — The time of handing in the message; — The MMSI (if the initial alert has been sent by DSC), the name and the call sign of the mobile station which was in distress; — The words "SEELONCE FEENEE" (pronounced as the French phrase "silence fini").

10. Urgency and Safety communications

1.	**Urgency and Safety communications relate to:** - Navigational and meteorological warnings; - Ship-to-ship safety of navigation; - Ship reporting services; - Support communications for SAR operations; - Medical advice and transports; - Other urgent or safety messages; - Navigation, movements and needs of vessels; - Weather observation messages (OBS) destined for an official meteorological service.
2.	**Urgency communications** specifically concern the safety of a vessel, aircraft, vehicle or person and have priority over all other communications, except distress.
3.	**Safety communications** concern important meteorological or navigational information and have priority over all other communications, except distress and urgency.

Continued on next page

4.	**Urgency and Safety Procedures.**

(a) The content of urgency and safety messages is usually best suited for transmission by voice, although text messages using narrow-band direct-printing (NBDP - i.e. telex) and voice/data messages over Inmarsat satellites can also be used. Because urgency and safety messages are often relatively lengthy, compared to distress messages, care needs to be taken to avoid overloading distress and safety traffic frequencies. Working channels should therefore be used where appropriate.

(b) Coast stations and vessels equipped to use DSC should also make an announcement by DSC before proceeding with the urgency/safety communications using RT. The DSC distress and safety calling frequencies listed in TABLE 1 above may be used by coast stations and ship stations to announce the impending transmission of urgency, vital navigational or safety messages by RT. The MF and VHF bands are the two most likely to be used for urgency and safety communication because such messages will tend to be of interest to a limited geographical area and for a limited duration. At VHF, the DSC distress and safety frequency 156·525 MHz/VHF Ch 70 is used to announce urgency or safety transmissions and, at MF, the DSC distress and safety frequency 2187·5 kHz is used.

(c) When announcing urgency and safety transmissions using DSC, care should be taken to avoid an excessive amount of DSC transmissions that could overload the DSC distress and safety calling frequencies or distract personnel on the bridge. In particular, safety messages transmitted by shore stations in accordance with a predefined timetable should not be announced by DSC techniques.

(d) Urgency or safety announcements by DSC may only be addressed either to "All Ships" or to individual stations and will denote which frequency is to be used to send the subsequent voice or NBDP transmission. An urgency or safety announcement by DSC from a shore station may also be directed to a group of vessels or to vessels in a defined geographical area. Vessels not equipped for DSC operations may make the initial urgency or safety call, by voice, on the frequency 156·8 MHz (VHF Ch 16). Coast stations or vessels outside VHF range will not receive the announcement.

(e) The urgency or safety voice transmission consists of a call sent on the appropriate RT distress and safety traffic frequency, for example, VHF Ch 16 or MF 2182 kHz, followed by the message on the same frequency or, when appropriate, on an RT working frequency in the same band as used for the announcement. In order to avoid obstructing more important communications, shore stations routinely use an appropriate RT working channel for long safety messages and, when circumstances require, have discretion on whether to continue using the RT distress and safety traffic frequency for urgency messages or to switch to a working channel.

(f) Voice transmissions of urgency calls and messages are preceded by the urgency signal "PAN PAN", spoken 3 times. The urgency signal "PAN PAN" and the urgency call format used for an announcement by DSC indicate that a very important message is to follow concerning the safety of a mobile unit or a person. However, urgency communications used in support of SAR operations do not need to be preceded by the urgency signal.

(g) Likewise, voice transmissions of safety calls and messages are preceded by the safety signal "SÉCURITÉ" spoken 3 times. The safety signal "SÉCURITÉ" and the safety call format used for an announcement by DSC indicate that an important meteorological or Navigational Warning is about to follow. |
| 5. | **Procedures for urgency transmissions.** Urgency transmissions consist of an initial voice call and a subsequent voice message, both identified as such by the urgency signal "PAN PAN". Urgency calls are normally preceded by sending a DSC announcement, using the DSC urgency call format.

(a) The urgency call and message should be transmitted on the appropriate RT distress and safety traffic frequency in the same band as the DSC announcement. However, in the case of a long message, a medical call or in an area of heavy traffic when the message is being repeated, then the urgency message should be sent on a working channel. The transmitting vessel's MMSI number should be included in the voice urgency message so that other stations can link the broadcast with the previously received DSC signal.

Note: Only VHF Ch 16, or 2182 kHz on MF in those areas around the world where the shore based authorities have declared its continued use, should be used for RT urgency calls because no other RT distress and safety frequencies will now be listened to on a continuous basis.

(b) An example of an urgency message in the required standard format shown below:

PAN PAN - PAN PAN - PAN PAN
ALL STATIONS – ALL STATIONS – ALL STATIONS
THIS IS NONSUCH - NONSUCH - NONSUCH
(MMSI NUMBER 123456789)
ONE ZERO MILES WEST OF SKERRIES
LOST PROPELLER DRIFTING WEST SOUTH WEST AT THREE KNOTS
REQUIRE TOW URGENTLY
OVER |

Continued overleaf

7.

Medical Advice.

(a) Many MRCC/RCCs or CRS around the world provide a medical advice service.

(b) Medical advice is classified as an urgent communication. Therefore the URGENCY category and call format should be used for a DSC announcement, and the urgency signal "PAN PAN" (spoken 3 times) should be used to introduce the associated call and message.

(c) Requests for medical advice should be addressed to the nearest MRCC/RCC or coast station using the published preamble shown in the ITU List of Coast Stations and Special Service Stations.

(d) The medical message should contain the following information:
— VESSEL'S NAME / CALL SIGN AND NATIONALITY
— POSITION
— NEXT or NEAREST PORT with ETA
— PATIENT DETAILS (i.e., name, age, sex, medical history, etc.)
— PATIENT SYMPTOMS and advice REQUIRED
— MEDICATION CARRIED ON BOARD

Note: The International Code of Signals contains medical (3 letter) codes which, when used, should be preceded by the word INTERCO. Where possible, patient name and personal details should preferably be passed over a non-broadcast communications system e.g. mobile/cell phone or satellite telephone.

(e) As part of the services provided ancillary to the GMDSS, all Inmarsat LES will provide a Medical Advice and Medical Assistance service using the 2 digit codes 32 and 38 respectively. In the UK SAR Region all requests for Medical Advice or Medical Assistance should be made to the nearest HM Coastguard MRCC who will link the caller to a specialist doctor free of charge.

(f) As noted in Recommendation ITU-T D90 (see the ITU Manual for Use by the Maritime Mobile and Maritime Mobile Satellite Services), no charge is raised against the originating maritime mobile station, for communications using the maritime mobile service which relate to medical advice provided that:

They are exchanged directly (i.e. without the involvement of any other coast station) between mobile stations and land stations shown in the ITU List of Coast Stations and Special Service Stations as providing such a service, or land stations which offer the service;

and

They are addressed in accordance with the conditions published in the ITU List of Coast Station and Special Service Stations, or as specified by the satellite service operator.

(g) Any land station and landline charges for medical advice communications will be billed to the appropriate shore authority.

Continued on next page

8.	**Medical transports.** (a) Distinctive signals may be used by medical units or transports for communications relating to persons protected in time of war. The term "medical transports", as defined by the Geneva Conventions and Additional Protocols, 12th August 1949, refers to any means of transportation by land, sea or air used to assist the wounded, the sick and the shipwrecked. Neutral vessels should provide such assistance when requested by one or other of warring parties and are afforded protection from any hostile action. (b) The announcement and identification of "medical transports" are classified as urgent communications and must follow the following procedures: (i) **Announcement of a medical transport:** When using DSC, the announcement of a medical transport must be broadcast on the appropriate DSC distress and safety frequencies either to "all stations", on VHF, or to a specified geographical area on MF/HF. The DSC call format used for DSC announcements must also indicate "Medical transport", as shown in the example below: — Format Specifier: "ALL SHIPS" — Category: "URGENCY" — Telecommand: "MEDICAL TRANSPORT" Voice calls and messages involving medical transports must be preceded by the RT urgency signal "PAN PAN" (spoken 3 times) and the initial urgency call must be followed immediately by the addition of the single word MAY-DEE-CAL (pronounced as in French "médical"). Medical transports may use one or more of the distress and safety traffic frequencies for the purpose of self-identification and to establish communications. However, as soon as practicable, communications should be transferred to an appropriate working frequency. (ii) **Identification of a medical transport:** The above signals indicate that the message which follows concerns a protected medical transport. The subsequent voice message serves to identify the medical transports concerned and must be preceded by the urgency signal "PAN PAN" and must convey the following information: — Call sign, MMSI and other means of identification — Position — Number and type of units — Intended route — Estimated time en route and of departure and arrival, as appropriate — Any other information, such as flight altitude, radio frequencies guarded, languages used and secondary surveillance radar modes and codes *Note:* In order to facilitate communications, one or more of the parties to a conflict may designate frequencies to be used for such communications.
9.	**Procedures for safety transmissions.** Safety transmissions consist of an initial voice call and a subsequent voice message, both identified as such by the safety signal "SÉCURITÉ". Safety calls may be preceded by sending a DSC announcement, using the DSC safety call format. However, in order to avoid overloading the DSC distress and safety frequencies or causing excessive receiver alarms on the bridge, CRS/MRCCs do not use DSC to announce safety transmissions that take place at scheduled times. (a) The safety call should be transmitted on the appropriate RT distress and safety traffic frequency (which would be in the same band as the DSC announcement, if made). The safety message may also continue on the same frequency but, preferably, should be sent on a working frequency, in which case a suitable indication to this effect shall be included on the DSC announcement or made at the end of the voice safety call. In particular, coast stations should always endeavour to send the message on a working channel in the same band as the initial safety call or DSC announcement. *Note:* If an announcement using DSC is used it should normally be sent on VHF Ch 70. Normally, VHF Ch 16 will be used for voice safety calls. VHF Ch13, the inter ship navigation safety channel, may be used instead of VHF Ch 16 for Navigational Warnings. Other channels may also be designated by local coastguard organisations for inshore warnings. The frequency 2182 kHz may also be used for safety calls and messages in those areas around the world where the shore based authorities have declared its continued use. The transmitting vessel's MMSI number should be included in the voice safety message so that other stations can link it with the previously received DSC signal. (b) An example of a safety message in the required standard format is shown below: *SÉCURITÉ - SÉCURITÉ - SÉCURITÉ* *ALL STATIONS - ALL STATIONS - ALL STATIONS* *THIS IS NONSUCH, NONSUCH, NONSUCH* *MMSI NUMBER 123456789* *LARGE RED CONTAINER SPOTTED AT 1030 UTC* *IN POSITION 52.02 NORTH 003.36 WEST* *VESSELS KEEP SHARP LOOKOUT AND REPORT* *OUT*

Continued overleaf

10.	**Transmission of Urgency and Safety Messages.** To summarise, the two stages in the transmission of Urgency and Safety Messages proceeds in the following stages: (a) Announcement of Urgency and Safety Messages When using DSC to announce broadcasts of Urgency or Safety Messages, the call format of the DSC announcement takes the following form: — Format Specifier: "ALL SHIPS" or the "MMSI" of the intended receiving station or group of stations — Category: "URGENCY" or "SAFETY" — Self Identification: "MMSI" of the transmitting station — Frequency: The CHANNEL to be used for transmission of the subsequent message — Subsequent Communications: Transmission mode for the message etc. - RT is the default mode. (b) The urgency or safety call, using RT, is then broadcast on the appropriate distress and safety traffic frequency in the following standard format, commencing with the urgency or safety signal, as appropriate: — The urgency signal "PAN-PAN" or the safety signal "SÉCURITÉ" (spoken 3 times) — The call "ALL STATIONS" or list of individually NAMED STATIONS (spoken 3 times) — The words "THIS IS" — The NAME of the station transmitting the call (spoken 3 times); — The CALL SIGN and any other IDENTIFICATION — The MMSI (if the initial announcement has been sent by DSC) Followed, where appropriate, by details of the radio channel to be used for the following message, e.g., — LISTEN FOR NAVIGATIONAL WARNING ON VHF CHANNEL 13 (c) The urgency or safety message is then broadcast, using RT, on the selected operating frequency in the following standard format, commencing with the urgency or safety signal, as appropriate: — The urgency signal "PAN PAN" or the safety signal "SÉCURITÉ" (spoken 3 times) — The call "ALL STATIONS" or list of individually NAMED STATIONS (spoken 3 times) — The words "THIS IS" — The NAME of the station transmitting the message (spoken 3 times) — The CALL SIGN and any other IDENTIFICATION — The MMSI (if the initial announcement has been sent by DSC) — [the text of the urgency or safety message]
11.	**Reception of Urgency and Safety Messages.** (a) Following receipt of a DSC Urgency or Safety call announcing a message addressed to "All Stations", the frequency or channel indicated for the message should be monitored until further information is received. If, at the end of the five-minute monitoring period, no Urgency Message has been received, a coast station should, if possible, be notified of the missing message. Thereafter, normal working may be resumed. (b) DSC urgency/safety "All Ships" announcements or RT calls to "All Stations" should NOT be acknowledged.
12.	**Termination of urgency traffic.** When an Urgency Message has been broadcast to more than one station, and once no further action is required, then the station responsible should terminate communications in respect of the event concerned by sending an "urgency cancellation" message using the format below: — The urgency signal "PAN PAN" (spoken 3 times); — The call "ALL STATIONS" (spoken 3 times); — The words "THIS IS"; — The NAME of the station transmitting the urgency message (spoken 3 times); — The CALL SIGN or any other identification; — The MMSI (if the initial announcement has been sent by DSC); — "PLEASE CANCEL URGENCY MESSAGE OF (time in UTC).

11. SAR arrangements in the United Kingdom

Search and Rescue operations are coordinated in the UK Search and Rescue Region (UK SRR) by Her Majesty's Coastguard through a network of Rescue Coordination Centres (RCC) which provide RCC and other maritime safety functions. A number of organisations provide resources and services to HM Coastguard to assist in delivery of maritime SAR and emergency response.

HM Coastguard (HMCG)

1.	HMCG is the authority responsible for initiating and coordinating all civil aeronautical and maritime SAR for aircraft and vessels and persons in need of assistance in the UK Maritime SRR. This includes coastal sea areas and the cliffs and shoreline of the United Kingdom. The UK Maritime SRR corresponds, where possible, with the International Civil Aviation Organization (ICAO) UK SRR and is bounded by latitudes 45°N and 61°N, by longitude 30°W and by the adjacent European SRRs.
2.	SAR services which HMCG can call upon in the UK SRR comprise of "declared" facilities which are available at short notice, including Coastguard rescue teams, helicopters and aircraft, lifeboats and hovercraft as well as additional facilities which include vessels which happen to be available and respond at the time.

Continued on next page

3.	The UK SAR coordination organisation is based upon a constantly staffed communications watch system at a number of RCCs located around the UK. Additionally, MRSC London based close to the Thames Barrier, covers the River Thames as far as Teddington.
4	HMCG is responsible for maintaining: (a) A loudspeaker watch at all times on 156·8 MHz (the VHF Distress, Urgency, Safety and Calling Frequency (VHF Ch16)). Coverage of the UK coastal waters is provided up to a range of at least 30 nautical miles offshore. (b) An electronic radio watch on VHF DSC Ch 70 around the whole of the UK coastline. (c) An electronic radio watch on MF DSC on 2187·5 kHz at selected stations. *Note:* The UK does not have a shore station for HF DSC. HF DSC alerts will be forward to the UK by the appropriate receiving HF DSC coast station.

Medical Advice Services

1.	Requests for medical advice from Masters and skippers of vessels at sea in the UK SRR should be made to the nearest RCC or callsign "UK Coastguard". On receiving a call, the operator will arrange a radio telephone call with the appropriate medical authorities. HMCG is guided by the advice of the doctor and is bound by that decision. There is no charge for this service. *Note*: Use of the Telemedical Advice Service (TMAS) in UK waters must be made through a Rescue Coordination Centre (RCC) and NOT direct to a hospital. To do so will introduce delay in the event of evacuation.
2.	Although advice should always precede assistance, a request for medical assistance sometimes requires immediate assessment and response without qualified medical advice. However, after alerting the appropriate service, the RCC will always seek medical advice. Once medical advice has been received, HMCG will make the necessary arrangements for the transportation of the person to shore by the most suitable means and/or arrange for a doctor to be transported to the vessel. Arrangements will also be made with local medical or ambulance services to provide appropriate assistance when the patient is landed.

Maritime Safety Information (MSI)

1.	HMCG is responsible for the distribution and transmission of MSI messages on the NAVTEX service. This is supplemented by set broadcast schedules on VHF and MF RT.
2.	Meteorological Services include gale warnings, sea area forecasts, inshore waters forecasts, 5 day extended outlooks and weather reports from coastal stations.
3.	Navigational Warnings include NAVAREA long range warnings which contain information concerning principal shipping routes which are necessary for the mariner to know before entering coastal waters, such as failure of and changes to major navigational aids, newly discovered wrecks or natural hazards in or near main shipping lanes and areas where SAR, anti-pollution operations, cable laying and other underwater activities are taking place. Navigational Warnings also include WZ Coastal Warnings which contain information similar to NAVAREA warnings but designed to assist the mariner in coastal navigation up to the entrance of ports. Both NAVAREA and WZ Navigational Warnings are transmitted by NAVTEX, but only WZ Navigational Warnings are broadcast by VHF and MF RT on receipt, thereafter, twice daily.
4.	Other information provided in MSI broadcasts may include Negative Surge Warnings, SUBFACTS and GUNFACTS (information relating to submarine and gunnery activity, in selected areas), ice warnings, and interruption to electronic navigational aids.
5.	MRCC Dover, which is also the station responsible for the Channel Navigation Information Service (CNIS), operates a radar surveillance system and maintains a constant liaison with its French counterpart at Cap Gris-Nez in monitoring the traffic flow through the Dover Strait. Regular broadcasts are made at 40 minutes past each hour on VHF Ch 11, with additional broadcasts in poor visibility or as circumstances dictate. CNIS operates an aircraft to identify vessels which appear not to be complying with the International Regulations for Preventing Collisions at Sea, 1972 (as amended). All its facilities are available for SAR operations or other maritime emergencies
6.	CALDOVREP is a mandatory vessel reporting system under SOLAS Regulation V/11 for the Dover Strait TSS and is operated jointly by the UK and France with vessels reporting to either MRCC Dover or CROSS Gris-Nez MRCC (CROSS standing for Centre Régional Opérationnel de Surveillance et de Sauvetage). This enables Dover and Gris-Nez to monitor shipping movements and provide improved advice and information about navigational hazards and weather conditions. Vessels operating the Ship Movement Reporting System (MAREP) should report to stations as shown in ALRS Volume 6(1) (NP286(1)).
7.	Radio and telephone traffic to and from RCCs is recorded for the purposes of public safety, preventing crime and to maintain operational standards of HMCG.

Continued overleaf

8.	Vessels may also make voluntary Position and Intended Movement (PIM) reports to MRCCs Falmouth, Shetland and Stornoway when on passage through their areas of responsibility.
9.	Inmarsat alerts and maritime and coastal EPIRB/PLB/ELT alerts on 406·0 - 406·1 MHz from within the UK SRR, and UK registered satellite distress beacons activated at sea outside the UK SRR, are received and processed at the UK Mission Control Centre (UK MCC).

Coastguard Rescue Service

The Coastguard Rescue Service is a declared facility operated by HMCG. It provides a national coastal network of professional Coastguard Rescue Teams (CRTs) made up of volunteers and managed by full time staff. CRTs are available 24 hours all year round for SAR purposes and deployable throughout the mainland and islands in the UK SRR, operating within the littoral area of the coast and certain designated inland waterways. All CRTs are SAR teams with training and equipment to deliver SAR operations, casualty care (first aid, casualty packaging, evacuation, rescue stretchers), land search, water safety and rescue. Where required, CRTs are equipped with additional technical rescue equipment to enable them to perform rope, mud and flood rescue. CRTs are trained, skilled and equipped to interact with all other UK SAR assets and will broadly support wider functions of HMCG in pollution response, vessel traffic management, maritime safety, maritime security, and emergency & disaster management.

SAR Helicopters

A number of SAR helicopters are available from bases around the UK. These helicopters normally have a maximum radius of action of 200 to 250 nautical miles and are available at 15 minutes readiness by day and 45 minutes by night. SAR rear crew are trained to a high level of first aid proficiency - often to paramedic level. The operating ranges of helicopters can be considerably increased by refueling at forward sites, from suitable vessels or offshore installations. These aircraft are tasked by the Joint Rescue Coordination Centre (JRCC UK). Some other military aircraft can also be utilised for SAR operations. JRCC UK is responsible for the management of all SAR tasked aircraft within the UKSRR (civilian and military). If necessary, JRCC UK will task an available aircraft as Aircraft Co-ordinator (ACO) for the management of the flight safety of airborne rescue operations. The ACO works in concert with the On Scene Coordinator (if one is appointed).

Fixed Wing Air Assets

Fixed wing assets are based at Doncaster Sheffield Airport and are tasked through the JRCC UK. These aircraft normally have a 6-hour endurance with and effective range of up to 1500 nautical miles (limited to 300 nautical miles from a forward operating base if required) and will be airborne at 45 minutes by day and 60 minutes at night. The aircraft are all weather capable and are fitted with a comprehensive communications suite and are capable of dropping small stores such as beacons or flares.

UK COSPAS/SARSAT Mission Control Centre

The United Kingdom Mission Control Centre (UK MCC) is co-located at the JRCC UK. In addition to analysing, evaluating, advising and transferring Cospas-Sarsat satellite distress-alert traffic to its three SAR Points of Contact (SPOC) (JRCC Long Range SAR, Police Services and Dublin MRCC), the UK MCC staff distributes globally valid 406 MHz distress-alert traffic received from its satellite tracking station in Southern England and/or from other MCCs around the world. The UK MCC staff also processes 121·5 and 243 MHz reports derived from terrestrial auto-triangulation systems and from high-flying aircraft, both initially coordinated and passed to the UK MCC by Distress and Diversion Cells at Air Traffic Control Centres (ATCC). The UK MCC staff correlates such information with that received from Cospas-Sarsat satellites and updates its SPOCs accordingly.

Air Traffic Control Centres (ATCC)

ATCCs are often the first to receive information about aircraft in distress. All commercial and many private aircraft are able to communicate with these centres by radio and, in certain circumstances, are under an obligation to do so. They may be requested to assist in the search for a casualty at sea; by keeping a look-out along or near their normal routes, by reporting the position of the casualty if they should find it and, if possible, by guiding vessels to the rescue. High-flying commercial and military aircraft routinely monitor selected aeronautical distress frequencies and the military Distress and Diversion Cells located at the Scottish and London Air Traffic Control Centres forward to the UK MCC any 121·5 and 243 MHz transmissions so reported. The Distress and Diversion Cell separately monitors aeronautical distress transmissions via a ground-based network of transmitting and receiving stations around the UK. They forward information to the UK MCC/JRCC UK as appropriate.

Rescue Boats - The Royal National Lifeboat Institution (RNLI)

The RNLI is a private charitable organisation supported entirely by voluntary contributions. The Institution operates a fleet of dedicated SAR surface craft around the coast of the UK, Ireland, the Isle of Man and the Channel Islands. The service is available 24 hours, all year round and is provided primarily by highly trained volunteer crews manning All-Weather Lifeboats (ALBs), inshore Lifeboats (ILBs) and inshore hovercraft. RNLI lifeboats are requested to launch by the coordinating RCC.

Every ALB is equipped with:

- Marine band VHF/FM RT and DSC equipment;
- Marine band MF RT and DSC equipment;
- HF RT and DSC equipment;
- VHF direction finding equipment capable of detecting and homing to marine VHF FM and 121·5 MHz for EPIRB, Emergency Locator Transmitters (ELT) and PLB transmissions;
- Radar, capable of activating and detecting SART transponders. S Automatic Identification System (AIS).

While on service these boats monitor all GMDSS DSC emergency frequencies appropriate to Sea Areas A1 and A2. Inshore lifeboats and hovercraft are fitted with marine band VHF/FM RT only and maintain a listening watch on VHF Ch 16.

Other Volunteer Lifeboat Services

Other voluntarily funded rescue boats and lifeboats are operated in various locations around the UK. The types and capabilities of these boats vary and will be tasked to SAR incidents on the request of the relevant RCC. Radius of action of such craft varies from near coastal to up to 50+ nautical miles offshore.

Lloyd's and tug brokers

Information about a casualty is sent by HMCG to a number of authorities and organisations including Lloyd's and tug brokers. Lloyd's List provides an overview of global casualty reports to subscribers. Tug brokers maintain an overview of tugs around the coasts of the UK and Europe and will advise HMCG of tug availability on request.

12. SAR Operations in the UK SRR

The SAR action taken when a distress or urgency incident occurs or is imminent depends on whether a vessel or aircraft is involved, its position and the circumstances.

1.	**Marine Casualties within UK SRR** (a) **Vessels distant from the UK coast:** If a vessel in distress transmits a distress alert or call, other vessels receiving the alert must proceed to their assistance. UK RCCs on hearing or receiving the distress alert will re-broadcast the distress message by all appropriate means, both terrestrial and satellite, to alert all shipping in the area and to Lloyd's. Immediate SAR action will be taken and, depending on the location and distance offshore, assistance may be requested from services and organisations which can supply SAR helicopters, aircraft or lifeboats (rescue boats). Mutual assistance from ships and vessels at sea may also be requested, wherever possible and/or appropriate, particularly for incidents outside the range of SAR aircraft and rescue boats. The RCC will coordinate SAR action until a successful conclusion is reached, or until the operation is called off, keeping all participants, including foreign SAR authorities, where necessary, informed. (b) **Vessels and Incidents close to and on the UK coast and shoreline:** HMCG may be informed of an actual or imminent distress situation in inshore waters or on the coast, by radio, satellite beacon alert, flare reports or 999 (or 112) emergency telephone call. In every case, the RCC receiving the initial distress call or report, automatically becomes the coordinating station for the incident, and takes action as in sub-paragraph (a) above, including the possibility of deploying the Coastguard Rescue Service and other inshore or coastal SAR assets. (c) **SAR co-operation plans:** Under Regulation 7 of the Merchant Shipping (Safety of Navigation) Regulations 2002, a plan for co-operation with the appropriate SAR Services must be drawn up and carried by all passenger vessels using UK waters. The plan must be agreed with the SAR Services relevant to the vessel's area of operation. Full details are available on the GOV.UK website: https://www.gov.uk/government/publications/international-sar-co-operation-plans-index. (d) In the UK a number of Off shore Renewable Energy Installations (OREI) have been constructed or are planned. These installations cover, in some cases many square miles of sea space. The emergency response implications of such installations have been assessed and processes and procedures are in place to respond to persons in distress, either on the installations or on vessels or in the water within or around them. Each OREI is required to have an Emergency Response Cooperation Plan (ERCoP) agreed with HM Coastguard. This document provides information of immediate operational use to the RCC coordinating the rescue operations and the owner/operator of the ORIE to ensure rapid, effective and cooperative response to emergencies.
2.	**Aircraft Casualties** In the case of an aircraft casualty at sea, the first indication that an aircraft is in trouble may be received by an Air Traffic Service Unit (ATSU) which will pass the information to the UK ARCC. The latter is responsible for the tasking and despatch of rescue aircraft and helicopters, and if it is suspected or known that the distressed aircraft is over the sea, will notify the appropriate RCC (if it is thought that Maritime SAR assets may be able to assist and a broadcast message to shipping may well be beneficial) and/or the appropriate Royal Navy authority. Coordination of Maritime SAR incidents arising from aviation accidents rests with the Rescue Authority, that initiates the response unit, until it is decided that the other is better placed to continue the response. However, there may be no regular communication between an aircraft and an ATSU, particularly for light aircraft who may fly outside of 'controlled' airspace and so aircraft may go missing over the sea with little clue as to their precise emergency location. In these situations, the UK JRCC and relevant RCCs (and foreign MRCCs) may have to conduct investigations similar to that for overdue vessels.

13. Guidance to Masters of Vessels

1.	Guidance to Masters on the assistance to be given during emergencies at sea is contained in the IAMSAR Manual obtainable from the International Maritime Organization, 4 Albert Embankment, London SE1 7SR. The carriage of the IAMSAR Manual Volume III aboard all SOLAS vessels became mandatory on 1 January 2004.
2.	There will be occasions when, perhaps due to mechanical, hull or other defect, a Master may have cause for concern for the ultimate safety of his vessel but which concern at the time does not, in the Master's judgement, require distress or urgency procedures. It would, in these circumstances, nevertheless be prudent for the Master to inform HMCG (or the appropriate SAR authority if outside the UKSRR) of the problem so that, should the situation subsequently deteriorate to distress or urgency, time is not lost ashore in assessing the situation and preparing or despatching the necessary assistance. In such cases a Defect Report (DEFREP) is to be sent to the nearest Coastguard Co-ordination Centre (see details on MAREP in ALRS Volume 6(1) (NP286(1))).
3.	Masters should not hesitate to use the urgency signal in situations where the imminence of danger to the vessel cannot be reliably established.

STATUTORY DUTIES OF MASTERS OF VESSELS

14. Duty of vessel to assist the other in case of collision

Merchant Shipping Act, 1995, Section 92 states:

1.	In every case of collision between two vessels, it shall be the duty of the Master of each vessel, if and so far as he can do so without danger to his own vessel, crew and passengers (if any). (a) To render to the other vessel, its Master, crew and passengers (if any) such assistance as may be practicable, and may be necessary to save them from any danger caused by the collision, and to stay by the other vessel until he has ascertained that it has no need of further assistance; and: (b) To give to the Master of the other vessel the name of his own vessel and also the names of the ports from which it comes and to which it is bound.
2.	The duties imposed on the Master of a vessel by subsection (1) above apply to the Masters of UK vessels and to the Masters of foreign vessels when in UK waters.
3.	The failure of the Master of a vessel to comply with the provisions of this section shall not raise any presumption of law that the collision was caused by his wrongful act, neglect, or default.

4.	If the Master fails without reasonable excuse to comply with this section, he shall
	
	(a) In the case of a failure to comply with subsection (1)(a) above, be liable
	    (i) On summary conviction, to a fine not exceeding £50,000 or imprisonment for a term not exceeding six months or both;
	    (ii) On conviction on indictment, to a fine or imprisonment for a term not exceeding two years or both; and
	
	(b) In the case of a failure to comply with subsection (1)(b) above, or be liable
	    (i) On summary conviction, to a fine not exceeding the statutory maximum;
	    (ii) On conviction on indictment, to a fine; and in either case if he is a certified Officer, an inquiry into his conduct may be held, and his certificate cancelled or suspended.

15. Duty to assist vessels or aircraft in distress

Merchant Shipping Act, 1995, Section 93 (as amended by SI no. 1691 - The Merchant Shipping (Distress Message) Regulations 1998) states:

1.	Subject to paragraph (2) below, it shall be the duty of the Master of a vessel, on receiving at sea a distress alert, to proceed with all speed to the assistance of the persons in distress, informing them or the appropriate SAR services, if possible, that he is doing so.
2.	The Master of the vessel need not so proceed if, having regard to the IAMSAR Manual: (a) The vessel is unable to do so; (b) In the special circumstances of the case, he considers it unreasonable or unnecessary to do so; or (c) He is released from the duty pursuant to regulations in paragraphs (5) and (6) below.

Continued on next page

3.	Where the Master of a vessel has received a distress alert at sea but does not proceed to the assistance of the persons in distress he shall: (a) Record in the vessel's log book the reason for not so proceeding; and (b) If the Master has responded to the distress alert by informing the appropriate SAR services that he is proceeding to the assistance of persons in distress, inform those SAR services as soon as possible of his decision not to proceed.
4.	Where the Master of any vessel in distress has, or the SAR services have, requisitioned any vessel that has answered a distress alert, it shall be the duty of the Master of the requisitioned vessel to comply with the requisition by continuing to proceed with all speed to the assistance of the persons in distress.
5.	**Release from duty** A Master shall be released from the duty imposed by Regulation in paragraph (1) above if he is informed (a) Of the requisition of one or more vessels other than his own; and (b) That the requisition is being complied with by at least one other vessel requisitioned.
6.	A Master shall be released from the duty imposed by Regulation in paragraph (1) above and any duty imposed by Regulation in paragraph (4) above, if he is informed by the persons in distress, by the Master of any vessel that has reached the persons in distress, or by the appropriate SAR services coordinating the rescue, that assistance is no longer required.

Penalties

If a Master of a vessel fails to comply with these Regulations he shall be guilty of an offence punishable on summary conviction by a fine not exceeding the statutory maximum and on conviction on indictment by imprisonment for a term not exceeding two years or a fine, or both.

Salvage rights

Compliance by a Master of a vessel with the requirements of these Regulations shall not affect his right, or the right of any other person, to salvage.

16. Reports of shipping accidents

1.	The requirements covering the reporting of accidents, including the definition of "accident", are given in Marine Guidance Note 564. (MGN 564) marine casualty and marine incident reporting.
2.	Masters should make themselves familiar with these requirements in order to take correct and prompt action should such an accident occur.
3.	Mariners are also reminded of their duty in compliance with the Merchant Shipping (Safety of Navigation) Regulations, 2002 No 473, to report to vessels in the vicinity and to the appropriate shore-based authority through a CRS should they encounter a dangerous derelict or other danger to navigation. Masters are also urged to report to the nearest CRS (RCCs in the UK) each time debris, which may be floating wreckage, is seen at sea.

17. Duties of Masters — official log books

1.	Stations on board vessels for which a GMDSS installation is required shall be provided with a log in which the following are recorded, together with the time of their occurrence, unless administrations have adopted other arrangements for recording all information which the log should contain: (a) A summary of communications relating to distress, urgency and safety traffic; (b) A reference to important service incidents; (c) If the vessel's rules permit, the position of the vessel at least once a day.
2.	All accidents should be entered in the official log book as required by the Merchant Shipping (Official Log Books) Regulations. A record of every signal of distress or a message that a vessel, aircraft or person is in distress at sea, observed or received should also be entered.
3.	In the UK, the requirements covering the recording of GMDSS communications in a dedicated Radio Log are given in Marine Guidance Note 530 (MGN 530).
4.	Where the Master, on receiving a signal of distress at sea or information from any source that a vessel or aircraft is in distress, is unable, or in the special circumstances of the case considers it unreasonable or unnecessary, to go to the assistance of the persons in distress (in accordance with the Merchant Shipping (Distress Message) Regulations 1998 which relate to a Master's obligation to assist vessels etc. in distress) a statement of his reasons for not going to the assistance of those persons should also be entered.

Continued overleaf

VESSELS IN DISTRESS
18. Statutory distress signals

1.	Annex IV of the Merchant Shipping Notice MSN 1781 Amendment 2 - Merchant Shipping (Distress Signals and Prevention of Collisions) Regulations 1996 and International Regulations for Preventing Collisions at Sea 1972, as amended, lists the signals to be used or exhibited either together or separately to indicate distress and need of assistance. These are: (a) A gun or other explosive signal fired at intervals of about a minute; (b) A continuous sounding with any fog signalling apparatus; (c) Rockets or shells, throwing red stars fired one at a time at short intervals; (d) A signal made by visual or by any other means consisting of the group ···— — — ··· (SOS) in the Morse Code; (e) A signal sent by RT consisting of the spoken word "MAYDAY"; (f) The International Code Signal of distress indicated by NC; (g) A signal consisting of a square flag having above or below it a ball or anything resembling a ball; (h) Flames on the vessel (as from a burning tar barrel, oil barrel, etc.); (i) A rocket parachute flare or a hand flare showing a red light; (j) A smoke signal giving off orange coloured smoke; (k) Slowly and repeatedly raising and lowering arms outstretched to each side; (l) A distress alert by means of DSC transmitted on: VHF Ch 70, or MF/HF on the frequencies 2187·5 kHz, 8414·5 kHz, 4207·5 kHz, 6312 kHz, 12577 kHz or 16804·5 kHz; (m) A ship-to-shore distress alert transmitted by the vessel's Inmarsat or other mobile satellite system which is part of the GMDSS (n) Signals transmitted by emergency position-indicating radio beacons; (o) Approved signals transmitted by radio communications systems, including survival craft radar transponders
2.	The use or exhibition of any of the foregoing signals except for the purpose of indicating distress and need of assistance and the use of other signals which may be confused with any of the above signals is prohibited.
3.	Attention is drawn to the relevant sections of the International Code of Signals, the IAMSAR Manual Volume III and the following signals: (a) A piece of orange coloured canvas with either a black square and circle or other appropriate symbol (for identification from the air); (b) A dye marker.
4.	The requirement for the carriage of vessel's distress signals for all classes of vessel including their associated survival craft, are contained in either: (a) The Merchant Shipping (Life Saving Appliances for Ships other than Ships of Classes III to VI(A)) Regulations 1999 as amended, SI No. 2721; (b) The Merchant Shipping (Life Saving Appliances for Passenger Ships of Classes III to VI(A)) Regulations 1999, as amended, SI No. 2723. (c) The Merchant Shipping (Passenger Ships) (Safety Code for UK Categorised Waters) Regs 2010 (SI2010/680), which implements MSN1823. (d) The Merchant Shipping (Passenger Ships on Domestic Voyages) Regs 2000 (SI2000/2687) which implements EC Directive 2009/45 as amended. (e) The Merchant Shipping (High Speed Craft) Regs 2004 (SI2004/302) which implements the HSC Code.

Continued on next page

5.	*Notes:* (a) Not less than twelve rocket parachute flares shall be carried by Classes I, II, II(A), III, IV, VII, VII(T), VIII, VIII(A), VIII(T), VIII(A)(T), IX, XI. (b) Classes VI, IX(A), IX(A)(T) and XII are allowed to carry alternative distress signals. (c) Survival craft are generally required to carry four rocket parachute flares, six hand flares and two buoyant smoke signals. (d) Class V vessels are not required to carry vessels distress signals. (e) For fishing vessels of 24m registered length and over built before 1st January 1999, the equivalent rules for UK registered fishing vessels are contained in Rules 76-81 and Schedule 18 of the Fishing Vessels (Safety Provisions) Rules 1975. For fishing vessels of 24m registered length and over built on or after 1st January 1999 should comply with the requirements of the Fishing Vessels (EC Directive on Harmonised Safety Regime) Regulations 1998 No 2998 and specifically requirements of Chapter VII of Annex II of the Torremolinos Protocol 1993. For fishing vessels of 15m length overall to less than 24m registered length, the requirements of Chapter 7 of MSN 1872 apply. For fishing vessels of less than 15m length overall, the requirements of the Annexes 1.1 to 1.6 of MSN 1871 apply.

19. Authority to use distress signals

1.	Rule 3 of the SI as amended 1996 No. 75, Merchant Shipping (Distress Signals and Prevention of Collisions) Regulations, 1996 provides as follows:
2.	The signals of distress which shall be used by vessels to which regulation 2(1)(a)[1] of these Regulations apply are those set out in Annex IV to the International Regulations[2].
3.	No signal of distress shall be used by any vessel unless the Master of the vessel so orders.
4.	The Master shall not order any signal of distress to be used by his vessel unless he is satisfied: - That his vessel is in serious and imminent danger, or that another vessel or an aircraft or person is in serious and imminent danger and cannot of itself send that signal; and - That the vessel in danger (whether his own vessel or another vessel) or the aircraft or person in danger, as the case may be, and requires immediate assistance in addition to any assistance then available.
5.	The Master of a vessel which has sent any signal of distress by means of radio or other means, shall cause that signal to be revoked by all appropriate means as soon as he is satisfied that the vessel or aircraft to which the signal relates is no longer in need of assistance as aforesaid.
6.	Masters and others in charge afloat are reminded of the importance of making a properly authorised signal of distress whenever a vessel or person is in grave and imminent danger, even when they believe that assistance has already been assured.
7.	Masters are also reminded of the need to cancel a distress call if the vessel is no longer in danger. Failure to do this has, on occasions, resulted in serious loss of time to other vessels and has in some instances caused needless anxiety to relatives and friends of those on board, because failure to find or establish communication with the vessel sending the signal has led to the belief that she has foundered. Attention is particularly drawn to the measures to prevent false alerts on GMDSS DSC frequencies given in Marine Guidance Note 294 (MGN 294) as amended.
8.	Vessels have also, on occasion, used red flares to warn off other vessels; the flares have been sighted from a distance and an extensive SAR operation has been mounted. This is illegal and it is also unnecessary: the use of warning signals is permitted provided that they are quite distinct from distress signals and for this purpose white flares are manufactured and are readily available through chandlers. A well trained Aldis lamp supplemented by the vessel's whistle or siren is also often effective.

[1] UK vessels wherever they may be, and other vessels while within the UK or territorial waters thereof.
[2] International Regulations for Preventing Collisions at Sea 1972 as amended.

20. Need for care in the use of certain distress signals

1.	Two of the statutory distress signals, namely "a continuous sounding with any fog signalling apparatus" and "flames on the vessel" could on occasions be misunderstood and it is recommended that where more easily recognised distress signals can be made the above mentioned signals should not be used.
2.	Distress signals should be as distinctive as possible, so that they may be recognised at once and assistance despatched without delay. Thus, instead of making an indefinite succession of blasts on the fog signalling apparatus when in distress, mariners should make the "continuous sounding" by repeating the Morse signal SOS (• • • — — — • • •) on the whistle or other sound signalling equipment. If this is done there can be no mistake as to the meaning of the signal. Similarly, by night, if signalling for help by means of a lamp or flashing light the same signal SOS should always be used.
3.	In the case of the "flames on the vessel" signal, unless the flames making the signal are sufficiently large to attract immediate attention, their chances of being recognised as a distress signal are very poor. The best visual distress signals are rocket parachute flares or hand flares showing red lights or rockets emitting red stars. Arrangements should be made to steady rockets to ensure their satisfactory flight when fired.

21. Maintenance of line-throwing rockets, distress rockets and smoke signals

1.	Line-throwing rockets, distress rockets, red flares, etc., are liable to deteriorate if kept for a long period, and they should be condemned and replaced immediately after a period of three years from the date of manufacture. Special care should be taken regarding the disposal of these obsolete pyrotechnics. On no account should they be used for testing or practice purposes, or landed for any purpose. They should be kept in a safe place until the opportunity occurs for disposing of them ashore by one of the following means: (a) Returning them to the supplier directly, or via their local representative; (b) Requesting a life raft service station in the UK or overseas to accept any of the vessel's out of date pyrotechnics when liferafts are being sent ashore for servicing; liferaft service stations deal with the disposal of expired pyrotechnics on a regular basis and have arrangements locally to do this; *Note:* Marine Guidance Note 419 (MGN 419) has been replaced by the link https://www.gov.uk/guidance/disposing-of-unwanted-marine-flares
2.	Lifebuoy smoke markers should also be replaced after three years. They should be examined carefully for corrosion or other defects and replaced earlier if necessary.

22. Emergency Position Indicating Radio Beacons (EPIRBs) and Personal Locator Beacons (PLBs)

1.	Vessels and mariners are increasingly carrying EPIRBs and PLBs either on a voluntary or mandatory basis. These devices operate on emergency frequencies between 406·0 - 406·1 MHz. The 406 MHz distress beacon alerts are detected by the Cospas-Sarsat satellite system and distress alert data is passed via ground tracking stations (Local User Terminals (LUTs)) to the Mission Control Centres (MCCs) which pass the alert data to the appropriate SAR authority. The UK MCC informs HMCG who coordinate SAR arrangements. In accordance with The Merchant Shipping (EPIRB Registration) Regulations 2000 and the guidance in MGN 665 (M+F) Registration of EPIRBs and 406 MHz PLBs used in the maritime environment, Owners, Masters and Skippers of all (UK) vessels that carry EPIRBs and/or PLBs must ensure that: (a) Any 406 MHz EPIRB fitted to a UK vessel or UK-coded PLBs carried by mariners must be registered with the UK Distress and Security Beacon Registration Database (UKDASBRD) held at MRCC Falmouth; as must all UK-coded 406 MHz PLBs used in the maritime environment; (b) Any changes regarding an EPIRB or PLB already registered must be notified; *Note:* It is an offence by the owner and/or the operator if either of the above requirements are not carried out.
2.	The above registration can be completed online at: https://www.gov.uk/register-406-beacons If you require assistance with registering your beacon online, contact the UK Beacon Registry team at: ukbeacons@mcga.gov.uk Although the aeronautical distress frequencies 121·5 MHz and to a lesser extent 243 MHz frequencies may be monitored by Air Traffic Service Units and by some aircraft, they are not routinely monitored by vessels or HMCG. It should be noted that Cospas-Sarsat satellite processing of the 121·5 and 243·0 MHz ceased on 1 February 2009.
3.	Once a 406 MHz satellite beacon alert signal has been received by the SAR authorities and a position provided, the homing transmissions on 121·5 and/or 243 MHz are essential as locating aids in connection with SAR aircraft or rescue boats and they can greatly reduce the time taken to locate the distress position (see paragraphs 31.6., 32.11. and APPENDIX B). 406 MHz EPIRBs/PLBS are equipped with either a 121·5 MHz homing transmitter (some with both 121·5 and 243 MHz) or another type of SAR locating device, e.g. an AIS Search and Rescue Transmitter or Search and Rescue radar Transponder (SART)for homing purposes. Many SAR aircraft are fitted with equipment which can identify and home in on signals on these frequencies at distances of up to (approx) 50 nautical miles. Although still in the minority, an increasing number of SAR-dedicated helicopters and a few fixed-wing aircraft have 406 MHz homing equipment, which promises even greater detection range. Cospas-Sarsat beacons are essential supplements to conventional maritime radio equipment. Once an EPIRB or PLB has been activated for a genuine SAR incident, it should not be switched off until the distressed vessel or person(s) have been located and rescued. It is important that, without unnecessary risk to rescuers, that the beacons of rescued survivors should be switched off as soon as possible, so that searching aircraft can concentrate on locating any other active beacons and remaining survivors without being confused by transmissions from rescued persons beacons being left adrift.
4.	It is recommended that the beacons be sited in accordance with the statutory requirements, where these exist, or the manufacturer's instructions. Great care should be exercised in finding suitable unencumbered sites to place float-free EPIRBs and considerations should also be given to the accessibility of all EPIRBs for transfer to survival craft and/or manual activation.
5.	It is very important that owners and potential users of the beacons are aware of the possible consequences of misuse. False beacon alerts cause the SAR services to respond as there is no immediate way of distinguishing genuine distress calls from false alarm beacon alerts. It is vital that any accidental triggering of an EPIRB, ELT or PLB be reported to the UK MCC, immediately. They will advise what to do with the beacon once they are alerted. Prompt and responsible reporting of accidental activation will be sympathetically received by the SAR authorities.
6.	**121·5/243 MHz satellite alerting services** (a) Since 1 February 2009, beacons primarily using 121·5 and 243 MHz have been rendered obsolete as those frequencies are no longer monitored by Cospas-Sarsat satellites. These older beacons have now been entirely replaced by 406 MHz beacons that uses the 121·5 MHz frequency only for the final stage of short-range homing to casualties. 121·5 MHz is mandated for homing. Further details may be found on the document C/SR.010, available for downloading from the Cospas-Sarsat website **(www.cospas-sarsat.org)** (b) In the UK, an aeroplane operating for the purposes of public transport, with Certificate of Airworthiness (CofA) first issued before 1 January 2002, needs either a portable or an automatic 406 MHz ELT with a homing frequency of 121·5 MHz. If the C of A is issued after that date it must have an automatic Electronic Locator Transmitter (ELT). Helicopters, according to their performance and type of operation, will be required to carry either an automatic or automatically deployable ELT. Schedule 4 of Air Navigation Order 2005 is the authoritative UK document on the subject. The Council of the International Civil Aviation Organization (ICAO) agreed that Cospas-Sarsat processing of 121·5 MHz ELTs could be discontinued from 2008. (c) EASA Air Operations Regulation (EU) No 965/2012 Annex VII (Part-NCO), (Non-commercial operations with other than complex motor-powered aircraft) rule NCO.IDE.A.170, states that an emergency locator transmitter (ELT) or personal locator beacon (PLB) needs to be carried on every aircraft for every flight; these must operate on 406 MHz.

23. Radio Listening watch procedures

1.	In accordance with the Merchant Shipping (Radio Installations) Regulations 1998 and the Merchant Shipping (Radio) (Fishing Vessels) Regulations 1999, all UK passenger vessels, cargo vessels of 300 GT and upwards and fishing vessels of 12 metres or more in length must maintain a continuous radio watch in accordance with the relevant provisions of ITU Radio Regulations and the SOLAS Convention appropriate to the sea area in which the vessel is sailing and the equipment fitted, namely that: (a) Vessels equipped for sailing in Sea Area A1 only will maintain a DSC watch on VHF Ch 70 with a dedicated DSC watchkeeping receiver; (b) Vessels equipped for sailing outside Sea Area A1 will also maintain a DSC watch as appropriate on the distress and safety frequency 2187·5 kHz with a dedicated DSC watch-keeping receiver and, if the vessel is fitted with an HF radio installation, on the distress and safety frequency 8414·5 kHz and, additionally, on at least one of the distress and safety frequencies 4207·5 kHz, 6312 kHz, 12,577 kHz or 16804·5 kHz, appropriate to the season, time of day and the geographical position of the vessel (this watch may be kept by means of a dedicated DSC scanning receiver); (c) Vessels fitted with a GMDSS compliant SES will maintain watch for satellite distress alerts.
2.	When practicable, every such vessel shall keep a continuous radiotelephone distress and safety watch on the frequency VHF Ch 16 and guard VHF Ch 13, for communications related to safety of navigation.
3.	A continuous watch for broadcasts of maritime safety information shall also be kept for the area in which the vessel is sailing, by: (a) NAVTEX (518 kHz) (b) Inmarsat C or EGC SafetyNET Receiver (c) Iridium EGC SafetyCast Service
4.	Any vessel which receives a distress message concerning a mobile station which is beyond any possible doubt in its vicinity must acknowledge receipt on the appropriate distress and safety working frequency. If however the mobile station in distress is beyond any possible doubt not in the immediate vicinity, a short interval of time must be allowed before acknowledging receipt, so that vessels nearer to the station in distress can answer and acknowledge receipt without interference. The radio operator on watch should alert the Master of the vessel and the radio operator designated as having primary responsibility for radio communications during distress incidents promptly to the receipt of a "Distress Alert" and the content of any subsequent communications. The radio operator designated as having primary responsibility for radiocommunications during distress incidents will then evaluate the situation and immediately assume responsibility for applying the relevant procedures of the ITU Radio Regulations and ITU-R Recommendations, having regard to the proximity of an RCC or CRS and the means of communication available. A summary of the distress traffic must be entered into the radio records (log book) as noted above in paragraph 17. Any vessel which is not in a position to render assistance and which has heard a distress message which has not been immediately acknowledged, must take all possible steps to attract the attention of the shore-based authorities or of other vessels which are in a better position to render assistance. Those coast stations maintaining a continuous watch on the DSC distress and safety frequencies are listed in the GMDSS Master Plan, the ITU *List of Coast Stations (List IV)* and in various national publications, e.g. ALRS Volumes 1 (NP281) and this Volume. The CRS in the UK are HMCG RCCs.
5.	Detailed radiocommunication watchkeeping requirements are set out in Parts A-VIII and B-VIII of the STCW Code.

Note: Meteorological and Navigational Warnings are also transmitted at fixed times throughout the day by coast stations on MF, HF and VHF. Further information is available in ALRS Volumes 3 (NP283) and this Volume and the ITU *List of Radiodetermination and Special Service Stations (List VI)*.

24. Survival craft equipment

Where vessels are provided with radio equipment, portable or otherwise, for use in the vessel's survival craft. This may be one or all of the following devices:

1.	Portable VHF radio apparatus for communications between survival craft and to/from rescue craft.
2.	406 MHz EPIRB and/or PLB, which can also be used for locating survivors (See Section 2).
3.	Search and Rescue radar Transponder (SART) for homing by vessels and aircraft (See Section 6) or;
4.	an AIS Search and Rescue Radio Transmitter for homing by vessels and some aircraft.

Continued on next page

25. Vessels reported missing or overdue

1.	**Other than fishing vessels.** Owners of vessels - other than fishing vessels - who are anxious for the safety of one of their vessels owing to the absence of radio or other reports or who fail to get in touch with the vessel directly or to obtain news of the vessel from other sources are advised to contact the nearest HMCG RCC. Action will then be taken to try to locate the vessel The following information about the vessel should be made available: (a) Name of vessel, call sign and MMSI Number (b) Port of registry (c) Type and size of vessel (d) Communications fitted (including mobile and satellite telephones carried by the vessel). (e) Last and next ports of call (f) Last known position including date and time (g) Anticipated track, course(s) and speed(s) if known (h) Number of persons on board (i) Any other relevant information - e.g. mobile telephones or such devices carried by any person on board.
2.	**Fishing Vessels.** HMCG is responsible for initiating SAR measures in relation to overdue fishing vessels. When an owner, or any other person, considers a fishing vessel to be missing or overdue, a report should be made directly to the nearest RCC, giving the following information about the vessel: (a) Name of vessel and Port letter and number. (b) Description. (c) What communications equipment is carried (including mobile and satellite telephones carried by the vessel). (d) Last known position. (e) Date last seen, or heard from. (f) Probable fishing area. (g) Full details of all safety equipment carried. (h) Number of persons on board. (i) Any other relevant information - e.g. mobile telephones or such devices carried by any person on board.
3.	Owners and/or agents should not delay in making the necessary report where they have any doubts concerning the safety of vessels.

26. Counter pollution and salvage

UK Maritime and Coastguard Agency (MCA) Counter Pollution and Salvage (CPS) is responsible for, and will respond to, oil and hazardous and noxious substance spills reported within UK Waters and the UK Exclusive Economic Zone (UK EEZ). It will assess reports of marine pollution and potential pollution both at sea and along the UK coastline and take appropriate action. It also provides scientific and technical advice on shoreline clean up and training for local government authority personnel on pollution response measures undertaken near shore and on the coastline.Further, MCA CPS will assess reports of vessels broken down within UK Waters and the UK EEZ, particularly those likely to cause serious harm to the environment and will ensure that appropriate recovery action is taken

The MCA maintains an Emergency Towing Vessel (ETV) off the north and north west coasts of Scotland, encompassing the Northern and Western Isles, which may be tasked to attend vessels broken down or in difficulty. This vessel is at 30 minutes notice to deploy to a casualty vessel incident and is available 24/7 - 365.

27. Intervention powers

The Secretary of State's statutory powers of intervention are now to be found in Schedule 3A to the Merchant Shipping Act 1995 as amended by the Marine Safety Act (MSA) 2003. This legislation has consolidated and extended the powers of intervention that were established in the original draft of the MSA 1995 and extended by the Merchant Shipping and Maritime Security Act 1997. The powers relate to incidents where there is a risk to safety (within UK territorial waters) and/or pollution by a hazardous substance (anywhere within the UK Exclusive Economic Zone). Hazardous substances include:

- Oil (defined in Section 151(1) of the MSA1995).
- Any other substance prescribed by Statutory Instrument (currently listed in The Merchant Shipping (Prevention of Pollution: Substances other than Oil) (Intervention) Order 1997 SI No 1997/1869).
- Any other substance which creates a hazard to human health, harms living resources or marine life, damages amenities or interferes with lawful use of the sea.

The "Trigger situation" which renders these powers exercisable is one in which an "accident" (e.g. collision of vessels, a stranding, another incident of navigation or another event, whether on board a vessel or not, which results in material damage to a vessel or its cargo or is an imminent threat of material damage to a vessel or its cargo) has occurred to or in the vessel and has created a risk to safety (in UK waters only) or a risk of pollution by a hazardous substance.

Directions for the purposes above can be given to anyone deemed appropriate including owners of vessels, persons in charge of vessels, Harbour Masters or harbour authorities. The nature of these directions could not be wider ranging and may require them to take, or not take, any action of any kind whatsoever in relation to a vessel or anything in, on or towed by the vessel, or any person on the vessel. Directions can also be given to persons in control of coastal land or premises requiring them to grant access to, or use of facilities in relation to a vessel or any person or thing which is, or was, on the vessel. This includes permitting persons to land, making facilities available for undertaking repairs or other works and making facilities available for the landing, storage and disposal of cargo or of other things.

In addition, if a person does not comply with a Direction, or if the Secretary of State feels that giving a Direction would be unlikely to achieve a sufficient result, the Secretary of State can authorise persons to take the action on his behalf. This includes entering premises on land, boarding vessels and making arrangements for the destruction of a vessel.

There are similar powers of intervention in cases where there is pollution, or risk of pollution, in relation to off shore installations. These are contained in The Offshore Installations (Emergency Pollution Control) Regulations 2002, SI no 2002/1861.

The UK has appointed the Secretary of State's Representative for Maritime Salvage and Intervention (SOSREP) to act on behalf of the Secretary of State in all matters of intervention and salvage. The SOSREP works closely with the MCA, HMCG and the Department for Business, Energy and \industrial Strategy (BEIS) and is contactable on a 24 x 7 basis through the MCA duty Counter Pollution and Salvage Officer system.

SOSREP has the sole authority to intervene and issue Directions. However, he may also take action himself, or authorise action to be taken by others in lieu of a Direction. The role of the SOSREP is to monitor salvage incidents, exercising the intervention powers if deemed necessary, in the over-riding interests of safety and the UK environment.

Once SOSREP has decided that the "trigger point" for intervention is nearing and it may be necessary to intervene, he will advise the parties in charge of the casualty, or to whom the Directions are likely to be given, accordingly. Initial intervention is likely to follow a prior warning to the casualty that the powers of intervention may be exercised. This will be accompanied by an offer of help from the MCA and a request for information about the Master's intentions.

Offences in relation to non-compliance with Directions and obstructing persons enforcing a Direction are set out in Paragraphs 5– 7 of Schedule 3A to the Merchant Shipping Act 1995 as amended by the Marine Safety Act 2003. Persons guilty of such offences are liable to a fine.

28. Visual signals used between shore stations in the UK and vessels in distress

In the event of a vessel being in distress off or stranded on the coast of the UK, the following signals may be used by life-saving stations when communicating with her, and by the vessel when communicating with life-saving stations.
a. Replies from life-saving stations or maritime rescue units to distress signals made by a vessel or person:

Signals	Signification
By day: Orange smoke signal or combined light and sound signal (thunderlight) consisting of three single signals which are fired at intervals of approximately one minute. **By night:** White star rocket consisting of three single signals which are fired at intervals of approximately one minute. Note: If necessary the day signals may be given at night or the night signals by day.	You are seen — assistance will be given as soon as possible (Repetition of such signals shall have the same meaning)

b. Landing signals for the guidance of small boats with crews or persons in distress:

Signals	Signification
By day: Vertical motion of a white flag or the arms, or signalling the code letter K (— • —) given by light or sound signal apparatus. **By night:** Vertical motion of a white light or flare, or signalling the code letter K (— • —) given by light or sound signal apparatus. A range (indication of direction) may be given by placing a steady white light or flare at a lower level and in line with the observer.	This is the best place to land

Continued on next page

By day: Horizontal motion of a white flag or arms extended horizontally or signalling the code letter S (•••) given by light or sound signal apparatus. **By night:** Horizontal motion of a white light or flare or signalling the code letter S (•••) given by light or sound signal apparatus.	Landing here highly dangerous
By day: Horizontal motion of a white flag, followed by the placing of the white flag in the ground and the carrying of another white flag in the direction to be indicated; and/or a white star signal in the direction towards the better landing place; or signalling the code letter S(•••) followed by the code letter R (• — •) if a better landing place for the craft in distress is located more to the right in the direction of approach; or signalling the code letter L(• — ••) if a better landing place for the craft in distress is located more to the left in the direction of approach. **By night:** Horizontal motion of a white light or flare, followed by the placing of the white light or flare on the ground and the carrying of another white light or flare in the direction to be indicated; and/or a white star signal in the direction towards the better landing place or signalling the code letter S(•••) followed by code letter R(• — •) if a better landing place for the craft in distress is located more to the right in the direction of approach; or signalling the code letter L(• — ••) if a better landing place for the craft in distress is located more to the left in the direction of approach.	Landing here highly dangerous. A more favourable location for landing is in the direction indicated

c. Signals to be employed in connection with the use of shore life-saving apparatus:

Signals	Signification
By day: Vertical motion of a white flag or the arms. **By night:** Vertical motion of a white flag or flare.	In general — "Affirmative" Specifically — "Rocket line is held" "Tail block is made fast" "Man is in breeches buoy" "Haul away"
By day: Horizontal motion of a white flag, or the arms, with arms extended horizontally. **By night:** Horizontal motion of a white flag or flare.	In general — "Negative" Specifically — "Slack away" "Avast hauling"

d. Signals to be used to warn a vessel which is standing into danger:

Signals	Signification
The International Code Signals U or NF. The letter U (•• —) flashed by lamp or made by fog horn or whistle, etc.	"You are running into danger"

If it should prove necessary, the attention of the vessel is called to these signals by a white flare, a rocket showing white stars on bursting, or an explosive sound signal.

29. Use of rocket line-throwing apparatus between vessels

1.	Where an assisting vessel proposes to establish communication by means of a line-throwing apparatus she should, before making her final approach, ascertain whether or not it is safe for her to fire the rocket, particularly if the other vessel is a tanker. If it is safe she should manoeuvre to WINDWARD before firing over the other vessel's deck. If not, she should go to LEEWARD and prepare to receive a line. EXTREME CAUTION must be exercised when firing line-throwing rockets between vessels when helicopters are in the vicinity.
2.	When a vessel in distress is carrying petrol spirit or other highly inflammable liquid and is leaking, the following signals should be exhibited to show that it is dangerous to fire a line-carrying rocket by reason of the risk of ignition: (a) By day: Flag B of the International Code of Signals hoisted at the masthead. (b) By night: A red light hoisted at the masthead.
3.	When visibility is bad the above signals should be supplemented by the use of the following International Code Signal made in sound: GU (— — • •• —) "It is not safe to fire a rocket."

30. Use of Fixed Wing aircraft in assisting vessels

1.	Aircraft (other than helicopters) dedicated to SAR duties may be able to assist a vessel in distress by: (a) Locating vessels when their position is in doubt and informing SAR helicopters and the shore authorities so that SAR assets in the vicinity going to a vessel's assistance may be given the precise position; (b) Guiding surface craft to the casualty or, if the vessel has been abandoned, to survivors in lifeboats, on rafts or in the sea; (c) Keeping the casualty vessel under observation; (d) Providing support for SAR helicopters and enhancing or extending communications between the vessel, the coordinating RCC and SAR helicopters and/or rescue vessels involved in the incident.
2.	Helicopters may be able to pick up survivors but their carrying capacity is limited.

3.	When a number of aircraft are engaged on a search for a casualty at sea, the procedure followed is to search an area which has been calculated to include the most probable position of the survivors or vessel, allowing for any movement due to water current drift and leeway since the incident occurred and during the period of the search. The common technique is for the aircraft to carry out "creeping line ahead" or "parallel track" searches to cover a calculated area or subarea, for as long as the aircraft's endurance on task will permit. An additional technique is the "square search" which is an expanding square centred on the most probable position of the survivor. The spacing between the tracks flown by the aircraft depends on the visibility, the characteristics of the object being searched for (e.g. lifeboat or lifecraft, etc.) and the type, if any, of locating devices or signals known to be available to the survivors. IAMSAR Volume III provides more details on search planning and area coverage.
	
	Actions by Survivors
	
	(a) Maritime aircraft may be employed to search at night for shipping known to be in distress or overdue, or for survivors in survival craft.
	
	(b) The aircraft will fly through the search area below cloud, and may fire a green flare approximately every five to ten minutes and at each turning point. When a green flare is sighted it is most important that the following actions are taken:
	  - Wait for the glare of the green flare to die out.
	  - Fire one red flare.
	  - Fire another red flare after about 20 seconds (this enables the aircraft to line up on your bearing).
	  - Fire a third red flare if the aircraft appears to be going badly off course.
	
	(c) Points to note:
	  - Each survival craft should carry at least three red flares, more is desirable.
	  - If the aircraft is diverted to the search from another task it may fire flares of another colour (except red) — reply to these as above.
	  - If all else fails, use any means at your disposal to attract attention.
	  - Survivors should ensure that pyrotechnics are not aimed directly at aircraft, particularly helicopters approaching overhead. Some rocket pyrotechnics have considerable energy and can hazard search aircraft.
	
	(d) SAR-dedicated aircraft are normally fitted with some or all of UHF, VHF, HF radio and satellite communications (voice and text) installations. UK SAR helicopters carry VHF/UHF equipment and either HF and satellite communications. SAR aircraft, aircraft engaged on SAR operations will usually maintain a listening watch on HF radio frequencies as allocated to them for that operation by the UKARCC which conducts a flight following function whilst they are on task.
	
	For the above purpose, the UKARCC therefore maintains a permanent watch on HF 5680 kHz USB, but may allocate to an aircraft any HF frequency, dependent on prevailing ionospheric conditions or operating criteria.
	
	(e) The following is included for information:
	  (i) SAR-dedicated helicopters can communicate on the principal VHF, FM, IMM channels including VHF Ch 16, with distressed and responding vessels, HMCG, RNLI and other SAR authorities. They can home on 121.5 and 243 MHz and 2182 kHz, using their DF equipment. Most UK SAR helicopters have good HF and UHF capability and can home on 2182 kHz and on 121·5/243 plus 406 MHz. Both aircraft types carry a Satcom terminal.
	  (ii) British military ships have VHF IMM channels installed, suitable for intercommunication with merchant vessels so equipped. British military ships also carry compatible VHF/UHF Airband equipment for communications with military and civilian aircraft. In cases where effective communications between merchant vessels and SAR aircraft cannot be established, British military ships, when present, may be used to link with these aircraft.
	  (iii) Most SAR aircraft of other nations carry communication installations similar to that of UK SAR-dedicated aircraft. Some are equipped to communicate and to home to transmissions on 121·5 MHz, 243 MHz and 2182 kHz. Some can home to radar SARTs in the 9 GHz band and AIS SARTs.
	  (iv) When operational on SAR missions, UK and most European SAR aircraft use voice call signs prefixed by the word "RESCUE".

31. Helicopter operations with merchant vessels

Helicopters based ashore in the UK and on military ships at sea may operate from time to time with merchant vessels at sea. The helicopter will establish contact with the vessel on VHF Ch 16 or, in the case of an emergency, the frequency assigned by the Coastguard to the emergency situation. During routine training, SAR helicopters may wish to practise winching to and from a vessel's deck. If this is intended, the helicopter crew will initially seek to make contact with the vessel's Captain on VHF Ch 16 to seek permission prior to switching to a working frequency. These operations can be hazardous unless the following safety precautions are taken:

1.	For helicopter winching, the vessel must be on a steady course giving minimum vessel motion, as directed by the helicopter pilot. As a guide, relative wind should be maintained as follows: 　　　For helicopter operating area: 　　　　　Aft - 30° on Port Bow. 　　　　　Midships - 30° on Port Bow or a beam wind. 　　　　　Forward - 30° on Starboard Quarter.
2.	An indication of relative wind direction should be given. Flags and pennants, illuminated at night, are suitable for this purpose. Smoke from a galley funnel may also give an indication of the wind but in all cases where any funnel is making exhaust, the wind must be at least two points off the Port Bow.
3.	Clear as large an area of deck (or covered hatchway) as possible and mark the area with a yellow dot 5 metres in diameter, Marine Guidance Note 325 gives guidance on the provision of permanent winching and low-hover areas). Whip or wire aerials in and around the area should, if at all possible, be struck.
4.	**All loose articles must be securely tied down or removed from the transfer area.** The down wash from the helicopter's rotor will easily lift unsecured covers, tarpaulins, hoses, rope and gash etc., thereby presenting a severe flying hazard. Even small pieces of paper, if ingested by a helicopter engine, can cause the helicopter to crash.
5.	If a clear area can not be provided, personnel can be lifted from a boat being towed astern on a long painter.
6.	On no account must the winch wire or load be secured to, or be allowed to foul any part of the vessel or rigging or structure. In the event of excess loading or the winch wire becoming snagged, the helicopter crew will cut the winch wire from the helicopter end.
7.	A helicopter can quickly build up a charge of static electricity which, if discharged through a person handling the winch wire, can cause a severe electric shock and so should be avoided if possible. The helicopter crew will normally discharge the static electricity before commencing the operation by dipping the winch wire (or the earthing lead attached to the hook and hanging below the winchman) in the sea or allowing the hook (or lead) to touch the vessel's deck. However, under some conditions sufficient static electricity can build up during the operation to give unprotected personnel a substantial shock.
8.	The helicopter will approach heading into the relative wind. For operating areas Aft and Midships the helicopter will approach from astern or abeam, and for operating area Forward it will approach from the bow. The maximum length of winch cable is normally about 90m (295ft)/75m (246ft) but may be less in some cases. A low-hover area may be practicable: the advantage of such an area is the reduction of time to transfer survivors because they can board the helicopter directly from the deck. This is particularly relevant in the case of a passenger ferry where there may be large numbers of persons to evacuate. A clear area sufficient to accommodate the helicopter is required: as a general guideline, a minimum diameter of 23 metres is essential (full requirements are detailed in Marine Guidance Note 325). The success of low-hover operations depends on the behaviour of the vessel. If any movement is taking place the operation may be dangerous. The decision on whether to use this technique will be made by the helicopter Captain. In any event, the operating area should be such that the helicopter pilot can have an unobstructed view of the vessel. The area should, as far as practicable, be clear of accommodation spaces, provide sufficient adjacent deck area for people to muster and provide safe access to the area from at least two separate directions.
9.	When being landed from a helicopter, personnel must obey the instructions given by the helicopter crew since there is a danger of inadvertently walking into the tail rotor which, due to its high speed of rotation, is difficult to see.
10.	**EXTREME CAUTION** must be exercised when firing line-throwing rockets or any pyrotechnics when low-flying aircraft or helicopters are in the vicinity.

Note: The IAMSAR Manual gives further guidance on working with helicopters and should be read in conjunction with this Annex.

32. Use of helicopters at sea for rescue and medical evacuation

1.	**General.** The use of helicopters has become commonplace to evacuate a limited number of persons from vessels following a casualty, for rendering medical assistance and for landing specialist personnel for fire-fighting, damage control and salvage purposes. Consequently, it has become important that provision be made on board vessel for such eventualities. Such provision includes the selection of an area or areas over which a helicopter can safely operate, the preparation of contingency plans for helicopter operations and the carrying out of drills. This is particularly important in the case of passenger vessels which operate within helicopter coverage from the nearest coast.
2.	Most helicopter operations are successfully executed due primarily to the skill of helicopter crews. However, these operations are often of a hazardous nature and their success can be better assured if owners, Masters and Officers have given consideration beforehand to making suitable provision and preparations.
3.	**Contingency plans, drills and communications.** In order that those on board are prepared for an emergency helicopter operation, contingency plans and check lists should be prepared and periodic drills carried out. An example of a shipboard safety check list is given at APPENDIX C.
4.	It is possible to communicate with a SAR helicopter on VHF Ch 16, or an agreed working frequency, as it is approaching the vessel. If difficulties are experienced, communications may be relayed by another unit on the scene - an Aircraft Co-ordinator if designated - or by the coordinating RCC. However, it should be noted that communications will be difficult when the helicopter is overhead due to engine noise unless the vessel's VHF equipment is fitted with headphones or other suitable devices for use in high ambient noise conditions. Face-to-face communications will be possible if a winchman is lowered onto the vessel.
5.	Guidance on the conduct of emergency helicopter operations will be found in the Department of Transport Merchant Shipping Notice 1506, the IAMSAR Manual and in the ICS publication "Guide to Helicopter/Ship Operations"

Continued overleaf

6.	When a distress message is received either visually or by radio from a vessel in distress, steps taken by the rescue authorities ashore may include asking the nearest RCC to despatch a helicopter to assist in the rescue.
7.	It is essential that the vessel's position should be given as accurately as possible if the original distress signal is made by radio. The bearing (state whether magnetic or true) and distance from a fixed object, like a headland or lighthouse, should be given if possible. The type of vessel and colour of hull should be included if time allows.
8.	The main types of helicopter employed on SAR duties in the UK have an automatic hover control system and so can conduct rescues at night and in limited visibility where there are no visual hover references. Typical maximum operating radius from base (or refuelling point) of the helicopters are between 180 and 250 nautical miles. These ranges can be extended by forward refuelling e.g. on offshore installations. The helicopters in their various configurations can carry between 8 and 21 survivors, but this number can usually be briefly increased for short durations if the emergency demands. The exact capability of all helicopters in given circumstances will be determined by the aircrew at the time.
9.	SAR helicopters are fitted with VHF FM and AM, UHF and HF RT; they do not normally carry MF. Communication between vessel and helicopter should normally be achieved on Marine Band VHF/FM. If contact is difficult, it can be achieved by relaying through a fixed-wing SAR aircraft if one is on scene, or through a lifeboat or the RCC.
10.	Once a helicopter has become airborne, the speed with which it locates the vessel and the effectiveness of its work depends to a large extent on the co-operation of the vessel herself. On long range incidents, a supporting fixed-wing aircraft is sometimes tasked as top cover and communications relay station. Using its speed and radar, it normally locates the vessel before the helicopter arrives in the area and directs the helicopter straight to it with the minimum of wasted time and fuel.
11.	From the air, especially if there is a lot of shipping in the area, it is very difficult for the pilot of a helicopter to isolate the particular vessel he is looking for from the many that may be in sight. To ease identification, the vessel's crew should read out their exact position and course on the radio. The vessel should then use a distinctive distress signal which can clearly be seen by the helicopter pilot. Any, or all of the following may be used: (a) An effective method, if the necessary equipment is installed on the aircraft, is by use of a radar SART, which responds to radar interrogation by transmitting a swept frequency signal which generates as a line of 12 blip code on a radar screen outward from the SART's position, along its line of bearing. (b) The use of an orange-coloured smoke signal during daylight or a flare at night, provide a very distinctive position indicator from the air. (c) A signal lamp can be seen except in very bright sunlight when the life boat heliograph could be used. It is not suggested, of course, that the signal lamp need necessarily be used to pass messages in Morse code. At night, other than at long/medium range, until the helicopter has identified the vessel, avoid shining lights directly at the helicopter. Once the helicopter has obviously turned towards the subject vessel, shine lights on the deck or super structure. Do not point 'laser pointers' or laser light-source devices at aircraft as this creates a flight safety hazard. If they have to be used, point them up into the sky. (d) The aircraft may request a VHF transmission e.g. a slow count from one to ten, for example for homing purposes. (e) The display of these signals will save valuable time in the helicopter locating the vessel (f) The crew of the vessel can often see and identify the SAR helicopter before the helicopter crew can identify them. Using radio, an efficient method of directing the helicopter to the vessel is to use the clock method where the nose and tail of the air craft is 12 o'clock and 6 o'clock respectively, and to state the location of the vessel relative to the helicopter. For example, "We are in your 2 o'clock, range 2 miles".
12.	If it is observed that the helicopter is going to pass by, or is on a course which will take it away, continued use should be made of visual distress signals, and at the same time, if fitted with radio, the fact reported to the helicopter, stating its present bearing and distance from the vessel.
13.	It is of great assistance to SAR aircraft if all fishing vessels were clearly marked on the top of their wheel houses or some other prominent horizontal surface with their Fishing Letter and Number as large as space allows and as described in Schedule 4 of the Merchant Shipping (Registration of Fishing Vessels) Regulations 1988.
14.	Whenever possible and when time allows, all the safety precautions in paragraph 32. above should be taken. However, in a distress situation it may not be possible to meet all the requirements. Under such circumstances the operation may necessarily be slower than a routine operation but, because of their operational limitations helicopters should not be unnecessarily delayed at the scene of the rescue. Cases have arisen where the rescue has been seriously hampered by survivors trying to take personal belongings with them when being rescued by helicopter. In distress situations, rescues are limited to people only.
15.	When cooperating with helicopters in SAR operations, vessels should not attempt to provide a lee whilst helicopters are engaged in winching operations as this tends to create turbulence for the helicopter.

Continued on next page

16.	The helicopter pilot and crewman are professionals in methods of rescue and well intentioned assistance from either the survivor himself or third parties in securing survivors invariably result in delays. The deck party should, therefore, remain stationary and allow the helicopter to move to them. The following rescue methods are employed: (a) The survivor, whether on deck or in the water, is rescued by means of the strop. Whenever possible the crewman is lowered from the helicopter together with the strop which is secured around the survivor's back and chest, and both are winched up into the helicopter. (b) On certain occasions it may be necessary for the survivor to position the strop himself. The following procedure should be followed: - Grasp the strop and put both arms and head through the loop. - Ensure the wide padded part is as high as possible across the back, with the two straps coming under the armpits and up in front of the face. - Pull the toggle down as far as possible. - When ready to be lifted, look up at the helicopter, put one arm out to full extent and give a "thumbs-up". - Put both arms down beside the body and keep them there. - On being winched up alongside the helicopter keep both arms down and do nothing until instructed by the helicopter crew. (c) If a survivor on a deck is injured to the extent that the use of a strop around his back and chest would aggravate the injury or cause suffering, a helicopter crewman will normally be lowered on to the deck with a stretcher. The survivor is placed in the stretcher, strapped-in in such a manner that it is impossible for him to slip or fall out, and both stretcher and helicopter crewman are winched up into the helicopter. If possible the helicopter will be carrying a doctor who will be lowered to the deck and will assist the survivors as necessary. If the patient is already in a stretcher this may be lifted straight into the aircraft or placed in the rigid frame stretcher or, the helicopter may require that the patient is placed in their specialist stretcher. It may also be possible to land a helicopter crewman with a portable radio for direct communication with the helicopter. (d) Hi-Line technique: In very bad weather it may not be possible to lower the crewman and/or strop directly on deck. In such a case a rope extension of the winch wire may be lowered to the vessel first. This should be handled by a member of the vessel's crew and the slack taken in as the helicopter pays out the winch wire. *Note:* This rope is not for lifting, it is only for control of the winch wire and to enable the winching to take place at an angle away from the overhead. The extension rope should be put in a bucket or coiled down on deck clear of snags but on no account should it be made fast or wrapped around any part of the body. When the winch wire is fully paid out the helicopter will move out to one side of the vessel and descend. As the descent is being made the vessel's crew should continue to take in the slack of the extension rope until the winch hook and strop are to hand. A winchman will usually be lowered with the strop. The earthing lead or winch hook must be allowed to touch the deck before the wire is handled. The casualty will then be secured in the strop and when he or another member of the vessel's crew signifies that he is ready, the helicopter will ascend and hoist in the winch wire. As this occurs, the extension rope should be paid out with enough weight on it to keep it taut until the end is reached when it should be cast clear of the vessel's side unless further lifts are required. If this is the case, the end of the extension rope should be kept in the hand if possible (but not wrapped around a limb or secured to the vessel) to facilitate the recovery of the strop for the next lift. Where a large number of persons are to be lifted, two strops may be offered simultaneously and one casualty should be placed in each strop in the normal manner.
17.	When being landed from a helicopter, personnel must obey the instructions given by the helicopter crew since there is a danger of inadvertently walking into the tail rotor which, due to its high speed of rotation, is difficult to see.

AIRCRAFT CASUALTIES AT SEA

33. Distress communications

1.	**Visual Signals.** An aircraft may indicate it is in distress by firing a succession of red pyrotechnic lights, by signalling SOS with signalling apparatus or by firing a parachute flare showing a red light. Navigation markers dropped by aircraft at sea, emitting smoke, or flames and smoke, should not be mistaken for distress signals. Low flying is not in itself an indication of distress.
2.	An aircraft which has located another aircraft in distress may notify vessels in the vicinity by passing a message in plain language by signalling lamp using the prefix "XXX" It may also give the following signals, together or separately, to attract a vessel's attention: (a) A succession of white pyrotechnic lights (b) The repeated switching on and off of the aircraft's landing lights (c) The irregular repeated switching on and off of the aircraft's navigational lights.

Continued overleaf

3.	If the aircraft wishes to guide a vessel to the casualty or survivors it will fly low round the vessel or cross the projected course of the vessel close ahead at a low altitude opening and closing the throttle or changing the propeller pitch. It will then fly off in the direction in which the vessel is to be led. British pilots are instructed to rock their aircraft laterally when flying off in the direction of the casualty. The vessel should acknowledge receipt of the signals by hoisting the Code and Answering Pennant close up, or by flashing a succession of "T's" on the signal lamp, and may indicate the inability to comply by hoisting the International Code Flag "N" or flashing a succession of "N's" on the signal lamp. It should then either follow the aircraft or indicate by visual or radio means that it is unable to comply. The procedure for cancelling these instructions is for the aircraft to cross the wake of the surface craft close astern at a low altitude, rocking the wings or opening and closing the throttle or changing the propeller pitch. These signals can be found in IAMSAR Volume III.
4.	In order to take advantage of the greater visibility of pyrotechnics by night, searching aircraft will fly a creeping line ahead or parallel track type of search, firing off green pyrotechnics at 5-10 minute intervals and watching for a replying red pyrotechnic from the survivor(s).
5.	Survivors from crashed aircraft in liferafts may give the following distress signals: (a) Fire pyrotechnic signals emitting one or more red stars or orange/red smoke. (b) Flash a heliograph. (c) Flash SOS or other distinctive signal by hand torch or other signalling lamp. Some life rafts may show a steady or a flashing light. (d) blow whistles. (e) use a fluorescent dye marker giving an extensive bright green colour to the sea around the survivors. (f) fly a yellow kite from the liferaft to support the aerial for the emergency radio transmitter. (g) Activate a 406MHz EPIRB, ELT or PLB, with locating signals on 121·5 MHz or 243 MHz.
6.	**Radio Signals.** Because aircraft often remain in two way radio contact with an Air Traffic Service Unit (ATSU) throughout their flights, a distress message may be transmitted on the frequency in use or alternatively on 121·5 or 243 MHz as appropriate. There are some classes of airspace (including areas over the sea) where no ATSU service or contact is required or possible. Therefore light aircraft in particular, can be flying without speaking to any ground ATSU service and if they suffer an emergency they may not be able to make an emergency transmission.
7.	There is close liaison between shore stations, including ATSU, JRCC UK and HMCG, and merchant vessels will ordinarily be informed of aircraft incidents at sea by Distress or Urgency broadcast messages from the HMCG RCCs made on the international distress frequencies and systems. Vessels may, however, become aware of the incident by: (a) Intercepting a distress signal from an aircraft using RT 2182 kHz (rarely) or VHF Ch 16. (The form of such messages is given in APPENDIX A), *or* (b) By picking up a message from a SAR aircraft. (c) Sighting an aircraft which appears or is in difficulty or is ditching at sea.

34. Action taken to render assistance

1.	Throughout their flight, civil commercial aircraft are normally in two-way radio contact with the ATSU appropriate to the area in which they are operating. In the British Isles there are two such centres; UK ATCC and the Shanwick Oceanic Control Area. In the case of aircraft in distress or overdue, JRCC UK will be alerted immediately by the relevant ATCC. The JRCC UK or HMCG is then responsible for initiating such action as may be necessary. Search aircraft may be sent, if necessary and practicable, to search for and fix as accurately as possible the position of the casualty. However, vessels at sea may be the closest to the aircrafts last known position or known flight track and may expect to be tasked to assist in rescue or search.
2.	Aircraft usually sink quickly (i.e. within a few minutes) and survivors may be injured or having difficulty in escaping from the aircraft so, vessels making for an aircraft in distress should consequently steam at full speed.
3.	Every endeavour will be made to give merchant vessels an accurate position of an aircraft casualty or lifecraft. The RCC will, if practicable and available, try to have an aircraft kept overhead survivors at least during daylight hours, until they are rescued. When given such a fix, vessels should at once consult other vessels in the area on the best procedure to be adopted. Vessels going to the rescue should answer the station sending the broadcast and give their identity, position and intended action.
4.	If a merchant vessel should pick up an SOS message direct from an aircraft or observe one in distress, they should respond and relay an alert to the nearest RCC or CRS. Moreover, a merchant vessel which has received an SOS message directly from an aircraft in distress and which is going to the rescue should take a bearing on the transmission or sighting and inform the nearest RCC or CRS and/or other vessels in the vicinity of the call sign of the distressed aircraft (if known) or general description of the type and the time at which the distress message was received or distressed aircraft was sighted, followed by the bearing and the position from which the bearing was taken and time at which the signal ceased or the aircraft disappeared from view.

Continued on next page

35. Action to be taken when survivors are picked up

1.	A survivor from an aircraft casualty at sea who is picked up by a vessel may be able to give information which will assist in the rescue of other survivors. Masters are therefore asked to put the following questions to rescued survivors of an aircraft incident and to communicate the answers to a RCC. They should also give the found position of the survivor(s) vessel and the time when the survivor was picked up. (a) Did the survivor bail out or was the aircraft ditched? What was the time and date? (b) If they parachuted out, at what altitude? (c) How many others did you see to leave the aircraft by parachute? (d) How many ditched with the aircraft? (e) How many did you see leave the aircraft after ditching? (f) How many survivors were in the water? (g) What flotation gear did they have? (h) What was the total number of persons aboard the aircraft prior to the accident? (i) What caused the emergency? (j) Did the aircraft have an ELT, PLB or EPIRB?
2.	Masters are reminded that survivors may, especially in colder climates, be suffering from hypothermia and may be at risk of secondary drowning, and that qualified medical advice should be provided at the earliest opportunity. Advice and guidance on the treatment of survivors and persons who have been in the water can be found in the IMO Pocket Guide to Cold Water Survival - ref: IMO Circular MSC1./Circ.1185/Rev.1
3.	If a survivor is recovered wearing an activated PLB or if there is an EPIRB in or attached to a life raft, it is important, without further risk to rescuers, that these be switched off as they may compromise the effectiveness of SAR homing to nearby survivors. The nearest RCC should also be informed of this action and the serial number(s) of the beacon(s).

NOTES

Maritime Search and Rescue Regions (SRR) and DSC Area Diagrams

The diagrams contained within this section are an amalgamation of the DSC and SRR diagrams contained in previous editions of NP285.

DSC Areas
The following diagrams depict the **approximate** ranges of all known operational VHF and MF DSC facilities world wide. The specific shaded areas are intended to be diagramatic only and should not be considered as accurate delimitations. Operational MF DSC stations are identified within the diagrams and the name of the station shown where it differs from any adjoining MRCC or MRSC. Areas not yet defined by Governments as a Sea Area A1 or A2 are as appropriate designated as Sea Areas A3 or A4.

The limits shown are, wherever practicable, calculated on the information contained in the IMO GMDSS Master Plan as amended. These limits are only an approximation.

Actual ranges may be limited by propagation fluctuation or atmospheric conditions. Communications are further affected by variations in geographical position and time of day as well as radiated transmitter power. Details of the formulae used to determine promulgated ranges with the recommendations of Governments to provide either individually or in co-operation with other Governments, the radio services deemed practicable, and necessary for the proper operation of the GMDSS, are contained in IMO Resolution A.801(19), adopted November 1995 (see the management of VHF section).

Maritime Search and Rescue Regions (SRR)
One of the major aspects of the GMDSS is the establishment of a Global Search and Rescue Plan. The International Maritime Organisation (IMO) and the International Civil Aviation Organisation (ICAO), the two agencies of the United Nations devoted to maritime and aeronautical transportation safety, respectively, are working towards this goal. IMO and ICAO are striving to foster co-operation between themselves, neighbouring states and maritime and aeronautical authorities to promote the harmonization of maritime and aeronautical SAR services, to ensure that persons in distress will be assisted without regard to their locations, nationality or circumstances.

As party to the International Convention for the Safety of Life at Sea (SOLAS), the International Convention on Maritime Search and Rescue or the Convention on International Civil Aviation, a State is obliged to provide certain maritime or aeronautical SAR coordination and services. The international community expects these commitments to be fulfilled.

An SRR is an area of defined dimensions associated with a Rescue Coordination Centre (RCC) within which SAR services are provided. ICAO Regional Air Navigation Plans (RANP), depict aeronautical SRRs for most of the world. States have agreed to accept SAR responsibility for an area which is composed of one or more aeronautical SRRs. The maritime SRRs published in the following diagrams are generally similar, but not necessarily identical, to the RANPs. The purpose of having an SRR is to clearly define who has the primary responsibility for coordinating responses to distress situations in every area of the world and to enable rapid distribution of the distress alerts to the appropriate RCC.

The delimitation of a Search and Rescue Region (SRR) is not related to and shall not prejudice the delimitation of any boundary between States. These areas are established to ensure that primary responsibility for coordinating Search and Rescue services for that geographical area is assumed by some State. In practice, SAR services may not necessarily be provided by the designated State. In such cases, SAR facilities are likely to be provided by the nearest country having the most appropriate SAR assets.

The Search and Rescue Regions shown in the following diagrams are based on IMO SRR diagrams.

KEY

●   Operational main MF DSC Station, indicates MF DSC only. Please refer to the DSC list of Coast Stations for Sea Area A1 and A2 for full station listings showing MMSI number, station location and range of both VHF and MF DSC stations.

▬   Link to remotely controlled station

■   Rescue Coordination Centre (RCC, ARCC, JRCC, MRCC, CGOC)

▲   Maritime Rescue Coordination Sub-Centre (MRSC)

───   Maritime Search and Rescue Region

───   Provisional Search and Rescue Region

───   No Data

– – – –   Approximate limit of Maritime Rescue Coordination Centre regional/district boundary

   Approximate limit of Operational VHF DSC for Sea Area A1

   Approximate limit of Operational MF DSC for Sea Area A2

   Approximate limit of Operational HF DSC for Sea Area A3

   Approximate limit of Operational DSC for Sea Area A4, North of 76°N and South of 76°S

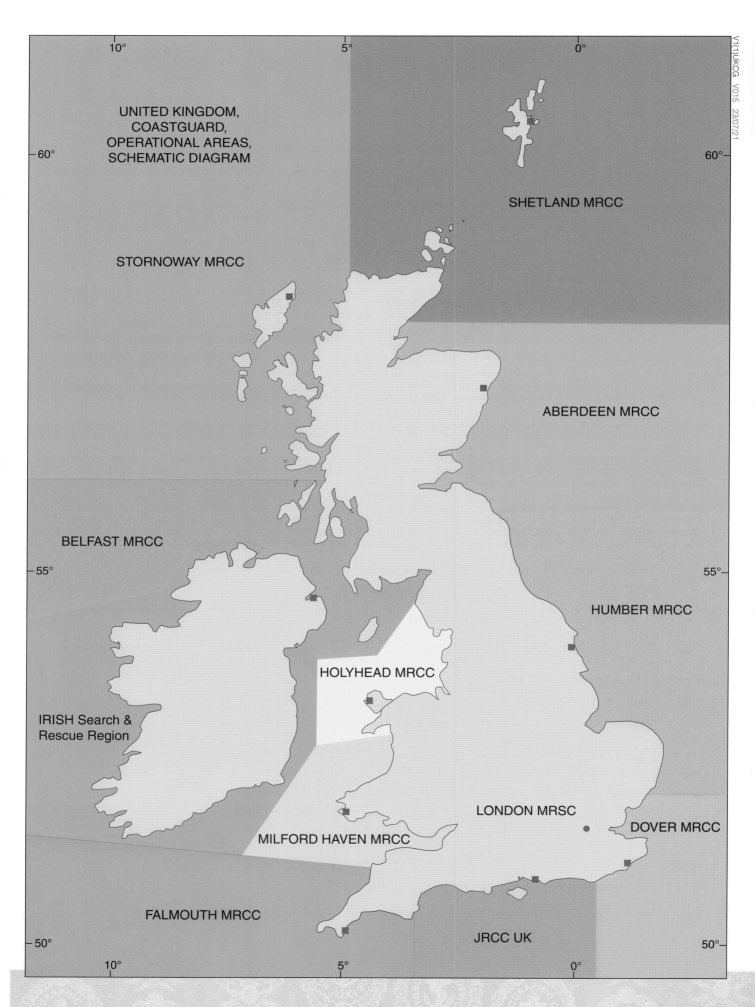

UNITED KINGDOM,
COASTGUARD,
OPERATIONAL AREAS,
SCHEMATIC DIAGRAM

STORNOWAY MRCC

SHETLAND MRCC

ABERDEEN MRCC

BELFAST MRCC

HUMBER MRCC

HOLYHEAD MRCC

IRISH Search &
Rescue Region

LONDON MRSC

DOVER MRCC

MILFORD HAVEN MRCC

FALMOUTH MRCC

JRCC UK

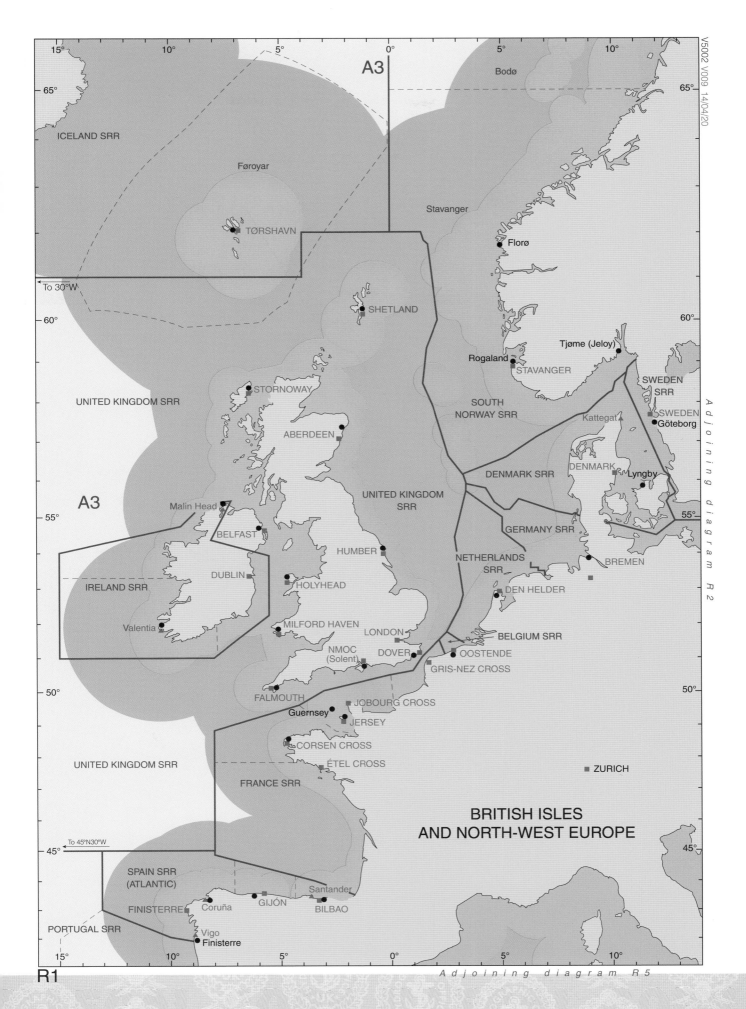

A3

Bodø

ICELAND SRR

Føroyar

TØRSHAVN

Stavanger

Florø

To 30°W

SHETLAND

STORNOWAY

ABERDEEN

UNITED KINGDOM SRR

A3

Malin Head

BELFAST

DUBLIN

IRELAND SRR

HOLYHEAD

Valentia

MILFORD HAVEN

FALMOUTH

Guernsey

JERSEY

CORSEN CROSS

ÉTEL CROSS

UNITED KINGDOM SRR

FRANCE SRR

To 45°N30°W

SPAIN SRR
(ATLANTIC)

FINISTERRE   Coruña   GIJÓN   Santander

Vigo   BILBAO

PORTUGAL SRR   Finisterre

UNITED KINGDOM
SRR

HUMBER

LONDON

NMOC
(Solent)   DOVER

JOBOURG CROSS

Rogaland

STAVANGER

SOUTH
NORWAY SRR

DENMARK SRR

NETHERLANDS
SRR

DEN HELDER

BELGIUM SRR

OOSTENDE

GRIS-NEZ CROSS

Tjøme (Jeloy)

SWEDEN
SRR

SWEDEN

Göteborg

Kattegat

DENMARK   Lyngby

GERMANY SRR

BREMEN

ZURICH

BRITISH ISLES
AND NORTH-WEST EUROPE

R1

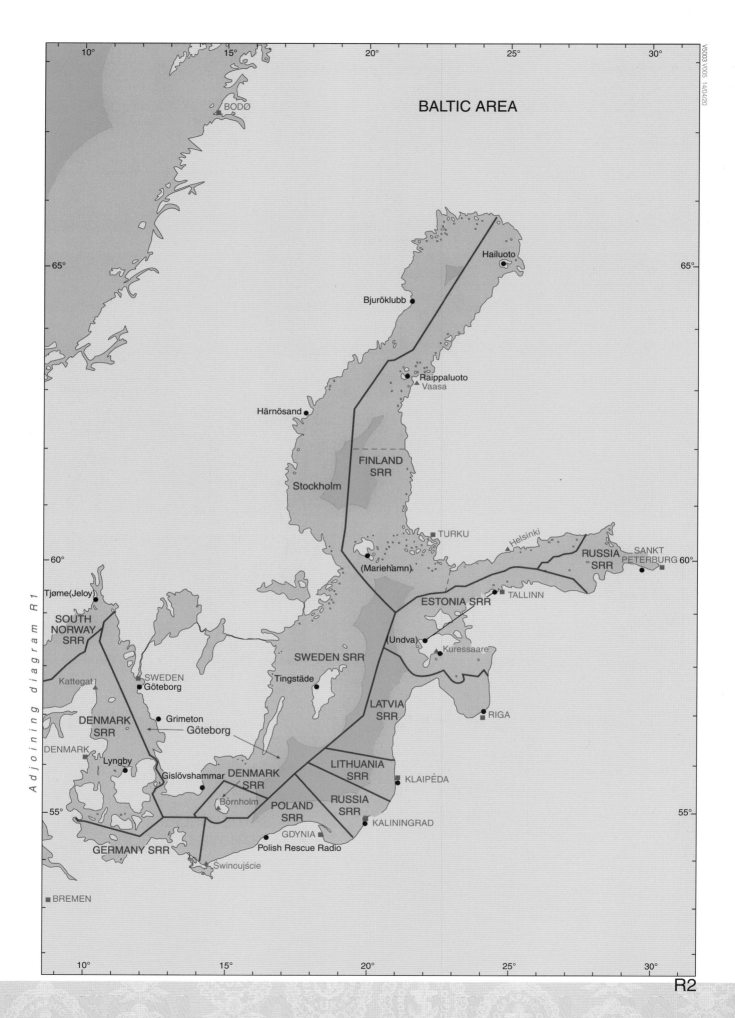

BALTIC AREA

BODØ

65°

Hailuoto

Bjuröklubb

Raippaluoto
Vaasa

Härnösand

FINLAND
SRR

Stockholm

TURKU

Helsinki

RUSSIA
SRR

SANKT
PETERBURG

60°

(Mariehamn)

ESTONIA SRR

TALLINN

Tjøme(Jeløy)

SOUTH
NORWAY
SRR

Undva

Kuressaare

SWEDEN SRR

SWEDEN

Göteborg

Tingstäde

LATVIA
SRR

RIGA

Kattegat

DENMARK
SRR

Grimeton

Göteborg

DENMARK

Lyngby

Gislövshammar

DENMARK
SRR

LITHUANIA
SRR

KLAIPĖDA

Bornholm

RUSSIA
SRR

POLAND
SRR

KALININGRAD

55°

GERMANY SRR

GDYNIA

Polish Rescue Radio

Swinoujście

BREMEN

Adjoining diagram R1

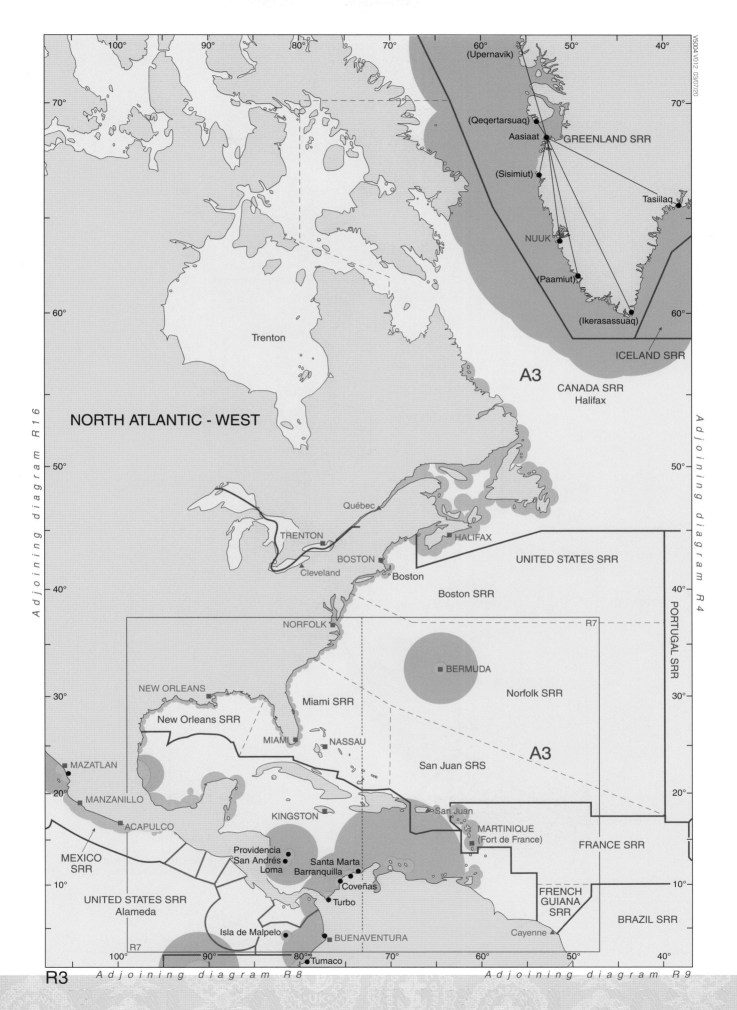

(Upernavik)

GREENLAND SRR

(Qeqertarsuaq)

Aasiaat

(Sisimiut)

Tasiilaq

NUUK

(Paamiut)

(Ikerasassuaq)

ICELAND SRR

A3

CANADA SRR
Halifax

Trenton

NORTH ATLANTIC - WEST

Québec

TRENTON

HALIFAX

BOSTON

Cleveland

Boston

UNITED STATES SRR

Boston SRR

NORFOLK

R7

BERMUDA

Norfolk SRR

NEW ORLEANS

Miami SRR

A3

New Orleans SRR

MIAMI

NASSAU

San Juan SRS

MAZATLAN

San Juan

MANZANILLO

KINGSTON

MARTINIQUE
(Fort de France)

FRANCE SRR

ACAPULCO

MEXICO
SRR

Providencia
San Andrés
Loma

Santa Marta
Barranquilla

Coveñas

FRENCH
GUIANA
SRR

BRAZIL SRR

UNITED STATES SRR
Alameda

Turbo

Isla de Malpelo

Cayenne

R7

BUENAVENTURA

Tumaco

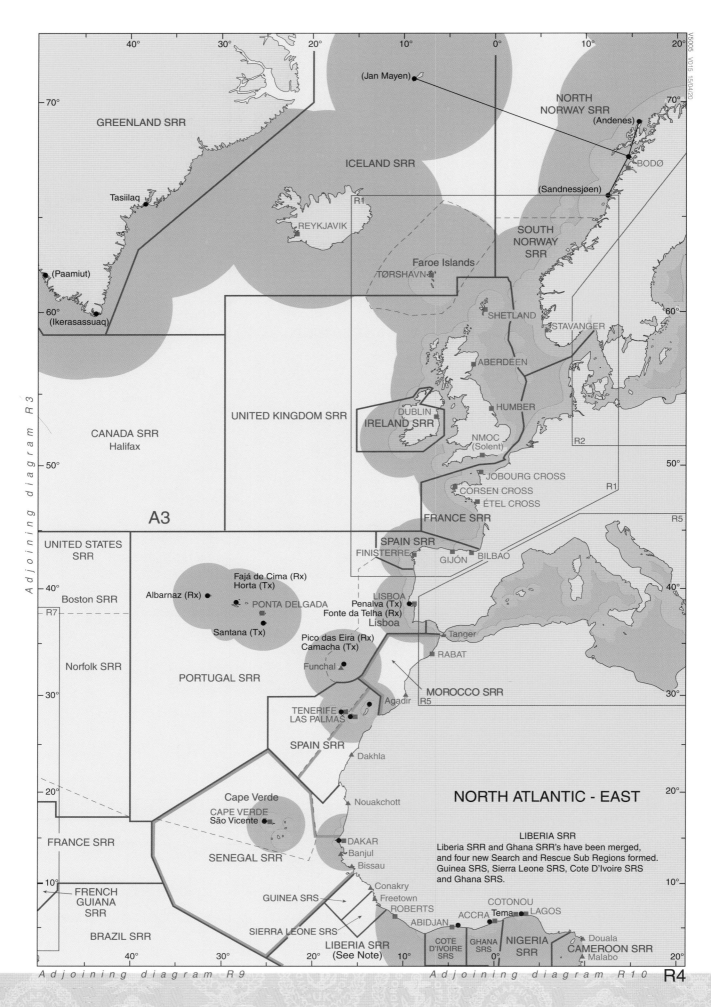

Adjoining diagram R3

GREENLAND SRR

Tasiilaq

(Paamiut)

(Ikerasassuaq)

(Jan Mayen)

NORTH
NORWAY SRR

(Andenes)

BODØ

ICELAND SRR

(Sandnessjøen)

REYKJAVIK

Faroe Islands

TÓRSHAVN

SOUTH
NORWAY
SRR

SHETLAND

STAVANGER

ABERDEEN

UNITED KINGDOM SRR

DUBLIN

IRELAND SRR

HUMBER

NMOC
(Solent)

JOBOURG CROSS

CORSEN CROSS

ÉTEL CROSS

FRANCE SRR

R1

R2

CANADA SRR

Halifax

A3

SPAIN SRR

FINISTERRE

GIJÓN

BILBAO

R5

R1

UNITED STATES
SRR

Boston SRR

R7

Norfolk SRR

Fajá de Cima (Rx)
Horta (Tx)

Albarnaz (Rx)

PONTA DELGADA

Santana (Tx)

LISBOA

Penalva (Tx)

Fonte da Telha (Rx)

Lisboa

Tanger

RABAT

MOROCCO SRR

R5

PORTUGAL SRR

Pico das Eira (Rx)
Camacha (Tx)

Funchal

Agadir

TENERIFE

LAS PALMAS

SPAIN SRR

Dakhla

NORTH ATLANTIC - EAST

FRANCE SRR

Cape Verde

CAPE VERDE
São Vicente

Nouakchott

LIBERIA SRR

Liberia SRR and Ghana SRR's have been merged,
and four new Search and Rescue Sub Regions formed.
Guinea SRS, Sierra Leone SRS, Cote D'Ivoire SRS
and Ghana SRS.

DAKAR

Banjul

Bissau

SENEGAL SRR

FRENCH
GUIANA
SRR

Conakry

Freetown

GUINEA SRS

ROBERTS

COTONOU

ACCRA   Tema   LAGOS

ABIDJAN

BRAZIL SRR

SIERRA LEONE SRS

LIBERIA SRR
(See Note)

COTE
D'IVOIRE
SRS

GHANA
SRS

NIGERIA
SRR

Douala

CAMEROON SRR

Malabo

Adjoining diagram R9

Adjoining diagram R10

R4

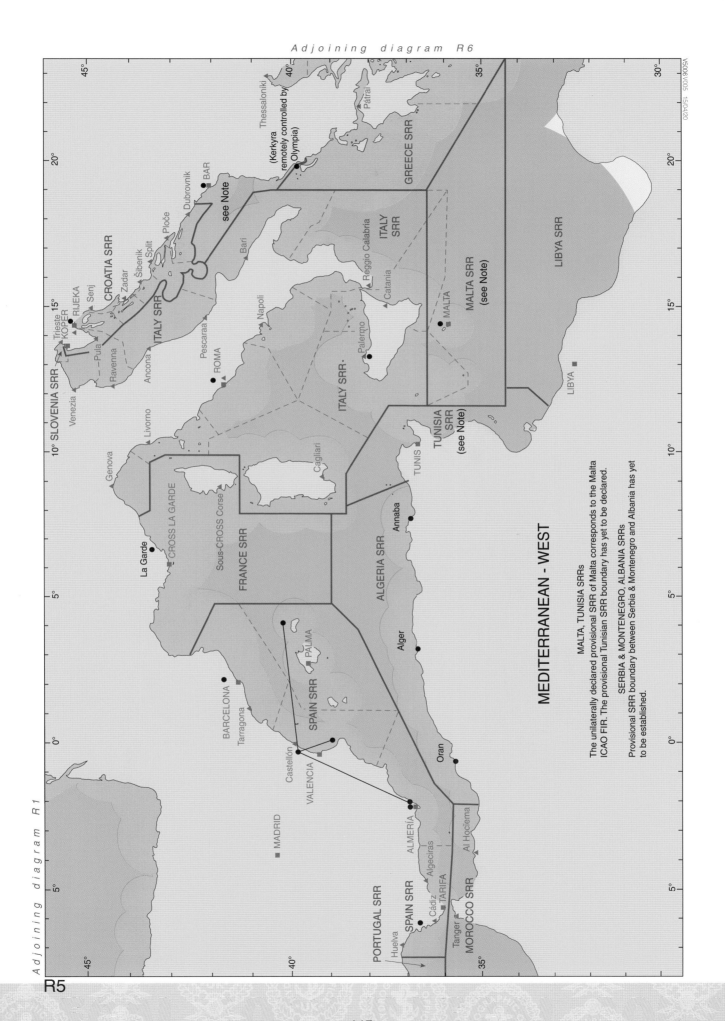

R5

MEDITERRANEAN - WEST

MALTA, TUNISIA SRRs

The unilaterally declared provisional SRR of Malta corresponds to the Malta ICAO FIR. The provisional Tunisian SRR boundary has yet to be declared.

SERBIA & MONTENEGRO, ALBANIA SRRs
Provisional SRR boundary between Serbia & Montenegro and Albania has yet to be established.

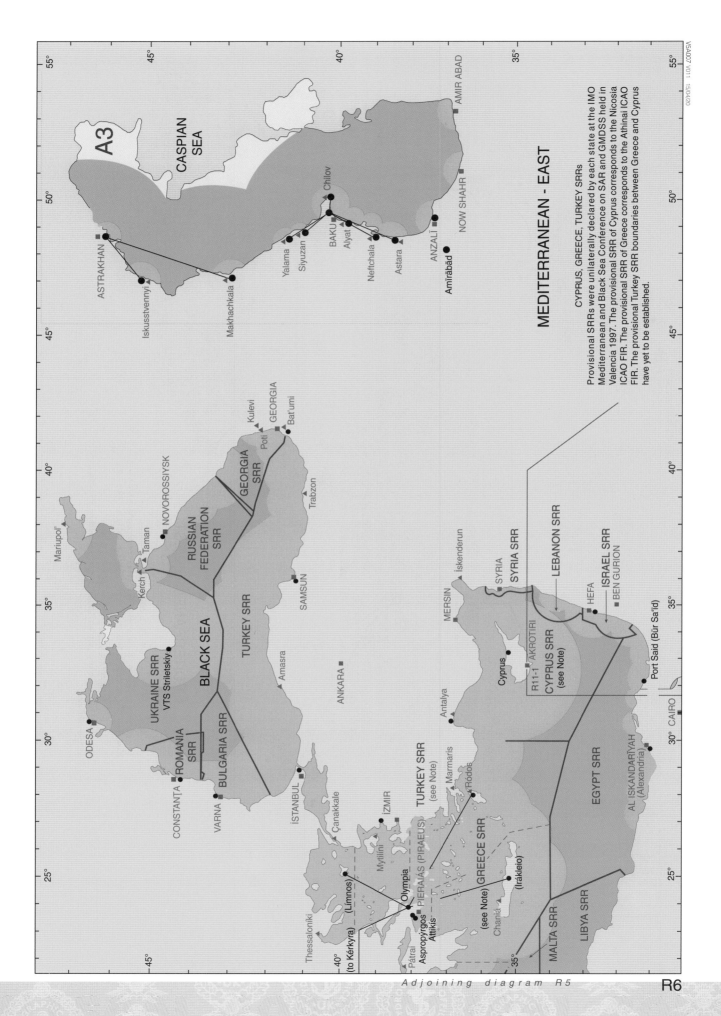

MEDITERRANEAN - EAST

CYPRUS, GREECE, TURKEY SRRs

Provisional SRRs were unilaterally declared by each state at the IMO Mediterranean and Black Sea Conference on SAR and GMDSS held in Valencia 1997. The provisional SRR of Cyprus corresponds to the Nicosia ICAO FIR. The provisional SRR of Greece corresponds to the Athinai ICAO FIR. The provisional Turkey SRR boundaries between Greece and Cyprus have yet to be established.

A3

CASPIAN SEA

AMIR ABAD

NOW SHAHR

ANZALĪ

Amīrābād

Chilov

BAKU

Alyat

Neftchala

Astara

Yalama

Siyuzan

ASTRAKHAN

Iskusstvennyi

Makhachkala

GEORGIA

Kulevi

Poti

Bat'umi

GEORGIA SRR

RUSSIAN FEDERATION SRR

NOVOROSSIYSK

Mariupol'

Taman

Kerch

TURKEY SRR

Trabzon

SAMSUN

Amasra

ANKARA

UKRAINE SRR
VTS Striletskiy

BLACK SEA

ODESA

ROMANIA SRR

CONSTANŢA

BULGARIA SRR

VARNA

İSTANBUL

Çanakkale

İZMIR

Mytilíni

MERSIN

İskenderun

SYRIA

SYRIA SRR

LEBANON SRR

HEFA

ISRAEL SRR

BEN GURION

AKROTIRI

Cyprus

R11-1
CYPRUS SRR
(see Note)

Port Said (Būr Sa'īd)

CAIRO

Antalya

Marmaris

Ródos

TURKEY SRR
(see Note)

GREECE SRR
(see Note)

Irákleio

Chaniá

PIERAIÁS (PIRAEUS)

Olympia

Aspropýrgos
Attikís

Pátrai

(Limnos)

(to Kérkyra)

Thessaloníki

EGYPT SRR

AL ISKANDARĪYAH
(Alexandria)

LIBYA SRR

MALTA SRR

V5A007_V011 15/04/20

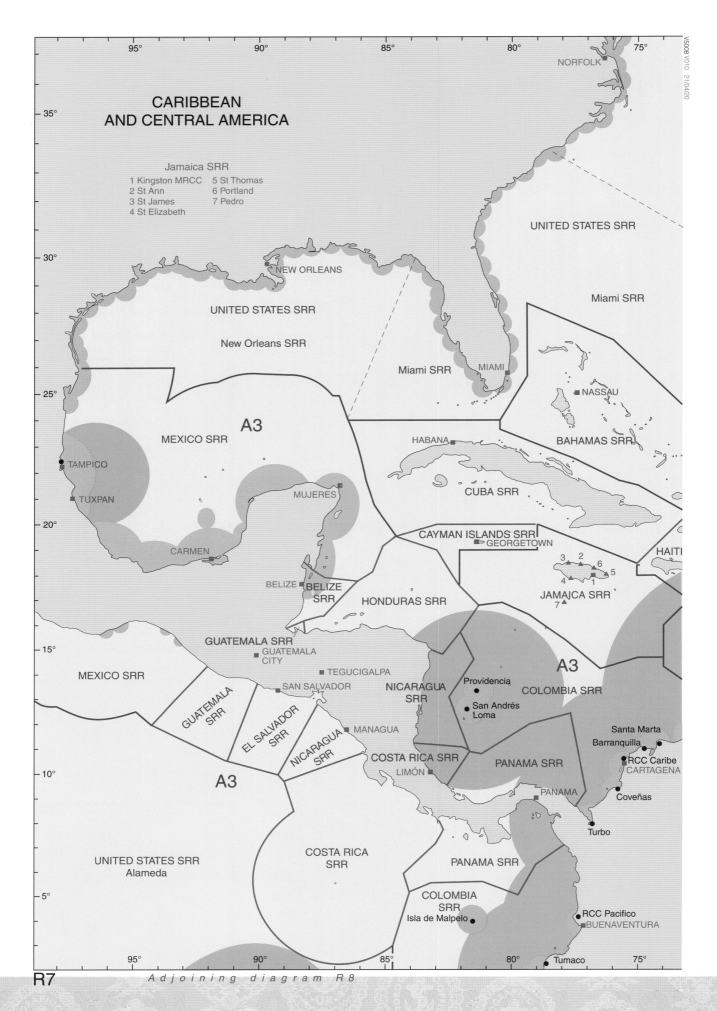

CARIBBEAN
AND CENTRAL AMERICA

Jamaica SRR
1 Kingston MRCC 5 St Thomas
2 St Ann   6 Portland
3 St James   7 Pedro
4 St Elizabeth

NORFOLK

UNITED STATES SRR

Miami SRR

NEW ORLEANS

UNITED STATES SRR

New Orleans SRR

Miami SRR

MIAMI

NASSAU

A3

MEXICO SRR

HABANA

BAHAMAS SRR

CUBA SRR

TAMPICO

CAYMAN ISLANDS SRR

GEORGETOWN

HAITI

TUXPAN

MUJERES

3   2   6

4   1   5

JAMAICA SRR

7

CARMEN

BELIZE BELIZE
        SRR

HONDURAS SRR

A3

GUATEMALA SRR

GUATEMALA
CITY

MEXICO SRR

TEGUCIGALPA

NICARAGUA
SRR

Providencia

COLOMBIA SRR

SAN SALVADOR

GUATEMALA
SRR

EL SALVADOR
SRR

San Andrés
Loma

Santa Marta

Barranquilla

NICARAGUA
SRR

MANAGUA

COSTA RICA SRR

PANAMA SRR

RCC Caribe
CARTAGENA

A3

LIMÓN

Coveñas

PANAMA

UNITED STATES SRR
Alameda

COSTA RICA
SRR

PANAMA SRR

Turbo

COLOMBIA
SRR

Isla de Malpelo

RCC Pacifico
BUENAVENTURA

Tumaco

R7   Adjoining diagram R8

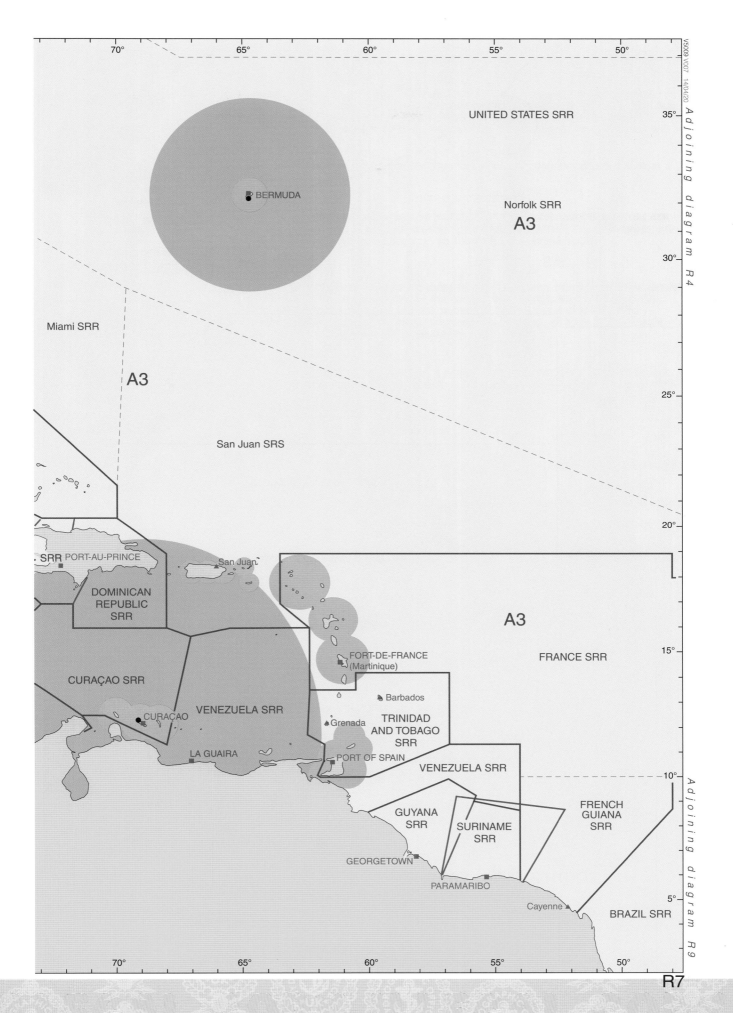

UNITED STATES SRR

Norfolk SRR

A3

Miami SRR

A3

BERMUDA

San Juan SRS

SRR PORT-AU-PRINCE

San Juan

DOMINICAN
REPUBLIC
SRR

A3

FRANCE SRR

CURAÇAO SRR

FORT-DE-FRANCE
(Martinique)

Barbados

VENEZUELA SRR

CURAÇAO

Grenada

TRINIDAD
AND TOBAGO
SRR

LA GUAIRA

PORT OF SPAIN

VENEZUELA SRR

GUYANA
SRR

SURINAME
SRR

FRENCH
GUIANA
SRR

GEORGETOWN

PARAMARIBO

Cayenne

BRAZIL SRR

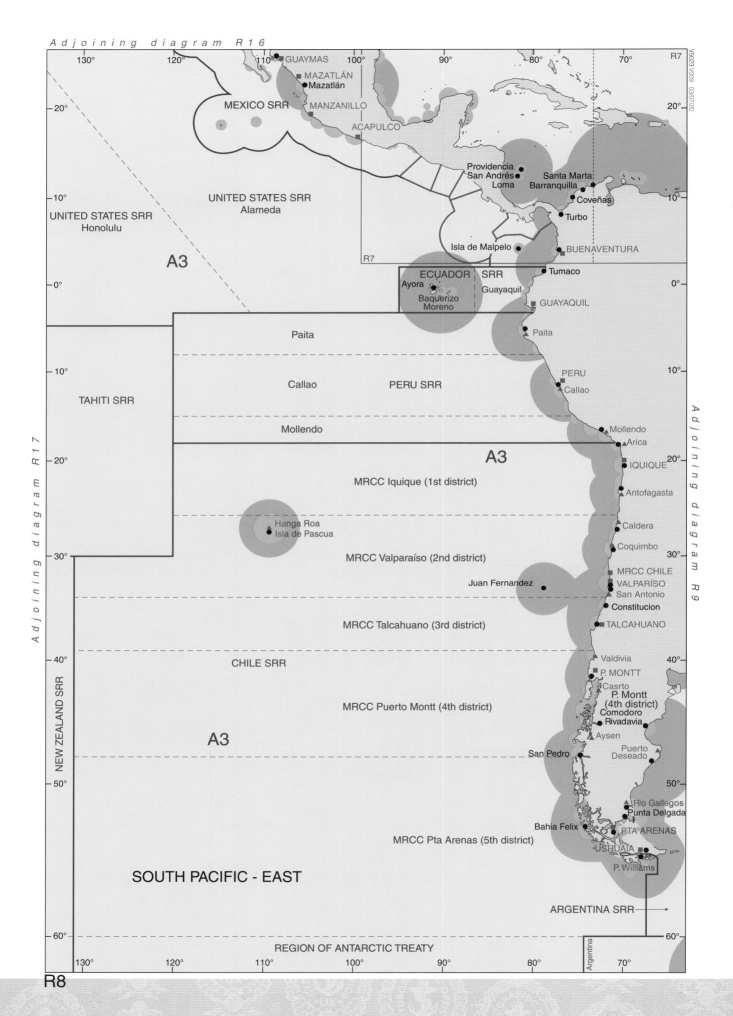

V5023 V009 03/07/20

GUAYMAS

MAZATLÁN
Mazatlán

MANZANILLO

MEXICO SRR

ACAPULCO

UNITED STATES SRR
Alameda

Providencia
San Andrés
Loma

Santa Marta
Barranquilla
Coveñas

Turbo

UNITED STATES SRR
Honolulu

A3

R7

Isla de Malpelo

BUENAVENTURA

ECUADOR   SRR
Ayora
Baquerizo
Moreno

Guayaquil

Tumaco

GUAYAQUIL

Paita

Paita

TAHITI SRR

Callao

PERU SRR

PERU

Callao

Mollendo

Mollendo

Arica

A3

IQUIQUE

MRCC Iquique (1st district)

Antofagasta

Hanga Roa
Isla de Pascua

Caldera

Coquimbo

MRCC Valparaíso (2nd district)

MRCC CHILE
VALPARÍSO
San Antonio

Juan Fernandez

Constitucion

MRCC Talcahuano (3rd district)

TALCAHUANO

Valdivia

CHILE SRR

P. MONTT

Casrto
P. Montt
(4th district)

MRCC Puerto Montt (4th district)

Comodoro
Rivadavia

A3

Aysen

San Pedro

Puerto
Deseado

Rio Gallegos
Punta Delgada

Bahia Felix

PTA ARENAS

MRCC Pta Arenas (5th district)

USHUAIA

P. Williams

SOUTH PACIFIC - EAST

ARGENTINA SRR →

NEW ZEALAND SRR

Argentina

REGION OF ANTARCTIC TREATY

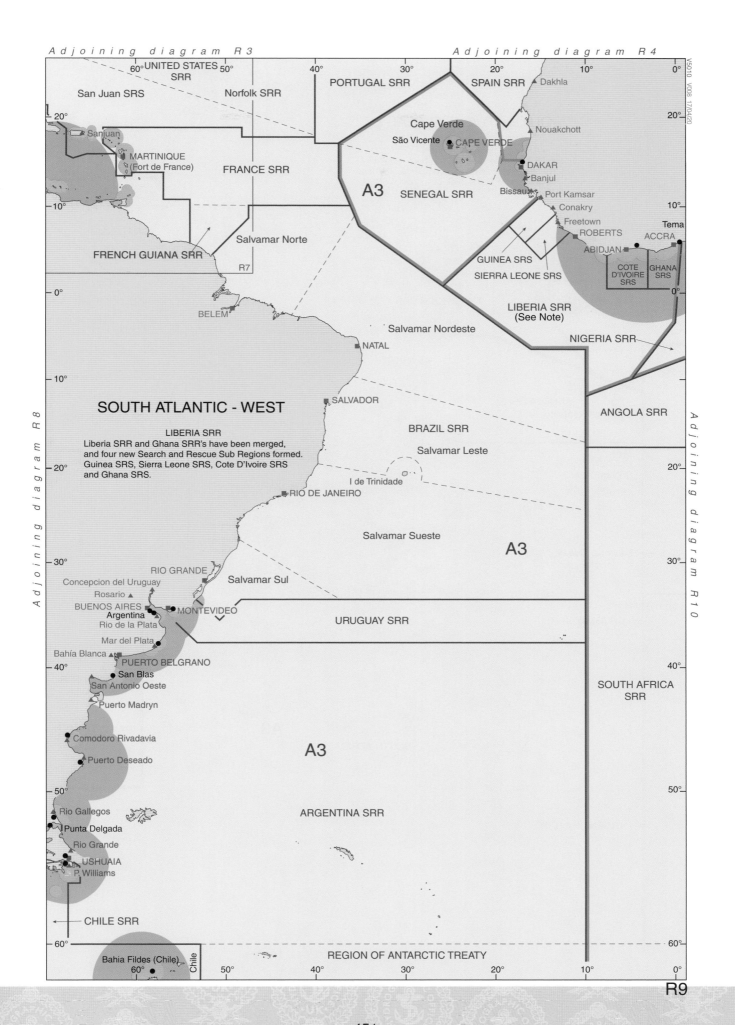

UNITED STATES SRR

60° 50° 40° 30° 20° 10° 0°

San Juan SRS

Dakhla

Norfolk SRR

PORTUGAL SRR

SPAIN SRR

20°

Cape Verde

São Vicente ● CAPE VERDE

Nouakchott

San Juan

MARTINIQUE
(Fort de France)

FRANCE SRR

DAKAR
Banjul

Bissau Port Kamsar

A3 SENEGAL SRR

Conakry

Freetown

ROBERTS

Tema

FRENCH GUIANA SRR

Salvamar Norte

R7

ACCRA

ABIDJAN

GUINEA SRS

SIERRA LEONE SRS

COTE
D'IVOIRE
SRS

GHANA
SRS

0°

LIBERIA SRR
(See Note)

NIGERIA SRR

BELEM

Salvamar Nordeste

NATAL

ANGOLA SRR

SALVADOR

SOUTH ATLANTIC - WEST

BRAZIL SRR

Salvamar Leste

LIBERIA SRR
Liberia SRR and Ghana SRR's have been merged,
and four new Search and Rescue Sub Regions formed.
Guinea SRS, Sierra Leone SRS, Cote D'Ivoire SRS
and Ghana SRS.

I de Trinidade

RIO DE JANEIRO

Salvamar Sueste

A3

RIO GRANDE

Concepcion del Uruguay

Rosario

BUENOS AIRES

Argentina

Rio de la Plata

Mar del Plata

Salvamar Sul

MONTEVIDEO

URUGUAY SRR

Bahía Blanca PUERTO BELGRANO

San Blas

San Antonio Oeste

SOUTH AFRICA
SRR

Puerto Madryn

Comodoro Rivadavia

A3

Puerto Deseado

Río Gallegos

ARGENTINA SRR

Punta Delgada

Rio Grande

USHUAIA

P. Williams

CHILE SRR

Bahia Fildes (Chile)

Chile

REGION OF ANTARCTIC TREATY

60° 50° 40° 30° 20° 10° 0°

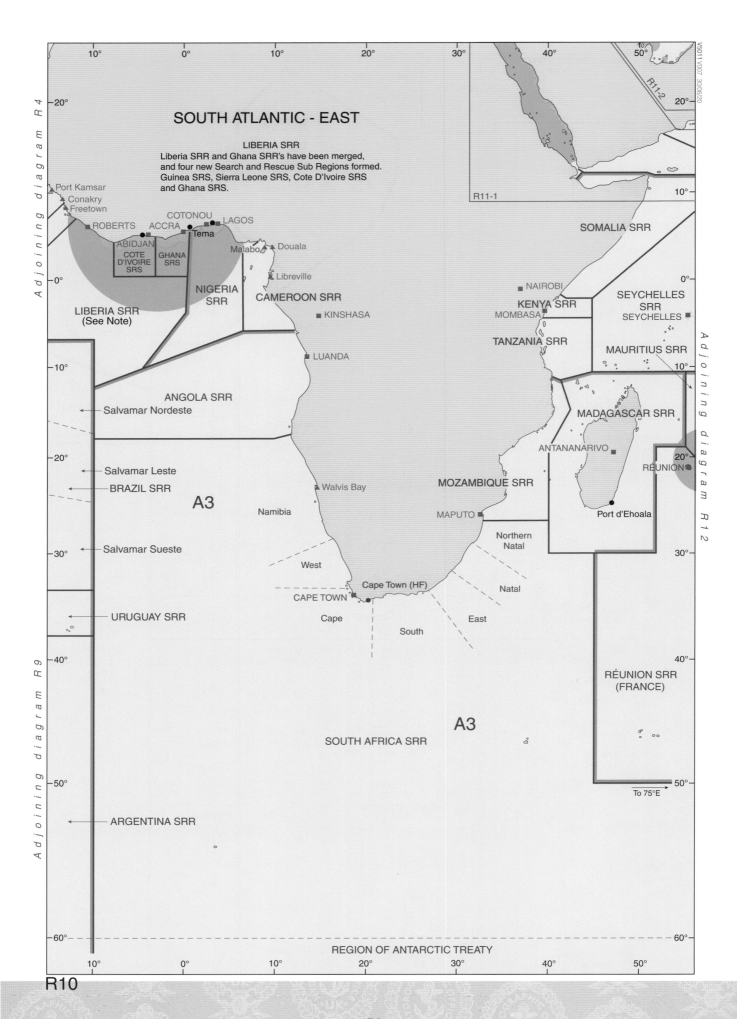

SOUTH ATLANTIC - EAST

LIBERIA SRR
Liberia SRR and Ghana SRR's have been merged,
and four new Search and Rescue Sub Regions formed.
Guinea SRS, Sierra Leone SRS, Cote D'Ivoire SRS
and Ghana SRS.

Adjoining diagram R 4

V5011 V007 30/06/20

R11-2

R11-1

Port Kamsar

Conakry
Freetown

ROBERTS   ACCRA   COTONOU   LAGOS
          Tema

ABIDJAN
COTE
D'IVOIRE   GHANA
SRS   SRS

Malabo   Douala

Libreville

LIBERIA SRR
(See Note)

NIGERIA
SRR

CAMEROON SRR

KINSHASA

SOMALIA SRR

NAIROBI

KENYA SRR
MOMBASA

SEYCHELLES
SRR
SEYCHELLES

TANZANIA SRR

MAURITIUS SRR

LUANDA

ANGOLA SRR

Salvamar Nordeste

MADAGASCAR SRR

ANTANANARIVO

RÉUNION

Salvamar Leste

BRAZIL SRR

A3

Walvis Bay

Namibia

MOZAMBIQUE SRR

Salvamar Sueste

MAPUTO

Port d'Ehoala

Northern
Natal

West

Natal

URUGUAY SRR

Cape Town (HF)

CAPE TOWN

Cape

East

South

RÉUNION SRR
(FRANCE)

A3

SOUTH AFRICA SRR

To 75°E

ARGENTINA SRR

REGION OF ANTARCTIC TREATY

Adjoining diagram R 9

Adjoining diagram R 12

R10

452

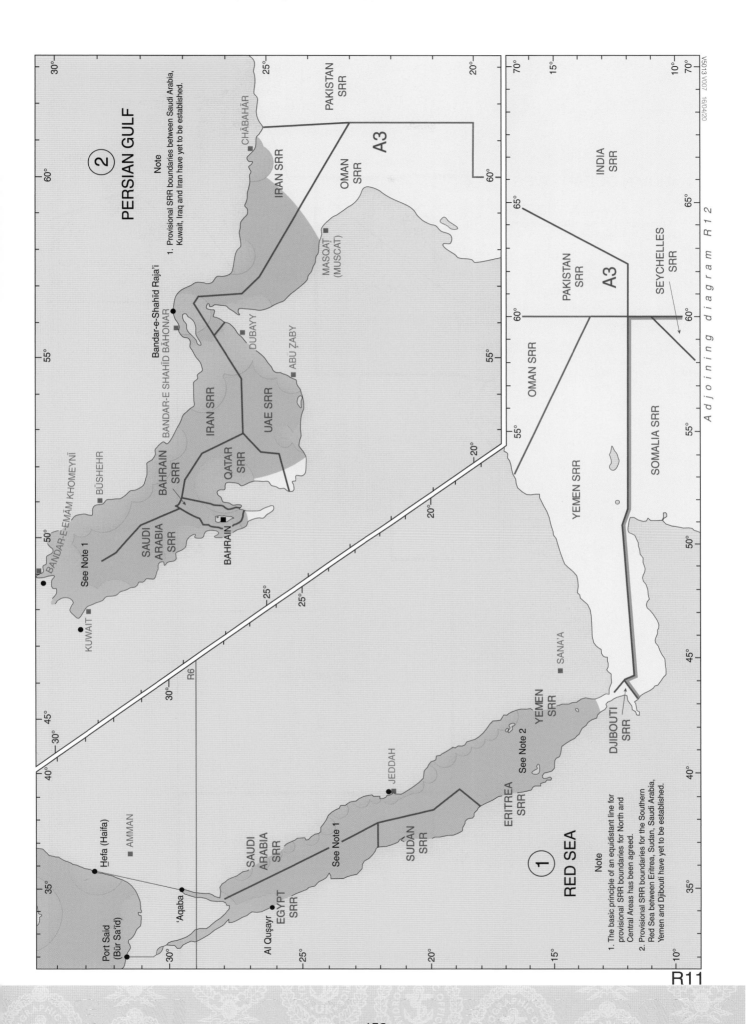

Adjoining diagram R12

PERSIAN GULF ②

Note

1. Provisional SRR boundaries between Saudi Arabia, Kuwait, Iraq and Iran have yet to be established.

CHĀBAHĀR

PAKISTAN
SRR

IRAN SRR

OMAN
SRR

A3

MASQAT
(MUSCAT)

Bandar-e-Shahīd Raja'i

BANDAR-E SHAHĪD BĀHONAR

DUBAYY

ABU ẒABY

BŪSHEHR

IRAN SRR

UAE SRR

QATAR
SRR

BANDAR-E-EMĀM KHOMEYNĪ

BAHRAIN
SRR

SAUDI
ARABIA
SRR

See Note 1

BAHRAIN

KUWAIT

PAKISTAN
SRR

INDIA
SRR

SEYCHELLES
SRR

A3

OMAN SRR

SOMALIA SRR

YEMEN SRR

SANA'A

AMMAN

Ḥefa (Haifa)

'Aqaba

Port Saïd
(Būr Saʿīd)

Al Quṣayr

EGYPT
SRR

R6

SAUDI
ARABIA
SRR

See Note 1

JEDDAH

SUDÂN
SRR

ERITREA
SRR

YEMEN
SRR

See Note 2

DJIBOUTI
SRR

RED SEA ①

Note

1. The basic principle of an equidistant line for provisional SRR boundaries for North and Central Areas has been agreed.

2. Provisional SRR boundaries for the Southern Red Sea between Eritrea, Sudan, Saudi Arabia, Yemen and Djibouti have yet to be established.

R11

453

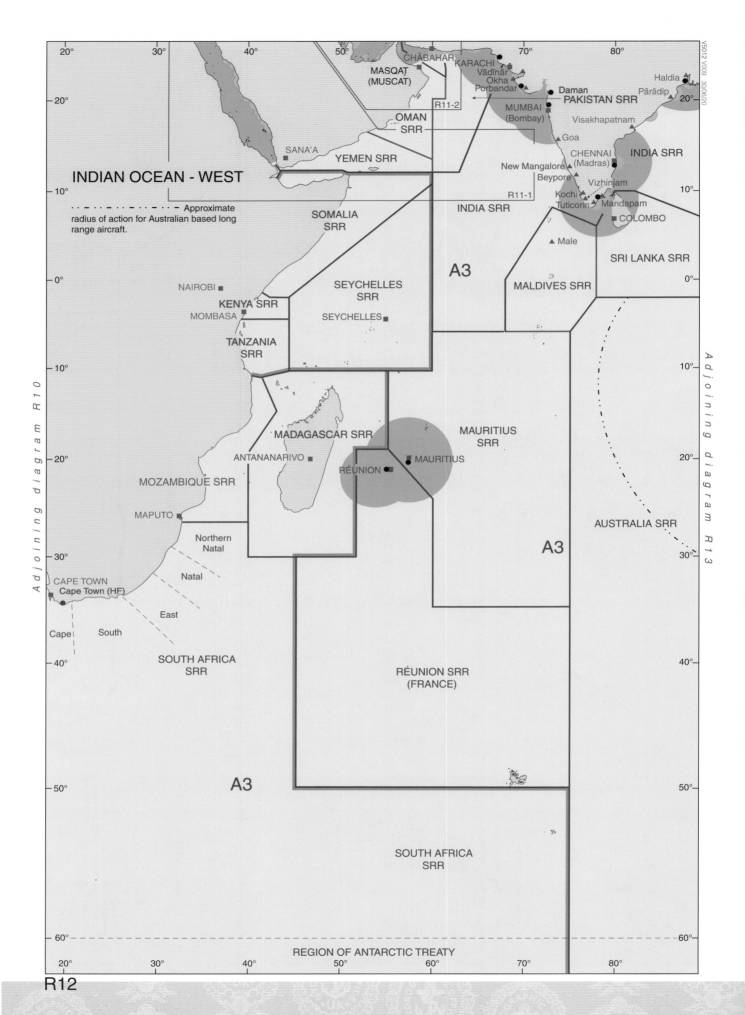

INDIAN OCEAN - WEST

∙ ∙ ∙ ∙ ∙ ∙ ∙ ∙ ∙ ∙ ∙ ∙ ∙ ∙ ∙ — Approximate radius of action for Australian based long range aircraft.

CHĀBAHĀR
MASQAT (MUSCAT)
KARACHI
Vādīnār
Okha
Porbandar
Daman
PAKISTAN SRR
Haldia
Pārādip
20°
Visakhapatnam
MUMBAI (Bombay)
OMAN SRR
R11-2
SANA'A
YEMEN SRR
Goa
New Mangalore
CHENNAI (Madras)
INDIA SRR
Beypore
Vizhinjam
R11-1
Kochi
Tuticorin
Mandapam
INDIA SRR
COLOMBO
SOMALIA SRR
SRI LANKA SRR
A3
Male
NAIROBI ■
KENYA SRR
SEYCHELLES SRR
MALDIVES SRR
MOMBASA
SEYCHELLES
TANZANIA SRR
MADAGASCAR SRR
MAURITIUS SRR
ANTANANARIVO
RÉUNION
MAURITIUS
MOZAMBIQUE SRR
AUSTRALIA SRR
MAPUTO
Northern Natal
A3
Natal
CAPE TOWN
Cape Town (HF)
East
Cape
South
RÉUNION SRR (FRANCE)
SOUTH AFRICA SRR
A3
SOUTH AFRICA SRR
REGION OF ANTARCTIC TREATY

Adjoining diagram R10

Adjoining diagram R13

V5012 V009 30/06/20

R12

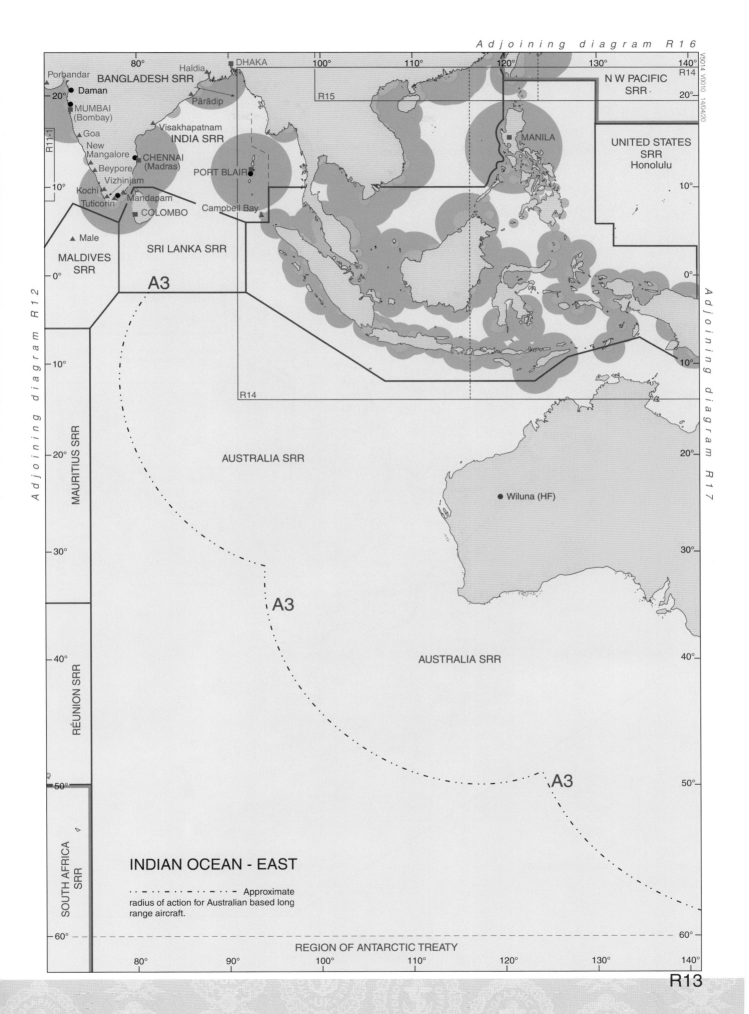

Porbandar
BANGLADESH SRR
80°
Haldia
DHAKA
100°
110°
120°
130°
140°
N W PACIFIC
SRR
R11-1
Daman
20°
MUMBAI
(Bombay)
Pārādip
R15
20°
Goa
New
Mangalore
Visakhapatnam
INDIA SRR
MANILA
UNITED STATES
SRR
Honolulu
CHENNAI
(Madras)
Beypore
Vizhinjam
PORT BLAIR
10°
10°
Kochi
Tuticorin
Mandapam
COLOMBO
Campbell Bay

Male
SRI LANKA SRR

MALDIVES
SRR
0°
A3
0°

10°
10°

R14
MAURITIUS SRR
20°
AUSTRALIA SRR
20°

Wiluna (HF)

30°
30°
A3
RÉUNION SRR
40°
AUSTRALIA SRR
40°

50°
A3
50°
A3

SOUTH AFRICA
SRR

INDIAN OCEAN - EAST

· — · · — · · — Approximate
radius of action for Australian based long
range aircraft.

60°
REGION OF ANTARCTIC TREATY
60°
80°
90°
100°
110°
120°
130°
140°

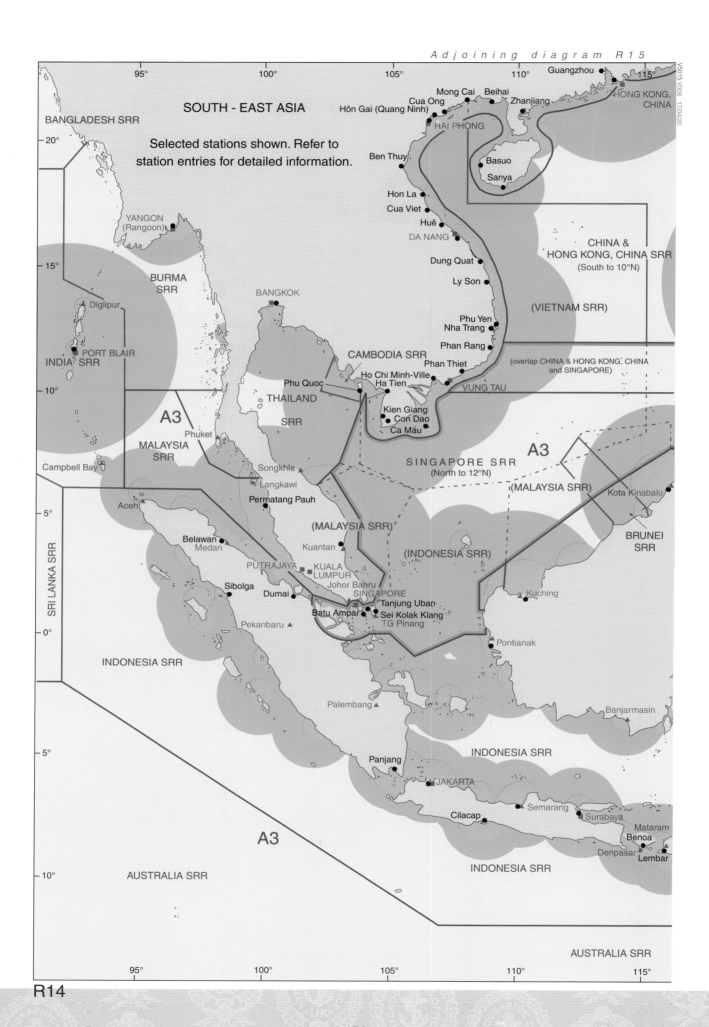

SOUTH - EAST ASIA

Selected stations shown. Refer to
station entries for detailed information.

BANGLADESH SRR

20°

YANGON
(Rangoon)

15°

BURMA
SRR

Diglipur

PORT BLAIR

INDIA SRR

10°

A3

MALAYSIA
SRR

Phuket

Campbell Bay

Songkhla

Langkawi

Permatang Pauh

5°

Aceh

Belawan
Medan

Kuantan

PUTRAJAYA

KUALA
LUMPUR

Johor Bahru
SINGAPORE

Sibolga

Dumai

Batu Ampar

Tanjung Uban

Sei Kolak Klang
TG Pinang

0°

SRI LANKA SRR

Pekanbaru

INDONESIA SRR

Palembang

5°

Panjang

A3

JAKARTA

Cilacap

Semarang

Surabaya

AUSTRALIA SRR

Mataram
Benoa

Denpasar

Lembar

10°

INDONESIA SRR

AUSTRALIA SRR

Guangzhou

Mong Cai
Beihai

Cua Ong
Zhanjiang

Hôn Gai (Quang Ninh)

HONG KONG,
CHINA

HAI PHONG

Ben Thuy

Basuo

Sanya

Hon La

Cua Viet

Huê

DA NANG

CHINA &
HONG KONG, CHINA SRR
(South to 10°N)

Dung Quat

Ly Son

(VIETNAM SRR)

Phu Yen
Nha Trang

Phan Rang

CAMBODIA SRR

Phan Thiet

Ho Chi Minh-Ville

Phu Quoc

Ha Tien

VUNG TAU

THAILAND

SRR

Kien Giang

Con Dao

Ca Mau

(overlap CHINA & HONG KONG, CHINA
and SINGAPORE)

SINGAPORE SRR

(North to 12°N)

A3

(MALAYSIA SRR)

Kota Kinabalu

(MALAYSIA SRR)

BRUNEI
SRR

(INDONESIA SRR)

Kuching

Pontianak

Banjarmasin

INDONESIA SRR

BANGKOK

95°   100°   105°   110°   115°

V5015 V008   17/04/20

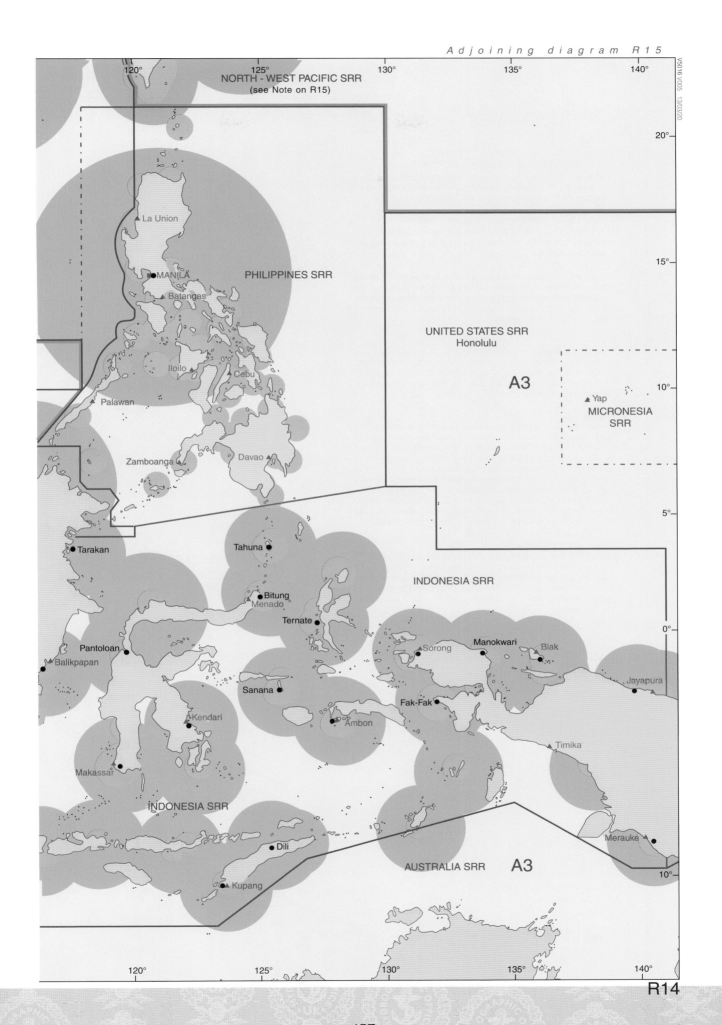

NORTH - WEST PACIFIC SRR
(see Note on R15)

20°

La Union

PHILIPPINES SRR

15°

MANILA

Batangas

UNITED STATES SRR
Honolulu

A3

10°

Iloilo

Cebu

Yap

Palawan

MICRONESIA
SRR

Zamboanga

Davao

5°

Tarakan

Tahuna

INDONESIA SRR

Bitung

Menado

Ternate

0°

Pantoloan

Sorong

Manokwari

Biak

Balikpapan

Jayapura

Sanana

Kendari

Fak-Fak

Ambon

Timika

Makassar

INDONESIA SRR

Dili

Merauke

AUSTRALIA SRR   A3

10°

Kupang

120°   125°   130°   135°   140°

R14

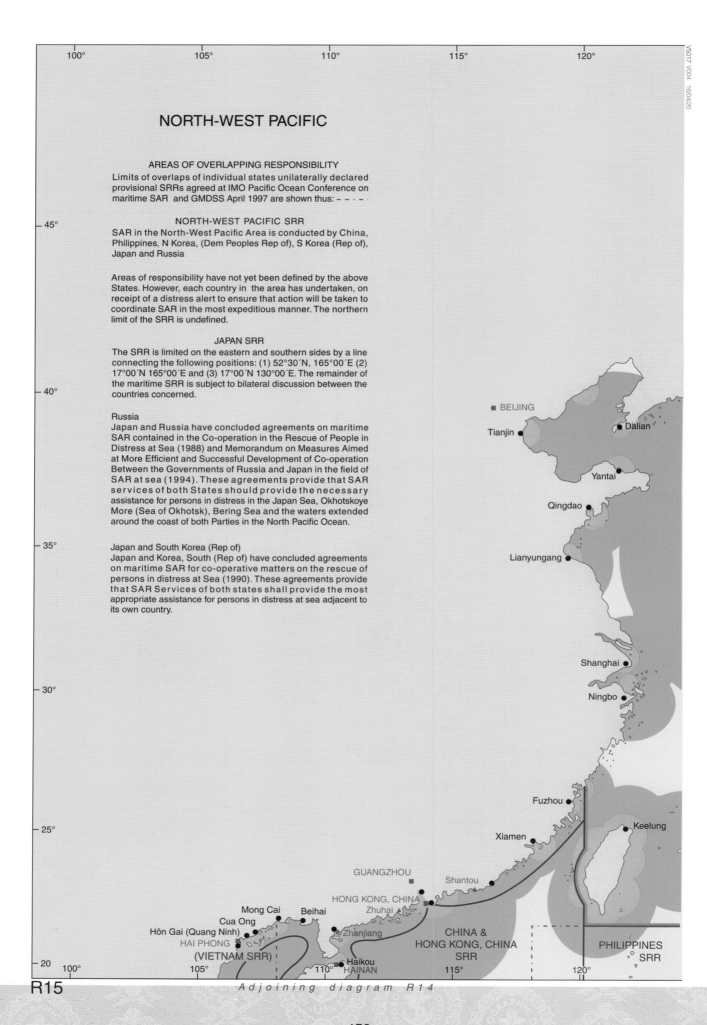

NORTH-WEST PACIFIC

AREAS OF OVERLAPPING RESPONSIBILITY
Limits of overlaps of individual states unilaterally declared provisional SRRs agreed at IMO Pacific Ocean Conference on maritime SAR and GMDSS April 1997 are shown thus: – – · –

NORTH-WEST PACIFIC SRR
SAR in the North-West Pacific Area is conducted by China, Philippines, N Korea, (Dem Peoples Rep of), S Korea (Rep of), Japan and Russia

Areas of responsibility have not yet been defined by the above States. However, each country in the area has undertaken, on receipt of a distress alert to ensure that action will be taken to coordinate SAR in the most expeditious manner. The northern limit of the SRR is undefined.

JAPAN SRR
The SRR is limited on the eastern and southern sides by a line connecting the following positions: (1) 52°30′N, 165°00′E (2) 17°00′N 165°00′E and (3) 17°00′N 130°00′E. The remainder of the maritime SRR is subject to bilateral discussion between the countries concerned.

Russia
Japan and Russia have concluded agreements on maritime SAR contained in the Co-operation in the Rescue of People in Distress at Sea (1988) and Memorandum on Measures Aimed at More Efficient and Successful Development of Co-operation Between the Governments of Russia and Japan in the field of SAR at sea (1994). These agreements provide that SAR services of both States should provide the necessary assistance for persons in distress in the Japan Sea, Okhotskoye More (Sea of Okhotsk), Bering Sea and the waters extended around the coast of both Parties in the North Pacific Ocean.

Japan and South Korea (Rep of)
Japan and Korea, South (Rep of) have concluded agreements on maritime SAR for co-operative matters on the rescue of persons in distress at Sea (1990). These agreements provide that SAR Services of both states shall provide the most appropriate assistance for persons in distress at sea adjacent to its own country.

Adjoining diagram R14

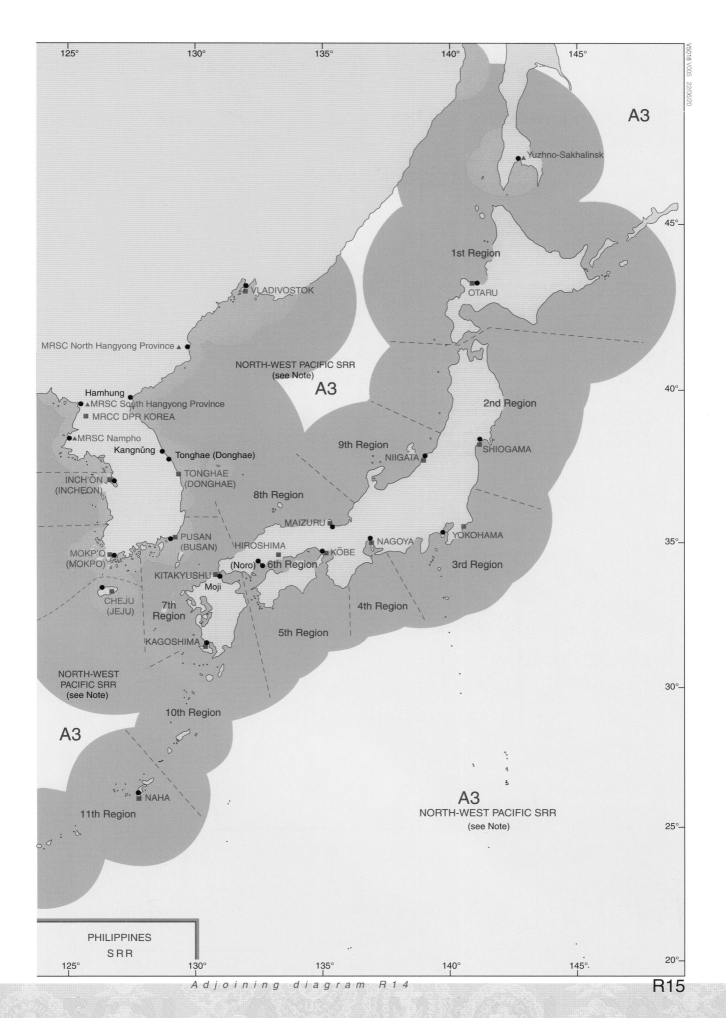

A3

125°   130°   135°   140°   145°

Yuzhno-Sakhalinsk

45°

1st Region

VLADIVOSTOK

OTARU

MRSC North Hangyong Province

NORTH-WEST PACIFIC SRR
(see Note)

A3

40°

2nd Region

Hamhung
MRSC South Hangyong Province

MRCC DPR KOREA

9th Region

SHIOGAMA

MRSC Nampho

NIIGATA

Kangnŭng   Tonghae (Donghae)

TONGHAE
(DONGHAE)

INCH'ŎN
(INCHEON)

8th Region

35°

MAIZURU

NAGOYA

YOKOHAMA

PUSAN
(BUSAN)

HIROSHIMA

KŌBE

MOKP'O
(MOKPO)

(Noro) 6th Region

3rd Region

KITAKYUSHU

CHEJU
(JEJU)

Moji

7th
Region

4th Region

KAGOSHIMA

5th Region

NORTH-WEST
PACIFIC SRR
(see Note)

30°

10th Region

A3

A3
NORTH-WEST PACIFIC SRR
(see Note)

NAHA

25°

11th Region

PHILIPPINES
S R R

125°   130°   135°   140°   145°

20°

Adjoining diagram R14

R15

459

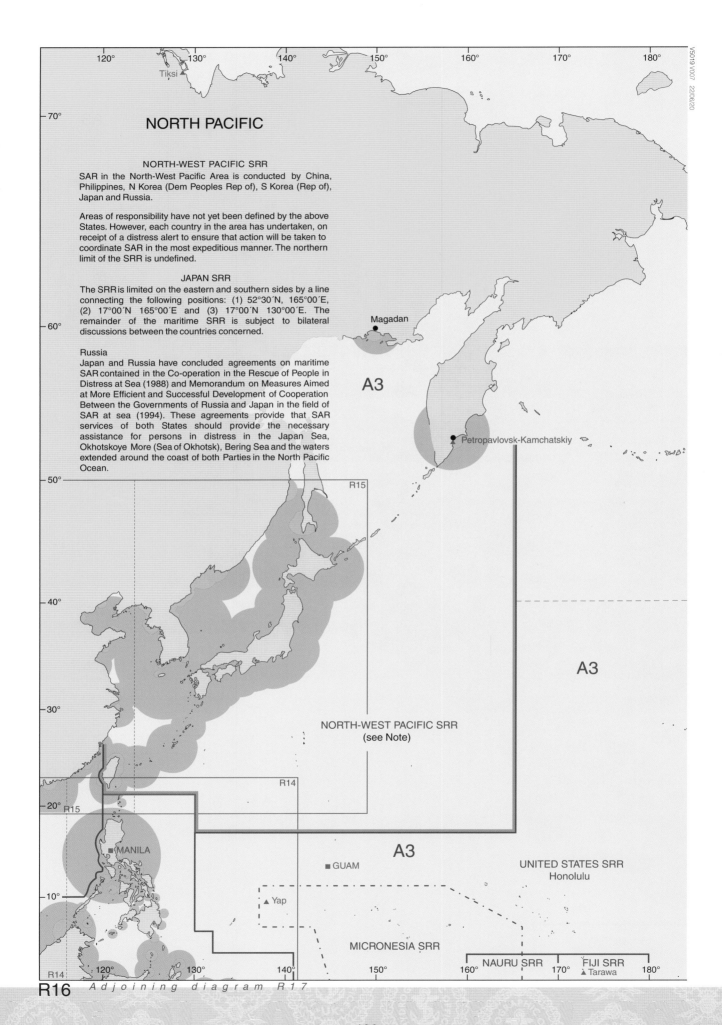

NORTH PACIFIC

NORTH-WEST PACIFIC SRR

SAR in the North-West Pacific Area is conducted by China, Philippines, N Korea (Dem Peoples Rep of), S Korea (Rep of), Japan and Russia.

Areas of responsibility have not yet been defined by the above States. However, each country in the area has undertaken, on receipt of a distress alert to ensure that action will be taken to coordinate SAR in the most expeditious manner. The northern limit of the SRR is undefined.

JAPAN SRR

The SRR is limited on the eastern and southern sides by a line connecting the following positions: (1) 52°30′N, 165°00′E, (2) 17°00′N 165°00′E and (3) 17°00′N 130°00′E. The remainder of the maritime SRR is subject to bilateral discussions between the countries concerned.

Russia

Japan and Russia have concluded agreements on maritime SAR contained in the Co-operation in the Rescue of People in Distress at Sea (1988) and Memorandum on Measures Aimed at More Efficient and Successful Development of Cooperation Between the Governments of Russia and Japan in the field of SAR at sea (1994). These agreements provide that SAR services of both States should provide the necessary assistance for persons in distress in the Japan Sea, Okhotskoye More (Sea of Okhotsk), Bering Sea and the waters extended around the coast of both Parties in the North Pacific Ocean.

Tiksi

Magadan

A3

Petropavlovsk-Kamchatskiy

R15

A3

NORTH-WEST PACIFIC SRR
(see Note)

R14

A3

MANILA

GUAM

UNITED STATES SRR
Honolulu

Yap

MICRONESIA SRR

NAURU SRR

FIJI SRR
Tarawa

R14

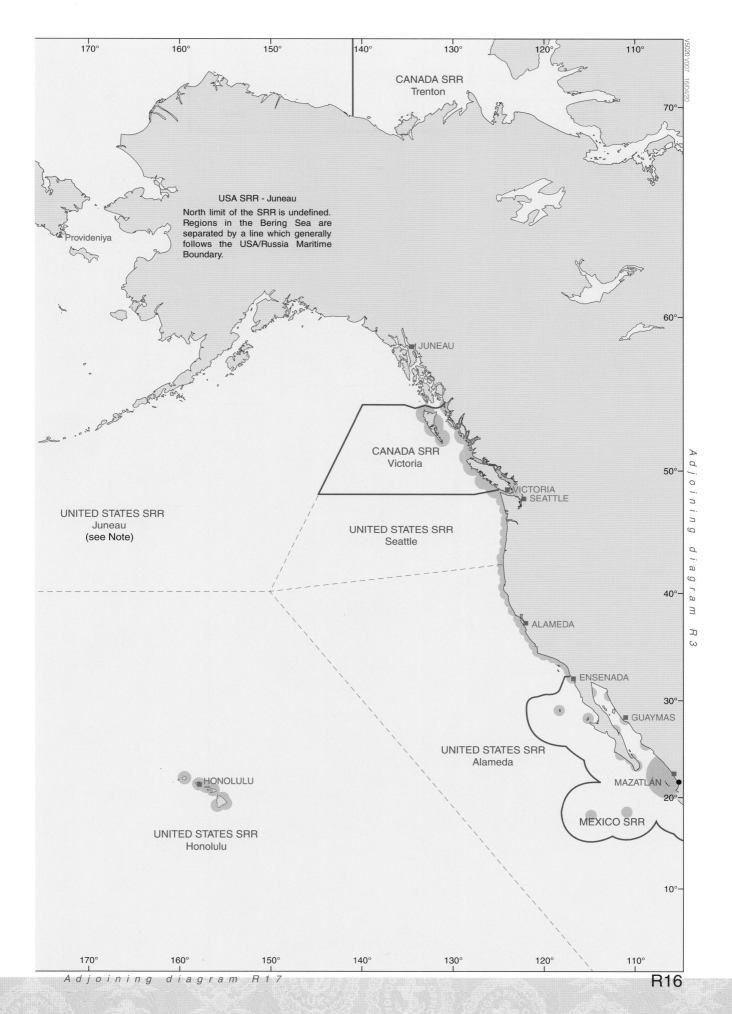

CANADA SRR
Trenton

USA SRR - Juneau
North limit of the SRR is undefined.
Regions in the Bering Sea are
separated by a line which generally
follows the USA/Russia Maritime
Boundary.

Provideniya

JUNEAU

CANADA SRR
Victoria

VICTORIA
SEATTLE

UNITED STATES SRR
Juneau
(see Note)

UNITED STATES SRR
Seattle

ALAMEDA

ENSENADA

GUAYMAS

UNITED STATES SRR
Alameda

MAZATLÁN

HONOLULU

MEXICO SRR

UNITED STATES SRR
Honolulu

Adjoining diagram R3

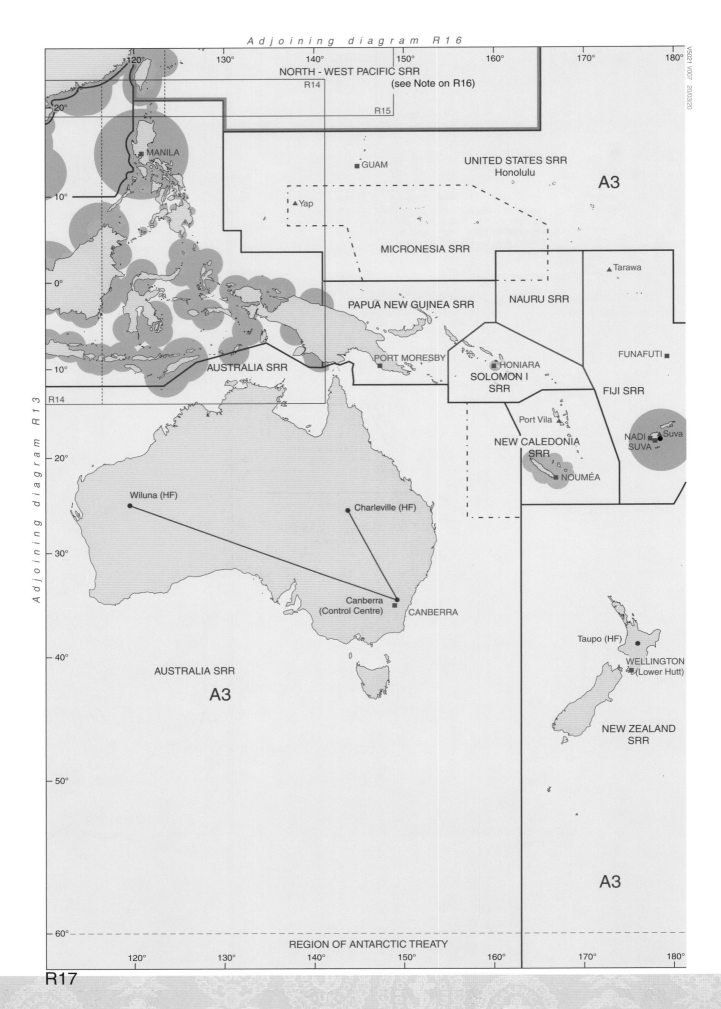

NORTH - WEST PACIFIC SRR

(see Note on R16)

R14

R15

■ MANILA

■ GUAM

UNITED STATES SRR
Honolulu

A3

▲ Yap

▲ Tarawa

MICRONESIA SRR

NAURU SRR

PAPUA NEW GUINEA SRR

■ PORT MORESBY

FUNAFUTI ■

■ HONIARA

SOLOMON I
SRR

FIJI SRR

AUSTRALIA SRR

Port Vila ▲

NADI ■ ■ Suva
SUVA ●

NEW CALEDONIA
SRR

■ NOUMÉA

Wiluna (HF) ●

Charleville (HF) ●

Canberra
(Control Centre) ■   CANBERRA

Taupo (HF) ●

WELLINGTON
■ (Lower Hutt)

AUSTRALIA SRR

A3

NEW ZEALAND
SRR

A3

REGION OF ANTARCTIC TREATY

R14

R17

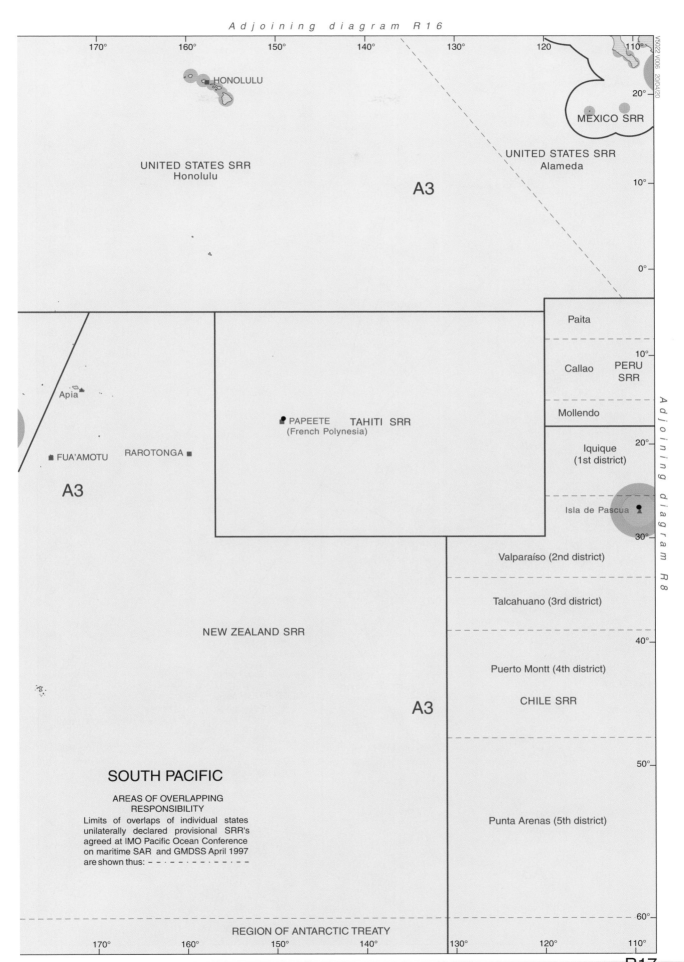

170° 160° 150° 140° 130° 120° 110°

HONOLULU

20°

MEXICO SRR

UNITED STATES SRR
Honolulu

UNITED STATES SRR
Alameda

A3

10°

0°

Paita

Apia

Callao   PERU
SRR

10°

Mollendo

PAPEETE   TAHITI SRR
(French Polynesia)

FUA'AMOTU   RAROTONGA

Iquique
(1st district)

20°

A3

Isla de Pascua

30°

Valparaíso (2nd district)

Talcahuano (3rd district)

NEW ZEALAND SRR

40°

Puerto Montt (4th district)

A3   CHILE SRR

50°

SOUTH PACIFIC

AREAS OF OVERLAPPING
RESPONSIBILITY
Limits of overlaps of individual states
unilaterally declared provisional SRR's
agreed at IMO Pacific Ocean Conference
on maritime SAR and GMDSS April 1997
are shown thus: – – – – – – – – – – – –

Punta Arenas (5th district)

60°

REGION OF ANTARCTIC TREATY

170° 160° 150° 140° 130° 120° 110°

R17

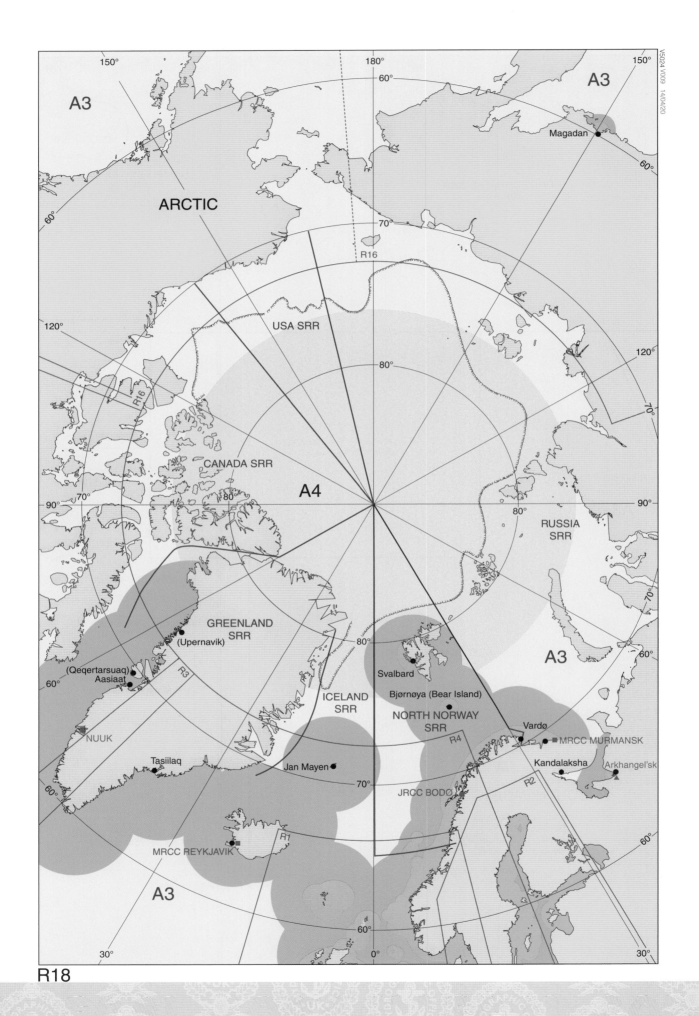

R18

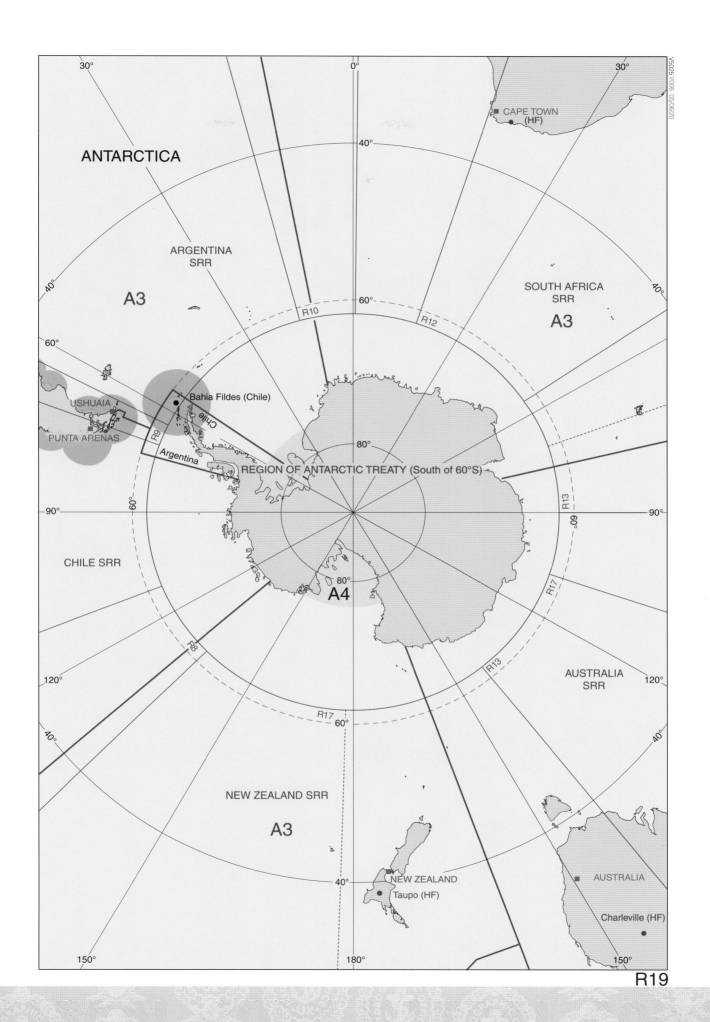

ANTARCTICA

ARGENTINA
SRR

A3

SOUTH AFRICA
SRR

A3

CAPE TOWN
(HF)

R10

R12

USHUAIA

PUNTA ARENAS

Bahia Fildes (Chile)

Chile

Argentina

R9

REGION OF ANTARCTIC TREATY (South of 60°S)

R13

CHILE SRR

A4

80°

80°

R17

R8

R13

AUSTRALIA
SRR

NEW ZEALAND SRR

A3

R17

NEW ZEALAND

Taupo (HF)

AUSTRALIA

Charleville (HF)

30°

40°

40°

60°

60°

90°

120°

40°

150°

0°

40°

60°

80°

180°

40°

60°

30°

40°

90°

120°

40°

150°

R19

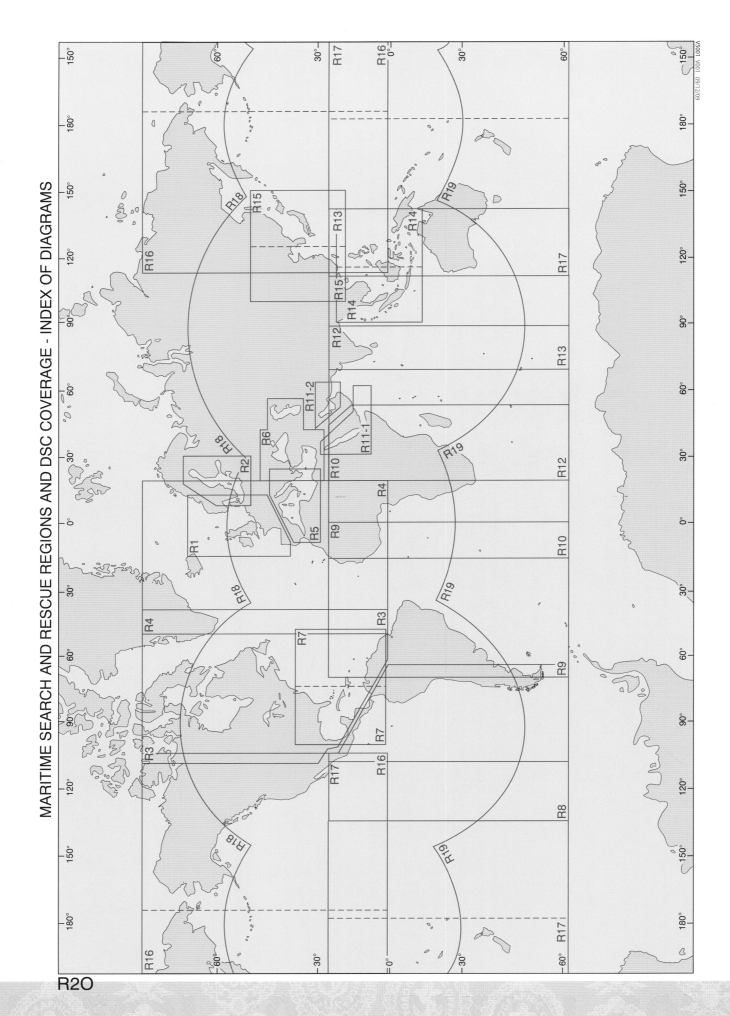

R2O

APPENDIX 1 - GMDSS Radio Log

EXTRACTS FROM MARINE GUIDANCE NOTE MGN 51 (M) ISSUED BY THE UK MARITIME AND COASTGUARD AGENCY, REGARDING GMDSS: RADIO LOG BOOK: GMDSS

1. Vessels complying with Part II of the Merchant Shipping (Radio Installations) Regulations 1992, namely those vessels operating under GMDSS, have a requirement under regulation 17 (1) that a Radio Log of matters specified in Schedule 3 of the Regulations shall be maintained and made available for inspection. The matters specified, to include the time of their occurrence, are:
   (a) A summary of communications relating to distress, urgency and safety traffic;
   (b) A record of important incidents connected with the radio service, and
   (c) Where appropriate, the position of the ship at least once a day.

2. In order to assist Masters and Officers in maintaining the necessary records, the Maritime and Coastguard Agency has produced a Radio Log Book (GMDSS). In the United Kingdom it is available from The Stationery Office, (TSO) or visit. www.tso.co.uk PUBLICATION DETAILS: GMDSS RADIO LOG BOOK

3. The Log incorporates instructions for its completion to meet the legal requirements and gives details of the periodic checks of the equipment which need to be carried out. The Log needs to be maintained in duplicate and for this reason it is produced in carbonized paper.

4. The Log, once full, shall be delivered by the Master to the appropriate Superintendent of a Marine Office or, if abroad, to the appropriate proper officer, at the same time as the offical Log Book; that is within 48 hours of the last person discharged from the crew agreement.

5. For illustrative purposes, an example of a typical day's log is printed overleaf.

30.6.01   M.V.   PORTISHEAD BAY

Call Sign   GKKA   M.M.S.I   232001000

DATE AND TIME UTC	STATION TO	STATION FROM	COMMUNICATIONS SUMMARY, TESTS OR REMARKS		CHANNEL OR SATELLITE
0100			*V/L departed Narvik bound Newport Watch commenced on all installations and on NAVTEX from stations G, P, T & L*		*Ch 70/16 2187·5/2182*
0105			*Performed self-test on all DSC facilities. Sp - Bus error on duplicate MF/HF Controller. All other facilities satisfactory. Telexed shore-based maintenance contractor with ETA Sullom Voe*		
0115			*Batteries tested, all ok*		
0145	*Shetland Coastguard*	*Portishead Bay*	*MF DSC 'test/safety call'*		*2187·5*
0146	*Portishead Bay*	*Shetland Coastguard*	*Acknowledged*		*2187·5*
0848			*Negative tidal surge warning via NAVTEX - passed to Master. Copy attached*		*518*
1222			*DSC Distress Alert. Ship's position 50·0°N.,2·50°W. ID Acknowledged by 002320014-No response required. Master informed*		*2187·5*
1506	*MV Benledi*	*MV Anne Faill*	*Channel 16 blocked due to lengthy correspondence*		*Ch16*
1815	*MV Stanley*	*MV Melville*	*Short call move to Ch06*		
1905	*MV Tweed*	*MV Berwick*	*Short call no response*		*Ch16*
1905	*MV Ibadan Palm*	*MV Al Shamiah*	*Short call move to Ch06*		
2020	*MV Peter D*	*MV Elizabeth L*	*Short call move to Ch06*		*Ch16*
2120	*MV Dunstanburgh Castle*	*MV Karina L*	*Radio check*		*Ch16*
			(Signed) Master	*(Signed) Designated Operator*	

COUNTRY NAME / Station	MMSI Number	VHF DSC	MF DSC	HF DSC	NAVTEX	SAR
A						
AÇORES (Portugal)			157		258	
CENCOMARACORES (SÃO MIGUEL)					258	
CENTRO DE COMUNICAÇÕES DOS AÇORES (CENCOMARACORES) & DELGADA MRCC	002040100		157			
ALBANIA						342
ALGERIA		131	158		260	342
ALGER	006052110	131	158			
ANNABA	006053814	131	158			
BEJAÏA	006053815	131				
BORDJ-EL-KIFFAN	006052110				260	
CHERCHELL	006052111	131				
DELLYS	006052112	131				
GHAZAOUET	006054119	131				
MOSTAGANEM	006054118	131				
ORAN	006054117	131	158			
SKIKDA	006053816	131				
TÉNÈS	006052113	131				
ANGOLA						373
ANGUILLA (UK)						356
ANTARCTICA		141	161			
BAHÍA FILDES (ANTÁRTICA CHILENA MRSC)	007250450	141	161			
BAHÍA PARAÍSO	007250470	141				
ANTIGUA AND BARBUDA						356
ARGENTINA		141	161	172	270	371
BAHÍA BLANCA	007100005				270	
BUENOS AIRES	007010001				271	
BUENOS AIRES (PREFECTURA NAVAL)	007010001	141	161	172		
COMODORO RIVADAVIA	007010008				271	
COMODORO RIVADAVIA (PREFECTURA NAVAL)	007010008	141	161	172		
MAR DEL PLATA	007010003				271	
MAR DEL PLATA (PREFECTURA NAVAL)	007010003	141	161	172		
RÍO GALLEGOS	007010010				271	
RIO GALLEGOS (PREFECTURA NAVAL)	007010010	141	161			
ROSARIO (PREFECTURA NAVAL)	007010004	141				
SAN BLAS (PREFECTURA NAVAL)	007010006	141	161			
USHUAIA	007010011				272	
USHUAIA MRCC (NAVY) & USHUAIA (PREFECTURA NAVAL)	007010011	151	167			
ZÁRATE (PREFECTURA NAVAL)	007010020	141				
ASCENSION (UK)						373
AUSTRALIA				173		384
JRCC AUSTRALIA (CANBERRA)	005030001			173		
AZERBAIJAN		131	158	170	260	342
BAKU	004231000 004232000	131	158	170		
BAKU (CHILOV)					260	

COUNTRY NAME / Station	MMSI Number	VHF DSC	MF DSC	HF DSC	NAVTEX	SAR
B						
BAHAMAS, THE						357
BAHRAIN					275	380
HAMALA					275	
BANGLADESH				172		375
DHAKA MRCC	405000236			172		
BARBADOS						357
BELGIUM		121	155		253	325
ANTWERPEN		121				
OOSTENDE	002050480 002050480	121	155		253	
BELIZE						357
BENIN		129	157			334
COTONOU	006100001	129	157			
BERMUDA (UK)		137	161		267	358
BERMUDA	003100001 003100001	137	161		267	
BJØRNØYA (Norway)		153	168			405
BJØRNØYA	002570000	153	168			
BRAZIL				171		370
MANAUS	007100003			171		
RECIFE (PERNAMBUCO)	007100002			171		
RIO DE JANEIRO (RENEC - EMBRATEL)	007100001			171		
BRUNEI						386
BULGARIA		132	158		260	343
VARNA	002070810 002070810	132	158		260	
BURMA		142	162	172	273	386
AYEYARWADY MRCC	005061411	142	162	172		
KYAUKPYU					273	
MYEIK	005060200	142			273	
YANGON	005060100	142	162	172	274	

COUNTRY NAME / Station	MMSI Number	VHF DSC	MF DSC	HF DSC	NAVTEX	SAR
C						
CAMBODIA						386
CAMEROON						334
CANADA						358 397
CANADA (Arctic Coast, Atlantic Coast and Saint Lawrence River)		137		171	267	
CARTWRIGHT	003160022				267	
CHEBOGUE	003160015				267	
HALIFAX (CANADIAN COAST GUARD)	003160016	137				
IQALUIT	003160023				267	
IQALUIT (NUNAVUT) (CANADIAN COAST GUARD)	003160023			171		
LABRADOR (GOOSE BAY) (CANADIAN COAST GUARD)	003160022	138				
LES ESCOUMINS (CANADIAN COAST GUARD)	003160026	138				
MOISIE	003160025				267	
PLACENTIA (CANADIAN COAST GUARD)	003160019	138				

COUNTRY NAME / Station	MMSI Number	VHF DSC	MF DSC	HF DSC	NAVTEX	SAR
PORT AUX BASQUES (CANADIAN COAST GUARD)	003160018	138				
PORT CALEDONIA	003160017				268	
QUÉBEC (CANADIAN COAST GUARD)	003160027	138				
ROBIN HOOD BAY	003160020				268	
SYDNEY (CANADIAN COAST GUARD)	003160017	139				
CANADA (Great Lakes)		139			268	
FERNDALE	003160029				268	
PASS LAKE	003160031				268	
PRESCOTT (CANADIAN COAST GUARD)	003160029	139				
SARNIA (CANADIAN COAST GUARD)	003160030	139				
CANADA (Pacific Coast)		150			283	
AMPHITRITE POINT (PRINCE RUPERT MCTS)	003160013				283	
DIGBY ISLAND (PRINCE RUPERT MCTS)	003160013				283	
PRINCE RUPERT (CANADIAN COAST GUARD)	003160013	150				
VICTORIA (CANADIAN COAST GUARD)	003160011	150				
CANARIAS, ISLAS (Spain)		129	157		258	
LAS PALMAS	002241026 / 002240995	129 / 132	157 / 158		258	
LAS PALMAS MRCC	002240995	129	157			
TENERIFE MRCC	002241007	129	157			
CAPE VERDE		129	157		258	335
SÃO VICENTE	006170000				258	
SÃO VICENTE DE CABO VERDE	006170000	129	157			
CAYMAN ISLANDS (UK)						359
CHANNEL ISLANDS (UK)		121			325	325
GUERNSEY COASTGUARD	002320064	121				
JERSEY COASTGUARD MRCC	002320060	121				
CHILE		141	167	175	286	403
ANCUD	007250240	151				
ANTOFAGASTA	007250050				286	
ANTOFAGASTA ZONAL RADIO STATION	007250050	151	167	175		
ARICA MRSC	007250010	151	167			
BAHÍA FÉLIX	007250370	151	167			
CABO ESPÍRITU SANTO, LIGHT	007250410	141				
CABO RÁPER, LIGHT	007250310	151				
CALDERA MRSC	007250080	151	167			
CASTRO	007250250	151				
CHAITÉN	007250260	151				
CHAÑARAL	007250070	151				
CONSTITUCIÓN	007250150	151				
COQUIMBO MRSC	007250110	151	167			
CORRAL	007250210	151				
HUASCO	007250090	151				
IQUIQUE MRSC	007250020	151	167			
ISLA DE PASCUA (EASTER ISLAND)	007250100				286	
ISLA DE PASCUA (EASTER ISLAND) AREA RADIO STATION	007250100	151	167	175		
ISLA DIEGO RAMÍREZ	007250440	152				
ISLA GUAFO, LIGHT	007250290	152				
ISLA SAN PEDRO	007250320	152	167			
ISLOTES EVANGELISTAS, LIGHT	007250350	152				
ISLOTES FAIRWAY, LIGHT	007250360	152				
JUAN FERNÁNDEZ	007250130	152	167			
LOS VILOS	007250120	152				
MAGALLANES ZONAL RADIO STATION	007250380	152	167	175		
MEJILLONES	007250040	152				
MELINKA	007250280	152				
PUERTO AGUIRRE	007250294	152				
PUERTO AYSÉN	007250300	152	167			
PUERTO CHACABUCO	007250298	152				
PUERTO EDÉN CAPUERTO		152				
PUERTO MONTT	007250230 / 007250230	152	167	175	286	
PUERTO NATALES CAPUERTO	007250340	152				
PUERTO WILLIAMS CAPUERTO	007250420	152	167			
PUNTA ARENAS (MAGALLANES)	007250380				286	
PUNTA CORONA, LIGHT	007250235	152				
PUNTA DELGADA	007250390	152	167			
PUNTA DUNGENESS, LIGHT	007250400	141				
QUELLÓN	007250270	152				
QUINTERO	007250125	152				
SAN ANTONIO MRSC	007250140	152	168			
TALCAHUANO	007250170 / 007250170	152	168	175	287	
TALTAL	007250060	152				
TOCOPILLA	007250030	152				
VALDIVIA MRSC	007250220	152				
VALPARAÍSO (PLAYA ANCHA) PRINCIPAL RADIO STATION	007251860	152	168	175		
VALPARAÍSO PLAYA ANCHA	007251860				287	
WOLLASTON	007250430	152				
CHINA		144	163	173	277	387 / 387
BASUO	004123600		163			
BEIHAI	004123400		163			
DALIAN	004121300 / 004121300	144	163		277	
FUZHOU	004122600 / 004122600	144	163		277	
GUANGZHOU	004123100 / 004123100	144	163		277	
HAIKOU	004123500	144				
HONG KONG	004773500				277	
HONG KONG MARINE RESCUE	004773500	144	163	173		
LIANYUNGANG	004122300	144	163			
NINGBO	004122400	144	163			

COUNTRY NAME / Station	MMSI Number	VHF DSC	MF DSC	HF DSC	NAVTEX	SAR
QINGDAO	004122200	144	163			
QINHUANGDAO	004121200	144				
SANYA	004123700 004123700		163		277	
SHANGHAI	004122100 004122100	144	163	173	277	
SHANTOU	004123200		163			
TIANJIN	004121100	144	163			
WENZHOU	004122500		163			
XIAMEN	004122700	144	163			
YANTAI	004121400	144	163			
ZHANJIANG	004123300	144	163			
COLOMBIA						359 397
COLOMBIA (Caribbean Coast)		139	161	171	268	
BARRANQUILLA	007300301	139	161	171		
CARTAGENA	007300501	139	161	171		
COVEÑAS	007300901	139	161	171		
PROVIDENCIA	007301201	139	161	171		
SAN ANDRÉS	007300701	139	161	171		
SANTA MARTA	007300401	139	161	171	268	
TURBO	007300801	139	161	171		
COLOMBIA (Pacific Coast)		150	167	174	283	
BUENAVENTURA	007300101	150	167	174	283	
TUMACO	007300201	150	167	174		
CONGO						335
CONGO (DEMOCRATIC REPUBLIC)						335
COOK ISLANDS (New Zealand)						401
COSTA RICA						360
CROATIA		132	159		260	343
DUBROVNIK	002380300	132				
DUBROVNIK MRSC	002387800	132				
PLOČE MRSC	002383350	132				
RIJEKA	002380200	132				
RIJEKA MRCC	002387010	132	159			
ŠIBENIK MRSC	002387500	132				
SPLIT	002380100	132				
SPLIT (HVAR I.)	002380100				260	
SPLIT MRSC	002387040	132				
ZADAR MRSC	002387400	132				
CUBA						360
CURAÇAO		139	161		269	360
CURAÇAO	003061000				269	
CURAÇAO (JRCC)	003061000	139	161			
CYPRUS		132	159	170	260	344
CYPRUS	002091000 002091000	132	159	170	260	

D

COUNTRY NAME / Station	MMSI Number	VHF DSC	MF DSC	HF DSC	NAVTEX	SAR
DENMARK		121	155			326
LYNGBY	002191000	121	155			
DIEGO GARCIA (BRITISH INDIAN OCEAN TERRITORY)						375
DJIBOUTI						380

COUNTRY NAME / Station	MMSI Number	VHF DSC	MF DSC	HF DSC	NAVTEX	SAR
DOMINICA						361
DOMINICAN REPUBLIC						361

E

COUNTRY NAME / Station	MMSI Number	VHF DSC	MF DSC	HF DSC	NAVTEX	SAR
EAST TIMOR			163			388
DILI	005250015		163			
ECUADOR		150			283	398
AYORA	007354757				283	
GUAYAQUIL	007354750	150				
EGYPT					261	344
AL ISKANDERÎYAH (ALEXANDRIA)	006221111				261	
AL QUŞAYR	006221112				275	
ISMAILIA (AL ISMÀ`ÎLÎYAH)					261	
EGYPT (Mediterranean Coast)		132	159	170		
AL ISKANDARÎYAH (ALEXANDRIA)	006221111	132	159	170		
PORT SAID (BÛR SA`ÎD)	006221113	133	159			
EGYPT (Red Sea Coast)		142	162			
AL QUŞAYR	006221112	142	162			
EL SALVADOR						361
EQUATORIAL GUINEA						335
ERITREA						380
ESTONIA		121	155		253	326
KURESSAARE MRSC	002760120		155			
TALLINN	002761000	121	155		253	
TALLINN NORTH	002760100		155			

F

COUNTRY NAME / Station	MMSI Number	VHF DSC	MF DSC	HF DSC	NAVTEX	SAR
FALKLAND ISLANDS (UK)						372
FAROE ISLANDS (Denmark)		121	155		253	326
TÓRSHAVN	002311000 002311000	121	155		253	
FIJI			167	174		402
FIJI MARITIME SURVEILLANCE RCC	005201100		167	174		
FINLAND		122	155			327
HELSINKI MRSC	002302000	122				
TURKU	002300230	122				
TURKU MRCC	002301000	122	155			
FRANCE						327 336 345
FRANCE (Atlantic and English Channel Coasts)		122	155		253	
CORSEN	002275300				253	
CORSEN (CROSS) MRCC	002275300	122	155			
ÉTEL (CROSS) MRCC	002275000	130	157			
GRIS-NEZ (CROSS) MRCC	002275100	122	155			
JOBOURG (CROSS) MRCC	002275200	122				
NITON (UK)					254	
FRANCE (Mediterranean Coast)		133	159		261	
CORSE (SOUS-CROSS) MRSC	002275420	133				
LA GARDE	002275400				261	

COUNTRY NAME / Station	MMSI Number	VHF DSC	MF DSC	HF DSC	NAVTEX	SAR
LA GARDE (CROSS) MRCC	002275400	133	159			
FRENCH POLYNESIA						402

G

COUNTRY NAME / Station	MMSI Number	VHF DSC	MF DSC	HF DSC	NAVTEX	SAR
GABON						336
GALAPAGOS ISLANDS (Ecuador)		150	167	174		
AYORA (ISLA SANTA CRUZ)	007354757	150	167	174		
CRISTÓBAL (BAQUERIZO MORENO - ISLA SAN CRISTÓBAL)	007354758	150				
GAMBIA, THE						337
GEORGIA		133	159		261	345
BAT'UMI MRSC	002130200	133				
GEORGIA MRCC	002130100	133	159			
KULEVI MRSC	002130400	133				
P'OT'I					261	
P'OT'I MRSC	002130300	133				
GERMANY		123	155		254	328
BREMEN MRCC	002111240	123	155			
PINNEBERG					254	
GHANA		130				337
TEMA	006270000	130				
GIBRALTAR (UK)		133				346
GIBRALTAR (VTS & SAR)	002361001	133				
GREECE		133	159	170	261	346
ASPROPÝRGOS ATTIKÍS (JRCC) (HELLENIC COASTGUARD)	002391000		159	170		
IRÁKLEION					261	
KÉRKYRA					262	
LÍMNOS					262	
OLYMPIA	002371000	133	159	170		
PEIRAIÁS JRCC (HELLENIC COAST GUARD)	002392000 237673000		159	170		
GREENLAND		161			254	361 405
AASIAAT	003313000	161 168				
GRINDAVIK (ICELAND)	002510100				254	
KOOK ISLAND (NUUK)					269	
SAUDANES (ICELAND)					254	
SIMIUTAQ					269	
UPERNAVIK					288	
GRENADA						362
GUAM (USA)			173	278		
GUAM	003669994			278		
GUAM SECTOR (US COAST GUARD)	003669994		173			
GUATEMALA						362 398
GUINEA						337
GUYANA						363

H

COUNTRY NAME / Station	MMSI Number	VHF DSC	MF DSC	HF DSC	NAVTEX	SAR
HAITI						363
HONDURAS						363

I

COUNTRY NAME / Station	MMSI Number	VHF DSC	MF DSC	HF DSC	NAVTEX	SAR
ICELAND			155		255	329
GRINDAVIK	002510100				255	
REYKJAVÍK (COAST GUARD RADIO)	002510100		155			
SAUDANES					255	
INDIA					274	376
BALASORE					274	
KEATING POINT					274	
MUTTAM POINT					274	
PORTO NOVO					274	
VAKALPUDI					274	
VENGURLA POINT					274	
VERAVAL					274	
INDIA (Andaman and Nicobar Region)		142	162	172		
CAMPBELL BAY MRSC	004194408	142				
DIGLIPUR MRSC	004194407	142				
PORT BLAIR MRCC	004194409	142	162	172		
INDIA (Eastern Region (Including Bay of Bengal))		142	162	172		
CHENNAI MRCC	004194401	142	162	172		
HALDIA MRSC	004194404	142	162	172		
MANDAPAM MRSSC	004194406	142	162	172		
PĀRĀDIP MRSC	004194403	142				
TUTICORIN MRSC	004194405	142				
VISHAKHAPATNAM MRSC	004194402	142				
INDIA (North Western Region)		142	162	172		
DAMAN CGAS	004192201	142	162	172		
OKHA MRSC	004192207	142				
PORBANDAR MRSC	004192202	142	162	172		
INDIA (Western Region)		142	162	172		
GOA MRSC	004192206	142				
KOCHI MRSC (COCHIN)	004192205	142				
MUMBAI MRCC	004192203	142	162	172		
NEW MANGALORE MRSC	004192204	142				
INDONESIA					278	388
AMBOINA (AMBON)					278	
JAKARTA					278	
JAYAPURA					278	
UJUNGPANDANG (MAKASSAR)					278	
INDONESIA (Bali)		144	163			
BENOA	005250014	144	163			
GILIMANUK	005251555	144	163			
INDONESIA (Halmahera)		144	163			
NAMLEA	005250096	144	163			
TERNATE	005250020	144	163			
INDONESIA (Jawa)		144	163	173		
CIGADING	005250033	144	163			
CILACAP	005250030	144	163			
CIREBON	005250032	144	163			
JAKARTA	005250000	144	163	173		
KALIANGET	005251514	144				
MENENG	005251518	144				

COUNTRY NAME / Station	MMSI Number	VHF DSC	MF DSC	HF DSC	NAVTEX	SAR
SEMARANG	005250008	144	163	173		
SURABAYA	005250001	145	163	173		
TEGAL	005251513	145				
INDONESIA (Kalimantan)		145	163	173		
BALIKPAPAN	005250009	145	163	173		
BANJARMASIN	005251520	145	163			
BATULICIN	005251523	145				
KETAPANG	005251503	145	163			
KUMAI	005251522	145				
PONTIANAK	005250016	145	163			
SAMARINDA	005251524	145	163			
SAMPIT	005251521	145	163			
SINTETE	005251565	145	163			
TANJUNG SANTAN	005251554	145				
TARAKAN	005250017	145	163			
INDONESIA (Kep Sula)		145				
SANANA	005250025	145				
INDONESIA (Lombok)		145	163			
LEMBAR	005250022	145	163			
INDONESIA (Maluka)		145	163			
SAUMLAKI	005251531	145	163			
TUAL	005251530	145	163			
INDONESIA (Nusa Tenggara)		145	163			
BIMA	005251516	145	163			
ENDE	005251517	145	163			
MAUMERE	005251518	145				
WAINGAPU	005251564	145	164			
INDONESIA (Papua)		145	164	173		
AGATS	005251532	145	164			
BIAK	005250031	145	164			
BINTUNI	005250026	145	164			
FAK-FAK	005250026	145	164			
JAYAPURA	005250007	145	164	173		
MANOKWARI	005250023	145	164			
MERAUKE	005250021	145	164			
SERUI	005251567	145	164			
SORONG	005250011	145	164	173		
INDONESIA (Riau)		145	164			
NATUNA	005251505	145	164			
INDONESIA (Seram)		145	164	173		
AMBOINA	005250006	145	164	173		
INDONESIA (Sulawesi)		145	164	173		
BAUBAU	005251526	145	164			
BITUNG	005250005	145	164	173		
KENDARI	005250019	145	164			
MAKASSAR	005250002	145	164	173		
MANADO	005251529	145				
PANTOLOAN	005250018	145	164			
PAREPARE	005251525	145				
POSO	005251527	145	164			
TAHUNA	005250024	145				
TOLI-TOLI	005251528	145	164			
INDONESIA (Sumatera)		145	164	173		
AIR BANGIS	005251558	145	164			
BATU AMPAR	005250012	145	164			
BELAWAN	005250003	145	164	173		
BENGKALIS	005250034	145	164			
BENGKULU	005250062	145	164			
DABO SINGKEP	005251559	145	164			
DUMAI	005250004	145	164	173		
GUNUNG SITOLI	005251556	146	164			
JAMBI	005251510	146				
KUALA LANGSA	005251562	146	164			
KUALA TANJUNG	005251504	146				
KUALA TUNGKAL	005251511	146				
LHOKSEUMAWE	005251503	146	164			
MUNTOK	005250546	146				
PALEMBANG	005251507	146	164			
PANGKAL BALAM	005251508	146	164			
PANGKALAN SUSU	005251563	146	164			
PANJANG	005250013	146	164			
RENGAT	005251560	146	164			
SABANG	005251501	146	164			
SEI KOLAK KIJANG	005250029	146	164			
SELAT PANJANG	005251561	146	164			
SIBOLGA	005250028	146	164			
SIPORA	005250047	146	164			
TANJUNG BALAI ASAHAN	005251552	146	164			
TANJUNG PANDAN	005251553	146	164			
TANJUNG UBAN	005251506	146				
TAPAK TUAN	005251502	146	164			
TELUK BAYUR	005250075	146	164			
TELUK DALAM	005251557	146	164			
INDONESIA (Timor)		146	164	173		
KUPANG	005250010	146	164	173		
IRAN		142	162	172	275	347 381
`ASALŪYEH	004225202	142				
ĀBĀDĀN	004224102	142				
ABŪ MŪSÁ	004225310	142				
AFTAB	004224311	142				
ARVAND KENĀR	004225106	142				
BANDAR-E EMĀM KHOMEYNĪ	004225100	142	162	172		
BANDAR-E SHAHĪD BĀHONAR	004224301	143				
BANDAR-E SHAHĪD RAJĀ'Ī	004225300	143	162	172	275	
BŪSHEHR	004225200	143			276	
CHĀBAHĀR	004225400	143				
DAYYER	004225203	143				
DEYLAM	004225205	143				
GENĀVEH	004225206	143				
JĀSK	004225308	143				
KHĀRK	004225201	143				
KHORRAMSHAHR	004225101	143				
LĀVAR-E SẠ̄HELĪ	004225204	143				
LENGEH	004224302	143				
QESHM	004224304	143				
QEYS	004224303	143				
TIĀB	004225309	143				

COUNTRY NAME / Station	MMSI Number	VHF DSC	MF DSC	HF DSC	NAVTEX	SAR
IRAN (Caspian Sea)		133	159	170	262	
AMĪRĀBĀD	004225601	133	159	170		
ANZALĪ	004225500	134	159	170		
FEREYDŪN KENĀR					262	
NEKĀ'	004224602	134				
NOW SHAHR	004225600	134				
IRAQ		143	162		276	381
UMM QAṢR	004250001	143	162		276	
IRELAND		123	155		255	329
DUBLIN (COAST GUARD MRCC)	002500300	123				
MALIN HEAD	002500100				255	
MALIN HEAD (COAST GUARD MRSC)	002500100	123	155			
VALENTIA	002500200				255	
VALENTIA (COAST GUARD MRSC)	002500200	123	155			
ISRAEL					262	347
HEFA (HAIFA)	004280001				262	
ISRAEL (Mediterranean Coast)		134	159			
HEFA JRCC	004280001	134	159			
ISRAEL (Red Sea Coast)		134	159			
EILAT	004280003	134	159			
ITALY		134	159		262	348
LA MADDALENA					262	
MONDOLFO					263	
PALERMO	002470002	134	159			
PIOMBINO					263	
ROMA RADIO	002470001	135	159			
SELLIA MARINA					263	
IVORY COAST		130	157	170		338
ABIDJAN	006191000	130	157	170		

J

COUNTRY NAME / Station	MMSI Number	VHF DSC	MF DSC	HF DSC	NAVTEX	SAR
JAMAICA						364
JAN MAYEN (Norway)		155				
JAN MAYEN	002570000	155				
JAPAN		164	173		278	389
HIROSHIMA (HIROSHIMA MRCC)	004310601	164				
HOKKAIDO (OTARU MRCC)	004310101		165			
KAGOSHIMA (KAGOSHIMA MRCC)	004311001		165			
KOBE (KOBE MRCC)	004310501		165			
KUSHIRO	004310102				278	
MAIZURU (MAIZURU MRCC)	004310801		165			
MOJI	004310701				279	
MOJI (KITAKYUSHI MRCC)	004310701		165			
NAGOYA (NAGOYA MRCC)	004310401		165			
NAHA	004311101				279	
NIIGATA (NIIGATA MRCC)	004310901		165			
OKINAWA (NAHA MRCC)	004311101		165			
OTARU	004310101				279	
SHIOGAMA (SHIOGAMA MRCC)	004310201		165			
TOKYO (JCG HQ)	004310001		173			
YOKOHAMA	004310301				279	
YOKOHAMA (YOKOHAMA MRCC)	004310301		165			
JORDAN						350

K

COUNTRY NAME / Station	MMSI Number	VHF DSC	MF DSC	HF DSC	NAVTEX	SAR
KAZAKHSTAN		135	159			
AKTAU		135	159			
BAUTINO		135				
KENYA						377
KIRIBATI						390
KOREA, NORTH		146	165	173	280	390
CHOLSAN (COAST RADIO STATION)	004451016	146				
HAMHŬNG					280	
HONGWON (COAST RADIO STATION)	004451009	146				
HWADAE (COAST RADIO STATION)	004451005	146				
KANGWON PROVINCE MRSC	004451013	146				
KIM CHAEK (COAST RADIO STATION)	004451006	146				
KOSONG (COAST RADIO STATION)	004451014	146				
KUMYA (COAST RADIO STATION)	004451011	146				
KWAKSAN (COAST RADIO STATION)	004451018	146				
MYONGCHON (COAST RADIO STATION)	004451004	146				
NAMPHO MRSC	004451021	146	165	173		
NORTH HAMGYONG PROVINCE MRSC	004451029	146	165	173		
NORTH PHYONGAN PROVINCE MRSC	004451015	146				
ONCHON (COAST RADIO STATION)	004451020	146				
ONGJIN (COAST RADIO STATION)	004451025	146				
ORANG (COAST RADIO STATION)	004451003	146				
PYONGYANG					280	
RASON MRSC	004451001	146				
RIWON (COAST RADIO STATION)	004451008	146				
RYONGYON (COAST RADIO STATION)	004451024	146				
SINAM (COAST RADIO STATION)	004451002	146				
SONCHON (COAST RADIO STATION)	004451017	146				
SOUTH HAMGYONG PROVINCE MRSC	004451012	146	165	173		
SOUTH HWANGHAE PROVINCE MRSC	004451027	146				
SOUTH PHYONGAN PROVINCE MRSC	004451019	146				
TANCHON (COAST RADIO STATION)	004451007	146				
TUNGAM (COAST RADIO STATION)	004451026	146				

COUNTRY NAME / Station	MMSI Number	VHF DSC	MF DSC	HF DSC	NAVTEX	SAR
UNRYUL (COAST RADIO STATION)	004451022	146				
KOREA, SOUTH		146	165	173	280	391
CHEJU (JEJU)		146	165			
CHEJU (JEJU) MRCC	004401005	146	165	173		
INCH'ŎN (INCHEON)		147	165			
INCH'ŎN (INCHEON) MRCC	004401001	147	166	173		
JUKBYEON					280	
KANGNUNG		147				
KUNSAN (GUNSAN)		147				
MOKP'O (MOKPO)		147				
MOKP'O (MOKPO) MRCC	004401003	147	166	173		
P'OHANG		147				
PUSAN (BUSAN)		147	166			
PUSAN (BUSAN) MRCC	004401004	147	166	173		
PYŎNSAN (BYEONSAN)	004401004				280	
SEOUL	004400002		166	173		
TONGHAE (DONGHAE) MRCC	004401002	147	166	173		
ULLUNG (ULREUNG)		147				
ULSAN	004400102	147				
YEOSU		147				
KUWAIT		143	162			381
AL KUWAYT (KUWAIT)	004472188	143	162			

L

COUNTRY NAME / Station	MMSI Number	VHF DSC	MF DSC	HF DSC	NAVTEX	SAR
LATVIA		123	155			329
RĪGA MRCC & RĪGA RESCUE RADIO	002750100	123	155			
LEBANON		135	159			350
BEYROUTH		135	159			
LIBERIA						338
LIBYA						350
LITHUANIA		123	156			330
KLAIPĖDA MRCC	002770330	123	156			

M

COUNTRY NAME / Station	MMSI Number	VHF DSC	MF DSC	HF DSC	NAVTEX	SAR
MADAGASCAR						373
MADEIRA (Portugal)		157			258	
CENCOMARMADEIRA (PORTO SANTO)					258	
FUNCHAL MRSC	002550100	157				
MALAYSIA					281	392
MIRI (SARAWAK)					281	
PENANG					281	
SANDAKAN (SABAH)					281	
MALAYSIA (Sabah)		147	166			
KOTA KINABALU	005330013	147	166			
LABUAN	005330014	147				
MALAYSIA (Sarawak)		147	166			
BINTULU	005330012	147				
KUCHING	005330011	147	166			
MALAYSIA, PENINSULAR		147	166			
BUKIT KEMUNING	005330008	147				
GUNUNG BERINCHANG	005330003	147				
GUNUNG JERAI	005330001	147				
GUNUNG LEDANG	005330005	147				
KUALA ROMPIN	005330007	147				

COUNTRY NAME / Station	MMSI Number	VHF DSC	MF DSC	HF DSC	NAVTEX	SAR
KUALA TERENGGANU	005330009	147				
KUANTAN	005330008		166			
MACHANG	005330010	147				
PERMATANG PAUH	005330002		166			
PULAU TIOMAN	005330006	147				
ULU KALI	005330004	147				
MALDIVES						378
MALTA		135	159		263	350
MALTA					263	
MALTA RCC	002150100	135	159			
MARSHALL ISLANDS						393
MARTINIQUE (France)		140				
CROSS ANTILLES-GUYANE (CROSS-AG) FORT-DE-FRANCE MRCC	003475000	140				
MARTINIQUE AND FRENCH GUIANA						364
MAURITANIA						338
MAURITIUS		142	162	172	275	378
MAURITIUS	006452700	142	162	172	275	
MEXICO						365 / 399
MEXICO (Caribbean and Gulf Coast)		140	161			
CAYO ARCAS	003450974	140				
CHETUMAL	003451120	140				
CIUDAD DEL CARMEN	003450710	140				
COATZACOALCOS	003450320	140				
COZUMEL	003451110	140				
ISLA CONTOY MRSC	003451175	140				
ISLA HOLBOX MRSC	003451174	140				
ISLA MUJERES MRSC	003451171	140				
LERMA MRSC	003450772	140				
MATAMOROS MRSC	003450172	140				
MEZQUITAL MRSC	003450173	140				
PLAYA LINDA MRSC	003451176	140				
PROGRESO	003450910	140				
TAMPICO	003450110	140	161			
TUXPAN MRCC (MEXICAN NAVY - 1ST REGION)	003450372	140				
VERACRUZ	003450310	140				
MEXICO (Pacific Coast)		150	167			
ACAPULCO	003451810	150				
ENSENADA MRCC (MEXICAN NAVY - 2ND REGION)	003450210	150				
LÁZARO CÁRDENAS	003451610	150				
MANZANILLO	003451410	150				
MAZATLÁN	003450810	150	167			
PUERTO VALLARTA	003451210	150				
SALINA CRUZ MRSC	003452071	150				
SAN BLAS MRSC	003450174	150				
MICRONESIA						393
MONACO						351
MONTENEGRO		135	159			351
BAR	002620001	135	159			
MONTSERRAT (UK)						365

COUNTRY NAME / Station	MMSI Number	VHF DSC	MF DSC	HF DSC	NAVTEX	SAR
MOROCCO						339 351
MOZAMBIQUE			162			374
MAPUTO MRCC	006501000		162			

N

COUNTRY NAME / Station	MMSI Number	VHF DSC	MF DSC	HF DSC	NAVTEX	SAR
NAMIBIA					272	374
WALVIS BAY					272	
NETHERLANDS		124	156		255	330
NETHERLANDS COASTGUARD	002442000				255	
NETHERLANDS COASTGUARD (DEN HELDER)	002442000	124	156			
NEW CALEDONIA (France)		144				384
NOUMÉA MRCC	005401000	144				
NEW ZEALAND				174		402
TAUPO MARITIME RADIO	005120010			174		
NICARAGUA						366 400
NIGERIA						339
NORWAY		125	156	175	256	330
BODØ	002570000				288	
JELØYA	002570000				256	
NORWEGIAN COASTAL RADIO NORTH	002570000	153	168	175		
NORWEGIAN COASTAL RADIO SOUTH	002570000	125	156			
ØRLANDET	002570000				256	
ROGALAND	002570000				256	
SVALBARD	002570000				288	
VARDØ	002570000				288	

O

COUNTRY NAME / Station	MMSI Number	VHF DSC	MF DSC	HF DSC	NAVTEX	SAR
OMAN					276	382
MASQAT (MUSCAT) (WATTAYA)					276	

P

COUNTRY NAME / Station	MMSI Number	VHF DSC	MF DSC	HF DSC	NAVTEX	SAR
PAKISTAN		143	162	172	276	382
KARACHI	004634060 004634060	143	162	172	276	
PALAU						393
PANAMA						366
PAPUA NEW GUINEA						385
PERU		152	168	175	287	404
CALLAO	007600125				287	
CALLAO MRCC	007600125	152	168	175		
CHANCAY MRSC	007600135	152				
CHIMBOTE MRSC	007600126	152				
HUACHO MRSC	007600128	152				
ILO MRSC	007600132	152				
MOLLENDO (MATARANI)	007600129				287	
MOLLENDO MRSC	007600129	152	168	175		
PAITA	007600121				287	
PAITA MRSC	007600121	152	168	175		
PIMENTEL MRSC	007600123	152				
PISCO MRSC	007600130	152				
SALAVERRY MRSC	007600124	152				
SAN JUÁN MRSC	007600131	152				

COUNTRY NAME / Station	MMSI Number	VHF DSC	MF DSC	HF DSC	NAVTEX	SAR
SUPE MRSC	007600127	152				
TALARA MRSC	007600122	152				
ZORRITOS MRSC	007600120	152				
PHILIPPINES		148	166	173	281	394
MANILA					281	
MANILA RESCUE COORDINATION CENTRE - NATIONAL HEADQUARTERS PHILIPPINE COAST GUARD (NHPCG) (MRCC PHILIPPINES)	005480020	148	166	173		
PITCAIRN ISLANDS						385 403
POLAND		126	156			331
POLISH RESCUE RADIO	002618102	126	156			
PORTUGAL		130	158		259	340
CENCOMAR (PENALVA)					259	
LISBOA MRCC	002630100	130	158			
PUERTO RICO (USA)				171	269	366
ISABELLA	003669992				269	
SAN JUAN SECTOR & RSC (US COAST GUARD)	003669992			171		

Q

COUNTRY NAME / Station	MMSI Number	VHF DSC	MF DSC	HF DSC	NAVTEX	SAR
QATAR						383

R

COUNTRY NAME / Station	MMSI Number	VHF DSC	MF DSC	HF DSC	NAVTEX	SAR
RÉUNION (France)			162			378
LA RÉUNION (CROSSRU) MRCC	006601000		162			
ROMANIA		135	160	170	264	352
CONSTANŢA	002640570 002640570	135	160	170	264	
RUSSIA						332 352 401 406
RUSSIA (Arctic Coast)		154	169		289	
ARKHANGEL'SK	002734414				289	
ARKHANGEL'SK MRSC	002734414	154	169			
DIKSON MRCC		154	169			
KANDALAKSHA	002733741	154				
MURMANSK	002734420				289	
MURMANSK MRCC	002734420	154	169			
PEVEK MRSC		154	169			
SABETTA					289	
TIKSI					289	
TIKSI MRSC		154	169			
RUSSIA (Baltic Coast)		126	156			
KALININGRAD	002734417	126	156			
KALININGRAD MRCC	002734417		156			
SANKT PETERBURG	002733700	126	156			
RUSSIA (Black Sea Coast)		135	160		264	
NOVOROSSIYSK					264	
NOVOROSSIYSK MRCC	002734411	135	160			
SOCHI	002731108	135				
TAGANROG	002734487	135	160		264	
TAMAN MRSC	002734446	135	160			
TUAPSE	002734413	135				
YEYSK	002734422	136				

COUNTRY NAME / Station	MMSI Number	VHF DSC	MF DSC	HF DSC	NAVTEX	SAR
RUSSIA (Caspian Sea)		136	160		264	
ASTRAKHAN					264	
ASTRAKHAN MRCC	002734419	136	160			
MAKHACHKALA	002734423	136	160			
RUSSIA (Pacific Coast)		151	167		285	
KHOLMSK					285	
MAGADAN	002733728				285	
MAGADAN (MRSC YUZHNO-SAKHALINSK)	002734416	151				
OKHOTSK					285	
PETROPAVLOVSK-KAMCHATSKIY	002734418				285	
PETROPAVLOVSK-KAMCHATSKIY	002733737		167			
PETROPAVLOVSK-KAMCHATSKIY MRSC	002734418	151				
PLASTUN	002734442		167			
VANINO	002734421	151	167			
VLADIVOSTOK	002734412				285	
VLADIVOSTOK MRCC	002734412	151	167			
YUZHNO-SAKHALINSK (REGIONAL CENTRE) MRSC	002733733	151	167			

S

COUNTRY NAME / Station	MMSI Number	VHF DSC	MF DSC	HF DSC	NAVTEX	SAR
SAINT KITTS AND NEVIS						366
SAINT LUCIA						367
SAINT VINCENT AND THE GRENADINES						367
SAINT-PIERRE AND MIQUELON (France)						367
SAMOA						403
SAUDI ARABIA		143	162		276	383
JEDDAH	004030000	143	162		276	
SENEGAL		130	158	170	259	340
DAKAR	006630005				259	
DAKAR MRCC	006631008	130	158	170		
SEYCHELLES					275	379
MAHÉ					275	
SIERRA LEONE						340
SINGAPORE		148			281	395
SINGAPORE (CHANGI)	005630002				281	
SINGAPORE PORT OPERATIONS CONTROL MRCC	005630002	148				
SLOVENIA		136				353
KOPER MRCC	002780200	136				
SOLOMON ISLANDS		144	173			385
HONIARA	005570001	144	173			
SOUTH AFRICA			172	272		374
CAPE COLUMBINE				272		
CAPE TOWN				273		
CAPE TOWN (INCLUDING DURBAN AND PORT ELIZABETH)	006010001		172			
DURBAN				273		
PORT ELIZABETH				273		
SPAIN				170	259	341 353
CABO DE LA NAO (VALENCIA)	002241004				264	

COUNTRY NAME / Station	MMSI Number	VHF DSC	MF DSC	HF DSC	NAVTEX	SAR
CORUÑA	002240992				259	
MADRID	002241022			170		
TARIFA	002240994				264	
SPAIN (Mediterranean Coast)		136	160			
ALGECIRAS MRCC	002241001	136				
ALMERÍA MRCC	002241002	136	160			
BARCELONA MRCC	002240991	136	160			
CARTAGENA MRCC	002241003	136				
CASTELLÓN MRCC	002241016	136				
TARRAGONA MRCC	002241006	136				
VALENCIA	002241024	136	160			
VALENCIA MRCC	002241004	136	160			
SPAIN (North Coast)		130	158	170		
BILBAO MRCC	002240996	130	158			
CORUÑA	002241022	131	158	170		
CORUÑA MRCC	002240992	131				
FINISTERRE MRCC	002240993	131	158			
GIJÓN MRCC	002240997	131	158			
SANTANDER MRCC	002241009	131				
VIGO MRCC	002240998	131				
SPAIN (South Coast)		131				
CÁDIZ MRCC	002241011	131				
HUELVA MRCC	002241012	131				
SPAIN (South West Coast)		136	160			
TARIFA MRCC	002240994	136	160			
SRI LANKA						379
SURINAME						368
SVALBARD (Norway)						406
SWEDEN		126	156		256	332
BJURÖKLUBB	002653500				256	
GISLÖVSHAMMAR					256	
GRIMETON					256	
SWEDEN JRCC	002653000	126	156			
SWITZERLAND						354
SYRIA		136	160	170		354
AL LĀDHIQĪYAH (LATAKIA)	004680011	136	160	170		
ṬARṬŪS (TARTOUS)	004680012	136				

T

COUNTRY NAME / Station	MMSI Number	VHF DSC	MF DSC	HF DSC	NAVTEX	SAR
TAIWAN		149	166	174	281	395
CHI-LUNG					281	
KEELUNG	004162019	149	166	174		
LINYUAN					281	
TANZANIA						379
THAILAND		149	166	174	281	395
BANGKOK	005671000	149	166	174		
BANGKOK (NONTHABURI)	005671000				281	
TONGA ISLANDS						403
TRINIDAD AND TOBAGO		140				368
NORTH POST (TRINIDAD)	003621001	140				
TUNISIA					265	354
KELIBIA					265	
TURKEY		137	160	170	265	355
ANTALYA	002713000	137	160			

COUNTRY NAME / Station	MMSI Number	VHF DSC	MF DSC	HF DSC	NAVTEX	SAR
ANTALYA (MEDITERRANEAN COAST)	002713000				265	
ISTANBUL	002711000	137	160	170		
İSTANBUL (MARMARA DENIZI)	002711000				265	
İZMIR	002715000		160			
İZMIR (AEGEAN COAST)	002715000				265	
SAMSUN	002712000	137	160			
SAMSUN (BLACK SEA COAST)	002712000				266	
TURKS AND CAICOS ISLANDS (UK)						368
TUVALU						385

U

COUNTRY NAME / Station	MMSI Number	VHF DSC	MF DSC	HF DSC	NAVTEX	SAR
UKRAINE		137	160		266	356
BERDYANS'K	002723672 002723659	137			266	
KERCH MRSC	002723632	137				
MARIUPOL' MRSC	002723650	137				
ODESA	002725613				266	
ODESA MRCC	002723660	137	160			
SEVASTOPOL MRSC	002723678	137				
UNITED ARAB EMIRATES		143				383
EMIRATES	004700000	143				
UNITED KINGDOM		127	156		257	333
ABERDEEN MRCC	002320004	127	156			
BELFAST MRCC	002320021	127				
CULLERCOATS					257	
DOVER MRCC	002320010	127	156			
FALMOUTH MRCC	002320014	127	156			
HOLYHEAD MRCC	002320018	127				
HUMBER MRCC	002320007	128	156			
JRCC UK	002320011	128				
LONDON MRSC	002320063	128				
MILFORD HAVEN MRCC	002320017	128	157			
NITON					257	
PORTPATRICK					257	
SHETLAND MRCC	002320001	128	157			
STORNOWAY MRCC	002320024	129	157			
UNITED STATES						369 396 400
UNITED STATES (Alaska)				174	283	
KODIAK	003669899				283	
KODIAK (US COAST GUARD)	003669899			174		
UNITED STATES (Atlantic Coast)		140		171	269	
BOSTON	003669991				269	
BOSTON RCF (US COAST GUARD FIRST DISTRICT)	003669991			171		
BOSTON SECTOR (US COAST GUARD)	003669901	140				
CHARLESTON					269	
CHARLESTON SECTOR (US COAST GUARD)	003669907	140				
COMMCOM (COMMUNICATIONS COMMAND) (US COAST GUARD)	003669995			171		
DELAWARE BAY SECTOR (US COAST GUARD)	003669905	140				
JACKSONVILLE SECTOR (US COAST GUARD)	003669962	140				
LONG ISLAND SOUND SECTOR (US COAST GUARD) (NEW HAVEN)	003669931	140				
MARYLAND NATIONAL CAPITAL REGION SECTOR (US COAST GUARD)	003669961	140				
MIAMI	003669997				270	
MIAMI RCF (US COAST GUARD SEVENTH DISTRICT)	003669997			171		
MIAMI SECTOR (US COAST GUARD)	003669919	140				
NEW YORK SECTOR (US COAST GUARD)	003669929	140				
NORTH CAROLINA SECTOR (US COAST GUARD)	003669906	140				
NORTHERN NEW ENGLAND SECTOR (US COAST GUARD) (SOUTH PORTLAND)	003669921	140				
PORTSMOUTH (COMMCOM)	003669995				270	
SOUTHEASTERN NEW ENGLAND (US COAST GUARD) (WOODS HOLE)	003669928	140				
VIRGINIA SECTOR (US COAST GUARD)	003669922	140				
UNITED STATES (Gulf Coast)		141		171	270	
CORPUS CHRISTI SECTOR (US COAST GUARD)	003669916	141				
HOUSTON-GALVESTON SECTOR (US COAST GUARD)	003669915	141				
KEY WEST SECTOR (US COAST GUARD)	003669918	141				
MOBILE SECTOR (US COAST GUARD)	003669914	141				
NEW ORLEANS	003669998				270	
NEW ORLEANS RCF (US COAST GUARD EIGHTH DISTRICT)	003669998			171		
NEW ORLEANS SECTOR (US COAST GUARD)	003669908	141				
ST PETERSBURG SECTOR (US COAST GUARD)	003669917	141				
UNITED STATES (Hawaii)		150		174	284	
HONOLULU	003669993				284	
HONOLULU RCF (US COAST GUARD FOURTEENTH DISTRICT)	003669993			174		
HONOLULU SECTOR (US COAST GUARD)	003669939	150				
UNITED STATES (Pacific Coast)		151		174	284	
ASTORIA	003669910				284	

COUNTRY NAME / Station	MMSI Number	VHF DSC	MF DSC	HF DSC	NAVTEX	SAR
COLUMBIA RIVER SECTOR (US COAST GUARD)	003669937	151				
HUMBOLDT BAY SECTOR (US COAST GUARD)	003669909	151				
LONG BEACH (CAMBRIA)	003669912			284		
LOS ANGELES - LONG BEACH SECTOR (US COAST GUARD)	003669912	151				
NORTH BEND SECTOR (US COAST GUARD)	003669911	151				
POINT REYES RCF	003669990		174			
POINT REYES RCF (SAN FRANCISCO)	003669990			284		
SAN DIEGO SECTOR (US COAST GUARD)	003669913	151				
SAN FRANCISCO SECTOR (US COAST GUARD)	003669926	151				
SEATTLE (PUGET SOUND) SECTOR (US COAST GUARD)	003669938	151				
URUGUAY		141	161	172	272	372
LA PALOMA					272	
MONTEVIDEO ARMADA	007703870	141	161	172		

V

COUNTRY NAME / Station	MMSI Number	VHF DSC	MF DSC	HF DSC	NAVTEX	SAR
VANUATU						386
VENEZUELA						369
VIETNAM		149	166	174	282	396
BAC LIEU	005743040	149				
BACH LONG VI	005741050	149				
BEN THUY	005741070	149	166			
CA MAU	005743070	149	166			
CAM RANH	005742090	149				
CAN THO	005743050	149	166			
CON DAO	005743060	149				
CUA ONG	005741020	149	166			
CUA VIET	005742010	149				
ĐA NANG	005742030 005742030	149	166	174	282	
DUNG QUAT	005742040	149				
HA TIEN	005743090	149				
HAI PHONG	005741040 005741040	149	166	174	282	
HO CHI MINH	005743030 005743030	149	166	174	282	
HON GAI	005741030	149	166			
HON LA	005741080	149				
HUÉ	005742020	149	166			
KIEN GIANG	005743080	149	166			
LY SON	005742050	149				
MONG CAI	005741010	149	166			
NHA TRANG	005742080 005742080	149	166	174	282	
PHAN RANG	005742100	149				
PHAN THIET	005743010	149	166			
PHU QUOC	005743110	149				
PHU YEN	005742070	149	166			
QUY NHON	005742060	149	166			
THANH HOA	005741060	149				

COUNTRY NAME / Station	MMSI Number	VHF DSC	MF DSC	HF DSC	NAVTEX	SAR
THO CHU	005743100	149				
VUNG TAU	005743020 005743020	149	166	174	282	
VIRGIN ISLANDS (UK)						370

W
X
Y

COUNTRY NAME / Station	MMSI Number	VHF DSC	MF DSC	HF DSC	NAVTEX	SAR
YEMEN						383

Z

TABLE OF INTERNATIONAL CALL SIGN SERIES (APPENDIX 42 TO THE ITU RADIO REGULATIONS)

Series	Allocated to:	Series	Allocated to:
2AA-2ZZ	United Kingdom	6OA-6OZ	Somalia
3AA-3AZ	Monaco	6PA-6SZ	Pakistan
3BA-3BZ	Mauritius	6TA-6UZ	Sudan
3CA-3CZ	Equatorial Guinea	6VA-6WZ	Senegal
3DA-3DM	Eswatini	6XA-6XZ	Madagascar
3DN-3DZ	Fiji	6YA-6YZ	Jamaica
3EA-3FZ	Panama	6ZA-6ZZ	Liberia
3GA-3GZ	Chile	7AA-7IZ	Indonesia
3HA-3UZ	China	7JA-7NZ	Japan
3VA-3VZ	Tunisia	7OZ-7OZ	Yemen
3WA-3WZ	Vietnam	7PA-7PZ	Lesotho
3XA-3XZ	Guinea	7QA-7QZ	Malawi
3YA-3YZ	Norway	7RA-7RZ	Algeria
3ZA-3ZZ	Poland	7SA-7SZ	Sweden
4AA-4CZ	Mexico	7TA-7YZ	Algeria
4DA-4IZ	Philippines	7ZA-7ZZ	Saudi Arabia
4JA-4KZ	Azerbaijan	8AA-8IZ	Indonesia
4LA-4LZ	Georgia	8JA-8NZ	Japan
4MA-4MZ	Venezuela	8OA-8OZ	Botswana
4OA-4OZ	Montenegro	8PA-8PZ	Barbados
4PA-4SZ	Sri Lanka	8QA-8QZ	Maldives
4TA-4TZ	Peru	8RA-8RZ	Guyana
4UA-4UZ	United Nations	8SA-8SZ	Sweden
4VA-4VZ	Haiti	8TA-8YZ	India
4WA-4WZ	Timor-Leste	8ZA-8ZZ	Saudi Arabia
4XA-4XZ	Israel	9AA-9AZ	Croatia
4YA-4YZ	ICAO	9BA-9DZ	Iran
4ZA-4ZZ	Israel	9EA-9FZ	Ethiopia
5AA-5AZ	Libya	9GA-9GZ	Ghana
5BA-5BZ	Cyprus	9HA-9HZ	Malta
5CA-5GZ	Morocco	9IA-9JZ	Zambia
5HA-5IZ	Tanzania	9KA-9KZ	Kuwait
5JA-5KZ	Colombia	9LA-9LZ	Sierra Leone
5LA-5MZ	Liberia	9MA-9MZ	Malaysia
5NA-5OZ	Nigeria	9NA-9NZ	Nepal
5PA-5QZ	Denmark	9OA-9TZ	Congo (Democratic Republic)
5RA-5SZ	Madagascar	9UA-9UZ	Burundi
5TA-5TZ	Mauritania	9VA-9VZ	Singapore
5UA-5UZ	Niger	9WA-9WZ	Malaysia
5VA-5VZ	Togo	9XA-9XZ	Rwanda
5WA-5WZ	Samoa	9YA-9ZZ	Trinidad and Tobago
5XA-5XZ	Uganda	A2A-A2Z	Botswana
5YA-5ZZ	Kenya	A3A-A3Z	Tonga
6AA-6BZ	Egypt	A4A-A4Z	Oman
6CA-6CZ	Syria	A5A-A5Z	Bhutan
6DA-6JZ	Mexico	A6A-A6Z	United Arab Emirates
6KA-6NZ	South Korea	A7A-A7Z	Qatar

Continued overleaf

Series	Allocated to:	Series	Allocated to:
A8A-A8Z	Liberia	EXA-EXZ	Kyrgyz Republic
A9A-A9Z	Bahrain	EYA-EYZ	Tajikistan
AAA-ALZ	United States	EZA-EZZ	Turkmenistan
AMA-AOZ	Spain	FAA-FZZ	France
APA-ASZ	Pakistan	GAA-GZZ	United Kingdom
ATA-AWZ	India	H2A-H2Z	Cyprus
AXA-AXZ	Australia	H3A-H3Z	Panama
AYA-AZZ	Argentina	H4A-H4Z	Solomon Islands
BAA-BZZ	China	H6A-H7Z	Nicaragua
C2A-C2Z	Nauru	H8A-H9Z	Panama
C3A-C3Z	Andorra	HAA-HAZ	Hungary
C4A-C4Z	Cyprus	HBA-HBZ	Switzerland
C5A-C5Z	Gambia	HCA-HDZ	Ecuador
C6A-C6Z	Bahamas	HEA-HEZ	Switzerland
C7A-C7Z	WMO	HFA-HFZ	Poland
C8A-C9Z	Mozambique	HGA-HGZ	Hungary
CAA-CEZ	Chile	HHA-HHZ	Haiti
CFA-CKZ	Canada	HIA-HIZ	Dominican Republic
CLA-CMZ	Cuba	HJA-HKZ	Colombia
CNA-CNZ	Morocco	HLA-HLZ	South Korea
COA-COZ	Cuba	HMA-HMZ	North Korea
CPA-CPZ	Bolivia	HNA-HNZ	Iraq
CQA-CUZ	Portugal	HOA-HPZ	Panama
CVA-CXZ	Uruguay	HQA-HRZ	Honduras
CYA-CZZ	Canada	HSA-HSZ	Thailand
D2A-D3Z	Angola	HTA-HTZ	Nicaragua
D4A-D4Z	Cape Verde	HUA-HUZ	El Salvador
D5A-D5Z	Liberia	HVA-HVZ	Vatican City
D6A-D6Z	Comoros	HWA-HYZ	France
D7A-D9Z	South Korea	HZA-HZZ	Saudi Arabia
DAA-DRZ	Germany	IAA-IZZ	Italy
DSA-DTZ	South Korea	J2A-J2Z	Djibouti
DUA-DZZ	Philippines	J3A-J3Z	Grenada
E2A-E2Z	Thailand	J4A-J4Z	Greece
E3A-E3Z	Eritrea	J5A-J5Z	Guinea-Bissau
E4A-E4Z	Palestine	J6A-J6Z	St. Lucia
E5A-E5Z	Cook Islands	J7A-J7Z	Dominica
E6A-E6Z	Niue	J8A-J8Z	St. Vincent and the Grenadines
E7A-E7Z	Bosnia and Herzegovina	JAA-JSZ	Japan
EAA-EHZ	Spain	JTA-JVZ	Mongolia
EIA-EJZ	Ireland	JWA-JXZ	Norway
EKA-EKZ	Armenia	JYA-JYZ	Jordan
ELA-ELZ	Liberia	JZA-JZZ	Indonesia
EMA-EOZ	Ukraine	KAA-KZZ	United States
EPA-EQZ	Iran	L2A-L9Z	Argentina
ERA-ERZ	Moldova	LAA-LWZ	Norway
ESA-ESZ	Estonia	LXA-LXZ	Luxembourg
ETA-ETZ	Ethiopia	LYA-LYZ	Lithuania
EUA-EWZ	Belarus	LZA-LZZ	Bulgaria

Continued on next page

Series	Allocated to:
MAA-MZZ	United Kingdom
NAA-NZZ	United States
OAA-OCZ	Peru
ODA-ODZ	Lebanon
OEA-OEZ	Austria
OFA-OJZ	Finland
OKA-OLZ	Czech Republic
OMA-OMZ	Slovakia
ONA-OTZ	Belgium
OUA-OZZ	Denmark
P2A-P2Z	Papua New Guinea
P3A-P3Z	Cyprus
P4A-P4Z	Aruba
P5A-P9Z	North Korea
PAA-PIZ	Netherlands
PJA-PJZ	Bonaire, Curaçao, Sint Eustatius and Saba
PKA-POZ	Indonesia
PPA-PYZ	Brazil
PZA-PZZ	Suriname
RAA-RZZ	Russia
S2A-S3Z	Bangladesh
S5A-S5Z	Slovenia
S6A-S6Z	Singapore
S7A-S7Z	Seychelles
S8A-S8Z	South Africa
S9A-S9Z	São Tomé and Principe
SAA-SMZ	Sweden
SNA-SRZ	Poland
SSA-SSM	Egypt
SSN-STZ	Sudan
SUA-SUZ	Egypt
SVA-SZZ	Greece
T2A-T2Z	Tuvalu
T3A-T3Z	Kiribati
T4A-T4Z	Cuba
T5A-T5Z	Somalia
T6A-T6Z	Afghanistan
T7A-T7Z	San Marino
T8A-T8Z	Palau
TAA-TCZ	Turkey
TDA-TDZ	Guatemala
TEA-TEZ	Costa Rica
TFA-TFZ	Iceland
TGA-TGZ	Guatemala
THA-THZ	France
TIA-TIZ	Costa Rica
TJA-TJZ	Cameroon
TKA-TKZ	France
TLA-TLZ	Central African Republic

Series	Allocated to:
TMA-TMZ	France
TNA-TNZ	Congo (Republic of)
TOA-TQZ	France
TRA-TRZ	Gabon
TSA-TSZ	Tunisia
TTA-TTZ	Chad
TUA-TUZ	Ivory Coast
TVA-TXZ	France
TYA-TYZ	Benin
TZA-TZZ	Mali
UAA-UIZ	Russia
UJA-UMZ	Uzbekistan
UNA-UQZ	Kazakhstan
URA-UZZ	Ukraine
V2A-V2Z	Antigua and Barbuda
V3A-V3Z	Belize
V4A-V4Z	St Kitts and Nevis
V5A-V5Z	Namibia
V6A-V6Z	Micronesia
V7A-V7Z	Marshall Islands
V8A-V8Z	Brunei Darussalam
VAA-VGZ	Canada
VHA-VNZ	Australia
VOA-VOZ	Canada
VPA-VQZ	United Kingdom
VRA-VRZ	China - Hong Kong SAR
VSA-VSZ	United Kingdom
VTA-VWZ	India
VXA-VYZ	Canada
VZA-VZZ	Australia
WAA-WZZ	United States
XAA-XIZ	Mexico
XJA-XOZ	Canada
XPA-XPZ	Denmark
XQA-XRZ	Chile
XSA-XSZ	China
XTA-XTZ	Burkina Faso
XUA-XUZ	Cambodia
XVA-XVZ	Vietnam
XWA-XWZ	Laos
XXA-XXZ	Macao SAR, China
XYA-XZZ	Burma
Y2A-Y9Z	Germany
YAA-YAZ	Afghanistan
YBA-YHZ	Indonesia
YIA-YIZ	Iraq
YJA-YJZ	Vanuatu
YKA-YKZ	Syria
YLA-YLZ	Latvia

Continued overleaf

Series	Allocated to:
YMA-YMZ	Turkey
YNA-YNZ	Nicaragua
YOA-YRZ	Romania
YSA-YSZ	El Salvador
YTA-YUZ	Serbia
YVA-YYZ	Venezuela
Z2A-Z2Z	Zimbabwe
Z3A-Z3Z	North Macedonia
Z8A-Z8Z	South Sudan
ZAA-ZAZ	Albania
ZBA-ZJZ	United Kingdom
ZKA-ZMZ	New Zealand
ZNA-ZOZ	United Kingdom
ZPA-ZPZ	Paraguay
ZQA-ZQZ	United Kingdom
ZRA-ZUZ	South Africa
ZVA-ZZZ	Brazil

MID	Country
[201]	Albania
[202]	Andorra
[203]	Austria
[204]	Açores - Portugal
[205]	Belgium
[206]	Belarus
[207]	Bulgaria
[208]	Vatican City State
[209] [210] [212]	Cyprus
[211] [218]	Germany
[213]	Georgia
[214]	Moldova
[215] [229] [248] [249] [259]	Malta
[216]	Armenia
[219] [220]	Denmark
[224] [225]	Spain
[226] [227] [228]	France
[230]	Finland
[231]	Føroyar - Denmark
[232] [233] [234] [235]	United Kingdom of Great Britain and Northern Ireland
[236]	Gibraltar - UK
[237] [239] [240] [241]	Greece
[238]	Croatia
[242]	Morocco
[243]	Hungary
[244] [245] [246]	Netherlands
[247]	Italy
[248] [249] [256]	Malta
[250]	Ireland
[251]	Iceland
[252]	Liechtenstein
[253]	Luxembourg
[254]	Monaco
[255]	Madeira - Portugal
[257] [258] [259]	Norway
[261]	Poland
[262]	Montenegro
[263]	Portugal
[264]	Romania
[265] [266]	Sweden
[268]	San Marino
[269]	Switzerland

MID	Country
[270]	Czech Republic
[271]	Turkey
[272]	Ukraine
[273]	Russian Federation
[274]	North Macedonia
[275]	Latvia
[276]	Estonia
[277]	Lithuania
[278]	Slovenia
[279]	Serbia
[301]	Anguilla - UK
[303]	Alaska - United States of America
[304] [305]	Antigua and Barbuda
[306]	Bonaire, Sint Eustatius and Saba - Netherlands
[306]	Curaçao - Netherlands
[307]	Aruba - Netherlands
[308] [309] [311]	Bahamas
[310]	Bermuda - UK
[312]	Belize
[314]	Barbados
[316]	Canada
[319]	Cayman Islands - UK
[321]	Costa Rica
[323]	Cuba
[325]	Dominica
[327]	Dominican Republic
[329]	Guadeloupe - France
[330]	Grenada
[331]	Greenland - Denmark
[332]	Guatemala
[334]	Honduras
[336]	Haiti
[338] [366] [367] [368] [369]	United States of America
[339]	Jamaica
[341]	St Kitts and Nevis
[343]	St Lucia
[345]	Mexico
[347]	Martinique - France
[348]	Montserrat - UK
[350]	Nicaragua
[351] [352] [353] [354] [355] [356] [357] [370] [371] [372] [373]	Panama
[358]	Puerto Rico - United States of America
[359]	El Salvador

Continued overleaf

MID	Country
[361]	Saint Pierre and Miquelon - France
[362]	Trinidad and Tobago
[364]	Turks and Caicos Islands - UK
[366] [367] [368] [369]	United States of America
[370] [371] [372] [373] [374]	Panama
[375] [376] [377]	Saint Vincent and the Grenadines
[378]	British Virgin Islands - UK
[379]	United States Virgin Islands - United States of America
[401]	Afghanistan
[403]	Saudi Arabia
[405]	Bangladesh
[408]	Bahrain
[410]	Bhutan
[412] [413] [414]	China
[416]	Taiwan
[417]	Sri Lanka
[419]	India
[422]	Iran
[423]	Azerbaijan
[425]	Iraq
[428]	Israel
[431] [432]	Japan
[434]	Turkmenistan
[436]	Kazakhstan
[437]	Uzbekistan
[438]	Jordan
[440] [441]	Korea South
[443]	State of Palestine (in accordance with Resolution 99 Rev. Guadalajara, 2010)
[445]	Korea North
[447]	Kuwait
[450]	Lebanon
[451]	Kyrgyz Republic
[453]	Macao - China
[455]	Maldives
[457]	Mongolia
[459]	Nepal
[461]	Oman
[463]	Pakistan
[466]	Qatar
[468]	Syria
[470] [471]	United Arab Emirates
[472]	Tajikistan
[473] [475]	Yemen
[477]	Hong Kong - SAR of China
[478]	Bosnia and Herzegovina
[501]	Adelie Land - France

MID	Country
[503]	Australia
[506]	Burma
[508]	Brunei Darussalam
[510]	Micronesia
[511]	Palau
[512]	New Zealand
[514] [515]	Cambodia
[516]	Christmas Island (Indian Ocean) - Australia
[518]	Cook Islands - New Zealand
[520]	Fiji
[523]	Cocos (Keeling) Islands - Australia
[525]	Indonesia
[529]	Kiribati
[531]	Laos, Peoples's Democratic Republic
[533]	Malaysia (includes Sarawak & Sabah)
[536]	Northern Mariana Islands - United States of America
[538]	Marshall Islands
[540]	New Caledonia - France
[542]	Niue - New Zealand
[544]	Nauru
[546]	French Polynesia - France
[548]	Philippines
[553]	Papua New Guinea
[555]	Pitcairn Island - UK
[557]	Solomon Islands
[559]	American Samoa - United States of America
[561]	Samoa
[563] [564] [565] [566]	Singapore
[567]	Thailand
[570]	Tonga
[572]	Tuvalu
[574]	Vietnam
[576] [577]	Vanuatu
[578]	Wallis and Futuna Island - France
[601]	South Africa
[603]	Angola
[605]	Algeria
[607]	Saint Paul and Amsterdam Islands - France
[608]	Ascension Islands - UK
[609]	Burundi
[610]	Benin
[611]	Botswana
[612]	Central African Republic
[613]	Cameroon
[615]	Congo
[616] [620]	Comoros
[617]	Cape Verde

Continued on next page

MID	Country
[618]	Crozet Archipelago - France
[619]	Côte d'Ivoire
[620]	Comoros
[621]	Djibouti
[622]	Egypt
[624]	Ethiopia
[625]	Eritrea
[626]	Gabon
[627]	Ghana
[629]	Gambia, The
[630]	Guinea-Bissau
[631]	Equatorial Guinea
[632]	Guinea
[633]	Burkino Faso
[634]	Kenya
[635]	Kerguelen Islands - France
[636] [637]	Liberia
[638]	South Sudan
[642]	Libya
[644]	Lesotho
[645]	Mauritius
[647]	Madagascar
[649]	Mali
[650]	Mozambique
[654]	Mauritania
[655]	Malawi
[656]	Niger
[657]	Nigeria
[659]	Namibia
[660]	Réunion - France
[661]	Rwanda
[662]	Sudan
[663]	Senegal
[664]	Seychelles
[665]	Saint Helena - UK
[667]	Sierra Leone
[668]	Sao Tome and Principe
[669]	Eswatini
[670]	Chad
[671]	Togo
[672]	Tunisia
[674] [677]	Tanzania
[675]	Uganda
[676]	Democratic Republic of the Congo
[678]	Zambia
[679]	Zimbabwe
[701]	Argentina
[710]	Brazil
[720]	Bolivia
{725]	Chile

MID	Country
[730]	Colombia (Republic of)
[735]	Ecuador
[740]	Falkland Islands - UK
[745]	Guiana - France
[750]	Guyana
[755]	Paraguay
[760]	Peru
[765]	Suriname
[770]	Uruguay
[775]	Venezuela

Note: This table will only be updated at the next new edition of this publication.

New MID codes may be issued by the ITU, please refer to the following website:

http://www.itu.int/en/ITU-R/terrestrial/fmd/Pages/mid.aspx

PHONETIC ALPHABET AND FIGURE CODE

(1) When it is necessary to spell out call signs, service abbreviations and words, the following table shall be used:

LETTER — SPELLING TABLE

Letter	Code word	Pronunciation of the code word	
		ENGLISH	FRENCH
A	Alfa	**AL** FAH	**AL** FAH
B	Bravo	**BRAH** VOH	**BRA** VOH
C	Charlie	**CHAR** LEE (or **SHAR** LEE)	**TCHAH** Li (ou **CHAR** Li)
D	Delta	**DELL** TAH	**DEL** TAH
E	Echo	**ECK** OH	**EK** O
F	Foxtrot	**FOX** TROT	**FOX** TROTT
G	Golf	GOLF	GOLF
H	Hotel	HO **TELL**	HO **TÈLL**
I	India	**IN** DEE AH	**IN** DI AH
J	Juliet	**JEW** LEE **ETT**	**DJOU** Li **ETT**
K	Kilo	**KEY** LOH	**KI** LOH
L	Lima	**LEE** MAH	**LI** MAH
M	Mike	MIKE	**MA** ÏK
N	November	NO **VEM** BER	NO **VEMM** BER
O	Oscar	**OSS** CAH	**OSS** KAR
P	Papa	PAH **PAH**	PAH **PAH**
Q	Quebec	KEY **BECK**	KÉ **BEK**
R	Romeo	**ROW** ME OH	**RO** MI O
S	Sierra	SEE **AIR** RAH	SI **ÊR** RAH
T	Tango	**TANG** GO	**TANG** GO
U	Uniform	**YOU** NEE FORM (or **OO** NEE FORM)	**YOU** NI FORM (ou **OU** NI FORM)
V	Victor	**VIK** TAH	**VIK** TAR
W	Whiskey	**WISS** KEY	**QUISS** KI
X	X-Ray	**ECKS** RAY	**ÊCSS** RÉ
Y	Yankee	**YANG** KEY	**YANG** KI
Z	Zulu	**ZOO** LOO	**ZOO** LOU
The underlined bold syllables are emphasized			

(2) When it is necessary to spell out figures or marks, the following tables should be used:

FIGURE — SPELLING TABLE

Figure or mark to be transmitted	Code word	Pronunciation of the code word	
		ENGLISH	FRENCH
0	NADAZERO	NAH-DAH-ZAY-ROH	NA-DA-ZE-RO
1	UNAONE	OO-NAH-WUN	OUNA-OUANN
2	BISSOTWO	BEES-SOH-TOO	BIS-SO-TOU
3	TERRATHREE	TAY-RAH-TREE	TÉ-RA-TRI
4	KARTEFOUR	KAR-TAY-FOWER	KAR-TÉ-FO-EUR
5	PENTAFIVE	PAN-TAH-FIVE	PANN-TA-FAIF
6	SOXISIX	SOK-SEE-SIX	FO-XI-SICKS
7	SETTESEVEN	SAY-TAY-SEVEN	SÉT-TÉ-SEV'N

Continued on next page

Figure or mark to be transmitted	Code word	Pronunciation of the code word	
		ENGLISH	FRENCH
8	OKTOEIGHT	OK-TOH-AIT	OK-TO-EIT
9	NOVENINE	NO-VAY-NINER	NO-VÉ-NAI-NEU
Decimal	DECIMAL	DAY-SEE-MAL	DÉ-SI-MAL
Full Stop	STOP	STOP	STOP
Each syllable should be equally emphasised			

SIGNAL TABLE

Signal	Pronunciation of the code word		Meaning
	ENGLISH	FRENCH	
Interco	IN-TER-CO	IN-TER-CO	International Code group(s) follow(s)
Stop	STOP	STOP	Full stop
Decimal	DAY-SEE-MAL	DÉ-SI-MAL	Decimal point
Correction	KOR-REK-SHUN	KOR-REK-CHEUNE	Cancel my last word or group The correct word or group follows

(3) Stations of the same country, when communicating between themselves, may use any other table recognized by their administration. For information about RT procedures etc, related to safety of navigation and persons, especially where language difficulties may arise, see International Code of Signals published by the IMO 1985.

SIGNALV001 09/12/09

Letter	Code	Meaning
ALFA	● ▬	I HAVE A DIVER DOWN; KEEP WELL CLEAR AT SLOW SPEED.
BRAVO	▬ ● ● ●	I AM TAKING IN, OR DISCHARGING, OR CARRYING DANGEROUS GOODS.
CHARLIE	▬ ● ▬ ●	YES (AFFIRMATIVE OR 'THE SIGNIFICANCE OF THE PREVIOUS GROUP SHOULD BE READ IN THE AFFIRMATIVE').
DELTA	▬ ● ●	KEEP CLEAR OF ME; I AM MANOEUVRING WITH DIFFICULTY.
ECHO	●	I AM ALTERING MY COURSE TO STARBOARD.
FOXTROT	● ● ▬ ●	I AM DISABLED; COMMUNICATE WITH ME.
GOLF	▬ ▬ ●	I REQUIRE A PILOT. WHEN MADE BY FISHING VESSELS OPERATING IN CLOSE PROXIMITY ON FISHING GROUNDS IT MEANS 'I AM HAULING NETS'.
HOTEL	● ● ● ●	I HAVE A PILOT ON BOARD.
INDIA	● ●	I AM ALTERING MY COURSE TO PORT.
JULIETT	● ▬ ▬ ▬	I AM ON FIRE AND HAVE A DANGEROUS CARGO ON BOARD; KEEP WELL CLEAR OF ME.
KILO	▬ ● ▬	I WISH TO COMMUNICATE WITH YOU.
LIMA	● ▬ ● ●	YOU SHOULD STOP YOUR VESSEL INSTANTLY.
MIKE	▬ ▬	MY VESSEL IS STOPPED AND MAKING NO WAY THROUGH THE WATER.
NOVEMBER	▬ ●	NO (NEGATIVE OR 'THE SIGNIFICANCE OF THE PREVIOUS GROUP SHOULD BE READ IN THE NEGATIVE').
OSCAR	▬ ▬ ▬	MAN OVERBOARD.
PAPA	● ▬ ▬ ●	**IN HARBOUR;** ALL PERSONS SHOULD REPORT ON BOARD AS VESSEL IS ABOUT TO PROCEED TO SEA. **AT SEA;** IT MAY BE USED BY FISHING VESSELS TO MEAN 'MY NETS HAVE COME FAST UPON AN OBSTRUCTION'.
QUEBEC	▬ ▬ ● ▬	MY VESSEL IS HEALTHY, AND I REQUEST FREE PRATIQUE.
ROMEO	● ▬ ●	(NO SINGLE LETTER MEANING)
SIERRA	● ● ●	I AM OPERATING ASTERN PROPULSION.
TANGO	▬	KEEP CLEAR OF ME; I AM ENGAGED IN PAIR TRAWLING.

Letter	Code	Meaning
UNIFORM	● ● ▬	YOU ARE RUNNING INTO DANGER.
VICTOR	● ● ● ▬	I REQUIRE ASSISTANCE.
WHISKEY	● ▬ ▬	I REQUIRE MEDICAL ASSISTANCE.
X-RAY	▬ ● ● ▬	STOP CARRYING OUT YOUR INTENTIONS AND WATCH FOR MY SIGNALS.
YANKEE	▬ ● ▬ ▬	I AM DRAGGING MY ANCHOR.
ZULU	▬ ▬ ● ●	I REQUIRE A TUG. WHEN MADE BY FISHING VESSELS OPERATING IN CLOSE PROXIMITY ON FISHING GROUNDS IT MEANS 'I AM SHOOTING NETS'.
1ST SUBSTITUTE		USED TO REPEAT THE FIRST FLAG OR PENNANT IN THE SAME HOIST.
2ND SUBSTITUTE		USED TO REPEAT THE SECOND FLAG OR PENNANT IN THE SAME HOIST.
3RD SUBSTITUTE		USED TO REPEAT THE THIRD FLAG OR PENNANT IN THE SAME HOIST.
CODE AND ANSWER		USED TO ACKNOWLEDGE A SIGNAL.

ONE	● ▬ ▬ ▬ ▬
TWO	● ● ▬ ▬ ▬
THREE	● ● ● ▬ ▬
FOUR	● ● ● ● ▬
FIVE	● ● ● ● ●
SIX	▬ ● ● ● ●
SEVEN	▬ ▬ ● ● ●
EIGHT	▬ ▬ ▬ ● ●
NINE	▬ ▬ ▬ ▬ ●
ZERO	▬ ▬ ▬ ▬ ▬

USED ON ALL OCCASIONS WHEN IT IS REQUIRED TO REPRESENT NUMBERS IN FLAG SIGNALLING

NOTE: SINGLE LETTER SIGNALS MAY BE MADE BY ANY METHOD OF SIGNALLING. THE LETTERS B, C, D, E, G, H, I, M, S, T, Z AND FIGURE 5 WHEN MADE BY A SOUND MUST COMPLY WITH INTERNATIONAL REGULATIONS FOR PREVENTING COLLISIONS AT SEA, RULES 34 AND 35. SIGNALS 'K' AND 'S' HAVE SPECIAL MEANINGS AS LANDING SIGNALS FOR SMALL BOATS WITH PERSONS IN DISTRESS.

CERTIFICATE OF AUTHENTICITY

ADMIRALTY
List of Radio Signals

Global Maritime Distress and Safety System (GMDSS)

NP285
Volume 5 3rd Edition
2022

FOR ADMIRALTY DISTRIBUTOR USE ONLY

DISTRIBUTOR STAMP
Your ADMIRALTY Distributor should stamp this certificate at the time of purchase.

DATE: ....
YYYY-MM-DD

NP285

ADMIRALTY LIST OF RADIO SIGNALS

VOLUME 5

THIRD EDITION

2022

GLOBAL MARITIME DISTRESS AND SAFETY SYSTEM (GMDSS)

IMPORTANT - SEE RELATED ADMIRALTY PUBLICATIONS

Notices to Mariners (Annual, Permanent, Preliminary and Temporary); **Symbols and Abbreviations used on Paper Charts** (NP5011); **ADMIRALTY Guide to ENC Symbols used in ECDIS** (NP5012); **The Mariner's Handbook** (NP100, especially Chapters 1 and 2 on the use, accuracy and limitations of charts); **Sailing Directions** (Pilots); **List of Lights** and **Fog Signals**; **List of Radio Signals** and **Tide Tables** (or their digital equivalents).

KEEP CHARTS AND PUBLICATIONS UP TO DATE AND USE THE LARGEST SCALE CHART APPROPRIATE

PUBLISHED BY THE UK HYDROGRAPHIC OFFICE